Product Strategy
and Management

▸▸▸▸▸▸▸▸▸▸▸▸▸▸▸▸▸▸▸▸▸▸▸▸▸▸▸▸▸

Product Strategy
and Management

▶▶▶▶▶▶▶▶▶▶▶▶▶▶▶▶▶▶▶▶▶▶▶▶▶▶

Edited by

THOMAS L. BERG

ABE SHUCHMAN

▶▶▶▶▶▶▶▶▶▶▶▶▶▶▶▶▶ *Graduate School of Business*
Columbia University

Holt, Rinehart and Winston, Inc.

New York   Chicago   San Francisco   Toronto   London

To RALPH S. ALEXANDER,
*friend, colleague, mentor,
and contributor of many of
the basic ideas that
shaped the development
of this book.*

2123701
2 3 4 5 6 7 8 9

Preface

This volume is an outgrowth of almost two decades of course development at Columbia University's Graduate School of Business. Its aim is to fill a gap in the marketing literature that has been among the more troublesome problems encountered in the development process. The fact is that despite general agreement about the importance of the new product function in business, few books devoted to this subject exist. Moreover, the books that are available suffer from numerous limitations that severely restrict their usefulness to the student, whether he be a tyro or a seasoned executive.

Perhaps the most significant limitation of the books to which the student has been able to turn is their highly circumscribed scope. They tend to be concerned with tactical and procedural issues and to ignore strategic or policy considerations. Also, they tend to concentrate attention exclusively on the problems of internal development and/or commercialization. And even within this narrow framework, the issues and problems are hardly ever dealt with in the context of the modern, multiproduct firm in which questions of product-line management are paramount.

This anthology differs, thus, from comparable books primarily in its scope. It is informed by a much broader, more inclusive conception of product management and it emphasizes the relationships between this function and other business policies and procedures. To achieve this, the book has been constructed in four principal parts. The first part describes the role of the product function in contemporary business and also sets out some basic ideas that should permeate managerial thought about product issues. The second part is concerned with the factors governing the development of multiproduct strategies and means for developing such strategies. The third part is devoted to the problems encountered in the process of internal development of products and procedures for guiding this process. And finally, the last part deals with the problems and methods of commercialization of new products. It can be seen, therefore, that this book is *not* concerned solely with new products and that it is *not* intended to be a manual for brand managers. Instead, it is addressed to managers at every level who are necessarily involved not only with new products as such but with the framework within which all products and product lines must be continually examined.

More specifically, it is hoped that this book will prove useful to a variety of audiences. Our own experience indicates that it can serve well both as a text for special courses in product strategy and management at colleges and universities and as supplementary reading for courses in general marketing management. In addition, the book may be of value in university and company executive development programs. Finally, staff and line executives directly involved in formulating product strategy and/or managing product development programs may find it useful either as a refresher course in fundamentals or as a source of relevant ideas. In any event, although the book has been designed primarily to fill a gap in the available college textbook literature, we have endeavored in its construction to take into account also the needs of a much wider range of people.

The book would not have been possible, of course, without the generosity of the many authors and publishers who granted permission to us for the inclusion of their materials in our anthology. A debt of gratitude is also owed to Susan V. Albach, Carol Carlisle, Ben Driver, Carol Fortin, Herbert Johnson, Judy Sandey, and Lottie Shuchman for their unflagging assistance in helping us to collect, copy, and prepare our source materials.

New York, New York   T. L. B.
August 1963   A. S.

Contents

Product Strategy
and Management

►►►►►►►►►►►►►►►►►►►►►►►►►►

part ▸ 1

Introduction

Among the numerous responsibilities of a firm's top management, the definition and development of the products to be marketed have steadily increased in importance. Over the past decade, in fact, it has become apparent that no other single management activity influences a firm's prosperity, in both the short and the long runs, as greatly as the planning and shaping of the product mix offered.

Of course, the product offer has long been recognized as an important instrument of marketing policy. Along with price, promotion, and channels of distribution, it has been regarded as a major competitive weapon. In recent years, however, there has been a growing realization that the product offer is not merely one of several equally important marketing tools but is, instead, of unique and crucial importance. There is an expanding awareness that it is, in fact, the key to competitive survival and success. Today, therefore, the design and implementation of a strategy that will result in products which will assure a profitable and healthy future has moved to or near the forefront of managerial tasks.

Some of the evidence on which the view just expressed is based makes up the first group of selections in this introductory segment. The selections have been chosen for three major reasons: (1) because they recount not only recent success stories but also the findings of careful and perceptive studies of the factors underlying business growth and business decline and so emphasize the significance of product planning and development for both the firm's immediate prospects and its long-term viability; (2) because they suggest some of the more important environmental forces and company experiences which have propelled product development to the top of the list of management's responsibilities; and (3) because they document the increased attention being given to product planning and development by the top executive teams of our more dynamic corporations. Together, therefore, these readings make manifest the singular need, in today's overproduced and highly competitive markets, for the rational and skillful management of a firm's product offering.

Rational and skillful product management is predicated, however, on an appropriate grasp and utilization of a number of fundamental ideas. To set out some of the more important of these ideas is the purpose of the readings in the second segment of this introductory section. Some of these ideas, it will be found, concern the environmental conditions which inhibit and foster innovation within the business context. They relate to the personal and organizational requirements for product innovation and the steps managers can take, both individually and collectively, to assure that these requirements are met. In addition, this segment includes ideas of another kind. These are ideas which provide a conceptual framework for the guidance and control of innovation. They are the foundation stones on which the strategy and tactics of product planning and development should be erected. More specifically, they involve the notions of planned obsolescence as a business creed, of the product life cycle as a determinant of business strategy, and of timing as a critical ingredient of new-product success.

In all, then, the readings in Part 1 are intended to achieve two ends. First, it is hoped that they will engender a keener appreciation of the special importance of effective product planning and development in the contemporary business world. And second, it is hoped that they will acquaint the reader with some of the essential ideas about business policies in general and the product planning function in particular which are crucial to profitable product innovation.

▶▶▶▶▶▶▶▶▶▶ A

The Significance of
New Products

▶▶▶▶▶▶▶▶▶▶▶ KEY FACTORS IN CORPORATE GROWTH

Management Consultant

If there is a pot of gold at the end of the rainbow, most businessmen would expect to find it through "growth." In fact, growth is a kind of American ideal; usually it is thought of in terms of size, and to grow in size is synonymous with achievement.

But the size of the pot may not reflect the amount of gold inside. Growth measured in sales volume alone has not always proved beneficial in the long run. The real growth companies are those which not only have increased their sales volume markedly, but have also significantly increased their net profits and, hopefully, the price of their common stock.

Viewing growth from this more balanced point of view, we can see that companies which are dissatisfied with current projections of their future profitability must bring to bear on their problems a broader based attack than that supplied by increased sales effort alone.

DIFFICULTIES OF THE
SALES APPROACH

There are a number of reasons why the sales route to the rainbow's end is becoming increasingly bumpy:

Reprinted with permission from Management Consultant, *Association of Consulting Management Engineers, 1962 Series, Number 2, pp. 1–4.*

1. Sales growth without new products is feasible but frequently unrewarding. A company enjoying a 10 per cent share of the market may find its marketing costs are trebled if it succeeds in building its share to 20 per cent. And this is wholly apart from the political and public relations problems which accompany dominance in a single field.

2. Partly for this reason, the most effective way to create growth in sales is through new products. But growth in profit is by no means automatic. Many companies' "new products" are in fact an invasion of someone else's backyard and contribute to overcapacity and weakness in price. Many "new products," similarly, are brought out for the sake of their newness alone and may actually be less distinctive, less compelling in the market place than previous products.

3. Growth through helter-skelter product diversification can be expensive to create. New product development is costly; unless it is planned, directed and efficiently conducted, development costs, and particularly the costs of failures, can consume in advance the entire profit potential of the new products created.

4. The cost of marketing new products can be prohibitively expensive, no matter how nicely they may fit into production capabilities. New markets or new channels of distribution may mean a new and separate marketing organization and very likely a series of critical marketing decisions outside of the experience of management.

Thus, true growth requires more than the "Get out and sell!" battle-cry of yesteryear, more than routine product development. At the root of growth in tomorrow's world are two all-important factors:

1. a recognition that constant change is our lot in this new scientific and technological world.

2. a setting of future goals which will capitalize on opportunities anticipated, followed by disciplined planning to marshal and strengthen the company's resources so that goals will be achieved.

RECOGNIZING CHANGE

To a great extent, the first of these factors is best explained by the total environment in which the company functions. The business exists, like a living organism, in an environment that constantly changes, oblivious of the very existence of any particular company. To adapt to this unconsciously hostile environment, companies must change also. Trying only to maintain present conditions and procedures is to stagnate. It is virtually impossible to stand still; thus, for most companies, the choice is between going ahead or going down hill.

In some ways, companies can actually create change rather than simply respond to change in their environment —and this is a worthwhile effort. But, for the most part, even the largest and most powerful corporations cannot influence the direction in which their environment as a whole will go. Take, for instance, some of the changes that have occurred in our society within the past decade:

Socially—more children and more elderly citizens; higher educational levels;

suburban growth; increased leisure time and recreational activities.

Economically—increased domestic and foreign competition; higher labor costs; widespread redistribution of discretionary purchasing power to the middle and lower-middle classes; changes in the distribution system.

Politically—greater military expenditures, shifting with each new defense emphasis; increased farm supports; tighter business regulation; increased state and local government spending.

Technologically—constantly accelerating rate of innovation; increased research spending and higher costs; development of company laboratories; constantly increasing need for scientists and engineers.

Obviously, there is not much any particular company can do to reverse trends like these. But if companies cannot alter the history of their society, there is no reason that they must sit idly by, hoping that the current of events will pick them up, like driftwood, and sweep them on to success. There is much that can be done and has been done by the more successful growth companies. And, thanks to a recent study done by Stanford Research Institute on growth businesses, some common denominators of success shared by most growth companies have been isolated. Here are the facts of that study which corporate planners ought to know.

1. *Necessity of being in a growth market* Short-sighted as it seems, many companies prefer to rely on gaining ever greater shares of existing markets (even when they are static or actually shrinking) than to seek out and enter growth fields. One such significant growth opportunity is afforded by government markets. In manufacturing industries, greater growth was registered by companies dealing with the government than those in consumer markets. Proof is the fact that 33% of the aggregate sales of high-growth companies were made to the federal government, largely in products and services for the defense effort. Low-growth companies, by contrast, reported only 2½% of sales of this type and over 50% to consumer markets. The significance of this is seen when manufactured defense products have shown a dollar growth of about 16% per year, while over-all consumer markets have grown only at a 5% clip. Therefore, companies in defense manufacturing have had three times the opportunity for growth in sales than those in consumer products only. Profits as a percent of sales are usually low; as a percent of investment, they may be highly attractive.

But this begs the question. We are dealing here in aggregates. There is nothing magical about being in defense production *per se*. In defense production, there are thousands of product lines that have lost ground or become obsolete. How then do the high-growth companies manage to emphasize the high-growth products? Are they merely lucky? Perhaps some are, but those which are leaders year in and year out must have relied on planning to spot a growing demand for certain products or (through top notch R & D efforts) have created the new products and stimulated the demand themselves.

If this point is true—that high-growth

companies do not just grow through luck, but through planning—there should then be evidence that these companies spot growth product areas and plan to get into them early. Such is the fact, reported SRI, using the rapidly burgeoning recreation field as its example. In the aggregate, high-growth companies devoted ten times as much of their consumer sales efforts to the leisure time product area than did the low-growth companies. Furthermore, the luck of being in the right place at the right time was ruled out by the fact that more than half of the high-growth companies in the recreation field had only been there for ten years or less.

2. *The more favorable growth potentialities of technically oriented products* There is a positive correlation between the growth rate of a company and the technical nature of its products. Once again, does this mean simply that companies with high technical proficiency merely rode the wave of the scientific revolution into success? Not by any means. Many companies, SRI reported, fought clear of the slow waters of static, non-technical areas and developed the proficiency to enable them to enter the faster moving current of technology.

3. *Diversification is undertaken more readily by high-growth than low-growth companies* Rather than diversifying in name only, the rapidly growing companies have shown a willingness to shift quickly and wholeheartedly into entirely new businesses, often unrelated to their original field. Today, nearly 30% of high-growth companies have diversified so completely that 50% of their total sales comes from their new

businesses—all this within ten years. By contrast, within the same period, 51 of the low-growth companies reveal that less than 10% of their aggregate business comes from new endeavors.

A further contrast is seen in that high-growth companies tend to diversify by acquisition of companies already established in their industries, while 60% of the low-growth companies elected to diversify by internal development of new businesses. Once again, in acquisition, planning for growth plays its part. High-growth companies tended to follow acquisition with a vigorous internal development program to build and solidify the growth potential seen in the purchased company. Also they tended to buy at the right time, after the point of greatest risk, but well before it became obvious to all that entry in a particular field was a wise move for future growth. Finally, the more harmonious acquisitions have resulted from the addition of potentially high-profit products to the acquiring firm's line, rather than short-term balance sheet benefits such as tax shields and the like.

PLANNING TO REACH GOALS

These are the points that high-growth companies have in common—a recognition of the necessity of being in a growth field, plus a willingness to diversify and to enter rapidly growing but hazardous technical areas. Here, then, is the pile of gold. But making sure that any one company can lay claim to the treasure requires the ability to plan effectively. This means not only long-range planning, but also planning *for change;* and its counterpart, planning necessitated *by change.*

Such planning requires foresight, imagination, discipline, and the whole-hearted cooperation of key executives in aspiring growth companies. Specifically:

1. Management must recognize the need for a definite growth program and be willing to support continued planned change—even when the excitement of the late nights and tough decisions wears off. It must further face up to the fact that this rigorous planning must become an executive way of life and realize that since constant change is inevitable it must be anticipated and the company's reaction to it controlled.

2. Next, planning must be done against a background of explicitly stated and thoroughly considered objectives, goals that challenge the company to far greater than normal effort. While objectives should be definite, they cannot be rigid and inelastic in a world of change. They should be subject to regular re-evaluation and modification in light of new developments. On the other hand, objectives that will not stand the test of even a few months time were probably poorly conceived in the first place. If too many changes of objectives are argued for, perhaps the planning procedure itself should be examined. But if objectives turn out to be set according to the best thinking possible, then alterations should be considered most carefully and acted upon, if at all, with deliberation.

3. Last, objectives should realistically stem from a matching of corporate resources against perceived opportunities. If the corporate resources (technical competence, financing, plant or equipment, and personnel) are lacking, yet the opportunity great and long-lasting, vigorous efforts to bolster these resources promptly should be made a prime objective.

Willingness to change and ability to plan are not in themselves enough, however. People are at the heart of a business. Basically, they are the cause of its growth or failure. Over a period of time, a company's ability to attract, develop and hold competent personnel will determine its success, not the theoretical proficiency with which it analyzes its environment or the skill with which it does its planning on paper—although these are assets which will help a company create the image of sophistication that will attract the best men. All three together, however —adaptation to a changing environment, sound planning, and top-notch personnel—will constitute a company whose continued growth should be assured.

CONCLUSION

Thus, the planning that is called for in connection with growth is similar to any long-range planning. That is, it involves the systematic analysis of company resources and opportunities, and the careful marshalling of all the regular functions like research, production, finance, and marketing. But it has four special characteristics:

1. It sets a goal that is higher than would be attained by simply planning to do better each year what the com-

pany already is doing. It sets an incentive goal, which may have to be scaled down on closer examination, but which in the meantime stretches the imagination of management people to see if they can't think of new ways of doing things.

2. Accordingly, it puts more than usual emphasis on the need for the company to organize, manage and innovate with the market as the focus. A growth company must shape itself to the consumer. It must orient itself to the market by producing what the market, and especially tomorrow's market, wants to buy.

3. In order to implement such an approach, it has to help people in the company to be more forward-looking and better prepared to deal with uncertainty, to consider each change in the environment as an opportunity and not an irritation. Personnel must learn that in making decisions for tomorrow they must be skeptical of today's facts, since today's facts may represent the results of yesterday's decisions, which may have been wrong, or even if right

then, may no longer be applicable. This puts all the more premium on using scientific techniques to figure out the best way to do untestable things.

4. There must be an attitude of calculated-risk taking, of willingness to make a few mistakes for the sake of many successes. The only way to avoid all mistakes is never to do anything new or different, to fail to create, to stop growing.

The winner is the company that is willing to make mistakes—but organizes to keep them fewer and less severe than competitors'. And one good way to do this is to keep them in line with the size of the opportunities and the probability of payoff. Sometimes this will mean deciding not to go ahead blindly, or to postpone action while building strength; sometimes it will mean accepting a challenge that otherwise would be overlooked or underestimated. For there is no such thing as a growth industry. There are only companies organized and operated to capitalize on growth opportunities.

►►►►►►►►►►►► MARKETING MYOPIA

THEODORE LEVITT*

Every major industry was once a growth industry. But some that are now riding a wave of growth enthusiasm are very much in the shadow of decline. Others which are thought of as seasoned growth in-

Reprinted with permission from Harvard Business Review, *July–August 1960, pp. 45–56.*

* *Lecturer, Graduate School of Business, Harvard University.*

dustries have actually stopped growing. In every case the reason growth is threatened, slowed, or stopped is *not* because the market is saturated. It is because there has been a failure of management.

FATEFUL PURPOSES

The failure is at the top. The executives responsible for it, in the last analysis, are those who deal with broad aims and policies. Thus:

The railroads did not stop growing because the need for passenger and freight transportation declined. That grew. The railroads are in trouble today not because the need was filled by others (cars, trucks, airplanes, even telephones), but because it was *not* filled by the railroads themselves. They let others take customers away from them because they assumed themselves to be in the railroad business rather than in the transportation business. The reason they defined their industry wrong was because they were railroad-oriented instead of transportation-oriented; they were product-oriented instead of customer-oriented.

Hollywood barely escaped being totally ravished by television. Actually, all the established film companies went through drastic reorganizations. Some simply disappeared. All of them got into trouble not because of TV's inroads but because of their own myopia. As with the railroads, Hollywood defined its business incorrectly. It thought it was in the movie business when it was actually in the entertainment business. "Movies" implied a specific, limited product. This produced a fatuous contentment which from the beginning led producers to view TV as a threat. Hollywood scorned and rejected TV when it should have welcomed it as

an opportunity—an opportunity to expand the entertainment business.

Today TV is a bigger business than the old narrowly defined movie business ever was. Had Hollywood been customer-oriented (providing entertainment), rather than product-oriented (making movies), would it have gone through the fiscal purgatory that it did? I doubt it. What ultimately saved Hollywood and accounted for its recent resurgence was the wave of new young writers, producers, and directors whose previous successes in television had decimated the old movie companies and toppled the big movie moguls.

There are other less obvious examples of industries that have been and are now endangering their futures by improperly defining their purposes. I shall discuss some in detail later and analyze the kind of policies that lead to trouble. Right now it may help to show what a thoroughly customer-oriented management *can* do to keep a growth industry growing, even after the obvious opportunities have been exhausted; and here there are two examples that have been around for a long time. They are nylon and glass—specifically, E. I. du Pont de Nemours & Company and Corning Glass Works:

Both companies have great technical competence. Their product orientation is unquestioned. But this alone does not explain their success. After all, who was more pridefully product-oriented and product-conscious than the erstwhile New England textile companies that have been so thoroughly massacred? The Du Ponts and the Cornings have succeeded not primarily because of their product or research orientation but because they have been thoroughly customer-oriented also.

It is constant watchfulness for opportunities to apply their technical know-how to the creation of customer-satisfying uses which accounts for their prodigious output of successful new products. Without a very sophisticated eye on the customer, most of their new products might have been wrong, their sales methods useless.

Aluminum has also continued to be a growth industry, thanks to the efforts of two wartime-created companies which deliberately set about creating new customer-satisfying uses. Without Kaiser Aluminum & Chemical Corporation and Reynolds Metals Company, the total demand for aluminum today would be vastly less than it is.

ERROR OF ANALYSIS

Some may argue that it is foolish to set the railroads off against aluminum or the movies off against glass. Are not aluminum and glass naturally so versatile that the industries are bound to have more growth opportunities than the railroads and movies? This view commits precisely the error I have been talking about. It defines an industry, or a product, or a cluster of know-how so narrowly as to guarantee its premature senescence. When we mention "railroads," we should make sure we mean "transportation." As transporters, the railroads still have a good chance for very considerable growth. They are not limited to the railroad business as such (though in my opinion rail transportation is potentially a much stronger transportation medium than is generally believed).

What the railroads lack is not opportunity, but some of the same managerial

imaginativeness and audacity that made them great. Even an amateur like Jacques Barzun can see what is lacking when he says:

I grieve to see the most advanced physical and social organization of the last century go down in shabby disgrace for lack of the same comprehensive imagination that built it up. [What is lacking is] the will of the companies to survive and to satisfy the public by inventiveness and skill.[1]

SHADOW OF OBSOLESCENCE

It is impossible to mention a single major industry that did not at one time qualify for the magic appellation of "growth industry." In each case its assumed strength lay in the apparently unchallenged superiority of its product. There appeared to be no effective substitute for it. It was itself a runaway substitute for the product it so triumphantly replaced. Yet one after another of these celebrated industries has come under a shadow. Let us look briefly at a few more of them, this time taking examples that have so far received a little less attention:

Dry cleaning This was once a growth industry with lavish prospects. In an age of wool garments, imagine being finally able to get them safely and easily clean. The boom was on.

Yet here we are 30 years after the boom started and the industry is in trouble. Where has the competition come from? From a better way of

[1] Jacques Barzun, "Trains and the Mind of Man," *Holiday*, February 1960, p. 21.

cleaning? No. It has come from synthetic fibers and chemical additives that have cut the need for dry cleaning. But this is only the beginning. Lurking in the wings and ready to make chemical dry cleaning totally obsolescent is that powerful magician, ultrasonics.

Electric utilities This is another one of those supposedly "no-substitute" products that has been enthroned on a pedestal of invincible growth. When the incandescent lamp came along, kerosene lights were finished. Later the water wheel and the steam engine were cut to ribbons by the flexibility, reliability, simplicity, and just plain easy availability of electric motors. The prosperity of electric utilities continues to wax extravagant as the home is converted into a museum of electric gadgetry. How can anybody miss by investing in utilities, with no competition, nothing but growth ahead?

But a second look is not quite so comforting. A score of nonutility companies are well advanced toward developing a powerful chemical fuel cell which could sit in some hidden closet of every home silently ticking off electric power. The electric lines that vulgarize so many neighborhoods will be eliminated. So will the endless demolition of streets and service interruptions during storms. Also on the horizon is solar energy, again pioneered by nonutility companies.

Who says that the utilities have no competition? They may be natural monopolies now, but tomorrow they may be natural deaths. To avoid this prospect, they too will have to develop fuel cells, solar energy, and other power sources. To survive, they themselves will have to plot the obsolescence of what now produces their livelihood.

Grocery stores Many people find it hard to realize that there ever was a thriving establishment known as the "corner grocery store." The supermarket has taken over with a powerful effectiveness. Yet the big food chains of the 1930's narrowly escaped being completely wiped out by the aggressive expansion of independent supermarkets. The first genuine supermarket was opened in 1930, in Jamaica, Long Island. By 1933 supermarkets were thriving in California, Ohio, Pennsylvania, and elsewhere. Yet the established chains pompously ignored them. When they chose to notice them, it was with such derisive descriptions as "cheapy," "horse-and-buggy," "cracker-barrel storekeeping," and "unethical opportunists."

The executive of one big chain announced at the time that he found it "hard to believe that people will drive for miles to shop for foods and sacrifice the personal service chains have perfected and to which Mrs. Consumer is accustomed."[2] As late as 1936, the National Wholesale Grocers convention and the New Jersey Retail Grocers Association said there was nothing to fear. They said that the supers' narrow appeal to the price buyer limited the size of their market. They had to draw

[2] For more details see M. M. Zimmerman, *The Super Market: A Revolution in Distribution* (New York, McGraw-Hill Book Company, Inc., 1955), p. 48.

from miles around. When imitators came, there would be wholesale liquidations as volume fell. The current high sales of the supers was said to be partly due to their novelty. Basically people wanted convenient neighborhood grocers. If the neighborhood stores "cooperate with their suppliers, pay attention to their costs, and improve their service," they would be able to weather the competition until it blew over.[3]

It never blew over. The chains discovered that survival required going into the supermarket business. This meant the wholesale destruction of their huge investments in corner store sites and in established distribution and merchandising methods. The companies with "the courage of their convictions" resolutely stuck to the corner store philosophy. They kept their pride but lost their shirts.

SELF-DECEIVING CYCLE

But memories are short. For example, it is hard for people who today confidently hail the twin messiahs of electronics and chemicals to see how things could possibly go wrong with these galloping industries. They probably also cannot see how a reasonably sensible businessman could have been as myopic as the famous Boston millionaire who 50 years ago unintentionally sentenced his heirs to poverty by stipulating that his entire estate be forever invested exclusively in electric streetcar securities. His posthumous declaration, "There will always be a big demand for efficient urban transportation," is no consolation to his heirs

[3] *Ibid.*, pp. 45–47.

who sustain life by pumping gasoline at automobile filling stations.

Yet, in a casual survey I recently took among a group of intelligent business executives, nearly half agreed that it would be hard to hurt their heirs by tying their estates forever to the electronics industry. When I then confronted them with the Boston streetcar example, they chorused unanimously, "That's different!" But is it? Is not the basic situation identical?

In truth, *there is no such thing* as a growth industry, I believe. There are only companies organized and operated to create and capitalize on growth opportunities. Industries that assume themselves to be riding some automatic growth escalator invariably descend into stagnation. The history of every dead and dying "growth" industry shows a self-deceiving cycle of bountiful expansion and undetected decay. There are four conditions which usually guarantee this cycle:

1. The belief that growth is assured by an expanding and more affluent population.
2. The belief that there is no competitive substitute for the industry's major product.
3. Too much faith in mass production and in the advantages of rapidly declining unit costs as output rises.
4. Preoccupation with a product that lends itself to carefully controlled scientific experimentation, improvement, and manufacturing cost reduction.

I should like now to begin examining each of these conditions in some detail. To build my case as boldly as possible, I shall illustrate the points with reference to three industries—petroleum, automobiles, and electronics—particularly petroleum, because it spans more years and more vicissitudes. Not only do these three have excellent reputations with the general public and also enjoy the confidence of sophisticated investors, but their managements have become known for progressive thinking in areas like financial control, product research, and management training. If obsolescence can cripple even these industries, it can happen anywhere.

POPULATION MYTH

The belief that profits are assured by an expanding and more affluent population is dear to the heart of every industry. It takes the edge off the apprehensions everybody understandably feels about the future. If consumers are multiplying and also buying more of your product or service, you can face the future with considerably more comfort than if the market is shrinking. An expanding market keeps the manufacturer from having to think very hard or imaginatively. If thinking is an intellectual response to a problem, then the absence of a problem leads to the absence of thinking. If your product has an automatically expanding market, then you will not give much thought to how to expand it.

One of the most interesting examples of this is provided by the petroleum industry. Probably our oldest growth industry, it has an enviable record. While there are some current apprehensions about its growth rate, the industry itself tends to be optimistic. But I believe it can be demonstrated that it is undergoing a fundamental yet typical change. It is not only ceasing to be a growth industry, but may actually be a declining one, relative to other business. Although there is widespread unawareness of it, I believe that within 25 years the oil industry may find itself in much the same position of retrospective glory that the railroads are now in. Despite its pioneering work in developing and applying the present-value method of investment evaluation, in employee relations, and in working with backward countries, the petroleum business is a distressing example of how complacency and wrongheadedness can stubbornly convert opportunity into near disaster.

One of the characteristics of this and other industries that have believed very strongly in the beneficial consequences of an expanding population, while at the same time being industries with a generic product for which there has appeared to be no competitive substitute, is that the individual companies have sought to outdo their competitors by improving on what they are already doing. This makes sense, of course, if one assumes that sales are tied to the country's population strings, because the customer can compare products only on a feature-by-feature basis. I believe it is significant, for example, that not since John D. Rockefeller sent free kerosene lamps to China has the oil industry done anything really outstanding to create a demand for its product. Not even in product improvement has it showered itself with eminence. The greatest single improvement, namely, the development of tetraethyl lead, came from outside the industry, specifically from General Motors and Du Pont. The big contributions made by the industry itself are confined to the technology of oil exploration, production, and refining.

ASKING FOR TROUBLE

In other words, the industry's efforts have focused on improving the *efficiency* of getting and making its product, not really on improving the generic product or its marketing. Moreover, its chief product has continuously been defined in the narrowest possible terms, namely, gasoline, not energy, fuel, or transportation. This attitude has helped assure that:

Major improvements in gasoline quality tend not to originate in the oil industry. Also, the development of superior alternative fuels comes from outside the oil industry, as will be shown later.

Major innovations in automobile fuel marketing are originated by small new oil companies that are not primarily preoccupied with production or refining. These are the companies that have been responsible for the rapidly expanding multipump gasoline stations, with their successful emphasis on large and clean layouts, rapid and efficient driveway service, and quality gasoline at low prices.

Thus, the oil industry is asking for trouble from outsiders. Sooner or later, in this land of hungry inventors and entrepreneurs, a threat is sure to come. The possibilities of this will become more apparent when we turn to the next dangerous belief of many managements. For the sake of continuity, because this second belief is tied

closely to the first, I shall continue with the same example.

IDEA OF INDISPENSABILITY

The petroleum industry is pretty much persuaded that there is no competitive substitute for its major product, gasoline—or if there is, that it will continue to be a derivative of crude oil, such as diesel fuel or kerosene jet fuel.

There is a lot of automatic wishful thinking in this assumption. The trouble is that most refining companies own huge amounts of crude oil reserves. These have value only if there is a market for products into which oil can be converted—hence the tenacious belief in the continuing competitive superiority of automobile fuels made from crude oil.

This idea persists despite all historic evidence against it. The evidence not only shows that oil has never been a superior product for any purpose for very long, but it also shows that the oil industry has never really been a growth industry. It has been a succession of different businesses that have gone through the usual historic cycles of growth, maturity, and decay. Its over-all survival is owed to a series of miraculous escapes from total obsolescence, of last-minute and unexpected reprieves from total disaster reminiscent of the Perils of Pauline.

PERILS OF PETROLEUM

I shall sketch in only the main episodes:

First, crude oil was largely a patent medicine. But even before that fad ran out, demand was greatly expanded by the use of oil in kerosene lamps. The prospect of lighting the world's lamps gave rise to an extravagant promise of growth. The prospects were similar to those the industry now holds for gasoline in other parts of the world. It can hardly wait for the underdeveloped nations to get a car in every garage.

In the days of the kerosene lamp, the oil companies competed with each other and against gaslight by trying to improve the illuminating characteristics of kerosene. Then suddenly the impossible happened. Edison invented a light which was totally nondependent on crude oil. Had it not been for the growing use of kerosene in space heaters, the incandescent lamp would have completely finished oil as a growth industry at that time. Oil would have been good for little else than axle grease.

Then disaster and reprieve struck again. Two great innovations occurred, neither originating in the oil industry. The successful development of coal-burning domestic central-heating systems made the space heater obsolescent. While the industry reeled, along came its most magnificent boost yet—the internal combustion engine, also invented by outsiders. Then when the prodigious expansion for gasoline finally began to level off in the 1920's, along came the miraculous escape of a central oil heater. Once again, the escape was provided by an outsider's invention and development. And when that market weakened, wartime demand for aviation fuel came to the rescue. After the war the expansion of civilian aviation, the dieselization of railroads, and the explosive demand for cars and trucks kept the industry's growth in high gear.

Meanwhile centralized oil heating—whose boom potential had only recently been proclaimed—ran into severe competition from natural gas. While the oil companies themselves owned the gas that now competed with their oil, the industry did not originate the natural gas revolution, nor has it to this day greatly profited from its gas ownership. The gas revolution was made by newly formed transmission companies that marketed the product with an aggressive ardor. They started a magnificent new industry, first against the advice and then against the resistance of the oil companies.

By all the logic of the situation, the oil companies themselves should have made the gas revolution. They not only owned the gas; they also were the only people experienced in handling, scrubbing, and using it, the only people experienced in pipeline technology and transmission, and they understood heating problems. But, partly because they knew that natural gas would compete with their own sale of heating oil, the oil companies pooh-poohed the potentials of gas.

The revolution was finally started by oil pipeline executives who, unable to persuade their own companies to go into gas, quit and organized the spectacularly successful gas transmission companies. Even after their success became painfully evident to the oil companies, the latter did not go into gas transmission. The multibillion dollar business which should have been theirs went to others. As in the past, the industry was blinded by its narrow preoccupation with a specific product and the value of its reserves. It paid little or no attention to its customers' basic needs and preferences.

The postwar years have not witnessed any change. Immediately after World War II the oil industry was greatly encouraged about its future by the rapid expansion of demand for its traditional line of products. In 1950 most companies projected annual rates of domestic expansion of around 6% through at least 1975. Though the ratio of crude oil reserves to demand in the Free World was about 20 to 1, with 10 to 1 being usually considered a reasonable working ratio in the United States, booming demand sent oil men searching for more without sufficient regard to what the future really promised. In 1952 they "hit" in the Middle East; the ratio skyrocketed to 42 to 1. If gross additions to reserves continue at the average rate of the past five years (37 billion barrels annually), then by 1970 the reserve ratio will be up to 45 to 1. This abundance of oil has weakened crude and product prices all over the world.

UNCERTAIN FUTURE

Management cannot find much consolation today in the rapidly expanding petrochemical industry, another oil-using idea that did not originate in the leading firms. The total United States production of petrochemicals is equivalent to about 2% (by volume) of the demand for all petroleum products. Although the petrochemical industry is now expected to grow by about 10% per year, this will not offset other drains on the growth of crude oil consumption. Furthermore, while petrochemical products are many and growing, it is well to remember that there are nonpetroleum sources of the basic raw material, such as coal. Besides, a lot of plastics can be produced with relatively little oil. A 50,000-barrel-per-day oil refinery is now considered the absolute minimum size for efficiency. But a 5,000-barrel-per-day chemical plant is a giant operation.

Oil has never been a continuously strong growth industry. It has grown by fits and starts, always miraculously saved by innovations and developments not of its own making. The reason it

has not grown in a smooth progression is that each time it thought it had a superior product safe from the possibility of competitive substitutes, the product turned out to be inferior and notoriously subject to obsolescence. Until now, gasoline (for motor fuel, anyhow) has escaped this fate. But, as we shall see later, it too may be on its last legs.

The point of all this is that there is no guarantee against product obsolescence. If a company's own research does not make it obsolete, another's will. Unless an industry is especially lucky, as oil has been until now, it can easily go down in a sea of red figures —just as the railroads have, as the buggy whip manufacturers have, as the corner grocery chains have, as most of the big movie companies have, and indeed as many other industries have.

The best way for a firm to be lucky is to make its own luck. That requires knowing what makes a business successful. One of the greatest enemies of this knowledge is mass production.

PRODUCTION PRESSURES

Mass-production industries are impelled by a great drive to produce all they can. The prospect of steeply declining unit costs as output rises is more than most companies can usually resist. The profit possibilities look spectacular. All effort focuses on production. The result is that marketing gets neglected.

John Kenneth Galbraith contends that just the opposite occurs.[4] Output is so prodigious that all effort concen-

[4] *The Affluent Society* (Boston, Houghton Mifflin Company, 1958), pp. 152–160.

trates on trying to get rid of it. He says this accounts for singing commercials, desecration of the countryside with advertising signs, and other wasteful and vulgar practices. Galbraith has a finger on something real, but he misses the strategic point. Mass production does indeed generate great pressure to "move" the product. But what usually gets emphasized is selling, not marketing. Marketing, being a more sophisticated and complex process, gets ignored.

The difference between marketing and selling is more than semantic. Selling focuses on the needs of the seller, marketing on the needs of the buyer. Selling is preoccupied with the seller's need to convert his product into cash; marketing with the idea of satisfying the needs of the customer by means of the product and the whole cluster of things associated with creating, delivering, and finally consuming it.

In some industries the enticements of full mass production have been so powerful that for many years top management in effect has told the sales departments, "You get rid of it; we'll worry about profits." By contrast, a truly marketing-minded firm tries to create value-satisfying goods and services that consumers will want to buy. What it offers for sale includes not only the generic product or service, but also how it is made available to the customer, in what form, when, under what conditions, and at what terms of trade. Most important, what it offers for sale is determined not by the seller but by the buyer. The seller takes his cues from the buyer in such a way that the product becomes a consequence of the marketing effort, not vice versa.

LAG IN DETROIT

This may sound like an elementary rule of business, but that does not keep it from being violated wholesale. It is certainly more violated than honored. Take the automobile industry:

Here mass production is most famous, most honored, and has the greatest impact on the entire society. The industry has hitched its fortune to the relentless requirements of the annual model change, a policy that makes customer orientation an especially urgent necessity. Consequently the auto companies annually spend millions of dollars on consumer research. But the fact that the new compact cars are selling so well in their first year indicates that Detroit's vast researches have for a long time failed to reveal what the customer really wanted. Detroit was not persuaded that he wanted anything different from what he had been getting until it lost millions of customers to other small car manufacturers.

How could this unbelievable lag behind consumer wants have been perpetuated so long? Why did not research reveal consumer preferences before consumers' buying decisions themselves revealed the facts? Is that not what consumer research is for—to find out before the fact what is going to happen? The answer is that Detroit never really researched the customer's wants. It only researched his preferences between the kinds of things which it had already decided to offer him. For Detroit is mainly product-oriented, not customer-oriented. To the extent that the customer is recognized as having needs that the manufacturer should try to satisfy, Detroit usually acts as if the job can be done entirely by product changes. Occasionally attention gets paid to financing, too, but that is done more in order to sell than to enable the customer to buy.

As for taking care of other customer needs, there is not enough being done to write about. The areas of the greatest unsatisfied needs are ignored, or at best get stepchild attention. These are at the point of sale and on the matter of automotive repair and maintenance. Detroit views these problem areas as being of secondary importance. That is underscored by the fact that the retailing and servicing ends of this industry are neither owned and operated nor controlled by the manufacturers. Once the car is produced, things are pretty much in the dealer's inadequate hands. Illustrative of Detroit's arm's-length attitude is the fact that, while servicing holds enormous sales-stimulating, profit-building opportunities, only 57 of Chevrolet's 7,000 dealers provide night maintenance service.

Motorists repeatedly express their dissatisfaction with servicing and their apprehensions about buying cars under the present selling setup. The anxieties and problems they encounter during the auto buying and maintenance processes are probably more intense and widespread today than 30 years ago. Yet the automobile companies do not *seem* to listen to or take their cues from the anguished consumer. If they do listen, it must be through the filter of their own preoccupation with production. The marketing effort is still viewed as a necessary consequence of the product, not vice versa, as it should be. That is the legacy of mass production, with its parochial view that profit resides essentially in low-cost full production.

WHAT FORD PUT FIRST

The profit lure of mass production obviously has a place in the plans and strategy of business management, but it must always *follow* hard thinking about the customer. This is one of the most important lessons that we can learn from the contradictory behavior of Henry Ford. In a sense Ford was both the most brilliant and the most senseless marketer in American history. He was senseless because he refused to give the customer anything but a black car. He was brilliant because he fashioned a production system designed to fit market needs. We habitually celebrate him for the wrong reason, his production genius. His real genius was marketing. We think he was able to cut his selling price and therefore sell millions of $500 cars because his invention of the assembly line had reduced the costs. Actually he invented the assembly line because he had concluded that at $500 he could sell millions of cars. Mass production was the *result* not the cause of his low prices.

Ford repeatedly emphasized this point, but a nation of production-oriented business managers refuses to hear the great lesson he taught. Here is his operating philosophy as he expressed it succinctly:

Our policy is to reduce the price, extend the operations, and improve the article. You will notice that the reduction of price comes first. We have never considered any costs as fixed. Therefore we first reduce the price to the point where we believe more sales will result. Then we go ahead and try to make the prices. We do not bother about the costs. The new price forces the costs down. The more usual way is to take the costs and then determine the price, and although that method may be scientific in the narrow sense, it is not scientific in the broad sense, because what earthly use is it to know the cost if it tells you that you cannot manufacture at a price at which the article can be sold? But more to the point is the fact that, although one may calculate what a cost is, and of course all of our costs are carefully calculated, no one knows what a cost ought to be. One of the ways of discovering . . . is to name a price so low as to force everybody in the place to the highest point of efficiency. The low price makes everybody dig for profits. We make more discoveries concerning manufacturing and selling under this forced method than by any method of leisurely investigation.[5]

PRODUCT PROVINCIALISM

The tantalizing profit possibilities of low unit production cost may be the most seriously self-deceiving attitude that can afflict a company, particularly a "growth" company where an apparently assured expansion of demand already tends to undermine a proper concern for the importance of marketing and the customer.

The usual result of this narrow preoccupation with so-called concrete matters is that instead of growing, the industry declines. It usually means that the product fails to adapt to the constantly changing patterns of consumer

[5] Henry Ford, *My Life and Work* (New York, Doubleday, Page & Company, 1923), pp. 146–147.

needs and tastes, to new and modified marketing institutions and practices, or to product developments in competing or complementary industries. The industry has its eyes so firmly on its own specific product that it does not see how it is being made obsolete.

The classical example of this is the buggy whip industry. No amount of product improvement could stave off its death sentence. But had the industry defined itself as being in the transportation business rather than the buggy whip business, it might have survived. It would have done what survival always entails, that is, changing. Even if it had only defined its business as providing a stimulant or catalyst to an energy source, it might have survived by becoming a manufacturer of, say, fanbelts or air cleaners.

What may some day be a still more classical example is, again, the oil industry. Having let others steal marvelous opportunities from it (e.g., natural gas, as already mentioned, missile fuels, and jet engine lubricants), one would expect it to have taken steps never to let that happen again. But this is not the case. We are now getting extraordinary new developments in fuel systems specifically designed to power automobiles. Not only are these developments concentrated in firms outside the petroleum industry, but petroleum is almost systematically ignoring them, securely content in its wedded bliss to oil. It is the story of the kerosene lamp versus the incandescent lamp all over again. Oil is trying to improve hydrocarbon fuels rather than to develop *any* fuels best suited to the needs of their users, whether or not made in different ways and with different raw materials from oil.

Here are some of the things which nonpetroleum companies are working on:

Over a dozen such firms now have advanced working models of energy systems which, when perfected, will replace the internal combustion engine and eliminate the demand for gasoline. The superior merit of each of these systems is their elimination of frequent, time-consuming, and irritating refueling stops. Most of these systems are fuel cells designed to create electrical energy directly from chemicals without combustion. Most of them use chemicals that are not derived from oil, generally hydrogen and oxygen.

Several other companies have advanced models of electric storage batteries designed to power automobiles. One of these is an aircraft producer that is working jointly with several electric utility companies. The latter hope to use off-peak generating capacity to supply overnight plug-in battery regeneration. Another company, also using the battery approach, is a medium-size electronics firm with extensive small-battery experience that it developed in connection with its work on hearing aids. It is collaborating with an automobile manufacturer. Recent improvements arising from the need for high-powered miniature power storage plants in rockets have put us within reach of a relatively small battery capable of withstanding great overloads or surges of power. Germanium diode applications and batteries using sintered-plate and nickel-cadmium techniques promise to make a revolution in our energy sources.

Solar energy conversion systems are also getting increasing attention. One usually cautious Detroit auto executive recently ventured that solar-powered cars might be common by 1980.

As for the oil companies, they are more or less "watching developments," as one research director put it to me. A few are doing a bit of research on fuel cells, but almost always confined to developing cells powered by hydrocarbon chemicals. None of them are enthusiastically researching fuel cells, batteries, or solar power plants. None of them are spending a fraction as much on research in these profoundly important areas as they are on the usual run-of-the-mill things like reducing combustion chamber deposit in gasoline engines. One major integrated petroleum company recently took a tentative look at the fuel cell and concluded that although "the companies actively working on it indicate a belief in ultimate success . . . the timing and magnitude of its impact are too remote to warrant recognition in our forecasts."

One might, of course, ask: Why should the oil companies do anything different? Would not chemical fuel cells, batteries, or solar energy kill the present product lines? The answer is that they would indeed, and that is precisely the reason for the oil firms having to develop these power units before their competitors, so they will not be companies without an industry.

Management might be more likely to do what is needed for its own preservation if it thought of itself as being in the energy business. But even that would not be enough if it persists in imprisoning itself in the narrow grip of its tight product orientation. It has to think of itself as taking care of customer needs, not finding, refining, or even selling oil. Once it genuinely thinks of its business as taking care of people's transportation needs, nothing can stop it from creating its own extravagantly profitable growth.

"CREATIVE DESTRUCTION"

Since words are cheap and deeds are dear, it may be appropriate to indicate what this kind of thinking involves and leads to. Let us start at the beginning —the customer. It can be shown that motorists strongly dislike the bother, delay, and experience of buying gasoline. People actually do not buy gasoline. They cannot see it, taste it, feel it, appreciate it, or really test it. What they buy is the right to continue driving their cars. The gas station is like a tax collector to whom people are compelled to pay a periodic toll as the price of using their cars. This makes the gas station a basically unpopular institution. It can never be made popular or pleasant, only less unpopular, less unpleasant.

To reduce its unpopularity completely means eliminating it. Nobody likes a tax collector, not even a pleasantly cheerful one. Nobody likes to interrupt a trip to buy a phantom product, not even from a handsome Adonis or a seductive Venus. Hence, companies that are working on exotic fuel substitutes which will eliminate the need for frequent refueling are heading directly into the outstretched arms of the irritated motorists. They are riding a wave of inevitability, not because they are creating something which is technologically superior or more sophisticated, but because they are satisfying a powerful customer need. They are also eliminating noxious odors and air pollution.

Once the petroleum companies recognize the customer-satisfying logic of what another power system can do, they will see that they have no more choice about working on an efficient, long-lasting fuel (or some way of delivering present fuels without bothering the motorist) than the big food chains had a choice about going into the supermarket business, or the vacuum tube companies had a choice about making semiconductors. For their own good the oil firms will have to destroy their own highly profitable assets. No amount of wishful thinking can save them from the necessity of engaging in this form of "creative destruction."

I phrase the need as strongly as this because I think management must make quite an effort to break itself loose from conventional ways. It is all too easy in this day and age for a company or industry to let its sense of purpose become dominated by the economies of full production and to develop a dangerously lopsided product orientation. In short, if management lets itself drift, it invariably drifts in the direction of thinking of itself as producing goods and services, not customer satisfactions. While it probably will not descend to the depths of telling its salesmen, "You get rid of it; we'll worry about profits," it can, without knowing it, be practicing precisely that formula for withering decay. The historic fate of one growth industry after another has been its suicidal product provincialism.

DANGERS OF R & D

Another big danger to a firm's continued growth arises when top management is wholly transfixed by the profit possibilities of technical research and development. To illustrate I shall turn first to a new industry—electronics—and then return once more to the oil companies. By comparing a fresh example with a familiar one, I hope to emphasize the prevalence and insidiousness of a hazardous way of thinking.

MARKETING SHORTCHANGED

In the case of electronics, the greatest danger which faces the glamorous new companies in this field is not that they do not pay enough attention to research and development, but that they pay *too much* attention to it. And the fact that the fastest growing electronics firms owe their eminence to their heavy emphasis on technical research is completely beside the point. They have vaulted to affluence on a sudden crest of unusually strong general receptiveness to new technical ideas. Also, their success has been shaped in the virtually guaranteed market of military subsidies and by military orders that in many cases actually preceded the existence of facilities to make the products. Their expansion has, in other words, been almost totally devoid of marketing effort.

Thus, they are growing up under conditions that come dangerously close to creating the illusion that a superior product will sell itself. Having created a successful company by making a superior product, it is not surprising that management continues to be oriented toward the product rather than the people who consume it. It develops the philosophy that continued growth is a matter of continued product innovation and improvement.

A number of other factors tend to strengthen and sustain this belief:

1. Because electronic products are highly complex and sophisticated, managements become topheavy with engineers and scientists. This creates a selective bias in favor of research and production at the expense of marketing. The organization tends to view itself as making things rather than satisfying customer needs. Marketing gets treated as a residual activity, "something else" that must be done once the vital job of product creation and production is completed.

2. To this bias in favor of product research, development, and production is added the bias in favor of dealing with controllable variables. Engineers and scientists are at home in the world of concrete things like machines, test tubes, production lines, and even balance sheets. The abstractions to which they feel kindly are those which are testable or manipulatable in the laboratory, or, if not testable, then functional, such as Euclid's axioms. In short, the managements of the new glamour-growth companies tend to favor those business activities which lend themselves to careful study, experimentation, and control—the hard, practical realities of the lab, the shop, the books.

What gets shortchanged are the realities of the *market*. Consumers are unpredictable, varied, fickle, stupid, shortsighted, stubborn, and generally bothersome. This is not what the engineer-managers say, but deep down in their consciousness it is what they believe. And this accounts for their concentrating on what they know and what they can control, namely, product research, engineering, and production. The emphasis on production becomes particularly attractive when the product can be made at declining unit costs. There is no more inviting way of making money than by running the plant full blast.

Today the top-heavy science-engineering-production orientation of so many electronics companies works reasonably well because they are pushing into new frontiers in which the armed services have pioneered virtually assured markets. The companies are in the felicitous position of having to fill, not find, markets; of not having to discover what the customer needs and wants, but of having the customer voluntarily come forward with specific new product demands. If a team of consultants had been assigned specifically to design a business situation calculated to prevent the emergence and development of a customer-oriented marketing viewpoint, it could not have produced anything better than the conditions just described.

STEPCHILD TREATMENT

The oil industry is a stunning example of how science, technology, and mass production can divert an entire group of companies from their main task. To the extent the consumer is studied at all (which is not much), the focus is forever on getting information which is designed to help the oil companies improve what they are now doing. They try to discover more convincing advertising themes, more effective sales promotional drives, what the market shares of the various companies are, what people like or dislike about service station dealers and oil companies, and so forth. Nobody seems as interested in probing deeply into the basic human needs that the industry might be trying to satisfy as in probing into the basic properties of the raw material that the companies work with in trying to deliver customer satisfactions.

Basic questions about customers and markets seldom get asked. The latter occupy a stepchild status. They are recognized as existing, as having to be taken care of, but not worth very much real thought or dedicated attention. Nobody gets as excited about the customers in his own backyard as about the oil in the Sahara Desert. Nothing illustrates better the neglect of marketing than its treatment in the industry press:

The centennial issue of the *American Petroleum Institute Quarterly,* published in 1959 to celebrate the discovery of oil in Titusville, Pennsylvania, contained 21 feature articles proclaiming the industry's greatness. Only one of these talked about its achievements in marketing, and that was only a pictorial record of how service station architecture has changed. The issue also contained a special section on "New Horizons," which was devoted to showing the magnificent role oil would play in America's future. Every reference was ebulliently optimistic, never implying once that oil might have some hard competition. Even the reference to atomic energy was a cheerful catalogue of how oil would help make atomic energy a success. There was not a single apprehension that the oil industry's affluence might be threatened or a suggestion that one "new horizon" might include new and better ways of serving oil's present customers.

But the most revealing example of the stepchild treatment that marketing gets was still another special series of short articles on "The Revolutionary Potential of Electronics." Under that heading this list of articles appeared in the table of contents:

"In the Search for Oil"
"In Production Operations"
"In Refinery Processes"
"In Pipeline Operations"

Significantly, every one of the industry's major functional areas is listed, *except* marketing. Why? Either it is believed that electronics holds no revolutionary potential for petroleum marketing (which is palpably wrong), or the editors forgot to discuss marketing (which is more likely, and illustrates its stepchild status).

The order in which the four functional areas are listed also betrays the alienation of the oil industry from the consumer. The industry is implicitly defined as beginning with the search for oil and ending with its distribution from the refinery. But the truth is, it seems to me, that the industry begins with the needs of the customer for its products. From that primal position its definition moves steadily backstream to areas of progressively lesser importance, until it finally comes to rest at the "search for oil."

BEGINNING AND END

The view that an industry is a customer-satisfying process, not a goods-producing process, is vital for all businessmen to understand. An industry begins with the customer and his needs, not with a patent, a raw material, or a selling skill. Given the customer's needs, the industry develops backwards, first concerning itself with

the physical *delivery* of customer satisfactions. Then it moves back further to *creating* the things by which these satisfactions are in part achieved. How these materials are created is a matter of indifference to the customer, hence the particular form of manufacturing, processing, or what-have-you cannot be considered as a vital aspect of the industry. Finally, the industry moves back still further to *finding* the raw materials necessary for making its products.

The irony of some industries oriented toward technical research and development is that the scientists who occupy the high executive positions are totally unscientific when it comes to defining their companies' over-all needs and purposes. They violate the first two rules of the scientific method—being aware of and defining their companies' problems, and then developing testable hypotheses about solving them. They are scientific only about the convenient things, such as laboratory and product experiments. The reason that the customer (and the satisfaction of his deepest needs) is not considered as being "the problem" is not because there is any certain belief that no such problem exists, but because an organizational lifetime has conditioned management to look in the opposite direction. Marketing is a stepchild.

I do not mean that selling is ignored. Far from it. But selling, again, is not marketing. As already pointed out, selling concerns itself with the tricks and techniques of getting people to exchange their cash for your product. It is not concerned with the values that the exchange is all about. And it does not, as marketing invariably does, view the entire business process as consisting of a tightly integrated effort to discover, create, arouse, and satisfy customer needs. The customer is somebody "out there" who, with proper cunning, can be separated from his loose change.

Actually, not even selling gets much attention in some technologically minded firms. Because there is a virtually guaranteed market for the abundant flow of their new products, they do not actually know what a real market is. It is as if they lived in a planned economy, moving their products routinely from factory to retail outlet. Their successful concentration on products tends to convince them of the soundness of what they have been doing, and they fail to see the gathering clouds over the market.

CONCLUSION

Less than 75 years ago American railroads enjoyed a fierce loyalty among astute Wall Streeters. European monarchs invested in them heavily. Eternal wealth was thought to be the benediction for anybody who could scrape a few thousand dollars together to put into rail stocks. No other form of transportation could compete with the railroads in speed, flexibility, durability, economy, and growth potentials. As Jacques Barzun put it, "By the turn of the century it was an institution, an image of man, a tradition, a code of honor, a source of poetry, a nursery of boyhood desires, a sublimest of toys, and the most solemn machine—next to the funeral hearse—that marks the epochs in man's life."[6]

[6] *Op. cit.*, p. 20.

Even after the advent of automobiles, trucks, and airplanes, the railroad tycoons remained imperturbably self-confident. If you had told them 60 years ago that in 30 years they would be flat on their backs, broke, and pleading for government subsidies, they would have thought you totally demented. Such a future was simply not considered possible. It was not even a discussable subject, or an askable question, or a matter which any sane person would consider worth speculating about. The very thought was insane. Yet a lot of insane notions now have matter-of-fact acceptance—for example, the idea of 100-ton tubes of metal moving smoothly through the air 20,000 feet above the earth, loaded with 100 sane and solid citizens casually drinking martinis—and they have dealt cruel blows to the railroads.

What specifically must other companies do to avoid this fate? What does customer orientation involve? These questions have in part been answered by the preceding examples and analysis. It would take another article to show in detail what is required for specific industries. In any case, it should be obvious that building an effective customer-oriented company involves far more than good intentions or promotional tricks; it involves profound matters of human organization and leadership. For the present, let me merely suggest what appear to be some general requirements.

VISCERAL FEEL OF GREATNESS

Obviously the company has to do what survival demands. It has to adapt to the requirements of the market, and it has to do it sooner rather than later.

But mere survival is a so-so aspiration. Anybody can survive in some way or other, even the skid-row bum. The trick is to survive gallantly, to feel the surging impulse of commercial mastery; not just to experience the sweet smell of success, but to have the visceral feel of entrepreneurial greatness.

No organization can achieve greatness without a vigorous leader who is driven onward by his own pulsating *will to succeed.* He has to have a vision of grandeur, a vision that can produce eager followers in vast numbers. In business, the followers are the customers. To produce these customers, the entire corporation must be viewed as a customer-creating and customer-satfying organism. Management must think of itself not as producing products but as providing customer-creating value satisfactions. It must push this idea (and everything it means and requires) into every nook and cranny of the organization. It has to do this continuously and with the kind of flair that excites and stimulates the people in it. Otherwise, the company will be merely a series of pigeonholed parts, with no consolidating sense of purpose or direction.

In short, the organization must learn to think of itself not as producing goods or services but as *buying customers,* as doing the things that will make people *want* to do business with it. And the chief executive himself has the inescapable responsibility for creating this environment, this viewpoint, this attitude, this aspiration. He himself must set the company's style, its direction, and its goals. This means he has to know precisely where he himself wants to go, and to make sure the whole organization is enthusiastically aware of where that is. This is a first requisite of leadership, for *unless he knows where he is going, any road will take him there.*

If any road is okay, the chief executive might as well pack his attaché case and go fishing. If an organization does not know or care where it is going, it does not need to advertise that fact with a ceremonial figurehead. Everybody will notice it soon enough.

▶▶▶▶▶▶▶▶▶▶▶▶ THE IMPORTANCE OF NEW PRODUCTS

BOOZ, ALLEN & HAMILTON

Long lists could detail the importance of new products, but in business strategy most of these can be grouped under three major headings; new products are: (1) a major contributor to company growth,

Reprinted with permission from Management of New Products, *Booz, Allen & Hamilton, 1960, pp. 5–7.*

(2) a primary influence on profit performance, and (3) a key factor in business planning.

1. THE IMPORTANCE OF NEW PRODUCTS TO COMPANY GROWTH

Business history demonstrates that growth industries have been heavily new product oriented. For example, Chart 1 compares R & D expenditures, which are a partial measure of new product effort, with the growth rates of selected industries. As can be noted, those industries spending the most for new product development have, in the main, experienced the greatest growth. Many other indices of growth in comparison with indicators of new product activity show similar relationships.

Within all industries, most growth companies attribute a large percentage of their sales and profitability to their new product lines. Industrial history documents many examples of this.

2. THE IMPORTANCE OF NEW PRODUCTS TO PROFIT MARGINS

New products have a characteristic pattern to their sales volume and profit margin curves as illustrated in Chart 2. While these two curves are similar in configuration, it is important to note that they do not have identical timing and phasing. The profit curve tends to start descending while the sales curve is still rising. The shape of the sales curve has been generally understood for many years and has often been the basis of planning for marketing strategy. However, identification of the out-of-

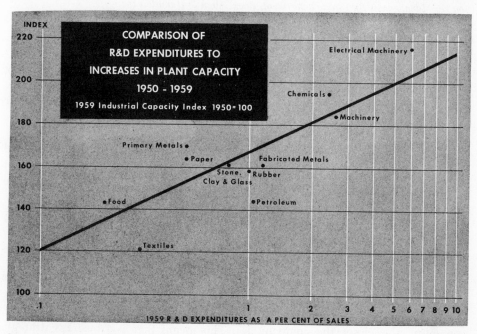

Source: Management Research Department, Booz, Allen & Hamilton Inc.

CHART 1

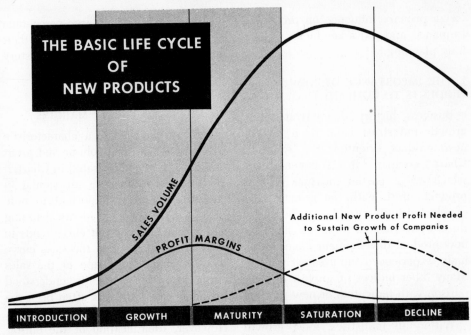

THE BASIC LIFE CYCLE OF NEW PRODUCTS

SALES VOLUME

PROFIT MARGINS

Additional New Product Profit Needed to Sustain Growth of Companies

| INTRODUCTION | GROWTH | MATURITY | SATURATION | DECLINE |

Source: Management Research Department, Booz, Allen & Hamilton Inc.

CHART 2

phase relationship between the profit curve and sales curve suggests that product strategy is better planned around the profit curve than the sales curve.

A primary economic conclusion, derived from analyzing the life cycles of numerous products, is that "sooner or later every product is preempted by another or else degenerates into profitless price competition." This inevitable fact makes clear the necessity of careful new product planning.

The sales volume-profit pattern and the timing of the product life cycle varies by product and industry. As a generality, the closer the company is to consumer goods and the market place, the shorter the cycle of its product. Conversely, as the product or

the company is closer to basic industry or producers' goods, the longer is the cycle. The position that a particular company has in the spectrum from basic goods to consumer goods may well dictate the amount of money, time, and management accorded the new product activity. However, it is clear that the time scale on almost all products is being more and more compressed now by accelerating research and technology, by changing markets, mass media and mass distribution.

Another key point is that business success tends to be governed not only by what you do, but what others do. This means that as a business strategy, a company must plan to run ahead of price competition by differentiating its products and introducing new products that can command better margins. Throughout history, the underlying secret of business success has been to be in the right business at the right time, and this strategy is expressed by the selection and development of company products. Over-all profits generally can be sustained in the long run only by a continuing flow of new products, not only to replace sales volume but also to bolster today's shrinking profit margins.

3. THE IMPORTANCE OF NEW PRODUCTS FOR BUSINESS PLANNING

Company plans are keyed to and made up of product plans. To project sales, costs, capital, facilities and personnel needs without clear product plans can only reflect broad estimates, not specific programs.

The plans for growth in sales and profits of a company are at the core of management interests. New products are a major factor in the growth of companies today. The impact of new products is clear even in short-term plans of United States manufacturing companies, as illustrated in Chart 3.

The length of the bars shows the dollars of sales growth expected in 11 industries. The shaded part of these bars is the share of this growth expected from new products in the period shown. As may be observed, this ranges from 30% to over 100% for these key industries. More and more the growth of the nation can be expected to come from new products. New product plans are the heart of corporate planning in most major companies today.

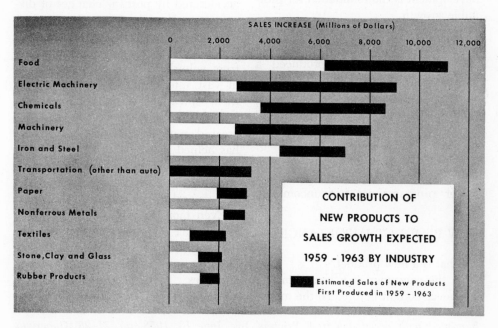

Source: *Federal Trade Commission and McGraw-Hill.*

CHART 3

►►►►►►►►►►►► WHAT NEW PRODUCTS MEAN TO COMPANIES:
growth, a longer life, bigger profits

Printers' Ink

One of the most significant developments of the marketing concept era is the growth of interest in new products.

American industry traditionally has been an innovator in products as a normal part of business growth. The essential difference today is that brutally fierce competition based on comprehensive marketing has given new products a special importance in the marketing operation. A PRINTERS INK survey reveals that:

For many companies, new product development is the foundation for profitable growth.

For some, it is actually the basic hope for *survival* in the market place.

Careful planning has produced a great number of profitable new product successes.

However, estimates of the failure rate of all new products run as high as 80 per cent.

Advertising is a key element of a new product campaign and blockbuster programs are not uncommon.

NEW PRODUCT IMPORTANCE

What is a new product?

To the consumer, it is something he has never bought before. To the manufacturer it can be a basically new product (frozen TV dinners, new "miracle" fibers, small cars). It can also be Marlboro cigarettes in a new flip-top package (backed by a spectacular advertising campaign). Or the addition of color to otherwise unchanged toilet tissue, a new ingredient (GL-70) in the same basic toothpaste, boron added to gasoline. For a manufacturer, a new product can mean any change in the form, content or package of the product, or even a new way of distributing it—a new market.

New product development has been accelerated by postwar changes of dizzying speed and magnitude. Markets have been and are shifting rapidly. People moving from city to suburb and from suburb to outer area have filled in vast interurban territories, making them spreading complexes of multi-economic-level consumers. The increased mobility of these consumers has helped kill off what formerly were major sales outlets and has led to new and bigger ones, including shopping centers and discount houses.

Even more important has been the broadening of the middle, upper middle and top income groups. More people have more money and more varied appetites. Their tastes have created markets within markets, specialized but big segments that offer many profitable opportunities.

For, in every segment of the market, the people—inspired by a zest for new and better living—are avidly seeking out new, and better products.

Technological advances have made it easier to produce what consumers want—at a rate faster than products can be sold.

A TIGHTENING MARKET

In the competition that arises from this tightening market, new products have been the most effective weapons. Few existing products can withstand the onslaught of competing new products, especially when these are accompanied by vast advertising and merchandising campaigns. Such programs are carefully researched in advance to take advantage of any weakness in existing products.

Nevertheless, some companies have only recently awakened to the importance of the new product phenomenon. Others started early. Giants like Du Pont, General Electric and RCA report that most of their current revenue is from products new since World War II. One study shows that seven industries within a relatively limited area expect that between 50 and 80 per cent of their growth between 1955 and 1959 will be from new products. Those seven industries: chemicals, machinery, electrical machinery, transportation (other than auto), iron and steel, textiles, rubber products.

Monsanto is reported working on a number of new products in the plastics field. U.S. Steel has had success in its work with Corten steel. Reynolds is among the pioneers in new aluminum products, including aluminum cans. Corning Glass has turned out many new glass products.

In the consumer field, P & G, General Foods and Johnson & Johnson are typical of companies who have scored outstanding successes with broad, well-planned new product campaigns.

That kind of activity requires tremendous investments. One authoritative estimate put the 1957 figure for research and development by American business at $7,000,000,000. Most of that went for new products. Experts expect the figure to increase.

Each company can explain its investment in new products in its own way. The general objective is summarized in the declaration made by the Purex Corp. when it established a new products division in March. Purex declared that the new division would be responsible for "The primary objective of aiding top management in formulating sound short-range and long-range product policies and objectives for future *corporate growth*" (emphasis added).

Carrying it one step further, Conrad Jones, partner and manager of new product planning for the management consultant firm of Booz, Allen & Hamilton, says a study of 2,000 companies shows that "new products hold the key not only to growth, but even to survival for many businesses." . . .

Too often, some entrepreneurs seem inclined to work at new product development as if they were playing a slot machine. They invest a little time and money and sit back to wait for jackpots. As in slot machines, jackpots in new product development are relatively few and far between.

Most new products fail. Estimates of the fatality rate range up to 80 per cent and more. This, of course, represents a great deal of waste. But, experts point out, most failures actually represent too little research, planning and preparation.

IMPRESSIVE PROFITS

On the other hand, a properly prepared and tested new product can be the basis for impressive profit performances. As one example of many: the Johnson's wax people carefully researched and tested the product, then invested more than one million dollars for advertising "Glade" in the year when the air freshener was introduced (with production handled by outside contractors). Johnson forecast average annual profits of $800,000 over a three-year period—and every indication is that this forecast is being met or exceeded. Such earnings can pay for a lot of new product failures (of which Johnson has had few).

That kind of success story has given new product development an irresistible impetus that not even failure can slow down—let alone stop. But the most successful developers approach new products with careful attention to the realities of the market.

Last year, an estimated 6,000 new grocery products were introduced: about 20 per working day, far more than any one buyer or buying committee could find time to consider. Of these, perhaps 80 per cent were doomed to failure. Even so, the survivors added hundreds of new items to already crowded store shelves.

FIGHT FOR SHELF SPACE

The traditional grocery used to stock between 500 and 1,000 items. The modern supermarket may carry as many as 15,000 items (though most carry a number closer to 5,000). The cascade of new products creates a fight for shelf space. What happens to the marginal products? They are displaced, with the resultant waste that accompanies such a process.

This situation is highlighted in the report on a 12-week study conducted by the Progressive Grocer last year in six midwestern Super-Valu supermarkets. The Super-Valu study showed that the six stores in the survey had handled an average of 867 items in 1928, and were carrying an average of 5,144 last year.

Excluding meat, dairy products, baked goods and produce from the 5,144 products, only one product in 10 sold as much as a case a week. Only 13 items of the thousands in the store sold more than 10 cases a week. The average item sold 10 units per week and grossed $2.67.

During the 12 weeks of the Super-Valu study, 1,152 new products were offered to the stores. Only one in four—288 items—were accepted, and of those accepted, the failure rate will be high. Meanwhile, for every eight new products accepted, five old ones are eliminated.

The Super-Valu people foresee an agonizing reappraisal of the shelf space and new product problems during the coming year.

Such reappraisal is a constant process for the more careful (and successful) new product introducers. For they must deal with the one underlying reality of new product development—the fact that even the finest products must be backed by constant innovation (in style, packaging, etc.) to survive. . . .

A *Printers' Ink* survey of the top 100 advertisers revealed that each respondent had new-product plans. The reports revealed a strong trend toward bigger new-product programs. A dry grocery company with a limited line reported that it had introduced one new product in the past two years, would introduce three more items in the next two years. A billion-dollar giant which brought out 275 new products in the past two years, had 350 planned for the next two. A major fabric company reported a steady new product pace: 15 new

products introduced during the past two years, 15 more to come by 1960. Typical is the planning of Scott Paper.

Scott Paper reported: "We have been emphasizing to an extraordinary degree our new product research program and are making intensive marketing investigations into ways of introducing and promoting new products . . . our budgets for this important activity will probably be increased by as much as 100 per cent over the next five years."

To accommodate new product growth, Scott is planning about $14,-000,000 in capital plant expenditures this year. More money is planned for a research center and office building. McCabe's comments and Scott's spending plans reflect the general attitude.

▶▶▶▶▶▶▶▶▶▶▶▶ NEW-PRODUCT   REVOLUTION: *is management*
organized for it?

Printers' Ink

. . . The importance of new products cannot be overemphasized. The potential benefits are indicated by the experiences of companies that reflect what is happening in wide areas of marketing today.

SUCCESS STORIES

In 1950, Haloid Xerox, Inc., sold $10,027,000 worth of duplicating and photographic equipment. By last year,

sales had grown more than 150 per cent to a new high of $25,800,000.

With pardonable enthusiasm and pride, the company announced in a special report to its stockholders that 60 per cent of that growth—$16,000,000 last year—had come from 64 new products introduced during the last seven years. The attractive 12-page brochure made the point that without new products the company's sales figures would have been virtually unchanged between 1950 and 1957.

More significantly, the special report cited figures to show that new products contributed heavily to increased profits. In 1950 profits were $1,048,000. By 1957 they rose to $3,399,000 and the profit ratio increased from 10.45 to 13.2 per cent. The report notes that new products, "compared to our conventional items, were more profitable for us to manufacture and sell."

Campbell's Soup had 26 products in 1945. It has 91 now. The new products, to a great extent, are responsible for the fact that Campbell's almost doubled its sales between 1950 and fiscal 1958, when revenue came to $501,385,653.

Pillsbury sales moved to a record of $350,000,000 largely aided by an active new-product program. Pillsbury's 211 current products include 125 items introduced during the last ten years. President Paul S. Gerot says, "We have at least 25 new products being readied for introduction during the coming year." Gerot forecasts a 100 per cent increase in sales during the next ten years.

AVERAGES, EXCEPTIONS

There are many other success stories that illustrate the role of new products in company growth. To get a general picture, PRINTERS' INK asked the companies it surveyed to estimate the part new products have played and are likely to play in company growth. The result is a dynamic picture of progress stimulated by innovation.

All companies (consumer and industrial) reported that an average of 43 per cent of their 1957 sales came from new products introduced during the last ten years. They forecast that an average of 56 per cent of sales ten years from now will come from products developed during that period.

Separating the industrial companies from the three consumer groups, the figures show that the surveyed industrials realized 48 per cent of their 1957 sales from new products; for the consumer companies it was 35 per cent. The industrials forecast that 56 per cent of sales in 1967 will come from products to be introduced between now and then; the consumer companies predicted 57 per cent.

Several companies in the appliance and health and beauty-aid fields reported that 100 per cent of their 1957 sales were attributed to new products and that 100 per cent of 1967 sales would come from new products. Those 100 percenters were *not* included in the general tabulation. They would have boosted new-product percentages considerably, but would obviously have distorted the general picture, which is bright enough.

It is significant that—precise figures aside—the fact of rapid new-product development and its contribution to growth holds true for all but a few companies. It is also significant that this is one area of marketing where some industrial companies are as ingenious and successful as many consumer companies. In fact, business-machine makers, chemical processors and other consumer-oriented industrial companies have shown more new-product initiative than some consumer-product companies.

Another statistical measurement of

the importance of new products to all kinds of companies is the amount of money invested in research, development and marketing preparations. Generally, and with relatively few exceptions, research and development expenditures have moved steadily upward, particularly during the last five years. Expert estimates of the total spent on research and development this year range between $7- and 10,000,000,000.

An American Management Assn. survey of 833 companies in 24 industries shows that they spent an average of 2.8 per cent of sales last year for development activities. Generally, research and development spending is up slightly this year. Of the 24 industries, 18 reported spending increases of up to 26 per cent (for the transportation equipment industry).

BUSINESS MACHINE BOOM

There is an obvious relationship between research and development investments, new products and company growth. How close this relationship is can be illustrated by the experience of the office equipment and business machine industry which—like other dynamic industries—has grown sensationally during the last ten years.

Most of the companies in this field do not issue statistics on their research and development spending. However, close analysis of data that are available provides the basis for some sound estimates. Thus, it can be estimated that IBM spending on product development and research has increased about 700 per cent in ten years, from less than $3,000,000 in 1947 to more than $25,000,000 in 1957. The Burroughs

Co. has increased its product development spending at an even more rapid rate, from probably less than $1,000,000 before 1948 to an estimated $14,000,000 this year. The Stromberg Time Corp., one of the smaller companies, will probably spend about $325,000 this year to develop new products, compared with less than $30,000 as recently as 1954.

The experience of other office equipment and business machine companies is similar. Together, the companies in the field have developed thousands of new products since World War II, many of them producing sensational sales figures.

Industry spokesmen estimate that new products account for all or nearly all of the industry's growth. An indication of that growth is available from the Office Equipment Manufacturers Institute, which represents about 90 per cent of the industry. Members report billings to the OEMI and the institute reports that in 1949 those billings came to $721,500,438 (excluding revenue from the data processing machines, which are usually rented rather than sold). In 1957 the billings rose to $2,433,531,604, an increase of more than 300 per cent.

Similar success stories are available for chemicals, textiles and other industries. They offer more than ample proof that growth for any company rests on its new-product program. . . .

NEW? HOW SO?

New products, or new-product programs, are not new. Historically, industry has been interested in developing new products, and such industries as autos, appliances and fashions have grown on them. What, then, is new about new products? The answer seems to be this: While new-product development has always been a function of marketing, today it is the prime function. Marketing today seems to mean new-product marketing.

It may, in this form, be described as a revolution that resulted from the other revolutions that have taken place in the national market since World War II. First was the "technological revolution" stimulated by the war. The new advances in techniques and materials opened unlimited new-product possibilities only vaguely thought of before the war. With that came the sociological revolutions: explosive population growth, the exodus to the suburbs, the spectacular rise of income levels.

Along with those developments radical changes occurred in the tastes, desires and demands of the consumer. Logically, in the drive to satisfy these changing requirements of the consumer most profitably, marketing has become increasingly competitive. In this new competition, new products proved themselves the most effective tools. With production capacity continuing to outstrip consumption, the recent recession stimulated competition further, and the importance of new products in the battle for the attention of the customer was heightened.

DEFINITIONS ABOUND

But what exactly *is* new? As a general rule, whatever the marketer considers a new product *is* a new product. More specifically, the definition covers several areas:

Most clearly, a new product is something basically new and different, something no one has ever made. In their debut, synthetic fibers, frozen foods and electronic computers filled that description.

A new product may be something a particular company has never made —for example, the frozen-food line added by Campbell's Soup when it acquired the Swanson Co.

A styling change or an improvement in form or content makes a new product. Autos and fashions are the obvious examples. But this kind of new product would also include the added filter in Tareyton's dual-filter cigarettes, the enrichment of various processed foods with vitamins, or the addition of lanolin to a hair dressing.

Packaging has become an important element. The aerosol container opened new-product opportunities for shaving creams, hair sprays, toothpastes and scores of other items. The king-size bottle gave Coca-Cola and other beverages a new product. And Marlboro, after its smashing success with the flip-top box, has rediscovered the ancient soft pack as a new-product possibility.

A new product can also mean a new market (Kosher wines expanding from the limited Jewish market to the national wine market); or a new brand in the same line, to be sold either as a premium brand or a low-price volume builder. It could also mean a significantly new advertising program or a new distribution pattern.

In short, by the broadest definition, a new product is anything that offers a sales peg on which to hang a new buyer attraction. . . .

A TRUE FAILURE RATE

Hanging over all discussions was the spectre of failure. By now every marketing man has been told that 80 per cent of all new products fail. In the face of such a high mortality rate it is understandable that there might be anxiety and confusion. The anxieties induced by this figure are, quite possibly, at the bottom of many product development problems.

For that reason, if for no other, a new look at the 80 per cent figure is in order. First, it must be remembered that while it is supported by some authoritative sources, it is only an *estimate*. It is commonly quoted, but has limited application, and it is not supported by anything resembling precise data for all industry.

There is one other factor that diminishes the effect of that estimate. A substantial part of the failure rate is made up of products that were withdrawn after test marketing. It would seem proper to consider test marketing a part of the development process and eliminate from success and failure calculations any product until it is launched commercially through normal distribution. Computing success rates solely on the basis of products that were placed in full distribution would alter the failure rate considerably.

In any event, the success rate can be (and is being) improved. The problems involved often suggest their own solutions. There are no organizational "packages" that guarantee success. However, the experience of successful companies indicated that there are some basic development principles that apply generally. . . .

B

Some Central Ideas

▶▶▶▶▶▶▶▶▶▶ MANAGEMENT OF INNOVATION: *key to the future*

Management Consultant

Management of change is perhaps the most critical and pervasive task facing our world today. Society is undergoing a profound structural revolution characterized by multiple and basic changes in our economies and our social and political institutions. The new forms that emerge will be shaped, in considerable part, by our skill in managing change and our ability to master the *process of innovation* through which science and technology are transformed into goods and services. For innovation is at the heart of scientific, technological, and social advance in a rapidly changing and competitive world.

In view of its tremendous appeal and importance to our free enterprise system, it is important to ask what the concept of innovation involves, why it must be managed, and how managers and management can promote it.

WHAT DOES IT INVOLVE?

The central fact about economic activity is that it commits present resources to an unknowable and uncertain future. In effect, it is a commitment to future expectations rather than facts. To take risks is, therefore, the essence of economic activity, and risk-making and risk-taking constitute the basic

Reprinted with permission from Management Consultant, *Association of Consulting Management Engineers, 1962 Series, Number 1, pp. 1–4.*

function of enterprise. These are the facts that define the role of innovation. *Innovation is purposeful, organized, risk-taking change introduced for the purpose of satisfying economic wants and resulting in increased profitability.* It means not only adapting to new conditions but creating new conditions; and it is as important in policies, goals, organization, marketing, and communications as it is in the technological areas of product and process.

Innovation is the basic inner law of business as we know it. It occurs in two forms: (1) exploration and improvement within certain limits or parameters; and (2) the questioning, testing, and establishing of the parameters themselves. Unlike some of the other central tasks of managing, it cuts across all areas of a business. It may take the form of a change in design, in product, in packaging, in price or service to the customer, or in marketing strategy; again, it may involve new knowledge, techniques, skills, organizational schemes or policies—or a new kind of insurance policy that makes it possible for management to assume new risks.

Hence, we can see the error of thinking that innovation is the same thing as creativity, change, improvement, product development, invention, or simply research. Each of these activities may, in fact, lead to innovation, but they are not so ambitious and sweeping in purpose. They are not major areas of executive decision for shaping the company's future through the management of change.

During the years ahead, the greatest need for innovation probably lies more in the social than in the technological area. For the technological revolution itself will be unproductive unless it is accompanied by major innovations in the nontechnological field. The most important need for innovation is in marketing. Also urgently needed are real advances in methods, tools, and measurements for doing the managerial job (since the development of competence, skill, and imagination among managers is the greatest necessity any business faces), as well as steps forward in the management of workers and in the organization of work. Despite the progress made in these areas to date, they may well have the greatest potential for increased productivity.

WHY MUST IT BE MANAGED?

One of management's most important responsibilities is to keep the organization alive, alert, and out of the rut of routine. This is not easy to do, and no substitute exists for the personal attention of top executives themselves. There are a number of important reasons why they must be very much "in the act" if the company is to be innovative. For instance:

Rationalization of decision making Marketing research, cost analysis, forecasting, statistical decision techniques, and other tools have become increasingly necessary—and valuable—in modern business. However, they tend to discourage the venturesome spirit unless management holds them in check by emphasizing other values that are important, too. For the new tools tend to focus men's attention on the avoidance of mistakes rather than on the taking of risks. An engineering-type viewpoint tends to dominate instead of an entrepreneurial one; decision makers try to see how close they can get to being 100% sure before moving ahead, overlooking that in a dynamic economy you are lucky in management if your tests and controls can make you even 75% sure.

Knowledge and tradition In many companies a large body of experience and tradition is building up. This knowledge can be extremely useful and has, in fact, accounted for many an edge that a veteran organization holds over competitors. At the same time, much of this experience is continually being dated in a changing industry and is a liability if not discarded. Therefore strong leadership is required to show which of the traditions are still valid, or valid with modification, and which are not. Turning away from an old and cherished policy can be a painful and agonizing job, as many businessmen know all too well, and it usually must be done from the top down.

Accounting conventions Modern accounting focuses a strong light on the profit-and-loss showing and has contributed notably to good management practice. It must also be said, however, that established accounting practices favor conservatism rather than risk taking. For instance, if the question is whether to build a factory that will produce 300,000 items or one that will produce 500,000, accounting conventions tempt the decision maker to err on the low side. If he decides on the

smaller plant, accounting will not show the profits he *could* have made with more production and more imaginative selling; whereas any excess capacity in the larger plant, if built, *will* show up clearly in the figures. Consequently, vigorous management is needed to support a "nonaccounting" viewpoint and keep accountancy in perspective.

Authoritarian emphasis A great many forms and practices in business management (as in the military) favor doing things as instructed and in a uniform manner rather than in an inventive way. This tendency, reinforced by certain traditions of scientific management, often carries over into areas where it is not wanted. In a sense, therefore, management must counter forces for conformity that it has set in motion itself. It is also significant that I.B.M. has made studies indicating that the development of management talent is retarded in departments which are highly organized and overformalized.

Automation and cost trends As we invest more money in automated plants and expensive distribution structures, pressures mount to freeze product design and marketing programs in the interests of further mechanization. Innovative ideas must survive a lengthening process of checking, double checking, revising, postponement, etc. Unless management is continually holding this process in check, mechanization may become its own worst enemy.

Operations myopia Ambitious executives naturally like to make a good showing on current operations. This is as it should be. But a kind of Gresham's Law can work here, with the motives for concentrating on operations driving out the motives for critical reflection, which are needed for innovation. If management does not worry about this danger, who will?

Cultural drags Chris Argyris of Yale and other behavioral scientists are concerned that certain values in contemporary culture (abetted often by management itself as well as by unions, bigness, and specialization of jobs) are infecting executive-employee relations. The tendency described is for the employee to agree, in effect, to report to work on time, stay busy, and follow instructions in return for fair pay and being left alone by his boss. Such non-involvement makes it difficult for an organization to do more than follow old routines.

Need for a flywheel If innovation and change were to proceed recklessly and unrestrainedly (as they might if only "idea men" dominated), an organization would weaken at the seams and fly apart. Tradition, custom, and routine all have value for their cohesive effect. Maintaining incentives for innovation and pressing for new thinking, while at the same time keeping the pace of change reasonable, calls for the most discriminating kind of leadership. As John Glover and Paul Lawrence noted in a study of the Air Force Department: "The process of change cannot be so fast that one set of forces which make the organization cohere are jettisoned before another set has developed to take its place. To move

from one point of view to another, to master a new technique, to develop new relationships, is a time-consuming educational process."

In short, management is needed at times to control the flood of innovation as well as to keep the stream of new ideas forming.

WHAT CAN THE INDIVIDUAL MANAGER DO?

In meeting a company's need for innovation, there is a good deal that executives can do acting individually. To be sure, only a part of the need can be met this way, for the problem is enormous and pervasive, as we have seen. But the things that *can* be done by a manager working on his own are indispensable to the creation of an over-all climate conducive to innovation. Thus:

1. *He must personally believe in innovation and risk taking* He must really want to take chances and not be content to move ahead securely and slowly. A useful analogy comes from bidding at bridge. If you don't go down on a bid once in a while, you will never win many rubbers because you won't be bidding the full potential of your hand. When the stakes are higher, the tendency is to be more careful in your bidding—yet this is the very time when you need courage and daring if you are going to come out ahead.

2. *He will not hesitate to ask for innovation* As Irving Reich, Director of Proprietary Research at Carter Products Company, has said: "A manage-

ment which really wants original ideas and achievement will be tough in demanding these things . . . and will not be satisfied with an employee merely because he obeys all the rules and speaks ingratiatingly to his boss."

3. *He must make innovation a matter of continuing concern* Innovation should not be thought of as a mere project in his organization. It should be seen as being more in the nature of a process than of a task. Efforts to innovate should come regularly, at a steady pace, and on a systematic basis.

4. *In appraising accomplishments he should look at the risks that were not taken as well as at the risks that were* Coming back to our factory example, suppose that the smaller plant is built and Pete, the manager responsible, comes in smugly after the first year with a nice P & L statement in hand. That's fine, and he deserves a pat on the back. But could he have done even better by going all out with a larger factory? It may be hard to account precisely for something like forgone profits (perhaps one reason is that we executives have not asked our controllers for such data), but that should not deter the boss from focusing attention on them.

5. *He can ask questions that stimulate thinking about innovation* For instance, a marketing head might ask of any department head, "How can we develop better ties with our distributors?" Of a sales manager he might ask, "Are we getting enough new accounts and enough business from old ones?" Of an advertising manager he might

ask, "What improvements in marketing goals would help you to set more specific advertising goals?" Of an assistant he might ask, "How can we improve two-way communications with the research department?"

6. *He can encourage argument, criticism, and discussion over goals, policies, products, etc.* To use Chris Argyris' term, the "psychological work contract" which he makes with assistants and subordinates can be one that welcomes innovative thinking rather than discouraging it. If he really wants new ideas and concepts, the cost—more spirited controversy, friction, interruptions, etc. —will be well worth it.

7. *He can assign men to jobs in new areas and give them ever more challenging responsibilities* A sales supervisor can be asked to look into an administrative production problem, or an engineer can be brought into an advertising program. The fresh viewpoint and challenge of a "change in scenery" have frequently kindled new ideas. And within the same function, a promising man can be given increasingly complex tasks. Says Texas Instruments' President P. E. Haggerty of the way his company tries to develop a manager, "His reward if he is successful [on a tougher new job] and masters his crisis is an even harder job. He is faced with another crisis at a more difficult level."

8. *He can look to the right people for innovation* There is no sense in pretending that men are equal in their capacity for innovation. Indeed, acting out the myth of equality can do more

harm than good, for the true innovators will not get enough depth of opportunity and the noninnovators will feel threatened or confused by the responsibility. Just as there are some people who revel in creativity, so there are others who delight in precision, discipline, and improvement through refinement rather than abrupt change—and still others, of course, who are "half of each." The more perceptively the executive can distinguish between these groups, the better he can maintain a dynamic balance of talent in his organization.

9. *He can himself set a good example for the innovative spirit* This does not mean that he personally must be extraordinarily creative, gifted in imagination, or a genius. What it means is that the more he can teach the *importance* of innovation by personal example, the more he can inspire others.

Murray D. Lincoln, pioneering head of Nationwide Insurance, once subjected himself to a battery of psychological tests that his executives were taking. The examiner asked him afterward if he knew what his outstanding characteristic was, according to the analysis. Lincoln said he had no idea. "Persistence," the psychologist answered. "The majority of people who have run up against the things you've met would have said, 'Oh, it can't be done,' and would have given it up. You didn't."

WHAT CAN MANAGEMENT AS A TEAM DO?

A good part of a company's need for innovation can be met only by management working as a team. There are many fine possibilities for collective action, and no executive group can pursue them all. It is enough to take the essential steps and add one or two of the optional ones as needed. These steps are valuable not only for their own direct results but also for their role in making individual efforts more effective:

1. ESSENTIAL STEPS

(a) *Set goals that management must stretch for* This means that the executive team deliberately sets somewhat visionary goals and then tries its damnedest to figure out how it can possibly attain them. Let's assume what we want five or ten years from now is so many dollars' worth of sales at such-and-such a margin. How could we get there? We think up ideas under that spur that we wouldn't have otherwise considered because without it our tendency is to project each future year as a little bit more of the preceding one. We never feel the need for a new breakthrough. "I would say," says Frederick R. Kappel, President of A T & T, "that part of the talent or genius of the goal-setter is the ability to distinguish between the possible and the impossible—but to be willing to get very close to the latter."

(b) *Keep policy statements fresh* Some corporate goals are so fundamental that they are important for many years—e.g., a goal to be the industry leader in research, or to be the small-company quality leader. If, however, the same words are used over and over, they become just a rote, losing their power to stimulate imagination. Hence management must keep restating and redefining its policies so that they stay fresh and meaningful in the minds of employees.

(c) *Support vigorous research efforts* There should be not only financial support for research but also "status support"; i.e., the professional technical people should have compensation levels, privileges, and the kind of administrative leadership that makes it clear without speeches how much aggressive research is valued.

(d) *Communicate the right image* If the company thinks of itself as constantly creating and innovating, it should make sure that the outside world knows this, too. The main reason for such an effort is not to impress the investment community (although that is important) but to impress the market of future employees. If the company is known as solid, traditional in its ways, and grooved, it will attract the kind of young men who will help to keep it that way. The innovative spirits will go where there is more challenge and excitement.

2. OPTIONAL STEPS

(a) *Employ "Management R & D"* This is the name for an approach used successfully at Schering Corporation and other companies. The idea, briefly, is that just as new products are researched and developed, so can new ideas and methods of decision making —the executive's most important product—be created and nurtured. Management R & D personnel work anonymously through operating executives,

helping them size up problems, questioning, analyzing, and giving them new knowledge to bring to bear on their work. Innovations are likely to result in such areas as planning, procedures, marketing research, and the use of creative outside consultants.

(b) *Set up executive task forces to examine key problems* For instance, A T & T charged such a group to examine the way the company was organized to provide communication services to other businesses. How was the job being done? Who was doing it? How were the responsibilities assigned? What were customers saying? What needed to be done? It should be clear that the group is *expected* to disturb old routines and set off chain reactions of new ideas. Firm top management support is essential.

(c) *Promote young aggressive managers into the top ranks of the company* This step had best be done boldly or not at all. If the young men are not moved up rapidly enough, some proponents of the idea believe, the old-timers are likely to convince them that the best ways are the safe, tested ones. The approach has obvious drawbacks, of course, because the executives over whom the newcomers are promoted may lose confidence—and get their toes stepped on besides. But at times this cost is small compared to the values to be gained.

(d) *Appoint a "Vice President in Charge of Innovation"* Under this scheme a responsible executive is freed from routine and given the job of picking holes in current procedures, challenging company policies, and in general stirring people up. There shouldn't be so many feelings of coziness, under this system, and there will probably be more discontent—both results conducive to innovation.

(e) *Establish a permanent "idea group"* This step calls for chartering a team of executives to consider and work out all ideas of fundamental long-range revolutionary potential for the firm, regardless of their present feasibility or profitability. The approach is similar in concept to the previous one but requires a greater organizational commitment. Proponents argue that in a typical firm the men in charge of operations are almost *necessarily* unreceptive to offbeat ideas and radical proposals, hence a fairly large and powerful counterthrust is necessary on behalf of innovation. The idea group should keep its doors open to suggestions from all levels, and its work should be widely and continuously publicized throughout the company.

CONCLUSION

In sum, there are many things we don't know about innovation. We can't predict well in advance which men of a group will be the innovators, and we know little about some of the social and cultural factors that affect the rate of innovation in a company. But there are also many things we do know about the subject. We know that:

Growth is the child of innovation, of creativity, of constant replacement of the old by the new, however successful the old may have been in the past or still is today.

Innovation is one of the central tasks of managing, and objectives or goals should be established for it on a short- and long-term basis.

Management itself must be creative if it is to meet successfully tomorrow's challenges.

Probably the most significant element in achieving employee creativity is management cooperation and backing. Management must assume responsibility for providing employees with opportunity, stimulation, climate, incentives, and recognition.

Management must learn how to fuse creative talent to an organization, mobilize it in a given direction—in a word, achieve the kind of innovation within the company which will serve organizational and social needs.

Hence, while innovation does not lend itself to a magic formula, it should not be left to chance. If we are to enjoy an increased rate of corporate growth, it is not enough to trust that random change, improvement, product development, invention, or research will do it. Management must itself take a hand in the process, giving full, vigorous, and continuous support to the work of technological and social innovation. Herein lies the key to an expanding economic system.

►►►►►►►►►► NEW "MANAGEMENT OF INNOVATION" MUST
FOSTER IDEAS, HALT BOREDOM, OVER-
CENTRALIZATION, DISTASTE FOR CHANGE

WILLIAM T. BRADY*

If the title of my talk ["The Management of Innovation"] doesn't include the words *advertising* and *marketing*, and if there is only infrequent mention of your profession during the course of these remarks, please appreciate the position I'm in. I would not presume to talk to architects about blueprints, to mathematicians about equations, lawyers about writs and torts, or marketing men about advertising and promotion. Because you are businessmen, though, and because it is your job to be especially creative, we share a common concern for the care and feeding of ideas, the management of change and innovation.

Each in his own way, within the context of his own work, we must find ways to encourage innovation and manage it properly. We *must* because the management of change is perhaps the most critical and pervasive task facing our world today. The shape of the world's population, the shape of our economies, of the social structure of our many societies, of politics and government, of education and of religion—all are in a state of flux of more than considerable pace and magnitude. And what new forms emerge will be, at least in part, shaped by our skills and knowledge of the process of innovation and our skill in managing change.

Just as energy is the basis of life itself, and ideas the source of innovation, so is innovation the vital spark of all man-made change, improvement and progress. If we believe our capacities are yet unfilled, that our business is still unfinished, we must then accept that our future, and that of mankind itself, depends first, last and always on innovation—on rearranging the known to create something new. This is my thesis.

The task is both awesome and challenging: Awesome in the sense that its scope is so wide and varied and the responsibility so great; challenging in the sense that a huge potential is yet underdeveloped. We must accept that challenge with vigor, confidently.

PROBLEM: CHANGING THINGS UPSETS PEOPLE

Let us turn now to the problem of change and of innovation and explore this together.

The problem is that most people seek a pattern of order and constancy in life—not change. They are not re-

Reprinted with permission from Advertising Age, *December 4, 1961, pp. 67–69.*

* *Chairman of the Board, Corn Products Refining Company.*

ceptive to rearrangements, and when these are suggested they are disturbed, upset, and sometimes even hostile.

You, of all people, are least likely to accept that nothing can be done about this. You have brought about many changes in consumer habits by informing, reasoning and inducing them into being. And despite all the overt and hidden persuasion that what you're doing is darkly sinister, you know that the world is in debt to you for what you have accomplished. You share, I'm sure, my conviction that innovation is the basic function of management, whether of industry, politics, science, or the arts, and that management must coax and coddle it into being.

We know painfully little about the process of innovation. We occasionally mine and refine previous innovation, but we often bungle the job of creating new sources, or even conserving those available to us. The answers seem to have escaped even the greatest of our enterprises.

Consider this fact: Of the 100 largest U.S. companies in 1900, only 36 were among the 100 largest in 1948. Industrial leadership is easily lost. Crowns are never tacked on securely. The majority of companies included among the top 100 today have reached their position within the last two decades. They are the companies which have developed and grown to meet changing conditions. They are the innovators. They are the ones who have started new industries. They have transformed old industries to meet consumer preferences—some of which their advertis-

ing helped create or influence. And, of course, it's not at all coincidental that most of them are also among the 100 top advertisers.

I don't mean to leave you with the impression that only a few enterprises are really innovating. From what I see and read, many are. But no one who can hear the clock ticking away on America's precious leadtime, who feels the urgency of human need, can be satisfied with our degree of progress.

I don't mean to suggest, either, that few people are innovating. From what I see and hear, there is no shortage of ideas, big and little, in all our organizations. But no one who has seen the way big ideas shrink into old familiar forms, as they pass through established channels, can be satisfied that our organizations are innovating as much as they could.

Not only is the search for innovation a significant one today, it is also urgent.

What time there is need not be spent in identifying and analyzing innovation or creative thinking. We know it when we see it. However, we do have to identify those things which stifle it, and root them out. Let me try, then, to put my finger on a few of the inhibitors to genuine creative thinking.

IS SOCIETY SHUNNING CHANGE, LIONIZING MEN OF FACTS, NOT IDEAS?

First, in our society there seems to be a basic cultural distaste for innovation. Years ago, we admired and rewarded innovation and creativity. We were continuously in search of new frontiers. The innovator was a hero, not a nuisance.

Today, however, in sharp contrast to the past, innovation goes frequently unrewarded. We appear to have developed a critical disapproval, a kind of snobbishness, that looks down on anything new. We are fearful—and so resent those who upset applecarts. Security is the slogan of our society.

Reacting against innovation, we lionize the sensible man, the man of facts, the practical realistic man, the man who "gets things done." The man of ideas is too often thought of as "out of this world." And too often we leave him there.

Perhaps our society has over-structured its systems and locked its people in. Perhaps we have insisted too much on getting everything regimented. In our efforts to be efficient, we have created systems which wear out but which we are loath to change or drop completely.

All this is characteristic of a society in retreat. These are dangerous and demoralizing attitudes for a nation on the new frontier.

COMPANIES GETTING TOP-HEAVY?

Further, any company, operating within a climate at best only lukewarm about innovation, produces some obstacles of its own to innovation.

There is the tendency in too many organizations to hold power and decision at the top. It is based on the mistaken notion that the only competent, intelligent, thinking individuals are those at the top. These people mo-

nopolize the power of decision. They coordinate, they direct, they do what little innovating they have time for—they work hard. In fact, their work becomes so consuming that they have little time for anything but the day-to-day tasks. The man whose eyes are focused only on today is not planning for the future. The long-term perspective is missing or woefully inadequate.

With this clustering of power comes the building of empires. Little cliques of "yes men" spring up. Innovation takes only the direction the leaders want it to take. And in the struggles for prerogatives and status, the creative thoughts of people all along the line are stifled.

More particularly, and unhappily, often too, the objectives of the company—that is, its purposes—are subordinated to the aims and goals of its most aggressive and colorful personalities. The real business of the company, as a whole, is either poorly defined or forgotten. Each division or functional unit develops its own narrow aim and perspective. Decisions, unfortunately, are made in terms of their parochial interests.

Moreover, in such an unhealthy environment, fear and anxiety all too frequently foul the atmosphere. Caught in the pull-and-tug of the top leaders, many people are never certain where they stand. In such a climate it is difficult for them to identify with the larger organization or to feel any sense of participation. Rather, they must, if they are to have any measure of security at all, find it within one of these cliques. And if, like most people, they wish for advancement and bigger rewards, they soon realize they must play along with its ritual. Oftentimes the advice given to newcomers in a department is to "find out what the boss wants and likes"—and do it.

In such a sterile system, lines of communication are a one-way street. Information flows from the top and usually never reaches the bottom. Even *that* information is oftentimes screened by the top and only what they think is fitting gets through.

These, then, are some of the *organizational* factors which inhibit innovation:

1. Overcentralization of power and control
2. Lack of planning
3. The building of little empires
4. The spreading of fear and anxiety
5. Limited loyalties
6. Poor communications

INDIVIDUALS "ORGANIZATION MEN"?

A third barrier to innovation centers in the individual himself.

We generally live far below our creative limits. Most people possess creative power they never use.

Too many people in business are bored stiff. They are apt to characterize all their work by the amount of routine it includes—and all our jobs include a good bit of it. Going through the motions, shuffling papers, their work day takes on the character of deadening monotony.

It is almost as if men were being paid by the pound for their work. Their effort is measured in terms of volume of work, none of which may be really productive or lasting. And far too often none of the work is truly innovative.

Too often when the individual in business has gotten all wrapped up in himself, he loses sight of greater goals and is content just to "coast by." There are those who resist change because they are unwilling to risk the amount of social status they've achieved where they are. They have little ambition and jealously guard their own job against any change whatsoever.

Under these patterns in many of our large organizations there is a tendency to develop organization men, men who are concerned primarily with following a pattern which others lay down. Highly sensitive to what others think of them, anxious to please, dependent, their own individuality is submerged. They are afraid to take responsibility for their own ideas. They hew too closely to the line, and until they find out what the line is, they don't hew at all.

While some measure of conformity is essential in any large enterprise, I for one believe the balance between individuality and conformity has swung too far away from individuality. Creative thinking has suffered or disappeared altogether, and we are all poorer for its loss.

The barriers, therefore, to innovation and creativity lie in three areas:

1. Within our society
2. Within the organization itself
3. Within the individual

If we are to liberate our creative forces, we must eliminate these inhibitors, substituting a climate that facilitates innovation and growth. Let's look at what can be done, first for the individual.

MORE TRAINING NEEDED
IN SKILLS TO CARRY THROUGH
ON IDEAS

For one thing, we can provide an atmosphere in which the individual's sensitivity can flourish, rather than wither away. Creativity or innovation comes from *awareness of a need or a problem*. The problem or need may exist within the individual himself or it may be present in the organization or in the public it serves. To solve it requires an openness of mind—a capacity for being receptive to new ideas.

We must also enlarge a man's knowledge about what's going on around him and encourage and assist him to learn more about his own field.

We can give him the opportunity to develop and improve the techniques and skills of his work. He should get the basic fundamentals of his job. For while the novice may generate insight, he usually is in no position to use it to his or his organization's advantage. He does not possess skills and techniques to follow through on ideas.

This is important. To be a good idea it must be carried through to its ultimate conclusions. Otherwise it is a passing fancy—a wish, a dream.

It must be communicated; it must be implemented; it must be placed into effect. And here's the rub. Some can come up with great ideas, but they cannot implement. They are "idea men" and either cannot or will not carry

them through. However, we need these people. It's pretty hard to bench a .400 hitter who can't field. We must develop, then, their ability to implement, or put others alongside them who have abilities in these fields. In short, create teams capable of supplementing thought with action.

We must also provide enough time for the innovator to create. He needs time for preparation, time for the incubation of ideas, time for evaluation and redefinition and time for complete double checking.

We must give the innovator a forum for his ideas. He must be part of a "community of creativity." Such a community of interaction stimulates; it serves as a catalyst to others. And in this forum there must be free exchange of ideas, constructive criticism and disagreement without penalty.

Further, we must give the innovator a sense of belonging to management. For only if he participates in the formation of goals and only if he is part of the broad creative effort of the entire organization can his contributions be real. And don't forget, "People support what they help create."

DON'T PUT PEOPLE
IN STRAITJACKETS

We must recognize the dignity of every person at every level, in every department, every type of work. As I have pointed out, every man has, within him, the potential for innovation, no matter how little formal education he may have, no matter how humble his background. We must use every resource of every man, for his sake and for society. We must be careful that we do not put people in straitjackets—that we do not try to make them over in our own image and likeness. For when we try, the individual becomes only the caricature of himself, a pathetic "Me Too-er."

These keen and sensitive words of Thoreau have long been a favorite of mine and are so appropriate here:

If a man does not keep pace with his companions, perhaps it is because he hears a different drummer. Let him step to the music which he hears, however measured or far away.

Now, the world's work must be done. Yet we must strive to permit differences and indeed to preserve them—well within the framework of constructive policy and direction. We can take no other course.

This is not a one-way street. The individual must give something in return. I refer to responsibility and a sense of dedication. Responsibility is primarily personal. It implies a sense of obligation for benefits received and a willingness to justify them by his own best efforts. Responsibility cannot be imposed. Rather, it must come from within the individual.

And most importantly, every individual must find his own sense of purpose, his area of dedication. He must develop a strong sense of what needs to be done, a constructive discontent. He must be concerned by what does exist and be excited about what could exist. Creativity comes only to those who are intensely committed—from men with a burning desire that every tomorrow be better than today.

These are the conditions which tend to stimulate the natural growth of creativity in the individual . . . an environment of freedom and participation on the one hand, and the prepared, responsible individual on the other.

Now let me try to distinguish for you between what we can—or must—do for individuals, and what I would call "the management of innovation." This, in effect, translates a number of these principles concerning the treatment of individuals into organizational terms.

First there is the relationship of supervisor to subordinate, of associate to associate.

It's probably quite true that a person's activity is geared in large measure to what his boss wants or expects him to do. The manager sets the stage, creates the role. And while one's associates are also important in setting expectations, in the end it is the boss who has the greatest influence.

Therefore, what the supervisor does or does not do in fostering innovation is crucial. He can crush it, stifle it, condemn it, or he can cultivate and encourage it. But all too often, he resists any creative effort by a subordinate, because for him change is disturbing. It may require more work on his part.

MANAGER'S SKILL IS PARTLY HOW WELL HE FOSTERS INNOVATION

The answer is that management must reward the supervisor who encourages innovation in himself, in his line and staff. The individual who innovates must be rewarded. So also, greater recognition must be given the supervisor under whom it takes place. Both are necessary.

In my company, for example, we are well along with just such a program. I receive periodic reports on all innovations. We investigate, and the superior of the person who made the innovation is rewarded. Our incentive program is directly geared in. A very important part of a manager's list of responsibilities is how well he fosters innovation. While this may not be the full and complete answer, results so far indicate that we are moving in the right direction.

Coupled with this is a strong program in long-range corporate planning. This involves establishing long-range objectives, the continued examination of what lines of business we should be in, intensive studies of our emerging economy and the formulation of plans well into the future. And while I have a top corporate staff on this, and devote a great deal of my time personally to it, the real responsibility for action rests with the operating divisions—with the line.

Further, our system of communication must be open. And when I say "open" I don't mean "loose." Communications have to be organized and properly channeled. But having done this, having taken care of the formal requirements, it is greatly desirable to get people in close touch with one another. The creative act thrives in an environment of mutual stimulation, feedback, and constructive criticism—in a community of creativity. Defensiveness and critical attack restrict and

inhibit. There is no place for either in an organization which is growing. Rather, the order of the day must be constructive and cooperative.

Organizationally we must provide for a system of sequential controls which will make certain that ideas are brought forward, evaluated, and carried through. As managers of innovation we must have a logical, orderly approach to new ideas. We cannot allow ourselves to become so infatuated with the idea of change that we are blindly uncritical of the merit and consequences of suggested changes.

FILL POSITIONS
WITH PEOPLE ON MOVE

And lastly, I would set this goal: "Keep the path open to talent." Key positions within an organization must not all be filled with individuals who have gradually risen by mere seniority, who plow the same worn-out acreage, year after year. If this happens, no fresh talent is brought to light and much is plowed under. There must be sufficient open positions filled with people on the move, to provide the necessary on-the-job training spots. For instance, an assistant department head should never be chosen who does not have the capacity to move into the top job. We must exert the strongest effort to bring individuals of ability to the fore, men possessing energy, clarity of thinking and strong will. We need people to carry the mail—and we need people to be looking for new routes!

But talent does not always stand up for the world to see. It is frequently a shy thing in itself. It must be developed and groomed. Therefore it is imperative that we initiate long-range programs and plans for development, that we employ accurate methods for evaluating individuals and that these programs and plans be pursued vigorously and continuously.

I've just about spoken "my piece." It's a quick excursion through a vastly complicated area, one full of gaps, unexplored subjects, unanswered questions, questions such as:

The nature of creativity in the individual.

The conditions which lead to its development—the environment of creativity, the stages of the creative process and how this can be managed.

The way to develop more know-how and insight into the task of blending in the new without shaking established foundations. This is a very real and significant problem. For innovation means more than developing something new. It means dropping the old, the useless. How do we determine what should be dropped? What criteria do we use? These are difficult questions. We need to know the answers.

We need to learn how to fuse creative talent to an organization, mobilize it in a given direction—in a word, to achieve creativity within an organization which will serve organizational and social needs.

I submit that these questions relate very directly to your calling. All the more because I've been speaking to you not merely as marketing managers

but as business managers. As such, the most important thing you do is manage innovation. How well you, and other trustees of progress, manage this —your greatest responsibility—will determine how well our world survives the convulsions of change.

NEEDED: OPPORTUNITY, STIMULATION, CLIMATE, INCENTIVE, RECOGNITION

During my discussion with you, I have drawn a more or less artificial distinction between the responsibility of the organization to the individual, and the individual's own responsibility to his company and to himself. I could argue, quite convincingly I think, that in the final analysis, all responsibility is personal—that any organization is built upon these many individual responsibilities—that no matter how they may be allocated, shared, blended, or merged, they rest on men, and not on something as abstract as an organization.

It is to those men who earnestly assume these responsibilities that we may confidently entrust the future of the world's people and their problems.

It is top management which must assume responsibility for providing these people with opportunity, stimulation, climate, incentive and recognition.

That done, we can be sure the very highest priority will be assigned to the endless pursuit of innovation, and that it will lead the way to a better life.

►►►►►►►►►►► PLANNED OBSOLESCENCE: *the setting—the issues involved*

GERALD B. TALLMAN*

The words "planned obsolescence" appear to have sufficient emotional content that they generate a bit of fire in response, even before definition. Response from people thinking in the framework of consumers shows they clearly sense something unfavorable to their interest. I have discussed the phrase with manufacturers, and seem to touch an area of decided sensitivity. Clearly the phrase carries connotations of something undesirable and unfair. I assume that part of our problem is to determine whether or not this is warranted.

On the other hand, planned obsolescence cannot be completely bad since I presume the purpose of this conference is a planned one to accomplish the obsolescence of some information and viewpoints which you and I have held. If we do not approve such obsolescence the simplest way to have prevented it would have been to have stayed away. This is also frequently true in the market place.

The word "obsolescence" is apparently derived from the Latin verb "obsolescere"—"to wear out, fall into disuse." It is further defined as "gone out of use, as a word, a style, a discarded fashion." The word "planned" suggests the purposeful arrangement of steps for the attainment of some object, scheme, method or design. Putting this in terms more specific to marketing, I will suggest that planned obsolescence is "a purposeful program of vendors to shorten the time span or number of performances over which a product (or service or even a way of life) continues to satisfy customers—thus presumably encouraging an early purchase for replacement."

Let us keep this replacement element clearly in mind. Without it, "planned obsolescence," whatever its definition, would have little attractiveness to the planner. The user of the obsolescent product must face the end of its acceptable usefulness with a friendly feeling toward the manufacturer and the product—or he may exercise his free choice to withdraw further patronage. My memory of the fragility of one model of a 1946 automobile is still so vivid that I consider it most unlikely that I will again purchase one of the same brand. This remains true even though I recognize that the lack of durability in this product was the result of the manufacturer's effort to reduce weight. This weight reduction was presumably part of a plan on the

Reprinted with permission from Advancing Marketing Efficiency (*Lynn H. Stockman, editor*), American Marketing Association, 1959, pp. 27–39.

* *Associate Professor of Marketing, Massachusetts Institute of Technology.*

part of the manufacturer to achieve for me, the user, a combination of better performance and economy in operation. Unfortunately, some of the engineering choices made in the design of that particular automobile were erroneous. The result was a customer who, having first been made very happy with the product, was subsequently inconvenienced and permanently lost to this vendor. It is difficult for me to believe that obsolescence of this particular automobile was planned. Rather I think it was the absence of adequate planning and testing which caused the trouble.

It is always possible that the acceptable use life of a product may be shortened by ineptness of the manufacturer in the choice of materials or methods of fabrication; but this common fault of products, however wasteful, is not planned obsolescence.

Perhaps the term "planned obsolescence" implies that at the time of design and manufacture, the producer has rather specific knowledge of the ways in which the product's period of acceptable usefulness will be terminated. Does it also imply that he so designs the product as to hasten this termination by a choice of less durable materials or methods of fabrication over other better ones equally available and no more costly to him? I doubt that in our highly competitive economy this type of malicious product life shortening is common—or very rewarding to its practitioners. It is possible that a producer might withhold fully developed attractive features whose present absence and subsequent introduction may be used to encourage an earlier replacement of the product

than would have occurred had he produced the most useful and attractive product that he knew how to—taking into account the many compromises between cost, quality and features that are a part of any product decision. In the absence of a very comfortable lead over competitors, exercise of this choice may be very risky.

It seems more reasonable to assume that the producer makes the most advanced product practical (according to his circumstances and knowledge) and then hastens to develop still more advanced products which will so intrigue consumers that the old product will be replaced before it is worn out. Perhaps it is the kind of bait that is used to so intrigue consumers that is really germaine to the unfavorable connotations which seem to be associated with the phrase, planned obsolescence.

The words "acceptable usefulness" may be helpful in indicating the combination of subjective and objective appraisals which define the life span of a product. It may also be helpful to consider for a moment the basic question of why people do in fact buy specific products or services or adopt particular living patterns whose fulfillment is enhanced by these products or services. Fundamentally we buy products or services to satisfy some want, to achieve some positive functioning such as comfort or enjoyment, or to avoid some negative experience, such as pain or boredom. For most people in this country the standard of living is too far removed from the bare necessities of life for the word "necessities" to have much meaning as a specific determinant in the selection among alternative purchases. We do require nourishment and in this climate we require both clothing and shelter, but our actual expenditures for these common examples of "necessities" are largely determined by some elaboration far beyond the bare necessity level. We do not always seek maximum food value per dollar nor maximum insulating economy in clothing or shelter.

Perhaps I can illustrate this by one purchase which my wife enjoyed. The purchase was of a bottle of perfume. The odor was one which she tested and found acceptable, but I am sure the controlling factor in the selection of this particular product was its advertisement as "the most expensive perfume in the world." The purchase was made, however, in what we believe to be the lowest priced retail market in the world for such a product, in the little country of Andorra, conveniently located for smuggling between France and Spain. You may ask, "What heights of irrationality is it possible to achieve?" but I would maintain that in perspective this was a highly rational purchase if you will consider the nature of the satisfactions sought in the purchase of any perfume at all. Now having suggested some subjectivity in the rationale of consumer expenditures, let us return more directly to the question of planned obsolescence.

The quality of obsolescence, or that of no longer having acceptable usefulness, may stem from one of three qualities:

1. The first of these is the physical incapacity of the product to continue performance of the service or function for which it was presumably created—assuming that when it was first created it would in fact perform the function. Its deterioration from this condition may have been due to breakage, wear, rot or corrosion.

2. A second kind of obsolescence stems from the new availability of other and presumably better means of performing the function for which the old product was designed. This is the meaning probably most commonly given to the term in industry.

3. There may also have been a change in the user's concepts of acceptable appearance. This aspect of obsolescence is obviously important with regard to such products as women's apparel and you recognize its impact on many other products—furniture, automobiles, houses, and even of men's apparel, to name but a few.

The presence of any one of these three circumstances—physical deterioration, the new availability of better ways of performing the function, or changed notions in acceptability of appearance—may cause a product to be obsolete and encourage the substitution of a replacement product.

Let us consider some of the factors which determine the rate of transition of a product from acceptability to non-acceptability.

PHYSICAL WEAR OR DETERIORATION

For most products the producer has available a wide range of choices as to materials, design and method of fabrication which in combination can provide substantial differences as to the durability of the product against the wear and tear of usage and its resistance to deterioration—as from corrosion. These same choices may have a bearing on cost, upon appearance, upon portability, or ease of use and upon the adequacy with which the product performs its primary function. No single choice is likely to maximize all the desirable elements and minimize all the negatives. Rather, some optimizing compromise is desirable.

In the case of the automobile it is entirely possible that some substitution of heavier gauge metals might add to durability but possibly with attendant higher production costs and less good performance in acceleration, in gas consumption, and possibly in riding qualities of the automobile. A motor designed for lower performance in relation to its weight might well achieve durability at the cost of sacrificing other qualities on which the consumer may place a higher value.

Not all in-built lack of durability is the result of complicated choices among incompatible characteristics. Some products are simply poorly made and use inadequate materials solely to the benefit of the manufacturer's initial production cost, uncomplicated by a balancing of other conditions of performance. I would assume that the ability of some manufacturers to fool some consumers by selling to them products unlikely to give the service promised, is not a sufficiently complicated issue to warrant our attention here. Taken in this form, it is a fairly clear case of wrong versus right. Not so easily categorized is the choice

which a manufacturer and his customers must make as to how much quality is optimum. Some products, by their nature, are desired to have a short life. If any of you don a crazy hat this New Year's Eve, your sober reflections of the morning after may not involve much concern over the hat's durability.

In the purchase of most products, the consumer is offered a choice between products of higher durability and lower durability and frequently makes that choice in a manner to minimize the initial expenditure while consciously accepting the risk of an earlier need of replacement. If the period during which we have need for a product is expected to be short—or if its expectancy of acceptability in style or method of functional performance is short—durability may be sacrificed to achieve low cost to the advantage of the buyer.

In the limited literature about planned obsolescence, I find several references to razor blades with the implication that manufacturers purposefully design them to give only a limited number of satisfactory shaves. I have discussed this particular example with a possibly biased, but certainly well-informed source, namely the president of a leading blade manufacturing company. This company is in active competition with several other manufacturers whose products can be readily substituted for its own. This president stated that their goal is to achieve an optimum balance between blade sharpness, durability and cost. It is their experience that the hardest steel can be honed to the sharpest edge and will give the most satisfactory shave. Because the amount of steel involved is small, they find it no serious hardship to pay a high price per pound to secure this quality of hardness on a uniform basis. These hardest blades are of carbon steel which rusts quickly. By and large these blades eventually achieve unacceptability in usefulness by losing their sharpness through corrosion at the cutting edge.

With the availability of various stainless steels, this factor of corrosion could be sharply reduced, but it is not possible to produce from stainless steel as hard and sharp and uniform a cutting edge as can be achieved with the carbon steel now used. We see, therefore, that the managers of this company have planned obsolescence of their product in the sense that they have made a decision among alternative materials which has emphasized one quality, the sharpness of the new cutting edge, versus another quality, that of corrosion resistance. This is something quite different from the alleged malicious use of a non-durable material solely for the purpose of shortening product life.

Another example might be drawn from the radio tube business. For many years RCA has offered customers a choice among tubes having similar transitory performance characteristics but differing life span. Much of their product is purchased by set manufacturers who in turn face intensive price competition in the sale of the finished assembled product. RCA finds that most customers prefer to pay the lower price for a product with shorter life and that the more durable tubes have found their principal application in military fields where dependability is of the greatest importance, and in certain industrial applications where the costs of non-performance and of servicing clearly overbalance the higher initial cost of the long-life tubes. In this tube illustration the economies of scale in production probably further unbalance the choice because of the higher costs involved in the small scale production of the long-life tubes versus the scale economies involved in making the shorter life tube.

Far from promoting planned obsolescence, many manufacturers, under the spur of competition, are planning and accomplishing a prolongation of product life. Tire manufacturers, for instance, are working towards a tire which will give 100,000 miles of service with but little likelihood that the owner will replace it before it is worn out despite continuing improvements in riding quality, appearance and safety. Without continued growth in tire usage this quality improvement policy would significantly reduce the total number of tires sold.

Even the automobile, with its much maligned style changes, its higher speeds and greater annual mileage, shows a persistent trend toward higher average life. The average age at time of scrapping has almost doubled in the last thirty years.

CHANGED NOTIONS OF USERS AS TO APPROPRIATE APPEARANCE

This aspect of obsolescence is most apparent in the so-called fashion industry and involves that phenomenon in which our wives tell us that they "have absolutely nothing to wear" despite the crowding of commodious closets with dresses which are neither tattered, faded, full of moth holes, nor suddenly inappropriate to the size and shape of the owner. Though it is true that the clothes budget which results from this complaint competes for other uses of our money, analysis by the mere male seems relatively fruitless. I find that though I often cannot distinguish one style from another, my wife seems happier, more assured and therefore more beautiful when attired in a dress that satisfies her sense of acceptable appearance. At the standard of living generally shared by the American public at least, this enhancement of self-confidence and beauty seems to be the satisfaction for which the product is desired and therefore basic to its utility.

It would considerably simplify our appraisal of the goodness or badness of planned obsolescence if we could clearly distinguish between products on the one hand in which the sole emphasis should be on dependable and durable performance of an objectively rational function, and products on the other hand whose primary usefulness is in the satisfaction of more frivolous wants. Perhaps the hidden foundations of a building would provide one of the pure examples of the former. I am quite unaware of any aesthetic pleasures which an occupant of a building might get from considering its foundations except in the knowledge that they would continue for the life of the building to hold it solidly in place. The satisfactions to be derived from the upper parts of the building may be at least

in part dependent upon its conformation to our transient notions of acceptable appearance; but I think that all we ask of the foundation is that it be durable and solid for its anticipated life. At the other extreme there are products in which much of the satisfaction in their use is derived from the fact that they are new and that their appearance and method of performance are appropriate to current notions of acceptability. A new necktie for the man, a new hat for the woman, a new toy for the child, a new sales story for the salesman may find in their very newness, and departure from the past, the principal reason for satisfaction in use or ownership. Here obsolescence might be said to be essential to the very purpose of the product. Perhaps here we might have recourse to more philosophical concepts concerning the purposes of consumption as part of our life pattern.

I think it will be generally agreed that the vast majority of products lie somewhere between these two extremes. The satisfactions which we as consumers gain from most products are complex. The automobile is one of the most commonly cited examples. Certainly a part of the satisfaction which we get from the ownership and use of an automobile results from the flexibility, speed, comfort and economy which the product provides in serving our transportation wishes. Any changes in the product which detract from this aspect of the car's performance are, by this valuation, undesirable. It is generally acknowledged, however, that the automobile is far more than a mode of transportation. In many instances it becomes a quite acceptable means of displaying to the world the fact of economic accomplishment and the owner gets a very real satisfaction in the knowledge that he is travelling, and is being seen travelling, in a vehicle which is consistent with current concepts of acceptable appearance. The driver may also gain satisfaction from a sense of mastery of great power. We may philosophically question the merit or appropriateness of the standards of value which automobile owners satisfy through the latest and longest and lowest assemblage of shaped metal; but there have been ample demonstrations in the market place that consumers do in fact vote with their dollars to satisfy these subjective values as well as to acquire dependable transportation. The recent growth in acceptance of smaller and simpler automobiles may suggest that until these cars became generally available the consumer did not, in fact, have fully free opportunity of choice, and that he therefore accepted the elaborated Detroit models under some degree of coercion. I have not been privy to the rather considerable amount of consumer research on this subject made in the last several years; but I strongly suspect that the choice of a smaller and simpler car is not wholly based on an overwhelming preference for economy in transportation, but rather includes, at least in part, a component of subjective satisfaction in being different—in this case being different by appearing to choose economy. We all recognize numerous instances in which financial success and the ability to spend is most acceptably demonstrated in refraining from conspicuousness in consumption.

If we attempt to identify those who have participated most heavily in the purchase of small cars (even excluding sports cars) we find that they are not drawn primarily from those segments of population in which the pressure of limited spending power weighs most heavily. My own observation suggests that the purchasers have been most heavily concentrated among people who in other aspects of their consumption exhibit a strong urge to differentiate themselves.

CHANGED TECHNOLOGY OF WAYS OF PERFORMING A FUNCTION

We live in an age of rapidly developing technology. The rate at which this technology can be brought to bear on products for industrial or consumer use is subject to wide variation depending upon decisions by manufacturers and upon the acceptance accorded the new by consumers. So long as this technological change continues, present products will be rendered obsolete by new developments. The rate of change is subject to planning and control. It involves both decisions as to amount of expenditure which should be made to develop the bases for product changes and decisions concerning the timing and the extent of changes to be incorporated into products as offered in the market. Acceptance by consumers is necessary if these decisions are to result in profits. Therefore, it behooves the planners of obsolescence to direct their efforts and expenditures along the lines which will be most acceptable to the prospective customers. In the discussion and literature concerning planned obsolescence I sense some criticism as to the stages of development at which products are solidified and brought to market. There are many examples in which early commercial models of a new development were rapidly rendered obsolete and replaced by improvements. An example would be that stage of the television industry development in which only very small picture tubes were available and in which the early purchasers quickly found that had they but waited, they could have subsequently purchased a set with a larger picture tube at the same or a lower price. Without these early purchasers, the commercial development of the television industry would undoubtedly have been markedly delayed. Was it desirable that the industry offer to innovating customers the opportunity to buy an early phase of the product which the manufacturer, and probably the customer as well, knew would soon be supplanted through the rapid development of the industry's technology?

There is another aspect of products in a changing technology about which we hear much criticism. This is the alleged rationing of introduction of changes or improvements in a manner that brings to bear at one time only a part of the available betterment and holds back other parts for future introduction. Stated in other words, this is a program under which a manufacturer designs into a product an early obsolescence which could have been prevented by the concurrent introduction of other improvements already known and proven operable. Without specific access to the research and planning conferences of specific manufacturers, it is difficult to know how frequent is this type of planned obsolescence. We can know that at any moment in time a manufacturer has before him a whole range of improvement possibilities, some of which are fully developed and tested in terms of market acceptability, and some of which are at present only a most tentative notion and require substantial further development. In the determination of how far along these series it is appropriate that a manufacturer should go at a given time, before freezing a design and offering it to the public, we would need to have information concerning the certainty of his technological information, a general understanding of production changeover problems and knowledge of the market risks involved in the introduction of varying degrees of innovation.

In our time-oriented society we seem to make some direct correlation between newness and desirableness. I have noticed that many publishers manage to delay publication of a new book until after the new year because of a habit which they recognize on the part of potential buyers to make a judgment partly on the year of publication. Some years ago I learned to my surprise that even in the publication of high school Latin textbooks, a book was believed to have a better chance of sales with a later rather than an earlier copyright date.

In seeking an over-all view of factors influencing obsolescence we should also recognize that sometimes with no change in product there is a change in the opportunity or the desire of potential users to make use of the functions which a product performs. In part this may be planned obsolescence, not through product change but through influence exerted on consumer values and activities.

In attempting to arrive at any value judgments concerning the desirability of consciously planned obsolescence it is necessary, though confusing, to recognize three views which may be in conflict with each other:

1. The first is the viewpoint of the user seeking satisfaction at a price. The attempt to maximize this satisfaction and minimize the sacrifice in gaining this satisfaction may result in differing views depending upon the circumstances of consumers and the nature of satisfactions sought from the goods. Perhaps the optimum general combination for consumers as such would be one in which products were introduced only after having achieved some reasonable degree of efficiency in performing the functions for which they were designed. Obsolescence, which is so largely subjective, could also be reduced by some repression of stimulants to dissatisfaction such as the publication of news of better, or at least different, ways of performing a function and the disquieting information that those with whom we are competing in our displays of conspicuous consumption have some new way of getting ahead of us. It is disquieting, however, to consider the effect of such repression on competition and the producer's striving for product betterment.

In considering the question of whether or not the consumer will find rapid product changes favorable or antagonistic to the achievement of his goals we may pose several questions:

a. Does the consumer have a relatively free choice as between products of greater or lesser durability?

b. Do competitive offerings provide an adequate opportunity to choose between products whose basically functional design is less likely to soon appear absurd and those which are more devoted to the styles of the moment in either function or appearance?

c. Does the consumer have adequate information to appraise product characteristics as to their suitability to provide satisfactory performance?

d. How well aware is the reasonably alert buyer of the acceptable use expectancy of the product?

e. A fifth and more difficult question is whether or not the market forces exert undue influence upon consumer's choice by sweeping him up in some almost compulsive acceptance of new functions to be performed or in new ways of performing familiar functions.

I see the whole problem of planned obsolescence as involved with our concepts of consumer choice. It is not difficult to identify widely accepted criticisms of the extent to which our way of life is product-oriented in a striving for more and more products without which we previously managed to get along quite well.

2. A second view is that of vendors, whose total benefits as a group are enhanced if rapid obsolescence does increase the total of purchases. Rapid product change may also divert competition from that focus on prices which businessmen seem to fear because of its self-amplifying tendency to spiral. On the other hand, rapid product change

greatly enhances the risks of product acceptability and the forward investments required to keep abreast of competition. In products like women's apparel there is little question that rapid style changes increase the total of consumer expenditures for the class of products; but in a product like the automobile, with its important second-hand market, there is room for serious question as to whether total industry sales over a decade are much increased by the phenomenon of annual style changes.

The individual vendor may have little option but to follow industry practice with regard to rapidity of product change if the aggressors in his industry are finding consumer acceptance of frequent product modifications.

3. A third view is that of society as a whole and here I believe there is a decided schism. The viewpoint of society in seeking maximum welfare for its members may be concerned on the one hand with a reduction in the effort which the members of society must expend in order to achieve the products which they consume and a maximization of the wholesome satisfaction in consumption. This aspect of the social view might favor moderation in the rate of obsolescence. The other social view is that of maintaining a dynamic economy, high employment levels and levels of profit suitable to stimulate growth in our capacity to produce. In these troubled times the merit of continually increasing capacity lies not only in our ability to produce the products for consumption but also in assuring the availability of production resources to provide an adequate supply of materials for our defense in times of emergency. From this view a certain amount of churning about in the making of products and continual obsolescence of equipment and methods may be very helpful in assuring the availability in time of emergency of resources and not only provide continued production of essential consumer products but take on the tremendous extra load for war material demand.

▶▶▶▶▶▶▶▶▶▶▶ TOP MANAGEMENT'S STAKE IN A PRODUCT'S LIFE-CYCLE

ARCH PATTON*

It is relatively easy for top management to recognize the profit implications of price reductions, design changes, product obsolescence, and other of the more obvious competitive weapons where a particular prod-

Reprinted with permission from The Management Review, *American Management Association, June 1959, pp. 3–26.*

* *Director, McKinsey & Co.*

uct is concerned. But executives have been slower to grasp the importance of a product's position in its life-cycle as a basis for planning the strategy of profitable product exploitation. Too often their attention is focused on day-to-day competitive situations, or company-wide problems, rather than on the opportunities to advantageously shape a product's destiny that result from trends inherent in its life-cycle.

The life-cycle of a product has many points of similarity with the human life-cycle: the product is born, grows lustily, attains a dynamic maturity, then enters its declining years. Like the human, a product that has not built up its potential during the formative years is likely to be relatively unsuccessful in its maturity. And just as each of us must manage our financial resources during maturity to take advantage of opportunities or protect ourselves against adversity, so executives who control the destiny of a product must optimize their use of capital and human resources in the latter stages of the product life-cycle.

There are critical differences between the product and the human life-cycle. Every person has an average life expectancy—his allotted "three score years and ten." But the life expectancy of a product varies widely. When a dress designer creates the "sack" style, he probably expects that it will have little more than a year of life; the design of a Chippendale chair may be "good" for generations. Aspirin is still aspirin after 65 years, but jet-prop engines were virtually obsolete by the time they came off the drawing board.

Although man has fruitlessly sought the elixir that will extend his own span on this planet, product life-cycles—or phases of the cycle—have been lengthened or shortened by a variety of causes. When patents on the tubeless tire did not stand up in court, the product moved through the introductory and growth stages to maturity in less than four years. The automobile industry lengthened its maturity period immeasurably by what has come to be called "planned style obsolescence," which made automobiles a symbol of success rather than a means of transportation. (The auto industry's short-cycle model change based largely on styling has been tried in other industries with relatively less success. Perhaps if TV sets, refrigerators, and washing machines were parked in our driveways, the result might have been different.)

THE LIFE-CYCLE CONCEPT

Essentially, the product life-cycle concept is a simple one. It has three key elements: (1) products move through the cycle of introduction, growth, maturity, and decline at varying speeds; (2) unit profits climb sharply in the growth phase and start to decline because of competitive pressures during the maturity phase, while volume continues to rise; and (3) the functional emphasis required for successful product exploitation—engineering and research, manufacturing, marketing, and financial control—changes from phase to phase in the cycle as shifts occur in the economics of profitability.

At the risk of over-simplifying the

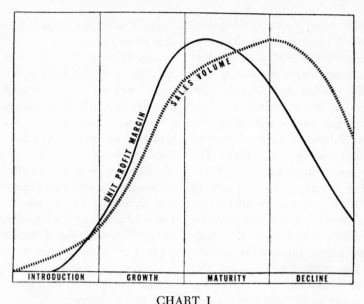

CHART I

PROFIT-VOLUME RELATIONSHIPS IN THE PRODUCT LIFE CYCLE

life-cycle concept, the chart on this page gives a view of the profit and volume relationships occurring in each phase of the cycle. The losses of the early introductory phase give way to soaring unit profit margins during the growth phase. Profits turn down—while volume continues to expand—in maturity, and both slump during the decline, or obsolescence, phase.

These profit-volume shifts, in turn, lead to changes in the relative importance of the various functions within a company from phase to phase. This is probably best described by a brief review of the distinguishing environmental characteristics in each segment of the product life-cycle.

THE INTRODUCTORY PHASE

The critical ingredient here is research or engineering skill in product development. However, skill in testing and launching the product ranks high as a factor in its ultimate success. Many a "better mousetrap" never saw the light of day because consumers did not know which door to beat a path to. Normally, losses are heavy in this period, for volume is too small to yield a profit in the face of high promotional costs.

THE GROWTH PHASE

The product having survived the introductory phase, the problem becomes one of getting a workable version on the market in sufficient volume to secure a brand franchise. This is of unusual importance for a consumer product, which must build acceptance at the distributor, retail, and consumer levels.

Thus manufacturing becomes the

key function. Many products have died in the growth phase because engineering or research tinkered with product design so long that competitors preempted the market by the time production got under way. Indeed, there is evidence that, under certain market conditions, volume is more important than product quality at this stage. The consumer apparentiy will accept uneven quality in a product's early growth period. However, it must be added that the extent to which a product provides real consumer satisfaction at this stage largely establishes the quality climate in which the product will live in later stages of its life-cycle.

This is a period of high and sharply rising profits for manufacturer, distributor, and retailer. Risks can be accepted that would be disastrous in a more competitive era, for soaring demand covers a multitude of sins involving hasty or ill-considered actions.

At some point in the growth phase, marketing decisions of great future importance are made. For example, agreeing to market the product through a specific distribution channel, or to sell only to the "quality" market, may become important restrictions on product maneuverability in the next, or maturity, phase.

THE MATURITY PHASE

As volume rises and the market becomes increasingly saturated, marketing steps to the center of the stage. Generally speaking, at this point all competitive products are reliable and there is less and less to choose between them. Improvements in the product tend to be small, with "selling features" or style changes dominant.

Profit margins begin to slip during this phase, despite rising volume. This results from each agency in the distribution process—starting with the retailer, moving back to the distributor, and finally reaching the manufacturer—giving up some profit in an effort to maintain or increase volume. This may take the form of one link in the chain absorbing costs that normally are borne by another (distributors handling credit and financing for retailers, manufacturers consigning stock to distributors), or taking over the functions of the other (as when manufacturers set up branches to replace distributors or retail outlets to by-pass both distributors and retailers).

Often overlooked in assessing product distribution costs at this juncture are the costs *beyond* the manufacturer's sales force—the profit margins of distributors and retailers. These costs loom large in the total product cost, lie closest to the consumer, and are the first to feel a price squeeze. If the experience of recent years is any criterion, price pressure on a "mature" product at the manufacturer level lags behind retail and distributor price pressures. This tendency underlies the movements among manufacturers to "get closer to the consumer" by establishing branches or retail outlets. Such a step is designed to protect the factory profit by accepting a break-even, or loss, if necessary, at the branch or retail level to move the product in quantity.

Creative selling may develop whole new markets for the product in the maturity phase, despite apparent saturation of the market. Cigarette manufacturers opened the female market when the sales to male smokers approached saturation; and deodorant makers reversed this procedure by turning to the male market after saturating the female market.

THE DECLINE PHASE

As a product becomes increasingly mature, the pressure to reduce costs in each step of the engineering-manufacturing-distribution process mounts. This results from growing price competition, as the difference between competitive products is reduced to the vanishing point and increasingly sophisticated consumers evaluate price and quality more effectively in their buying. The advantages of the "old" product versus the attractiveness of the "new" products coming on the market also play a part in the consumer's assessment of product value at this point.

The need for controlling costs, which normally starts while volume is still rising, becomes a matter of survival as the product moves into the decline phase. The few manufacturers of street cars, steam locomotives, and windmills still in business are the last of a long list of competitors; they survived by withstanding price pressures of the decline phase longer than the others, or by developing other products.

The dominant role of marketing at product maturity gives way in the final phase of the product life-cycle to the need for a coordinated control over all product costs: engineering, manufacturing, and marketing. The functional emphasis in a product's decline—and in the later maturity phase—thus becomes one of "managing" product expenditures to optimize the return on each dollar of cost.

The product can no longer afford

a marketing-, or manufacturing-, or engineering-oriented management. It cannot afford, for instance, to have the engineering department spend 90 percent of its development budget on marginal improvements with little consumer attraction; or to have a manufacturing department "under run" a seasonal product 30 percent to protect itself against being overstocked at the year end; or to have a sales department overestimate product requirements by 20 percent to ensure prompt delivery.

Each of the above decisions (they actually occurred) appeared reasonable to the functionally-oriented executives who made them, and, had the products involved been in the growth phase, the chances are good that these errors in judgment would have been buried under the rising tide of demand. However, each of the products faced the severe price pressures of late maturity, and company profits were sharply reduced by these unilateral decisions.

As the necessity for "managing" the exploitation of a product grows more acute, financial controls become increasingly important. So do the skill, resourcefulness, and courage of the financial executive. He becomes, in effect, the chief of staff to the executive with over-all profit responsibility, who alone has the authority to insist that functional executives develop a coordinated program to optimize product profitability.

So functional control comes full cycle in the decline phase. The executive with over-all responsibility saw to it that the product was successfully introduced; then he yielded a measure of influence to the manufacturing and marketing executive as the cycle unfolded, only to reassert his authority in the final phase.

SOME BIG QUESTIONS

There are those who believe that so many exceptions can be found to the product life-cycle that it has questionable validity. They point out, for example, that many products of venerable vintage—such as steel, brick, coal, cement, bread, copper, shoes, and window glass—fluctuate with the economy rather than conform to the traditional product life-cycle pattern. Similarly, a broad range of consumer and specialty items appears to be impervious to the normal life-cycle pressures. These include such products as drugs, patent medicines, branded packaged foods, printing presses, roller window shades, drill presses, saws, bicycles, and the like.

Some products appear to be less subject to price competition at maturity than others for reasons that are not always readily explainable. One segment of this fortunate group consists of relatively low-priced products with pleasure- or health-giving properties that people have come to believe in— and have little basis for judging. Products of this type are generally bought emotionally, frequently from habit or simply liking the product, as distinct from purchases that are made after a more or less judicious comparison of the merits of competing products.

The whole range of proprietary and ethical medicines, and certain proprietary specialties—Angostura Bitters and Hershey chocolate, for example—fall in this category. Another segment includes a large group of products that so dominate the market that their manufacturers are in a position to exercise great influence, if not actual control, over prices.

Durable consumer products, which are more subject to price competition than emotionally-bought consumer items, appear to have certain life-cycle advantages over products bought by industry. These largely reflect the franchise that a refrigerator, or shoe, or furniture manufacturer has at both the retail and consumer level. The new producer of a durable consumer item (radio, refrigerator) faces the costly prospect of building brand acceptance among retailers and consumers, even with a vastly improved or new product. Industry's hard-headed purchasing agents, on the other hand, are willing to buy a new product—or drop an old one—in short order if the reason is demonstrable. With less emotion involved in the buying decision, the advantage of innovation is quickly lost in an industrial product.

Much of the doubt about the validity of the life-cycle concept appears to stem from two basic sources: the economics of the production-distribution process, and the definition of what constitutes a new product.

For instance, anthracite coal does not exhibit the price weaknesses associated with a product in its decline phase. Yet domestic output of anthracite has been cut 50 percent during the past 15 years as a result of the competitive inroads made by oil and gas. The reason coal prices did not decline, of course, lies in rising union-controlled labor rates, the failure of a large number of marginal producers that were forced by declining volume to close down, and lower production costs stemming from mine mechanization.

In other words, the fact that anthracite coal does not behave like a product in its decline phase results from a combination of economic factors that made it possible to maintain prices, despite a large drop in demand, by curtailing output.

A substantial number of products that do not follow the typical life-cycle pattern are protected by the economics of their production-distribution process. Patents, a limited number of producers willing to live and let live, heavy brand-advertising expeditures, and a dominant market share by a single producer —all help a product negate the facts of the life-cycle.

However, the most complex element to untangle in understanding the life-cycle concept involves the question: What is a new product? For example, are stereo records a new product or simply an improved variation of the conventional monophonic record? How about the steam iron versus the dry iron? Or filter cigarettes versus the original nonfilters? Or fluorescent versus incandescent lamps? Or color television versus black-and-white TV?

The difficulty of determining under what conditions a new product moves into its own cycle and when it is a variation of an old product that merely fluctuates around the life-cycle of the "mother" product is a major factor in doubts regarding the product life-cycle.

There appear to be few universally recognized characteristics distinguishing the new product from an improved variation of an old one. Indeed, examination of a good many products indicates there may be several degrees of "newness."

1. *The unquestionably new product* Stereo records show all the signs of a new product at introduction: high price, severe performance problems, spotty distribution, and the like. As another example, the transistor does certain things better than radio tubes, and at a lower cost.

2. *The partially new product* The steam iron satisfies a consumer need— for dampening fabric—that the original dry iron cannot. However, the steam iron can do everything the dry iron does, hence competes as a general-use iron with the latter. Another example might be the portable radio, which does everything the table radio does and, in addition, can be readily carried about. The key here appears to be a product that extends the market, but also competes with the old product.

3. *The major product change* Basic technological changes may yield a new product that becomes a mature product virtually overnight by simply replacing the old product. LP records and tubeless tires are cases in point. The principal manufacturers switched from the old to the new product so quickly that the new product had virtually no life-cycle of its own.

4. *The minor product change* Power steering, remote-control TV tuning, and the like may give the product a short-term competitive edge, but they do not alter the life-cycle pattern of the product.

These examples indicate that a new product can reasonably be described in these terms:

A new product is a product that opens up an entirely new market, replaces an existing product, or significantly broadens the market for an existing product.

Since there are many marginal situations where—even with the advantage of hindsight—it is difficult to distinguish the new product from the variations in an old one, there is obviously considerable risk of error in assessing the future of an existing product. For many years prior to the war, for example, telephone installations fluctuated with building construction and the economic cycle. The telephone showed every characteristic of a mature product during those decades. Yet in the postwar years, telephone installations zoomed and far outstripped new construction.

Why? The answer lies in a change in the promotional philosophy of the telephone company after the war. The gaily colored phones, the advertising about the use of these phones in the den, kitchen, and so on, contributed to an upward push that renewed the growth pattern of what appeared to have become a mature product.

ECONOMIC FORCES AT WORK

Some industries have found it essential to *count* on relatively short life-cycles for their products. Ethical drug and package-cereal manufacturers discovered that sales of new products normally enter a declining phase in three to five years. Therefore, if product-development programs are not planned around this short life-cycle, company profits become unrealistically high for a short period and then slump drastically.

A patent-protected product may stay in the high-margin growth phase for years after an unpatented item of identical vintage has been subjected to profit-slashing price competition in its maturity phase. When the Ronson lighter patents expired a few years ago, the product switched from what appeared to be its growth phase to a highly competitive maturity phase virtually overnight.

Fundamental economic forces are constantly at work changing the life-cycle pattern of products. For example, the farm market is in the process of a major shift from small operators who look at farming as a way of life to large farmer-businessmen (and even farm corporations). Such a move is likely to mean that the distribution mechanism for selling the farm market will tend toward fewer and larger outlets. This, in turn, may well speed up the life-cycle of farm products as the more aggressive manufacturers sense the opportunity to gain an advantage by stepping up the tempo of marketing change and product development.

Studies of the product life-cycle face the problem that the four major phases of the cycle do not divide themselves into clean-cut compartments. At any given point in time, a product may appear to have attained maturity when actually it has merely reached a temporary plateau in the growth phase prior to its next big upsurge, or an economic recession can give a growth-destined product temporary symptoms of maturity. This means that it is frequently difficult to judge with accuracy the phase of the cycle in which the product currently finds itself.

THE LIFE-CYCLE AT WORK

Perhaps the best means of breathing life and reality into this concept is to trace the life-cycle of a product with which all of us are familiar. While the black-and-white television cycle is by no means completed, it course has been so spectacular as to put the spotlight on the economic forces involved in all except the final phase—and the economic pressures of this phase are clearly foreshadowed. The basic elements of the black-and-white TV life cycle have a bearing on all but the economically "sheltered" products, with patent or some other built-in protection.

TV'S INTRODUCTION

The first commercial TV set was sold in 1947. These early sets had small picture screens and huge performance problems, but the demand for television receivers overwhelmed all obstacles. Consumers were preconditioned to poor set performance, and scarcity gave them little opportunity at this stage to compare between brands.

The TV set manufacturers' major problem in the opening phase of the cycle was continuous product improvement. This involved both the elimination of performance weaknesses and the evolution of a more attractive and practical product.

TV'S GROWTH

The manufacturers had little idea, in the early days, of the set characteristics that consumers would ultimately de-

mand. There were round screens and rectangular ones. The early 7-inch screens expanded to 10 inches, then in rapid succession to 12, 14, 16, 17, 21, 24, 27, and finally 30 inches. Tuning systems ran the gamut from relative simplicity to Rube Goldberg complexity.

But one thing was clear: The consumer would pay a lot of money for almost *any* TV set. This fact touched off one of the greatest product booms in history. Within two years after the first set was sold, 60 manufacturers had TV sets on the market. By 1951—four years after introduction—the speculative floodgates had been opened and an estimated 100 manufacturers had climbed aboard the TV bandwagon.

All these companies did not start from scratch; some had great advantages. The major radio producers, for example, had a ready-made distribution system for their TV sets. Their problem was to maintain this advantage. The primary need of all manufacturers during the growth phase was to put a sufficient number of sets in the distribution channels to establish the company's identity as a TV producer with the retailer and the consumer. Otherwise, the producer had no franchise with either the seller or the buyer.

Profits skyrocketed in all distribution channels during this period. In fact, the clamor of retailers for sets to sell was a major factor in tempting many manufacturers into the field. The huge demand at this stage made for full margins in every step of the selling process and concealed the economic realities that would eventually assume control.

The principal claim to fame of a

sizable proportion of the entries in the "Great TV Handicap" was engineering skill, so it is not surprising that the basic necessity of producing sets in volume went unrecognized by a large number of the early manufacturers. Instead of turning out sets in volume for the hungry distribution channels, many manufacturers sought to perfect their product. But technology and styling were changing too fast, and a large number of entrants in the race never got beyond the starting gate—the design, or introduction, phase.

As the race for dealer and consumer recognition became more intense, the eager consumer acceptance of the early days turned to a more critical judgment of product performance. There was a growing insistence among consumers that TV sets should *work*. Performance problems had actually been reduced, but competitive pressure forced manufacturers to recognize—and do something about—consumers' complaints. Production still held the key to building a brand's franchise, but marketing was beginning to make its early moves in preparation for the coming struggle at the retail level.

Wittingly or unwittingly, all manufacturers were developing a product "image" with dealers and consumers during this stage. Some took steps to become known as producers of "quality" sets, coordinating their engineering, quality control, advertising, and distribution to this end.

Other manufacturers aimed at the volume market. This called for large production, adequate quality and servicing, and a saturation coverage of retail outlets. If distributors could not achieve the outlets necessary to meet share-of-market and volume objectives, other means of achieving these goals—such as company-owned branches—were tried.

Another group began developing an image with dealers and consumers as "price" manufacturers. Since few companies consciously set out to develop a "price image," it is probably fair to assume that those in this category had no product image objective to begin with. It's likely that they became "price" manufacturers to all concerned because they reacted on a price basis when confronted with problems in the market place.

The distribution strategy of some producers started to crystallize in the growth phase. The "quality" set makers began to pre-empt the "quality" outlets, often with selective distribution and price protection as a weapon. The volume manufacturers set about to force distribution by heavy advertising and promotional outlays, as well as by an increasing use of company-owned branches to secure adequate retail coverage.

TV'S MATURITY

As the product approached maturity, the "image" of various manufacturers became increasingly fixed in the minds of both retailers and consumers. The "quality" set maker was recognized as being different from the "price" manufacturer. This, in turn, led to a limiting of the number and quality of brands a retailer carried. In other words, the selection process began to shake down into a pattern that reflected consumer needs and retail economics.

With production rolling in high gear, and supply beginning to exceed demand, keeping the flow of sets moving into consumer hands became the manufacturer's dominant problem. Price pressures developed rapidly as distributors and retailers resorted to price-cutting to move sets. Normally, price-cutting moves like a wave—from retailer to distributor to manufacturer—and the impact of the price-cutting wave on the various distribution channels is partially obscured by the tendency of one element in the distribution process to "take over" responsibilities usually assumed by the other rather than cut prices. The reduction in total profit, however, is just as real.

At this juncture, many retailers simply stopped selling TV sets. They had entered the field because of its high early profits, found the servicing problem costly, and dropped out when profit margins plunged. An industry study estimates that one out of every five retailers handling TV sets at the peak had given up by 1958.

The dwindling number of retailers—and the growth of large, low-margin, high-volume discounters—coincided with the mounting need for factory volume and greatly increased the competition among manufacturers for a balanced representation among the remaining retailers. The sales job, which had been largely one of product allocation during the growth phase, now became one of securing outlets. This took salesmanship of a high order. However, it became increasingly evident that the distribution problem was not to be solved by salesmanship alone. Indeed, evidence began to appear that undue concentration on the sales and promotional aspects of the marketing process resulted in high costs that did

not yield a commensurate improvement in market share. An increasing number of marketing executives, noting this fact, began to reassess their positions. From this probing emerged conclusions that challenged old concepts and pointed to new approaches in strategic planning:

The complete internal and external redesign of the manufacturer's TV line each year is enormously expensive, and there is little to indicate that the consumer demands a complete overhaul. It was necessary in the early years because of the continuous flow of technological advances, but this is no longer true.

The large number of models and chassis required by the numerous early engineering improvements has become an expensive anachronism. Reduction in length of the line offers substantial manufacturing and engineering cost savings. And retailers favor shorter lines.

There is a widespread reliance among TV manufacturers on privately owned distributorships in big-city markets to sell their product, despite clear-cut evidence that the objectives of the distributor and the manufacturer in such a situation are frequently not compatible. As an individual entrepreneur, the distributor requires a profit on his sales to stay in business. Because of the marginal profit inherent in high volume, however, the manufacturer's profit interest is often best served by a break-even or even a slight loss on sales by the distributor (or branch) if this increases volume substantially.

These few examples emphasize the growing need for product expenditures to be "managed" to optimize the overall profit of the company rather than reflect the presumed requirements of a single function, however important. Thus, savings generated in engineering and manufacturing by reducing the number of models and chassis, or by stretching out the restyling cycle, might be used in bolstering the distribution process or as an increment to profit.

During the growth phase, a company could afford a light control over costs, since errors resulting from poor planning were offset by mounting volume. But this luxury is fast disappearing from TV manufacturing. Today there are 35 manufacturers left of the 100 who were in business at the peak seven years ago. A third of these concerns do 75 to 80 per cent of the industry's volume. Thus the need to "manage" the marketing of this product is apparent.

TV'S DECLINE

If the portable TV set is a "new" product, the console may well be in its decline phase today. Prior developments in radio set manufacturing—with the portable and clock radios reducing the market share of table models—indicate this is a possibility. Commercial exploitation of color TV, when that occurs, is likely to reduce the market for black-and-white TV.

The need for tighter cost controls and "managed marketing"—key characteristics of the decline phase—is clearly evident in television today. There have been sharp reductions in the number of models and chassis by leading producers. There is evidence that model-line planning is being better coordi-nated. Significant moves are being made to get control over the distribution function, to secure balanced dealer structures, and to provide the retail foundation for volume. Efforts to reduce manufacturing costs have found some producers taking steps to make or buy parts at lower cost in Europe or Japan. If black-and-white TV is not yet in its decline phase, all the signs indicate this may not be far off.

VALUE OF THE CONCEPT

Despite the many unanswered questions, the life-cycle concept has proved to be a sound planning tool when properly used. An appliance manufacturer was considering an expensive advertising and promotional campaign designed to create a "quality image" for its product. A survey showed that this particular appliance was in the late maturity phase of the life-cycle. Competition was keen, and the company's product had spotty distribution (rarely in "quality" outlets); it was considered a "price" item by retailers, and recent models had had serious performance deficiencies. If this product had been in the growth phase, attempting to change a "price" image into a "quality" image might have been practical. The fact that this product was in the maturity phase, however, argued that, in the short term, funds could be used to better advantage in other directions. The reason, of course, was that both the consumer and retailer image of this and competing products had "hardened." Any material change in this image would require a huge advertising and promotional expenditure over many years—and years were too long to wait for improvement.

Another manufacturer was considering eliminating wholly-owned branches in large cities because they were losing money. However, the product was a mature one, and field surveys indicated that gaining tight control of retail distribution in big cities was essential to maintaining volume. This pointed to the need for *more*, not fewer, branches, and led to a careful investigation of the whole distribution process. It was found that (1) company-owned branches had consistently captured a higher market share than the best independent distributors, (2) the *manufacturing profit* on branch volume easily offset branch losses, and (3) in spite of branch losses or break-even results, the company was generating substantially greater profits in branch markets than distributor markets having similar potentials—enough to make the return on large branch investments very attractive. In this case, a major decision was reversed because the life-cycle position of the product forced a more intensive study of the problem.

The life-cycle concept has been valuable in planning the future product exploitation strategy of many companies. For example, General Motors' early decision that a strong dealer organization was essential to its future success gave this company an important competitive edge as the automobile attained maturity. The decision of companies like Stewart-Warner, CBS, Raytheon, and Stromberg-Carlson to withdraw from television set production early in this product's maturity phase points to their recognition that

life-cycle pressures were working against them.

On the other hand, many companies have made decisions damaging to their product's position in the market, indicating that they did not fully understand the forces at work at various stages in the product's life-cycle. Servel, for instance, decided to switch distribution of its gas refrigerators from local gas companies to the more typical distributor-dealer channels during the product's maturity phase. The loss of sales momentum at this critical juncture in the gas refrigerator's life-cycle is regarded as an important factor in the company's ultimate withdrawal from refrigerator production.

PROFITS AND PERSONNEL

To be sure, much remains to be learned about the economics of the product life-cycle. But studies to date have shown that two critical management areas are best understood in terms of this cycle: (1) product profitability, and (2) the personnel requirements of product management.

PRODUCT PROFITABILITY

The fact that product profits are greatly influenced by their life-cycle position points to the wisdom of taking this into account in product-exploitation strategy. Great risks can be taken in the growth phase. Indeed, time is so critical at this juncture that such risks often *must* be accepted. However, a careful husbanding of resources is essential in the later maturity phase, when profit margins are so low that losses become very difficult to recoup.

Underlying any discussion of the product life-cycle is the pressing need for management effort to ensure the generation of new products to provide stability of company profits. This is particularly vital in industries where product life-cycles are characteristically short. The role of the research and development functions, and the strategy of merger, cannot be overestimated as elements in long-term profitability—or even survival.

PERSONNEL STRATEGY

The perspective that the life-cycle concept provides top management in the development of executive personnel can greatly influence company profits. When General Motors chose Harlow Curtice as its chief executive in 1953, the directors' action undoubtedly reflected the maturity of the automobile itself and the need for a strong marketing executive.

The shifting of functional job skills that are required in the several phases of the product life-cycle makes it possible for top management to assess future personnel needs with some accuracy. Research and engineering are the key in the introductory phase, manufacturing in the growth phase, marketing in the maturity phase, and financial and over-all management judgment in the decline phase.

However, since phases of individual product life-cycles are constantly changing and usually overlap phases of other products, there is evidence that a *balanced* group of functional executives is of prime importance. This need is attested to by the expanding product line of the average company. This means that more and more individual products are likely to be in different phases of the life-cycle at a given point. For example, the major TV producers also sell radios and high-fidelity equipment. Each of these products is in a different phase of the life-cycle: hi-fi is rapidly growing, TV is at maturity, and table radios are close to the decline phase. Thus each has different problems and opportunities and requires executives with somewhat different talents.

In the long run, since all products get older and the maturity and decline phases constitute the longest portion of the life cycle, a growing demand for executives who can accept full profit responsibility is clearly forecast. How these men are to be identified and trained is one of the problems that many companies, with an eye on the life-cycle of their products, are wrestling with today.

►►►►►►►►►►►PRODUCT STRATEGY AND FUTURE PROFITS

C. F. RASSWEILER[*]

In conversation among management people and in business forums the expression "product strategy" is heard more and more often. Among those responsible for long-range business planning, there is growing recognition of the fact that decisions regarding future products must be made as much as six to eight years before the products will actually become profit producers. Consequently, the mechanics of product strategy are demanding more and more attention.

Against this background, two aspects of the role of products in planning for maximum profits in the future will be discussed: the *importance of product planning in any growth program* and the *product life cycle* as a tool for product planning. This discussion will consider the kind of products Johns-Manville sells—products that are essentially materials. Concepts would necessarily differ in a discussion of equipment or assembled products such as automobiles or TV sets.

PRODUCT PLANNING IN GROWING PROGRAMS

PROFIT FORMULA

A simple formula involving the principal factors contributing to profit would be:

$$\underset{\text{A good product}}{\underset{A}{}} \times \underset{\substack{\text{Efficient} \\ \text{manufac-} \\ \text{turing}}}{\underset{B}{}} \times \underset{\substack{\text{Effective} \\ \text{marketing}}}{\underset{C}{}} = \text{Profit}$$

All three factors are essential for profit. Planning for B and C is dependent on prior planning for and decision-making about A in four ways:

1. The product must come first. There can be no manufacturing or sales without a product.
2. The nature of the manufacturing and sales effort must be adjusted to the requirements of the product.
3. The magnitude of the manufacturing and sales efforts is determined by the market potential of the product.
4. The ceiling on possible profit is set by customer acceptance of the product.

As manufacturing and sales efforts are improved, profit approaches the maximum potential of the product. Profitability can be further increased only by a change in the product, substitution of a new product, or addition of a second or third product.

TIME ELEMENT IN PRODUCT DEVELOPMENT

The substantial period of time required for product development further

Reprinted with permission from Research Review, *April 1961, pp. 1–8.*
[*] *Vice President for Research, Development and Engineering, Johns-Manville Corporation.*

emphasizes the key role of products in profit planning.

To be of value, a plan for profit growth must have as its objective the guiding and stimulation of *present* action. Merely predicting what may be sold in 1965 and 1971 has little value compared with looking into the future in order to decide what must be done *now* to achieve maximum sales and profit in 1965 and 1971.

The time cycle between decision and accomplishment is shortest in making changes in sales effort. Decisions made now about changes in sales activity can be effectuated quickly enough to influence even 1961 profits. Specific sales plans for 1965 need not be made until 1963 or even 1964.

The time cycle between decision and completed action is intermediate in connection with changes in manufacturing effort. Changes in manufacturing effort planned now may proceed quickly enough to affect 1961 profits; they are much more likely to be delayed in accomplishment until 1962, however, or if they involve major capital expenditures, even until 1963. The plan for 1961 production cost savings was completely formed before the year started. Broad directions of manufacturing effort should be considered now, but even rather major plans can be started as late as 1963 or 1964 and still be effective in 1965.

The lead time required for a major product change is longer, however. Between the decision to initiate development of a specific product and the start of commercial production and sale of the finished product from three to eight years elapse. Most of the new or improved products that will affect 1965

profits are either already under development or will develop from research already programed. Development of modifications of some existing products may be initiated as late as 1963, but by that time it will be too late to start planning radically new products to bolster 1965 profits.

It may seem unrealistic to consider six years as a normal period for development of a new product. But some examples will be enlightening.

Development of a plastic-coated asbestos-cement sheet was well along in 1946; and the corrugated window separators in the Johns-Manville Research Center represent one of the early plastic-coated products that did not hold color as well as might be desired. In 1950 acrylic coatings were among many plastic materials being investigated. Acrylic-coated shingles began making profit in late 1959, nine years after work was started on the specific type of coated product now being sold.

Terraflex vinyl-asbestos floor tile was first manufactured and sold in 1945, but the product was sufficiently developed at the time of the Chicago World's Fair in 1933 to permit Johns-Manville to lay the first commercially successful vinyl tile floor at that exhibition.

Seven years elapsed between the time Johns-Manville started to adjust European asbestos-cement pipe to American needs and the time the pipe business became profitable.

More and more companies are becoming conscious of the long time between the start of research and the realization of profits. As a result, planning in industry has become more and more a matter of long-range product strategy, the objective of which is to initiate *now* the actions necessary to provide the products that will be marketed four to ten years from now.

PRODUCT LIFE CYCLE

For intelligent product strategy, some method of surveying the behavior of products over a period of time is necessary, as well as a method for pre-senting graphically the best predictions of how decisions reached *now* will affect the future product situation. This has led to a new concept of thinking about products in terms of life cycles.

What is a product life cycle? What does it look like?

The first question is a simple one to answer. A product life cycle is the history, presented graphically, of what

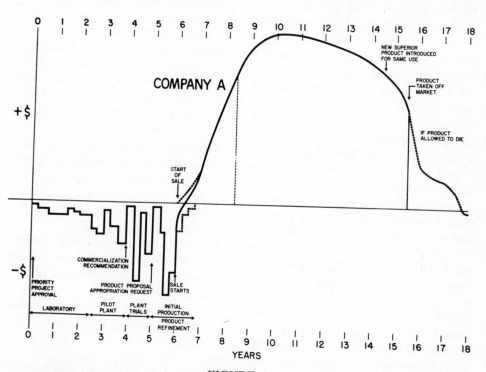

FIGURE 1

Hypothetical life cycle of a product assumed to be distinctly new and requiring substantial development expense. The life-cycle line, at the right, traces the rate of profit production on an annual basis. The development period, at the left, is plotted as a block chart showing the amount of expense by quarters. Since this is not a mathematical reproduction of an actual product history, exact dollar amounts on the vertical axis have been omitted. The horizontal line represents zero expense and zero profit, however. The area between this horizontal line and the line below it represents the amount of gross expense. The area between the horizontal line and the line above it represents the amount of gross profit. An overlap of profit and expense occurs at the point where sale is initiated, with the solid line representing the cumulative effect of these two factors. On the profit side of the curve, the area from start of sale to the vertical dotted line represents the amount of gross profit necessary to balance the preceding gross cost of development.

the product has done to increase or decrease company profits during the periods of development and sale.

The second question, "What does a product life cycle look like?" is more difficult to answer. However, a hypothetical life cycle (Fig. 1) will serve to illustrate the various stages involved and to permit discussion of their significance as well as possible modifications to improve profit potential.

In this hypothetical life cycle, the product is assumed to be distinctly new, therefore requiring substantial development expense. It is further assumed that ready market acceptance is achieved. The product rises rapidly to maximum profit and, characteristic of an item that satisfies a basic need, has a longer life cycle than could be expected if the product were vulnerable to styling changes.

In Figure 1 the life-cycle line, at the right, traces the rate of profit production on an annual basis. The development period, at the left, is plotted as a block chart showing the amount of expense by quarters. Since this is not a mathematical reproduction of an actual product history, exact dollar amounts on the vertical axis have been omitted. The horizontal line represents zero expense and zero profit, however. The area between this horizontal line and the line below it represents the amount of gross expense. The area between the horizontal line and the line above it represents the amount of gross profit. An overlap of profit and expense occurs at the point where sale is initiated, with the solid line representing the cumulative effect of these two factors. In practice, this overlap may sometimes cover a considerable period. On the profit side of the curve, the area from start of sale to the vertical dotted line represents the amount of gross profit necessary to balance the preceding gross cost of development.

Figure 1 plots the major phases of the hypothetical product's life cycle:

Laboratory development.

Pilot-plant activity designed to establish a practical process for large-scale manufacture.

Trials during which methods are worked out for duplicating the pilot-plant results on a plant scale.

Plant start-up and initiation of sale.

Growth as the product achieves market acceptance.

Topping off, dictated partly by market potential and partly by competition from similar products.

Gradual decay in profit production under pressure from similar competitive products.

Beginning of accelerated decline under the impact of some new or superior product intended for the same use.

Eventual death either by removal from the market or by gradual decay.

It must be emphasized that the life cycle under discussion is that of a single product, one which is a material, and not of an assembled product such as an automobile. Each time a product is introduced that differs sufficiently from previous materials to affect customer acceptance, the product must be considered as having its own life cycle. This is true for an improved product as well as for a new one. The life history of the asbestos-shingle business, for example, would be represented by a succession of overlapping life cycles of asbestos-shingle products each of which differs in a major characteristic from the others.

THE DEVELOPMENT PERIOD

The development period before commercial sale of a product is started is surprisingly long. It is generally accepted that the average product requires about six years for development and has a profitable life of about the same length of time. The hypothetical product under consideration here was given a six-year development period and a nine-year life span.

In planning product strategy these factors concerning the development period must be considered: availability of technical information, definition of market requirements, and promptness of management decisions regarding risks.

Availability of technical information The most important factor in determining the length of a product's development and the expense involved is the extent to which technical information is already available. The following sources of such information must be drawn upon:

Educational background of the professional staff.
Available scientific literature.
Basic research aimed at an understanding of physical laws and the properties of materials in fields of company interest.

Exploratory research, the objective of which is to discover "what kinds of things" might be made from certain materials.
Information accumulated during the development of earlier products.
Information made available by materials suppliers.

Every company has pools of knowledge in specific fields. Among the company's most valuable assets are its files of research reports and memoranda that record technical information collected over the years. To keep research costs at a minimum, the company must take advantage of this storehouse of knowledge, while continuing to record new material.

Since the life cycle depicted in Figure 1 and Figure 2 assumes entry into a relatively new technical field, the development cost is fairly large in relation to its eventual profit production. In magnitude, development cost might be approximately $350,000; sales, $1,000,000 a year; and gross profit, a maximum of about $350,000 a year.

On the other hand, life cycles that draw largely on existing technical knowledge show a more favorable ratio between development cost and profit. The first five years of the profit curve in Figure 1 are an approximate plotting of the record for a specific product. The actual development cycle for this product was only four years instead of six, and the total development cost was approximately $30,000. A shorter development period and consequent lower development cost were possible because product strategy called for a product that could be based on an existing pool of technical knowledge.

Profit and growth in the shortest possible time with minimum research and development expenditure is achieved by placing special emphasis on new-product possibilities and new-market possibilities that can be developed by drawing upon the richest pools of technical knowledge and manufacturing know-how the company possesses.

Definition of market requirements The second product-strategy factor affecting the development period is the accuracy with which the market and customer needs for a new product are defined. Lengthy development cycles and increased research costs are often the direct result of research activities pointed toward poorly defined market requirements, necessitating a change in objectives after large sums of money have been spent going in the wrong direction. Proper project strategy and adequate project definition avoid the waste of time and money.

Two approaches must be considered in a discussion of market requirements and growth planning: one, the necessity of serving present customers with a wider diversity of products; two, the importance of finding wider markets, new uses, and more customers for existing products and for products that can be developed from present technical and manufacturing know-how. Often the tendency is to place too much emphasis on serving present customers. Research and development programs frequently become so dominated by what the customer wants that the research staff finds itself in the position of a chef trying to supply orders taken by waiters who ask the customer what he would like to have without showing him the menu.

Prompt management decisions regarding risks A third factor in development involves the promptness of management decisions, especially as to whether the potential life cycle of a product justifies risks to get to the market quickly or whether circumstances make it desirable to sacrifice speed in order to minimize annual research expense and to avoid making capital installations that may have to be altered later.

In Figure 1 the development curve shows a number of flat resting points that represent periods in which actual technical development is essentially at a standstill while such management decisions are being made. A decision point appears, for example, in the laboratory development section where disappointing results led to work stoppage while the continuation or abandonment of the project was determined. Another decision point appears at the end of the laboratory period where it was decided whether or not to start pilot-plant expenditures. During pilot-plant operation, unsatisfactory results or the need for revised equipment and additional expenditure caused a stoppage, and again a decision was made on continuation or abandonment. At the end of the pilot-plant period the undertaking of technical project activity in the plant was decided upon. The first factory runs were not entirely successful, and there is a period for decisions

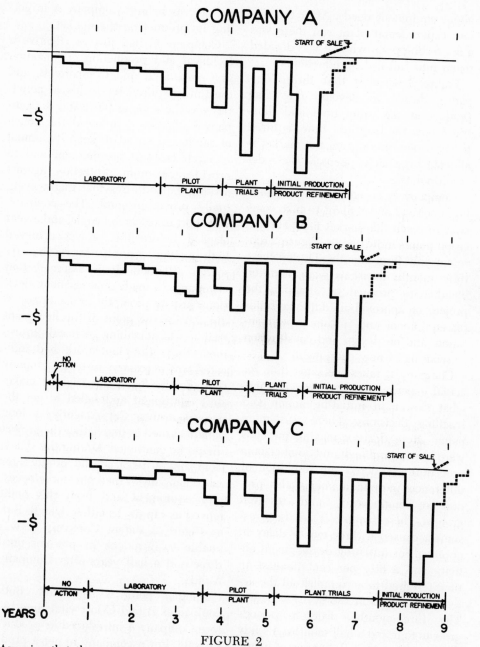

FIGURE 2

Assuming that three companies decide to develop the same product at the same time, the graph represents the length of time required for each to get the product on the market.

about equipment needs. After the second experimental plant run there was a flat resting point while it was decided to go into full-scale production.

Figure 2 assumes that three companies decide to develop the same product at the same time and illustrates how the length of time required to get a new product on the market is affected by what happens at these decision points.

Company A is aggressive, fast-moving, decisive, and willing to take some risks to reach the market first. The decision points indicated on Figure 2 represent only three months. During these three months decisions were made on whether to proceed or abandon the project, on approval of additional funds for equipment and further experimentation, and on design and construction or securing of new equipment.

Company B takes the same time for actual experimental work but is somewhat slower in initiating action and reaching decisions. There was more paper work; decision-making methods were less streamlined; and cumbersome procedures hindered the resolution of differences in opinion among sales, production, engineering, and research groups. These factors, it has been assumed, caused a three-month delay in approval for initiating development activity and a fifty per cent increase in time required to accomplish all the activities involved at the decision points. The three-months decision periods grew to four and a half months. A study of the chronological history of many developments will show that this is still a very good average performance. Yet, as a result of its looseness, Company B

was a year behind Company A in getting its product on the market.

Company C had just as effective a technical and production organization as Company A and Company B, and the time required for technical activities was the same as for A and B. Company C, however, followed the policy of sacrificing speed to keep its annual research costs at a minimum and to provide maximum protection against making expenditures that might eventually prove unsound. The company was short of research people, and a year elapsed before the project achieved high enough priority to receive research attention. It is assumed that Company C made management decisions just as promptly as Company B did. But at the point of the first plant trial it was unwilling to install equipment that pilot-plant work had indicated was necessary. Instead Company C made the first plant trial on makeshift equipment and failed to get the desired results. Consequently, a long debate ensued as to whether the project should be continued. During this delay, Company A released the product for sale. Company C then put in the necessary equipment and from this point moved as rapidly as either A or B. But, as Figure 2 shows, Company C was unable to introduce its product until three and a half years after Company A did.

Another point is significant. Both companies B and C lost vital time before Company A introduced its product for sale. For a company to get a product on the market as quickly as its competitors do, crucial management decisions must be made before the company knows about its competitors' activities.

FOLLOWING START
OF COMMERCIAL SALE

Now let us consider the portion of the product life cycle that follows the start of commercial sale. Ultimate profit following initial appearance on the market will be influenced by three elements of product strategy: ability to reach the market first with the right product, sales promotion, and product replacement.

First on the market with the right product In Figure 3 the development periods for companies A, B, and C are combined to present a hypothetical illustration of how delays in initiating production and sales affect the profits the three companies realize from the same product (equal selling effectiveness assumed). You may have your own ideas as to how the first part of their curves might run, but the important fact revealed by Figure 3 is that companies B and C cannot regain the profit lost in early years by extending the life of their respective products. Profit from the original product disappears for all three companies when any one of them introduces the "new, superior product for the same use."

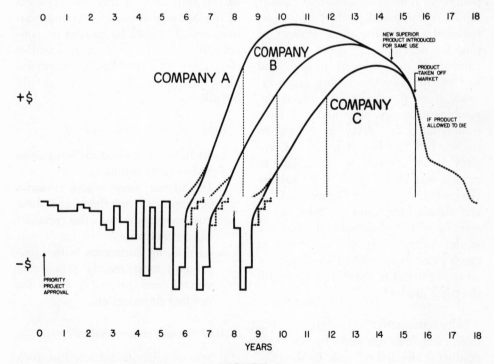

FIGURE 3
The product development periods for three companies, A, B, and C, are combined to present a hypothetical illustration of how delays in initiating production and sales affect the profits the three companies realize from the same product.

	A	B	C
Excess of gross profit over gross development expense	$2,295,000	$1,618,000	$927,000
Net cash produced by product after tax credit for obsoleting equipment at the end of product life	$1,091,000	$ 587,000	$442,000
Rate of yield on wearable equipment	12%	10%	8%

According to the curves shown on Figure 3, the financial results achieved by the three companies with the same product are as shown above.

The difference in results realized by the three companies was purely a matter of management decisiveness and policy. All three companies had equally skilled research and production people, required exactly the same amount of time for development, spent the same amount of development money, and had equally effective selling organizations. Even if caution had saved development money, it would not have compensated for delay in getting to the market. The loss of profit to Company B as a result of being late to market was almost twice the total development cost. For Company C it was almost four times the total development cost. No amount of economy in development expense can yield as much profit as spending enough money promptly to get to the market first with the right product.

Sales promotion The gross profit three companies can make from a given product is affected not only by the relative rapidity with which they get the product introduced, but also by the aggressiveness and effectiveness with which the product is promoted and sold after it is released for sale.

To achieve rapid market acceptance, activity directed toward establishing sales policy and selling plans for a new product should start long before it is released for sale. Such activity should start no later than the approval of the commercialization recommendation, and it should be carried on concurrently with the production activities concerned with establishing successful plant production. This activity should include:

Before starting commercial sale

1. Identifying and studying potential markets and uses.
2. Identifying areas where research is necessary to determine how customers can use the product most effectively.
3. Identifying customers with highest and most readily procurable volume and preparing them for product introduction.

After starting commercial sale

1. Special promotional activities such as advertising and press conferences.
2. Extra incentive compensation.

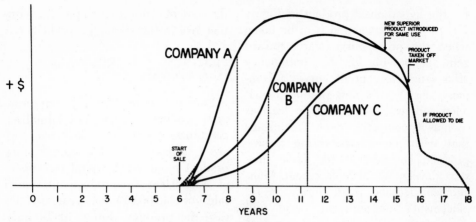

+ $

COMPANY A

NEW SUPERIOR
PRODUCT INTRODUCED
FOR SAME USE

PRODUCT
TAKEN OFF
MARKET

COMPANY B

COMPANY C

IF PRODUCT
ALLOWED TO DIE

START
OF
SALE

YEARS

FIGURE 4

One concept of the respective profits three companies, A, B, and C, might realize from the same product released for sale at the same time by all three. Company A has carried on the most effective prerelease activities and promoted the product with maximum aggressiveness. Company B has carried out much the same program, but has done so less effectively, and Company C has been content to ride on the coattails of competitors' promotion.

3. Specialized selling.
4. Technical services to customers.

Figure 4 depicts one concept of the respective profits three companies might realize from the same product released for sale at the same time by all three. Company A has carried on the most effective prerelease activities and promoted the product with maximum aggressiveness. Company B has attempted much the same program but has done it less effectively. Company C has, for the most part, been content to ride on the coattails of competitors' promotional activities. On the basis of the curves of Figure 4, the returns to the three companies are as shown below.

Even if Company A had spent considerably more on promotion, it would still have been better off than B and C, especially C.

Product replacement A third aspect of product life cycles can be illustrated by referring again to Figure 1. The most important product-strategy factor

	A	B	C
Excess of gross profit over gross development expense	$2,295,000	$1,656,000	$942,000
Net cash produced by product after tax credit for obsoleting equipment at the end of product life	$1,091,000	$ 873,000	$444,000
Rate of yield on wearable equipment	12%	11%	6%

for the hypothetical product in Figure 1 is to plan what action is to be taken when the profit curve starts toward zero. To provide for the continuance of a satisfactory profit curve, a company must have a new product developed and ready for release at least as soon as its competitor does. This means that when one starts selling a new product, he must at the same time start developing its replacement. Management decisions made during the replacement's development cycle will determine whether the new product becomes available when the life cycle of the first product starts to fall or three years later, when the product becomes obsolete, with consequent loss of market position. Again, vital decisions must be made before competitive activities are known.

Thus far, the life cycle for a single product has been considered. Obviously, any growth program must be based upon a group of products, each of which has its own life cycle. The objective of product strategy, therefore, is not simply to provide a replacement to take over when a product dies; rather, strategy should be directed toward providing as many supplementary similar products as possible so that the cumulative effect of a group of such products represents a constantly advancing profit curve without any aging decline. In the case of Johns-Manville Colorlith, it is interesting to note that the Industrial Insulations Division is doing exactly this. The profit curve for Colorlith itself is apparently topping off. However, Colorchip Colorlith is being introduced, which is expected to open an entirely new market in the furniture field and which, with the present Colorlith, will provide a further rise in the combined profit curve.

PLANNING CAPITAL INVESTMENT

Finally, the relation between products, product strategy, and capital expenditures should be considered. Figure 1 is based on a hypothetical new product requiring a capital investment of $1,000,000 to produce maximum sales of $1,000,000 per year. In this case the product, during its lifetime, produced net cash of $1,091,000. If, instead, this were a new product to be produced on idle equipment already in place, the product during its lifetime would have produced net cash of $2,308,000.

Two conclusions are obvious: First, the quickest and surest way to make future profits is to find markets and customers for new products that can be manufactured on existing idle equipment with minimum capital expenditures. Second, justification of a capital investment on the basis of the profits anticipated from a single product is difficult. Capital investment, to be really attractive, must have a strong likelihood of continued usage for the equipment over a period longer than the normal life of a single product. Hence, the prime objective is a product that will be profitable itself, but in addition will generate related products. The original investment will thus produce continually growing profits from an expanding family of products all related to and generated from the starting product.

Good investment possibilities must not be missed by thinking of one product only in estimating profitability, since the initial product development might well yield a questionable return. Rather, kindred products must be considered—products that may logically be developed once the field is opened.

SUMMARY

A major objective of growth planning is to guide the actions that must be taken *now* to achieve the results desired for the future. Products to be sold in 1965, and in some cases as far away as 1970, must be planned now. For entirely new products, more than six years are usually required to progress from initiation of research to profitable commercial manufacture and sale. Development of modifications of existing products without major new-process developments usually requires three or more years. To achieve maximum profit from new and improved products, the period between the initiation of development and full profitable sale must be shortened. Promptness of management decisions and management policies regarding risks to be taken play an important part in determining the length of the development cycle. To achieve short development cycles and low research-development costs, new customers and new markets must be discovered for products that can be developed with available pools of technical and manufacturing know-how and that can be manufactured on existing equipment. One of the major responsibilities of product-strategy planners is to find profitable opportunities for the accomplishment of these results. Finally, particularly in cases involving major new capital investment, high priority should be given to products that will not only be profitable in themselves, but will also lead to the development of a whole family of closely related, salable products based on the same technology and capital investment.

►►►►►►►►►►►► HOW TO USE "PRODUCT LIFE CYCLE" IN MARKETING DECISIONS

ROBERT N. WHITE*

If you know where your products are now in their individual "life cycles," you can sharpen your marketing decisions.

For example, awareness of product life cycles will help you decide whether to:

Push hard now for diversification.

Increase advertising expenditures this year.

* R. N. White & Co., Management Consultants.

Chop down your research director's budget.

Hire a manager of market research.

Set up a new product planning committee.

Every product has a life cycle. The product goes from its birth to its prime to its death, in various stages. Cycles vary in length—from weeks to generations—but every product or service has one.

AN EXAMPLE

I know a company whose chief product is past its prime, but the managers don't realize it. Many bold actions have been taken to stop the profit decline. But nothing has worked, and nothing will work short of product innovation. Many companies drain away profits waging a battle for markets they can never win.

Let's look at some rough "rules of thumb" about product life cycles, then use one of your own products in an example of how to determine where a product is right now in its cycle.

STAGES IN THE CYCLE

The *stages* in the life cycle are basically the same regardless of product. They are the stages through which the product passes from its inception as an idea, to "degeneration"—loss of market acceptance. The length of the cycle—and the length of each stage within the cycle—will vary with the product and its market situation, but these stages stages are constant:

1. *The introduction phase* where costs are high and profit often low.

2. *The growth phase* into which the product emerges as soon as it has developed market acceptance; sales and profits are on the upswing.

3. *The competitive phase* when profits and prices are stabilizing, new competition enters the field, and the sales curve is leveling off or declining.

4. *The obsolescence phase* when the market has been overstayed with the old product, and sales and profits are heading decidedly down, despite intense sales efforts.

5. *The drop-out phase* when it is time to bid farewell to a good money-maker that has run its course. Only sentiment keeps these burned-out products in the catalog. And sentiment and profit are poor bedfellows.

Different industries, of course, have products with different life cycles. Chemicals normally have long, gradual "curves" to their cycles. Toys (with exceptions like "Monopoly") have short, staccato cycles. Containers have many variations in cycles within the industry, i.e., cardboard boxes versus aerosol cans.

Let's take just one product in your product line. Can you identify where it stands in its life cycle at the present time? Let's see.

Note that the stages of a product's life cycle are stated in marketing terms. Properly so, because we are considering the product in relation to its market—to competition, to customer acceptance. Where a product stands in its life cycle is arrived at by *market* analysis.

LINING UP FACTS

Let's apply this market analysis by lining up some "easy to determine" facts.

What is the history of your product's life?

Has there been a fast or slow initial growth in sales volume?

Did the product design "hit" right off the bat, or were there bugs that had to be ironed out?

Were dealers or distributors hard to sign up?

What is the history of allied products, those similar in general character or function, as well as those directly competitive?

How long have they been on the market in their present form?

Has their growth pattern been similar to that of your product?

Have there been many "casualties" that you can recall?

ITS PRESENT

Having looked at the product's past, now look at its present.

Are your sales on the upswing, leveled out for the last couple of years, or heading down?

What about the directly competitive products? Is something moving up to take the place of your product?

Are customers becoming more demanding on price, or service, or special features?

Is more sales "push" required to keep volume up—because of competition on some items or on different products performing the same function?

Is it harder to get dealers or distributors?

THE COMPETITION

Now for some general considerations.

How profitable a business is this for you today?

Is it less or more so than a couple of years ago—despite close control of manufacturing and selling costs?

Is it so profitable that competition is still moving in—or are they starting to drop away due to lack of profits?

How easy is it for a new firm to get into this business?

Does it require a big initial investment which keeps almost everybody out?

What's the life cycle of the industry itself? For example, the electronics industry is obviously in the second or "growth" phase of its cycle, whereas the cast-iron stove industry is somewhere between obsolescence and the drop-out phase. A realistic consideration of the industry as a whole will often set the pattern of your analysis of your product line.

When you have jotted down answers to these questions, turn back to the definitions of product life cycle stages. If you have been able to put down even approximately correct answers to the questions, you will now begin to see a picture of the life cycle of your product—and the point in that cycle where you stand today. For this data is arrived at by *analysis of the impact of market growth, competition, profitability, distribution,* and the related factors represented by the above questions.

FUTURE IN FOCUS

By going through this process of analysis, crude as it may be for many, an image of the future for your product starts to come into focus. What can you do about this picture?

A soul-searching "think" about your product and its life cycle may well reshape the foundation on which you are going to base your marketing decisions for the next year, or two, or even longer.

Many executives have never stopped to realize how many of their decisions are keyed to their product's life cycle. Another word to describe life cycle is— the future. And where you are going with your product in the future depends in part on where it has been in the past, and where it is today.

►►►►►►►►►► TIMING: *how marketing masters it*

EDWARD A. MALLING[*]

In marketing there are only three kinds of timing—too soon, too late and just right. The decision as to just when the market is ready for a new product or design rests with the marketing executive, and the astuteness of his judgment usually determines whether the innovation scores a marketplace touchdown or falls flat on its face.

Timing in marketing can involve a couple of years or, in a seasonal business, the margin for error can dwindle to months, weeks and even days. Unless the marketing executive has a "feel" for timing, he may make costly errors. On the other hand, the executive who has the knack of sensing impending change usually enjoys a relatively long time span in which to prepare for shifts in market conditions or receptiveness.

Mastery of the art of time involves the ability to plan far enough ahead so that sufficient time is allowed for preparing a coming move with thoroughness and without error-begetting haste. The marketing executive must be able to decide whether he has time to plan slowly and carefully or whether the situation calls for immediate action even at the risk of by-passing certain desirable details.

EFFECTS OF TIMING

Good timing is surely an executive skill of great importance, and one that demands an almost prescient knowledge of the fluctuations of the market barometer. When this particular ability is lacking in a marketing executive, the result is often the launching of a new product or some marketing innovation either too soon or too late; examples abound in both of these categories.

Reprinted with permission from Printers' Ink, *April 20, 1962, pp. 60, 63.*

[*] *Vice President of Marketing of Titeflex, a Division of Atlas Corporation.*

An ancient example of premature innovation is the jet steam "engine" devised by the Greek mathematician and philosopher, Hero of Alexandria, around the first century A.D. It would have been an engine, had there been anything for it to drive.

The modern classic of "too soon" timing is probably the case of the Chrysler Airflow design in 1934. This new design was an imaginative breakthrough away from the boxy car styling of the period, and it could hold its own even today—one might take it for an off-beat import. But in 1934 the public wouldn't have it. The Airflow certainly was ahead of its time, but how far? Would it have sold in 1939? In 1946? Chrysler didn't get a second chance.

Also in the automotive field, the diminutive Rambler, introduced by Nash in 1950, had rough going in the beginning. The trend was toward bigger cars and more powerful engines, and the little Rambler didn't sell impressively until consumer reaction set in and "compact" became the most important word in the industry. From 1950 until that time, the Rambler hardly justified its existence—another example of too-soon marketing.

The automobile industry also has its problems with "too late" timing. There can be little doubt that Henry Ford's insistence on retaining the black-only Model T in the face of competition from the more stylish Chevrolet offered by General Motors made it possible for GM to break what had been Ford's firm grasp on the low-priced field. Furthermore, Ford's antipathy to change paved the way for the appearance of Plymouth, rounding out the "low-priced three" class. Around 1927, Ford sales dropped about 60 per cent through loss of business primarily to Chevrolet. And Ford's belated reaction, the introduction of the Model A, must be assigned to a niche in the "too late" hall of fame.

This timing error was a monumental one and, to a great extent, canceled out the advantage that Ford had won through its founder's genius for production.

Marketing executives have also scored some resounding successes based largely on their inherent "feel" for timing.

During World War II the great reduction in the availability of peacetime materials and equipment naturally hampered maintenance and repair operations in the electrical power industry. Unable during the war years to modernize their power-producing equipment, the utilities were ready to buy when an important innovation in turbine design hit the market in 1945. The ideally timed introduction of the reheat principle resulted in one manufacturer's selling about 30 turbines for every one sold by his major competition. Had the new design been delayed until after the post-war re-equipment boom was over, utilities probably would have adhered to their normal policy of dividing business among major suppliers.

PORTABLE TV
AT THE RIGHT TIME

The television manufacturing industry also has some success stories. Just as screen size was stabilizing at 17 and 21 inches, General Electric caught competition off guard by introducing the first really new TV concept since color —portable TV with a 14-inch screen. GE's head start in this field improved its market position considerably. Had the portable set been introduced a year earlier, it would have had to buck the still-current trend toward wider screens. A year later, a competitor or even the entire industry might have been high-lighting some other innovation.

Well-timed changes need not be limited to the product alone. Often a new idea in packaging may bring good results if the market is ripe for the idea.

The medical X-ray field shows a case in point. For more than 20 years improvements in this area were concentrated on the X-ray product itself, and the ever-increasing problems of too little space in the laboratories and problems associated with the usage of the film prior to use in X-ray equipment had gone unnoticed.

Through their long familiarity with the X-ray medical field, Ansco product planners began to sense problems associated with the laboratory storage of X-ray film and the time required to open and dispose of the elaborate light-safe packages. Because these packages were designed to contain only small quantities of the product, the frequency of the job itself was a burden.

A careful study by Ansco of the problems revealed that the customers themselves were becoming concerned about the limited space in the hospital X-ray laboratory and the high cost of delaying skilled specialists through the handling and disposing of many small boxes. In addition, improvements seemed to be indicated that would

reduce the cost of packaging by eliminating the elaborate interleaving between each film.

Once the customers' needs were crystallized, it was apparent to Ansco that it had the opportunity for a profitable change in packaging that might not present itself again for a long period of time. The Ansco marketing manager, working through the company's scientists, packaging designers and manufacturing personnel, succeeded in presenting a new concept in packaging that solved the customers' pressing problems.

To increase the customers' storage efficiency, Ansco eliminated interleaving and, at the same time, provided double capacity of film per box. Also, to improve the customers' handling efficiency, Ansco completely scrapped its previous packaging design and presented a pouch-designed, humidity-sealed, light-safe envelope packed within an over-pack and readily opened by pulling a rip-strip.

TOOK COMPETITION BY SURPRISE

With this well-timed and carefully anticipated change in packaging, Ansco succeeded in enhancing its product acceptability without changing the product, and sales climbed to a new high.

Competition, caught off balance, followed suit, but considerable time elapsed before it was able to devise a package offering equal benefits and, meantime, Ansco had placed itself firmly on a higher plateau of sales and profits.

Marketing executives, whose responsibility it is to decide the if, how and when of releasing a new product or a product innovation, might well take as starting points for deeper investigations the following considerations of timing:

Has the field been deluged lately by innovations, real or simulated? The need to counter developments by competitors must be weighted against the danger of having customers register nothing but apathy at a costly new change inaugurated primarily to make the manufacturer appear progressive, but bearing little relation to the customers' real needs.

Is the nature and present state of the particular industry such that competition will be able to react quickly, allowing little time for a marketing "edge"? Can an advantage be retained long enough to justify the cost of the innovation?

The effect of the innovation on the rest of the line must be considered. Does it make other items obsolete or unprofitable and, if so, can the old customers be serviced? If so, for how long?

How is the business climate in the particular field under consideration, and the climate in general? Are people in a mood to try something new? If the industry involved is in the doldrums, is it advisable to wait for an upturn or should an attempt be made to seize leadership while competition lags?

Even if the industry is not a seasonal one, subtle or little-considered elements should be sought that could, taken together, dictate a change in projected timing.

What is the trend of a particular trade? Should it be followed, led, ignored—or should an effort be made to change it?

How long can the new design be marketed before still another change becomes advisable or necessary? Could a further advance be made now, or would the result be too "far out" for the customers?

How long will the advanced product have to be on the market before the costs of redesign, retooling, sales training and higher overhead are recovered?

If the innovation seems inevitable, is it advisable to let the competitor take the risks and bear the costs, then move in strongly after market acceptance has been established? Or would too large a share of the present market be lost in the process, as well as prestige?

Timing can be a make-or-break factor in marketing a new product, a revised one or a new packaging scheme. Poor timing—too soon or too late—can bury fine and useful products in total market oblivion, whereas timing as an asset can be one of the most important tools in the hands of the marketing executive. Astute marketing men recognize its importance in organizing planned actions and assuring effective use of time, money and manpower.

part 2

Developing
a Product Strategy

Although it is possible to develop and commercialize new and improved products by proceeding in a hit-or-miss fashion, the odds against achieving success on the way are rapidly mounting. Staggering product mortality rates and the huge losses such misfires can entail, as the cases of Ford's Edsel and Du Pont's permanent antifreeze—Telar—show, point to the need for development procedures that will minimize the risks involved.

Much can be accomplished by way of risk reduction through a rationalization of the process of product development. And this rationalization can be achieved by the definition and, over time, the redefinition of a product line policy which specifies the firm's product objectives, the types of products and/or services the firm should seek to supply, and the markets or consumer groups which are to be served. Such a policy provides a strategy or framework which gives direction to effort and establishes a set of criteria on which to base decisions concerning additions to and deletions from the company's product offerings. It focuses attention, therefore, on the types of innovation which hold greatest promise for the firm and makes possible a far more consistent and systematic examination of proposed changes in the firm's product lines.

Success in the management of a firm's product offerings is largely a matter of skill in matching the firm's capabilities to market opportunities. Of course, this means only that in the direction of effort and in the making of particular product decisions a company should seek to do only those things which it can do well *and* which supply an unfulfilled consumer want. To be effective, therefore, a product strategy or product line policy must arise from a thorough and objective appraisal of the company's situation and a sensitivity to market needs. It must derive from a full recognition of the firm's strengths and weaknesses as well as from a careful and continual monitoring of consumer requirements. Why and how this recognition and monitoring must and can be achieved and how the information thus acquired can be used to design a product strategy which emphasizes the firm's unique skills and assets while minimizing the burden of its weaknesses constitute the subject matter of Part 2 of this book.

More specifically, Part 2 has been organized around these four topics:

1. *General factors in product strategy design* In developing product policy for a specific company, awareness of certain broad but fundamental considerations can be an important aid. These considerations are not in themselves the elements out of which product policy is compounded. Rather, they are factors which should underlie and guide policy deliberations. They are concepts and perspectives which, although general in nature, nevertheless throw into bold relief the nature of the problem and of the factors which should be taken into account in designing product strategy.

Among the considerations of this type discussed in the first segment of Part 2 are (1) the dual nature of the problem of product management; (2) the forces tending to alter a firm's product mix; (3) the principal avenues of product development and the influence of corporate climate and structure on the choice of avenue; and (4) the problem involved in defining profit objectives and estimating the probability of their achievement.

2. *Internal aspects of product strategy design* As has been suggested, one important element of a product policy is a set of criteria governing product decisions. These criteria are of two kinds. First, there are the criteria which reflect company capabilities—its financial and technical resources; its research, production, and marketing facilities; its pool of specially skilled manpower; and so on. Beyond these, however, there is another criterion which reflects the alternative investment opportunities open to the company or, in some cases, its aspirations. This criterion is expressed as some acceptable level of profits or, more appropriately, as a desired return on invested capital.

In the second segment of Part 2 types of criteria are dealt with. Procedures for appraising both a company's capabilities and the relationship of existing products and product line to these capabilities are discussed. In addition, the utility of the contributions-margin or incremental profit concept as the profit criterion in product evaluation is described and illustrated.

3. *External aspects of product strategy design* It is dangerous and often fatal for a company to base product and product line decisions on its capabilities alone. Examples of product failures that have resulted from such decisions abound, as the first two selections in the third segment of Part II demonstrate. After all, a company's skills and assets have value in our economy only to the

extent that they can provide want-satisfaction for some significant segment of our industrial or consumer population. Success in product development depends, therefore—probably above all else—on speedy recognition of market opportunities. It depends on rapid identification of new wants and of the spread of known wants to new and unserviced consumer groups. It is predicated, in very large measure, on the ability to discover and fill significant gaps in the spectrum of products available to consumers. For this reason, the bulk of the readings in this third segment of Part 2 are concerned with emphasizing the directions that consumer wants appear to be taking, the methods that are available for determining the general nature of consumer wants as well as the want-satisfying ability of a particular product, and the difficulties involved in determining a product's potential.

Knowledge that a product yields significant and unique benefits to a sizable segment of consumers does not, unfortunately, ensure its success. The actions of competitors and of intermediaries in the distribution process can prevent the attainment of satisfactory volume and profits. It is important, therefore, that the definition of market opportunity be based not only on consideration of consumer or user wants but also on careful consideration of the desires of distributive organizations and the behavior of rivals. To drive home this point, the readings in this section include discussions of the competitive and distributive factors that are relevant and procedures for evaluating these factors.

Finally, careful study of consumer behavior can provide clues to product design and marketing tactics which can revitalize the sagging sales and profit of a company's mature products. In the last two selections of this segment some suggestions are made about both how to find these clues and how to exploit their implications.

4. *Product development and diversification strategies* In the five articles comprising this last section of Part 2 a classification of product strategies is proposed and procedural suggestions for the design of two of these strategies— product development and diversification—are made. The purpose of this section is to give the reader a comprehensive view of the process through which the design of an effective product policy can be achieved. It is included in order to demonstrate the manner in which the general, internal, and external considerations previously stressed can be integrated to provide management with a coherent and powerful tool for the making of decisions about what to sell.

A

General Considerations

SOME BASIC CONCEPTS UNDERLYING
COMPANY [PRODUCT] STRATEGY

PHILIP MARVIN[*]

Those responsible for advancing technology and maintaining company operations provide leadership not only by exhausting inner-directed resources but also by borrowing the best from the experiences of others. A process that proceeds from observation to analysis, synthesis, testing, and evaluation and then begins all over again with more observation is fundamental to future growth and development.

Failure to capitalize on new concepts can be just as disastrous as failure to capitalize on growth opportunities. One is related to the other. Growth opportunities inherent in a changing business climate generate a need for new concepts. If the business is to take advantage of growth opportunities as they appear on the horizon, these needs must be met.

Industry leaders of the future, as in the past, will be those who have noted these new needs and acted to meet them as they arose. Keeping up with the Joneses isn't enough in business operations. "Firstness" can be an asset. Real leaders don't deal in averages—they set averages for others to achieve. Their acute awareness aids them in developing a sensitivity to situations

Reprinted with permission from Developing A Product Strategy (*Elizabeth Marting, editor*), *AMA Management Report No. 39, American Management Association, 1959, pp. 11–24.*

[*] *Division Manager, Research and Development, American Management Association.*

and details. They detect ways and means of turning opportunities into profits.

There are no secrets of success in the sense that they are inscribed on a parchment and safely secured in the inner recesses of a vault owned by one of the more prosperous companies. Most successful executives will admit that many of the keys to prosperity for their organizations would only have unlocked doors to disaster in other businesses. The important thing to determine, these men add, is what's good for the individual company.

But one suspects that there are certain clues or guidelines having more or less universal applicability that will help management profit from the lessons learned by others in planning for growth. These guidelines are highlighted by synthesizing the experiences of executives that reveal the causal factors underlying success or failure. They disclose no new managerial concepts and no radically different techniques. Rather, they reveal common shortcomings that have cropped up when management's time and thought have been diverted by a myriad of matters demanding attention. Revealing, as they do, some serious pitfalls, they might justifiably be called secrets of success.

Some specific questions provide keys to these clues:

1. Are the basic ingredients of growth recognized?
2. Are profit-producing responsibilities clearly positioned?
3. Are performance-measurement areas known and understood?
4. How does the product plan fit into the risk spectrum?
5. Is size growing faster than earnings?

BASIC INGREDIENTS OF GROWTH

In planning ahead, it is important to have a clear concept of the factors that contribute to business growth. Companies that have developed in size, strength, and income have capitalized on four opportunities for growth. These are (1) growth markets, (2) capital accumulation, (3) technical advance, and (4) creative merchandising.

The first—growth markets—calls attention to opportunities that are created by population increases, bringing about the demand for different products as our way of living expands and develops new needs. Capital accumulation gives a business a resource to work with and the opportunity to multiply management's effectiveness as a profit producer. Technological advances reveal new directions that product and process exploitation can take. Creative merchandising provides the opportunity of acquiring a greater share of customers' dollars.

Each of these opportunities is open in varying degrees to every business man. All must be combined with the ability to turn opportunities into a profitable return on the investment involved.

PROFIT-PRODUCING RESPONSIBILITIES

An important ingredient of success is the fixing of profit-producing responsibilities. The effectiveness of the over-all profit picture in a going business is considerably enhanced if these responsibilities can be delegated to individuals who will have the authority to take effective action.

General Electric's Ralph J. Cordiner, in his *New Frontiers for Professional Managers,* makes these observations about the situation that faced the company some time ago:

Unless we could put the responsibility and authority for decision making closer in each case to the scene of the problem, where complete understanding and prompt action are possible, the company would not be able to compete with the hundreds of nimble competitors who were, as they say, able to turn on a dime.

In addition, General Electric faced the need to develop capable leaders for the future; the need for more friendly and co-operative relationships between managers and other employees; the need to stay ahead of competition in serving the customers; and the very human need to make the work of a manager at all echelons of the organization more manageable. The work had to be made more manageable so that it could be understood and carried out by people of normally available energy and intelligence, thus leaving no requirement for the so-called indispensable man.[1]

Decision making authority, to be most effective, should fall into clearly discernible performance-measurement areas that, taken in total, create the return on investment that characterizes managerial leadership in growth corporations. In any operation, eight of these areas are important: (1) profit-

[1] Cordiner, Ralph J., *New Frontiers for Professional Managers,* New York: McGraw-Hill Book Company, 1956, pp. 45–46.

ability, (2) productivity, (3) position, (4) products, (5) planning, (6) personnel, (7) policies, and (8) progress.

Self-examination, or performance measurement, is the basis of business health and growth; it should be a continuing practice. The eight performance-measurement areas provide focal points that facilitate this process. Certain of them assume a magnitude that overshadows others. This, however, in no way impairs their usefulness as performance-measurement guides.

The primary purpose of the eight performance-measure areas is to aid in the evaluation of the effectiveness with which a business operates and so justifies its existence. Privately owned businesses exist to produce a profit on invested capital by selling a product. That product may be a tangible commodity or an intangible service. Whichever it is—and it may be both—the product is the basis of a growing business. In the course of time, a single product grows into multiple products and product lines. These "product centers" provide a point of application for performance measurement.

CURRENT AND POTENTIAL PROFITABILITY

The profitability of a product center is one of the first factors to be measured in evaluating total performance. Judgment must be exercised in striking a balance between the current and the potential profit producer; one is as important as the other to the success of a business. Similarly, today's runners-up are as important as today's winners in the product scene from a total and a long-range view, the only meaningful position in analyzing product lines.

In their declining days, products fall below breakeven points that they passed during the growth phases of their existence. Generally no little attention is devoted to determining when a product passes the breakeven point on its way up, but the significance of the breakeven point of a product with declining sales is often overlooked. Despite this contrast in executive interest, however, products with established records of declining sales make just as many demands on management's time and the corporation's resources as products with better long-term outlooks. Unless cognizance is taken of this fact, and unless action is taken to eliminate the poor performer, profitability will suffer.

Profitability as a performance-measurement area calls for a three-sided or stereo-dimensional concept encompassing height of profit levels, breadth of base, and profit trend, upward or downward.

PRODUCTIVITY OF EACH FUNCTION

Every function the business performs in the course of the operations associated with each product center should be subjected to an analysis to determine the degree to which it approaches maximum effectiveness. This is the only way of determining how closely actual income approaches the upper limits of potentially procurable levels.

A common error that leads to loss through unrealized income results from the acceptance of certain profit levels as satisfactory without any basis for the implicit assumption that these levels are the best that can be achieved. Measuring the productivity of each function forms the only basis for establishing criteria of acceptability. Hidden opportunities for greater profits have been revealed by taking a new look at operations to measure productivity on a functional basis across the board. The productiveness of research, engineering, manufacturing, and sales alike is evaluated in this process.

Two questions are important in examining each operation from the product-idea to the ultimate dollar-profit stage: (1) Are we doing this job as well as it can be done? And (2) how sure are we of the accuracy with which we are measuring the relative productivity of this operation?

Productivity measurement is more than a detailed analytical process. It has diagnostic and therapeutic overtones as well. In establishing performance criteria, new standards and improved procedures are inevitably developed or acquired. These by-products represent money in the bank in a very real sense.

Productivity as a performance-measurement area has two dimensions: one of quantity and one of quality. Depending on the demands of the particular situation, each must give some ground to the other. Determining how much ground to give might be considered to add a third dimension.

POSITION IN THE INDUSTRY

Industry position is an important yardstick of performance. Each product should be rated against its competitors with respect to significant factors—including sales volume, market coverage and penetration, style, design, consumer acceptance, price, and manufacturing cost.

The results of such measurements are useful in determining strengths and weaknesses in each product center. Data should not, however, be regarded as absolute. If it is found, for example, that sales of a particular product surpass those of others in the industry, this fact by itself does not prove that market opportunities are exhausted. Only by a study of market potentials can this conclusion be reached.

A product's relative position with reference to each factor measured serves to highlight areas where further analysis and action are indicated. Analysis is needed to compare industry position with optimums that could be obtained through more productive operations. Action is needed to achieve these optimums. Measurement of performance in the industry provides, in many cases, a clue to the priority and sense of urgency which should attach to specific programs undertaken to develop added strength in each product center as a base for future profits.

PRODUCTS: THE COMPOSITE PICTURE

Measurement of performance in the product center should determine the degree to which products meet the test of design for (1) consumer acceptance, (2) satisfactory performance, (3) economical production, (4) distribution, depth, and breadth, (5) effective merchandising, (6) ease of installation, (7) adequate servicing, and (8) ultimate replacement.

Beyond these considerations, each product should be examined with respect to its own individual life cycle and the basic objectives of the business. The composite picture reveals the degree to which the company is meeting these objectives and protecting its future earnings by assuring a continuing supply of new products to replace those that become obsolete. For products pass through ten distinct stages during their life span: the prospective, speculative, potentially profitable, scheduled, development, introduction, growth, competitive, obsolescent, and drop-out periods.

The composite picture also tells whether or not the company is taking full advantage of every opportunity to introduce lower-cost products, restyled items, and products designed for improved performance, as well as new markets and uses.

INITIAL AND SUBSEQUENT PLANNING

Effective planning determines to a large degree the profitability of each product center. By the time products are passed on to the consumer, such a long interval has elapsed that initial plans have been forgotten. Yet to these initial plans, as well as subsequent planning, should accrue credits for successes and debits for failures.

One of the significant measures of performance is the effectiveness of the planning process itself. Product planning calls for programs encompassing research and engineering, resource development, commercial development, plant and equipment development, staff development, and return on capital investment. Plans, moreover, should meet three important needs: (1) They should state targets to be achieved. (2) They should provide timetables for the achievement of important targets. And (3) they should spell out detailed techniques for reaching the desired end results.

MANAGEMENT SKILLS AND SPECIALIZED TALENTS

The degree to which manpower has been developed is another important yardstick of over-all performance. Measurement of performance in this area should be broad in scope yet penetrating.

For example, the background and interests of the directors of the corporation should be considered. These men have the last word in determining the destiny both of proposed programs and of those which are actually undertaken. At the managerial and operating levels, the interests, background, and experience of those identified with individual product centers also should be subjected to careful analysis. And, in addition, it is necessary to know the availability of the specialized talent and skill required to put new programs into motion and achieve the objectives of current projects.

In measuring manpower performance, five points are important: (1) the ability of the individual to perform his presently assigned function, (2) his capacity for increased responsibility, (3) specific action taken to prepare for the increased responsibility, (4) the degree to which the individual subordinates his personal interests to the job at hand, and (5) his ability to inspire associates to higher levels of performance.

POLICIES AS GUIDES TO ACTION

Policies are governing guides that make it possible for managers to exercise initiative and at the same time operate within established organizational concepts as conceived by top-level management.

When men must make decisions, they must know not only the limits of their authority but the general rules of action to which top management wants them to adhere. Policies make top management thinking known and so guide action into compatible channels for effective over-all operations. Each product center should therefore be studied to determine the policies that are applicable, their adequacy to cover specific needs, their relationship to the needs of other product centers, the degree to which policies are generally known, their clarity of statement, and their stability over a period of time.

The formulation and statement of policies is a top management responsibility. Performance, however, is measured at the product center. This is where the full impact of policy making is felt. The effectiveness of decisions, and the effort called upon in making these decisions, is directly related to the availability of sound policy guides.

PROGRESS COMPARED WITH POTENTIAL

The eighth and final performance-measurement area directs attention to the evaluation of the progress made in each product center. In making this measurement, the important question to be answered is a simple one: To what degree have growth opportunities been capitalized on?

Performance should be measured against the results that could have been achieved if every available opportunity had been exhausted. Our question therefore breaks down into two parts: (1) How much progress *has been made?* (2) How much progress *could have been made?* It is of no particular consequence to know what competitors have accomplished unless the information serves as a partial indication of levels of potential achievement. The real test is what could have been accomplished by high-level talent supplied with adequate resources within the period of time that is being considered.

THE RISK SPECTRUM

Risk is an inherent ingredient in business operations. Notwithstanding the general acceptance of this fact, business risks—and particularly those associated with product planning—are not always viewed in their full perspective. Product risks can, in fact, be arrayed in a spectrum ranging from readily acceptable products sold in reasonably well defined and developed markets to radically different products that must pioneer new markets.

Profits are often—and not unreasonably—associated with risk taking, but it would be a mistake to assume that high profits and high risk are inseparable. Rather, from a product-planning position there are speculative profits and there are calculable profits. Speculative profits call for a high degree of imaginative ability and pioneering spirit. Calculable profits are premised on the adequacy and availability of historical data as a basis for projections into the future.

Any undertaking brings into play opportunities for both speculative and calculable profits. Executives charged with product responsibilities should evaluate these, using the risk-spectrum concept as a tool and re-examining each product's position in the risk spectrum from the standpoint of three significant factors: (1) relative risk, (2) acceptability of risk, and (3) access to funds. These three aspects of risk in product planning are indissolubly linked: Management must know, in the most accurate quantitative terms possible, how much risk is involved in a particular undertaking in order to arrive at a conclusion as to whether or not it is an acceptable level of risk in the light of the funds that will be required.

SIZE—LIABILITY OR ASSET?

Size can be a liability as well as an asset. "Bigness" in itself is a hazardous height of achievement unless the added resources can be utilized effectively to offset the dangers inherent in size. It is part of the American dream to want to be big, and product planners should think big. But they should examine the problems associated with growth to make certain that programs capitalize on size and turn it from a millstone into a milestone.

If size turns out to be truly a millstone, the company may flounder and sink as have so many successful smaller businesses when they crossed the threshold into the world of big business. In sharp contrast, those have prospered who have recognized the problems as well as the advantages. For this group, crossing into the big-business category was a milestone in forging ahead.

Where growth is revealed more readily by the statistics of size than by the profit position, clues to causal factors are commonly revealed by answers to four questions that have proved useful in probing into this troublesome twentieth-century symptom of business success:

1. Is product addition matched by product deletion?
2. Do high profits hide high costs?
3. Do profit leaders get as much attention as loss leaders?
4. Is responsibility for trouble shooting and problem solving shifted to consultants?

PRODUCT ADDITION
VS. PRODUCT DELETION

Both product addition and product deletion are important. New products maintain the vitality of product centers through lowered costs, better styling, improved performance, additional markets, and new uses. Any one or any combination of these factors is vital in developing and expanding product centers. But it is equally necessary to make certain that products are dropped from the portfolio when they cease to be profit producers.

Developing new products requires both imagination and initiative. So does dropping products that have become obsolete. Of the two functions, however, product deletion is the more neglected. It's difficult to drop products from the line; as long as any sales volume exists, it's only human to follow the easiest course of action and let things coast along. Add to this the fact that when products are dropped there are always a few customers who are vociferous in their objections.

Every product in the portfolio exhausts a portion of the company's resources with its demands on funds, managerial time, technical personnel, equipment, and facilities. Profits result from striking the best possible balance between value paid and value received in using these resources. Many times specific products make greater demands than are justified by the return on the basis of comparison with alternate product programs. The fact that an item produces a profit is not enough. The test is, does it produce a greater profit than could be gained by using the equivalent resources in another way?

When profits fail to keep pace with growth, it's time to check up on the number of products that have been dropped from the line, as well as the number that have been added. Carrying products beyond the period when the rate of return falls behind that of others is a major cause of slippage in profit position.

THE PITFALL OF HIDDEN COSTS

Growth and prosperity make managers complacent. When this happens, costs rise disproportionately.

One of the focal points of excessive costs is hidden in high-profit lines. When profits are high, almost everyone seems to feel that it is no longer necessary to be cost-conscious. This, of course, is a sheer absurdity. The only justification for any element of cost lies in its ability to improve the profit position. When profits are high, costs should be scrutinized even more carefully because more dollars are involved.

The gamble may be great in attempting to improve the profit position of product lines in the high-profit category by incurring new costs. Cost increments too often exceed profit increments. In fact, one of the real opportunities for effective cost reduction centers around high-profit lines.

ATTENTION TO BOTH PROFIT AND LOSS LEADERS

Do profit leaders get as much attention as loss leaders? This question merely serves to amplify the problem of the hidden costs that may lurk in high profits. Product lines in the red attract attention immediately; those showing a profit aren't examined as closely. Yet the real losses from profit leaders operating at levels below maximum efficiency may be greater than the total losses from all the lines that are operating in the red.

No one wants losses; it's obviously bad business to have red figures on the books. But what is really important is to maintain the total profit at the highest possible level. The best way to accomplish this may be to direct attention to lost efficiency in high profit lines first and to look at low-volume loss

leaders last. Why? Because, generally, profit leaders are high-dollar-volume lines. Where this is true, small economies exert a tremendous impact percentagewise on the profit position.

Operating economies, time aside, should not be spent on loss leaders if it means failure to capitalize on the full potential of profit producers. These proven performers should be given every opportunity to exploit their full usefulness as contributors to the company's profits. They should have first call on every resource available. In the profit centers which they represent every phase of the product's life cycle and every function from planning through production to promotion should receive the attention needed to take full advantage of the product's potential capacity to produce profits. To repeat: Time and resources directed to the further development of profit producers can be substantially more productive than time spent troubleshooting loss leaders.

Again, this should emphatically not be construed to suggest that loss leaders should be neglected. The point to keep in mind is that resources—administrative, technical, and operating, as well as capital—should be deployed so as to produce the greatest profits. Too often, profits are sacrificed while putting out brush fires in a forest of loss leaders.

TROUBLE-SHOOTING AND PROBLEM-SOLVING RESPONSIBILITY

When profits fail to keep pace with growth, administrative talents may be spread too thin. Well-managed companies grow in size. This is inevitable. But, as growth takes place, the management team must grow as well. If the technical and administrative group that initiates growth doesn't expand, progress is stifled and profits suffer too.

One of the symptoms indicating that management development isn't keeping pace with growth is the employment of outside consultants. Consultants can serve a useful purpose in providing extra legs and arms in special situations that arise from time to time. The need for such extra help should be studied carefully to make sure that this will be a non-recurring need and that it has grown out of a special situation which in no way reflects on the capacity of the management team in technical and non-technical areas. If, on the other hand, a consultant is hired to do a job because management didn't act promptly or competently enough, this is symptomatic of failure to grow with expanded operations.

At best, no group assembled by a consulting firm from available staff members can ever approach the effectiveness of well-integrated company management. First, there is the risk that personnel assigned to the job by the consultant have been drawn from on-the-shelf staff rather than the most highly qualified members, who may already be working on other projects. Then, too, the consultant must develop a familiarity with the company situation before he can even start work. None of this necessarily reflects on the desire or willingness of most consultants to do the best possible job. After all, consultants are in business to sell a commodity, and this commodity— staff time—must be productive if the consultant is to stay in business. Consulting staffs put in long hours, at the customer's expense, in an effort to overcome these obstacles in performing the job they have been hired to do. The fact that they cannot operate at higher levels of effectiveness is not usually attributable to lack of effort—but profits to the company are measures of results, not effort.

The guidelines that will serve to aid management in capitalizing on the experience of others in planning for growth are best highlighted, in summary, by five questions that managers should ask in opening expanded vistas and establishing new concepts. They are important enough to warrant repeating:

1. Are the basic ingredients of growth recognized?
2. Are profit-producing responsibilities clearly defined?
3. Are performance-measurement areas known and understood?
4. How does the product plan fit into the risk spectrum?
5. Is size growing faster than earnings?

Each should be the subject of careful analysis. Each focuses management attention on fundamental issues. Each directs management attention, both directly and indirectly, to the need for a highly developed and integrated product planning program that will provide a basic operating guide and lead to the establishment of product centers which will yield a satisfactory profit.

The development of a philosophy for product development that combines clear-cut concepts, well-defined objectives, and properly assigned responsibilities is fundamental to business success in the years ahead.

► ► ► ► ► ► ► ► ► ► ► ► BASIC PATTERNS OF NEW PRODUCT STRATEGY

MICHAEL J. O'CONNER *

This represents a summary of experiences in the involved and frustrating, fascinating and important work of developing new products for sale through grocery stores. For the sake of organization, we will talk first about the three main avenues of approach, and then we will touch on the three most important factors for successful new product development. There are three ways a company can expand its business through the marketing of new products. They are: invention, improvement, and acquisition.

INVENTION

First, let us review *invention*. This category deals exclusively with the development and production of products which are entirely new in *form, formula*, and, to some extent at least, consumer use. Some classic examples in this category are Coca-Cola, Corn Flakes, Kleenex, Kotex; and in more recent years frozen concentrated juice, the detergents, and Metrecal.

Now stop and think for a minute.

How many *really* new consumer products can you name which have been successfully introduced through grocery stores in the past ten years? The list is surprisingly small. Of those which have survived, we can find less than twenty, and, although I am sure there are some we have missed, the list is still very, very limited.

Before World War II when advertising was much less powerful in its ability to reach great concentrations of people in quick time, and when competition was less able and less likely to copy a new product, and when the private label activities of the retailer were practically nil in most categories, product *invention* seemed to bring greater and longer lasting rewards than it does today. Coca Cola was virtually unopposed until 1935. Kellogg's Corn Flakes has had things pretty much its own way even though it was copied early in its existence. Kleenex was the only major brand in its field from 1924 to about 1955, and Campbell's Soup built such a powerful franchise it still

Reprinted with permission from Marketing Precision and Executive Action *(Charles H. Hindersman, editor), American Marketing Association, 1962, pp. 387–396.*

* *Vice President and Director of Merchandising, Foote, Cone & Belding.*

dominates a major category of the food business.

But today things are different. New ideas, unprotected by law, are quickly copied. The original heavy duty detergent was copied in less than a year, and overpowered almost immediately. Today the innovator of heavy duty detergent has less than one-seventh the volume enjoyed by the leading brand in the field. The first cake mix now has less than 3 per cent of the market. The original brand of instant coffee has less than ⅟₃₀ the volume of the industry leader. And the first liquid detergent for washing dishes now ranks third in sales nationally with heavy competition from ten other national brands and scores of private labels. To give you some idea of how private label has moved into this new product category, Table 1 shows some figures from a midwest chain with 100 stores showing brand share for '60-'61 by national and private label products.

In reviewing the facts and the history of important inventions in the grocery products field, it is also interesting to learn that product invention does not seem to be a big corporations game. Although, according to a review of annual reports, big grocery manufacturers spend millions on research, a check of ten of the largest grocery manufacturers shows only a half a dozen successful new product inventions made by all these firms in the last ten years. Invention seems to thrive best in the hands of the independent entrepreneur. I should not want you to conclude that *invention* is no longer a desirable factor in corporate business development. However,

I think it is important to realize that *invention* offers the innovator no insurance for success even though the product category may become highly popular with the consumer.

TABLE 1

SHARE OF MARKET OBTAINED BY LIQUID DETERGENTS IN MIDWEST CHAIN OF 100 STORES, 1960–1961

	1960	1961
Private Label	25.6%	30.9%
Lux	17.4	15.2
Ivory	13.7	15.0
Joy	11.9	9.2
Trend	10.8	8.5
Vel	7.6	6.5
Fels	4.8	4.4
Chiffon	4.4	1.9
Swan	2.5	7.2
Shina Dish	1.3	1.2

In summary, *invention* seems to be a desirable factor, but has some serious limitations. First, it is a rare thing—it cannot be programmed or scheduled, and the chances are, if it is successful, it will be copied quickly. So, if the innovating manufacturer is not prepared to spend heavy amounts of advertising and promotional funds to build a brand franchise, he should think twice about investing the time and money it takes to develop a completely new item. And certainly, no growth-minded company in the grocery products field today can rely exclusively on *invention* as a means for expansion.

IMPROVEMENT

For the sake of clarity, I would like to break this broad general category into two sub-categories: (1) product improvement for *general* use, and (2) market fractionalization, i.e., the change or improvement of an existing product to appeal to a specific or special group of consumers, or for a very specialized purpose.

First, let us review improvement for general use. In the past ten years we have seen a tremendous number of product improvements. Through processing alone we have seen frozen fruits, vegetables and prepared foods climb at a meteoric rate. Ten years ago national retail volume in all frozen foods was approximately five hundred million dollars. Today the grocery business sells over three billion dollars in frozen foods. In the dry grocery or packaged foods business there are also many good examples. Procter & Gamble's Mr. Clean came on the market four and a half years ago and in two short years took over leadership. This was done by making a product that was *demonstrably* better in the eyes of the consumer. They also stayed in their test markets *long enough* to be sure the product was everything it should be from a standpoint of repurchase.

Johnson's Wax has done a superb job of marketing new products during the past ten years. Based on a completely consumer-oriented philosophy of marketing, this company made furniture polish easier to apply with Pledge and attained leadership in that field. They improved the packaging and performance of auto cleaners and polishers with notable results, and they kept pace with changes in floor finishes with products like Klear, which now leads all others in that field. They made insecticides better by combining elements

to give the consumer a product with much broader usage—and they gained leadership in that field. A year and a half ago they developed a shoe polish in a radically new container which made application easier, cleaner and more efficient; and they appear to be on their way to leadership in that field.

In every instance they followed one simple formula which Mr. Sam Johnson outlined in a speech to his executives, and I would like to read his formula to you. Mr. Johnson said, "We intend to concentrate company research, production and sales efforts on . . . chemical specialties with at least one point of demonstrable superiority recognized by the consumer over competitive products, either in performance or in method of use." This to me is the essence of success in product improvement.

On the negative side of the ledger, one of America's great names in the food business tried to enter two new fields; both seemed to be natural expansion opportunities—both were closely allied to their basic category. The products they developed were good products, no better or worse than others already in the field, but they had the advantage (so thought the manufacturer) of his good name and brand franchise. The results were disastrous and in two years both products were out of distribution and out of business. This example is not unique; many manufacturers have found that a well established franchise in one field cannot substitute for product benefits in another category.

Now let us talk about the growing art of market fractionalization. This technique of product development involves the alteration or change of a basic product so that it will have greater appeal to a fraction or specific segment of the consuming public. Detergents with bluing added, detergents with bleach added, and detergents with low sudsing characteristics for use in automatic washers are classic examples of segmenting or fractionalizing the market.

This technique is best applied in larger categories where volume is sufficient to profitably support a brand or brands which appeal to only a part of the market. Dial Soap is a good example of market fractionalization. Dial is a deodorant soap. It began as a specialty product sold at a much higher than average price through drug stores. Today Dial has expanded its distribution to all outlets which sell soap and is the leader in dollar sales of *all* toilet soaps. In this instance the specialized product worked *so* well it became the industry leader even in the face of some of the toughest competition in the entire grocery products field.

Another good example of market fractionalization began right here in Cincinnati two years ago. Since about 1955 Kleenex and Scott, two general purpose brands of tissues, dominated the tissue business. Then a new product entered the field. Instead of a broad general appeal this new brand, Puffs, was a decidedly feminine product. It was soft and scented and its advertising made no secret that it was a female through and through. Although it is too early to tell conclusively, it would appear Puffs is here to stay with a very respectable share of the special market it chose to concentrate on.

And no discussion of market fraction-alization would be complete without at least a mention of the cigarette business. Dominated by three brands holding better than 64 per cent of the total market ten years ago, this industry has been cut to ribbons with new products offering special appeals. The same three brands today account for only 24 per cent of the market and new products continue to enter the scene almost monthly.

ACQUISITION

Now let us move on the third avenue open to the company with new product ambitions. Let us take a quick look at the record. In the past ten years the following acquisitions occurred.

Procter & Gamble acquired: Duncan Hines Mixes, Charmin Paper Mills, and Clorox.

General Foods acquired: Kool Aid, S.O.S., Good Seasons, and Open Pit.

General Mills acquired: O'Cello, Puffin Biscuits, Spratts Dog Food, and Three Little Kittens Cat Food.

Campbell Soups acquired: Swanson and Pepperidge Farms.

Corn Products acquired: Best Foods, Knorr Soups and Skippy.

Pillsbury acquired: Ballard and Tidy House.

Gillette acquired: Toni and Papermate.

And there are many more. As corporations get larger, the route of acquisition seems to become an increasingly attractive means of growth. Money, management personnel, and the advantages of low cost group advertising buys make this route an efficient one for many companies.

It has also become advantageous for

the small businessman to sell out to the big corporation. The problems of getting expansion capital, the tax advantages and the security of big corporate stock holdings has served to stimulate sale on the part of the individual entrepreneurs. But all is not necessarily rosy—there are real problems in this area too.

The biggest single problem in acquisition might be termed incompatibility. Frequently you see a successful company lose volume and momentum after it has become a part of a larger corporation. What usually happens is that the dominant company attempts to conform the new company's marketing and production policies to those which have been developed for their own business. And all too frequently the policies and procedures which are successful in one business simply will not work in some other line. The most successful operators do not attempt to force an alien business to their basic pattern of operation. Instead, they operate their new acquisitions as separate divisions of the company or reorganize their divisions so that only those compatible products are grouped together.

Many problems of compatibility develop in the areas of sales and marketing management. To demonstrate the point, let us suppose Company "A" is operating in a category of the grocery business where trade deals such as special allowances and free goods are not offered. Company "A" then acquires Company "B." "B" operates in a category where promotional allowances and one case free with ten is considered common practice. Company "A" is faced with a problem. Should it force

its new acquisition to change its ways and suffer an inevitable loss in volume, or should it corrupt its own sales force and teach them new bad habits by putting free goods and case allowance in their hands?

Another problem concerns the flexibility of management personnel. It is not at all unusual for marketing and production executives to be strongly influenced by their early successes. And, as long as they stay in that same basic industry, the instincts which were developed as a result of those early lessons are valuable and productive. But when they are given a new company in a new industry, problems frequently arise.

Some time ago a client of ours made tremendous gains as the result of a competitor being acquired by a larger corporation. The parent company attempted to absorb their new acquisition into their existing marketing organization. And because the big corporation sold most of their product on a direct basis, they had little respect and even less understanding of the wholesale business. As a consequence, they changed their new division's discount policies to conform to their own, and as a result gave us, their competitor, a four million dollar gift in sales volume that we could never have hoped to achieve on our own. It is for these reasons that most big companies today tend to keep major acquisitions in separate divisions.

NEW PRODUCT DEVELOPMENT

Now, in addition to these three avenues for growth through new products, there are three other important factors which have consistently strong effects on new product development programs. Two of the factors have to do with corporate frame of mind, and one relates to organization.

CONSUMER PREFERENCES

The first of these factors deals with consumer preferences. One of the greatest common denominators in the development of new products is the respect, at all levels of corporate management, for consumer preference. In the developmental stage, many compromises must be made between manufacturing and marketing. In our experience those corporations where final decisions are based on consumer preference, the odds definitely favor success. Conversely, in those corporations where important decisions are made in favor of manufacturing efficiencies or trade considerations, success is much less consistent.

One prime example of the importance of consumer preference comes to mind. It relates to an important segment of the grocery products field. Ten years ago two competitors squared off and began the new products race. One competitor, which we will call Company "X," had nine products and a share of the total industry market slightly over 30 per cent. The other competitor, Company "Z," had three products and held approximately 19 per cent of the market. During the intervening ten years, Company "X" brought out twelve new products. Company "Z" brought out thirteen new products. "X's" share went from 30 per cent to over 40 per cent. "Z's" share

went down from 19 per cent to 17 per cent. The reason for the great difference between these two companies was simple. "X" brought out products which consumers wanted; "Z" made products best suited to their manufacturing operation.

There is also a tendency on the part of some marketing men to consider low price more important than other product benefits, and in many cases this is not true. In case after case a new product with a demonstrable consumer benefit has sold at higher prices and has been successful. Obviously the price cannot be out of reason and it must be carefully market-tested; however, if the consumer feels it is worth the money, we have learned she will pay the price. Another important competitive advantage accrues to the marketer who has the product advantages and the nerve to increase his price— he has marketing margins which provide the added advertising and promotion which are essential to get quick consumer action and trade support.

FISCAL POLICY

Our second factor for success in marketing new products concerns fiscal policy. Because today's market moves so rapidly, it is becoming more and more essential that product introductions be done with sufficient power to gain a strong share of market quickly. This is necessary to minimize competitive intervention and to insure the best possible trade support. As we have seen in the examples cited earlier, innovating brands are vulnerable to competitors who make improvements on the basic product and then make heavy investments in advertising and promotion to gain leadership.

And from a standpoint of trade support, involving such important factors as distribution, pricing, and featuring in displays and advertisements, the slow pay-as-you-go introduction generally fails to produce satisfactory results. The retailing trade has a hearty respect for the consumer franchise, and a new product which quickly achieves strength in this area is most likely to gain their cooperation. Conversely, the new product which is introduced on a slow pay-as-you-go plan is usually relegated to a "wait and see" status.

PLANNING AND ORGANIZATION

The third factor for success in new product development concerns planning and organization. Good technical libraries can provide a wealth of material on this subject which I will not attempt to cover here. However, I would like to touch on some of the basic common denominators for success which we have had an opportunity to observe during the past ten years.

The most important single thing in organizing for new products seems to be direction. Companies which have been consistently successful in the new products field have all worked with a plan. A good example of this is Johnson's Wax; as you recall, Mr. Johnson said to his executives, "We will concentrate . . . on chemical specialties." This provided his research and development people and everyone else involved in new product work with a set of guidelines. Without such direction it is very easy for any organization to wander into fields which could not conceivably prove profitable or practical from financial, manufacturing or marketing standpoints. A statement of direction which is based on a thorough understanding of the corporate fiscal and marketing philosophy, and which is tempered with an honest evaluation of the limitations and capabilities of the manufacturing and sales organizations is essential to success in new product development programs.

Another area of organization which is important concerns facilities, both manpower and physical — without a separate staff, new product development programs tend to get pushed aside during heavy work periods. As one highly successful new products developer put it: new products in the development stage, like children, need great patience and tender loving care. To provide this kind of attention a separate staff, well isolated from day-to-day competitive pressures, is highly essential.

Also of great importance is the inclusion of practical marketing experience in the new product development process. All too often marketing personnel and their advertising agencies are brought into the new product development program too late. In most successful operations we know anything about, a marketing executive gets into the program at or very near the beginning. And while the chemists and other manufacturing and development specialists are working with the problems of formula, fabrication and packaging, the marketing man, with the aid of his own market research people and his advertising agency, studies the market, the industry, the consumer, the trade and the competition to determine the best practical ways and means of getting the product into distribution and the consumer's hands.

SUMMARY

Now let us summarize. The effective new product development program must have these elements:

1. Executive direction
2. A staff protected from day-to-day competitive pressures
3. Consumer orientation at all levels in the corporation
4. The services of a marketing specialist
5. Financial backing sufficient to permit the early dominance.

And from the standpoint of approach, all evidence would seem to indicate that *improvement* and *acquisition* are the best corporate routes to success, while pure *invention* is best for the individual entrepreneur or the manufacturer of basic raw materials where patents offer a better promise for return on investment.

➤➤➤➤➤➤➤➤➤➤➤➤ DETERMINANTS OF PRODUCT MIX

RALPH S. ALEXANDER, JAMES S. CROSS, AND ROSS M. CUNNINGHAM[*]

Product planning implies a course of action which has been thought through in advance so as to result in a consistent pattern of decisions regarding the product mix. Careful attention by top management to the formulation of product-planning policy is still the exception rather than the rule. Lacking such a policy, decisions regarding additions to or deletions from the product mix of a company are likely to be based upon the pressures of the moment. Although such decisions usually take into account the dominant characteristics of the company, they often do so on an intuitive basis and incompletely.

The following discussion identifies the fundamental determinants of the product mix of a company in order to provide an understanding of the basic forces which are at work. The diffi-

Reprinted with permission from Industrial Marketing *(Revised Edition), Richard D. Irwin, Inc., 1961, pp. 124–129.*

[*] *Ralph S. Alexander, Philip Young Professor Emeritus of Marketing, Columbia University; James S. Cross, Manager, Statistical Research Division, Sun Oil Company; Ross M. Cunningham, Associate Professor of Marketing, Massachusetts Institute of Technology.*

culties faced by management in formulating a sound product policy will become evident. Management's role consists of adjusting to these forces as skillfully as possible in the light of the resources of the enterprise and of guiding the enterprise along product paths which will lead to future growth and profit.

So far as possible, the determinants discussed are limited to those of a fundamental character and no effort has been made to treat in detail the various specific reasons or motivations underlying product action. There is a growing literature on the subject of diversification in which the emphasis is placed upon reasons for diversification.[1]

GENERAL DETERMINANTS TENDING TO CHANGE PRODUCT MIX

Changes in the product mix of a company stem from changes in the design or variety of present product lines, from the addition of products which are new to the company, and from the elimination of products which had formerly been in the product mix. A new product is one which is new to the particular company and which usually involves significant tensions, difficulties, and adjustments during its assimilation by the manufacturing, sales, and other departments within the company. Under this definition, a new product need not be new to the market, only to the company.

[1] See particularly H. Igor Ansoff, "Strategies for Diversification," *Harvard Business Review,* September–October 1957, pp. 113–124, and Thomas A. Staudt, "Program for Product Diversification," *Harvard Business Review,* November–December 1954, pp. 121–131.

TECHNICAL RESEARCH AND DEVELOPMENT

Approximately three quarters of the total annual dollar volume of national research and development effort in recent years has been performed in the laboratories of American industry. Such expenditures grew from $3.6 billion in 1953 to $9.4 billion in 1959, an increase of 161 per cent in current dollars, and it was expected that the figure for 1960 would be over $10 billion.[2] The largest part of the increase since 1954 was represented by federal funds which jumped from $1.4 billion at the beginning of the period to $5.4 billion in 1959. Much of this research was done by business firms under government contracts. Business-financed research during this period increased from $2.2 billion to $4.0 billion. More than one half (55 per cent) of the 1959 total was spent in the aircraft and parts industry and the electrical equipment and communication industry, while chemicals and allied products, machinery, motor vehicles, and other transportation equipment added another 29 per cent.

Basic research designed to uncover new knowledge represented $344 million or 4 per cent of the total. Thus by far the greatest industrial use of research and development is in the application of existing knowledge to development of new products and processes. For example, the maser (microwave amplification by simulated emission of

[2] National Science Foundation, "Funds for Performance of Research and Development in American Industry 1959–A Preliminary Report," *Reviews of Data on Research and Development,* No. 24, December, 1960.

radiation) promises to have many important applications in communications as well as in other fields. The rate of technological change is accelerating, and technical research is unquestionably the most basic force affecting the product mix of the individual company. It underlies a number of the other determinants of product mix which will be treated.

CHANGES IN COMPETITORS' PRODUCT MIXES

A second important determinant of the product mix of a firm is found in the changes in product offerings of competitors. Closely related to this is the introduction of competitive products by companies not now considered to be competitors. This has happened increasingly in recent years, with the growing tendency of industrial firms to enlarge their product mixes and to include some product lines which represent entries into fields and markets not previously served. Changes in competitive products represent a direct challenge to the company, and if the change is a truly significant improvement, it may prove disastrous unless it can be matched or surpassed within a reasonable length of time. In addition to changes in design of competitive products, competitors may make changes in their over-all product mix which put the manufacturer at a competitive disadvantage. As will be pointed out later, there are important forces favoring a product mix of reasonable breadth. Broadening the grouping of product lines may be a real advantage in distributor relations and in lowering selling costs.

In addition to changes in competitors' products or breadth of product mix, there may be important changes in the numbers of competitors. Usually an increase in numbers is likely to result in keener competition and lowered profit margins. Significant increases in numbers of competitors is possible in those industries in which the capital investment necessary for entry is of modest size. In such situations a product enjoying a rapid increase in sales, by virtue of widespread market acceptance, is likely to attract many new entrants into the field, only a portion of which will survive the period of consolidation or "shakeout," as it is sometimes called. In industries requiring large investment, increases in the number of competitors are less dramatic, although when such an increase does occur even a limited number of additional sellers may have a very important effect upon the sales and profits of present suppliers.

CHANGES IN MARKET DEMAND FOR PRODUCT LINES

Although declines in demand are the most disturbing to management and may result in an expansion of the product mix in an effort to replace loss of business, upward changes are also of significance. It is management's responsibility to capitalize as fully as possible upon expanding product fields just as much as it is to meet the challenge of declining markets. These changes in product demand are of various types.

Shift in customer's product mix The industrial marketer by definition is selling his products to other businesses either for incorporation in their products or for use in running their businesses. Items which enter customer products are therefore vulnerable to changes in the product lines manufactured by customers. If the customer is himself an industrial goods producer selling to other industries, his shift may be derived from shifts which his customers have found it necessary to make. Such a chain reaction may have several links, all within the field of industrial marketing. In contrast, the immediate customer may be a manufacturer of consumer goods, and a change in his product mix will have repercussions because of his efforts to satisfy ultimate consumers more precisely with his offerings. The widespread use of annual models in the consumer field introduces a regular periodicity to changes and intensifies the need for planning ahead. Many annual models are designed years before they appear, and the seller who is not alert to the need for establishing and maintaining sales contacts and providing materials or equipment to facilitate such changes may find his product lines partially obsolete.

In addition to the product demand shifts brought about by customers' changes in product-line design to meet their own customers' needs, some customers may engage in diversification programs which expand their product mix and offer opportunities for sale of additional quantities, or for modification of the product mix to capitalize on additional business available from regular customers. Since diversification programs are often premised either on a decline in business which has taken

place or the fear of a future decline, there may well be concurrent drops in demand.

Some customers may pursue a policy of simplification of product mix. If this is confined simply to the dropping of low-volume items, the decline in their purchases will not be large. A drastic simplification of the total product mix, however, involving the elimination of some product lines which are selling in substantial volume, will cause an important shrinkage in purchasing requirements.

Changes in manufacturing processes
Changes in manufacturing methods by customer firms may affect the demand for the company's product. This would be most striking for manufacturers of major special purpose equipment since a drastic change in the manufacturing process might render such equipment obsolete. A producer of processed or raw materials could also be affected because of the considerable freedom of choice which exists today between the materials of which a product may be made.

Shifts in location of customers
Transportation costs are important for many types of industrial goods. These costs limit rather definitely the geographical extent of the market which can be profitably served by an industrial marketer, and any shift of customers out of this market area can result in major declines in sales and the necessity for replacing this lost business with other products. Sometimes migration of customers or poten-

tial customers into the area economically served by a producer helps offset losses from outward migration. Some manufacturers, however, have been so closely tied to particular industry groups, as, for example, textiles, that large-scale migration becomes a possible death sentence unless the producer also moves.

Changes in levels of business activity The examples just given of changes in product demand are based upon market changes of various types. There may also be changes in demand which result from seasonal fluctuations in the industries served. Nearly every producer faces some type of seasonal pattern of sales and also is vulnerable in greater or less extent to major shifts in the level of general business. Some companies have extended their product mix, by adding lines whose seasonal patterns offset those of their present lines, and thus obtained a reasonably even rate of total production and sales activity throughout the year. This consideration also applies to distributors who may feel the need for a product mix which evens out seasonal fluctuations. In somewhat similar fashion, some companies have sought to add product lines which are less sensitive to business-cycle variations than their existing lines. Many manufacturers of machinery, particularly in the major equipment groups, are concerned about their sensitivity to cyclical drops in demand and would like to meet this through diversification.

In addition to changes in national business activity, there may be variations at any given time in the levels of business activity in particular local or regional markets.

Government controls The last two decades have been a period of active war and general tension in international relations. It seems certain that for many years in the future there will be a high level of government spending for national defense, coupled with the possibility of limited-scale military action. Under such conditions certain materials are of great strategic importance and the government may take steps to limit their usage for civilian purposes in order to manufacture military material or to build stockpiles. Such government controls have widespread ramifications upon industry and tend to cause major changes in sales volume for particular product lines. Where there is no possibility of substituting materials, little product action can be taken. Frequently, however, such a tight material situation may encourage experimentation and research on substitute materials which will perform the function adequately. This leads to changes in product offerings.

Difficulties in predicting product demand changes Although marketing research is of great assistance in measuring trends in demand for products and thus aids in prediction of future demands, there will always remain considerable uncertainty. This has led some managements to diversify product lines in order to lessen the risk of unpredicted declines in demand for particular items.

►►►►►►►►►►► PRODUCT PLANNING AND ADAPTATION

ALBERT HARING*

During the 1950's, marketing began to play an important part in product planning and the development of a product line. . . . This article will summarize the issues and conclusions that appeared in discussion and case analyses.

CORPORATE POLICY

Considerable emphasis was placed upon the fact that a company must have a broad corporate policy to avoid many pitfalls of improper product development. The following eleven points were considered:

1. The first step is to evaluate the company's present line of products. Are the current lines shrinking in importance and volume or do they show signs of a promising future? Even though a product or line of products may have a favorable volume future, the question of profits must be carefully considered. There has been a distinct tendency during the last decade for established products to have greater competition and, consequently, declining profits. Thus, the evaluation of the current line must include not only future volume but profit possibilities.

In a rapidly changing economy with a tendency toward unused capacity, the profit squeeze may be the most significant factor in examining the future.

2. Management must set its broad goals for at least the next decade. The volume forecast for 1970, for example, must be carefully analyzed. The next step is to match the probable sales and profits provided by the current line for 1970. Then the question of expansion or contraction arises. If the current line will not provide the goals for 1970, then the problem is to set clearly the goals for facilities, sales, and profits. The development of a product line to attain these goals then becomes much more clear. In most cases, new products or additions to old lines will be essential to attain any goal that involves significant expansion.

3. A profit goal is also vital in evaluating new products. If the profit goal should be 10 per cent of sales, some products will be eliminated and others will appear promising. The existing line should be carefully examined with respect to its profit ratio by age of product. In some industries, the long-established products have much lower profit ratios than successful newer ones. In looking ahead, many companies will

Reprinted with permission from First International Seminar on Marketing Management, Business Horizons, *Indiana University, February 1961, pp. 74–77.*

* *Professor of Marketing, Indiana University; Past President, American Marketing Association.*

find that their established products are contributing significant profits in dollars but an undesirable profit ratio.

One of the functions of the new products is to yield above-average profits during their early years so that the company average reaches the desired level. To evaluate the situation properly, products may have to be segregated not by age alone but by whether they are staples or specialties. In addition, a division by type of market may also be required. Currently, this analysis of products is very helpful in evaluating the areas that offer the greatest promise of adequate profits in the future.

4. Where a new product may require sizable investment in either equipment or a new plant, the problem of the time necessary to recover the new investment is significant. This is directly connected with profits but has additional implications. For plant expansion and large equipment investment, the corporation should set a specific number of years as the write-off period so that new product ideas can be evaluated against a standard. In a rapidly moving industry where innovation is common, special equipment might require a one-year write-off. On the other hand, in a relatively stable industry with broad markets, a ten-year write-off might be considered appropriate.

5. In what areas is the company willing to expand? One company in the chemical field chooses to limit its activities to chemical products derived from and serving agriculture. A second company may desire to limit its new products to those that are purchased by consumers through druggists and sim-

ilar retailers. A third company may be completely opportunistic and feel that it can afford to expand wherever the profit potential is adequate and the write-off of new equipment is within its goals.

Most companies are not very successful in what might be called "scrambled" additions, although in some instances the profit motive alone has apparently caused illogical additions that turned out very well. The concensus, however, is that a corporation should have a definite policy as to which areas are most desirable for expansion. If the research and development division comes up with products that do not meet this requirement, the tendency would be to sell or license such products rather than to change the form of the corporate picture. For example, the National Cash Register Company sought a method to eliminate carbon paper in making copies of sales slips, cash register receipts, and similar duplications. The company developed "encapsulment," a process that has many uses far removed from the business machine and business machine supply field, but chose to license its use in other industries rather than to change the company's basic pattern. Such a policy would appear to be desirable for all except the most unusual operations.

6. For both existing lines and proposed new products, markets should be carefully examined. After analyzing the market according to the use of product and channels of distribution (an approach called market segmentation), companies often find that they are not covering the total market.

Product planning involves an advance decision as to which market segments a company should serve, a process that involves careful research and raises many problems. Should a private brand be made? Should large retailers be sold direct? Should the direct distribution of industrial goods be supplemented by industrial distributors? Should an inferior quality of a standard product be fabricated? Market segments and the products that they require vary so much that many companies have found it essential to create special departments to serve each major market segment.

7. The proven ability of executives and personnel of a company to operate profitably in a limited area is no guarantee of success in an unfamiliar area. Stated in another manner, no new activity should be undertaken that is not controllable by the management and managers upon the basis of their past performance. For example, members of a firm that has had great success in producing top-quality items at a premium price may be completely unable to make the mental adjustment necessary to produce a low-quality product for the mass market where no premium price can be justified. Where a company's experience has been largely in the handling of metallic products, a jump over to an industry that is based on woodworking would seem to involve an unnecessarily large risk.

One company will have greater marketing strengths through certain types of channels. A second company may be very strong on research and development. A third company may be excellent in its production techniques. If a company decides to expand, it should get executives experienced in the new areas.

8. In considering new products and growth, a company must weigh the advantages of acquisition against construction. Acquisition offers speed and secures personnel for a new line. Construction and expansion offer more modern facilities. Some sort of criteria must be developed to choose between these, so a broad company policy is usually most helpful.

9. Every organization that is successful over a period of time develops some type of company or corporate personality. This personality may be synonymous with quality at a premium or with competitive prices. A company may have a reputation for leadership or innovation, or producing staple products at competitive prices. A company may be in good favor with individual consumers and the public, or have an excellent industrial reputation. One major requirement in product planning is to recognize the company personality and to consider limiting product development and production to those areas where the company personality is strong and favorable. Certainly, the personality and thinking of the company is a key to determining the areas where success with new products is most promising.

10. The next major step is to evaluate the present product line. Should the company drop scrambled additions made during the 1950's or earlier, or products whose sale has been falling? Certainly, in considering a new product the existing line should be carefully examined to determine whether plant

and equipment should be made available for the new product by eliminating an old one, or whether new facilities should be created. From the discussion, the general feeling was that many poor decisions have been made to expand plant and equipment when weak and fading products should have been dropped from the line.

The sales of fading products tend to be overstated because they are never in short supply, while the sales of new and rising products tend to be understated because of shortage and inability to ship. The latter condition suggests that unfilled orders are as important as shipments in analyzing the position of products now being made.

11. No new product is likely to fit a list of criteria perfectly. As a result, the assumption must be made that every new product will involve compromising some of the criteria. The problem is to choose products that best fit the test criteria and offer the greatest probability of success. Practical compromise thus becomes basic in product decisions.

PRODUCT POLICY

The criteria that have been discussed provide an incomplete list. With another group of participants, a somewhat different emphasis might have developed. To develop a sound product policy, each company must draw up its own list of criteria for evaluating product ideas and product planning.

Two points, however, should be emphasized. First, every business will have to evaluate impartially its own competitive strengths and weaknesses.

To be realistic is very difficult; in fact, numerous companies hire consulting firms to ensure impartial analysis.

In adding Paper Mate ball-point pens and Toni hair preparations to supplement its razor and blade line, Gillette appears to have decided that its marketing skills should be concentrated in consumer products that required substantial investment in advertising and promotion. Container manufacturers, as more and more containers have shifted from tin to aluminum and plastic (and other materials), have broadened their lines to cover the container field. Automobile parts manufacturers serving the original equipment market alone have entered the replacement or "after-market." Specialty manufacturers of major appliances have expanded or combined to offer full lines. Kaiser, after securing the Jeep line, has shifted market emphasis mainly to industrial, commercial, and farm use, the areas in which its corporate picture is most favorably known. General Motors has entered the diesel-powered truck field to round out its line of trucks. Each of these companies, as well as many others, has expanded where the company management believed its competitive strengths were close to a maximum.

Second, organization for effective product planning and product development was recognized as possibly the most difficult mixture of line-and-staff relationship in today's business management. User- and market-oriented product development requires close cooperation among market research, sales, product and development engineering, engineering, production, and service (as a minimum) before the proper product, its probable market, and its profitable price can be determined. Where a new plant must be built, finance and other areas of the company become involved. In a large company, many of the executives carrying on the work are below top level, yet must deal frequently with top level men who must have the vision to treat them as equals, possibly as experts, in the particular issues under consideration. Discussion highlighted this problem, but did not suggest any easy solution. The needs for adequate early market analysis, for testing new products under actual use conditions, and for test marketing were, however, consistently emphasized.

One additional point should be made. The need for educating company executives and personnel about new product policy, once it has been established, appears to be vital. When basic policies concerning new products, product lines, and product development have been established, the people concerned must be indoctrinated with such policies and their importance. This area appears to have been so nebulous in many companies that executives interpret new product policy in diverse ways or do not regard such policy changes as significant. To implement new product policy appears to require as much effort in communications as a basic change in compensation methods. And, since many companies will rely upon products not now produced for the bulk of their profits in 1970, adequate understanding warrants whatever effort may be needed. . . .

►►►►►►►►►►► PRODUCT-LINE POLICY

JOEL DEAN[*]

INTRODUCTION

A company's conscious competitive actions have three facets: (1) product policy, (2) promotional policy, and (3) pricing policy. Product policy commands not only managerial attention, because of rapid changes in technology and demand; it is also significant for the entire economy, since it is the mainspring of economic progress and hence an important test of a company's social contribution.[1]

[1] Although most modern firms make several products, economic theory has been developed on the premise that each firm makes only one product. The reasons for such an inadequate premise are to be found partly in the historical origins of theory and partly in

Reprinted from Journal of Business, *October 1950, pp. 248–258, with permission of* The University of Chicago Press.

[*] *Joel Dean Associates and Professor of Business Economics, Columbia University.*

The purpose of this article is to examine, from an economic standpoint, the managerial problems of product coverage in a multiple-product firm. We are concerned with only one phase of product policy, namely, product coverage—that is, decisions on what end products the company will make and sell. Product improvement—the other phase of product policy—is not examined here. We shall attempt to sketch a framework for a policy approach to product coverage, that is, a set of standing answers to recurring product proposals.

The term "product" in this discussion will mean an end product offered for sale by the firm. Intermediate products produced as a consequence of vertical integration and parts and components purchased for inclusion in final products are excluded from this analysis.

The term "product line" will be used here in a broad sense to include all the products manufactured by the firm. The term can be used in a narrower sense to refer to groups of products that are related either on the marketing side as being complements or substitutes or on the production side as being made from the same materials or by similar processes.

In a dynamic economy, where prod-

uct monopolies are characteristically transient and where product development is a major facet of competitive rivalry, economically sound decisions on additions to the company's product coverage are obviously of great importance. Three important problems encountered by top management in formulating policy on adding new products are: (1) scouting out potential product additions, (2) appraising these proposals and making the product selection, and (3) launching each new product venture in a way that gives it a maximum chance of success.

The first, development of a flow of promising proposals for candidate additions to the company's product line, is fundamental to sound product additions. For many companies product research is the main instrument. Others license new product inventions or buy them directly from independent inventors and corporate research departments or through professional "product-finders." Product proposals also come from customers, from the company's marketing staff, from small companies that want to sell out, and from independent inventors.

The third top management problem —launching the new venture—involves questions of refinement of the product design, selection of market targets, methods of distribution, pricing the new product, and making capital expenditures for production and marketing facilities.

Top management's second problem— the appraisal of candidate product additions—is the central concern of this article. Even in large, well-managed companies the methods used in select-

---

the simplicity of theoretical analysis when it is confined to single-product output. Determination of the costs of individual products in a multiple-product company is both conceptually and empirically difficult. The neglect of these problems may also be due to the notion that management views each product as a separate business activity with the characteristics of a single-product firm, but this approach has little theoretical and no practical support.

ing product additions leave much to be desired. A survey of the experience of two hundred leading packaged-goods manufacturers in the postwar development of new products revealed that only 20 per cent of the products put on the market actually turned out to be money-makers.[2] For most of these products, expectations had been far too optimistic. This dismal experience showed that product innovation required more careful selection and more deliberate planning than these companies had anticipated. A rich mixture of market research, product testing, adequate financial resources, and persistence was needed.

POLICY PROPOSALS

Management needs a rational routine for this appraisal in the form of a set of criteria to guide its analysis. In this section we consider what questions management should ask and what criteria it should establish. The discussion has three parts: (a) standards of prospective profits from the candidate product; (b) considerations of product-line strategy; and (c) specific criteria of acceptability of new products.

STANDARDS OF PROFITABILITY

Usually the most important question about a new product is its prospective profitability. If the sole objective of the enterprise were to maximize profits in a strict sense, all considerations affecting additions to the product line could be subsumed under profitability; to a

[2] "The Introduction of New Products," a survey made by Ross Federal Research Corporation, for Peter Hilton, Inc.

degree, the nonprofit considerations are merely indicators of long-run profit prospects. Yet, business motivations are more complex than has been assumed in economic theory. They encompass objectives such as external corporate life, market share, volume growth, comfortable cash reserves, assured tenure for management, and pleasant employee relationships. These purposes can be forced into a concept of long-range profit maximization; but, when this is done, the concept evaporates for analytical applications.

Prospective profitability, in the narrow, cash-return sense, is nevertheless the key consideration. Candidates for addition to the product line should be ranked in a priority ladder according to profitability and should be selected from the top down, except in unusual strategic circumstances. But a profitability ladder raises four questions: (1) What concept of profits is relevant? (2) What form of profit standard should be used? (3) How should profit prospects be measured? (4) What rejection level should be established?

Profit concepts The relevant concept of profits for product-line additions is not always clear; it depends on circumstances. The basic choice lies between some notion of incremental profits and the concept of net profits over full cost. Incremental profits refer to the difference in the firm's profits with and without the addition of the product in question. It thus credits the new product with the whole increase in profitability of existing facilities that its introduction produces. In contrast, the use of net profits means that some of the fixed overheads are loaded onto the new product, and cost burdens of existing products are correspondingly lightened.

If they are extended over a long enough period to encompass the probable life-cycle of the new addition, incremental profits are the relevant concept. Sometimes product additions are so short lived that incremental profits are the difference between price and short-run marginal cost. Examples are subcontracting work, war work, and production of specially designed products in a job shop. In this special case the usual strategic considerations that enter into product-line additions are rather unimportant. But here, as in a longer-range setting, incremental profits must be measured against the profits that could come from the best alternative use of money, time, and facilities. If the alternative is idleness, then presumably any incremental profits will justify the addition of the product. If, as is more common, the alternative is to use resources on some other product, the alternative return sets the standard of minimum incremental profits.

For more durable additions to the product line, short-run marginal cost is not the correct concept for estimating the added profitability of the new product. The adoption of a new product carries with it explicitly or tacitly the commitment to stay with the new venture at least until it has had a fair trial, and possibly longer. Additions to common costs that are often unforeseen at the time of the introduction of the new product are likely to occur, so that the businessman's rule of thumb of loading on the new product its full share of

common overhead is often the most appropriate method after all.[3]

Form of profit standard In order to compare the profitability of alternative uses of facilities, profit standards must be stated in a form that is relevant for ranking them. What form should a profit estimate take—unit margins, return on investment, aggregate dollar profits? The most general form is the total dollar income over the whole life of the product minus the total outlay to produce it. But in cases where the new product is a permanent addition, it may be easier to measure the profit return per unit of some fixed, bottleneck factor of production absorbed by the new product. Such a bottleneck factor might be executive time, machine time, or materials (e.g., steel during the postwar period of shortage and private rationing by producers). In the most usual case it is strictly limited funds for capital outlays on the new product (e.g., those available from retained earnings). In this case, return on incremental investment is the best measure. This form of profit measures the income-producing efficiency of the product relative to alternative uses.[4]

[3] The experience of many business organizations is that new products added to mop up overhead actually produce new overheads and, in addition, incur untraceable costs, such as added drain on executive time and energy. These costs make their incremental profits quite different from those indicated by short-run marginal cost estimates.

[4] In the extreme case, where all resources are idle and there is just one candidate product which itself cannot absorb any resource completely, the rate-of-return form is inapplicable, since efficiency is not a consideration in production.

Measuring profit prospects The major problem in estimating profitability is to make decent projections of revenues and costs. Ideally, these should cover the expected life-span of the product; in practice, three to five years is the limit of visibility. Forecasts of demand and costs are extremely speculative for new products; indeed, they are much more so than many firms realize. In explaining the failure of new products, the two hundred companies mentioned at the beginning of this section put particular emphasis on (a) inadequate market research and (b) underestimated selling-cost requirements.

The hardest cost estimates to make are estimates of development and selling expenses. Pressure to get the product onto the market may cut short the research that is needed to work all the bugs out of the product. This can be an expensive short cut, since the bad impressions made on the first venturesome customers may cause delays and perhaps foreclose market acceptance.

Products vary widely in forecastability; for some products no refined calculations are possible at all. Consequently, any use of profit standards for appraising the candidate product is precluded. Going into some products is like making a bet on the horses. Decisions then must rest more completely on grand strategy and on criteria of acceptance like those discussed later in this section.

Level of profit standards To determine how large an incremental profit should be to justify the addition of the product to the line requires some standard of adequate return. Ideally, the market cost of new capital should always be the criterion, but it is not widely used. One alternative standard is supplied by the competition of rival product additions and rival internal investments of all sorts for the company's limited resources. Under such a plan, a candidate product will be rejected unless it promises a rate of return that exceeds the next best use for funds. Another standard (where resources are not limited) is in terms of some historical return on investment. Thus some companies require a minimum return equal to the company's ten-year average; others develop an arbitrary standard of adequate profits of this type that is not specifically related to anything. For example, a large automobile manufacturer, for unknown reasons, has adopted 30 per cent before taxes as a standard. Sometimes the standard is formulated in terms of unit net profit margins at some normal output rate. One company, for example, in the drug field, has a minimum 50 per cent margin. Presumably, such a high standard reflects competition of highly profitable alternative products; thus it is likely to be an opportunity cost standard.

Summary The pivotal test for the addition of a new product is its profitability. If profit maximization were the sole goal of the enterprise, this test would encompass all others, but pluralistic motivation makes the other goals relevant as well. The relevant concept of profits is incremental returns over the appropriate time period, that is, what addition the product makes to enterprise profits over its life-span. The profit prospects must be expressed in a form that allows significant comparison with alternative uses of labor, plant, and time. It is common practice to establish some standard of minimum acceptable earnings, but this floor should really be determined by profitability of alternative opportunities, that is, by external conditions.

PRODUCT STRATEGY

Supplementing tests of profit prospects are general considerations of strategy. These are to a degree composed of the specific acceptance criteria discussed in the next subsection.

Multiple-product "strategy" is a shorthand name for the company's long-run purposes in product diversity. Although strategy is usually focused on profits in the long run and is confined by economic limitations, it is also affected by the technical abilities and personal preferences of management. It is a position consciously taken to simplify decision-making at crucial points. Presumably, under an enterprise system, the purpose of strategy is to make money, in the long run at least. Yet, as we have seen, this is not the whole story. In a going concern, product-line strategy usually has historical roots—sometimes in the company's original purposes but often later in a basic merger or an empire-builder's dream.

Companies with no clear product-line strategy have been conspicuously profitable, and many mergers have grown in spite of the seeming lack of kinship among the products of the merging companies. Other companies say they have a product-line policy, although they are simply rationalizing a product line that grew without pattern. Yet considerable evidence indicates that many well-managed, mature, multiproduct enterprises do have a logical product-line policy that serves as a real guide to action, as is demonstrated by both product surgery and acquisitions that are consonant with announced product policies.

A few examples will show the general character of product-line strategy. A leading electrical manufacturer conceives of its broad product-line policy as a beneficent circle. Its apparatus line generates and transmits electricity; its industrial products and its lamps and home appliances build up the demand for power and help lower the public utility companies' costs; as a result, the price of current is reduced and the demand for its industrial apparatus to produce more current is expanded.

A large producer of insulating materials views its product-line strategy in terms of a complete coverage of the full thermal range, with adequate alternatives throughout the range. The company wants to be considered a specialist in insulation, able to deal with any insulation problem impartially. It assumes that if it sells various alternative devices itself, customers will rely on it to select the most effective technique or material for their particular uses. The product line is an implement for selling a complete insulation service.

Product lines are sometimes conceived in terms of a framework of know-how. Thus one company views its know-how as essentially papermaking techniques. The pivotal machine converts wet pulp into dry, flat products. The company refuses to add products that depart significantly from this framework of know-how (e.g., products that involve intricate metal stamping or assembly operations). A leading automobile manufacturer looks upon its product line as essentially motive-power units and incidentally produces the bodies and wheels that use the power. Chemical companies sometimes conceive their product-line boundaries in terms of the equipment and processes that have been peculiar to the chemical industry. But the constant stream of discoveries in by-products and methods has recently made these borders quite elastic. Chemical companies have been led toward textile and paper processes, and oil companies into chemical industry research and processes.

Sometimes product-line strategy is strictly defensive. One of the building material companies, for example, has in the last twenty years been guided in its product acquisitions by the broad line of building materials offered by the two giants in the industry, whose coverage of building materials was formerly far more comprehensive than the company's own. This policy was in part based on the belief that basic distribution economies were possible in selling a broad and related line of products all handled by the building materials dealer.

The outer limits of a product line (like the outer limits of an industry) are typically framed in terms of common raw materials, production processes, distribution channels, or final uses. These criteria—which are alternative and occasionally contradictory—

are often less fundamental for determining product-line strategy than are the competitive relationships in terms of tactics for increasing profits and rivals' reactions to these tactics. Thus considerations of product-line strategy reflect technical as well as competitive limitations on management. They thus become the groundwork for that nebulous but real part of the company—"grand strategy."

ACCEPTANCE CRITERIA FOR NEW PRODUCTS

Because estimates of probable profits from new products have wide margins of error and cannot be projected far into the future, and because maximizing financial profits is not the only strategic objective of the company, supplemental standards of acceptability for new products are needed. In theory, these standards are not so fundamental as are direct estimates of profits. They rest on empirical characteristics of the firm. Nevertheless, since they are frequently easier to appraise than are profitability standards, they have much value in themselves. A candidate product can be compared with the existing product line in terms of:

1. Interrelation of demand characteristics with the existing product line
2. Use of the company's distinctive know-how
3. Use made of common production facilities
4. Use of common distribution channels
5. Use of common raw materials
6. Benefits to existing products

These criteria can supplement estimates of the direct profits from adding the product.

Interrelation of demand characteristics An important factor in considering new products for the product line is the relation of their demand characteristics to the characteristics of the existing group of products. Since the right combination of products in the product line has powerful promotional value, this interrelation is a primary criterion of acceptable product additions.

What are the kinds of demand relationships between the candidate product and the existing product that will improve its chances of success? Two kinds may be distinguished: the new product may be a substitute, or it may be a complement. Rigorously speaking, the distinction may be framed in terms of cross-elasticity of demand. The candidate product is a substitute if its sales fall when the price of an existing product is reduced (other things equal). If its sales gain, then it is a complement.

There are various kinds of substitute relationships in demand that favor admission of the candidate product. Sometimes the new product, by extending the range of coverage, acts as a hedge against uncertainties and shifts in consumer demand. The garment industry provides many examples of product diversity to reduce risks that stem from buyers' ignorance and style change. Addition of paper, glass, and plastic containers to the product line of manufacturers of tin cans is probably partly a hedge against a revolution in container materials. Another

type has to do with innovations. The acceptance of a new product which makes obsolete the company's existing product is justifiable, primarily because obsolescence is inevitable. The present product would be displaced by new ones in any event—by competitors, if not by the company itself.

Complementarity is the other general kind of demand relationship that is important in testing product additions. Typically, the question is whether the new product can fit into the pattern of demand so that the company's name established by the present products can help to sell the new one. In a sense, this condition shows excess capacity in advertising. Occasionally, another type of complementarity exists when a spectacular new product adds prestige to the existing line. Closely related to the promotional assistance of a new product, and more fundamental and common in most businesses, is the ability of a new product to make the present product line either operate or sell better. Thus the addition of fine-grain film to the product line of a camera manufacturer who sold high-speed lenses brought out the full usefulness of the high-speed lens.[5]

A second demand characteristic is the entity of the product group as a whole. The promotional advantages of a full line often make the whole greater than the sum of its parts. The tactical advantage of a full line of sizes, grades,

[5] Accessories and extras, particularly in the early days of the automobile industry, served both as promotional balloons and as functional improvements. For example, the roof of the 1905 Stanley Steamer was an extra, and the self-starter remained an extra for most cars for years.

and supplementary products in getting good dealers and in merchandising high-margin specialties makes this kind of interrelationship of demand a commonly used basis for product-line policy. Some would go so far as to deny the validity of analyzing sales performance for any individual member of a product group, because each member contributes to the sales and profits of the other members and because the economic unit of merchandising activities is the whole group of products.

A "full line" may be defined as the broadest coverage of related products successfully sold by a rival manufacturer. This concept brings out the defensive nature of a full line policy. By carrying a broad product line (relative to rivals), a manufacturer has advantages in getting good dealers and in efficiently aiding in their merchandising activities by training, co-operative advertising, and "point-of-sale" materials. Consequently, whether the candidate product is needed to match a competitor's breadth of line is an important criterion.

Distinctive know-how Sometimes the determining consideration in making product-line decisions is that new products must make use of the company's distinctive and almost personal source of differential advantage. An example is the M. W. Kellogg Company, which sells engineering skill in the design of giant processing equipment for chemical and petroleum industries. Fabrication and construction are carried on but are subsidiary to the principal product—technical pioneering skill. One of the company's product-line specifications is that products must fully utilize this asset and must be suitable vehicles for the sale of this service.

One of the large electrical manufacturers uses this same test in an indirect fashion. Only products that are highly engineered and that call for intricate manufacture and assembly methods are regarded as suitable, partly because the market that is developed for such products will be protected from easy invasion by these know-how requirements.

Sometimes the distinctive asset is research power. It is a fairly conscious policy of one of the large chemical companies to choose only those new products that have been developed by its product research organization and that are distinctive enough in both chemical and manufacturing requirements to be protected for some time to come. The counterpart of this policy is to abandon products when they have degenerated to the status of commonly produced commodities. The company advances to new monopoly positions as fast as economic progress wears down the walls of the old.

For many companies, research capacity and experience is the major phase of its distinctive know-how. In such a case an admissibility standard should be framed in terms of whether the candidate product is susceptible to the kind of improvement that will put the research capacity of the company to its highest and noblest use.

Another test that may fall into this category is the volume potential test. Many large companies scorn product additions that would meet other tests but that do not promise a sufficiently large volume of sales to use the powers of a large company fully or to overcome its disadvantages of inflexibility. They look upon small-volume new products as requiring an organization that is quicker on its feet than a large company can expect to be.[6]

Common production facilities The requirement that the candidate product use existing or highly similar production facilities is a widely used test of admissibility. When applied strictly to the use of existing facilities, it depends on economies of mopping up excess capacity, which are short lived. Hence, to this extent, the test has perils of using short-run incremental cost when long-run increments are involved.

When the test is framed in terms of requiring similar production facilities, it does not run these risks, since it is not then short run in concept. In this form it bears a close resemblance to the test of distinctive know-how. Similar production facilities are, in large part, a monopoly return on specialized knowledge and concentrated effort.

Most product additions fall somewhere between the extremes of idle capacity and familiar production methods. They normally make use of unused capacity of some facilities, at least common overheads, but often require additional facilities that, though different, have much in common with those for existing products.

Common distribution channels Another popular test of the admissibility of a new product is that it must permit effective marketing through the same distribution facilities used by the company's existing products. In economic terms this criterion is sometimes used to mop up unused capacity. More often, the economies result from savings of specialization or of large scale.[7]

The test is most applicable when the company has a single or a clearly dominant distribution mechanism. A company whose only channel is direct sales to retail stationers might require that a new product be the kind that could be handled by stationery stores and sold by the sales force that serves them. Manufacturers' postwar experience with new products traveling through unfamiliar distribution channels and requiring a different sales organization was, on the whole, quite disappointing.

Even though a product meets this distribution test, there are limits to the number and variety of products that can be efficiently sold by a salesman if he is to be more than a mere order-taker.

Sometimes the selling power rests on no more than a blanket brand name. Products that can be sold compatibly under a well-known company label are sometimes added even though they are

[6] A systematic search for products developed by large research organizations whose volume prospects were too small for the developing company to commercialize was made recently by an outfit which has shown considerable success in developing fairly diverse small businesses. Professional "product-finders" also prospect here for their 5 per cents.

[7] A special case of distribution mechanism economies are the savings of carload mixed-shipment rates for products that come under common freight classifications. This economy has been an important one in inducing building materials manufacturers to broaden their product lines.

sold through different channels and require a specialized sales force.

In addition to savings of specialization and scale, established marketing organizations of salesmen and distributors constitute a source of monopoly advantage. Frequently the dealer organization is the company's most valuable and hardest to duplicate asset. Development of adequate distribution is sometimes a major barrier to entry. Hence the selection of products that will most happily utilize this facet of monopoly power is an important element in successful product-line development.[8]

Common raw materials Many companies look for product additions that use the same basic raw material or its by-products. The rubber industry's product lines exemplify the application of this test. A company with extensive asbestos mining properties has directed its product research toward developing new products that will use not only asbestos but also the short fibers and other wastes that are left after the regular asbestos products have been manufactured.

The economic rationale for this test rests on two points: First, the basic source of raw material is controlled by the company (e.g., asbestos mines or bauxite deposits); the addition of products that use the common raw material

may help develop the market for that material. They can also put the company in a position to exploit differentials between the prices of raw materials and finished products. Second, important savings result from intimate familiarity with intricate processing methods. For this reason the petroleum companies rely heavily upon the common-material test.

Benefits to present product line The foregoing tests depend largely on the contributions that existing products and facilities can make to candidate new products. This "benefits" test, in contrast, asks what the new product can offer to existing products. Contributions through interrelationship to demand have already been mentioned; contributions through experience in new types of production methods which have applicability to old products have received much attention as a result of the peacetime lessons of war production. Similarly, postwar "defense" research and pilot production supported by the military organization illustrate this educational contribution of some new products. Private ventures into new products simply for educational benefits in producing old products are long bets which few companies can take. Old products are a generic class subject to continual evolution. The educational benefits from an added product, either in research, production methods, or even demand interdependence, apply not only to the present products. Often, more importantly, these benefits apply to the projected path of development of these existing products. Remington Rand's recent acquisition of a company mak-

---

[8] The question is not whether the new product can be distributed at all through the company's marketing organization but rather whether it can be distributed economically, both as compared with alternative candidate products, which might otherwise use these limited distribution facilities, and as compared with selling the product to other distributing organizations, while itself manufacturing it.

ing a new type of "electronic brain" computing machine may illustrate this kind of contribution along the paths of projected development of existing Remington equipment.

DROPPING OLD PRODUCTS

The problem of determining what products should be dropped is, in general, the converse of the problem of selecting products for additions. There are, nevertheless, certain differences.

Broadly speaking, when a product's profit or sales behavior is absolutely or relatively unsatisfactory, there are four choices: (1) improve the present operation and keep the product; (2) keep on making it but sell it in bulk for others to market; (3) keep on selling it but buy it from others who can produce it more advantageously; and (4) stop manufacturing it and stop selling it.

The first three are outside our present discussion. The criteria for eliminating a product altogether are substantially the opposite of those for product additions. One approach, therefore, is to screen products that look sick enough to be candidates for deletion through the same kinds of suitability tests discussed above. Another approach is to appraise the product in terms of profits and sales results, such as whether it is slipping in market share, whether it accounts for a trifling percentage of the company's sales, and whether its net or incremental profits are satisfactory as compared with other products or with products that might be produced if it were eliminated. A product that fails the suitability tests and also shows up badly in profit results is more clearly a candidate for

total elimination than one that is inherently suitable but temporarily sick.

In applying the profit tests, a distinction must be made between the long-run and the short-run profits. Products that show comparatively low or negative net profits may still have incremental profits, that is, they may make contributions to general overheads that would not be made if the product were dropped. This sort of short-run consideration can lead to serious errors if it is projected too far into the future. Presumably, the growth of more profitable products should soak up the excess capacity that produces these incremental profits, and the continual stream of candidate products may in the long run produce a greater contribution to overheads than the old product that is retained because of its incremental showing.

The main economic difference between dropping and adding a product is, of course, sunk costs. Deletions that are decided upon solely on the basis of net profit, with no consideration given to the fact that costs are sunk, can lead to short-run losses. But, again, it may be that this is a more valid criterion than it appears to the economist, because executive time squandered on the squeaky wheel and on passed-up opportunities to substitute new and better products overbalances the sunk-cost element.

SUMMARY

1. Product-line composition is a major facet of modern competition, and a company's achievements in new and improved products are an important test of its social contribution.

2. An underlying reason for adding a new product to the line is that it utilizes excess capacity. Broadly conceived, excess capacity occurs when it would cost the multiple-product firm less to make and sell the new product than it would cost a new company set up to produce only that product. Vertical integration and research also promote multiple-product lines.

3. Prospective profitability, in the narrow, cash-return sense, is a key consideration in the selection of product-line additions. The relevant concept is incremental profits over the probable life-cycle of the candidate product. Some standard of adequate incremental return is needed for this profitability test. Ideally, it should be the firm's market cost of new capital with allowance for special risks. In practice, different standards are used, including some average of the company's past return, return from the best alternative investment, or some arbitrary profits goal.

4. Product-line strategy is a semi-independent consideration, though presumably the purpose of strategy is to make money in the long run. Strategic considerations reflect personal, technical, and competitive limitations on the range of product diversity. This policy short cut may center on putting the firm's distinctive strength to its highest and noblest use.

5. How the candidate product's demand dovetails with that of existing products is an important selection criterion. Complementary or substitute relationships or the tactical advantages of a full line underlie the more conventional test of common distribution channels.

6. A candidate product which is made from common raw materials, uses existing production facilities, and/or can be effectively sold through the same sales organization is likely to mop up excess capacity and use the company's distinctive know-how.

7. The problem of deciding on what products to drop is the converse of adding products, except that long-run cost functions are not reversible and that specialized capital is not perfectly mobile. Hence the possibility of salvaging product-line mistakes by partial retreat should be explored before considering total elimination.

►►►►►►►►►►► PRODUCT INVESTMENTS

JOEL DEAN[*]

This chapter discusses the problems of estimating capital productivity on investments in product improvements and additions of new products to the product line. Product investments are essentially par-

Reprinted with permission from Capital Budgeting, *Columbia University Press, 1951, pp. 128–139.*

[*] *Joel Dean Associates and Professor of Business Economics, Columbia University.*

ticular kinds of replacement and/or expansion investments, and rate-of-return estimates for them follow the same basic procedures. Nevertheless, in practice, product investments have sharp peculiarities that distinguish them as a separate estimating problem.

DISTINCTIVE ESTIMATING PROBLEMS

In the first place, the incremental revenues and costs are trickier to identify for product investments than for replacements and expansion. A basic purpose in adding new products is to mop up excess capacity somewhere in the organization—to make better use of one or several existing facilities. Cost changes caused by the addition are more difficult to predict than incremental costs of expansion in present operations, partly because simple expansion usually comes when capacity is filled up. Moreover, product-line changes usually make inroads into the markets of the older products of the company, either intentionally or inadvertently, but there is a question of whether old products would not have been displaced by rival companies in any case.

The second peculiarity of product investments is that they are steeped in strategic benefits for other parts of the product line—intangible effects that are often as important as the measurable profit estimate in the decision to invest. But since direct profitability is usually the first consideration in product-investment decisions, they do not fall into the class of pure strategy investments, . . . where there is no visible profit that can be measured.

The third peculiarity is that changes in product line have greater uncertainty about their outcome; they are ventures into unexplored territory where much depends on natural ability of executives rather than on specific skills they have learned.

TYPES OF PRODUCT INVESTMENT

Product investments can be classified into two types, improvement of existing products and addition to the product line. Product-line additions are either well-known products that are new only to the company or innovations that are new to the world. In this chapter, this breakdown will be followed in discussing product investments.

There is no clean dividing line between a new product and a product improvement, but for our purposes it is enough to say an improvement is intended to displace an existing product immediately, while a new product is intended to augment the product line, at least in the short run.

Product-line policy is an area of management problems that goes much beyond the scope of this book. This chapter is concerned only with product investments that take the form of cash outlays for fairly long-term commitments and thus fit into the capital budgeting program. The most important investment in products is frequently not cash at all, but rather some bottleneck factor such as a limited supply of steel or limited management time. The basic product-line problem is to maximize return on whatever factor is most limited in supply. Cash is usually not the bottleneck for products with very short life expectancies when no long-term outlays are contemplated; nor is it the bottleneck in the longest run when the capital markets will provide funds. But for a middle range of product-line planning, cash availability may frequently be the major supply consideration. It is with this kind of product problem that the present chapter is concerned.

PRODUCT-IMPROVEMENT INVESTMENTS

Investments for improving the usability of existing products may take the form of research activity, engineering design, retooling of equipment, promotional expenses, or frequently only better quality control in production.

For capital budgeting, there is a difference between defensive improvements, that is, those required to bring the product up to competitors' products, and aggressive improvements, that is, those which improve the product beyond competitive standards. The dividing line is often hard to fix clearly, because in many industries competing products are better in some respects and worse in others. But the distinction is useful when it can be clearly drawn, because there is a compulsion to make capital expenditures which bring the product up to competitive par that is much stronger than the need to put it ahead of the parade.

Strategic considerations may be quite different on these two kinds of improvement and may depend on what position the company is aiming at in the industry quality ladder. For example, a major oil company is under strong compulsion to make whatever research and equipment investments are necessary to bring its house-brand gasoline up to the standard of major competitors, since deterioration of its brand reputation can be very costly to repair. The first department store in Chicago to put in escalators hoped that they would pay for themselves by attracting business away from competing stores. Once escalators were commonly accepted, a store with a reputation for premium service would be under strong compulsion to make this modernization investment. The source of capital productivity was the same—namely, its effect upon shifts of patronage—only the probability differs. The certainty of losing prestige and sales from below-par products and service standards is a much stronger incentive to invest than the problematic returns from aggressive improvements in products.

Investments required to keep abreast of styles are in some products even more compelling because customers can distinguish style in most products more easily than they can quality. The tremendous capital outlays of the automobile manufacturers for model changes exemplify this kind of investment. How can the rate of return of such investments be estimated? In principle, the method is clear enough. First, estimate the difference in sales with and without the contemplated product improvement; second, estimate the added net profit from this sales differential; third, relate this added profit to the capital expenditure that produces it, recognizing the limited economic life of this investment (e.g., one year for some dies);[1] fourth, estimate the added long-run profits that will result from the company's reputation for keeping abreast of styles.

In practice, forecasting sales with the precision required for this kind of rate-of-return estimate is seldom attempted. Instead, the practical course of action for most companies whose marketing strategy requires standard-quality products and services is to view investments that are required to bring products or services up to competitive par as having such high capital productivity (in view of the disastrous consequences of not making them) that they go automatically to the top of the capital productivity ladder. Investments that better competitive standards should come under review, and some kind of guess on how much short-run and long-run sales advantage will be obtained by how much capital outlay should be an integral part of the decision.[2]

[1] From the viewpoint of the annual income statement, an investment for a style that is certain to be usable for one year only is not properly a capital expenditure, but rather a current cost of production.

[2] A high order of judgment is required for decisions about product improvement necessary to meet competitive goals, and capital expenditure is a part, and only a small part, of the general over-all decision of what is required to keep the company competitively ahead. For example, in a new body design for an automobile, the top brains of the company participate in decisions on design from the standpoint of what is needed to attain a market share goal and keep the company's reputation for being abreast of styles. Then the top production men determine what kinds of equipment are required to produce this specified model on an economical basis. In this there is little leeway

NEW-PRODUCTS INVESTMENTS

In estimating the productivity of new-product investments, it is, in principle, desirable to construct what amounts to a long-term conjectural income statement. Such a statement requires, first, a forecast of probable sales and probable prices over a period of years; second, a projection of outlays for market development, including initial losses and the costs of redesigning the product to adapt it to demand; third, a projection of production costs that foresees as well as possible the size and technology of plant needed to supply a fully developed market. This income projection should, of course, cut across business cycles and envisage the long-term trend of prices and costs. In estimating costs, there is danger that some will be omitted and that some will be overstated. In general, all the costs of a going concern should be included, but they should be computed on a long-run incremental basis in the sense that they involve only the added cost of having the new product. Similarly, the investment on which the return is computed should include the added working capital, such as inventory and receivables, as well as fixed equipment. When existing land, buildings, and equipment are diverted to the new product, this investment should be included. Strictly speaking, these costs of occupation, together with other kinds of manufacturing overhead,

given the design of the product. Thus, the capital expenditures required for new-model equipment follow more or less automatically, particularly when the capital expenditures that will be required to carry it out are small.

ought to be estimated on a long-run incremental basis, but in practice such costs may be approximated by accounting allocations of full overheads. A big part of the investment outlay is the executive time, research time, advertising, and marketing work needed to develop the new product. Since these are largely fixed costs, it is in general their opportunity cost that is relevant. Although the value of forgone opportunities is hard to determine, a guess might be made by charging against the new product the cost of time devoted to it by top planners and marketers. In practice, these costs are usually treated as current expenses in the financial accounts and can only be chopped out to capitalize by meat-axe estimates.

KINDS OF NEW PRODUCTS

New-product investments may be subdivided in various ways. An important distinction, as already mentioned, must be made between established products that are new to the company and pioneering products that are new to the world. The appraisal of these two kinds of investment involves different strategy, risk, and estimating techniques. Introducing a new product necessarily entails considerable risk, and profit estimates of the kind outlined above have wide error margins. Since there are substantial differences in the estimating problems for mature-product additions and for new-product additions, they will be discussed separately below.

Mature-product additions The problems of estimating return on invest-

ment in adding mature products to invade established markets differ from those for pioneering products. Some big companies show a cavalier and confident neglect of the costs and the profits of the market occupants in deciding whether to add the product. Primary emphasis is placed on prospects for large sales volume, long-run future, and appropriateness to the facilities and special skills of the company.

The early stages of such an investment are analogous to an investment in a research laboratory or a prestige advertising campaign. It is largely a matter of faith that earning power can eventually be developed in this area by the company—a faith reached by the combined judgment of the high command. Since the initial investment in the new venture is pretty much a gamble, no precise rate-of-return computation is made. After the venture has been going for a few years, however, and additional capital is needed for further expansion, rate-of-return criteria can be applied. Even at this stage and, more particularly, in the early stages, the pivotal estimate in the projection is not profitability, but the ultimate size of the market and the company's probable market share. A projected income statement and estimated rate of return on the new venture are never any better than this sales forecast.

The objective in invading established markets is not always aggressive. Sometimes it is primarily defensive. The most common kind of defensive move is the addition of certain basic established products that a major company thinks it needs in order to meet broad-line competition. It may be willing to make the additions even though the investment required does not show a satisfactory return directly from these products. Similarly, market rescue investments needed to hold a particular market until a more fundamental solution can be reached are sometimes justifiable even though the direct return is low. When the cost of recapturing the lost market by selling outlays would be great, a subnormal return on the market rescue investment might be justified if the forgone returns were less than the selling costs of recapture. An example of protective investment in product improvement is that made by one company to develop and produce a specially designed electric motor for window air conditioners. The company knew that the special motor would be made obsolete in two years by basic improvements then being worked out, but in the short run it faced substantial loss of business to a competitor who was using a motor of this kind. It made the investment to prevent having to spend even more money later to get back into the market.

In general, for such investments the threatened segment of the market should be regarded as marginal business, and the earnings on it should be regarded as the additional return that would be obtained by making the improvement as opposed to dropping the product. The investment should be made only if it passes the company's rejection-rate tests. If grand strategy calls for an eventual share of the market, the costs of recapture should be the minimum standard for an acceptable return on the short-run investment.

That is, with this strategy, some out-of-pocket loss may be acceptable.

New-product additions The uncertainties and hazards of introducing a true innovation to the product line are far greater than those of mature-product additions, and rate-of-return estimates are made with different considerations in mind.

The mortality rates for such products are terrifying. The experiences of organizations with venture capital to invest, such as J. H. Whitney & Company, are instructive here. This company reported that of 2,100 propositions studied, only 17 were sufficiently meritorious for the company to put money into them, and, out of this 17, only two were conspicuously successful. Five were moderately so, six were borderline failures, one was a clear failure, and three were still too young to appraise.[3] Even new products introduced by large and successful companies have high mortality. Only about one out of five such products is successful, according to a recent study.[4]

Several specific sources of uncertainty need attention in capital budgeting. First, the product itself may not be as good technically or from the consumer's standpoint as it appears. Protracted field testing is a necessary prelude to commercialization. The instances of premature introduction are

[3] "Volume and Stability of Private Investment," Subcommittee on Investment of the Joint Committee on the Economic Report (81st Congress, 2d Session, March, 1950), p. 26.
[4] "The Introduction of New Products," a survey made in 1949 by Ross Federal Research Corporation, for Peter Hilton, Inc.

numerous. The Chrysler Air-Flow design was a glaring example. Second, initial low-volume production methods are subject to rapid and unpredictable technical changes. Cost projections—the most reliable element of most profit forecasts—have wider error margins, therefore, for new products than for established products. Third, the impact of cyclical swings and fashion cycles is harder to guess, as is underlying demand. Fourth, the costs of developing the market for a striking innovation are great and hard to predict. The innovator usually has to carry the main burden of consumer education, at least in the early stages.[5] Fifth, the rate of competitive entry and imitation is hard to predict. Distinctive specialties tend to degenerate into ordinary commodities, with a corresponding deterioration of profit margins, as competitive encroachment wipes out the salient of monopoly innovation.

These various technological, economic, and competitive uncertainties are often accentuated by the long gestation period between the basic research and the final profits of full commercialization, and these uncertainties make capital productivity estimates so

tenuous that strategic considerations are often determining.

An important strategic consideration in product-line additions is to develop goodwill for other products. For example, a large electrical company recognizes that its investment in the production of betatrons and industrial X-ray equipment and its basic research in atmospheric electricity are largely justified by the contribution that these activities make to the company's general reputation. Like investments in research laboratories, these new-product investments have invisible payouts that are primarily promotional for the new-product investments.

Another kind of strategic consideration in new-product investments is the desirability of getting in on the ground floor in a pioneering area that appears likely to become important in the future. The experiments of Boeing Aircraft with trucks driven by gas turbines fall into this class.[6]

SUMMARY

Product investments include both improvements in existing products and additions to the product line. Defensive product improvements have a higher order of productivity (stemming from the strategic importance of holding market share) than aggressive improvements, and capital budgeting considerations are quite different for the two types of improvement.

Investments to add products to a company's line are of two main kinds

---

[5] An example of error in estimating the time and the amount of specialized education and corporative experiment required to induce buyers to substitute new products for existing ones is found in a large company's investment of $12 million in a plant to manufacture a newly developed silicone. The plant lost money over a much longer period than had been estimated. Part of the delayed development was due to the company's failure to realize that highly specialized chemical engineers were needed to introduce the product. It originally tried to market through its regular sales organization.

[6] A more complete analysis of product-line strategy is found in Joel Dean, *Managerial Economics,* Englewood Cliffs, N. J.: Prentice-Hall, Inc., 1951, Chapter III.

—investments for established products that are new to the company and investments for pioneering products that are new to the economy.

To measure the return on such investments involves projection of complete income statements over a period of years. These statements require forecasts of sales, prices, market development costs, and production costs.

Prospective profitability can be measured for investments to manufacture an established product somewhat more reliably than for new products. For most large companies, however, the pivotal estimate is the long-run future size of the market, and the companies are willing to take their chances on designing an acceptable product, getting its costs down to competitive levels, and grabbing an adequate market share. Thus, precise estimates of prospective return are probably not controlling considerations, at least in the initial stages.

For pioneering products, profit projections have such wide error ranges by reason of the technical, marketing, and competitive uncertainties that forecasts of rate of return give a false impression of precision. Consequently, in making such investments, a high order of judgment of the critical forecasting factors is required. And the *reliability* of these estimates is often the pivotal consideration, rather than the *level* of return calculated from these uncertain estimates.

For both mature and pioneering products, most of the factors in the product-line decision come to a focus in prospective "profits" in some comprehensive sense of the word. But the factors are so difficult to measure that a consideration of their size and the weight to be given them throws many new-product investments out of the arena of rate-of-return competition.

Strategic considerations then become dominant. New-product investments may serve several kinds of strategic ends besides making money on the new product itself: they may be primarily defensive, as in the addition of products to meet full-line competition; they may be predominantly aggressive in staking out a claim in new areas such as television or nucleonics that promise a big future, or they may be primarily promotional in that a large part of their prospective return is invisible and takes the form of increased goodwill for added sales of other products. The strategy of mature-product additions is usually either defensive or a deployment of forces for aggressive action.

B

Company Considerations

▶▶▶▶▶▶▶▶▶▶▶ APPRAISAL OF COMPANY STRENGTHS AND WEAKNESSES

RALPH S. ALEXANDER, JAMES S. CROSS, AND
ROSS M. CUNNINGHAM [*]

In many respects a manufacturing enterprise may be compared to a human being. Definite flows of activity and rhythms are observable. A company has a physical structure of certain size dimensions and a power to perform which reflects its strength and endurance. Intelligence of a certain level is brought to bear in the combined efforts of the people constituting its management and work-ers. It has certain behavior patterns which are the product of past environment and policy and which do not change rapidly. A company may display imagination in its activities, or the reverse; the degree of alertness and response to both internal and external challenge varies widely among firms. Perhaps the firm's chief difference from the human organism is that a corporate form of organization makes possible

Reprinted with permission from Industrial Marketing (Revised Edition), Richard D. Irwin, Inc., 1961, pp. 132–136.

[*] Ralph S. Alexander, Philip Young Professor Emeritus of Marketing, Columbia University; James S. Cross, Manager, Statistical Research Division, Sun Oil Company; Ross M. Cunningham, Associate Professor of Marketing, Massachusetts Institute of Technology.

146

an indefinite life span assuming capable management, whereas the life span of a human being is finite.

The many forces that influence the particular product mix offered by an industrial marketer to buyers make it especially important that management policy regarding product planning be developed with the greatest care. Not only will such a policy guide the addition of new products which mesh well into the company's accustomed practices, but it will indicate the general directions in which management should move to correct practices, which if unchecked will limit seriously its earning power in future years. A well-conceived product policy also is a helpful chart of the general course which the company is to follow and thus enables research personnel as well as others throughout the organization to move in directions which give promise of profitable returns. In the absence of such a chart, there is significant danger that considerable amounts of manpower and funds will be committed to projects which are later abandoned when management really faces up to its decision to move the product into semiworks or full-scale manufacturing and sales. Such abandonments are not only unnecessarily costly to the enterprise but can have unfortunate effects upon the morale of the organization.

A sound product policy must be thought through for several years in advance because a substantial period of years may often elapse between the decision to move ahead on a promising idea and the actual time at which a resulting new product is earning profits for the company. In fact, there is no

area of business management decision in which so long a time lag exists between an initial green light to explore a new idea on a limited scale and the final fruition of the process.

The general policy guides for product planning which will develop as a result of the appraisal processes being discussed find their application in defining the general areas of product search. In considering specific new product ideas, however, as will be developed in the last section, management does not always keep these general product policies in sufficiently sharp focus to aid in the screening process. For such applications, these guides should be translated into a series of questions or check lists which will make certain that all aspects of product suitability are taken into account in arriving at a decision.

PROCEDURE FOR APPRAISING COMPANY CAPABILITIES

The general method of appraising company capabilities is to make an inventory of its present position and to trace the route by which it has reached the present situation. An important part of this procedure is to make continuous comparisons with the situations of competitors. Such comparison is not limited to industrial marketers who make comparable product lines but should also be extended to those who make industrial goods which can serve as satisfactory substitutes in the eyes of the buyer. Although the yardstick of competitive practice is reasonably adequate for most situations, there may be special circumstances in which competition is so weak that other yardsticks must be found in order to make sound appraisals of company capabilities. Such yardsticks may have to be adapted from analogous situations and, while necessarily crude, are none the less useful.

A detailed appraisal of capabilities is beyond the scope of this discussion because it would involve an extent and depth of coverage which is not necessary to illustrate the general philosophy. It will suffice to consider the appraisal in terms of product mix, production facilities, processes, materials and labor, research and development, technical service, marketing organization and activities, financial resources, executive groups, and ownership groups.

Product mix audit The first step here is to analyze sales and gross profits (and net profits when available) for the most recent annual accounting period available and for a period of several years prior to that time. A ten-year period would normally be adequate, while anything less than a five-year period would not present a very complete evolutionary picture. The exact period chosen would depend not only upon the availability of records but also upon the timing of any major fluctuations in business levels of the industry in which the company operates, as well as major fluctuations in United States business.

The amount of detail in which such an analysis of sales should be made depends upon the character of the product mix itself. Certainly, product lines should be shown separately, and it may be desirable to show the sales by

at least the most important items within each line. In addition to analyses by product lines and some items within each line, important additional information would be gained if the distribution of such product sales could be shown by industry markets. Another dimension of sales experience that can be very useful in appraising the present product line relates to the end-uses of different product lines. Thus, the sale of electric motors is spread among a wide range of industries. Yet the end-uses of these motors would represent a considerably smaller listing.

The type of sales analysis just sketched is incomplete as a reflection of the adequacy of the product mix unless it can be compared with similar information about competitive companies. Although at times it may be possible to obtain detailed information about individual competitors, the more usually accessible information consists of estimates of most industry sales. This makes it possible to calculate the shares of market figures by various product lines, and in some cases to analyze them by industry markets, and at times by end-uses. Such shares of market figures are a measure of total company performance for particular product lines. This performance includes not only the product but the price at which it is sold, the amount and quality of the marketing effort expended, and similar factors. Because the product is so important in the total result, it becomes necessary to separate this from the total picture of sales results and to analyze product attributes in comparison to similar attributes for competitive product lines. This makes it possible to render judgments concerning the skill of the company in keeping abreast of or ahead of competitive product offerings. In such comparisons the effect of warranties and guarantees offered should be considered.

Coupled with analyses of these types, a field survey measuring the attitudes of customers and prospects regarding the company and its product offerings can be very helpful.

Production facilities, processes, materials, and labor For a time period similar to those used in the product-mix audit, there should be an analysis of production activities of the company in terms of equipment and other facilities used, processes of manufacture, materials used, and labor force. This analysis would likewise be historical in order to assess the behavior of the company in the past. Past behavior is often the most accurate foundation on which to forecast future behavior. In addition to a detailed description of the plant and equipment devoted to various product lines, the study should include measurement of the degree of utilization and some indication of production efficiencies.

Comparisons with competitors' practices in production should also be made, and the historical picture presented in adequate detail. Much can be learned about the alertness of a company by studying the degree to which it has been an innovator of new methods of production or has been quick to adopt such improved methods.

Comparisons of production costs by product lines with competitive costs, when available, would reveal both strengths and weaknesses. It is rare that a company is equally efficient in the production of its various products, and this pattern often suggests promising areas for new product expansion.

Research and development The present size and types of activities carried on by the research and development staffs, in conjunction with the history of changes which have taken place over a period of several years, provide an indication of the growth or lack of growth and the activities in which these groups have concentrated. Of even more importance, however, is the record of the actual accomplishments of the research and development staffs over a period of time in terms of product improvements, development of new products, and assistance in uncovering new applications of old products. It is difficult to establish meaningful yardsticks to measure the efficiency of research. One of the most useful comparisons is to study the research activities and research accomplishments of competitive companies. Such comparisons will reveal the role which management expects its research and development group to play in each of the companies covered.

Technical service Many industrial products require some degree of technical service in the selling program. For products which are highly technical or for markets which require individualized application of products to technical production methods, the need may best be met by hiring salesmen with a technical education and by training them in the particular problems faced in selling the company's line. When the need for technical service becomes less, either because the product is less technical or less technical knowledge is required for satisfactory selling, the use of sales engineers becomes an expensive means of meeting this problem. It is very common, therefore, to have technical service staffs who are on call at the request of salesmen and customers. The size and competence of such a technical service staff can be an important resource to a company in considering product lines which could be handled successfully by the existing technical staff, or which they might handle given suitable training. The history of this staff and its present capacity in relation to the demands made upon it are important factors in assessing its value to the company. As with most of the aspects of a manufacturing enterprise which are being considered in this appraisal process, comparison with the technical service offered to customers by competitive concerns may prove particularly meaningful.

Marketing organization and activities
The function of the marketing operation within a manufacturing company is to maintain adequate contact and communication with customers and prospects and with the various types of distributors which handle the company's product lines. It is important to know how the sales force is organized in terms of product lines handled and markets served. Changes which have been made in this organization

over past years sometimes yield clues as to the effectiveness of the sales force or sales forces. The quality of the distributor organization may be a source of major strength and sometimes a major weakness. There are never enough competent and aggressive distributors to satisfy all competing sellers, and some companies have been much more successful than others in attracting and holding a strong distributor organization.

Although advertising in industrial marketing does not represent as important a selling method as it does in certain types of consumer products, it still can be an effective helpmate to the sales department. The skill that is displayed by industrial advertising managers and industrial advertising agencies varies widely, and this potential resource justifies careful assessment.

Marketing research has been increasingly adopted by industrial companies in the last few years and has proved an effective means of aiding management in making better decisions. The present size and the history of the marketing research department will provide some indication of its value as a source of company strength.

Finally, a very important marketing resource may be present in the goodwill which the company has earned among customers in many markets. This goodwill is intangible and difficult to measure but may be very important in facilitating the successful introduction of new products.

Throughout the evaluation of these various aspects of the marketing structure of the company, comparisons with competitive practices will make possible more meaningful judgments as to strengths and weaknesses. Another factor of especial importance is the degree to which the marketing organization and the distributor organization are currently working at capacity. As earlier pointed out in this chapter, one of the important forces tending to broaden the product mix is that buyers prefer to purchase several product lines from one salesman and that salesmen are able to sell several product lines with reasonable effectiveness. In many instances one of the real strengths of a company may be found in excess capacity which exists in some phase of its marketing activities and the opportunity which this offers to the efficient marketing of new product lines.

Financial capabilities The present financial capabilities of a company and its financial history are relatively easy to measure, and they represent one of the most important controlling factors in planning for new products. The successful introduction of a new product may require a substantial investment in research and development work, in various types of technical and marketing studies, in a careful program of product evaluation, in the construction of a semiworks manufacturing plant, and eventually in the addition of new plant and equipment for the production of a new product. Besides knowledge of the funds which might be available for allocation to new products, it is vital to assess the willingness of the management to spend them in this fashion. This is particularly true in companies whose stock is closely held. The owner-ship interest may not wish to assume the risks of new ventures, even though substantially higher rates of return might be secured.

The scale of investment necessary to add a new product line to the established product mix varies widely. Production of some types of chemicals and of certain metals demands a large-scale investment and makes it impossible for a company with limited resources to consider entry into such fields. In contrast, entry is relatively easy in industries in which capital requirements are low. Such industries tend to be characterized by keen competition and low rates of overhead expense. Companies which are accustomed to operating in high investment industries are justifiably cautious about entering all low investment fields, because experience has shown that they may have great difficulty in competing effectively on price.

As with the other aspects of the resources of an enterprise, evaluation requires comparison with competitive financial resources. For example, if a manufacturing company were to embark on a particular new product program, the financial ability of competitors to adopt effective countermeasures would be an important consideration.

Capabilities of the executive group One of the most important strengths which may be found in appraising a business is the judgment, skill, imagination, alertness, and physical vigor of the top executive as well as the midzone executive group. In part, this will have already been revealed through a consideration of each aspect of the company's activities over the recent period studied. A certain amount of good fortune, however, may have been present to aid an otherwise mediocre team of executives, and it is desirable to be coldly objective in assessing the capabilities of this group. One important characteristic is to be found in the age distribution of the executive personnel. If this distribution is bunched at certain age levels, the company may face serious problems of retirements in a short span of time. Another factor to be investigated is the extent to which the company has a definite and well-thought-out program for uncovering and developing executive talent.

Finally, there is the question as to how nearly the executive group is working at capacity levels. In some instances it may be found that the key executives are spread thinly over a vast range of problems and responsibilities. This may be a serious limiting factor in considering additions of new products for which success depends upon careful executive attention and follow-through. Naturally, such an appraisal of executives would be broken down into the various functional groups within the company, because different patterns of competence and capacity may well exist in different departments. In order to secure the most realistic interpretation of executive strengths and weaknesses, some consideration should also be given to the situations which prevail among competitors' executives.

►►►►►►►►►►► AUDITING PRODUCT PROGRAMS

PHILIP MARVIN[*]

It can't be emphasized often enough—the only reason for being in business is to produce products at a profit. The products on which profits are based deserve more attention than they usually receive. Prosperity and growth are results of soundly planned product "portfolios," reflecting a smooth flow of products throughout the various phases of the process of creating, producing, and distributing products.

It isn't enough to create products. These individual products must fit into product portfolios. These portfolios, in turn, must be re-examined to evaluate the effect of new products on older products and to sense both needs and opportunities.

For effective appraisal of product portfolios, the whole product spectrum must be scrutinized, from the beginning of the product cycle with the creation of product ideas through each

Reprinted with permission from Machine Design, *January 8, 1959, pp. 107–111. Copyright 1959 by The Penton Publishing Co., Cleveland 13, Ohio.*

[*] *Division Manager, Research and Development, American Management Association.*

step to the final sale. Increasing technological complexity of the contemporary industrial scene and growing intensity of competition that surrounds its products demand that those responsible for the development of new products accept also the responsibility for assuring balanced portfolios.

Where is the starting point? The admission by one engineer that he had been under severe criticism for concentrating on products that were troublemakers rather than those that were profit producers reflects the misplaced emphasis frequently encountered. In filling the role of troubleshooter, engineers can and should provide the type of leadership and direction to product programming that prevent problems from arising by eliminating them at their source.

Errors of judgement are too common. The only sure way to know where to concentrate efforts is through continuing analysis of the company's product portfolio.

DEVELOPING A PLAN OF ATTACK

The basic ingredient of success in any undertaking is a well-organized plan of attack. To reveal strong and weak points in different product lines, performance of individual product lines must be examined separately.

A company's image in the eyes of its customers is usually established on a product-line basis. The multiple-plant manufacturer in the electrical industry may be a producer of household appliances to one group of customers, and construction materials to another. The large machinery company, similarly,

may be a supplier of automatic lathes to one and textile machines to another. To strengthen product programs the customer-centered product line offers the starting position.

To point up fundamental facets of product-line analysis, the accompanying case study, *Troubleshooting A Product Program,* reconstructs a typical situation. The problem faced at the close of the fiscal year by a hypothetical company will serve to illustrate the way in which a product portfolio can be thrown into significant perspective.

BALANCING A PRODUCT LINE

Favorable or unfavorable returns from a product line over any significant span of time reflects the degree of balance achieved in the portfolio of products identified as the product line. At a given time, a low return on invested capital in a particular product line may be due to the introduction of new products to strengthen the line. Another cause of poor returns may be the fact that one or more products have become obsolete but are being carried until replacements can be generated. These and other circumstances may justify a low return on invested capital. Unusually high returns are attributable to equally transitory factors.

To analyze individual product lines, each product in production, as well as those in development and predevelopment phases, should be positioned with respect to its own individual life cycle, and with respect to the basic objectives of the product offerings of the business.

The composite picture reveals the degree to which the company is meeting objectives and protecting future earnings by assuring a continuing supply of new products to replace those becoming obsolete. It also reveals the degree to which a company is taking full advantage of opportunities to introduce lower-cost products and restyled items, as well as those designed for improved performance, new markets, and new uses.

SYNCHRONIZING PRODUCT EFFORTS

In the life cycle of a product, ten distinct phases are recognizable. These include five pre-market categories,

1. Prospective
2. Speculative
3. Potentially Profitable
4. Scheduled
5. Developmental

and five in-market categories,

1. Introductory
2. Growth
3. Competitive
4. Obsolescent
5. Drop-out

One of the important indicators of a soundly planned program is the presence of several or more products in each phase. The fundamental importance of each of these individual phases to overall profits will be reviewed, starting first with the competitive phase of their life cycle.

COMPETITIVE PHASE

In most companies it would be expected that the bulk of the product effort would be classified in the competitive phase. These products would be well-established in markets that would have proved attractive. As a consequence of this attractive market, others in the industry would have similar product offerings.

Prices and profits would normally have reached rather well-defined upper limits as the opportunity for exploitation of the market was curtailed and opportunities to reduce costs through greater volume became more difficult. The competitive phase of a product's life would normally reflect a growth of volume and profits followed by a leveling off and some mild decline.

OBSOLESCENT PHASE

Products should be regarded as having passed from the competitive phase of their life cycle into the obsolescent phase when a pronounced downward trend in sales volume is clearly indicated. For as long a period as steps can be taken to prolong the time before this downward trend becomes established, products should be regarded as competitive. As soon as it becomes evident that all of the available resources that can be used to maintain healthy sales have become exhausted, it should be recognized that the forces of obsolescence have taken control of the situation.

Classification of a product in the obsolescent phase does not imply that there are no further profit opportunities inherent in the product offering. Profitable sales may be enjoyed for a considerable period of time after a product is classified in the obsolescent phase.

Steps should be taken to project the probable time at which individual products will become unprofitable. Dropping products from the line calls for careful planning. Dropping products merely because they are unprofitable may have very far-reaching effects on the sale of other products. Even though they are unprofitable, certain items, because they round out the total product line, should be carried until replacement items can be introduced.

DROP-OUT PHASE

Classification in the drop-out phase serves as a reminder to management that specific products have been assigned scheduled dates on which they are to be dropped from the line. In some instances, the date may be set 30 or 60 days ahead; in others the drop-out date may be set months ahead. The selling organization must prepare dealers and distributors for the discontinuance of these items. At the same time, this classification calls to the attention of those responsible for the product portfolio the necessity of scheduling replacement items that should be available prior to the scheduled drop-out dates.

INTRODUCTORY PHASE

In another phase of the product life cycle are those new products which are being placed on the market for the first time. These products should be classified in the introductory phase. Here it is important to note not only the products themselves but specific reasons why these new products are being introduced.

New products are introduced into the line to increase sales and profits and to replace products that are dropping out of the product portfolio.

Five major competitive opportunities should be capitalized upon by new-product offerings. Soundly planned programs should reflect new-product offerings falling into each of the following categories:

1. *Lower cost* Any redesign resulting in a substantial cost reduction should be regarded as an important new-product offering. Lower cost usually changes the profit position of the product either as a result of increased margin per unit of sales or as a result of potentially greater sales volume at the lower selling price.

2. *Restyling* The redesign of a product, resulting in greater sales appeal and added consumer acceptance, is a major competitive opportunity for the introduction of a new product.

3. *Improved performance* Re-engineering existing products for improved performance or introducing newly engineered models featuring improved performance offer a fertile and commonly exploited area of competitive opportunity.

4. *New markets* Exploiting new markets may be accomplished by extending the usefulness of existing products into new areas or by introducing radically new products.

5. *New uses* Another major competitive opportunity is that of adapting products to new uses. These new uses may represent an extension of the area of application of present products or they may represent a radical departure from existing products.

These five major competitive opportunities overlap and any consideration of the category of new uses provides an example of such overlap. But this is not a serious limitation of the system of classification because it forces product planners to stretch their imagination somewhat and the result can only be for the good. The category of new uses directs attention specifically to capitalizing on opportunities to extend the usefulness of present products.

Many products can be used for more than one purpose. Exploitation of these new uses increases sales. For example, the tongue depressor the physician uses in throat examinations can also be effectively used to mark the location of plants in the garden. Such extremes of usefulness apply in the case of many products. To detect these new uses, product planners must exercise both their ingenuity and imagination.

These five major competitive opportunities have been explored in some detail because they are important not only in planning new products but in auditing product programs once they are underway. The five categories stimulate thinking in the planning stage by calling attention to the full spectrum of opportunities that are open. Beyond this they provide a reference framework for measuring the effectiveness of product offerings in accomplishing these specific end purposes.

GROWTH PHASE

As soon as a product has proved its ability to capture market acceptance and to increase volume saleswise, it should be classified in the growth phase. This is another reason why the introductory phase will seldom if ever show a net profit.

DIVIDING LINE

Up to this point, only those phases in the product cycle where products are offered for sale have been considered. In these five categories, in-market items in the product portfolio are classified.

The second group of pre-market items is of a less tangible nature. Nevertheless, these are an equally important group of products from the long-range position of the company.

PROSPECTIVE PHASE

Each proposal for a new product falls in the prospective phase until such time as it can be appraised. The products in the prospective phase form a stockpile of ideas which should be part of a continuing process of finding, screening and appraising new ideas. Unless the hopper of new ideas is full at all times, the screening and appraising function grinds to a halt for lack of raw material. Once halted, this operation is hard to get going again. A healthy stockpile of unappraised ideas is a positive sign of a vigorous product-development program.

Prospective-product proposals should be found classified under each of the five major competitive opportunities previously discussed. Unfilled classifications on the chart (see case study) may reveal a lack of vigorous action on the part of those who hold the responsibility for developing ideas for new products.

SPECULATIVE PHASE

In the process of evaluating product proposals, a preliminary screening eliminates those of little or no apparent value to the company. Those remaining should be classified as speculative. As such, they are subject to more intensive analysis of their value to the company.

POTENTIALLY PROFITABLE PHASE

Ideas that are appraised as potential profit producers should be placed with other proposals awaiting their turn on the development schedule. Positioning these in a special category calls attention to the fact that they have not been assigned a place in the development group's schedule. This is important. Good ideas, ones on which time and money have been spent in assessing their potential as profit producers, have failed to get into development schedules as a result of neglect and oversight. Positioning these in a special category reduces this risk.

SCHEDULED PHASE

In the analysis of a product portfolio, projects awaiting development are a sign of management vigor in promoting new product programs. When too many projects are awaiting development, this fact may point up organizational weaknesses such as inadequate development appropriations or staffing.

DEVELOPMENTAL PHASE

This is the phase in which ideas are turned into commercially feasible products. Everything that must be done to produce a saleable product takes place here. Known facts are applied in developing the new product. Research is undertaken to supply new understand-ing to enhance product development. These facts and this understanding should encompass both the physical sciences as well as economics and fundamental knowledge of customer motivation if a complete job is to be performed.

Ideas and information are the raw materials in the development process. Saleable merchandise is the end product of effectively applied technical talent. In between these two, the success of the business is largely determined. Second or third-rate talent here will be reflected in competitive weaknesses of final products. Products leaving the developmental phase should be ready for sale in every respect and, until ready, should remain under development.

PLANNING FOR TOMORROW

Positioning individual products properly with respect to their own place in the life-cycle will do more to reveal to engineers new needs than any other step that can be taken in evaluating the soundness of product programs.

In this age of steadily advancing technologies, top-management is becoming increasingly aware of the rapidly growing need for dynamic product-portfolio management. Product-portfolio analysis is the starting point in planning for profits. The insight revealed by such analysis joined to that gained by perusing financial statements provides the perspective that turns words and numbers into meaningful facts and figures. It can be a potent tool both in positioning the present and projecting the future.

TROUBLESHOOTING A PRODUCT PROGRAM

Details of a Typical Product-Portfolio Analysis

At the close of the fiscal year, sales of the XYZ Co. had increased steadily to a peak figure of $80,241,000. Contrasted with increased sales, after-tax profits were less than 6 per cent. This was the poorest profit position company management had ever faced. To isolate factors contributing to declining profits, the performance of individual product lines themselves will be examined. Comparing individual product lines on the basis of their capacity to produce profits provides insight in interpreting profit trends.

INCOME ANALYSIS

Overall product program of the company is built around ten basic product lines. Sales, profits and other significant data for each product line are summarized in *Income Analysis by Product Line*. Analysis of profits by these individual product lines is a basic management control, each product line being revealed as a profit producer or profit reducer. This analysis tells where to concentrate efforts in improving the overall profit position.

Overall profits of the company for the year are 5.4 per cent of sales. Product line D is the most profitable, six product lines show losses, three contribute negligible returns.

Each product line makes use of company resources which should be deployed in the most productive manner. Here, more than half of the funds are seen to be unprofitably invested. Over 45 per cent of the company's money is invested in product lines producing an unattractive return. In sharp contrast, the funds invested in a single product line produced the unusually favorable return of 45.3 per cent on that investment.

PRODUCT-PORTFOLIO ANALYSIS

Finding the problem areas will require a more probing analysis of each basic product line. To illustrate this approach, product line A will be examined in detail here. Product-life phases will be considered in the same order as discussed in the article text.

Product line A consists of a group of the company's mechanical goods, centering around a line of reel-type mowers and including certain other auxiliary products to round out the product portfolio. Product life-cycle relationships in this product line are depicted in chart form in *Product Program Analysis*.

Competitive Four models of reel-type mowers are currently regarded as being in the competitive phase. These are models 72, 36, 85, and 29. They are positioned in the chart with respect to their own individual life cycle. Collectively, these four products account for a net income of $60,000. The net income attributable to each individual product is shown by the solid black bars in the lower section of the chart, just below the individual model. Figures at the top of each bar show the specific amount in thousands of dollars. For example, an $18,000 net income is allocable to the model 72 mower.

Obsolescent Two products are classified in the obsolescent phase: Models

TABLE

INCOME ANALYSIS BY PRODUCT LINES

Product Line	Share of Market (%)	Sales Volume ($1000)	(% of total)	Manufacturing Costs ($1000)	(% of total)	Administrative and Sales Costs ($1000)	(% of total)	Profit or Loss ($1000)	(% of sales)	(% return on invest-ment)	Capital Investment ($1000)	(% of total)	Turnover of Investment†
A	8	3,600	4.5	3,052	4.6	497	5.1	51	1.4	3.2	1,593	4.1	2.3
B	7	9,845	12.3	9,694	14.6	1,592	16.4	-1,441	-14.6	-49.6	2,903	7.5	3.4
C	12	9,700	12.1	8,228	12.4	1,700	17.5	-228	-2.4	-3.8	5,990	15.6	1.6
D	21	36,900	46.0	26,356	39.8	3,388	34.8	7,156	19.4	45.3	15,800	41.0	2.3
E	16	4,845	6.0	4,030	6.1	909	9.3	-94	-1.9	-11.5	819	2.1	5.9
F	14	2,200	2.7	1,851	2.8	347	3.6	2	.1	.1	1,795	4.7	1.2
G	18	1,975	2.5	1,829	2.8	141	1.4	5	.3	.4	1,259	3.3	1.6
H	15	5,925	7.4	5,587	8.4	513	5.3	-175	-3.0	-4.3	4,033	10.5	1.5
I	11	2,950	3.7	3,327	5.0	368	3.8	-745	-25.3	-26.9	2,774	7.2	1.1
J	8	2,301	2.8*	2,226	3.5*	280	2.8*	-205	-8.9	-13.3	1,540	4.0	1.5
Total		80,241	100.0	66,180	100.0	9,735	100.0	4,326	5.4	11.2	38,506	100.0	2.1

* Adjusted to total 100%. † Ratio: Sales volume/capital investment.

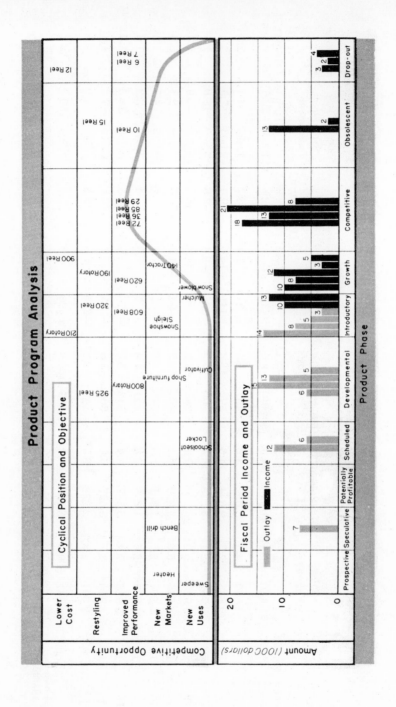

Product Program Analysis

10 and 15 reel-type mowers. Together, they represent an income of $15,000.

Drop-out Products classified in the drop-out phase account for $9,000 of the net profit from sales.

Introductory New product offerings by the company cut across the range of competitive opportunities.

Lower Cost: Model 210 rotary mower is a redesign of the Model 190 rotary and provides a comparable product at a lower cost, reflected in the selling price of the new items.

Restyling: Model 320 reel-type mower, which is being introduced to the market, represents a restyling of the Model 6 reel unit, which is scheduled for drop out.

Improved Performance: The Model 608 reel-type mower represents a re-engineering of the Model 15 reel unit which is classified in the obsolescent phase. A drop-out date has not yet been scheduled for the Model 15.

New Markets: An attempt is being made to enter new markets having different seasonal characteristics. Snowshoes and sleighs are being added to the line to provide items in the product portfolio which will have off-seasonal characteristics. Both snowshoes and sleighs have seasonal patterns running directly counter to the products in the present line, all of which are used during the summer.

New Uses: Prior work with lawn mowers gave the company's engineers the experience needed to extend the usefulness of this product to leaf mulching.

Products in the introductory phase represent an outlay in excess of income of $7,000. Two of the products yield a profit of $23,000 but this is offset by the $30,000 outlay for the four remaining products in the introductory phase. It should be expected that products in this category will not show a profit. This is a market development phase.

Growth Five products have entered the growth phase: A snowblower, a tractor, two reel-type mowers, and one rotary mower. In the current period shown in the chart, each of the five major competitive opportunities discussed previously are being exploited by products in the growth phase. This reflects the fact that considerably greater attention is being paid to product development in current periods than was the practice in earlier years. From a study of the classification of older products in the competitive, obsolescent, and drop-out periods it is apparent that no attention was given to products for new markets or new uses. Primary emphasis was in the single direction of performance improvements in existing models with one attempt at restyling and one at design for lower cost.

Products in the growth phase currently yield an annual return of $38,000. Growth in sales is anticipated for each of these five items. The net return is expected to exceed $100,000 within a short period of a few years. New product development is not only making substantial contributions to the profits of the company but is broadening the profit base, and contributing to stability.

Turning now from the in-market

categories to the premarket items gives a further insight into the long-range strengths and weaknesses of the company's product program.

Prospective In this program, there is a relative dearth of new ideas awaiting appraisal. Both a driveway and sidewalk sweeper have been proposed, as well as a workshop heater, but ideas for lower costs, restyling, and improved performance are noticeably lacking.

Speculative The company has already spent $7,000 in evaluating a bench drill that would enable the company to enter new markets. As yet, available evidence is inconclusive as a basis for either accepting or rejecting the proposal.

Potentially profitable Analysis of this product portfolio shows that there are no unscheduled proposals. Those ideas that have appeared to be potential profit producers have been scheduled. Other than to accommodate the normal time required to process an idea into the development schedule, there isn't any good excuse for a backlog of unscheduled projects. Even though it may not be feasible to commence work on a project for several years, it should be scheduled. This in itself will call management's attention to the need for action to relieve the backlog of scheduled projects.

Scheduled Two projects are in the scheduled phase, a school seat and a locker. An expenditure of $18,000 has been allocated to these two proposals. This money was actually disbursed in evaluating the merit of these respective proposals. Since the proposals themselves have moved into the scheduled phase, expenditure figures move with them.

Developmental Four products are under development, a cultivator, shop furniture, a rotary mower, and a reel mower. An outlay of $39,000 has covered this development work during the period under review. It should be noted that no attention is being given to new products that will take advantage of cost-reduction opportunities in the present program. This neglect could have rather far-reaching consequences in the event that competitors plan to capitalize on such opportunities.

▶▶▶▶▶▶▶▶▶▶▶ CRITERIA FOR EVALUATING EXISTING PRODUCTS AND PRODUCT LINES

D'ORSEY HURST*

There are few elements of a company's marketing operations which, when subjected to critical, objective, and systematic appraisal, afford a greater opportunity for improving over-all marketing effectiveness than the company's existing products and product lines. However important tomorrow's products may be—and, make no mistake, they are very important indeed—it is *today's* products that are closest to the cash register, and upon which a company's chance to market tomorrow's products ultimately depends. The challenge to marketing today is to find ways of dealing more effectively with current products under current conditions.

The product-line audit represents very little that is new in terms of the elements involved, but it represents something quite new indeed as a formal approach for the critical, objective, and systematic appraisal of the company's product lines. The company that uses it today will almost certainly gain an edge on its competitors, for the chances are good that they are not making a regular audit of their product lines. Although most of the companies covered in our recent study exhibited great interest in the subject, few had anything approaching a continuing, comprehensive audit program.

There are, no doubt, as many reasons for this lag as there are marketing executives, but the following are certainly among the most significant:

Lack of time We have come a long way since the days of order taking. Marketing and sales managers today are so busy that they have no time to analyze objectively, to review systematically, or to sit back and take a broad perspective.

A false sense of security Some executives believe that they are making "informal" marketing audits simply by reviewing the profitability of their product lines from time to time. These men honestly feel that profitability is the only measure of success. If a product is not profitable, they drop it immediately from the line, but they keep any product that is profitable on any basis because they are afraid to "rock the boat."

"New-babyitis" Let's face it, existing products are simply not as interesting or fascinating as new ones. Like the new baby in the house, the new

Reprinted with permission from Analyzing and Improving Marketing Performance, *AMA Management Report No. 32, American Management Association, 1959, pp. 91–101.*

* *D'Orsey Hurst Inc.*

product seems to get all the attention while the rest of the company's products are pretty much neglected.

Internal organizational problems Even in companies where an audit is considered desirable, it must be decided who is going to do the auditing: division or corporate staff, outside consultants, or a combination in the form of a task force.

Resistance to change in the status quo The executive vice president of a building-supply firm told us of his attempt to audit a product line of shingles. "My office had no sooner raised the question," he said, "than all the product managers got busy defending their positions."

In view of these barriers to the use of marketing audits for the evaluation and improvement of existing product lines, how can the marketing audit concept be made more understandable and more acceptable? Although there are certainly any number of valid approaches, that which we in Market Planning Corporation consider most useful is a division of the marketing audit concept according to the following ten categories of criteria used in evaluating a product line:

1. Profitability
2. Scope of product line
3. Marketing efficiency
4. Production efficiency
5. Cost
6. Price
7. Value
8. Quality
9. Service
10. Competition

For the remainder of this paper, we shall consider each of these categories in detail.

CRITERIA OF PROFITABILITY

Standards of profitability vary not only from industry to industry and from company to company but also, within any given company, from division to division and from product line to product line. In general, however, product-line profitability is measured in terms of percentage of profit on sales or investment, as compared with company or industry averages.

Specifically, the questions we suggest asking are these: How does the product line's profitability compare with the company's general profit objective? How does it compare with the company's actual average? How does it compare with the industry average? Answers to these questions will assist in evaluating current performance and also provide clues for predicting future performance. If, for example, a product is low on all counts, there is certainly room for improvement. Such a rating is the signal to find out what is wrong with the product and improve it, since others in the industry are making money with comparable products. If, on the other hand, the showing is below the company average but above the industry average, it may be that even the best producer is not doing very well, and this raises the question of whether it is desirable to stay in the field.

Although profitability is obviously the most important consideration in determining whether to make a modification or deletion in a product line, it is not the *only* consideration. Unfavorable profitability may sometimes be nothing more than a signal for review and evaluation. It is also vital to find out what contribution the product is making to overhead. High-volume, low-profit items are frequently continued in a product line because they are carrying a substantial share of the line's overhead and because dropping them would adversely affect the corporate or divisional net profit. There may also be other compelling competitive or policy reasons for retaining the product.

Products which make a below-average contribution to profits should be reviewed at least annually to avoid continuing them on an overvalued rating of their contribution to overhead. The pertinent question is: What overhead facilities, manpower, and other related costs could be cut if the product were dropped? Continuing review of the fixed/variable cost relationship against the product's volume potential and pricing may open up the way to increased profitability. Breakeven points should be carefully reviewed with an eye to the prospects of increased volume. Consider, for example, George Romney and his Rambler: Volume increases took this product from a loss position to that of an extremely substantial profit earner.

CRITERIA OF PRODUCT-LINE SCOPE

Even when a product contributes no profit, it is often retained to round out the company's line, to satisfy distributors or customers, or to prevent competitors from getting their foot in the door. There is at least one dog in every manufacturer's line, but it stays there year after year because the company feels that the losses incurred by having a hole in the product line would be greater than the cost of keeping the dog. Basically, this is because every company is striving to attain or maintain a position of dominance in its industry, and the industry leader is ordinarily expected to carry a full line.

It is possible, however, to concentrate in profitable areas without offering a complete line. Magnavox, for example, a highly respected manufacturer of phonographs and television receivers, has successfully managed to avoid both the cut-price production and distribution headaches at the low end of the line and the complications of the hi-fi specialty-components market by concentrating on cabinetry and tone quality in the upper price ranges. In another instance, two producers in the automotive supply market have the same total volume but vastly different profit pictures: The low-profit operator tries to ape his giant competitor in size of product lines, while the high-profit operator limits both his product lines and his territories, concentrating on long runs and low marketing costs.

Something else to consider in relation to the scope of the product line is the need for the company to maintain its position with distributors, dealers, and customers. This factor can increase the attention given certain items which are not inherently profitable. Service and franchise factors should be reevaluated regularly and continuing efforts made to bring about ingenious solutions to the problems which exist.

Corporate-image considerations sometimes dictate continuance of unprofitable products. Thus, although every other manufacturer of color television receivers has dropped out of the business because of the sizable losses incurred, RCA continues to manufacture color receivers, partly because its patent position gives it a greater stake in color television but also because it wishes to maintain its image of leadership in the fields of radio and television. The losses incurred in color television are therefore actually an investment in institutional prestige.

A company may also find it necessary to delete profitable items from its line because they are not compatible with the public's image of the company and its products. A major manufacturer, for example, cannot generally afford to be associated with items having an unfavorable social or psychological connotation. It is for this reason that major packers of food products hesitated for years to become associated with dog foods, and that Johnson & Johnson, which wishes to preserve its image as a producer of surgical products, established a subsidiary company, Personal Products Corporation, for the merchandising of feminine-hygiene products.

There are two tested approaches for checking on the continuance of existing products which have not achieved or maintained the desired level of profitability. One of these is the periodic *"profit detractor"* review. A major manufacturer of consumer durables, for example, makes a review every six months of all products whose profitability is less than the corporate average; for each such product, the manager responsible is required to recommend action for improving earnings or elimination of the product. The second approach, the *test of substitutability*, is especially useful in checking on large product lines, in which a multiplicity of items may be included for either merchandising or service reasons. Too often, in such lines, duplication results in more items than are actually necessary. Even though every item in the line can pass the profit test, it may be advisable to eliminate some to reduce production, inventory, and marketing costs. For industrial customers, especially, it may be desirable to supply low-volume, low-profit items in order to obtain orders for large items. A systematic check of the line should be made frequently, however, to see whether less expensive items could be substituted to do the job.

CRITERIA OF MARKETING EFFICIENCY

The evaluation of marketing efficiency involves a number of individual assessments. To begin with, does the product first of all create special handling, shipping, or storage problems which disrupt normal marketing operations? The "wraparound" auto windshield, for example, has caused a gigantic increase in shipping costs, storage space requirements, and the number of sizes which must be carried in stock.

Are the size, shape, and material of the package well suited for handling in the normal channels of trade? The difficulty of stacking beer bottles on crowded store shelves, for example, was an important consideration in the development of the beer can.

Is the product sold through special channels of distribution or by a special sales force which is not justified by volume alone? For years, one company sold a single line to the shoe-repair trade by a direct sales force, while competitors sold through jobbers and distributors. The company's theory was that direct selling gave it better control of the market, but the plain fact was that the low frequency and volume of the purchases made by most shoe repairmen made it uneconomical to call on them directly. Only jobbers and distributors who could supply *all* the repairman's needs—soles, heels, laces, polish, thread, nails and so forth—could afford to call on him directly.

Is the item being penalized by being distributed through the same channels as company products which require high-cost distribution? National Biscuit Company's breakfast cereals and dog foods, for example, were being distributed direct to retailers through the same channels as the company's fresh crackers and cookies. The freshness requirement of breakfast cereals and dog foods, however, does not call for such high-frequency, high-cost, direct distribution as does the freshness requirement of crackers and cookies, and when the company switched to wholesalers for its cereals and dog foods it was able to cut its prices considerably.

Does the product divert selling effort from other, more profitable items in the line? Sales drives on certain items are often successful at the expense of other items in the line.

Are market-share goals for the product consistent with profit goals? Frequently, certain items in the line can go for a "free ride" and make money. When ambitious penetration objectives are set, however, the cost of driving sales up does not justify the program. In the parts business, for example, "skimming the cream" can be quite profitable, but competing with cut-price marginal producers is unrewarding.

CRITERIA OF PRODUCTION
EFFICIENCY

Even under the new "marketing concept," you can't ask the factory to make just *anything*. It may be just plain uneconomical to make a certain product, perhaps because of the high quality requirements or because existing capital equipment cannot be converted. In the textile business, for example, the mill that could not produce flawless woolens for the solid pastel shades which were in vogue a couple of years ago is probably going great guns today on the currently popular bulky-looking tweeds.

There are many other considerations. A merger may bring in additional production facilities that will allow the company to compete in a new geographical area or a new product area. Or perhaps it can change its warehousing and inventory setup because new equipment, operating more efficiently on short runs, has eliminated the necessity for longer runs and bigger inventories. These are just a few of the marketing possibilities that can be revealed by a serious examination of production efficiency criteria.

It is essential, then, to review for compatibility continually; the product must fit in with the company's engineering and production know-how as well as its facilities. Also important are unusual seasonal variations, style changes, and size requirements, which complicate the production task and cut down efficiency and quality.

CRITERIA OF COST

The application of cost criteria to existing products should be a continuing effort and should include criteria of *design* cost as well as criteria of manufacturing cost.

An important new tool in auditing the product line for design cost is value analysis, the essence of which is the question: Is the weight, dimension, or strength of this part really necessary? Many serviceable parts are produced more simply and at lower cost today through the value analysis approach. The application of value analysis does not, however, imply a lowering of quality. The use of a cardboard back on certain television and radio sets was unfortunate, for example, because the customer could *see* the cheaper part, and the public's image of the brand suffered accordingly. The test of any value analysis recommendation should be this: Does it represent a reduction in cost to the manufacturer without a reduction in value to the consumer?

Frequently, the best audit of manufacturing cost can be made by soliciting outside bids to manufacture the product or component in question. Besides being a useful cost criterion, this sometimes serves as the basis of a make-or-buy decision. The facts must be examined extremely carefully, however, before deciding to buy from an outside producer. The total contribution to fixed charges, rather than the cost applicable to the specific component, must be considered, for overhead costs continue.

CRITERIA OF PRICE

Pricing is an extremely complex process. Balancing prices with such factors as profit yield and competition requires all the skills of marketing management. In this connection I should like to emphasize four points.

First, the primary test of any price should be: Is it yielding sufficient profit? It is a mistake to be bound by the pricing tradition of an item, such as historical relationships between grades or between basic units and parts or accessories. If profits have shrunk, these relationships may have to be altered. There are often items in the line that can command a higher-than-normal markup because of their patent protection, tooling requirements, or other factors. Such profit opportunity items may be overlooked in formula pricing and should be sought for diligently in auditing the product line for price.

Second, it is essential to be wary of pricing formulas based on cost. Each of the components of cost—engineering, processing, and materials—should be checked to insure that profit margins will yield the required return on investment. Where there is virtually no processing cost—as in a retail supermarket operation, for example—margins can be low and profits adequate; where processing costs are high, however, margins must be greater. Many a company has been trapped by single-line competitors who understood this simple distinction while it was working under a blanket cost formula applied to widely different items.

The product's patent situation must also be considered in auditing for price. Minnesota Mining and Manufacturing Company, for example, maintains a very favorable profit margin on a patented product until a few years before the patent expires, then reduces it quickly in order to avoid providing a profit umbrella which would invite competition.

Third, both fixed and variable cost elements should be examined when making pricing decisions. If there is a high element of fixed cost, curves of estimated volume should be developed for a range of prices and the point of optimal price/volume relationship chosen. If there is a high element of variable cost, any price reduction should be weighed carefully.

Finally, price leadership opportunities should be sought aggressively. Most business men say they set prices to meet competition, yet somebody ultimately must lead on price. Leadership usually varies by line, not by company. One key to price leadership opportunity is the company's share-of-market position. A dominant company may choose not to raise prices on its most profitable line because its competitors, whose costs are probably higher as a result of their lower volumes, will welcome a price increase and gladly follow the lead.

CRITERIA OF VALUE

Value analysis is a major key to marketing success. One of the most significant contributions of the new marketing concept has been its basic injunction to ask: What are the customer's criteria of value—that is, what does the customer believe that he is getting for his money? With a view toward possible improvement, the next question that logically occurs is: Why is any given product regarded by the customer as being "different" or "better"? The marketer should constantly aim to develop points of distinction or uniqueness. There is great opportunity for creativity in devising new ways to present a product to the public through the media of advertising, promotion, and direct selling.

Value is not necessarily a function of the cost/price relationship. Engineers often "overdesign" products. The first aerosol bombs, for example, were quite expensive because of the heavy-gauge steel of which they were made. Thus, though their high price was justified in terms of cost, it was not justified in terms of value to the consumer. When lighter metals and different pressures were used, the price of aerosol bombs was brought down to a point where the product represented good value to the consumer.

Often features can be added to a basic product at low cost which will greatly increase its value and appeal to the customer. The leaf-mulcher attachment on power lawnmowers, for example, increased consumer value considerably at a small increment in manufacturing cost. Mail-order houses are especially adept at this technique of value enhancement.

The multi-use factor is related to this question of value to the consumer. A manufacturer of small radios, for example, decided that the customer wanted not merely small size but greater flexibility for use under all conditions. The company subsequently manufactured a small unit which could be run by batteries as well as by house current and secured a handsome share of the radio market.

There are, then, some obvious questions for a company's management to ask itself: Have our customers discovered new applications for our product which are of value to them? Are there any features we can exploit? Are we learning of these quickly? How adequate is our communication with the marketplace? The role of continuing market research in determining a product's value to the user is clear.

CRITERIA OF QUALITY

The perennial question in connection with quality is: What is meant by "quality" and who measures it? The marketing man must concern himself with three different standards and perceptions of quality: (1) the producer's, (2) the competitor's, and (3) the customer's. Marketing research makes an important contribution to the integrated assessment of existing products by providing a feedback of data from the field on customers' and competitors' quality standards which can help manufacturing and engineering establish quality specifications and maintain quality control. In short, marketing should relate value analysis to quality standards. Too often, however, a manufacturer resists quality changes because field intelligence either is not presented to him at all or is not presented persuasively.

Quality is, of course, subjectively related by the user to *service*. Minor annoyances, such as difficulty in opening a jar, can downgrade quality assessments. In the end, the only important criterion of quality is what the customer thinks it is.

CRITERIA OF SERVICE

Service requirements are designed into a product. Although design, engineering, and manufacturing should anticipate most parts needs, there are usually some unanticipated problems, particularly with complex products. Careful planning has resulted in a great deal of progress in this area in recent years. Service training schools have been established in many industries—the most notable, perhaps, being the mechanics' courses which companies in the automotive industry have set up.

A number of questions must be considered in auditing a product for service. How frequently should the product be serviced? Are service facilities available? Are parts and components available, and for how many years must they be provided? What is the user's viewpoint on such problems as replacements and repairs? Obviously, the service audit can be an important guide in designing the next model of the product.

Guarantees and warranties should be reviewed regularly. Is the warranty needed? Is it meaningful? What does the customer want? Can the guarantee be made self-liquidating? Answers to these questions lead to improved service.

CRITERIA OF COMPETITION

Competition seems to spring from new and unsuspected sources every day. The traditional sources of competition, of course, are always ready to upset an unwary opponent, and this under-your-nose type of competition must always be watched carefully. Today, however, competition can barrel in from many new directions: new materials, new processes, new distribution channels, and new buying practices, to mention only a few. It is therefore extremely important to know *why* a product is losing ground; the right answer may help bring it back up among the high-profit producers.

In our audits, we ask questions like these: Is the product losing ground because of quality, price, or demand? If quality characteristics are under review, have thorough and objective laboratory analyses been made of the product and competitive products to highlight differences and weaknesses? Are competitive products really better, or have the customers merely been convinced that they are better? When the criteria suggested above are used on a continuing basis, weaknesses in terms of profit, performance, and competitive position become evident sooner than they otherwise would.

The basic considerations in evaluating traditional and direct competition are cost, price, and value (as perceived by the customer). Perhaps even more significant, however, is the threat of encroachment by new materials and processes, planned product innovations, and technological explosions in research and development. These can create new, dynamic competitive situations both for consumers and for industrial producers. Examples of such "supplantive" competition from alternate processes and materials are transistors versus electronic tubes and sheet plastics versus paper and foil laminates.

When competition hits a company in the cash register, there are only three things to do: meet it, whip it, or get out. Needless to say, there are circumstances under which each of these alternatives may be the best solution.

When a competitor develops a new process or product that cuts into a company's sales, this competition can be met in either of two ways: by matching the product or by beating the price. There is, however, one basic rule which always applies: If the company decides to stay in the market with the existing product, it should never let its competitor maintain an advantage over a long period of time.

Product modifications and improvements should be carefully weighed in terms of the additional competitive strength they will provide in the marketplace and the comparative cost of introducing a new product. A sales increase can often be accomplished by redesign, new packaging, or new colors. Although such modifications may be less expensive than anticipated, they do require careful planning.

The time may come, however, when investigation of all sales, manufacturing, and distribution elements, as well as of the possibility of modification, indicates that the product must be deleted. How can the death of one of its products be made less painful for the company? It is first necessary to determine whether the product's withdrawal from the market should be carried out in a manner that will dry up demand abruptly or gradually. Factors to be assessed in timing include the state of field inventories and the effect of withdrawal on trade channels and customers. For instance, how many users will be inconvenienced if not supplied?

Another question is whether the product should be maintained on an inactive basis. In consumer sales this is known as "milking." All sales efforts and promotions are stopped, and the product is dropped from the sales sheets but continued in limited production. After what is usually a sharp decline following upon the withdrawal of promotion, the momentum from previously satisfied users may permit the product to continue indefinitely. For example, Procter & Gamble's Teel, a liquid dentifrice, is still selling profitably on a no-promotion basis. Such products will, of course, ultimately wind up in the obituary columns when the minimum-volume point is reached.

There are other cases where a sharp cut-off, or what is known as "abandonment," is dictated. For instance, where a product has been purchased, a legal time limit may have been established in order to earn a tax write-off within the company's fiscal year. . . .

The product-line audit offers a company new opportunities to stay on top of its market by judging its products objectively and accurately against all pertinent criteria. The audit should be made at least once a year for profitable products and every six months for less profitable products. Applied consistently on such a basis, the audit will soon be needed only once a year—for *all* the company's products will be profitable.

►►►►►►►►►►►► HOW TO DECIDE WHICH PRODUCTS TO JUNK

LYMAN J. HOUFEK*

Since World War II many companies have added new products—assuming that more profit automatically would follow. Their sales forces fought for new products and for new packs of various sizes on established items. Product innovation seemed to be a mark of progress and success in a market steeped with competitive rivalry.

Certain advantages in maintaining extensive product lines do exist—especially lines with wide profit margin items. But during the post-war realignment of products and product lines a system of controls was rare, and many product lines were overexpanded.

Management, fast becoming acutely aware of these excessive marketing costs, is more and more pointing an accusing finger at product line growth and giving the order, "Cut the line; set

Reprinted with permission from Printers' Ink, *August 1, 1952, pp. 21–23.*

* *Printers' Ink.*

up controls!" With that directive, interdepartmental problems immediately emerge.

These conflicting interests are best reconciled through the committee approach. Product line simplification and control is a problem of interdepartmental coordination. The function of the committee is to develop, and after development to police a product line that will:

produce maximum long-range net profits by . . .

satisfying trade and consumer requirements with . . .

the greater efficiency of long uninterrupted production runs on standardized products.

The basic steps in cutting the product line are:

1. Tabulate sales by product for the most recent 12-month period.
2. Calculate composite cost including:

direct material costs (including all raw material necessary to complete the finished product)

direct labor costs covering all activity of labor engaged in completing the finished product

variable factory overhead, consisting of variable (or volume) factory costs that include that part of the indirect labor, supplies and other expenses which bear a direct relationship to the volume of a product passing through a department or factory

marketing costs, when a drastic reduction in product line is anticipated or when a candidate product is part of a limited line or requires unique marketing effort.

3. Subtract composite cost from sales value, product by product, and the result is *incremental profit*.
4. List all products in a product line according to their incremental profits and consider in terms of incremental profit which ones are logical candidates for elimination from the line.

The committee is composed of the sales manager, market research manager, controller and plant superintendent, together with his production control manager and his product engineer. This management team studies each item in terms of its *incremental profit*. It evaluates the effects that such hypothetical changes as price reduction, revised profit margins, improved quality and utility and change in packing specifications might have on the candidate product's sales performance. All products not contributing or not likely to contribute to the profit picture, to trade-consumer requirements and to manufacturing standardizations are cut from the line.

The sales executive must exercise seasoned judgment in keeping the product line to a minimum. In the face of a line simplification program, he will vote for a new product only after he is convinced that it has these qualifications:

Customers need the product.

Product is an improvement over competitive product or over similar product being eliminated from the line.

Potential volume could be at a profitable level at a specified date.

HOW IT WORKS OUT IN PRACTICE

In a typical case the committee, functioning as a management team, made considerable changes in the structure of their product line. It eliminated 109 products which had accounted for 6

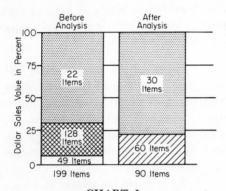

CHART I

STRUCTURE OF PRODUCT LINE

Note: 109 items were cut from the line, leaving 90 items—30 of which accounted 80 percent of the remaining sales value.

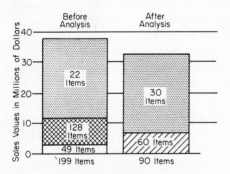

CHART II

STRUCTURE OF PRODUCT LINE

Note: Sales value amounting to 6 millions was eliminated by cutting 109 items from the line. The remaining 90 items left in the line represented 32 of the 38 million sales value for the calendar year just ended. Of the remaining 90 items, 30 represented 25.6 million sales value and 60 accounted for 6.4 million.

million dollars sales or 15.8% of total sales value. The revised structure (as shown in Charts I and II) contained 30 products accounting for 80% (25.6 millions) of the remaining sales value and 60 products representing the other 20% (6.4 millions). In this typical analysis the committee decided to reconvene at the end of the next 12-month period to re-evaluate the product line and to give special attention to the 60 products that represented only 20% of sales volume. No additions to the line were to be authorized without joint approval by the committee.

THE CASE OF PRODUCTS NO. 150 AND NO. 151

During committee discussion of product No. 150 (shown in Table A), the sales manager noted that product No. 150 along with product No. 151 produced small incremental profits. He reported that these two products were very similar in function to product No. 143, and that he felt all sales effort should be centered on product No. 143 rather than make any further effort to develop the market for No. 150 and No. 151. The market research manager submitted sales test data (Chart III) showing that No. 150 and No. 151 sales dropped when the price of No. 143 was cut, demonstrating that these two products were substitutes for No. 143. The plant superintendent reported that production was needed badly in the department where No. 150 and No. 151 were made, and that these products were produced during slack periods. He felt that the products should be retained and perhaps be promoted more strongly as they helped to stabilize production. In spite of the

CHART III

DEMAND RELATION BETWEEN PRODUCTS IN THE LINE
Consumer purchases during sales text demonstrated products No. 150 and No. 151 to be substitutes for No. 143. (Product No. 143's price was cut at end of sixth week.)

production problem, the committee decided that the similarity of the products to No. 143 made it desirable to eliminate them from the line.

TABLE A

INCREMENTAL PROFIT, THE RETENTION-
ELIMINATION FACTOR

Product Number	12-Month Sales Value	12-Month Incremental Profit
142	$102,000.00	$9,100.00
143	98,000.00	8,900.00
144	94,000.00	8,200.00
145	82,000.00	7,800.00
146	75,000.00	7,200.00
147	58,000.00	6,000.00
148	43,000.00	1,200.00
149	28,000.00	480.00
150	13,000.00	420.00
151	7,000.00	240.00
152	5,000.00	230.00
153	2,800.00	102.00

Note: 1. Incremental profit in this analysis was related to an item's annual sales value and not to a unit of sale. It was felt that the criterion for profit generation should not be the profit per unit of sale, as the profit per unit was of significance only when related to volume over an extended period of time.

PRODUCT NO. 153—A NEWCOMER

In the committee discussion of product No. 153, the market research manager pointed out that this product was on list for only 6 months. Its incremental profit of $102 for 12 months was an estimated figure. Two division sales managers had been pleading for this product for years, but during the six-month trial period the product failed to take hold. The market research manager re-read the product tests results that showed the product had just average consumer acceptance, and he again recommended that the product be improved before any additional effort was made to sell it. The production control manager said the product was a nuisance in the packaging phase, and he hoped it would be removed from the product line.

Product No. 153 was placed on the list principally to satisfy the two division sales managers. Including the product in the line served as a sales test for it. Nobody had expected the product to backfire as it did. Even in the two sales divisions where demand supposedly was greatest sales were limited. It was decided to drop the product from the line; and because tests showed only a limited acceptance, to have the sales force ship back all stock of the item they could find in customers' inventories. Then the item was returned to the market research department for further development.

PRODUCT NO. 152—GOOD POTENTIALLY

The controller led the discussion on product No. 152. He reported that it was on list for 18 months with an encouraging monthly rise in sales. It was one of a few products that was consumer-tested in its development. The package was developed out of a series of package design tests, and finally the product was sales-tested and shown to have a satisfactory repeat purchase rate and volume level when compared with competing products in its classification.

The controller stated that if the product reached its estimated sales volume by the end of the next 12-month period, the volume would be sufficiently large to permit unusually low manufacturing costs. It was decided to retain the product on list but to review its performance one year later.

PRODUCT NO. 149—NOT MOVING

When product No. 149 was reviewed by the committee, it was reported that it had been marketed for 3½ years with annual sales for each of the last two years about the same. Last year's sales at $28,000 produced the incremental profit of $480.

In the discussion of the product the plant superintendent explained there was no production problem. The product was somewhat perishable, however,

and could not be stock-piled. As a result periodic short runs were required, but the runs fitted into the production picture very well by using a full 8-hour shift for each run. The package materials were easily handled at the production line and required limited storage space.

According to a purchasing department report, buying advantages could not be obtained in purchasing the package materials because of the limited annual quantities involved, and current package materials would last another eight months at the present production rate.

The market research manager explained that reports from salesmen conclusively indicated that several important customers were finding it difficult to move their inventories of product No. 149, and that the product's potential was limited. The sales manager agreed with the market research report. It was decided to remove the product from the line even though it had produced an incremental profit of $480.

THE CRITICAL QUESTION— HOW TO FIGURE INCREMENTAL PROFIT

The critical question for committee action on line simplification is: *What is the criterion for determining whether a candidate product is to be retained or eliminated?*

A desirable criterion would be a precise profit or loss figure for each product. Such a figure, however, is not often available because only a limited number of companies have developed their budgetary controls so precisely. And for those companies supplying a profit and loss figure per product, it should be remembered that there is an enormous element of judgment involved in prorating sales and administrative overheads and certain fixed costs to each specific product for a profit or loss figure.

An acceptable and more easily attainable figure, the *incremental profit,* is available for each product, and its calculation requires little, if any, judgment. Part of the judgment required is confined to determining whether a particular factory overhead cost is variable or fixed.

The *incremental profit* for each product is figured by subtracting from a product's sales value its composite cost (see Table B) consisting of (1) direct material costs, (2) direct labor costs, (3) variable factory overhead costs and, in some cases, (4) marketing costs.

Composite cost used in arriving at incremental profit can be determined precisely. Direct material costs is an accounting figure. The direct labor component cost is fixed per product, based on direct labor cost or on piece-work figures. In some companies, the components that go to make up the composite cost are precisely related, with limited judgment, to each product by developing a correlation of manufacturing expense to a production index (such as cost per machine hour, piece-work labor, etc.) through standard cost accounting, through variable budgeting control or on some other basis. This technique provides an equitable allocation of variable factory overhead to a product.

The retention-elimination factor, as developed here, is presented as a handy tool to *expedite* more intelligent evaluation of each candidate product separately and in terms of its relation to a

TABLE B

THREE CANDIDATE PRODUCTS, SUGGESTING:

	Retention	Retention	Elimination
Sales	$10,000	$10,000	$10,000
Composite cost			
Direct material	4,800	6,000	5,000
Direct labor	1,500	1,000	1,800
Variable factory overhead	1,000	300	2,600
Total composite cost	7,300	7,300	9,400
Incremental profit (retention-elimination factor)	2,700	2,700	600
Amount remaining for fixed factory cost, selling, administrative, and profit	2,700	2,700	600
Percent fixed factory cost, selling, administrative, and profit to sales	27%	27%	6%

Note: Variable selling and administrative costs, which customarily are relatively small, are subject to judgment when allocated to a specific product. Therefore, they are excluded from the composite cost figure even though they are volume costs and do bear a direct relationship to product passing through the sales and administrative departments.

company's over-all operating problems. It facilitates from committee members statements of facts that can be more specific and contain more certainty. It shows which products are contributing disproportionately more or less to selling and administrative expenses, to fixed costs, and to profits.

As a concept, it requires the bread-and-butter products in the line to carry the selling, administrative and fixed cost burdens as they will necessarily do after the line is simplified. It requires skillful and joint handling by committee members in terms of both critical evaluation of each product's incremental profit and the requirements of the company.

▸▸▸▸▸▸▸▸▸▸▸▸ A METHOD FOR MAKING PRODUCT-COMBINATION DECISIONS

ROBERT K. JAEDICKE*

The manager of any business firm faces at least three important classes of decisions. They are (1) how to produce; (2) how much to produce; and if more than one product is involved, (3) what combination of products to produce. The first class of decisions involves the problem of choosing that combination of men and equipment which will produce a given quantity of output at the least cost. The second class of decisions has to do with the choice of the most profitable quantity of output to produce and sell. Inherent in the output decision is the third class of decisions, what combination of products should be produced and sold.

Product-combination decisions constitute a very broad and important group. Such decisions range from whether to make or to buy a part or subassembly to the best allocation of floor space among departments of a department store. Yet, as important as this type of decision is to the firm manager, if he were to turn to existing accounting techniques and to accounting literature for a complete and definitive answer, he would probably be quite disappointed. The purpose of this article is to set forth a sound approach to product-combination problems which might be used as a basis for managerial decision making.

THE CONTRIBUTION-MARGIN APPROACH

The contribution margin of a unit of product is defined as the excess of the selling price over the variable costs of

Reprinted with permission from Business News Notes, *A Publication of the School of Business Administration, University of Minnesota, No. 38, April 1958, pp. 1–4.*

* *Professor of Accounting, Stanford University.*

producing and selling the product. Variable costs are those costs which will change in total as a result of changes in output. However, the variable cost *per unit* is assumed by the accountant to be constant. Hence, the contribution margin, with a given selling price, is also constant per unit of product. The total contribution margin for any accounting period, however, depends on the number of units sold. The assumption that the variable costs and the contribution margin are constant per unit is probably valid as long as the firm produces within the normal operating range. Once the normal operating range is exceeded, the variable costs per unit may increase as the number of units increases. This same qualification also applies to the unit selling price. If the number of units sold is to be increased by any significant amount, the selling price per unit will undoubtedly have to be decreased.

The contribution margin concept is an attempt to focus the attention of management on variable costs rather than full costs. The contention is that the contribution margin per unit is more significant for decision making than the net profit per unit. The latter would be computed by deducting fixed costs from the contribution margin. This approach would be used primarily for internal profit reporting: for example, to show performance by department or other subdivisions of the company. The form of the aggregate income statement sent to the stockholders and creditors need not be affected by the contribution-margin concept.

If internal reports are submitted to management on the conventional or full-cost basis, the income statement would appear as shown in Figure 1. This example represents a hypothetical department store with three departments. The Cost of Goods Sold consists of the purchase price of the goods sold together with adjustments for freight costs, etc. Assume that Selling Expenses represents sales commissions, which are 5% of sales, and Administra-

FIGURE 1

INCOME STATEMENT BY DEPARTMENTS
FOR THE YEAR 195X

	Totals	*Department 1*	*Department 2*	*Department 3*
Sales	$100,000	$50,000	$30,000	$20,000
Cost of Goods Sold	80,000	45,000	25,000	10,000
Gross Margin	$ 20,000	$ 5,000	$ 5,000	$10,000
Other Expenses:				
Selling Expenses	$ 5,000	$ 2,500	$ 1,500	$ 1,000
Administrative Expenses	6,000	3,000	1,800	1,200
Total Other Expenses	$ 11,000	$ 5,500	$ 3,300	$ 2,200
Net Profit or Loss	$ 9,000	$ (500)	$ 1,700	$ 7,800

tive Expenses are the rental charge on the building. The rent, although fixed, is allocated to the departments as a percentage of the sales volume of each department.

The conventional income statement by departments, as given in Figure 1, has serious limitations if the data are to be used in decision making. The Gross Margin, for example, cannot be used as a measure of departmental profitability because there may be variable expenses of operating a department other than the cost of the goods sold. Also, in a manufacturing firm, some fixed costs may be included in Cost of Goods Sold. In a retailing operation, this criticism may not apply. The net profit has limited usefulness because of the allocation of fixed expenses to the departments. Referring to Figure 1, it may be unwise to eliminate Department 1, which operates at a $500 loss, because the over-all profit of the store will be decreased if the building rent is a fixed cost.

Limitations in the conventional income statement, such as those mentioned above, have set the stage for the contribution-margin approach. This approach concentrates the attention of management on sales, variable costs, and the contribution margin rather than emphasizing the departmental gross margin and net profit. A contribution-margin income statement by departments using the same data as given above is shown in Figure 2.

The justification for this type of report is that in planning decisions regarding the object of costing (in this example the object of costing is the department) the pertinent cost is the variable cost rather than the total cost. Fixed cost, therefore, is not distributed to the departments but is reported as a total for the entire operation. In a question regarding the proper combination of departments, the contribution margin rather than the net profit of each department is considered to be the important figure. *Thus, each department is judged by its ability to contribute a margin toward fixed cost and profit.* The major criticism of this presentation by most businessmen and accountants is

FIGURE 2

CONTRIBUTION-MARGIN INCOME STATEMENT BY DEPARTMENTS
FOR THE YEAR 195X

	Totals	Department 1	Department 2	Department 3
Sales	$100,000	$50,000	$30,000	$20,000
Variable Costs:				
Cost of Goods Sold	$ 80,000	$45,000	$25,000	$10,000
Selling Expenses	5,000	2,500	1,500	1,000
Total Variable Costs	$85,000	$47,500	$26,500	$11,000
Contribution Margin	$15,000	$ 2,500	$ 3,500	$ 9,000
Fixed Costs:				
Administrative Expenses	$ 6,000			
Net Profit	$ 9,000			

that, in the long run, fixed costs must be covered and therefore deserve proper consideration. This criticism will be examined later in the article.

PROFIT-VOLUME ANALYSIS

The contribution-margin approach, as outlined above, forms the basis for profit-volume analysis. This can best be described by discussing the profit-volume graph (Figure 3). As has been pointed out, the variable cost and the contribution margin per unit are assumed to be constant. The ratio of the contribution margin to the selling price is called the profit-volume ratio. This ratio, when expressed as a percentage and multiplied by the dollar sales, will give the total contribution margin at that particular level of sales.

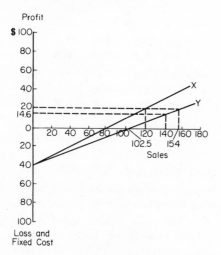

FIGURE 3

In Figure 3, sales in dollars are plotted along the horizontal axis. The vertical axis is used to plot dollars of profit and loss and the fixed costs. Line Z represents the relationship between sales and profit when the fixed costs are $30 and the profit-volume ratio is 15%. The profit-volume ratio will be 15% if the unit of product sells for $1 and the variable costs of producing and selling the unit are 85¢. With this set of data, the contribution margin per unit would be 15% (15/100).

Profit and loss are read from the Y axis. For example, at sales of $300 the profit is $15; at sales of $100 the loss is $15; the loss at zero sales is $30, the amount of the fixed costs. The point at which line Z intersects the sales axis ($200) gives sales at the breakeven point: namely, the point of no profit or loss. Sales at the breakeven point can be computed by dividing the fixed costs by the profit-volume ratio. The explanation for this computation is as follows:

1. The profit-volume ratio gives the percentage of each sales dollar that can be used to cover fixed costs.

2. Breakeven sales give the level of sales at which fixed costs are covered: that is, the level of sales where the contribution margin is equal to the fixed costs.

3. Therefore, breakeven sales can be computed by dividing the fixed costs by the percentage of each sales dollar available to cover the fixed costs: namely, the profit-volume ratio.

ADVANTAGES
OF PROFIT-VOLUME ANALYSIS

Profit-volume analysis has proved to be helpful in demonstrating the effects of a change in product combinations. Therefore, it has been used primarily to report the effects of a change rather than to decide what the proper combination of products should be. The reporting advantages will be examined first, and the decision-making advantages will be discussed later.

Assume that a company sells two products, A and B, whose selling prices, variable costs, etc., are given below:

Product	A	B
Selling Price Per Unit	$10	$8
Variable Costs Per Unit	$ 7	$3
Contribution Margin Per Unit	$ 3	$5

Fixed costs in total—$40,000.

If the two products are sold in the ratio of 2 B to 1 A, the profit-volume ratio for the product "package" is computed as follows:

```
Sales
  1 A @ $10    $10
  2 B @ $ 8     16    $26
Variable Costs
  1 A @ $7     $ 7
  2 B @ $3       6    $13
Contribution Margin    $13
Profit-Volume Ratio: $13/$26 or 50%
```

For this sales mix, the profit-volume relationship is shown graphically (line X) in Figure 4. If the sales of the firm are currently $120,000 per year, profit is $20,000 provided the sales mix remains 2 to 1 in favor of product B. Assume, however, that during the following year the firm's sales increase to $140,000, but profit actually decreases because of a change in sales mix from 2 B to 1 A to 2 A to 1 B. Also, assume that everything else remains the same; that is,

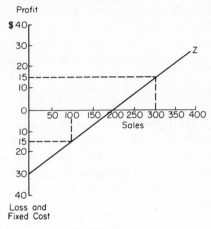

FIGURE 4

there is no change in selling prices or costs. The new profit-volume ratio is computed below, and the new profit-volume relationship is shown graphically by line Y in Figure 4.

```
Sales
  2 A @ $10    $20
  1 B @ $ 8      8    $28
Variable Costs
  2 A @ $7     $14
  1 B @ $3       3    $17
Contribution Margin    $11
Profit-Volume Ratio: $11/$28 or 39%
```

With fixed costs of $40,000, the new breakeven sales are $102,500 compared with $80,000 under the previous sales mix. Although actual sales have increased to $140,000, profit is decreased from $20,000 to $14,600 ($140,000 × 39%−$40,000). The decrease in profit is caused by a change in sales mix in favor of product A which has a lower profit-volume ratio than product B. The profit-volume graph illustrates this situation quite effectively. The decrease in the profit-volume ratio (for the new product package) is shown by a decrease in the slope of the profit line. Also, if the $20,000 profit line is extended to line Y, the level of sales necessary to produce the same absolute dollar profit under the new sales mix is shown to be about $154,000.

The primary advantage of the contribution-margin income statement and the profit-volume graph in reporting the results of operations stems from the regrouping of the variables which affect profit. In the conventional profit report, fixed costs are merged in several accounts while in profit-volume reporting the fixed costs are reported in total. In contribution-margin reports, the selling price of the product, the variable costs, and the sales mix are considered as a package; hence, all three variables must be considered in explaining profit changes. If profits change as the result of a change in the profit-volume ratio, the manager knows immediately which variables he must investigate in order to explain the change. Furthermore, he need not waste time looking at the level of the fixed costs; if there is a change in fixed costs, it will be apparent immediately simply by glancing at the graph or the income statement.

DECISION-MAKING ADVANTAGES AND LIMITATIONS

The proponents of contribution-margin analysis claim various decision-making advantages for this tool. For example, it is pointed out that variable costs might be used in pricing the product particularly in a "dumping" situation. Some writers even say that variable costs may be used for regular pricing decisions if a markup is added which will cover a portion of the fixed costs and a satisfactory profit margin.

At this point, a storm of protest is usually forthcoming, primarily from businessmen who point out that the fixed costs must be considered in pricing the product. Many people view the allocation of fixed costs among the units as the only "safe" approach to cost-plus pricing. The fear is that if variable cost information is given to the sales personnel, the price actually quoted will gradually slip down so close to the variable cost that in the long run the sales revenue will not cover the fixed costs.

Turning now to product-combination decisions, what are the advantages and limitations of contribution-margin and profit-volume analysis? First of all, it must be recognized that the prices of the products are assumed to be given. Hence, the question is, with given prices, what product mix should be adopted? Actually, product-combination decisions are much broader than the above question indicates. When a firm is deciding whether to make or to buy a particular subassembly or part, the problem involved is essentially one of product combinations. Furthermore, the entire realm of distribution or marketing decisions consists essentially of product-combination problems. For example, the question of the proper combination of sales territories or customer classes is very similar to the question of what combination of products should be produced and sold. The same general approach should be used for all of the above-mentioned problems. The desirability of a customer class, like the desirability of a shoe department, should be judged on the basis of its contribution to the over-all operation.

For illustrative purposes, the example given above will be used in the following discussion. The firm sells two products, A and B, whose prices are $10 and $8 and whose variable costs are $7 and $3 respectively. If the contribution-margin approach is used to determine the best combination of products, the fixed costs of $40,000 will not be allocated to the two products. Fixed costs, although necessary for the operation of the firm, will not change as a result of choosing various combinations of products. The decision to be made is one of choosing the best use of the firm's facilities. Those costs which do not change no matter what use is chosen are irrelevant.

For any given level of dollar sales, the best combination of products is that combination which will give the highest contribution margin. With this restriction on sales, the choice can be made by looking at the profit-volume ratio for each different sales mix. Thus, if sales are estimated at $200,000 for the coming year, the firm will make more profit if the sales mix is 2 to 1 in favor of product B than if the mix is 2 to 1 in favor of product A. The following calculation supports this conclusion:

Product Mix	2 B-1 A	2 A-1 B
Dollar Sales	$200,000	$200,000
Profit-Volume Ratio	50%	39%
Contribution Margin	$100,000	$ 78,000
Fixed Costs	$ 40,000	$ 40,000
Net Profit	$ 60,000	$ 38,000

However, if the sales restriction is dropped, it is not safe to conclude that 2 B for 1 A is a better combination of products than 2 A for 1 B. In other words, the problem of product mix cannot be solved in every situation by using only the profit-volume ratio.

If the products are examined individually, the profit-volume ratio for A is 30% ($10-$7/$10) and for B is 62.5% ($8-$3/$8). It may appear, therefore, that product B is the most profitable product and thus should be pushed by the firm. However, such a conclusion overlooks one very important principle of profit maximization—in order to maximize profits the firm must maximize the rate of return with respect to *the scarce operating factor*. The contribution margin is the proper measure of the rate of return for each product, but a statement of the scarce factor is not a part of the contribution-margin approach. Hence, the method is incomplete. More information is needed in order to use this approach in product-combination decisions.

Assume that the scarce factor in this case is production time; that is, the firm can sell more units of A or B than it can produce at the present level of capacity. In such a situation, even though product B has the highest contribution margin and profit-volume ratio, product A may still be the more profitable product. This may be the case if product A takes less production time than product B. For example, assume that it takes only 1 man-hour to produce a unit of A and 4 man-hours to produce a unit of B. If the capacity of the plant is 200,000 man-hours per year, profit would be maximized by producing only product A. The following calculation brings out this point:

Product	A	B
Units of Production		
Possible	200,000	50,000
Contribution Margin		
(200,000 × $3)	$600,000	
(50,000 × $5)		$250,000
Fixed Costs	$ 40,000	$ 40,000
Profit	$560,000	$210,000

In this example, the scarce factor is production time. Actually, the scarce or limiting factor depends on the situation. In choosing the size of departments within a department store, the scarce factor may be floor space or the necessary capital investment. Using the contribution margin as a measure of the rate of return, the pertinent computation is the contribution margin as related to the scarce factor, e.g., the contribution margin per hour of production time, per square foot of floor space, per dollar of capital invested, etc. In the above example, product A is more profitable than product B since the contribution margin per hour of production time is $3 ($3/1 hour) for product A and $1.25 ($5/4 hours) for product B.

The contribution-margin approach combined with a statement of the scarce factor of production is a useful approach for solving product-combination problems. The profitability of the unit can be judged by its rate of return as related to the scarce factor. To criticize the contribution-margin approach because it overlooks fixed costs, as is sometimes done, is not justified. In-stead, the criticism should be that this approach may be incomplete because of its failure to consider properly the scarce operating factor.

Actually, allocation of fixed costs to products *may* give an indication of the relative profitability of each of the products if the allocation is based on the scarce factor. For example, if the scarce factor is 200,000 man-hours of production time and the fixed costs are $200,000, a charge of $1 per hour might be allocated to each product. The relative profitability of the two products can be calculated as follows:

Product	A	B
Contribution Margin		
Per Unit	$3	$5
Hours of Production		
Time Per Unit	1	4
Fixed Cost Per Unit	$1	$4
Profit Per Unit	$2	$1

This solution does not hold in *every* case however; thus, this procedure may be very misleading. For example, when the fixed costs are only $40,000, the charge based on 200,000 man-hours is 20¢ per hour and product B appears more profitable than product A—$2.80 profit for A as compared with $4.20 for B. Hence, in this case the allocation of fixed costs leads to a wrong conclusion. The reason for allocating fixed costs is to convert the scarce factor to dollars. However, unless the fixed cost rate is sufficiently high, the procedure is invalid. The reason is that the value of an hour of production time depends on the contribution margin per hour of the respective products. There is no logical reason why the fixed costs per hour should be any indication of the value of an hour of production time.

The contribution-margin approach for choosing product combinations may appear to be applicable only to short-run problems. This, however, is not the case. In the long run, the firm may face decisions which involve expansion of facilities. Such an expansion might involve additional capital investment and the question of what area or part of the firm should be expanded. For maximum profit, the department which should be given the additional floor space is the one which will give the highest contribution margin per additional square foot of floor space. Likewise, if the firm is choosing new sales territories as part of a market expansion program, the territory chosen first should be the one which will give the highest contribution margin as related to the scarce factor—which in this case might be capital invested or hours of salesmen's time. Hence, the contribution-margin approach is useful not only for decisions regarding the best use of existing facilities but also for decisions involving an expansion of existing facilities.

CONCLUSIONS

In approaching the problem of product combinations, fixed costs should be ignored. Even if the fixed costs increase, the most profitable product mix will not be changed. The pertinent information regarding each product, department, sales territory, customer class, etc., is the contribution margin. This requires a knowledge of selling prices and variable costs. However, it is also necessary to have a statement of the scarce operating factor. The profitability of each product can then be judged by relating the contribution margin to the scarce factor. The information required may be difficult to compute. It may be that the firm faces many alternatives, and an estimate of each may be required. However, a careful estimate of the pertinent information should give a better solution than various short-cut methods which use readily available but meaningless data.

►►►►►►►►► ADVANTAGES OF DIVERSIFICATION

LEO C. BAILEY[*]

Whatever the underlying reasons, company diversification has been clearly one of the most distinctive characteristics of American business development during the past ten or fifteen years.

Reprinted with permission from Battelle Technical Review, *September, 1956, pp. 38–43.*

[*] *Investors Diversified Services, Inc.*

Almost every issue of the leading business magazines and newspapers headlines another move of some well-known company to merge, integrate, or diversify. Certainly merger and integration are neither new nor novel. They have been characteristic methods for corporate expansion during almost every prosperous period for which we have records. But diversification, with its objectives of attaining both growth and stability, is not synonymous with either merger or integration. A brief definition of terms may help clarify the point that diversification is different.

Integration generally implies a policy for greater coverage of a given business field by participation in more of the stages between raw material and ultimate market or more intensive coverage of a single stage. As such, it is a policy of control, one that gives a company greater control over supply, production, or markets. Because of the different characteristics of an industry at different stages, integration achieves one form of diversification. It carries all the risks and opportunities of dependence on a single industry.

Merger, on the other hand, is merely a method of corporate combination, which may or may not achieve diversification and integration. Generally, a merger involves a purchase of one company by another under various arrangements so that the purchased company loses its corporate existence.

Diversification, as the name implies, is a policy or management philosophy of operating a company so that its business and profits come from a number of sources, usually from diverse products that differ in market or production characteristics. In an extreme case, the component parts of a diversified company may have no direct logical relationship to each other except those resulting from financial strengths or managerial ability. Commonly, other more tangible and definable relationships do exist, although they may not be obvious.

DIVERSIFICATION— A LONG-RANGE POLICY

If the forces favoring policies of integration and the practice of mergers are segregated temporarily, there are still several strong reasons to explain the widespread current business interest in diversification. Among these reasons are (1) the conduct and results of basic and applied research, which provide the product opportunities necessary for many diversification ventures; (2) growth and change of the American economy, which provide many of the needed market opportunities; (3) the inflexibility of marketing and staff costs relative to those of production; (4) social pressures from both labor and management for stability and security; and (5) persistent general shortage of top management talent which encourages a strong company to broaden its activities. Of course, these are general and underlying reasons for diversification that may not be apparent in an analysis of a particular diversification venture. Similarly, the immediate and obvious reasons—eliminating seasonality or cyclical fluctuations, expanding sales, increasing profits, and opening new growth channels—are usually traceable to one or more of the five basic and persistent factors cited above. This point is made to emphasize the author's belief that diversification is no passing fancy or offspring of World War II but is here to stay. The methods for accomplishing it may change with fluctuations in the business cycle or shifts in government policy, but there is strong evidence that certain forms of diversification are becoming a permanent part of the American business scene.

RESEARCH AND PRODUCT CHANGE

Consider research as one of the five foster parents of diversification. Not too many years ago there was no synthetic fiber except rayon. There were no plastics of commercial importance except celluloid and Bakelite. There were few electronic products except radios. Organic chemicals were confined pretty much to pharmaceuticals. And iron, steel, copper, tin, lead, and zinc were the materials that the man in the street would mention if asked to name our important metals. Research has changed that picture drastically, not only for the broad, basic materials of industry but for a host of their end products. Just as effectively, research-developed machinery and production methods have changed the ways by which even old, familiar products are manufactured. The effects on industry have been enormous. No existing field is safe from technological obsolescence, and that force alone will foster continued interest in diversification.

Research and change are almost synonymous. Organized team research and development has emerged as the "safest" way to assure a steady flow of new processes and products, whatever their purpose. Organization for stability, the Maginot Line of business thinking, is being replaced by organization for flexibility and change.

ECONOMIC CHANGE

Simultaneous with the development of new processes and products, the world's economy itself is changing. The two go hand in hand to make and absorb the products of industry and to encourage diversification.

Confining discussion to the United States, whose size, diversity, and natural wealth emphasize changes effective elsewhere, there are a number of noteworthy facets to the picture. First, as production becomes more and more based on inanimate energy, it becomes cheaper in terms of human effort. In other words, the absolute essential needs of man are satisfied with less and less effort. In this situation, we are turning constantly to the production of less essential but pleasure-giving products and to working less. The nonessentials that man can make to satisfy his wishes or to complicate his life are apparently limitless. Fortunately for industry, the bounds of his wishes also seem to have a high upper limit. Certainly the possibilities for altering color, form, quality, and variety of products has provided a steady supply of diversification opportunities for companies making such things as automobiles, small and major appliances, paints, and textiles. This basic consumer philosophy of shifting his purchases of nonessentials among a wide range of products and of increasing his standard of living is not going to cease unless war or other catastrophe reduces us to a subsistence level.

DISTRIBUTION AND STAFF COSTS

Although engineering, science, management, and labor seem continually capable of increasing productivity in manufacturing, there are several areas of business where the man-hour input stays relatively high, where the resultant costs are less flexible, where change takes more time, and where feeling still dominates fact. The chief of these areas is distribution. Another is in the use of supporting staff. Both bear importantly on diversification.

In an economy that can absorb growing quantities and varieties of nonessential products, the opportunities for sales success can be exploited best by companies having a highly developed, sophisticated marketing and staff organization. Market research becomes necessary to detect subtle product preferences, to guide marketing and production strategy, and to anticipate shifts in buying habits. Advertising and sales promotion specialists utilize skills, experience, and contacts that can be transferred from one product line to others without a proportional increase in staff size or costs. The same applies to such line and staff activities as fund raising, architecture, plant location, site selection, layout, purchasing, and many phases of industrial engineering. From the standpoint of management, there are cost-saving and control advantages in spreading these skills among a variety of products. Although highly developed staff organizations exist primarily in large companies, the tendency to spread costs and abilities over a wider line of products is important to companies of all sizes.

It commonly takes longer to develop management and markets than to develop products. Wartime experience with new products and the performance records of companies with a long history of diversification by internal growth have established the feasibility of using existing management organizations, sales forces, and dealer or customer contacts to handle a variety of more-or-less related products. In fact, the performance of such companies as American Home Products, Borg Warner, General Motors, General Dynamics, American Machine and Foundry, W. R. Grace, Textron, and The Borden Company seems to indicate that top-management philosophy, policies encouraging quite autonomous decentralized operations, and well-established marketing organizations contribute much more to the success of diversified operations than do similarity of materials and production processes in widely varied product lines.

STABILITY AND SECURITY

A fourth factor creating pressure for continued industrial diversification is the general trend among many segments of society and government to improve economic stability and security. Without going into detail, it is obvious that there is a general trend toward fringe benefits for all types of employees, toward stockholder interest in both consistent dividends and appreciation of investment values, toward labor union emphasis on some form of "guaranteed annual wage," toward

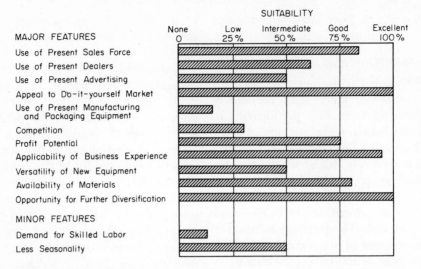

This suitability rating scale shows the extent to which a hypothetical product, shaped plastic drop covers for furniture, satisfies diversification criteria set by a paintbrush manufacturer.

management and government dedication to avoiding either a major business depression or runaway inflation, and toward general recognition of the advantages of a stable, predictable high level of income. When these are added to existing and expected shortages in many categories of professional and hourly employees, the poor future of an unstable business becomes evident.

It is a paradox that business rigidity seems to germinate economic instability. These factors explain much of the interest in diversification among parts suppliers, construction and capital equipment manufacturers, and companies traditionally associated with a single material or market. While diversification undoubtedly creates new management problems, it is coming to be viewed as the best method of insuring growth or at least stability of employment, sales, and earnings over

a long period. Interestingly enough, many of these companies are seeking stability in new and rapidly changing fields where a consistently large research effort is almost as necessary to maintain current position as it is for growth. It appears that this in itself will force a new stability in research activity that has been lacking historically, except in the most far-sighted organizations.

MANAGEMENT SCARCITY

A fifth force pushing toward long-range adoption of diversification by American industry is the perennial scarcity of top-management personnel. This is a problem quite separate from the widely discussed shortage of technical manpower. In fact, as technology and other fields of special knowledge carve firm footholds in business organizations, the need for good general management to plan, direct, and control their use increases. As staff activities grow, the role of a business manager becomes more and more like that of a military commander. He must understand and use an ever-increasing variety of special skills, keeping all in the best balance for attack on changing problems and conditions. The need for this high level of ability in planning, organizing, staffing, and control puts a premium value on utilizing qualified management people over as broad an area as possible. Where top management is strong but not fully utilized, there is a powerful incentive to acquire or develop new products, new divisions, and even new affiliated corporations. In a company where top management is deficient, acquiring it by hiring or merger may also be accompanied deliberately or incidentally by diversification.

STAGES IN DIVERSIFICATION PLANNING

Whether diversification is desired for better stability, survival, better profits, greater growth potential, or more effective utilization of management, resources, and facilities, its inclusion as a basic company policy needs careful consideration and planning. No matter what methods are chosen as the most suitable ways to diversify, each can be expected to absorb a good share of management attention and company funds before it begins to pay off.

Reduced to simplest terms, there are only three or four ways of diversifying. The quickest, but not necessarily the least expensive or easiest, is by merger with or acquisition of a going concern. The slowest may be development of new products internally through research, but its time requirements and small scale start permit management to meet and solve many small problems before they mushroom. Intermediate in speed are the development of new uses and markets for existing products and the entry with established products into fields already covered by competitors. It is clear that each of these approaches to diversification has its own peculiar problems of organization, management, finance, and profit structure.

COMPANY SOUL SEARCHING

Any subject as much in vogue as diversification needs particularly sharp analysis when it is suggested as the cure for company troubles or the road to some utopian state not presently enjoyed. Rather, it seems that poor profits, declining sales, organizational unrest, and failure to keep pace with the growth of general business should be tried for size against many other possible causes before they are blamed on lack of diversity. Even seasonality of sales can often be traced to a lack of imagination in exploiting all possible markets or in changing established use patterns. Thus the first stage in any sound form of diversification planning has two elements of self-appraisal:

1. Determination of strengths and weaknesses in the company's present business, including policies, organization, personnel, products, production, markets, costs, and profits.

2. Determination of the degree of ability and interest in diversifying including:
   a. unity of management support
   b. financial resources
   c. production facilities
   d. marketing organization and experience
   e. research organization
   f. engineering and service organization

ESTABLISHING OBJECTIVES

If defensive or growth strategy still indicates the need and strong desire to diversify after such an analysis, the next logical phase of planning is the establishment of specific objectives. What is expected of diversification? What problems *must* it solve? What *compromises* would be acceptable in meeting lesser goals? If company policy is one of taking advantage of financial opportunities almost without respect to the product involved, this phase is not a difficult one. Objectives can be defined in strictly financial terms—a certain volume of business, certain investment in plant, certain rates of return on sales and investment, definable tax position, and similar conditions. Commonly, however, there are more complex problems relating to such elements of the business as:

1. Seasonality or cyclical nature of sales.
2. Channels of distribution.
3. Definition of desired market position.
4. Prestige of company and brand names.

5. Utilization of idle buildings and equipment.
6. Utilization of sales contacts, organization, and staff.
7. Location of raw materials, production, and markets.
8. Time schedule of expected returns.
9. Profit and cost patterns.
10. Growth potential.
11. Research requirements to achieve and maintain position.

Even these do not exhaust the full range of objectives that may be pertinent or even essential for a given company to define what it expects from diversification and to fit these wishes into a realistic relationship with its current strengths and weaknesses. As a final consideration, flexibility should be built into the plan. At its best, a company intending to make diversification a lasting, successful element of its management philosophy should be ready to exploit unplanned and unexpected opportunities when they arise.

DIVERSIFICATION CRITERIA

With objectives defined, the next phase is to develop methods for measuring opportunities against the stated objectives. For many aspects, suitable measurements exist in regular reports, charts, and financial statements or special analyses prepared from them. Others can be compiled from market statistics, production cost estimates, and sales records, when these are available. Still others (particularly those relating to intangible similarities or differences in production, markets, products, and organization) can be ranked, if not accurately measured, by imaginative use of bar charts, rating scales, index numbers, or other means.

METHODS OF DIVERSIFICATION

The prime methods of diversification were mentioned earlier as: (a) internal research and development; (b) acquisition of companies or patents; (c) developing new use patterns and markets for existing products; and (d) broadening product lines to include items already made by competitors. Each has its own merits and difficulties. In actual practice, a company with firm plans to diversify may be wise to include elements of all four.

The chances for innovation, strong patent protection, and high profits are generally best if diversification is achieved by research and development. It has the added advantages of permitting the company to grow with the problems, studying or solving them in steps as developments progress from laboratory, through pilot operation, to full production. A strong technical position can also make it easier to obtain outside financial help, if needed, or to justify retention of earnings for expansion. Opposed to these definite advantages, successful development of new products to the point where a return is realized may take years—or may never be achieved at all. It is this risk and time lag that force many companies that have never supported a continuing research program and that are faced with a survival problem to seek diversity by other routes.

Acquisition of patents or merger with other going concerns are much quicker ways to diversify. Superficially, it would seem that investment requirements might be higher and per cent returns lower than for a company willing to face the risks and delays of an internal development program. This is not always true. The purchased company may have excellent products and technical position but may lack capital, sales organization, general management ability, or other things that make it a bargain for a purchaser who can supply the missing elements. Similarly, business conditions in the industry of the purchaser or seller may enhance the value of time. The chance to launch and "digest" a new building products division during several years of peak construction volume may more than compensate for a high initial purchase price. However, this need for digestion —the time and problem of fitting the new organization into the old—is one of the greatest drawbacks of diversification by merger. Another, which often results from the speed necessary to negotiate purchase of an attractive and available going concern, is that there are no intermediate steps from which to change course or to turn back. As insurance against this risk, a number of companies with successful merger histories have organized teams skilled in quick analysis of opportunities to acquire new business or patent rights. In one case the team, headed by the comptroller, is supplemented by representatives from the technical and legal staffs, commercial research, production, and general management.

Another company, which prides itself in ability to acquire good management as well as good product lines, depends largely on a personal appraisal of the prospective business by a top executive, who can then negotiate purchase quickly if he believes it advisable.

Finding new uses and markets for existing products is a very real and effective method of diversification. It is one that should be considered seriously during the first phase of diversification planning. While generally most applicable to a basic material, there are numerous examples to demonstrate its potency in other fields. Among these are fiberboard, adhesive-coated tapes, various types of packaging, power lawn mowers, home power tools, and a wide range of home appliances—all adapted from specialized industrial or commercial application to broader consumer markets.

Manufacture of unpatented products already made by competitors is a familiar and unspectacular form of diversification. But it, too, requires planning and has its share of risks. For example, it seems quite a logical step for a producer of refrigerators to initiate a new line of electric ranges or for a manufacturer of automotive supplies to begin making appliance parts. However, as many companies have learned by bitter experience, brand reputation, sales organization, and consumer acceptance are not so easily developed as a production line. And often the characteristics of one industry are too much like those of another for real diversification to be achieved by a relatively simple addition of new products or new customers.

It is critically important to recognize the immediate and long-range features of these different methods of diversifying. None is a panacea, but each has advantages in particular situations that can be exploited by management fully cognizant of how they apply to company policies, objectives, and capabilities.

SEARCHING AND SCREENING

Searching for and screening diversification opportunities is much like any other research undertaking. The obvious possibilities are generally highly competitive—otherwise they would not be obvious. The best opportunities for spectacular returns are highly speculative, usually requiring a long period of business or laboratory development with uncertain chances of success. And, in between, are a large number of more-or-less attractive opportunities, usually each demanding some compromise of objectives with reality and especially needing the same type of imaginative, dedicated follow-through that makes any company stand out in its field.

The sources of diversification ideas are too broad for thorough description here. From a strictly technical viewpoint, the engineers and scientists of a large, versatile research laboratory are one of the best sources of educated opinion on the future of new materials, products, and processes on probable competition to be encountered; and on the technical needs of the industries they serve. This applies more to industrial products than to those slanted toward consumer markets, where salesmen, designers, advertising specialists, and consumer opinion researchers may be better at idea generation. Similarly, while all of these groups may recognize certain types of needs and products, they are not usually familiar with the business problems that must be faced in satisfying these needs or making and selling the products.

For these reasons, specialized teams of men from the company's own staff or from consulting organizations are often successful in spotting promising opportunities from a variety of sources, culling out the obviously unacceptable ones, and preparing reports on the well-screened remainder. From these reports, management can either make selections and take action or request further information in the form of more detailed reports. It is seldom worthwhile to develop such detail before a preliminary screening. Out of several hundred product or company suggestions, often less than a dozen will merit full investigation. Finally, the de-

cision of management is often a negative one on all possibilities, and the general broad search may be continued for an indefinite period. Continued scanning is well worth while for any company dedicated to long-range growth and diversification.

ACTION AND FOLLOW-UP

Just as a successful laboratory experiment is only the first step in the development of a new product, the immediate steps toward diversification are only the beginning. Each new product line should be followed and developed—but dropped if necessary—with the same interest and enthusiasm that are too often confined to the initial search and acquisition. Certain fields of business may always remain specialized, but a company that plans to diversify successfully will find that the policy is not one to be applied once and then dropped after a finite series of steps.

C
Market Considerations

MANY NEW PRODUCTS FIZZLE
DESPITE CAREFUL PLANNING, PUBLICITY

BURT SCHORR*

New York — One breezy May morning in 1958, a bus load of magazine editors from Manhattan rolled up to the Huntingdon Valley Country Club north of Philadelphia. As the editors assembled inside, each received a glossy green brochure proclaiming: "You are looking at 1965. Philco takes the most spectacular forward stride in television history. . . ."

Thus began the elaborate unveiling of a new Philco Corp. product line—Predicta television sets.

If distinctive appearance guaranteed brisk sales, the Predictas seemed destined for success. They were unusually slim, utilizing a picture tube considerably shallower than any previous type. Some models featured a screen unit—little more than a picture tube with a metal base—that was separate from the rest of the set; the screen could be placed across the room from the cabinet containing the receiving and tuning gear and could swivel to face any direction.

"For the first time, we had designed TV sets as instruments, distinct from furniture," recalls Armin Allen, Philco vice president in charge of products. Sipping highballs and munching hot

Reprinted by special permission from The Wall Street Journal, *April 5, 1961. Copyright, 1961, Dow Jones & Co., Inc.*

° *Staff Reporter of* The Wall Street Journal.

crab cakes following the presentation, the editors were inclined to agree that Philco's innovations were indeed bold and striking, and they later said so in a rash of copy acclaiming the Predicta line.

PUBLIC UNIMPRESSED

But the public apparently was unimpressed. Though an initial burst of dealer enthusiasm led Philco to double production at the start of 1959, orders began to dwindle by the middle of that year. They kept falling, and last year —long before such a basically revamped product line could normally be expected to expire—Philco stopped shipping Predicta models to dealers. The Predicta line, for which Philco had exceeded development and retooling budgets by 25% and on which profits had been negligible, was clearly a flop.

Though the splashy promotion accompanying the launching of the Predictas may have made their subsequent troubles especially conspicuous, Philco's unhappy experience is far from unusual. Many firms are bringing forth new products these days in an effort to hold their own against ever stiffening competition. In some cases, of course, they pay off handsomely; U.S.-made cars provide a conspicuous example. But more often the new products turn out to be duds as far as consumers are concerned.

Lippincott & Margulies, a New York industrial design concern, underscores the high casualty rate. The firm says its research indicates that of every 26 new products introduced by industry, 23 fail. Similarly, McCann-Erickson,

Inc., a large advertising agency, reports that of every 25 products test marketed, only one succeeds.

SPOTTING A FLOP

Sometimes a product destined for failure can be spotted early, perhaps at the test-marketing stage, and killed off quickly. Other times, as in the case of Ford Motor Co.'s Edsel fiasco, they may grow into full-fledged, costly enterprises before it becomes evident they have no future. Commenting on the tendency for some new product projects to move ahead inexorably once they get under way, a psychologist employed by a design firm observes: "Products can take on a life of their own. When the wheels of an organization get going, there's often no turning back."

No matter when a firm cancels a new product, however, a failure costs money, either in the form of losses or narrowed profit margins. This consideration spurs efforts to diagnose past flops in hopes of avoiding similar mistakes in the future.

The theories put forward to explain failures are as varied as the products themselves. Pondering the passing of the Edsel, experts in the art of hindsight have called it a case of a product with the wrong name, the wrong price and the wrong design which was introduced at the wrong time. As for the Predictas, the merchandising manager of one retail chain that bought large quantities suggests that "the price was too high and the design was too extreme. People said the sets were nice to look at, but they wouldn't want to have them in their own homes."

MISJUDGING A MARKET

Richard J. Coveney, vice president of Arthur D. Little, Inc., an industrial consulting firm which assesses more than 2,500 new products annually, contends failure to appraise demand carefully is the biggest single cause of flops. Mr. Coveney tells of a manufacturer who allotted $50,000 to develop a new optical instrument and $5 million to produce it. "After five years, he came to us to find out what was wrong with sales," Mr. Coveney relates. "The answer was simple. There's no market for that kind of instrument. We advised him to sell off his patents and give up."

Market researchers claim they often can determine the size of the market for a product and in addition can help steer firms to the right choice of name, package and advertising. But manufacturers frequently shy away from such market studies. Some are reluctant to expose new ideas to public testing because they want to keep their plans from competitors. Others lack confidence in samplings of consumer tastes.

Explaining Philco's decision not to pre-test Predicta styling, Mr. Allen, the vice president, declares: "The one true test of a product is to price it, put it on the market place and then—and only then—will you get an idea of what the public is buying."

One designer reports consumer surveys have repeatedly shown a strong preference for wide-mouthed catsup bottles that don't require vigorous thumping to get the catsup out. But when bottles with broad openings are placed on supermarket shelves, house-wives invariably reject them and reach for the old narrow-mouth bottles.

THE PILL THAT FAILED

Additional evidence that consumer research isn't foolproof is provided by the story of Bristol-Myers Co.'s Analoze, a combination analgesic, or pain killer, and antacid, or stomach sweetener. The executives who conceived the product a few years ago were impressed by the fact that Americans were gulping record quantities of analgesics such as Bufferin and Anacin. Since this was true, they reasoned, wouldn't an analgesic that could be taken without water have a ready market? Mindful of the success of antacids such as Tums and Rollaids, they later decided to make Analoze a combination tablet.

The company's laboratories came up with the desired product—a cherry-flavored combination tablet. Working with Young & Rubicam, a New York advertising agency, Bristol-Myers submitted samples of Analoze and competing products to a consumer panel. The verdict: Panel members overwhelmingly preferred Analoze.

Young & Rubicam copy writers then developed ads boosting Analoze as the combination analgesic-antacid that "works without water." Tests showed the ads had strong impact. Bristol-Myers also was confident that the package was well designed and that the price—eight tablets for 35 cents, slightly higher than competing products—was right in view of Analoze's reputed advantages.

Backed by heavy advertising outlays, Analoze moved into test markets—Denver, Memphis, Phoenix and Omaha. Dealers were enthusiastic, and prospects appeared bright. Then the sales results began to trickle in. Despite all the careful preparations, the public was buying only small quantities of Analoze. Weeks went by with no improvement, and Bristol-Myers glumly withdrew Analoze from the test markets.

FINDING THE FLAW

What happened? After months of post-mortem probing, it was concluded that the fatal flaw was the "works without water" feature. Headache sufferers, so the theory ran, unconsciously associated water with a cure and consequently had no confidence in a tablet that dissolved in the mouth.

A market study also led General Mills, Inc., astray when it launched its meringue mix in the fall of 1958. Polls of housewives had shown they were eager to buy a powder which, among other conveniences, eliminated the egg yolks always left over in the making of meringue, a blend of egg whites and sugar. But after spending "several hundred thousand dollars" on magazine and TV advertising, the company reluctantly concluded housewives have perfectly good uses for left-over egg yolks and don't mind whipping up meringue ingredients themselves. Sales never attained a profitable level, and General Mills dropped the mix last summer.

Another big food processor, General Foods Corp., took a more spectacular tumble with its Gourmet Foods line, introduced in the summer of 1957. General Foods' decision to sell high-priced, fancy foods was based mainly on a careful study of the competition in the field. "We found literally hundreds of producers of fine foods, but no producer with a comprehensive line under one label," says a General Foods executive. Most of the companies were small, and "both distribution and marketing techniques seemed primitive." In short, says the company official, there appeared to be "a clear opportunity for an aggressive marketer to do a real merchandising and selling job in a relatively uncrowded field."

BISCUITS AND LINGONBERRIES

General Foods scouts sampled unusual and expensive foods from many countries, and the company put together a product line that included imported biscuits and Swedish lingonberries. The company first tried marketing the line in specialty and department stores, and later it experimented with supermarket sales and reduced prices and with mail order sales. None of these tactics were successful, however, and General Foods recently dropped the Gourmet line.

One marketing analyst's theory: Gourmets in search of unusual, exotic foods shied away from products turned out by a big, well-known American company such as General Foods.

An ad campaign that miscarries or a name that doesn't strike quite the right note can sometimes play a major role in the downfall of a product. Most marketing authorities consider these factors largely the troubles that have beset Hit Parade cigarets, which was American Tobacco Co.'s first entry in the filter tip market.

According to a survey conducted by

Brown & Williamson Tobacco Co., a competitor, American poured $40 million into Hit Parade advertising and promotion during the three years following the introduction of the cigaret in late 1956. While American labels this estimate "much too high," it's known the company paid over $17 million for air time and publication space alone during those years.

SLIPPING SALES

At first, Hit Parade responded to the advertising hypo. Harry M. Wootten, tobacco industry analyst, estimates that distribution totaled 4.5 billion cigarets in 1957, the first complete marketing year; there's no breakdown, however, on how many of these were given away for promotional purposes and how many were sold. But in 1958 the total dropped to 3.2 billion, and last year, after American cut off the flow of advertising dollars, a relatively insignificant number of Hit Parades—500 million—were distributed.

Advertising executives suggest American got its new filter smoke off to a bad start when it chose the name Hit Parade. Later research showed the rock 'n' roll takeover of the TV program of the same name, which was sponsored by American, soured many smokers on the cigaret. Some adult smokers also told pollsters they thought it was morally wrong to associate a program for adolescents with a cigaret. Moreover, the adolescent aura surrounding the cigaret bothered people worried about the possible relationship between smoking and lung cancer; they indicated they felt Hit Parades weren't "mature"

enough to assure a safe smoke. Public confidence in the cigaret was further weakened by a July, 1957, Reader's Digest article ranking Hit Parade high in tar and nicotine. Though ad men say the Digest article was a serious blow to Hit Parade, they argue the blow could have been overcome if the cigaret had not been faced by its other problems. They cite the case of L&M, which the Digest rated higher in nicotine and tars than Hit Parade. L&M's sales last year were up nearly 37% from the level of 1956, the year before the article appeared.

Hit Parade advertising did little to improve the cigaret's image, ad men now agree. The first magazine ad, which pictured a group of adult smokers performing a variety of contorted dance steps, drew this acid comment from Advertising Age, a trade publication: "We have seldom seen so unfortunate an advertisement featuring a cigaret with so unfortunate a name in so dismal a fashion." Advertising Age went on to predict "a most difficult future" for Hit Parade.

Word-of-mouth criticism is sometimes enough to eliminate a new product, according to B. F. Michtom, chairman of Ideal Toy Corp. This was the case with an Ideal doll which was sold along with a supply of cosmetics. Little girls from three to five would love to daub lipstick and eyebrow make-up on the doll's face, Ideal reasoned.

As it turned out, little girls did enjoy smearing the cosmetics on the dolls. But they also thought it was fun to apply them to wallpaper, floors and drapes, and this diversion was not appreciated by mothers. Their adverse comments caused demand to plummet, and the company had to drop the cos- metic doll after selling a relatively small number. Mr. Michtom figures the company lost $200,000 on the product.

▶▶▶▶▶▶▶▶▶▶▶ THE SHORT HAPPY LIFE

Time

Ｎew products are the lifeblood of U.S. business, but many a company in 1963 uses up a lot of its own lifeblood in the race to bring them out. Once, U.S. corporations had only to develop a few new products every year or so, confident that they would dominate the market long enough to show a healthy profit. No longer. Today's new products not only take more time, effort and money to develop, but face a far shorter life at the hands of the fickle consumer. There are plenty of companies to woo him; so many firms now have fast-moving research labs and trigger-ready marketing techniques that few new products are far ahead of competing copies or improvements. "Lead time is gone," laments Du Pont Chairman Crawford Greenewalt. "There's no company so outstanding technically today that it can expect a long lead in a new discovery."

LESTOIL SYNDROME

Du Pont had the nylon market to itself for 15 years, and did well with Dacron too. But when it went into production of its tough new Delrin plastic—a breakthrough it considers as important as nylon—hardly two years passed before competing Celanese Corp. hit the market with an almost identical plastic developed by its own chemists. U.S. Steel recently developed a new, economical "thin tin" plate— only to find other steel companies out in six months with a thin tin that customers liked better because it gleamed brighter; Big Steel is now copying some of its competitors' gleam-making methods. Sunbeam's new electric skillet was imitated so widely that the market was saturated within a few years, and Squibb's electric toothbrush is getting the same treatment.

Rivals are so quick to follow in the wake of any successful product that smaller, weaker originators are frequently swamped. In industry, this is now known as the Lestoil syndrome because of the experience of Lestoil Products of Holyoke, Mass. Lestoil scored a hit with its liquid household cleanser and gleefully watched sales climb to $25 million. Then Lever Brothers followed with Handy Andy,

Procter & Gamble with Mr. Clean; recently Colgate weighed in with liquid Ajax. Lestoil's sales have fallen to $16 million, and the company has had to stop paying dividends.

Britain's Wilkinson Sword Ltd. has had such success in the U.S. with its long-lasting stainless steel razor blades that American Safety Razor and Schick have produced copies, and Gillette is now preparing to assault the market. Finding themselves unable to keep up the pace against competitors with greater resources, some companies have chosen to sell their new ideas to larger firms. Even giant Monsanto, first into the market with a soap for automatic washers (All), eventually got out of the hotly competitive market rather than try to match the budgets of soap-makers.

LITTLE PROTECTION

Sometimes company research moves so fast that it makes a company's own products obsolete. Du Pont's Dacron is giving tough competition to the company's nylon and rayon, and Du Pont has decided to give up making rayon altogether. General Electric's recently announced silicon transistor will sell for half the price of its own germanium transistor.

Patent protection often means little; copycat firms know that a copied product may have spent its life cycle by the time lengthy litigation is finished. Westinghouse recently found a company copying its new hair dryer so exactly that even the instruction book was the same. In desperation, many inventive companies now license their competitors before they can copy, hoping at least to collect some royalties.

Companies that once simply devised a new product and then offered it to the public now go to the consumer before-hand to find out what products he wants designed, or old ones changed. Even such basic industries as steel, which once sold products only to fabricators, now try to recognize the uses new alloys or materials can be put to, and aim their research at end products for the consumer. Says Edward Green, vice president of Westinghouse Air Brake: "Companies must become more oriented not only to what the customer wants today but also to what he'll want five years from now."

TRIBUTE TO VIGOR

In many ways, the short, happy life of new products is a tribute to the vigor of free competition, but it inevitably means a harder life for companies. Big companies often suffer a profit cut or even a loss on a new product that is quickly copied or improved upon, and even the copiers frequently cannot recover the expense of tooling and production before the product succumbs to newer, better or flashier things. The race to get to the consumer first has forced companies to shorten their product development time, and in some cases has actually made the product secondary in the sweat to sell it. Chicago's Alberto-Culver was so eager to beat Procter & Gamble's Head and Shoulders shampoo to market that it filmed the TV commercials for its Subdue shampoo even before it had developed the product.

►►►►►►►►►►► NEW PRODUCTS: *Boon or bust*

HANS L. CARSTENSEN, JR., AND NORMAN H. MCMILLAN*

Carstensen: Business' fascination with new products does not end with *producing* them. Someone has to buy them! This is, of course, the root of new product successes and failures. And to get at the root we have to look to the consumer.

For every 1,000 new product ideas a company starts with, only a small fraction ever reach the market. And of those which do get out where the big money gets laid on the line, four out of five are destined for rejection by consumers. These are very poor odds. But in this gloomy picture let's not forget the tremendous rewards of success.

I think the greatest single challenge for marketing men can be stated quite simply: How can we bring home more successes—fewer failures?

Management wants an answer. If new products are to be the number one preoccupation of management then the second major preoccupation of management must be *risk reduction* in new product development. The odds for success are not good enough now. The costs of failure are staggering and will get more so.

There are a variety of reasons for the poor batting average on new products so far. But none is more important than what we call "management blinders." Horsemen use blinders to keep their steeds running straight and true. But the two "management blinders" I have in mind focus attention on the *wrong* targets.

The first of these blinders is the practice of overconcentration on what competition is doing. It is human nature in a competitive situation to fight back. The trouble is we usually fight back with the same weapons our competitor is using—whether it be pistols at 40 paces, bare knuckles, six-ounce gloves, boxes of corn flakes, or tubes of tooth paste. In a marketing fight this practice leads to products that are not really new. They are imitative, simply "me-tooing" other products already available to the consumer. The focus is on doing *just as well* as our scrambling to *catch up with* or *matching* competition. Not on developing something new and different that the consumer wants or will buy.

There are times when you must match competition. But this is not the road to leadership.

Surprisingly, there is a lot of this "me-tooing" going on. But the lesson is clear: Products which are new to the manufacturer, but not really new to the consumer, only land smack against the fiercest kind of competition—precisely as the market reaches saturation when profits are at the low point.

We have a phrase that we use in our

Reprinted with permission from Madison Avenue, *November 1961, pp. 26 ff.*

* *Vice Presidents, N. W. Ayer & Son, Inc.*

new product work for our clients—*the wanted difference.* If a new product doesn't have a wanted difference, to borrow from Winston cigarettes, it simply doesn't have it and it isn't going to get up front.

The second "management blinder" is the practice of paying more attention to our own internal problems than to our customers' problems. The fact is we are all far too introspective. We think and worry about production, processing and distribution problems. We don't spend half as much time thinking about our customers. Introspection is necessary, of course, in many businesses just to survive. But I think we can all agree that too much of this "tunnel vision"—looking inward at ourselves instead of outward at the customer—is a bad habit that none of us can afford.

It results in thinking like this:

because we can produce it, somebody ought to buy it.

because it makes good economic sense to run that $30,000 machine another two hours a day, the consumer will apply the same logic and solve our problem for us.

because the president's or vice president's wife, or even you or I, like this new product, so will hordes of consumers.

The result of this kind of thinking is usually what we call a "who needs it" product. Sure, *we* may need it, but who else?

There is one set of blinders that management *should* be wearing. It is the set that focuses attention on the one essential ingredient common to new product successes and the universally

missing ingredient in the flops. It is an ingredient that can be summed up in these simple words—*find out what consumers want and give them more of it. Find out what they don't want and give them less of it.*

Constantly keeping your sights on the consumer will avoid such common failures as:

the product that is just great, but is too much work for the consumer, so she doesn't bother.

the product that is too far ahead of the market.

the product that is just too costly relative to the alternatives the consumer can choose from.

the product that solves only *your* problem.

the product that had all the necessary elements for success, but failed simply because consumers never heard of it. It was under-promoted because the manufacturer forgot the importance of telling the consumer.

But looking to the consumer in any of the traditional ways isn't going to be good enough. What consumers have done, what they think about existing products, and what *they say* about their plans for the future will be helpful, but most of this is based on hindsight.

Looking ahead is what is needed. That is where the real risk reduction will come in—*anticipating* consumers' needs and wants, or *anticipating* the opportunity to create new needs and wants.

If we can find ways to do that successfully we obviously will succeed, because the consumer is on the side of the innovator. Consumers are strongly loyal to the first brand on the market with a really new product and to the brands that keep improving.

Obviously, improved research techniques will be very important in developing ways to look ahead. But there is a way to do so right now without spending a cent of money. Yet it gets surprisingly little use. We call it "trend watching"—seeking out the *trends* in consumer thinking, behavior, and buying habits—trends that create the opportunity for new products—trends that create the tailwinds to push new products along to success. A jet pilot gets there faster with a tailwind. You'll improve your new product batting average riding the favorable winds of consumer trends.

McMillan: Let me try some questions on for size with you:

How come instant coffee, which in this man's opinion isn't even remotely as good as the real thing, has (nonetheless) captured a sizeable chunk of the coffee business?

How come something like half the cakes baked in this country are built from a box, not from scratch?

How come a product like aerosol starch, which costs 15 or 20 times as much as the kind bought in a box or a bottle, is suddenly showing up on the ironing board in an awful lot of homes all over the country?

In fact, how come almost anything sold in aerosol seems to have had a little magic associated with it?

I am sure you see the common thread running through these questions. This is the trend to *convenience* that is so evident in almost every packaged goods category. People want it—and usually (but not always) they are willing to pay for it. And any new product that offers noticeably more convenience starts with a leg up. Maybe this is the most basic of the trends we're going to list here. Certainly it is the most obvious. So you may wonder why we bother to discuss it. The reason is that all too often people in marketing are getting pinned with a steely stare by top management and asked questions like these—

How come we struck out on three products in a row?

How come sales aren't up to forecast?

How come we spent so much in advertising for such a puny result?

Finally, *how come* we aren't making any money around here?

And the reason we are being asked questions like that, surprisingly often, traces to *our* forgetting the ABC's: Build convenience into the package, or the form of the product, or through combination with others, or through size, or take the work out of it—and we build in a tailwind.

Stack your own new product experience up against these trends—and see if the big successes you like to talk about haven't usually had the trends *with* them. See if those little beauties you would just as soon forget weren't involved in an uphill struggle *against* them.

TREND 2

Here is the second trend—and another batch of questions for you.

How come almost all of the product categories that are sold for personal grooming have boomed, and are booming?

How come men nowadays are dousing themselves with all sorts of sprays and tonics—stuff that until recently was considered sissy?

How come women now have electric shavers all their own?

How come deodorants (a word that was scarcely mentioned a few years back) now come in several hundred sizes, shapes, brands, or product forms?

All of these relate to another inexorable trend—the desire to look better (or maybe smell better).

If you say, "*That* trend is centuries old," you're right. But it is coming stronger all the time as more people have the time, and the money, to indulge themselves.

Now if you are in the food business you may think this trend has no bearing on your business—but let me point out that these items are competing hard for food dollars in the supermarket right now. And if you are in the toiletries field I don't have to tell you that at all.

TREND 3

How come filters keep coming so strong in the cigarette business?

How come vitamin pills sell in such astounding quantities—particularly with so much of the medical profession lukewarm?

How come big supers have whole sections of dietetic food?

What we are getting at here is the desire to feel better, or maybe it is the fear of disease. Personal health is one of the big trends. There is more aware-ness of vitamins, of minerals, of calories, of things that are good and bad for our hearts, our lungs, our *everything*. And it is a trend that is having important consequences in many businesses.

TREND 4

The look-better and feel-better trends merge into the fourth—the diet trend. People want to lose weight chiefly for cosmetic reasons. Then their resolve to lose a few pounds is backed up by all sorts of outstanding medical authority —the *Ladies' Home Journal*, *Good Housekeeping*, and *McCall's* to name a few. Even the doctors think it is a good idea. The results in some cases are startling. Whole industries have had to adjust.

People want lean meat, and lard-type hogs go out of style. And a lot of farmers have been asking, "How come?"

Skim milk, not so many years ago, could hardly be given away. Now it sells for about the same price as whole milk—and dairymen are delighted saying, "How come?"

The same dairymen—not so delightedly—are also looking at declining cream sales, and asking "How come?"

And let's not forget Slenderella, wheat germ, yogurt, Vic Tanny, and dozens of others.

Finally, the stockholders, the directors, and the management of any number of food and drug companies who could have come out with a diet product are looking at Metrecal and asking, "*How come?*"

TREND 5

Most of the examples I am using relate to food, simply because food is so basic. I want to point out, however, that what we are really talking about is *people*—they cause the trends. So don't be misled. No matter what kind of a consumer product you are selling, these affect *you*.

More questions:

How come buffet-style entertaining is in—and seven course dinners for 12 are out?

How come so much food gets eaten around the TV set?

How come last week I was able to count 52 different kinds of crackers at a super market?

How come when you go to put the dishes in the dishwasher you have to collect them from every room in the house—*not* just the kitchen or dining room?

. The answer is the trend to more informality in our lives, and the way we behave around foods. You see it in almost any meal. The old idea of three squares a day at the dining room table is giving ground fast to casual eating. This fact of informality in our eating habits has caused a lot of new items to take off like a sky rocket. It has also caused some to fizzle—and it has led to a few conversations that began. How come———?

TREND 6

Let me ask you:

How come so many of us stand around our back yards with smoke in our eyes, singeing the hair off our knuckles, burning otherwise delicious meat over charcoal?

How come many of us go on from there and douse the chicken or steak with a concoction of wine and herbs?

How come many of our wives like to add a fresh egg to a cake mix— when the manufacturer says plainly that nothing needs to be added except water?

How come practically any big super-market, anywhere you go in the country, suddenly has to stock dozens and dozens of different spices, most of whose names I can't even pronounce?

This is the urge many of us have to express ourselves more creatively. This is an important trend in my book. It is of more recent vintage. It is coming fast. It provides a clear-cut warning as you apply convenience to a product.

The point is that it is okay to take the work out of meal preparation, but definitely not okay to take the fun out of it.

TREND 7

The seventh trend is closely related to creativity. This is the *increasing level of taste*. Partly this is more money. Partly more time. But we have an idea that it is mostly a reflection of an increasing education level, and along with it an increase in the demand for products which reflect educated tastes.

Bringing this back, or down, to foods, you find these interesting things happening:

The Swedes in Minnesota buying items like lobster, French pastries, pizza, prosciutto ham, sour cream—and so on—in the supermarkets. These were strictly East Coast specialties until just a few years ago. Now they're available in about any supermarket in Minneapolis, or Chattanooga, or El Paso.

Hormel is just completing introduction of a line of Around the World Foods—beef stroganoff, chicken cacciatore, garbanzo soup, etc. It sells for about a buck a throw, and it sells surprisingly well in some fairly surprising places.

Cornish game hens, once confined to fancy New York menus, can now be bought across the country.

A lot of the low-income staples like sowbelly, fatback and lard, to name three that vitally affect the meat industry, are not even handled in neighborhoods where only ten years ago they were tonnage items.

And, of course, many of us have learned the lessons of ordering in a restaurant. We want Beefeater martinis, 15 to 1, with a twist of lemon. We want *very* rare steaks. We want Roquefort dressing on the salad. We want sour cream on the baked potato. We tamp it all down with Irish coffee.

These are not just Manhattan sophisticates ordering. This is happening all over the country. We used to figure that tastes or fashions were set in the East, and the rest of the country was a few years behind. Maybe taste is still set here (although I am not so sure any more), but I can assure you the rest of the country is no more than 15 minutes behind now.

How come? The tastes of the country are on the ascendancy. More manufacturers are likely to recognize this in the Sixties and profit in the process.

TREND 8

We have skimmed briefly through some pretty familiar territory in our look at the first seven trends. We want to pause on the eighth and last one because we think it has far-reaching implications for anybody associated with marketing. And it slices through and combines with some of those already listed.

It reflects the fact that our population has become really huge. It reflects our increasing level of taste. And as taste goes up so does the desire for distinction—the very opposite of "mass." It also reflects a growing ability to pay.

We label this the trend to *miniature-mass markets*.

This, we think, is a threshold trend. We expect that all of us are going to become increasingly involved with it in the next several years. We will be thinking increasingly in terms of the miniature-mass markets.

There are special markets within markets now. Baby foods are, of course, an obvious example—a specialized market for canned foods within the total market. The growing above-65 population is another—now big enough to make specialization in this area possible and profitable for some lines.

I can't help wondering if there isn't a wide open opportunity to *think small*, to think in terms of the *miniature-mass markets*.

I am pretty sure there is. But let me warn you, it requires that you re-orient your thinking. There seems to be a built-in mechanism in most of us that tells us that we should go for broke in the big mass market every time we look at a new product. If more money can be made with a 5 per cent share of market than with 20 per cent, we will have to be smart enough to recognize it.

Let me illustrate what happens when you think small. Suppose you and I are partners and we have a new product—egg white in an aerosol can for meringue pie toppings. We know that the product has the consumer tailwinds with it. We have our corrosion and keeping problems all worked out so we know the product is okay. So we put it on the market.

Now if we start with the assumption this will sell in the volume eggs do, we're destined for disappointments. If we calculate our marketing investment on the assumption that every home in America will buy a can per month, we'll be bankrupt. And if we price it like eggs we're crazy. But if we start with the assumption that inside the big mass market for eggs there is a market in miniature for egg whites in an aerosol bomb, if we think small about this product, we will evaluate our results differently. And we will plan differently.

We will find out just who the immediate prospects are—and we will sell to them, ignoring the rest. If we find the prospects are all over 60, we will design the package and advertising to suit their tastes. If they are all under 25 we will design it differently. Or, if the language they understand best is Sanskrit, we will use that language. You

see, we don't care about the *mass* market. We don't need to straddle the tastes of *everybody*. We are not trying to reach an average consumer. We are aiming for a very precise target.

Now, maybe egg whites in an aerosol bomb is a poor idea, but you get the point, I am sure. When you begin to think small, many things begin to look possible. When you begin to plan with the miniature mass market concept in mind, you may start out after a 5 per cent market share rather than 25 per cent. And as you do, a couple of interesting things happen.

First, you increase your chances for success simply because you are shooting for a much more specific target, and you can more often arrive at a precision fit of the product and promotion to the prospect. So you should improve the odds considerably.

Second, because you scale your investment to the size of the market you are shooting for, you risk less on any given new product.

The point is this. Increasingly, it will be possible to do a sizeable amount of business—enough to get all the efficiencies of mass production within specific population groups and within restricted geographic areas.

And increasingly it will be more profitable to think small, to think about the miniature mass market, to think about nailing down, *really* nailing down, a smaller piece of business and making a profit—rather than constantly going for big casino, and too often missing.

The implications for marketers, for agencies, and for media are obviously important.

►►►►►►►►►► RESEARCHING THE NEW PRODUCT

WILLIAM J. STOKES*

BEFORE-&-AFTER RESEARCH

In general the marketing research to be done on a new product can be separated into two major classifications:

1. Pre-production research (that work done before the decision to produce is made, the major purpose of which is to provide a sound factual basis for that decision).

2. Follow-up research (the research done after the product is on the market, to keep top management informed of the product's health and to provide a running check on the rightness of previous decisions).

This article will deal only with the first of these categories.

Pre-tooling research, to reach its ultimate in economic effectiveness, must be properly planned. And to plan properly at this stage requires a thoughtful analysis of the major factors, the principal influences in the market, which tend to increase or decrease the inevitable risks. Only when these factors are understood and their importance realized can plans be developed leading toward greater chances for success.

These critical influences on saleability are not necessarily of equal importance for every new product. Perspective is needed in assessing their relative importance for your new product. However, regardless of the product, there are certain primary factors which are sufficiently important for every new product to warrant their further discussion.

IS THE NEED REAL?

First in importance for any new product is the *need factor*. Before the new item even reaches the drawing board stage an honest and unbiased answer must be obtained to this question: "Does a need exist for this product?" Only a "yes" answer can justify further consideration of the product and expenditures for designing and engineering. The answer, to be honest and valid, must be arrived at by a realistic appraisal of the market. Are you sure it is a genuine need and not one based on circumstances peculiar to the operation of one or two customers?

Is the enthusiasm for the product within your own organization founded on a knowledge of the market or is it engendered by personal ambitions and desires for greater power in the company? Is someone in the organization looking for a chance to test his ideas at the stockholders' expense? If data which is adequate, which is up-to-date, and which has a broad enough base, is not available then it should be dug up in

Reprinted with permission from Industrial Marketing, *June 1948, pp. 33, 135 ff.*

* *Research Director, G. M. Basford Company.*

the field. Guesses and hopes aren't enough. Facts are essential.

When there is no longer any doubt as to the existence of a need for the product, then two other questions must be considered:

1. Is the product planned to fill a known need, or
2. Is it planned to fill a need of which the market is not actively aware?

For example, in many metal working industries there is a need for protective coatings. The need is being filled by existing products or methods. A new coating which does the job faster, or better, or more economically will fill this known need of which the market is aware. Here the manufacturer must capture a share of a known market.

POTENTIAL NEED TAKES EDUCATIONAL SELLING

On the other hand, let us consider a mythical low cost television attachment for telephones. There is no demand at present, certainly, for such a product but if preliminary research indicates that such a product could contribute to more profitable business operation, more comfortable living, or more pleasant recreation, then a demand could be created. A need thus exists without the market's being actively aware of its existence. The manufacturer must, in this case, be prepared to do an entirely different selling and promotion job with considerable emphasis on education of potential users.

At this preliminary stage of new product planning then, marketing research in the case of the *known* need, should be used:

1. To determine whether or not the market is large enough to justify the expenses to be incurred.
2. To determine whether or not the planned product improvements are sufficiently important to buyers to capture an adequate share of the potential volume.
3. To analyze the competitive situation with respect to sales volume, brand loyalties, promotion and product advantages.

If a need is *not known* to exist but is suspected, then the immediate objectives of the field research should be:

1. To confirm or disprove the suspected need.
2. To define that need in terms of benefits to the buyer.
3. To arrive at a practical estimate of the minimum size of the market in terms of unit sales at various possible price levels.

In many cases this is only part of the research work to be done on a new product. In other cases it may be the whole job. Perhaps the product's advantages are not strong enough to make it really new from the viewpoint of users but only competitive with existing products. Perhaps the advantages, again from the users' angle, do not justify the price. If careful examination of cost estimates indicates that a lower price is impossible further consideration should be passed up. Perhaps the field work indicates that no real need exists, that it would be wise to forget this particular product and concentrate on another. Up to this point field work has been limited and research costs held down to a minimum.

RESEARCH BRINGS IDEA
DOWN TO EARTH

Now is the time to analyze and evaluate the results obtained and to use these results in deciding whether or not additional expense is justified. For example, our organization recently made a very limited field study for a manufacturer who was planning the production and sale of an electronic valve control. Certainly there is a need in many process industries for a valve control and this control could do some things better than any control then on the market.

Interviews in depth were conducted with engineering personnel in plants where large numbers of controlled valves were used, and some harshly realistic facts were brought into the open.

1. The things the proposed control could do better were not the things users wanted improved.

2. There were no markets for the proposed control beyond those being adequately serviced by existing controls.

3. The proposed control would have to be sold for a price approximately 50% above the price of existing controls doing a satisfactory job.

4. Proper servicing of the new control would require field service branches which the manufacturer did not have.

5. Replacement parts inventories would have to be maintained at each field service branch.

When these facts were weighed against the cost of tooling for the new product, producing it, promoting it and selling it, the product was abandoned. The decision was certainly wise, and outstanding evidence of good management can be seen in the fact that the field work was done and the results analyzed, evaluated and applied *before* the big expenditures were made.

On the other hand the preliminary field work may support the thinking which prompted plans for the new product. The research man in the picture may have brought back the necessary proof that a need exists, that the potential volume is attractive, and the competitive and profit picture quite favorable. Should he then bow out to rest on his laurels? Hardly. In many cases it is necessary at this time to examine product quality in relation to the desires of the market.

SHIFTS SCENE TO
PRODUCT'S REAL MARKET

The product, as planned thus far, may require more engineering to make it really good enough for the job it will have to do. Or it may be found that the product is too good for the market at which it is aimed. A large electrical manufacturer recently developed a variable speed motor control that was really a honey. Its range was extraordinary and control was actually hairline. All through the development stage the company had a particular processing industry in mind as the logical market.

Field research, on a small scale but very intensive, punctured a bubble again. The processing industry did not need speed control of greater than 5:1 ratios and this type of control could be had by mechanical means at very low cost. For a while it looked like another stillborn product but the same field research had indicated that other industries offered better possibilities. A little more work showed that a very definite and substantial market did exist. Promotion plans were changed and sales efforts directed more realistically.

Today the product is making money and profits are not being eaten up by writing-off the cost of badly aimed promotion and futile sales efforts. The product is clear evidence that quality must be tailored to the needs of the market. Pre-production research is low premium insurance against the over-engineered or under-engineered product.

Now let us assume that the preliminary investigation has assured the manufacturer that he is on firm ground so far. He must at this time consider the distribution of the new product. Selection of the proper distribution channels is of paramount importance, important enough to make examination and consideration of all the possibilities essential. A wrong decision may actually make it hard for the most logical prospects to buy the product, and certainly a good decision goes a long way toward making the sales job easier. The fact that a firm has built up a fine distribution system for some of its products should not be allowed to obscure the problem. These channels opened up through the years may not be best for the new product. A good example of this came to our attention recently.

FRIENDS WOULDN'T TELL HIM

A manufacturer had spent substantial sums in producing a new addition to his line. He was puzzled and alarmed by the lack of repeat orders from his distributors. Almost ready to write it off and try again. Remember that he was an old hand at the game and had worked for years with his distributors building up a really enviable relationship. It was at this stage that research came on the scene.

Distributor-dealer level interviews quickly proved that the new product was the victim and not the beneficiary of the manufacturer's distributor friends who expansively assured him of their ability to sell the product. Changes were recommended and made and the product is today moving in gratifying quantities through other channels. The ending here is happy, but it could have been even happier if the research on distribution had been done before production.

So before production begins, certain questions regarding distribution must be answered without the inescapable bias present in the company's sales personnel and distributors.

1. From what sources of supply will most prospective users seek to buy the new product?

2. If it appears desirable to open new distribution channels what will be the effect on present distributors of the company's line?

3. Will a change in distribution necessitate a change in the discount structure which might have repercussion among existing distributors?

4. Had the firm's previous experience given it any recognition among the new distributors? Are they friendly, unfriendly or unbiased?

5. Are the company's present sales-men familiar with the new channels? Will they be able to meet the task of selling the new distributors or must plans be made for special training or an expanded sales force?

Up to this point the research job has been small, inexpensive and fast. It has brought home facts to replace conjec-ture and wishful thinking. Research has not replaced business judgment, it has provided the factual knowledge of ex-isting conditions which is the founda-tion of sound judgment. Top manage-ment has some assurance that the risks are not too great. Tooling expense can be incurred with a greater ease of mind than would have been possible without the research work.

▸▸▸▸▸▸▸▸▸▸▸ FINDING OUT WHAT CUSTOMERS WILL BUY

Steel

Above the cash register in a small-town hardware store is a sign: "The Customer Is King."

He is. He can make you or break you. It all depends on whether he wants what you produce.

That's why it's imperative to find out what the customer will buy.

The concept of finding out what the customer wants sounds so elementary it's hard to realize that it has not been more widely practiced. Perhaps the reason for the neglect is expressed by James H. Jewell, vice president of mar-keting, Westinghouse Electric Corp., Pittsburgh: "For too long we have re-garded the customer primarily in terms of our needs to influence him favorably toward our products. Our marketing concept requires that we recognize him as an important source of information on needs and desires—with this infor-mation serving as the basis of planning and controlling our entire business operation."

Many people contend that the art of moving goods to the consumer lags at least a decade behind our ability to produce goods.

What with the concurrent disappear-ance of the sellers' market and the completion of a big expansion in our industrial capacity, we are forced to turn from a philosophy of production to one of marketing.

Its doctrine: Marketing is more than selling. It must precede production, rather than follow it. It encompasses the functions concerned with finding out what is wanted, measuring the de-mand, planning the product, and mov-ing it to the consumer.

Too many times companies have built a new product, then set out to see how they could sell it. Under the new concept, you find out exactly what

Reprinted with permission from Steel, *July 14, 1958, pp. 101–108.*

prospective customers want, where and when they want it, how many or how much they want, and how much they'll pay. Then you make it.

The editor of one of the nation's leading marketing magazines said: "There is abundant evidence that many businesses are still organized on the principle of 'we make it; you buy it.'"

HOW TO FIND OUT

How do you find out what the customer wants? Ask him. The process of finding out can range from the simplest of procedures to the complex. You can do it yourself, or you can hire it done.

You have three ways to ask: 1. By mail. 2. By telephone. 3. By face-to-face interview.

If you use the mails for finding out, you'll use a questionnaire. If you use the telephone or the personal interview technique, you'll find it helpful to have a questionnaire before you as a guide.

A CASE STUDY

The Heil Co., Milwaukee maker of truck equipment, set out to learn prospective customers' wants before building a product.

It wanted to know how much demand there'd be for plastic truck bodies and what features and qualities the prospective customer would want. Getting such large products into production requires large equipment and a considerable capital outlay. The company had to be sure there was a market, and to put in the right kind of equipment, it had to know precisely what the market wanted.

The Heil Co.'s manager of commer-

cial research, K. C. Sanders, handled the job of finding out.

His department prepared and mailed 3,000 two-page questionnaires. Half went to meat packers, half to dairies.

Only objective questions—those asking for a "Yes" or "No"—or quantitative figures were used. Wordy and subjective questions which might be difficult and time consuming to answer were avoided. One question asked the respondent whether the doors of his truck were hinged or sliding, and which type he preferred. Meat packers were asked whether they hung meat from the truck ceiling and whether any special reinforcement was used.

The return was 15 per cent. The only spur used was a follow-up letter to those who had not responded within two weeks.

Before questions were used, they were pretested on transportation experts outside the Heil Co. This gave assurance that recipients would not be wasting their time and that their intelligence would not be insulted.

ROOM FOR IMPROVEMENT

Mr. Sanders had an experience common to many researchers. He says he would make a few changes if he were doing the job again. He thinks a little more pretesting of questions would have been beneficial.

"After a survey is finished and interpreted, every researcher has experienced the feeling that he could now construct a better questionnaire if only he had a second chance," says the noted market researcher, Alfred Politz, president of Alfred Politz Research Inc., New York. "This," he explains, "does not necessarily mean that mistakes were made the first time; but every question is based on assumptions, and after the survey is finished, some of the assumptions are proved, while others appear to be unsupported. With the knowledge gained, one could always design a more efficient questionnaire," Mr. Politz declares.

ASK THE PEOPLE

Another company that went to the people to find out what they wanted is Market Forge Co., Everett, Mass.

Samuel B. Sheldon, vice president of sales and operations, was dissatisfied with the back rest in his automobile. He put his company's research and engineering department to work devising an adjustable model that would be more comfortable and one that would contribute to a proper and healthful posture.

When his researchers and developers believed they had a prototype that would fill the bill, Mr. Sheldon sent it to leaders in the medical profession and to many of his prospective customers for their opinions.

They liked the seat. It was put into production. Customer response was immediate. As a result, the plant had to go on three shifts in March. On April 1, it moved production up to 10,000 seats a month—and this was during the depth of the nationwide recession.

A GUARD AGAINST FAILURE

A market test doesn't always show there's demand for a product. Sometimes, it shows the reverse, an equally important piece of information.

General Electric Co. received many requests from the trade for a new type night light—one with a low light output, low wattage, long life, and a prong-base which could be plugged into a convenient outlet. One of GE's competitors had introduced such a light.

To find out what prospective customers wanted, GE wrote to 6,000 people and asked whether they burned a light at night. To GE's surprise, about 16 per cent did. A sizeable portion used ordinary lamps.

GE included a page that showed all of the common types of night lights in use and asked respondents to check the kind they used.

GE sent about 1,000 of the proposed lights to those who used them, with a request that they try them out and give their reactions.

GE found that the users were firmly wedded to the type now on the market. They liked the shield, the switch, and the replaceable bulb—none of which were features of the proposed product.

Also, the price which the people thought was reasonable was lower than what GE could sell it for.

GE did not introduce the new product, and within a year the competitor who had brought out a similar product withdrew it from the market.

Finding out what the customer wants is a way of protecting your company from the failure of new products. New products are the life blood of any successful business, but the road is rough. Studies show that four out of five launched by 200 major manufacturers since World War II have flopped.

One company that seeks to guard

against product failure through customer research is International Business Machines Corp., whose world headquarters are in New York. In an extreme case, IBM will spend the equivalent of 20 man-years to study a bold new concept and its possibilities of application.

A good example of an IBM product designed and engineered with the user in mind is the IBM 305 RAMAC. (Pronounced RAM-ACK, it stands for random access method of accounting and control.) The new electronic data processing machine makes it possible for records stored in the machine to reflect the business picture as it is at any moment.

The 305 RAMAC sells for $189,950 or rents for $3200 a month. Around 70 RAMACs have been installed, and 1200 are on order.

WHAT DO YOU WANT?

Whether you make a survey by mail, telephone, or face-to-face interview depends on whether you want quantitative or qualitative research, or both.

Quantitative research develops information of a numerical type, such as how many and what proportion. A questionnaire which deals with limited subject matter is often used.

When you want to dig deeper and find out why, what kind, or how, you use qualitative research.

In quantitative research, you usually deal with a large number of people. In contrast, qualitative research usually deals with fewer, but you spend more time with them.

General Motors Corp., Detroit, uses both quantitative and qualitative research. For quantitative research, it de-

pends on mailed questionnaires. GM's researchers recognize that certain types of information can best be obtained by personal interview. It makes considerable use of this method at auto shows to get public reaction to new models before they are put on the market.

GM Motoramas are an excellent means of obtaining public reaction to new models, especially "dream cars." In some cases, they are not intended as "cars of the future." But they often have certain features—such as a fender treatment or a windshield design— which are so well received that they are translated into designs for production models.

By talking to thousands of people at these shows and asking them the right questions, it is possible to learn rather quickly which items are worth pursuing and which should be discarded.

GM sends questionnaires to car owners throughout the country, and the results are usually broken down by areas because varying conditions can cause differing viewpoints.

THREE WAYS TO ASK

The mail survey is probably the most widely used method of asking a customer what he wants. It has these advantages: (1) It's economical. The cost per person contacted is far less than that of the telephone or personal interview method. (2) A wide geographic area can be reached—and you do it quickly. (3) There is no interviewer to influence the interviewee and produce a bias in the reporting. (4) The questionnaire gets beyond the interviewee's door. (5) Hard-to-reach people, such as those who are away much of the time, can be contacted. (6) Respondents can take enough time to answer carefully.

The telephone survey provides some of the personal contact of the face-to-face interview and does it faster. The method includes these advantages: (1) Travel is eliminated. (2) You can probe for answers.

The face-to-face interview yields more information than a mail or telephone survey, and the interviewer can do more probing to arrive at attitudes, desires, opinions, or facts. The interviewer can show samples or examples to help elicit reactions.

All three methods have their disadvantages. You can ask only a limited number of questions in a mailed questionnaire. You run the risk of "hang-ups" in a telephone survey. Face-to-face interviews take time, cost money.

Choose the method or methods that you think will have the most advantages and the fewest disadvantages in each survey you make. What may be considered a heavy disadvantage in one case may be less so in another.

HANDLE WITH CARE

Choice of words in a questionnaire is important. A. Marsden "Tommy" Thompson, director of GM's customer research section, distribution staff, points to an early survey question asking whether customers wanted a car with radical or modified streamlining. "At that time 'radical' was an unpopular word and it would have distorted our replies," he explained.

If you do your own job of finding out, you ought to make sure that every one of your surveys is conducted across a representative sample. Otherwise, you will get a distorted picture.

Sometimes, this question arises: How many answers are needed to be sure that they are representative? A number of considerations are involved, including subject matter, type of questions, and breakdowns required. A note of caution: The total may be adequate for a nation-wide picture but inadequate if attempts are made to break the results down by areas or size of community.

WHERE TO GET HELP

If you aren't set up to do your own job of finding out, there are many outside sources of help. They range all the way from the one-man consultant to the large research agencies. They can do any portion of a job, or an entire project. They can be engaged for a one-shot job, or put on retainer. . . .

There are advantages and disadvantages of doing customer research with your own people. The same holds true of outsiders. Your own people know your company and its field; an outsider has to become acquainted with them. But closeness to your problems may hinder your own people. An outsider can come in with a fresh and objective approach.

Finding out what the industrial customer wants is often more difficult than finding out what the users of consumer products want. Those who buy consumer goods usually don't have to take anyone else into consideration, but the industrial customer may. What the machine operator wants, for instance, may conflict with what the maintenance chief wants.

Also, it's impractical to take big

machines to prospective industrial customers to check their reactions. The alternative is to use models or blueprints. Blueprints were used by Robert E. Sanford, design engineer of Erie Foundry Co., Erie, Pa., in finding out what improvements were wanted in forging presses. . . .

Market research for specialized industrial equipment requires an expert with intimate knowledge of the proposed product — in the case of Erie Foundry, Mr. Sanford had those qualifications. It's usually easier to teach an engineer or designer the fundamentals of customer research than it is to train the market researcher for such a role.

Customer research often requires more data than the research department's staff can collect. Because salesmen are out in the field, there's an inclination to saddle them with the job of data collecting and interviewing. The value of the sales force in gathering data has long been a subject of controversy. A frequently heard objection is that most salesmen are not qualified to do market research. It has been pointed out that their qualities differ sharply from those of researchers. Also, a salesman is inclined to feel that the extra duty takes too much time from selling and cuts his commissions.

W. C. Graham, a principal of McKinsey & Co. Inc., New York, a management consultant firm, points out that salesmen find it more difficult to get in to see people than market researchers.

DON'T EXPECT TOO MUCH

There's a limit to what you can get from customer research. You generally can't expect them to tell you what new products you should make. They don't know. They can help you, though, in the redesign or further development of your products. The consumer thinks only in terms of what he is acquainted with, says Researcher Politz. . . . GM's market researchers concur: "The average person cannot project his thinking beyond the things he can see and use. He can have positive opinions about the design and construction of equipment now available, but it would be hopeless to get completely accurate expressions of opinion on what might be desired several years in the future."

It is still the job of the stylist and technical people to do the forward looking and to conceive the big ideas, the GM researchers aver.

In GM's case, it considers the average car owner as an expert on the use of the product, and it is in that area that the company seeks his opinions.

WANTS VS. NEEDS

In polling the customers or prospects, we are trying to find out what they want. Wants should be distinguished from needs. You may not need a new automobile, but if you want one, a potential sale is created for the auto manufacturer. Sales are made by satisfying wants, not needs.

CONTINUITY PAYS OFF

Customer research should be a continuing project, the experts say. At least, it ought to be done often enough to catch any significant changes in trends. A rule of thumb for the frequency of checking follows this order: (1) Consumer products. (2) Large products like stoves and refrigerators. (3) Large industrial products.

Some of the Politz clients use four studies a year; supplementary surveys are made when a situation requires it.

Louis Cheskin, director, Color Research Institute, Chicago, says that a number of consumer attitude studies it made "show clearly that consumer attitudes toward many products are not as they were a year ago, two years ago, or even three, four, or five years ago.

"For example, as recently as last year, our tests showed that people reacted favorably to elaborate ornamentation, gaudy color combinations, and extensive chrome trim on cars and other steel products, although the favorable attitudes were not generally admitted in direct interviews.

"Recent studies show that people are reacting unfavorably to such ostentatious ornamentation. They reveal that people who only a year ago were attracted by frills now react unfavorably to functionless objects."

One reason for the continuing approach is that attitudes never stand still. For example, several years ago most people would have answered "No" to this question: "Do you want an automatic transmission or power steering on an automobile?" In the early days of both developments, a frequent comment was: "I can do a lot of shifting for that amount of money," or "I wouldn't pay that much for some help in steering."

The devices were offered for those who wanted them. Through an evolutionary process, they came into such wide use that the manufacturer who doesn't offer them now will lose sales.

Researcher Politz points out that "some kind of change is involved in most marketing situations, and a second survey in the same area often reveals more than the first one because it indicates progress, or lack of it. But even beyond this is the fact that the logic of question-making favors a sequence of surveys.

"Research has little in common with the one-shot survey procedure, which so often is characterized by overexpectation and underproductiveness," Mr. Politz declares.

TIME FOR DECISION

Completion of a survey brings the need for interpretation of results and for exercise of executive judgment. But judgment is no better than the information upon which it is based. That's why it's so important to find out what the customer will buy. The better the information, the better the executive judgment.

WHY WE MUST FIND OUT WHAT THE CUSTOMER WILL BUY

1. The challenge is to market. Production is no longer a problem. Industrial capacity is overexpanded.
2. You have a better chance to sell when you make what the customer will buy. Too many manufacturers bring out a product before seeing whether it will sell.
3. It's more important than ever before to keep your plant busy. Heavy investment in plant and equipment makes idleness costly. Once upon a time, you could cut costs by laying

off men. You can't lay off today's automated machines.

WHAT WE MUST FIND OUT

1. Who would be a customer.
2. What he would buy.
3. How much he would pay.
4. How much or how many he'll buy.
5. When he'll buy.

FINDING OUT PAYS OFF

1. SALES ARE BOOSTED:
   a. By offering products that will be in big demand.
   b. By uncovering new markets.
   c. By helping you get into a market before it is saturated.

2. COSTS ARE CUT:
   a. By making volume production possible.
   b. By reducing the risk of new product failure.

WHO WILL FIND OUT WHAT THE CUSTOMER WILL BUY?

I. YOUR OWN COMPANY:

1. By using its full-time market research department.
2. By using other members of its staff.

II. OUTSIDE ORGANIZATIONS, INCLUDING:

1. Market research agencies.
   a. Complete-service type (they can do the whole job).
   b. Limited-service type (they may do only tabulating or interviewing).
   c. Specialized-service type (they specialize in certain phases and may offer a standardized service).
2. Market research consultant (he is a specialist).
3. Management consulting firm.
4. Advertising agency (when it does such work, it's usually for advertisers it serves).
5. Advertising media (their services are usually available only to advertisers or potential advertisers).
6. Government agencies.
7. Educational institutions (some colleges and universities do market research).

WHY "OUTSIDERS" ARE USED TO FIND OUT

1. To get a fresh and objective approach.
2. To supplement your staff with specialized talents and services.
3. To carry you over a peak in customer research.
4. To help you speed up a project.
5. To do the entire job when you don't have a customer research staff.

THERE'S A LIMIT TO WHAT THEY KNOW

The consumer thinks only in terms of what he is acquainted with, says the noted market researcher, Alfred Politz, president of Alfred Politz Research Inc., New York, whose list of clients reads like a bluebook of American industry.

"If, in the 1800s, you would have

asked a person what improvements he wanted in lighting, he might have suggested a bigger wick or a light that didn't smoke. He would have thought in terms of a kerosene lamp, for that's all he was acquainted with," Mr. Politz explains. "He couldn't have been expected to say the improvement he wanted was electric lights. He had never heard of them."

New things must come from inventors and industry, Mr. Politz implies. At best, the consumer can tell you what he would like to achieve, or how you can improve a product.

Even when a person has heard of something new, he may not have built up wants for it. Wants have to be stimulated, Mr. Politz says. He illustrates the point this way: "Suppose you took cigarets into a country where the people had never heard of them. They would not know whether they wanted them. Their wants would have to be built up."

HOW TO GET THE MOST OUT OF A QUESTIONNAIRE

IMAGINE YOURSELF AS THE RECIPIENT

He isn't nearly as excited about the questionnaire as you are. You must win a favorable reaction from him. Ask yourself: "How would I react to this? Would I be inclined to answer it?"

KEEP IT SHORT

A long one reduces the quality of answers and the quantity of return.

MAKE IT EASY TO UNDERSTAND

Avoid wordiness. Use words people understand. Make questions simple.

Ask only one thing per question. Phrase your questions so they will not be misinterpreted. Remember: It is not enough that a thing can be understood —it must be so clear that it simply cannot be misunderstood. Sometimes, an illustration will help express what you have in mind.

MAKE IT EASY FOR RESPONDENT TO ANSWER

The less writing he'll have to do, the more returns you'll get. If a check mark won't serve, make it possible for him to answer with only a few words.

MAKE IT EASY TO RETURN

Provide the respondent with an addressed, postage-paid envelope or card for making the return.

TAKE CARE IN ORGANIZING IT

The sequence of questions often influences the quantity and quality of answers. Questions presented in a logical order are easy to answer. Any inflammatory questions should come last to prevent getting distorted answers to the other questions. If you must include hard-to-answer questions, place them last to avoid discouragement. Keep ease of tabulation and analysis in mind when you're formulating your questionnaire.

DON'T CROWD IT

A jam-packed page is repelling. Space the questions so they can be read easily. Leave enough room for answers, whether they are check marks or words.

MAKE RESPONDENT FEEL IMPORTANT

To promote response, enclose a brief note explaining how much he is helping you. Chances are, you'll bolster his ego, get his co-operation.

POLISH IT . . . PRETEST IT ON YOUR ASSOCIATES

When you believe you have the questionnaire in tip-top shape, try it out on your associates. They often can spot bugs in it.

HOW TO SPEED UP AND ENLARGE THE RESPONSE

Another way to boost the odds in your favor is to send a pencil, pen, or similar gimmick with your questionnaire, or offer to supply a copy of the results. (Sometimes, you can shake loose additional replies with a follow-up letter.)

BE SURE YOUR MAILING LIST IS REPRESENTATIVE

If your questionnaire is going to only a portion of the people who are qualified to answer it, select a cross section. Otherwise, you may get a distorted picture.

TIME THE MAILING

For best response, mail questionnaires at the right time. One season may be better than another for your purposes. Summer vacations and year-end holidays can cut the returns.

► ► ► ► ► ► ► ► ► ► ► PREDICTING CONSUMERS' NEEDS: *can tastemakers point the way?*

Printers' Ink

Economists predict that a decade of prosperity lies ahead. The forecasts, based on sound economic projections, are undoubtedly valid for the economy in general—but what about specific products and companies?

To plan for profits, marketing men must know today what particular products will succeed tomorrow where others will fail. Is there some way to learn now what consumers will want sometime in the future?

Progress demands that the answer be "yes." And "yes" is the answer that marketing research now is learning to provide. Researchers, armed with the approach of the scientist and the knowledge of the social-psychologist, are now probing the future for the profitable path to tomorrow's markets. PRINTERS' INK presents an exclusive report on their progress.

THE FIRST STEP

Marketing research as now practiced already meets the first challenge posed by the demand for accurate predictions. To understand today, historians have long argued, you must know what has happened in the past. Likewise, to predict what will happen tomorrow, you must have some understanding of the events of today. Marketing research, with its new and improved techniques, is helping to meet this need.

Modern store auditing methods permit the manufacturer an up-to-the-minute report on the progress of his goods in the field. Mail, telephone and personal interview surveys enable him to locate the consumers of his products for information about rate of consumption, methods of consumption and the reasons that govern them.

Government and industrial agencies are at work improving the production and income indices that serve as a backdrop against which we can gauge individual consumption. Such independent organizations as the Survey Research Center at the University of Michigan are personalizing the general government statistics with particular data on individuals.

All these data, when combined with still more information obtained from other arms of marketing research, provide the manufacturer with the tools for understanding the markets and the consumers that he must deal with today. They also provide the marketing researcher with the gauges needed for measuring change as it occurs.

The most far-seeing marketing analysts believe, however, that these data need not be only touchstones, not merely bases with which future change can be compared. Somewhere within that mass of tables and charts and graphs, somewhere within that endless record of interviews, they say, must be a clue to future intentions, future decisions, future actions.

Extracting these elements is the problem of the day.

PROJECTING TO WHAT?

Many of the clues to future marketing have long been recognized, isolated and projected. It takes little imagination, for example, to foresee that the infants of the war-time baby booms must some day grow up to become purchasing adults with families of their own. More imaginative but equally sound are the predictions of 1.7 per cent as the average annual increase in the nation's population.

Long-range forecasts of gross national product, personal income, personal per-capita income also have been refined to a high degree. The Econometric Institute of New York, for example, fed some 80 equations into an IBM 650 computer to come up with an electronic model of the U.S. economy, a model so sensitive that in 1956 it was able to forecast the recession of 1958. The institute now predicts that the rate of industrial production will climb about 35 per cent by 1970.

Many of these long-term predictions of population, production and income have proved reasonably accurate over past years. For marketing men they provide excellent guideposts to the general tenor of the economy in the decade ahead. They are, however, only general guideposts. They can hardly answer the needs of a manufacturer who wants to know what particular products will sell and at what rate.

An experiment in projecting the future market for a specific product was made by the Stanford Research Institute of Menlo Park, Calif. But the prediction of automobile ownership by spending units in 1969 was, as the institute itself admitted, little more than a "first approximation." The institute assumed that if 70 per cent of the spending units with an income of $5,000 each owned one automobile in 1958, 70 per cent of the spending units with similar purchasing power in 1969 (and there would be more then) also would own one automobile. Using this technique, the institute estimated that the total ownership of automobiles for all income brackets would climb from 45,540,000 in 1958 to 56,439,000 in 1969.

The institute recognized the obvious flaw in its simple projection: The failure to take a multitude of variables into account. It added hopefully, however, that the findings "could be modified in light of expectation concerning other factors that might be thought to influence automobile ownership, including any expected change in the impact of income." But just what these "other factors" are supposed to be, the institute failed to specify.

Other researchers have suggested that the inclusion of an historical approach in the Stanford technique might prove more helpful in estimating a future market. If, for example, 67 per cent of the spending units with a $5,000 income owned one automobile in 1956 and 69 per cent owned one automobile in 1957, the 70 per cent figure for 1958 would be revealed not as a static ratio, but as one point in a climbing curve. A projection of the curve could show that 75 per cent of the units with a similar purchasing power would own an automobile by 1970, resulting in a still higher market penetration.

But even this refinement, combining the simple mathematical projection with an historical analysis, fails to take into account possible changes in values, motives and ways of life which could severely affect any long-range marketing outlook.

To predict future consumer reaction to a specific product, it is obviously not enough simply to ask: What will the economy be like in ten years? The vital question is: What will the people be like in ten years?

THE CULTURE: A CLUE

In some other culture at some other time, marketing specialists, perhaps, might have found it easier to penetrate and comprehend the enigma of consumers.

In an ancient patriarchal society, for example, the dominant male adult set the thinking and mores of his family. By noting change, if any, in the patriarch's reactions, a researcher could reasonably predict how the entire culture would act for the next several years. Only a breakdown in the basic social culture could throw the prediction off, but this, too, could be guarded against by measuring the "obedience" level at lower rungs of the family hierarchy.

Similar predictions, with similar checks, also could have been made in a theocratic society, where the priest was law; in an aristocratic culture, where the royal court set the pace; in a matriarchal society, where the men may have decided the important issues of church and state, but the women ruled the house and every man in it.

What about now? Do we have some form of pace-setter today?

Dr. Paul Lazarsfeld of Columbia University suggests that some 20 per cent of the community's population may be classed as opinion leaders. Their influence, however, is not uniform in all areas of public and private life. Some women influence fashions while others set the pace for a parents' organization. Some men decide the fate of a political candidate while others establish a teen-age fad.

These people, it can be theorized, are thinking and acting now in some areas the way the general public will think and act in later years. Their attitudes, by dint of their influence, will become majority attitudes. To carry the theory one step further to a marketing application: Their reaction to specific products now may well determine the reaction of the mass consumer market at some later date.

These opinion leaders, if they exist, would seem to be our searched-for index of future consumer reaction. They are the sources available today for predicting with reasonable accuracy what will happen tomorrow.

But how can we locate these individuals? How can they be identified with those areas of behavior in which they do exert an influence? How can their pace-setting attitudes be collected and used?

By definition, if we have opinion leaders in our contemporary American society, they must collectively embody the characteristics of the society they mold. What characterizes the society must characterize the minority that leads.

What is the unifying thread of modern American culture? What is our one constant?

Historians, sociologists and philosophers, those who have long pondered the question, have been able to conclude only that the one *constant* of our society must be *change*.

If that is true, then those who most embody the concept of change are the ones who must be our opinion leaders, and the marketing man's guides to the future actions of society as a whole.

If we can accept this concept of change, our problem is reduced to a matter of technique, a problem of developing the methodology for locating these individuals and extracting from them whatever information can be of help.

One such technique is proposed by Opinion Research Corp. of Princeton, N. J.

AN APPROACH

Opinion Research Corp. accepts the concept of change as "perhaps the common denominator" of American culture.

"America's mobility," ORC holds, "is set forth in its significant dimensions—geographically across land and sea, in its occupational structure, in its economic life, in the range and variety of human associations, in its mercurial politics, its educational system, its changing family relations and ethnic composition, its intellectual and cultural life."

ORC accepts a leadership concept in what it calls "The Tastemaker Theory." The hypothesis: "The central thread of our modern society is mobility. The leadership elite is that group of people who possess this quality in greater degree than do other people." That group is made up of what Opinion Research calls "The High Mobiles." In relation to the rest of our society:

They travel more and change residence more often.

They show more movement through the occupational structure.

They are more likely to change their economic status.

They associate with a wider variety of people, of different types.

They move through more educational levels and institutions.

They move through more intellectual influences.

They are more selective and variable in their politics.

In these various dimensions, they have moved a greater distance from their family of birth.

Those are the distinguishing elements of both our society and the High Mobiles. But, ORC stresses, "the High Mobiles are not to be identified by any one or two main characteristics. It is the *pattern* of their mobility that serves to distinguish them."

Once identified, how can they be used? ORC continues its theory: "The distinctive character of a society consists in the pattern of such choices made by the individuals who compose it. And the unfolding pattern of the marketplace is the result of an ever-changing kaleidoscope of choices." At the first stage of any choice, ORC holds, are the values brought to the marketplace. These values lead to styles and tastes. The third stage is the ultimate for marketing: product choice.

By identifying the High Mobiles, ORC asserts, it is possible to determine the changing pattern of their values. It is further possible to relate these value patterns to the ways in which they are expressed in styles, tastes and, ultimately, product preference.

"If the High Mobiles perform as posited by the theory, they should give us advance notice of change in time to prepare for it. . . . If the theory is sound, we should expect that the prevailing tendency would be for the High Mobiles to dominate the early market for new products. That is, they should represent a disproportionate part of the market for goods and services that are moving toward mass acceptance. They should operate to:

"Form the early market for new products and services before acceptance has become widespread, or before prices have been lowered to broaden demand;

"Act as idea disseminators on what to buy; through their example, their interests and their influence on the rest of society."

ORC, in an extensive pilot study in well-to-do suburban Ridgewood, N.J., found what it considered substantial evidence to indicate that both the theory and techniques met a predictive need. The organization now is planning to widen its research to a national study.

ORC never claims, it must be pointed out, that the pilot study has proved that the Tastemaker Theory is right. Black and white judgment can never be applied to any scientific theory. And scientific must be the approach of marketing in predicting the actions of consumers a decade ahead.

THE SCIENTIFIC APPROACH

A scientific theory is not supposed to be a definitive statement of cause and effect and the relationships in between. In even the purest of sciences, no physicist or chemist can state a theorem with finality. He can say, at best, that such an effect probably will result under such and such controlled conditions.

A theory never is right or wrong. It is only useful. And we do not necessarily have to understand all the ramifications of a theory to use it effectively. We do not have to understand and explain all the whys of consumer action, for example, if only a partial explanation will give us sufficient clues for predicting that action. A scientific theory is, in the long approach, only a method to gain insight.

As ORC explains it: "A scientific theory is a particular set of spectacles we put on to see what we can see. The spectacles may be simple or they may be complicated, microscopic or telescopic, wide angle or narrow angle, but a scientific theory remains a particular way of looking at things."

How can we judge the usefulness of a theory, any scientific theory?

Primarily, the theory should be able to generate prediction that can be verified by tests. The theory also should permit us to see new relationships between facts, and help us learn some new facts. It should generate further research, possibly back into the basic assumptions used to formulate the theory in the first place.

The theory, in the long run, should enable the researcher to fit together into a larger, consistent and workable framework that miscellaneous knowledge already possessed. But, most importantly, as ORC notes, the theory should limit "the amount and kind of information that we must try to deal with" lest we be "overwhelmed by the sheer volume of collected data."

The theories of market research must be as productive as the theories in any pure science. Opinion Research believes its Tastemaker Theory meets the test of usefulness. The theory permits some method of predicting what the market will be like in the years ahead.

Only time, however, can tell whether the ORC predictions are accurate to the point where they really can be of use to marketing men. But there is no need to wait for the test of time to begin work on other theories of marketing which might prove more useful, more productive and more accurate.

This is the challenge that marketing research must answer today on the threshold of what many hopefully believe will be a decade of affluence. We must be able to predict with accuracy.

To predict, we must create a theoretical framework, a marketing theory, from which a forecast technology can be evolved.

As many serious-thinking marketing men realize, if we fail to meet this challenge, if we fail to provide the tools for prediction, the prosperous decade ahead might, through misdirection and misconception, prove to be not so prosperous after all.

▶▶▶▶▶▶▶▶▶▶▶ THE NEW PRODUCT BOOM

Sales Management

TRADE ACCEPTANCE

One of the biggest hurdles for the new product to overcome these days is trade resistance. With supermarket and industrial distributor shelves fairly bulging with goods, the middleman can pick and choose as he pleases.

Ten years ago the average supermarket carried 3,000 items; today it carries 6,000. And out of the 40 new products offered each week, the buying committee picks up 15, and drops 5 previously stocked, for a net addition of 10.

The industrial distributor is just as overcrowded, although in a slightly different way. Industrial outlets usually stock the lines of only a few manufacturers. Rather than carrying a wide number of competitive products, they tend to stock a wide number of models from the same manufacturer.

Nevertheless, the shelves of the average distributor of residential heating and cooling controls—to choose a random example—sag under the weight of as many as 18,000 different models.

MIDDLEMEN HOLD REINS

This kind of selection, coupled with the physical limitations of the respective outlets, means that the middleman will get even choosier—indeed he is forced to become so. Consequently, manufacturers will have to dream up more generous promotion deals in the future, and these will help force the cost of new product introduction up still further.

Many industrial distributors have turned to electronic data processing techniques to help weed out their less profitable lines, and supermarkets and discount houses are making noises that suggest they might follow suit. Generous deal or not, there is nothing so hard to convince as an electronic brain.

An area that has long gone begging for improvement is trade advertising. Since it costs less—and consequently provides the agency with smaller commissions—it is often treated as second in importance to consumer advertising. Some firms, however, have learned to adapt the selling points of their consumer ads to trade promotion. Occa-

Reprinted with permission from Sales Management, *August 3, 1962, p. 45 ff.*

sionally a change in copy is all that is needed to make an ad serve in both consumer and trade fields.

One solution to trade resistance is to build up demand at the grass roots level. Industrials might use a technique similar to the one used by Cargill—hitting all their customers in one big promotion while they attend a convention.

Consumer products could take a page from the Lestoil book. When Jake Barowsky, the company's former president, came to New York after a successful New England campaign, he found supermarket doors closed to him. Trade acceptance was obviously going to be slow in coming, and competition would probably know before the retailers did that it was profitable to hop on the Lestoil bandwagon. Me-too products could hit him before he was established. Undaunted, Barowsky went ahead with his famous spot TV promotion.

Consumers were quick to react, but when they trotted down to the stores with pocketbooks open—lo, no Lestoil! It didn't take many consumer requests to supermarket personnel before the buying committees went looking for Barowsky.

He unwittingly gave them a little extra cause for concern by hiring an answering service instead of renting an office. The buyers were frantic trying to locate him. And the product was advertised for fully six weeks before it appeared on the shelves.

It was an expensive side road, but it paid off. When the supers bought, they bought well, and the Lestoil success story is well known. Incidentally, Barowsky's faith in spot TV is well illustrated by his plunking down $18,132,030 (by objective measurements) for this medium in 1959.

But however successful the Lestoil and Cargill . . . introductions were, they obviously will not work for every product. It is the new, the revolutionary, the untried idea, the dramatic way of supplying an undiscovered need that benefits most from such swashbuckling tactics.

The innovations on old products have to stick to the tried and safe methods, but they will have to think in a similar vein about one important factor in both of the above campaigns—the time factor. The biggest benefit these campaigns provided their respective products was time. The products were apparently good in that they supplied a real need, and they would have sold eventually in any case. But they got off to a roaring start and were able to pile up plenty of profits before they felt the hot breath of competition on their necks.

ME-TOO EROSION

Me-too products and private labels follow hard on the heels of any success, and while the effects of their efforts are not usually felt until well into the life cycle, they can do a lot to shorten it. The only real advantage a new product has over its competition is lead time. As soon as it is apparent that the product is filling a need, competitors will try to fill that need more cheaply, with gimmicks, novel packages, or simply a better product.

Sometimes they are inordinately fast in picking up a hot lead. The Lever

Bros.–General Foods buttered pancake syrup battle makes a classic case. Lever was supposed to be first with its Mrs. Butterworth, but you couldn't tell that from the marketplace. GF dressed up an old buttered syrup from its institutional line so quickly that it actually beat Lever into some markets.

The me-too's are not necessarily products of inferior quality either. As Campbell Soup's President Murphy points out, "When the 'me-too' product is a higher-quality, higher-value product, the scorn [of marketers] turns to admiration with a measure of wonder as to why the originator did not keep his lead."

LESTOIL'S LOST LEAD

Lestoil lost out to such products, which beat the liquid detergent innovator simply because they took the offensive odor out of it. The subsequent improvements in Lestoil keep it in the running, but with nothing like the terrific lead it had before.

Private labels have come of age in the last few years. In the '30's and even later, they were considered "cheap imitations" and outlaw products. But through the efforts of mass retailers, they had become recognized as quality brands by the end of the '50's.

The Nielsen 10-year study . . . shows that between 1951 and 1961 the annual share of market accounted for by nationally advertised brands in 38 food store commodity groups ran between 74% and 76%. These figures would indicate that the national advertisers are more or less holding their own, but they represent the broad perspective.

There are any number of single cases that show the national product taking a terrific beating, and show what can happen when a local product or a private label really gets the formula, or when the national product doesn't stay well ahead in market strategy.

The Milwaukee beating given Pepsi-Cola (18.5% share of market) and Coca-Cola (16.2%) by the local soft drink, Graf's (26.4%), is a good example. Just let the national advertisers relax a little and this could get more prevalent.

Pressures of follow-after competition have given rise to two major changes in corporate thinking. For one thing, marketers are now expecting their products to become obsolete—not deliberately planning to make them outmoded in order to bring out new annual models, but realistically expecting that competition will drastically reduce the life cycle and planning well in advance to offset this reduction from a profit point of view.

Perhaps Charles Mortimer of General Foods expressed it best when he said, "The very moment you put a new product on the supermarket shelf it is out of date—and you should already be thinking about developing the next one."

Such a policy would have saved Lestoil much lost ground. A simple consumer complaint like the offensive odor of the product should have been uncovered in the introductory stage. The competition uncovered it. The reason Lestoil didn't is simply that it didn't expect obsolescence—it was product, rather than market, oriented.

The importance of the time factor

in the early stages of new product life has also made marketers conscious of the need to cover as much ground as possible. The imminent entry of competition prompts them to get as many customers as possible using the product in as short a time as possible. Consequently, sampling has come in for wider use in the consumer goods field— another factor, incidentally, which drives the cost of introduction continually upwards. . . .

. . . As Peter Hilton [president of Kastor, Hilton, Chesley, Clifford and Atherton] sees it:

. . . New products themselves are not the problem in the years ahead. Most major manufacturers I know have a backlog of new products, so the bottleneck is not in the laboratory or in the research and development department—the bottleneck is in the marketing area.

I am as impressed as you are when they [manufacturers] recount the percentage of their earnings that are devoted to new product development. . . . How much more constructive it would be if these same men allocated a percentage of corporate revenue, no matter how modest, to the development of new marketing techniques to break the log jam of new product introduction.

In spite of Hilton's apparent deep conviction that the marketing structure is not up to the task of providing these new products, it would be a little less than naïve to say that no one is doing anything about it.

First, the old criterion for evaluation of a new product is gone. In the former production-oriented economy, companies brought out new products when they corresponded to the conveniences of the production line. Later a product was deemed marketable if it fit the distribution patterns of a company's present products.

Now even this criterion has gone by the board. The only consideration is whether the company can make a profit on the new product. A new channel of distribution is merely another expense factor to be worked into the formula.

Already we have seen industrial companies slip into consumer fields and vice versa. This is a pattern that will grow in the future as marketers discover new markets for the by-products of their research and development.

Since the expense of bringing out a new product has become so high— and will undoubtedly go higher—the old methods of introduction can no longer be relied upon. The pay-out period stretches out interminably, and before profits start to roll in the competition is usually eating into the market.

Thus the time factor has become all important. This factor is driving the preparatory work for product introduction back into the earlier developmental stages. Sales and advertising strategy planning is being undertaken earlier, developed along with the product.

Marketers are constantly looking for ways to get the product off the ground sooner. Sampling, couponing and other booster devices are being used more frequently, and their popularity will continue to grow.

RESUSCITATING THE PRODUCT

Marketers are beginning to plan for the demise of their own products. They are either building defensive weapons into the product in the form of prestige components, laying plans for launching a promotional counter attack when competition hits a certain level, or lining up product No. 2 to lay the competition flat.

Instead of concentrating on revolutionary changes in big markets, marketers increasingly are directing their research people toward products that will satisfy the fractional markets. Here they will have little or no competition for a longer period of time. In order to attract competition one has to be in a lucrative market. The fringe areas that get only one or two producers provide companies with breathing space and a relatively stable income.

This characteristic of big company research is reflected by the fact that so many of the really revolutionary products brought out in the recent past were introduced by small companies or companies entering a market for the first time. . . .

To say that marketers are not doing anything about the new dilemmas is selling them short. It has been impossible for them to ignore the host of problems the new product boom has brought, and their activities are breaking down the old marketing patterns.

This is a time of transition. New rules are being drafted; new techniques are being designed; new ways of doing the old things are being found. And all because the new product boom has made marketers hop and hop and hop.

►►►►►►►►►►► ANALYZING COMPETITIVE FACTORS IN NEW-PRODUCT DEVELOPMENT

I. INDUSTRIAL GOODS

GORDON H. WEHRLY*

Competitive success depends to a great extent upon the fundamental company approach to new-product development and product modification. An effective new-product program generally involves the following basic steps:

Determine over-all company objectives and goals.

Integrate all product research and marketing activity into management plans.

Organize a system to facilitate getting ideas for products.

Obtain, evaluate, and select useful ideas and information.

Design, build, and test the product.

Produce and market the product.

Evaluate the product continuously.

Reprinted with permission from Establishing a New-Product Program, *AMA Management Report Number 8, American Management Association, 1958, pp. 109–124.*

* *Business Research Manager, International Division, Vickers Incorporated (A Division of Sperry Rand Corporation).*

There are still a few rugged individualists who say that they don't care what competitors are doing; that if you are on the ball you will lead and others will follow; and that you should let *them* worry about what *you* are doing or planning to do. Needless to say, these persons are generally not marketing people. Business has become huge, complex, and perhaps overcommunicated. Management decisions must now be based on the work of groups of specialists, and among these are the people whose primary job it is to keep management aware of anything that can affect the growth and profit of the company.

The saying goes, "Never underestimate the power of a woman." It can be equally well said, "Never underestimate the power of a competitor." Knowledge of competitors' plans and activities, with regard to both products and markets, can often result in decisions that influence future plans. Following is a statement made in a report published by the Bureau of Labor Statistics for the National Science Foundation a few years ago.

Competition apparently provides the underlying stimulus for company financial research and development. Virtually all company officials interviewed reported that the competition their companies face is a major factor in determining the scale of their research and development programs.

This report also notes that 75 per cent of the companies were thinking in terms of, and adjusting the size of their research programs and budgets to, long-range plans for company stability and growth. This planning generally falls into one of two areas: (1) new-product development and (2) diversification of the product line. It is therefore obvious that competition influences all facets of a business and so becomes one of the basic considerations in any management decision.

Industrial-goods firms have a much more difficult job of evaluating competition accurately than do consumer organizations. For one thing, they generally deal with highly technical products that require factual data rather than opinions. In addition, they work with skilled engineers and professional buyers who base their decisions on a very close scrutiny of how much money the use of a product will *make* them, and how much money it will *save* them. Market information of all types thus tends to be harder to obtain and more difficult to interpret and apply.

FACTORS OF COMPETITION

Since competition must be considered in almost any course of action, it is difficult to classify. There are several major competitive factors, however, that usually should be emphasized: (1) definition of competition, (2) competitors, (3) products, (4) information sources, (5) prices and discounts, (6) industries and applications, and (7) distribution methods.

DEFINITION OF COMPETITION

What is competition? The definition varies somewhat according to the company, but basically it includes the following elements:

Present manufacturers of products comparable to the products you are making.

Potential manufacturers of these products.

Competitors' methods or techniques.

The known competitors probably account for most of a company's effort. The evaluation of potential competitors becomes increasingly difficult, particularly in a period of diversification and acquisition, when a company pegged as a catsup manufacturer can very well be making sputniks next month. It is necessary to keep abreast of the market activity of people whose products are in the same general areas of application, but who use an essentially different method or engineering principle. For example, our business is the manufacture of oil hydraulic equipment. Oil hydraulic equipment is one of the most flexible and successful means of transmitting power, but there are other types of equipment that can be used, such as electrical or pneumatic.

COMPETITORS

Who are the competitors, how many are there, and what is their relative strength and position in the industry? Where possible, the historical background of each company—particularly as to organization, financial strength, reputation in the industry, and similar factors that help determine why they have been successful—should be investigated. Also important is an estimate of competitors' share in the industry business, any statistical data on their sales earnings and profit history, and an evaluation of their strong and weak points.

It is sometimes difficult to estimate the share of the market that each major company in the field accounts for. In some instances, Government figures or association statistics can be used as a guide to make a reasonable estimate. Occasionally, this market share can be determined by a review of statistical and financial corporation reports; this approach, however, can become complicated in the instance of large companies whose financial statements are consolidated for all of their member companies.

Consumer goods organizations can measure fairly accurately the strength of any company in any given market by means of a customer or dealer brand survey. This approach can be supplemented to a certain degree by a physical inventory of equipment in the plants of industrial-goods manufacturers, although it is an expensive and oftentimes inconclusive method of estimating a competitor's strength. Even a carefully chosen survey sample of manufacturers may not give an accurate result.

Another approach that has been used with some degree of success is to have the field sales organization estimate the percentages of the business that a company and its competitors are getting in a particular area. This approach, of course, is based principally upon knowledge of the existing and potential business in a particular territory and frequent contact with key customers or prospects in order to find out or approximate which brands, and how much of them, the customers are buying or using. This method is admittedly subject to error, since it is based mainly on a district manager's or salesman's opinion of the competitive situation in his particular area. The procedure is simply for the salesman to list the major competitors in each geographical area and to estimate the percentage of business that they are doing in this area for comparison with his own company's percentage. For example, if a firm's sales in a particular area are $2 million and its field man's estimate is that it is doing about one-third of the business, the total business in the area would be $6 million. The percentage of the $4 million going to competitors can then be estimated according to competitive makes. This procedure, by the way, calls for an experienced (and honest) field man.

PRODUCTS

Competitive products on the market must be studied thoroughly, both quantitatively and qualitatively. For example, the following questions should be asked:

What are the current competitive products on the market?

Who is making them?

What advantages or disadvantages do they have as compared with your own product?

How good are these competitive products?

Can they be improved?

How complete is your competitor's line as compared with your line?

What is the market strength of indirect competitors?

Is the market for a new product so good that other manufacturers are likely to produce it themselves?

Are there any other competitors working on a similar product? If so, how soon are they likely to have a successful development on the market?

Once your new product is on the market, how long will it take competitors to copy it?

Are there any legal restrictions or disadvantages to the new product?

What share of the market is immediately available, and what can be expected in the future?

In adding a new or modified product to the existing product line, there are really only three approaches: (1) to invent a completely different product for an untried and unproven market, (2) to adapt a product to a market that already exists, or (3) to copy an existing competitive product. The choice made governs the thoroughness and amount of activity necessary in checking competitors. Of course, everyone would like to come on the market with a completely *different* new product. Whether or not this can be done depends to a large extent upon the nature of the particular product and upon the possible limitations of its design and manufacture.

A very useful basic method of evaluating competitive models on the market is a comparison chart which simply lists all competitive makes and models. For example, across the top of the sheet are listed the data to be compared, and down the left side the competitors. These comparison charts can be based on one or a combination of factors, such as specifications, performance characteristics, prices, primary applications, and advantages and disadvantages of each feature. The sources used to obtain these data might include competitive catalogues and literature, advertising and publicity releases, trade shows, technical journals and special association reports (for example, the new-product sections of certain trade magazines), and the firm's own field force's contact with customers.

The comparison sheet mentioned above lists data on the existing products of all firms in the market. It is fundamental, of course, to know what is already in use before seriously considering a new product. A thorough analysis of what is available on the market often points up possibilities for different sizes, features, operating characteristics, performance ranges, and so forth when related to current knowledge of customer problems and needs.

INFORMATION SOURCES

For many manufacturers, the field sales organization is a primary source of information on competitive products and activity. District managers and sales engineers are frequently consulted on new-product possibilities. Some of this information can be based on their personal opinion and experience; some of it involves direct contact with customers and prospects. In the course of getting a customer's opinion on a proposed new product, it is inevitable that the latter will compare it right down the line with any competitive makes on the market.

In addition to the specific and rather detailed field surveys noted above, we have found it advisable to check with major users of a particular product or model before making any radical design changes that might not be acceptable to the customer. Records tell who the major customers for a particular model in question are and in what quantities they use the product. If the

proposed change is acceptable to the customer, it is made on the product. The extent of the inquiries made depends largely upon the importance of the design change. A very detailed personal visit with the major customers may be necessary to get the answers, or letters or postcards may be used in the case of minor engineering changes.

After all available product information has been obtained and evaluated—not only on the proposed product but on those of all significant competitors—sketches are made up and sent to the manufacturing department for a cost estimate. These cost estimates are usually double the figure that the sales department thinks it can sell the product for. When and if the sales and production people agree on a cost figure based on annual production quantities, the manufacturing department must find out how much of the anticipated new design could be handled with existing tooling and what the expense would be for new tooling.

PRICES AND DISCOUNTS

Price is always a critical factor, although perhaps not so much for industrial-goods manufacturers as for consumer goods firms. Of course, the higher the price of the article or product, the less critical is the exact price. For many industrial-goods manufacturers, price is often secondary in importance to quality, durability, customer service facilities, sales engineering assistance, and so forth. These factors are all considered by most purchasing agents in addition to the product price. For this reason, it is often the policy of industrial-goods manufacturers to base their prices on a markup over cost which will allow them a satisfactory margin of profit.

Nevertheless, it is important to keep close watch on competitors' prices; if a company's price should happen to be out of line on a particular model, competitors will soon recognize this and may come on the market with the same or a similar product at a reduced price. As previously mentioned, purchasing agents are professional buyers, and on engineered products they demand—and get—high value.

There are no routine methods for obtaining price information on competitors except, of course, where they make their prices available in printed lists. Marketing people have occasionally been known to get hold of competitors' price lists, but there are certain G-2 aspects of this procedure that are occasionally distasteful.

INDUSTRIES AND APPLICATIONS

Products are often designed for or related to specific industries and applications. This is particularly true in our case: We serve many customers in the aircraft, machinery, marine, and mobile-equipment fields. Many of our pumps, valves, motors, cylinders, and so forth are specially designed for the customer's equipment. It is obvious that before getting into an extensive and time-consuming design program for an anticipated new model, a thorough check should be made of all possible competitive models and all other companies which might be selected as the supplier. If a certain prospect is now using a competitive product, a thorough evaluation of the product in terms of the customer's need should be made. This investigation may include all factors of design, performance, cost, availability, and service, and is usually done cooperatively by the field sales engineer and home office personnel. We, like most manufacturers, are constantly searching for new industries and new applications, and we use all sources of information to accomplish this end.

DISTRIBUTION METHODS

Ours is basically a direct-to-the-customer selling organization. Consequently, we have in many cases a close working relationship with our customers through our sales engineers located in the various branches throughout the country. Other manufacturers use different forms of distribution, such as industrial and specialized distributors or manufacturers' representatives.

We try to keep a fairly close watch on the sales and distribution techniques used by our major competitors, since these can often result in sales or service advantages of great value to a customer. For example, an adequate parts and units warehouse stock in the field means quick availability and replacement in the event of emergency breakdowns. The speed and quality of product service in the field to the customer is a prime consideration for many manufacturers who cannot tolerate any down time. We are constantly broadening and improving our field facilities and, of course, are always interested in knowing about any competitor's activity that has proved successful.

The basic procedure, then, begins with the idea, which may come from many possible sources. The idea is subsequently evaluated in terms of the market and the company's plans; engineering research and design lead to the building of a pilot model; laboratory or field tests are carried out on the pilot models; and finally production quantities are released for sale to customers. One aspect of this procedure is the purchase and laboratory testing of competitive models. This is a routine procedure for most companies. Although expensive, it is the only way to evaluate a competitive product properly from the standpoints of design and performance. We have extensive laboratory test facilities which are, of course, used primarily for our own products. We also constantly evaluate competitive designs which we feel might cut into our sales for a particular industry or application. Field testing for our products does not involve a proving ground or a racetrack; it is always carried out on the customer's machinery or equipment operating under the actual usage conditions for which the application is designed.

A year is not an unusual length of time for these tests, and often the evaluation and correction of deficiencies takes another year after the test model has been returned to us by the customer. Although competitive models are not field-tested by us, field test conditions are simulated as closely as possible in our laboratory.

APPROACHES OF OTHER COMPANIES

Marketing men are well aware of the need for systematic research procedures in analyzing competition. At the same time, however, the majority of these men have no formalized approach. For the most part, they get as much information on the subject as they can through associations, publications, meetings, and reported case histories outlining the experience of comparable companies in the field.

On the basis of both published remarks and responses to personal inquiries on the subject, there is considerable reason to believe that the majority of industrial-goods firms have no routine procedure or system of checklists to use when studying the competitive aspects of new-product development. Whether this is good or bad I do not know. It would seem that complete coverage of all possible information sources as well as market research techniques would result in more accurate programing; there is admittedly a high mortality rate in new-product introduction. Actually, failures are probably more numerous than quoted figures indicate, if all those products that never reach the production stage are included. The systematic use of checklists might improve this batting average.

INTRA-COMPANY ASPECTS

The research climate in a company has much to do with the success or failure of its competitive studies. All department heads must recognize the importance of this activity and work cooperatively with the marketing people through all phases of the program. If they do not, the program may be slowed down, and it may be impossible to achieve the integrated and coordinated effort necessary to do the job.

Before embarking on a new-product

program, there must be some understanding of company policy with regard to competitive products. First, a complete study of the existing product line is necessary, the primary objective being standardization and simplification of the present line. This study should streamline procedures, reduce expense, clear management's thinking, and make time available for the study of completely new products (as opposed to minor product modifications and engineering changes).

Another factor which occasionally has some bearing on whether or not a new product is put on the market is a firm's relationship to its most significant customers. The advantages of bringing out a new product can sometimes be counteracted by the ill will of major customers whose areas of the market are being invaded.

Another limitation is that basic design principles may be completely different from those of products built and sold in the past. Once a particular design principle or method has been put into effect and used successfully for many years, it can be a blow to the prestige and morale of the sales department to release a product of different design simply because a competitor has made a success of it.

The timing involved in introducing a new product is a key factor. On some occasions, a firm may have the product and a ready market, but it may not have vision enough to take advantage of the situation. The item may be shelved somewhere among engineering records, never reach the pilot model stage, and not be brought out of mothballs until the market demand has been satisfied by a competitor. This process

can also work in reverse. In its eagerness to scoop competition, a firm's R&D group may come up with a product, have the vision to foresee its use, but find out that the market is not immediately available.

Any firm can learn much from its competitors. Yet, as previously noted, this is just one phase of over-all marketing activity. Basically, our company planning is broken down first into annual programs, and then into projects within each of these programs. These breakdowns are written and defined. They are also subject to periodic review by top management for integration into over-all company plans. The status of each product is reviewed in terms of expense allocation, technical or engineering progress, and the current competitive or market situation. At reviewal times, a project may be accelerated or perhaps given a lower priority in the budget; if competitive or other factors indicate the need for speed, we step up the activity.

Wherever possible, the best approach is to develop a unique product which is new to the market and which will satisfy either a current or a future market demand. This does not, however, bar the possibility of further development of an item already on the market, if we believe that we can build a better product at less cost and sell it at a price equal to or less than our competitors' prices. Often, the nature of the product line may impose certain design limitations on a product; functionally, for instance, a valve is a valve and there is just so much you can do with it. In certain cases, therefore, emphasis is necessarily on product modification and improvement.

One essential feature to consider in reviewing competitive models is their simplicity of design. Simplicity means lower cost and fewer manufacturing and service problems. Patent review can establish a firm's position on possible usage of a good competitive design feature, but quality should never be sacrificed for simplicity. Strict quality control measures are especially vital for products in which a system failure could cause loss of life.

One final aspect of marketing which, in my opinion, does not receive enough emphasis is the human element. Research of products, markets, and selling methods is routine, but many firms do not know much about their competitors' management. The quality of these people is important, for, after all, ideas and products originate with people. The implications of this aspect of marketing should be discussed with the personnel manager. Pirating of competitors' personnel is frowned upon, yet it is a common approach, particularly in certain industries such as the automotive industry in Detroit.

The policy and direction of any organization is reflected by the ambitions of the man at the top. Review of the printed articles or the speeches of important executive personnel can often shed light on this matter. A VIP file can be very useful. Also, it is good to know who in the company is on a first-name basis with key executives in other companies—whether customers or competitors.

A high new-product failure rate is costly to any company. Competitive evaluation is only one of the many cost-saving aspects of new-product development, but it is an important one. Broad areas of management interest lie in product acquisition or internal product development; both require thorough study of all competitive influences. Too few companies are doing this, and those who do not are paying the long price. Recent international events have forcibly brought home to us the importance of knowing our competition. It is costly not to, and we can no longer afford the waste of money, time, and manpower.

II. CONSUMER GOODS

JOHN T. CAHOON *

Even when it has been determined who the potential purchasers of a new product are, what the trends of the industry in question have been in the past, how the product will be bought and used, where the product will be sold, and how potential users may be contacted to evaluate customer acceptance of the product's size, shape, color, odor, packaging, and other vital features, the process of marketing research is not yet complete. It is still

* *Manager, Marketing Research Department, The Firestone Tire & Rubber Company.*

necessary, just as in war, to size up the "enemy." This paper will deal with the various ways of analyzing competition in the marketplace.

Basically, there are four important areas of competition to investigate:

1. The number of competitors, and the importance of each, in the field the new product will enter.
2. The quality of the new product as compared with the quality of competing products.
3. The portion of the market which can be taken away from competitors.
4. The effect competition has on the company's policy for the new product.

COUNTING COMPETITORS

The first step in the investigation of competition is to determine the number of competitors in the field. Knowing how many "fronts" it will be necessary to fight on is important in marketing plans. If the new product is closely related to the firm's existing line, and if the potential customers are similar to the present customers, the sales force can get a good indication of who the competitors will be.

There are, of course, many other ways to get this information. For example, Thomas' Register lists manufacturers by product line, and Moody's Industrials shows the products of various companies. These data should, of course, be supplemented. There are many directories which break down whole industries into product groups, then name the producers within each group. At Firestone, for example, we use the *Rubber Red Book* and *Modern*

Plastics Annual. Publishers of trade journals or secretaries of trade associations can be consulted for the names of firms in the field; both of these are excellent sources for information of this type. The Department of Commerce will in some cases furnish the names of producers of new items.

Actually, most competitors become known in the course of other work that is necessary to introduce the new product. For example, a consumer survey made to find out what the customer wants can at the same time determine what brands he now buys and how much of each brand he buys.

SIZING UP COMPETITORS

Several of the sources used to find out who the competitors are may also be used to determine the relative importance of each. In addition to these, there are several valuable sources of free information on the size of competition. Magazines sometimes conduct surveys among subscribers as a service to advertisers. The information gathered is often made available to all competitors, but it is still helpful. Often, the supplier of a basic material will undertake studies that are of value to others. Du Pont's service station studies, which include brand information, are prime examples.

The Consolidated Consumer Analysis, a summary of brand preference surveys made by more than 20 newspapers throughout the United States, is an important source of information on many products. A number of these surveys made over a period of years show how various competitors have fared in respect to one another. This service was helpful to Firestone when a decision was being made on a brand of appliances to be added to our line of home and auto supplies. Top Ten Brands is another brand-preference compilation of newspaper studies. The *Look* (formerly Crowell-Collier) automotive and tire surveys have been extremely helpful to car and tire manufacturers in measuring competition.

Much can be learned at a price. Nielsen's Food and Drug Index, Market Research Corporation's Consumer Panel Reports, and Audits & Surveys' National Total Market Audit are all fine ways to keep tabs on competitors in the lines they cover.

Other light can be shed on this sometimes dark picture through the use of general indicators of company size— that is, factory size, number of employees, total assets, total sales volume, total profit, and so forth. If the company produces only one product, this information will be of prime value; even if it produces many products, the data will tell whether or not it is an important adversary. General information of this kind can be obtained from local chambers of commerce, state labor departments, annual reports, and financial source books.

Another important indicator of the extent of competition is the amount of money spent for advertising. *Advertising Age* annually lists 100 leading advertisers, and the Publishers' Information Bureau publishes national advertising investments by product and manufacturer and by medium twice a year. The annual advertising issue of *Printers' Ink* gives valuable data on advertising expenditures.

To obtain this information, then, a firm will find it necessary to rely on one or more of the following sources:

Its own sales force.
Financial source books.
Industry directories.
Magazines (trade and consumer).
The U.S. Department of Commerce.
Trade associations.
Its own consumer surveys.
Newspaper and magazine preference surveys.
Continuing audits.
Local chambers of commerce.
State labor departments.
Advertising-expenditure source books.

EVALUATING COMPETITORS' PRODUCTS

Having discovered the identity of its potential competitors, a firm must find out many things about their products—in particular, whether its own product will meet or beat this competition. Work on these problems should begin in the company's development department. The scientists and technicians there can analyze the competing product, determine how it is put together and what it is made of, and give an opinion as to how well it answers the need for which it was made. The firm can also go to an independent testing laboratory, such as Underwriters' Laboratory, to find out how the competition stacks up. In the rubber industry, Smithers' Reports give the exact specifications of competing tires.

Two organizations have been set up to test products for consumer members: Consumers' Union and Consumers' Research. Most products are tested by one or both of these groups and reported upon in their publications (available in libraries). If the company has not already done so, it is almost invariably necessary to make a consumer survey to get information about competing products. Some of the questions which demand accurate answers are as follows: In what ways do these products meet the desires of the new product's potential users? What particular features do the consumers like and what features don't they like? What additional features would customers like to have? How much more would the customer be willing to pay in order to obtain such features? Is there a part that has been prone to failure, leads to inconvenience, or makes for difficulty in use?

DETERMINING CONSUMER ACCEPTANCE

At this point the firm can list the good and bad features of competing products and compare them with its own new product's characteristics. As yet, however, it does not know what consumers will actually think, for the product has not been tested under conditions of actual use. Laboratories cannot provide a natural environment, and home economists are often far too professional in their handling of a product to anticipate all the "bugs" that the consumer will find. Housewives, for instance, often complain that the perforated flaps on soap or sugar boxes fail to puncture easily, even with sharp knives. Deft professional home economists may know just the angle at which to jab or cut to make entry into the plastic bags and cardboard boxes, but many a housewife is helpless when confronted with such "conveniences."

An effective first step is to set up a comparison test. The product can be put into consumers' homes or the homes of the employees—who, after all, are also consumers. Firestone often "uses" employees for this purpose. The tester may be paid to write out a report on the strengths and weaknesses of the product and to suggest improvements. As an alternative, he may be provided with a checklist of questions or interviewed by trained investigators.

Consumer-testers can be selected at random, or a regular "jury" can be maintained. General Electric maintains a consumer panel of housewives for testing many of its new products. There are, of course, regular commercial services available for testing consumer products, such as National Family Opinion and Home Testing Institute. If the products are too large or too expensive to test in a great number of homes, other means can be used. Appliances can be taken in trailers to housewives (General Electric), or consumer laboratories can be operated (Corning Glass).

Not to be overlooked are the various by-products of such research, many of which are most helpful in marketing plans. Some of these by-products are as follows:

Ideas for advertising campaigns.
Special merchandising possibilities.
New uses for products.
Competitive practices.
Types of product distribution.
Price information.

Ideas for improving the availability of products.

Packaging ideas.

Development of brand loyalty.

Once it is known how the new product compares with competitors' products, the next decision is whether or not to put it on the market in its present form. If, on the one hand, it has shown up badly, the firm may want to make some changes, test them, and then go on from there—particularly if consumers have voiced the need for a new entry in the product group in question. If, on the other hand, the product appears ready for the market, there is an intermediate step that should be considered: test-marketing. An article in a recent issue of *Chemical Week* points out quite dramatically the benefits of test-marketing:

In the past few weeks, Lever Brothers has taken a low-sudsing powdered detergent off the market and replaced it with a liquid low-suds detergent. Yet the whole operation, rather than being a costly and consumer-ruffling grand maneuver, looked more like a move in a calm game of chess. Because both products—the now-discontinued dry Vim and the newer liquid Hum—have been sold only in test markets. Lever, by closely observing their performance in these carefully chosen, geographically limited fields of action, has learned enough to make its decision—a decision based on information far more sound than that provided by a simple consumer survey and obtained at far less risk than that from a full-scale national marketing attempt. Lever, like many other specialty makers, finds test-marketing the best way to learn the public's reaction to a product.

Test-marketing, then, not only shows whether the product will sell but also indicates how much of the market can be captured.

ANTICIPATING MARKET PENETRATION

Test-marketing and consumer surveys help to determine how large a portion of the total market a new product can be expected to command. These data indicate the percentages of the consumers preferring the new product and that of each competitor, as well as which competitors will be easy prey and which will be tough opponents. Consumers are seldom easily swayed from their "tried and true" purchasing habits. Initial enthusiasm for the product is to be expected; this will, of course, fall off toward the already established pattern. The company's reputation in related fields sometimes helps to make the new product successful.

An important factor to consider is whether competitors will strike back—and, if so, how soon. Will they be able to come up with an improved, or perhaps a completely new, product? Some industries are committed to specialized approaches to the market from which they cannot depart to meet new-product ideas. The Nash Rambler is an example of a new product which no company as yet is willing to challenge.

Reports on competitors' past performances can be gathered through company personnel and other contacts. Are they fast-moving or relatively sluggish? Are they the methodical, testing kind who try to make certain that every last detail is perfect before marketing a product? How active are they in development and research? What sort of capital position are they in—that is, can they go ahead with a new- or improved-product expenditure, even in view of its usual delayed return? Annual reports can be helpful in this investigation.

Competitors' distribution and pricing setups have a real bearing on how much of the market can be captured. Even gilt-edged information on competitors and data on how the new product fares in test markets will not enable a firm to estimate its share of the market until it has formulated definite distribution and pricing policies for the product. Knowledge of competitors' policies helps a firm with a new product develop its own plans. Ordinarily the system of distribution for a product will be rather rigidly established, and it will not be possible to vary greatly from it. Many times, however, the gimmick that will sell the product may be found in the distributive setup.

Customers and potential customers are often able to furnish ideas for competitive pricing setups. It may be possible to read prices in industry catalogues, retail outlet lists, or newspaper advertisements. Customary terms and discounts must be known, and customers and potential customers are the best sources. Which competitors give additional discounts, and why? Who are the price cutters? Are there quantity discounts? It is often possible to get some history of competitors' pricing moves through the sales force or possibly from dealers.

This information, coupled with ac-curate knowledge of the facts of competition, will enable a firm to estimate how much of the market it can take from its competitors.

COMPETITION AND COMPANY POLICY

Among the matters to consider in setting up a company policy for a new product are retail prices, wholesale prices, type of selling, service provisions, advertising techniques and approaches, advertising allowances, dealer and consumer financing, and freight allowances. The first task is to pinpoint how much to charge for the product. For instance, the market value of each feature can be estimated separately. Test-marketing provides an opportunity to try out different prices for the new product and to see what price will bring the optimum return. Comparison testing gives an indication of the price the consumer would be willing to pay for the new product. The discount structure is of prime importance in obtaining and retaining good dealers. In all of these areas, marketing research can be used to good advantage.

The channels through which the new product will move are an important marketing consideration. By studying competitors' methods, it is possible to learn their weaknesses and make improvements on their setups. Sometimes it is feasible to market through an entirely different channel; the decisions to sell insurance, encyclopedias, and women's hosiery in grocery stores are examples. Distribution is in a state of constant flux today—a fact which makes it all the more likely to hit upon an entirely new and more effective way of getting a product to the consumer. Perhaps a firm can give faster delivery service by means of more sensible warehouse locations, or improve supply by setting up a good system of inventory control for its customers. Better time-payment terms than competitors offer may be established. Containers may be designed in handier or more popular sizes which are easier to store and to stack. Repair service is fertile ground for improvement, and salesmen can do missionary work to simplify the customer's inventory problems. Through research, for example, Firestone helped solve an inventory problem that has plagued merchandisers of batteries for years: battery aging. The company developed and pioneered the Dri-Charge storage battery. Batteries no longer age on dealers' shelves; their "birthday" is the day they are sold to the consumer. The acid is not added until the battery is in the consumer's car, and the car owner no longer buys "aged in acid" batteries.

A thorough investigation of the advertising carried on by competitors may point out a slightly different mix which will give broader or more effective coverage. Advertising allowances or special merchandising programs can often help steal the march on competitors. The company's policies with respect to collections, returned goods, order cancellations, retail price maintenance, freight allowances, and dealer financing must also be decided upon with care. Can competitors be surpassed in these areas, or should they be "joined"?

Before company policy based on competitive factors is finalized, it is necessary to determine whether the new product would fare better from a competitive standpoint by relating it in name, packaging, and other such features to a line of products already made. If not, it should be able to stand on its own with an unrelated brand name, a separate sales force, and different channels of distribution. The cost involved in building a new brand name is, of course, important. The advertising department can be helpful on this point; it should have good ideas on the cost of building brand awareness. It must also be determined whether the new product will fit in with the currently existing distribution setup, or whether costly rebuilding and training of the sales force will be necessary. It is important in this connection to know if competitors use an exclusive sales force or are able to spread selling costs over a variety of related products.

When the research for a new product has been completed, all competitive factors must be weighed to decide on the most advantageous marketing policy. Drawing a perfect bead on all competitors is, of course, no substitute for *judgment* and *experience*. The information gathered about competitors must be put to work intelligently to win battles in today's competitive markets.

►►►►►►►►►►►► FUNCTIONAL FEATURES IN PRODUCT STRATEGY

JOHN B. STEWART*

In recent years styling and brand image have come to occupy a prominent spot in marketing managers' concern for creating and maintaining brand preference. Meanwhile, marketing strategists continue to employ functional product features as a means of achieving differentiation, just as they have over the years. Advertisers vigorously promote the features to the public, whether they be filters and flip-top boxes, razor blade dispensers that change with a "push-pull, click-click," or push-button gear shifts.

But for all their getting and using of features, does management have an understanding of the role of product features in the over-all marketing plan? Actually, in spite of their continued use, surprisingly little attention has been devoted to refining the art and strategy of using these features in the marketing effort.

This article presents some findings from a study of approximately 5,000 functional claims made by 206 companies over a period of some 26 years. Some of these features were trivial product modifications, while others were basic improvements; but they all represent attempts by businessmen to gain preference for their brand through functional product differentiation.

The study not only sheds light on the marketing use of functional features but also points up some of their advantages over such other kinds of product differentiation as styling and brand image. There is also the suggestion that the use of this and other kinds of differentiation, either collectively or individually, may raise the problem of *limiting* rather than *building* markets and the concomitant challenge to marketing managers to make the best strategic use of their preference-building elements.

RANGE OF PRODUCTS

It is not always easy to draw a clear distinction between functional product features and other differentiating devices. For the purposes of this study, however, a feature is *a physical and functional characteristic or component of the basic product that may be used to distinguish it from competing products of similar quality.* For example, the basis of a feature may be:

1. Material of construction (e.g., the glass-lined water heater).

Reprinted with permission from Harvard Business Review, *March–April 1959, pp. 65–78.*

* *Assistant Professor of Marketing, Harvard University.*

2. Method of construction (e.g., the "unitized" automobile chassis).
3. Kind of performance (e.g., the television console combined with radio).
4. Method of performance (e.g., the refrigerator working on gas rather than electricity).
5. Construction or performance of one part (e.g., power steering).
6. Arrangement of component parts (e.g., the freezer at the bottom of the refrigerator).

To get a perspective on how the manufacturers of consumer durable goods can employ functional features, this study sought to learn what kinds of features have actually been used in the past, by whom, and when. It also examined general patterns of relationship, such as:

How many features has the typical firm used, and have the manufacturers of some product types found it advantageous to use more features than other firms have?

Have increased research expenditures raised the number of new features introduced in the market each year?

And, most important, when a firm succeeds in developing a successful feature, *how long* will it be able to enjoy the benefits of its research expenditure and the risk it has sustained?

In order to answer these and similar questions about use of features, an examination was made of magazine advertisements of eight types of consumer durable goods selling for $50 or more. Studied were automobiles, 35-millimeter cameras, domestic refrigera-

tors, television sets, gasoline-powered rotary lawn mowers, vacuum cleaners, electric water heaters, and jeweled wrist watches. These range from relatively mature products (wrist watches) to young products (television sets, rotary mowers); from highly personal products (cameras) to products of low individual interest (water heaters); from a broad market (refrigerators) to a more specialized market (cameras); and from the $50 price range (some watches, cameras, rotary mowers) to several thousand dollars (automobiles).

INDIVIDUAL PATTERNS

Some interesting differences in the average number of features claimed per company among the various product types are shown in EXHIBIT I. Advertisements for wrist watches and water heaters contained, on the average, only half as many features as did those for cameras and refrigerators. What accounts for these differences? The statistics themselves cannot reveal the reasons, but by comparing the nature of the products it becomes possible to suggest some logical reasons.

NATURE OF PRODUCTS

For the products included in this study there appear to be two particularly important characteristics that influenced the profitable number of features a company could use. One is the amount of *operational effort* that is required to use the product in terms of skill, work, and frequency. For example:

The smallest number of features were utilized by manufacturers of

EXHIBIT I

AVERAGE NUMBER OF FEATURES ADVERTISED PER COMPANY

Year	Auto-mobiles*	Cameras	Refrig-erators	Rotary Mowers	Television Sets	Vacuum Cleaners	Water Heaters	Wrist Watches	Average for All 8 Industries
1930	4.3	3.0	0†	—	—	0	0	0	3.6
1932	5.4	8.0	3.3	—	—	4.2	1.7	0	4.5
1934	5.3	4.2	5.2	—	—	4.5	0	0	4.8
1936	6.9	2.7	6.8	—	—	4.3	0	0	5.2
1938	7.5	—‡	4.0	—	—	2.6	2.8	1.7	3.7
1940	4.9	0	4.6	—	—	6.7	3.0	4.0	4.6
1941	4.3	—	5.2	—	—	4.4	2.7	2.8	3.9
1946	2.2	3.6	3.2	—	—	5.0	1.5	2.2	3.0
1947	3.0	4.6	2.2	—	—	3.6	3.0	1.4	3.1
1948	1.6	5.3	4.7	0	2.7	6.3	1.9	2.3	3.5
1949	2.8	6.8	3.7	5.0	2.1	2.0	2.9	2.6	3.5
1950	4.8	7.4	3.5	5.0	2.8	1.7	2.1	2.1	3.7
1951	4.6	6.6	5.6	3.2	3.3	3.8	1.9	2.9	4.0
1952	4.8	5.5	5.2	4.0	3.1	4.2	2.4	2.8	4.0
1953	6.4	6.4	6.4	4.9	2.8	4.8	2.8	3.2	4.7
1954	4.0	5.1	8.8	4.4	3.1	5.4	2.8	4.7	4.8
1955	6.3	6.4	9.1	5.1	3.1	6.0	3.7	3.4	5.4
1956	6.1	5.3	9.6	4.6	4.5	4.6	1.7	2.8	4.9
Average	4.9	5.4	5.4	4.5	3.1	4.4	2.5	2.8	

* In 1957 the average was 8.8 for automobiles.
† The figure zero indicates that less than two companies advertised.
‡ The dash indicates insufficient data available.

water heaters and wrist watches in their advertising. Water heaters require the least work to operate of any of the products studied. Wrist watches require little more operation.

Television sets require more varied operation and have had a few more features advertised.

Vacuum cleaners and rotary lawn mowers require still more operation, and their advertisers have found it advantageous to utilize substantially more features.

Automobiles not only require a great deal of skill and effort in operation, but the circumstances of operation vary widely. They have had still more features advertised.

The largest number of features were employed by the advertisers of cameras and of refrigerators. The correct use of a good, flexible 35-millimeter camera requires precise operation to match the circumstances of use. As for refrigerators, although the range of service is limited to storing various types and sizes of food, the high frequency of use by the housewife makes operation important; also, there are few good alternative methods of obtaining differentiation.

Another factor which appears to have been a pertinent determinant of the number of features used is the *degree of interest* consumers have in the "output" of the various products. While few people get excited about hot water (unless they do not have it), nearly every amateur photographer takes a keen interest in the quality of his pictures. His pictures are an expression of his ability—almost an extension of his personality. Advertising managers have been well aware of this and have taken advantage of the photographer's willingness to notice and to remember specific differentiating features.

RATE OF INNOVATION

In view of the expanded research budgets of manufacturers in recent years, it would be logical to expect both more new features and an improvement in feature quality. Figures published by the Resources Division, Office of the Secretary of Defense, show a fourfold increase in total United States research expenditures from 1941 to 1952.[1] While a large part of that rise is accounted for by government-sponsored projects, the same figures indicate that company-financed research by industry tripled from 1945 to 1952. And since the Korean War—from 1953 to 1957—business research expenditures have nearly doubled.[2]

Did a rash of new features result from these research dollars? Apparently not.

EXHIBIT II . . . shows the cumulative number of *new* features advertised each year for the eight consumer durables studied. While there are significant differences between the rates at which the various product types adopted new features, there are almost no differences between their prewar and postwar rates of adoption. Indeed, the rates of feature development appear to be so constant that they suggest an inherent feature adoption rate

[1] From Howard S. Turner, "How Much Should a Company Spend on Research?" HBR May–June 1954, p. 102.

[2] Robert P. Ulin, "Thinking Ahead: What Will Research Bring About?" HBR January–February 1958, p. 27.

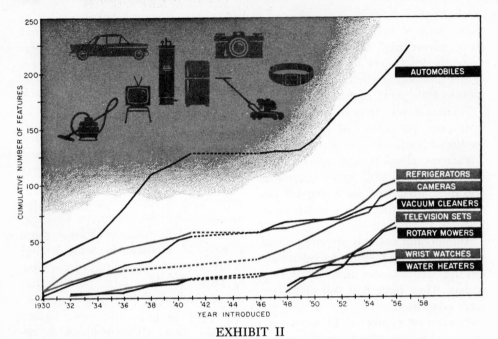

EXHIBIT II

CUMULATIVE NUMBER OF NEW FEATURES INTRODUCED TO THE MARKET

for each of the separate industries, perhaps determined by the nature of the product itself.

The study reveals that the automotive industry was by far the most prolific innovator during the period studied, averaging 10 new features per year. The closest rival was the television industry, averaging 7½ new features per year. The averages for all the industries were:

	New Features per Year	
	1932–1956	1948–1956
Automobiles	10.5	8.8
Television sets	—*	7.6
Rotary mowers	—*	6.9
35-mm cameras	6.0	6.2
Refrigerators	5.8	4.7
Vacuum cleaners	5.1	2.7
Wrist watches	2.4	2.0
Water heaters	1.9	1.2

* Not comparable

It is interesting to note that the number of new features advertised each year in the various industries does not correspond to the number of competing firms within the same industry. One might suspect that in an industry characterized by a number of small producers, such as the camera industry, the large number of separate organizations and viewpoints would result in a wider variety and larger number of product developments. The figures above do not support this hypothesis.

Nor can it be said that those industries with a few large firms will necessarily have a high rate of feature development. Many of the same large firms that produced television sets and refrigerators, with a fairly high rate of new feature adoption, also produced electric water heaters, with very few new features. Again, the nature of the product itself would appear to have been one of the major determinants of the rate of product development.

NEWNESS OF PRODUCTS

The two newest products, television sets and rotary power mowers, both had relatively rapid rates of functional feature innovation. Did this result from a greater need for functional differentiation, or from more opportunity for improvements? New products generally have been accompanied by numerous consumer dissatisfactions, and this creates an initial opportunity for rapid improvements. In addition, new products have tended to be accompanied by vague and flexible demand specifications. In the field of rotary power lawn mowers, for instance, consumers have been willing to accept an extremely broad variety of product configurations. For example:

In 1956 rotary mowers were being offered with one, two, or three cutting blades; with gasoline engines or electric motors; with two-cycle engines or four-cycle engines; with dozens of different transmissions and clutches. Some had to be pushed by the user, some were self-propelled, and others were built to be ridden on. Of the riding mowers, some had steering wheels, some had handle-bar steering, and one used a joy stick like an airplane's.

Judging from these variations the producers did not feel limited to a narrow array of product specifications. The product was so young that consumers had not developed rigid conceptions of what they wanted. This flexibility in the nature of demand presented mower manufacturers with many opportunities for functional product variation—far more, for instance, than the wrist watch industry had during the period under study or is ever likely to have in the future; it went through the innovation stage earlier. Thus, it would seem that the maturity of a product has had an important influence on the number of new features brought to the market by manufacturers.

OPTIMUM NUMBER

Turning now to the question of how many features a company should advertise, we find that there are conflicting opinions about the proper number of features to advertise at one time. One school of thought has held it best to concentrate attention on one or two product features and thereby make a definite and lasting reader-impression. An opposing school has suggested the virtues of scattering the shots—reasoning that if enough features are pointed out, at least one will appeal to almost everyone. How many in fact have been used?

The survey results show that within each industry there were strong differences of opinion as to the optimum number of features to use. It is not possible to say that after 25 years of experience all companies selling vacuum cleaners found it most advantageous to use x number of features simultaneously. It *is* possible, however, to show that most industries had certain central tendencies.

The distribution of the average number of features used by the individual companies is shown in EXHIBIT III, and

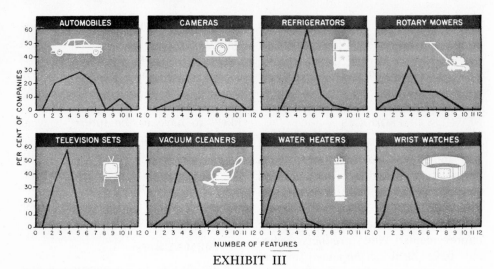

EXHIBIT III

DISTRIBUTION OF THE AVERAGE NUMBER OF FEATURES USED PER ADVERTISEMENT
BY COMPANIES IN THE VARIOUS INDUSTRIES

it is apparent that the strength of these central tendencies varies. Apparently the individual manufacturers of automobiles, cameras, and rotary mowers found it desirable to deviate considerably from the average of their industry. The nature of those products enabled a large number of features to be used effectively, and yet there were many companies that chose to use only a few. This would suggest that specific companies within each of the industries had their own peculiarities which played an important part in determining the best strategy for them to follow.

In contrast, companies producing refrigerators tended to follow quite similar paths, as did television manufacturers. Apparently the nature of the product itself was a large determinant in selecting the best number of features to use; or, perhaps equally likely, even though the character of the companies themselves was important, they were so similar in size, goals, and customers that what was best for one company was best for all.

It is interesting to compare the strategy followed (in regard to the number of features used simultaneously) by some of the well-known companies. One might suspect that in an established industry, such as automobiles, the largest number of features would be employed by the smaller, struggling firms, while the older, more sedate firms such as Cadillac would use few features and concentrate on prestige building — institutional type selling. As EXHIBIT IV . . . demonstrates, the established firms did tend to use more, but the reverse was not true. For instance:

Buick used more features per advertisement than any other make of automobile, and did so almost continuously throughout the ten years its advertisements were studied. Likewise, Chrysler maintained a high average during the twelve-year survey period. Neither company could be described as being new or struggling, at least not relative to the small independent firms.

It is difficult to make any safe correlations between the number of features used and company characteristics. For instance, it would be hard to find two companies more similar in size, age, product, price level, and method of distribution than the Oldsmobile and Buick divisions of General Motors. Yet their strategies concerning the number of functional features to use were at opposite ends of the spectrum. Buick, with an average of 10.3 features per advertisement, used more than two and a half times the 3.9 features averaged by Oldsmobile.

Which company was more successful? Apparently each company believed its strategy to be successful, for each continued its practices. Their averages for the period from 1950 to 1957 were 10.2 and 3.3 features, respectively— almost the same as their over-all averages from 1930 to 1957. The only hint of dissatisfaction came from Oldsmobile, when in advertising its 1957 models it jumped to 10 features.

However, while Oldsmobile's sudden shift in the number of features used was unusual for it, sudden changes were common among most of the companies studied. As Exhibit iv shows, Chevrolet dropped from 16 features in 1955 to 2 in 1956; Plymouth dropped from 13 in 1955 to 4 in 1956; De Soto dropped from 10 in 1955 to 3 in 1956, and then jumped to 17 fea-

tures in 1957. Such large changes indicate that there were not only wide variations between the different companies' opinions as to the best number of features to employ, but also equally large variations within a given company over a short period of time.

It is possible that the nature of the particular features available each year plays an important part in determining how many features are advertised. For example, it might be assumed that during those years when a company had more *new* features it would be inclined to advertise more features in general. As it turns out, the data do not support any such conclusion; there were simply too few new features to account for much of the fluctuation discussed above.

The companies either did not know what was best and made changes to experiment, or the determinants that guided their decisions were so complex as to defy visual correlation.

COMPETITIVE RATIOS

One of the problems the use of functional features raises for management is the ease of duplication by the competition. How quickly in fact do competitors follow in adopting new product features? The answers to this question are summarized in Exhibit v, both in terms of all features (the lower curve) and of successful features (the upper curve). For example:

The lower curve shows that when the typical company included in this study brought out a new feature—any feature at all—it was advertised at least once by an average of one competing

EXHIBIT IV

NUMBER OF AUTOMOBILE FEATURES ADVERTISED IN MEDIA SURVEYED

Company	1930	1932	1934	1936	1938	1940	1941	1946	1947	1948
Auburn	2		2							
Buick	6	12	9	15						
Cadillac	6	1		2		1				
Chevrolet	6		4			8	6			
Chrysler	6		5	8	17	3	3			
Franklin	1	2								
Hupmobile	8			10						
La Salle	6			2	2					
Lincoln	1									
Nash	8		8	9	3	7	10	4	3	1
Oldsmobile	4		3	14	10	3	3	1	2	1
Packard	1	4		1	8					2
Plymouth	1	8	5	6	14	6	4			3
Pontiac	8			6	3		1			
Reo	1			6						
De Soto		3	3	6	6	4	3			
Hudson		8		8	4	2				
Dodge			9	5	1		2			
Studebaker				4	14	5	8		2	
Ford				9		6	2	2	5	1
Mercury						9	5	2		
Henry J. Kaiser										
Kaiser										
Imperial										
Rambler										
Total features advertised	65	38	48	111	82	54	47	9	12	8
Number of companies	15	7	9	16	11	11	11	4	4	5
Average number of features per company	4.3	5.4	5.3	6.9	7.5	4.9	4.3	2.2	3.0	1.6

company within two years after its introduction.

After the new feature had been on the market four years, an average of 1.5 competitors had advertised or were advertising it; and after nine years an average of 2 competitors had used it.

Many of the features were not followed because they were not judged to be worth duplicating. In fact, in each of the product types, almost half of all the features introduced to the market were not followed. The percentages of features not followed at all were: auto-

EXHIBIT IV (*Cont.*)

NUMBER OF AUTOMOBILE FEATURES ADVERTISED IN MEDIA SURVEYED

1949	1950	1951	1952	1953	1954	1955	1956	1957	Total Features	Total Years	Average per Year
									4	2	2.0
			12	13	8	5	11	12	103	10	10.3
						2	4	4	20	7	2.9
	6	9	7			16	2	4	68	10	6.8
			6	6	5	8	6	12	85	12	7.1
									3	2	1.5
									18	2	9.0
									10	3	3.3
						3	11	6	21	4	5.2
4	8	6	7	1	10	2	11	13	115	18	6.4
1		1	1	3		3	2	10	62	16	3.9
			3		1		7		27	8	3.4
5		8		7	3	13	4	9	96	15	6.4
	5		3			4	1	4	35	9	3.9
									7	2	3.5
	3		7	6	5	10	3	17	76	13	5.8
		4		6	4		6	12	54	9	6.0
	2	6	2	8	4	6		10	55	11	5.0
1	3	2			1		10	3	53	11	4.8
2	7		5	8	3	8	6	5	69	14	4.9
4	4	3			2	7	10	10	56	10	5.6
		5	3						8	2	4.0
		2			2				4	2	2.0
						1	3		4	2	2.0
			1			7		9	17	3	5.7
17	38	46	57	58	48	95	97	140	1,070		
6	8	10	12	9	12	15	16	16		197	
2.8	4.8	4.6	4.8	6.4	4.0	6.3	6.1	8.8			5.4

mobiles, 54%; 35-millimeter cameras, 46%; refrigerators, 49%; television sets, 47%; rotary lawn mowers, 48%; vacuum cleaners, 48%; electric water lowed by any competitors simply be- heaters, 47%; and wrist watches, 50%. Furthermore, the vast majority of these unimitated features were quickly dropped by the originating company.

SUCCESSFUL FEATURES

Since the more pertinent question is, "How quickly will competitors follow the *better* features?" separate analysis

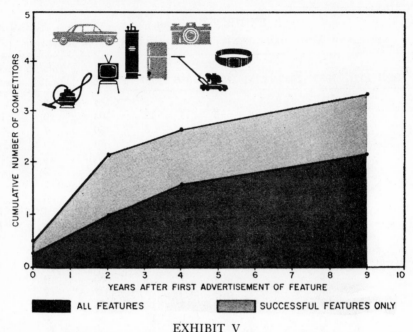

EXHIBIT V

AVERAGE NUMBER OF COMPETITIVE ADVERTISERS FOLLOWING
A FEATURE'S INTRODUCTION

is needed of the follow rate on features which appeared to be "successful." This analysis excludes all features that were not advertised a second year (not necessarily a successive year) by some company—either the originator or a competitor. By examining the upper curve in EXHIBIT V, it may be seen that the number of competitors duplicating these features each year is one and a half to two times the over-all average.

VARIATIONS BY INDUSTRY

For each of the product types there was a slightly different pattern of competitive behavior, as shown in EXHIBIT VI. The exhibit brings out the following observations:

Among automotive manufacturers nearly all the competitors who were destined to follow had done so by the time the feature was two years old.

Among refrigerator manufacturers the number of followers increased at a uniform rate through the fourth year of use.

In the case of both electric water heaters and wrist watches, even during the tenth year of use a substantial number of new competitors were giving the feature a try.

In the television industry not only was the number of followers greater than in any of the other industries, but the competition followed more quickly. In fact, the typical company in the television industry which innovated a feature had as many competitors duplicating its feature after two years as an innovating company in the automobile

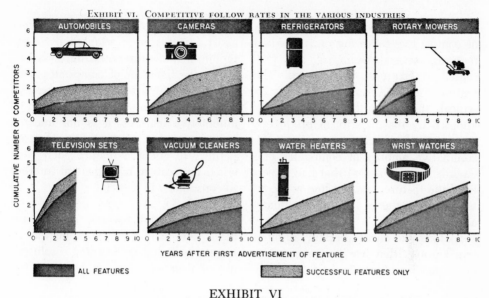

EXHIBIT VI

COMPETITIVE FOLLOW RATES IN THE VARIOUS INDUSTRIES

industry usually had after ten years. While it may have been easier for the television set producers to initiate new features (because of technological progress and lower tooling costs), it was apparently more difficult for them to maintain whatever functional differentiation they achieved.

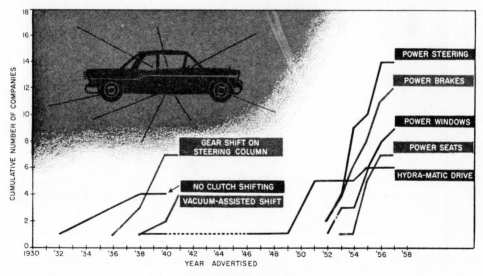

EXHIBIT VII

COMPETITIVE FOLLOW RATES ON SELECTED AUTOMOTIVE FEATURES

To give some idea of the patterns of competitive following on individual features, several examples are presented in EXHIBITS VII and VIII. The features selected are not necessarily typical, though most were eventually adopted by the majority of producers. The curve for each feature gives the cumulative number of companies (including the originator) that had advertised the feature, and the line was continued as long as at least one company advertised it.

EXHIBIT VII covers certain automotive features that are designed to reduce driving effort. It is particularly interesting to note how rapidly power-assist features were adopted by automobile manufacturers. EXHIBIT VIII . . . shows the behavior of competitors following several wrist watch features. As may be seen from both the watch and automotive features, it is not uncommon for two or more additional competitors to adopt a feature each year when the feature is of general interest to consumers. In short:

Out of all 715 features studied, no more than half a dozen appeared to have succeeded in keeping exclusive use of a general interest feature. One

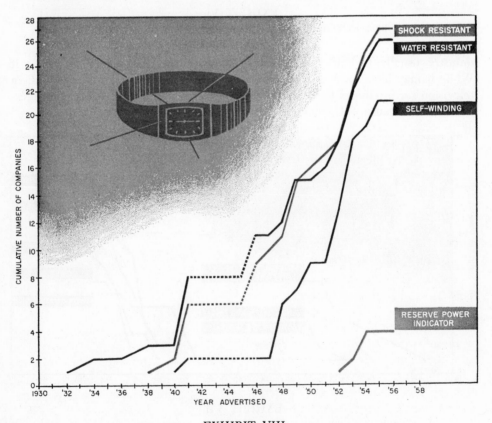

EXHIBIT VIII

COMPETITIVE FOLLOW RATES ON SELECTED WRIST WATCH FEATURES

of these was Crosley's "Shelvador" feature, wherein a patent was granted on the idea of storage shelves built into the refrigerator door. But within two years after the patent expired, 15 competing companies adopted the feature.

STRATEGIC ADVANTAGES

In view of the high probability that competitors will quickly follow a firm's better features, why is so much money still spent developing new features? Why is so much emphasis put on features in selling and in advertising? One does not have to look very far to find marketers who advocate placing the major selling effort elsewhere. Writing on the virtues of a strong and clear company image to boost sales, Pierre Martineau recently said:

. . . it is taken for granted that all products will perform their functions. But in my experience there are far too many mental "DP's" at the management level who cannot shift their perspective from the long-gone days when there were distinctive product differences to dramatize.[3]

Is this kind of thinking really justified? What can be said in defense of relying heavily on functional features to gain consumer preference?

First, it would seem reasonable that the development of new functional features is one of the most effective means of *building* a company image of progressiveness and leadership. Further, the aura of leadership so established is apt to last long after competitors have duplicated the feature. But the most outstanding virtues of

[3] "Sharper Focus for the Corporate Image," HBR November–December 1958, p. 56.

functional features in the strategy of achieving product superiority are more direct:

1. Functional features are an extremely flexible competitive tool.
2. They can gain the intense preference of a preselected market segment.

Features are a flexible tool because they can be adapted quickly, dropped quickly, and often can be made optional at very little expense. In contrast, trying to obtain an equal amount of brand preference on the basis of a distinctive company image usually takes years to accomplish. Once established, moreover, the image is expensive and time-consuming to change. These characteristics make differentiation through an image almost useless for a new company just entering the market. They also make it dangerous for the company to develop a distinctive image which may have to be changed as market conditions change.

Probably the safest image that a company can cultivate is one that is "good" in general—"You can be sure if it's Westinghouse." No one can argue against the desirability of having such a good-in-general image, but it should be recognized that intense consumer preference is not likely to result.

SHORTCOMINGS OF STYLING

Distinctive product styling is a great deal more flexible than an image is, but it is usually *not* as flexible as functional features. Styling can be adopted or dropped quickly, but it usually cannot be made optional as easily as functional features. You cannot buy a 1959 Edsel without the distinctive grill! Extreme styling variations are dangerous when they cannot be made optional.

Also, more often than not, it is difficult to predict the degree of acceptance a new styling will obtain, and it is still more difficult to predict what kind of people will prefer the style. Will the group preferring the style be the kind you wish to sell? With functional features, in contrast, it is often easy to fit features to segments with some degree of sureness. For example, a refrigerator without a freezing compartment appeals specifically to what, in this instance, turns out to be two distinct markets: (1) high-income families that already have a deep freeze as a separate unit, and (2) large families of lower income that need maximum storage space at minimum cost.

The fact that functional features can be used to develop an intense preference within a preselected market segment may or may not be important to a company. It is certainly not important if the strategy is to try to be all things to all people. On the other hand, it is rarely possible to produce a product that *is* better in the eyes of *all* consumers. If you are only going to capture 5% or 10% of the market anyway, why not recognize it and produce a product that *is* better to one or more segments of the market?

MARKET SEGMENTATION

Let us consider this matter of segmentation at greater length because of the implications it bears for marketing planning. As a market grows in size, it becomes increasingly feasible for man-

ufacturers to specialize the appeal of their product. Wendell R. Smith has noted the value of market segmentation and offered additional explanations for the increasing interest in this type of specialization:

There appear to be many reasons why formal recognition of market segmentation as a strategy is beginning to emerge. One of the most important of these is decrease in the size of the minimum efficient producing or manufacturing unit required in some product areas.

. . . Present emphasis upon the minimizing of marketing costs through self-service and similar developments tends to impose a requirement for better adjustment of products to consumer demand.

. . . It has been suggested that the present level of discretionary buying power is productive of sharper shopping comparisons, particularly for items that are above the need level. General prosperity also creates increased willingness "to pay a little more" to get "just what I wanted."

. . . Many companies are reaching the stage in their development where attention to market segmentation may be regarded as a condition or cost of growth. Their *core* markets have already been developed on a generalized basis to the point where additional advertising and selling expenditures are yielding diminishing returns. Attention to smaller or *fringe* market segments, which may have small potentials individually but are of crucial importance in the aggregate, may be indicated.[4]

Still another reason for the increasing interest in market segmentation may stem from the development of more

[4] "Product Differentiation and Market Segmentation as Alternative Market Strategies," *Journal of Marketing*, July 1956, pp. 6–7.

sophisticated market research techniques. Marketing research may reveal that management has *unintentionally* brought out a product which has appeal only to a specialized market. For instance, a company may learn that most of the customers preferring its product are elderly people, yet it may have been spreading the selling effort equally over a market composed of many age groups. Thus the company may have been suffering from the disadvantages of a limited market size while undertaking the expense of promoting a product of general appeal. The other side of this coin is that the company is not taking advantage of the potential benefits of a specialized appeal to a specialized market—the market economies of reaching a homogeneous group of consumers.

DIFFERENT DIMENSIONS

If management decides to pursue a course of market segmentation as a means of improving efficiency, there are several dimensions which provide specialization. For instance:

1. Geographical segmentation—such as northern, southern, and western markets; urban and rural markets; and similar divisions according to climatic differentiations.
2. Cultural segmentation—according to race, language, or cultural mores.
3. Socioeconomic differences—income, occupation, education, or family size.
4. Personal differences—including sex, age, interests, and various psychological differences (e.g., introverts or extroverts).

Although there may be many potential dimensions for market segmentation, not all of them are equally useful. One rather obvious limitation is the size of the segment. Many possible segments are simply too small to warrant the design of products to match their individual needs. Other segments may be large enough in size, but their particular needs are not *acute* enough to make possible the development of an intense preference. As an example of the latter effect, consider this:

In 1950 a television manufacturer promoted a product feature which consisted of a switch that would instantly magnify what was on the screen, so that if the viewer wished to view a particular scene in greater detail, by turning this switch the center portion of the picture would be magnified to full-screen size. Now while most people might occasionally make use of such a feature, it is not one that is used often enough to promote any compelling preferences. As a result, the feature was dropped after one year.

Much less obvious, but of extreme importance, is the "accessibility" of the segment. Can the segment be reached *efficiently* through existing channels of distribution and through existing advertising media? For instance, if a product were differentiated to appeal strongly to left-handed customers, how could it be advertised efficiently through existing media? For every potential customer covered, there would be multitudes who were not potential customers.

In contrast, specialization which is based on geographical segmentation can be much more efficient. If a product can be developed to do an unusually good job of meeting the needs of a given area, all of the local channels of distribution and advertising media may be used without covering market segments which have no advantage to be gained from the product specialization.

In short, the more efficiently the selected segment can be reached, the greater the specialization can be and still yield an acceptable volume of sales.

Once an attractive market segment has been selected, management may proceed to formulate a product with characteristics that will meet the needs of the segment. Although this formulation should not be difficult, it is surprising how often management needlessly overspecializes the product.

CAVEAT SEGMENTER

All too frequently management (1) selects a group of functional features which "are rated highly by consumers" when tested individually; (2) combines these with a style which is not too expensive to produce and is thought to be preferred by the largest number of consumers; (3) sells the product under a brand that has an image which has been built up over a period of years—partly without conscious guidance and partly according to what an advertising agency thought the image should be. And yet when these three elements—each of them strong—are combined in the strategy, the result, as often as not, is a product with rather low over-all consumer preference. The problem is this: the group of consumers that liked the features may be different from the group that liked the style, and the

group that liked the image may have been different from either of the first two groups!

The problem becomes increasingly acute as more distinctive—and hence possibly more market-limiting—characteristics of the product are combined. Accordingly it is highly essential that great care be used in coordinating the means of differentiation.

GENERAL OR SPECIAL?

Distinctions may be made between the alternative means of differentiation on the basis of their effect on the market. Aside from whether the means of differentiation happens to be quality, style, brand image, or functional feature, is the effect a *general* increase in preference or is it only a *specialized* increase in preference, i.e., does only a part of the market consider the differentiation to be preferable?

Combining general preference changes is not dangerous. They may not be efficient to use—either because of high development costs or because all competitors can advantageously follow them—but they cannot limit the breadth of preference for a brand.

In contrast, combining specializing means of differentiation may be dangerous, depending upon their specific effects. Some consumers will be enthusiastic and others will be indifferent or show an active dislike. For example:

Electronic flash synchronization on a camera appeals strongly to some customers but is not apt to bother or please those who do not need it.

A reflex type view finder is preferred by some camera purchasers, while others insist on having an eye-level view finder. The latter type—potentially market-limiting—may in some case be made optional in order to add value for some consumers yet not detract value for any consumers.

Still other market-limiting feature types cannot be made optional at reasonable costs, and hence are inherently market-limiting.

Despite the danger of using inherently limiting means of differentiation, it is sometimes desirable or necessary to do so. It may well be the least expensive method of achieving an intense preference within a smaller part of the market. Because of their market-limiting effect, such features may be less attractive for large competitors to follow. It may also be necessary for management to accept an existing market-limiting characteristic of its product (or its brand image) and to build additional differentiation around this existing characteristic.

PARALLEL OR DIVERGENT?

For purposes of discussing the problem of combining two or more market-limiting means of differentiation, two terms may be helpful, defined as follows:

Parallel means of differentiation refers to any and all distinguishing characteristics of the product which appeal to the same market segment.

Divergent means of differentiation refers to any and all distinguishing characteristics of the product which appeal to segments of the market that bear no clear relationship to one another, i.e., only by sheer chance are the members of one segment also members of another segment, which usually means

that those who belong to both segments are few.

To illustrate, take a hypothetical manufacturer of automobiles. Suppose that this manufacturer is one of the smaller producers and decides it would be advantageous for him to specialize his brand to avoid direct competition from the larger firms. To do this, the manufacturer may develop a small, lightweight automobile with an engine of small displacement. These characteristics are limiting, but they *parallel* one another in building an appeal to the economy-minded segment of the market. But then suppose the brand is also given a divergent "distinctive" styling. Now note what may result:

If only 10% of potential automobile purchasers are economy-minded enough to prefer this type of automobile over larger, more powerful, and softer-riding makes, and if also only 10% of the total market is willing to accept the "distinctive" styling, the result is apt to be an over-all preference by only 1% (0.10 × 0.10) of the market.

When there is no reason to believe that the market segment preferring one type of differentiation also tends to prefer a second type of differentiation, then the two characteristics will be cross-dimensional or completely divergent. In the above example, the 10% of the market preferring an economy-type automobile is no more likely to prefer the brand's styling than any other segment of the market taken at random. If a styling cannot be developed which will appeal to economy-minded consumers, then care should be taken to ensure that the style is not market-limiting. And if additional means of differentiation are used which are also market-limiting in nature, the size of the remaining group that prefers the brand continues to drop at a geometric rate.

In practice, most differentiating devices are neither exactly parallel nor completely divergent. There probably is *some* degree of overlap between the segments being appealed to. However, management is hardly safe in assuming that the segments will overlap *enough* to eliminate the dangers of overspecialization. To ensure that a product is not overspecialized, management must know *who* the consumers are that prefer certain characteristics of their brand —not just how many consumers prefer each of the characteristics.

The rapid rate at which a product may become overspecialized puts a heavy premium on those means of differentiation which are not inherently market-limiting *or which can be made optional*. Considerable emphasis must also be placed on those means which— if they are limiting by nature—can be focused to parallel the existing dimensions of a product's specialization. Finally, the geometric rate at which a product can become overspecialized sets particular value on those means of differentiation which can be changed rapidly if the need arises. The use of functional features as a means of differentiation can meet all of these requirements.

CONCLUSION

Besides directly bolstering consumer preference, new features often bring the innovator undreamed-of free publicity, step up the enthusiasm of salesmen, and do more toward building an outstanding brand image than words alone can ever do. Moreover, they offer management freedom and flexibility to a degree that images and styling can never match. But, unfortunately, all of this is a two-way street. A poorly engineered "improvement" rushed into production can quickly destroy a reputation for product quality or undermine sales enthusiasm.

As a higher level of sophistication develops in the art of product strategy, it is not going to be enough for management to simply sort out the "good" feature ideas for development and adoption. Managements will be forced to pick features appropriate to their company's size and goals. For instance:

Small companies should think twice before pouring research and development funds into features of general interest to consumers. They rarely have sufficient advertising funds or retail distribution to capitalize fully on the value of such features. Further, these general interest features are the very ones which are most likely to be rapidly duplicated by large companies.

As for large companies, when they introduce new general interest features, the managements must have enough market research information available to recognize in advance the potential of the features and be prepared to make the most of them quickly.

Features which are of intense interest to only a segment of the market can do wonders for a company—especially a small company. The high consumer interest makes advertising dollars go further and will help to draw consumers to sparsely scattered retail outlets. At the same time, more planning is needed here also. Market research must have identified those who *now* prefer your product and who *will* prefer it with the new feature. Will the feature build up loyalty among existing customers or shift it to a new segment? The identification of this new segment is vital for efficient advertising, selling, and distribution.

This, then, is the role of functional features in marketing strategy:

In the struggle for the creation and preservation of brand preference, the product features are a potent, flexible element offering greater maneuverability to management than the more stable or general dimensions of style and image.

Successful features are most likely to be followed in the absence of strong patent protection, but again the flexible nature of functional features continually presents new opportunities.

When employed in combination with style and image, or with other features, management must combine with care lest the net effect be a dilution of the market.

As the economy and the total market grow, and as management seeks to serve specialized segments more efficiently, the characteristics of functional features make them an especially powerful ingredient in the marketing mix.

Management must recognize, however, that intelligent use of the advantages depends to a large extent on how well it knows its market, both present and potential, and how well it can deliver products that really are better . . . if not to all of the people all of the time, at least to a lot of the people a lot of the time.

►►►►►►►►►►►►► NEW-PRODUCT "MIDDLE AGE":
the dangerous years

KENNETH M. REISS[*]

The party's over. That no-longer-new product, lately the talk of the industry, has been matched by competition, undersold, overpromoted, and is now more likely to draw a yawn than an order.

The breakthrough has become a broke-through. The product is afflicted with middle-age spread: as it becomes more profitable to produce and sell, it becomes less and less promotable.

In most cases, this is the signal to fish or cut bait, to relegate the product to a modest niche in the company's line or

Reprinted with permission from Sales Management, *November 2, 1962, pp. 37–39ff.*
[*] Senior Associate Editor, *Sales Management.*

to pour new time and money into temporarily promotable "new features."

But this painful and uneconomical decision need never be made.

For, as marketing molds the fire and life into a new-product plan, it can also, at the same time, build in middle-age promotability.

The secret: Put a "difference" into your product, even when there are no competitors from whom to be different. This can take several forms. The product can be designed to incorporate key components (Timken ball bearings or Talon zippers). Or it can be made of brand-name ingredients (Formica, Owens-Corning Fiberglas). Or it can incorporate other materials that are easily recognizable, are thought of as superior, and are therefore promotable.

When a product is new, buyer attention usually focuses on function: what the product does, how well it does it, and why what it does is necessary or desirable. In this department, marketing really has command. It researches the need, the market, the probable demand. The product is designed to appeal to this market by filling its need. The package (if there is one) is designed to attract attention, and the promotion is created to bring demand to a boil and to prove that the product will satisfy the demand.

This is the extent of product planning as most marketers know it.

But it covers only the first phase of the product life-cycle.

Once the function of a product becomes known, accepted, even commonplace, buyer interest also shifts—and it shifts clear out of marketing's traditional product planning scope.

It shifts away from function to the product (brand) itself. Instead of "What does it do?" the buyer asks, "Why should I buy this brand? How does it differ?" and, of course, "How fast can we get it and what can you do on price?" He wants to be shown why the product will perform better, last longer, give greater value.

Too often, the marketer is backed into a corner. There really is no convincing reason why the customer should buy his particular brand or model. His product really isn't enough different to sway a buying decision. He is stuck with talking price, or with offering the moon in service deals, or with inventing watery claims of superiority. Or he may even have to rush to the factory to add the famous "pink screw" to make his product stand apart from the rest.

To cope with this problem, he must extend the scope of his product planning interest.

He must build a "difference" into his product at the beginning.

This is not so easy as it may appear.

The marketer must put himself in a position of control over specifications within his own company. He must be able to determine what will be promotable, which parts or materials—and what kinds of these—will have the magic influence. And, in certain cases, he must encourage the suppliers of high-quality ingredients to beat their own drums more loudly, to build the reputation that will make the finished product more salable.

Then, after all, there is no guarantee that buccaneering competitors will not cancel out the sales advantage by copying the promotable components in their own products. But this is not too likely, for at least three reasons: (1) well-known, reputable competitors will balk at exact duplication; (2) fly-by-night or lesser-known competitors often must go to brand "X" ingredients in hopes of obtaining a price advantage; and, possibly most significant, (3) the sales value of the promotable ingredient generally does not emerge until the middle age of the product, well after most competitors have thrown their hats in the ring.

This, incidentally, is one of the most important differences of building in salability with components rather than with functional or design features; the latter can and will be copied almost immediately.

None of the problems is insoluble. In fact, they all must be beaten down if marketing's role in product planning is to include making the product more salable, more advertisable, later as well as at the beginning of its life cycle.

The very heart of the full-cycle product-planning concept is the highly controversial question of how basically sound it is to specify and promote well-known materials or components.

As a practice, this is neither new nor especially popular. There are advantages and drawbacks. But, as a practice, it may be necessary.

THE MARKETER'S ROLE IN SPECS

For years, smallish, little-known companies making, say, power lawnmowers, have known the value of a component like the Briggs & Stratton engine as a hypo for customer confidence. Many firms, both large and small, have added sales-fire to their products by talking up the fact that they were made from USS steel, were fabricated from Alcoa aluminum, or were blended with the finest Turkish tobaccos.

Now, with exclusivity all but gone from even the most famous finished goods lines, the specification of built-in brands is of key importance to an ever-widening segment of marketing.

For purposes of closer examination, this concept can be broken down into three key areas: Why should marketing become involved in specification? What specific advantages are to be gained from promoting such specified material? Exactly what role should marketing play in this process?

First, the "why":

Only marketing can know which components or materials will be most appealing to the customer, which will attract him and make him feel that the whole product is superior. This is basic, and it is the single biggest reason why marketing should play an active role in this part of product planning. In fact, it is reason enough.

But there are other reasons, too, and these make an active marketing role in parts specification even more imperative.

INFLUENCE OF SUPPLIERS

For example, materials and components suppliers are today becoming more and more active in hawking their own wares to end users, or customers' customers. Because of this, Robert W. Williams, general marketing manager of American-Standard, told *Sales Management,* "Consumers and specifiers are much more knowledgeable today about materials and their advantages." He adds, "We believe marketing must recognize these buyer attitudes."

In some businesses, as a matter of course, the spotlight on the individual components or materials that make up a product will be brighter than in other, more functionally oriented fields. It will be brightest in industries where emphasis is on sales of custom equipment or systems. In such cases, comments like this one by Walter E. Blake, sales manager of Stewart-Warner Corporation's heating and air conditioning division, are not unusual: "The marketing of our products requires promotion of design and materials to a great degree. Therefore, the sales department has a strong voice in determining such things as color, dimensions and materials used."

It's no secret that the most enticing components or materials are often those that cost the most. This means that somewhere a line of maximum marketability must be drawn. Philip B. Schnering, assistant to the president of McCormick & Co., explains the function in this way: "A major question is one of eye appeal and motivation of consumer impulse to purchase. This is generally offset by an increase in cost. Only marketing can evaluate the appeal advantage against the pricing disadvantage."

In other words, there are a number of good, solid reasons for marketing to get into the specifications act. These include making the product more attractive to customers, protecting the product against imitations, evaluating price-versus-salability questions, and so on—all of which add up to a stronger, more promotable product on hand for when the sales track is muddiest.

This brings up the second point. There are any number of marketers who do get involved in specifying components and materials . . . but who do not go on to promote the fact that these are built into their products. This may enable them to keep a tight grip on product quality—or meet certain high minimum market demands—but it does not pay off particularly well in extra sales of the middle-aged product.

CAPITALIZING ON THE NAME

Before it will add any special benefits, the famous name must be promoted.

There are a number of strong objections to this, some of them quite valid under certain circumstances. But, for the most part, the marketer must get mileage out of every real feature he has —or can get. Clayton Visnaw, v-p sales for the match division of Universal Match Corp., goes even further. He says that "Whenever sales finds a component or product with a name, we should capitalize on that name in our marketing—even if it means paying a premium for the product to use the name."

Promoting a brand-within-a-brand does more than simply add a glimmer of sales appeal to a tired product. For example, E. H. Holt, sales v-p of Barber-Greene Co., points out that "it can be beneficial to cite quality components when selling a prime quality product against lower-priced competition." And that's precisely the kind of competition that so often leeches onto a successful new product.

In some cases, of course, the quality component can add a crown of prestige to a product that may be otherwise unknown to the consumer. For years the garment industry, for instance, has made use of such awe-inspiring trade names as DuPont's Dacron and Chemstrand's Acrilan to lend acceptability to little-known brand names.

C. B. Ramsey, general sales manager of the Ready-Hung Door Manufacturing Co., offers this example: "For some years we had used various types of hinges in the assembly of our Ready-Hung door. It was largely the voice of our sales people that brought about the decision to standardize on Stanley hinges, because of that company's reputation in this field, and to promote the Stanley name in conjunction with other features."

Or, materials can be promoted specifically to show certain outstanding characteristics of the finished product: durability, water repellency, rigidity, flexibility or whatever.

Thus, the promotion of built-in famous names can be made to do much more than just provide a sales point. It can be used as proof of performance or as justification for a price. The name can be used to enhance eye appeal or to call attention to a feature which the buyer might otherwise miss. Exactly how it is used would differ greatly from company to company. It would depend on sales problems, on customer needs.

DANGERS IN PROMOTING PARTS

Of course, just as there are many individual advantages to promoting components or materials in certain ways, so, too, there are cases in which it is disadvantageous. For the most part, which it is depends on company peculiarities. This individuality is what tends to make the whole concept somewhat controversial: Executives tend to project their own company's situation across the whole business world, and wind up generalizing about something which is purely an individual matter. *Here are some of the ways certain marketers could weaken themselves by promoting ingredients:*

If the part is weaker than the whole. An extreme example might be if Cadillac chose to advertise the fact that it uses a good but fairly mundane brand of window glass or paint. This situation will occur in cases where the finished product's halo is shinier than the ingredient material's.

Along the same line, the maker whose price reflects above-average craftsmanship (and not just materials) would leave himself open to promotional borrowing by less careful competitors. Lester Frankenstein, president of B. Kuppenheimer & Co., illustrates: "Being a manufacturer of a high-priced, high-quality product, we are reluctant to use the name of a specific brand of material because competitors who produce a lower quality product of the same material will attempt to undersell us [by using that point]."

If being tied to one supplier would be impractical or undesirable. In cases where it is advisable to have many sources of supply for a particular component, or where reciprocal deals make this necessary, it is, of course, impossible to use a single brand name in a promotion. Note, however, that this would not apply to the promotion of generic names of materials.

Where changing technology makes it important to keep the make-up of a finished product flexible. M. R. Wingfield, v-p of paintmaker Benjamin Moore & Co., has this attitude: "The promotion of components of a branded product tends to freeze its formula or composition. We look on such advertising as a short-term benefit to be avoided."

THE DIPLOMATIC MARKETER

Now, what about the role the marketer must play in his own company in order to obtain or specify promotable ingredients? Chances are, if he is not already doing this, he will have to expand his influence somewhat to get in on the act. This could easily result in bruised egos, not to mention a crushed toe here and there. Purchasing agents, design engineers, research technicians, production executives are among those who could resent what may look like an intrusion by sales. For this reason it is important that the marketer go no further than is absolutely necessary and exert no more pressure than is truly needed.

Just what role marketing will play is often determined by the nature of the product manufactured and by the nature of the component or material desired. A look at the three main classes of promotable ingredients shows why:

There is the broad general category of unbranded materials which would be promoted by generic name: stainless steel, douglas fir plywood, galvanized steel, aluminum, Colombian coffee, wool, or whatever other material might offer significant advantages to a user in any particular product. In this area, the marketer could be concerned with the very design and structure of his product . . . or simply with a piece of trim or single part. He may "suggest" that R&D see what could be done with aluminum for basic structural use, or "demand" that a stainless steel trim strip be used instead of a plastic one.

Second, the marketer may wish to deal with specific, branded materials, such as Owens-Corning Fiberglas, Du Pont Mylar, 3M's Scotchgard repellent, Union Carbide Bakelite plastics, and so on. Here, the marketer could encounter both development and purchasing executives, and the toughness of the row he has to hoe will be different for every product in the book.

The third type, branded components or manufactured parts, resembles the second in degree of difficulty. The marketer might upset a P.A.'s buying relationships, a designer's personal or professional preferences or plans, both —or neither—in the attempt to get his product equipped with a General Electric motor, a Goodyear power drive, a Worthington pump, or whatever.

DEGREES OF INFLUENCE

It is impossible to generalize, to pin down the exact way in which marketing should influence product specifications. Because of this, it may be helpful to look at a cross section of comments from marketing executives. They range from the active and emphatic to the cautious and hesitant. They may be right or wrong; in any case, they are typical:

"In certain cases it is logical for

marketing to recommend materials and/or components which will make a product superior to competition and make it more salable. This doesn't happen too often in the electronics business, but it does occur in some instances and it's good business practice. However, marketing should not try to take over the product engineering function; instead, there should be a free flow of communications between marketing and the design engineers."—Stuart D. Cowan, v-p, commercial marketing services, Raytheon Co.

"Marketing would primarily select and promote complete components used in a product package, such as the motors in a gear motor."—John V. Moynes, v-p, sales, Morse Chain Co.

"Marketing management plays a major part in decisions of this type. Close cooperation exists between marketing, purchasing, research and manufacturing in trying to arrive at the best product to meet the needs expressed by architects, general contractors and our customers."—D. S. Miller, v-p, marketing, E. F. Hauserman Co.

"The marketing group must define the product image that the market will accept and make appropriate recommendations as to how this can be achieved. Mainly, however, it acts to veto product changes which would affect the acceptability of a product image."—Amos L. Ruddock, general sales manager, The Dow Chemical Co.

"In our company, the marketing area enters into choice of material and components only from a standpoint of a suggestion, though as an intimate part of all new product planning activities, ours is probably a reasonably important

voice in such decisions."—Fred E. Schuchman, Jr., general sales manager, Homestead Valve Manufacturing Co.

"We have a development committee which passes on all new products and on changes to existing products. All departments are represented on it, but marketing is the most influential voice unless its desires are impractical."—Edward C. Hewitt, v-p, sales, The Thomas and Betts Co., Inc.

Other shades of participation included specifying type but not brand of a material, demanding a promotable component for a certain use but not insisting on one specific brand and, of course, virtual "last word" authority over what goes into a new product.

THE BUILT-IN DIFFERENCE

If there is one clear danger to marketing from within, it is the sameness of product, price and promotion which at times appears to dominate—and stupefy—modern selling. Little relief can be expected from time alone in a competitive world like this.

Relief must come in the form of uniqueness, difference, especially for products which have been on the scene awhile. About the only kind of difference available to the marketer is that which can be built into the product.

It is imperative that marketing have "differences" to sell; it is equally imperative that marketing create and control these differences.

Help is available from the growing numbers of components and materials makers and trade organizations that are beginning to zero in more on end-user markets. And, because of this promotional build-up, customers will be reacting more and more to the names that are built into the product.

Everything—supplier promotions, customer demands, sales and promotional needs—points to the rapid growth of marketing-oriented specification and components promotion. Now it's up to marketing to make it work.

➤➤➤➤➤➤➤➤➤➤➤➤ PLANNING NEW USES OF PRODUCTS

LEWIS K. JOHNSON*

An important but neglected aspect of product planning is that of analyzing and determining new uses of the product. New uses lead to new markets, improved merchandising methods, improved old products, and even new products. Promotion of new uses increases the consumption of present users and also attracts new users.

Manufacturers are often not aware of all their product's uses; in some cases not even the most important ones. Consumers often find ingenious ways unknown to the manufacturer of using a product. Effective sales planning, however, requires that manufacturers be aware of and exploit all possible uses of their products.

A number of companies have capitalized upon the new use idea. The Lambert Pharmacal Company is a classic example. Listerine was promoted initially as an antiseptic to remove odors from the breath. Over the years, however, the company has advertised the product as a dandruff remover, as a cure for athlete's foot, as a cold preventive, as a deodorant, and for other uses. The Scott Paper Company advertises paper towels for a number of uses among which are the removal of grease from foods and pans, and in laundrying. The Johnson Wax Company inadvertently discovered that the company's floor wax was being used for polishing furniture and automobiles. This led the company to develop special waxes for these uses. Salt companies are promoting salt for use as a dentrifice, in beer, in grapefruit juice, and on citrus fruits. One widely known company that recently started capitalizing upon the new use idea is the Minnesota Mining and Manufacturing Company, promoting new uses of Scotch Brand Cellophane Tape. New uses advertised by the company include sealing sandwiches and food and drink items to be taken on picnics, sealing shakers to prevent spilling, taping wax paper covers on foods for preservation in refrigerators, and labeling canning jars.

The search for new uses of a product can be approached in a number of

*Professor of Marketing, Washington and Lee University.

ways. The possibility of extending use of the product to the opposite sex should not be overlooked. The toilet goods industry, for example, is successfully promoting the sale of toilet items —deodorants, lotions, cleansing creams, powder—for use by men. A profitable market has been developed among women for cigarettes and razors. Opportunities should be explored for the product's use among children. The manufacturers of umbrellas and cosmetics have introduced their products to the juvenile market. Studying the product's ingredients often suggests new uses. Sloan's Liniment, for instance, was originally developed for use on animals and later promoted for use by human beings. Baking soda is recommended for relieving insect bites, for preventing colds, and for relieving indigestion. A brushless shaving cream is claimed to be useful as a shampoo, as a utility soap, and for treating sunburn, chapped hands, and insect bites. Analyses of the uses of a product with other products should be investigated. For example, Sunkist, Incorporated, and the Tea Institute are jointly advertising the use of lemons and tea. The manufacturers of beer, cheese, pickles, and crackers have exploited the opportunities of promoting the sale of these products together.

Opportunities for promoting the sale of products in new markets should be sought. For example, the Fairbanks Scale Company developed a profitable home market in addition to its industrial market by designing a practicable bathroom scale. A manufacturer of carpenter's tools also added the home market to his industrial market by packaging tools in a special kit for home use. Studies indicate that a product used in one part of the home might be used in another part. The floor covering industry, for instance, persuaded a sizable segment of the consumer market that linoleum and congoleum are as attractive and desirable in the living room and bedroom as they are in the kitchen and bathroom. Radios are advertised for use in the kitchen, bedroom, and playroom as well as in the living room. Analyses should be made of slightly different applications of the product's current use. Clorox is recommended for use as a stain remover, as a deodorant, as a disinfectant, and as a bleach. Log Cabin syrup is suggested for use on ice cream sundaes and cakes.

Studies of new products, of types of entertainment, recreation, games, and sports, of modes of travel, and of occupational and living habits, provide leads for a product's new use. The Coca-Cola Company has successfully promoted the use of Coca-Cola at bridge games and parties. The popcorn industry is promoting its product to television viewers. The makers of cocktail glasses, anchovy paste, and caviar are profiting by the increasing popularity of cocktail parties. The public's increasing sunbathing and automobile traveling has opened up lucrative markets for sun glasses. The continuing popularity of swimming provides an excellent opportunity to promote the sale of cigarette lighters for beach use.

The entire personnel of an organization can be made "new use minded." A company's experimental and testing laboratories are good sources of new use suggestions. The advertising agency retained by a company might investigate and recommend the promotion of new uses for a product. Surveys among consumers are one of the best methods of uncovering such uses. Premiums and prizes might be offered consumers for their suggestions. Even dealers and trade associations might be approached for suggestions.

The promotion of a product's new uses does not increase sales as effectively as other methods of sales expansion. Such promotion increases the sales of the entire industry—competitors profit from the promotional efforts of the manufacturer who initially stressed the new uses. Competitors can easily appropriate new use ideas for their own sales promotion activities. Product improvements cannot be copied and exploited by competitors whereas new uses can. However, the promotion of new uses requires no change in the product and production facilities whereas changes in the product often disturb production methods.

Manufacturers should not take the uses of their products for granted. Some years ago the Borden Company assumed that the most important use of condensed milk was for feeding babies. A market survey revealed, however, that only 40 per cent of the market used the product for this purpose, and that 60 per cent used condensed milk for cooking purposes.[1] The Corning Glass Company for some years advertised Pyrex for use in cooking and serving certain foods which a market analysis later revealed were seldom cooked or served in Pyrex. Illustrations that formerly were carried in the company's advertising featuring these foods were then changed to conform with the more popular uses of the product. It is a waste of time, money and effort to stress the promotion of wrong and occasional uses of a product when appeals to the most important, logical and popular uses are easily discovered and more profitably promoted.

[1] Lyndon O. Brown, *Sales and Market Analysis: A Text with Selected Reading Materials* (Northwestern University School of Commerce, unpublished, 1934).

▶▶▶▶▶▶▶▶▶▶ D

Designing the Product Strategy

▶▶▶▶▶▶▶▶▶▶▶ PRODUCT PLANNING: *key to changing conditions*

Acme Reporter

When the thoughtful businessman squeezes a moment for reflection from the hammering demands of daily decisions and deadlines, he can hardly help wondering where his company will be five or ten years from now. Given the quick-paced society in which we live, he is wise to be concerned with this question.

Looking back over the past fifty years at the nation's top 100 firms, one notes a startling turnover. Of the leading companies in 1909, two-thirds have since disappeared; of the top-rank enterprises of 1919, over half are now gone. To look at it the other way, of those that make up the 100 leaders today, the majority have arrived during the last 25 years. The ups-and-downs have been just as violent throughout the whole business community—small and medium-size companies as well as big companies.

Obviously the successful companies are those that were created or altered to meet the rapidly shifting demands of the market. In a dynamic economy, which bids fair to be dominated over the next decades by a rate of change far greater than that of the past, the enterprise that is not constantly on the move will be left by the roadside.

KEEPING UP WITH CHANGE

Are today's managers trying to meet this situation by fiddling around on the

Acme Reporter, *Association of Consulting Management Engineers, Inc., 1959 Series, Number 2, pp. 1–4.*

periphery of the problem? Many of them are trying sales gimmicks, tricky new packages, advertising approaches based on unverified speculations of untrained "social scientists," and so on . . . when they should be taking a sharp look at their products and their markets.

For the fact is that people's wants are changing. Technology is making new items possible all the time. Even the functions which products serve for the customer are shifting. Automobiles, for example, may gradually be turning into mere means of transportation again, instead of symbols of power and prestige; while boats and swimming pools, once far out of reach for most families, are becoming devices to gain status as well as facilities for recreation.

So products, like humans, may have a life cycle from conception to death, and the company that relaxes because of the sales and profits of today could find itself with warehouses full of hula hoops or Davy Crockett hats tomorrow.

Success and failure   How can a company manage to keep up? Obviously, by pruning out dead products and adding new products; by diversifying; by concentrating or broadening the appeal; by defining markets more clearly or expanding their boundaries— in short, by not being content with the *status quo*. More importantly, it can strengthen its basic situation by bringing into the management of the company the point of view of the customer and a real understanding of what the company and its products have to be and do for him.

If management attention today is more intensely concentrated on the development of new products than ever before, the reason is simply the tremendous potential profit and volume in new products. Studies in a number of industries indicate that new products are expected to contribute from 30 per cent to 80 per cent of total volume over the next five years.

But while the development and marketing of new products promise important volume and profits to those who succeed, the odds against the success of a new product today are higher than most businessmen realize. In fact, a frequently quoted observation that 80% of new products fail greatly underestimates the odds, since competitive pressures are becoming stronger all the time and the company that falls behind has farther and farther to go to catch up.

There are many reasons for a high rate of duds and misfires. Lack of coordination, especially between marketing and engineering, is a major cause. The failure of production-oriented top executives to measure the marketing needs of the product against the resources of the company; changed economic conditions or public tastes; poor executive judgment on the size or nature of the market; internal management rivalries and jealousies; too many decisions based on "intuition" without evidence or solid argument to back them up—any or all of these can be involved.

Need for policy   Underlying many of these difficulties is the lack of a clearly and generally understood method for selecting among the many alternative courses of action. In other words, there is no over-all policy with built-in, specific measures by which management can determine whether to drop product X, pick up item Y by diversification, or continue with the development of project Z through R & D.

What is a "product policy," and how does management go about putting one together? Essentially, it is a statement of the characteristics of successful items, both now and in the future, for the particular company concerned which can be used as a measuring stick for additions, subtractions, and multiplications.

Before building such a list, managers have to come up with answers to three questions:

1. What do we think lies ahead for our company and industry, particularly in the market place?
2. What are the objectives of our firm, both short-range and long-range?
3. What are our particular strengths and weaknesses?

Let us look at each of these three areas in turn.

GAUGING THE FUTURE

The first category of information managers have to assemble if they are to construct a viable product policy deals with what the future will bring. This is essentially forecasting, but looking around for the "building materials" for this purpose is a little different from pure economic predicting. The initial step is a sales forecast which rests on a consideration of general business trends, political and international developments, characteristics of the industry as a whole, the position of the particular firm in the industry, the direction of manufacturing costs, and, above all, the wants and needs of con-

sumers and users. A five-year period is a useful one to choose, always remembering that the farther you get from the present, the shakier the estimate.

It is wise to rough out two predictions, one high and one low, since this kind of forecasting is hardly precise and most of us tend to weight our judgment on the optimistic side.

In today's world, sudden events can upset careful predictions with surprising rapidity. A far-reaching technological breakthrough may well occur in some industries during the next five years; or it may be a change in public tastes, another recession, or a major shift in the international picture. For "insurance" purposes, real thought should be devoted to the effect of developments like these, or others especially applicable to a particular company or industry. What, specifically, would they do to sales curves, and how quickly would their impact show up after the event?

Forecasting of this kind, one can complain, is not much more than educated guessing—and maybe not so educated at that. This is true, but it has to be done all the same since the decisions on product policy have to be based on expectations for tomorrow as well as the facts of today. The rough outlines of what is down the road are going to play a major part in determining the kinds of questions and answers in the area of objectives and company characteristics. If the possibility of different conditions has been foreseen, managers can plan for necessary adjustments in product policy, and can have alternative programs ready for implementation.

Furthermore, the exercise of looking

ahead carefully is a healthy one, and may protect a company from being ambushed by a totally unexpected development along the way. Thus, predictions form the broad framework within which the product policy is set and implemented.

One final comment on forecasting: it calls for a high degree of executive skill and perception. Spotting all the possibilities, balancing them against each other, determining what policy shifts should be made in the event of major changes in the over-all picture—all these demand judgment of a distinguished order.

SETTING OBJECTIVES

Once the general conditions and possible variations have thus been determined, the objectives of the firm should next be added to the data from which the product policy will be drawn.

What does a company want to accomplish by changes in products or product lines? Generally speaking, growth, flexibility, and/or stability are the objectives. But a simple concern with any one or a combination of these three, even if weighted on the basis of the sales predictions, is not precise enough to be the basis of a product policy.

Some of the statements of goals which various companies have found useful as a basis for planning are these:

1. We want to make up for the coming obsolescence of existing items.

2. Our demand is sharply cyclical; we need to flatten it out.

3. We ought to be utilizing waste or by-products.

4. We have management, marketing, or production resources we are not using to the full.

5. We should be spreading our risk by reaching into several markets.

6. We foresee a change in the strategy plans of the government and want to be prepared to shift from defense work.

Some such specific objectives have to be pinpointed if a company is to have a sophisticated and really meaningful product policy which will serve as a firm guide in selection of new items and elimination or alteration of old ones.

WEIGHING RESOURCES

Finally, a look at company resources is called for. What do we have to work with? To start with the tangible factors, an examination of the financial situation is important. How much money is available or obtainable? If a large amount of cash is within reach, new products or functional changes which demand heavy investment are appropriate; if it cannot be had, a firm has to content itself with items that do not require much by way of new facilities. It is interesting to note, incidentally, that even though a large concern has the capacity to take on low-investment projects, experience indicates that it will do better to leave such ventures to the small operator. Its heavier overhead and reduced flexibility may make it a poor competitor in a field where sales are small or margins are slim.

Another significant resource to study is the company's distribution channels.

Too often production-oriented executives assume that salesmen can take on "one more product," or that the best test of a new product is whether or not it dovetails wih available manufacturing facilities. Yet some specialists feel that it is far more important in launching a new item to make sure that existing marketing machinery is workable for it than any other single factor. Often the merchandising and distribution system is nowhere near as flexible as top managers believe.

Then, there are intangible assets: the flexibility of managers, the imaginativeness of researchers, the quality of personnel across the board. Closely interwoven here is the breadth and type of interests of executives. An art supplies company, for example, might find it economically feasible to go into the house-painting equipment business; but its executives could well be uninterested in that kind of endeavor.

FINDING THE PRODUCT

Once this material has been assembled — forecasts, objectives, resources—a pattern begins to emerge. A series of requirements for products and product lines, varying in importance, can be ascertained as company needs and capabilities become more clear. Some firms have found it helpful to draw out (a) a list of "required" characteristics for a product and (b) a list of "desirable" ones. Such a listing might look like this:

Required characteristics (in order of importance)

Can be sold through current marketing channels.

Will counter our present cyclical trends.
Does not require large investment.
Will give us at least 20% of market.

Desirable characteristics (in order of importance)

Will take advantage of current unused manufacturing capacity.
Will tie present customers to us more closely.
Will utilize present raw material suppliers.
Will give us broader product base in case of unexpected early obsolescence of present items.
Will stimulate sales of existing products.
Takes advantage of and will strengthen brand image.
Requires low-precision production.
Medium bulk size.
High value added by manufacture.

A policy like this can be stated as a check list, a series of questions, a formal policy statement, a series of brief definitions, or in various other ways. Some firms have prepared a comprehensive statement of their product policy, and supplemented it with a check list for ready use.

Implementing the policy The policy itself, however, is not enough; it has to be backed up with a process of implementation. In putting the product policy to work, a number of companies have found it advisable to ask themselves first, "Is this a situation in which product is the central issue?" With all the current popular talk about new products, diversification, and functional features, it is all too easy for a company to assume that one of these tools will open the locked box of treasure. Actually, cost control, greater efficiency, reshuffling of executives, or new marketing methods may be a more appropriate jimmy.

It is safe to say, however, that applying the litmus paper of a product policy to the existing line is a good idea under any circumstances. One company with annual sales of $40 million did just that, and eliminated 16 different items with a $3 million volume. Over the next three years, sales increased by one-half and profits by a factor of 20%.

Another corporation, one of the nation's largest, checked over its line only to discover that it was manufacturing one product with a market of $200,000 but a break-even sales volume of $216,000. Interestingly enough, the break-even point for a small firm on the same product was $55,000. The big company consequently let the item go.

Assuming that top management has concluded that new or changed products—acquired either through diversification, purchase, or internal R & D —are called for, the search begins. The executive judgment and talent has been geared into the process in the setting of the basic policy; the exploration can now be turned over to specialists who have been equipped with map and compass. They would do well to start off with as wide a selection of ideas as possible, narrowing the list down steadily by matching it against the measure provided by the policy. Stiffer research and tests have to be applied at each step, until finally a handful of

changes or products remain as candidates.

At this point, a more quantitative analysis in terms of the criteria is called for. To what extent does product X fit the standards established in the product policy? Does it meet the demands of the more important standards closer than it does the less significant? How much closer? Finally, some sort of test of return on investment might well be applied in an effort to make the final decision.

New features   A word might be said about the particular problems associated with the development of new features or improvements for existing products. The same kind of rigorous thinking is called for here, since even what may seem like minor changes may have the effect of either expanding or shrinking the market for the product. Characteristically they have an impact on the market for the parent item which may or may not be in the best interests of the company itself.

Assuming of course that the feature is well engineered and will perform as the advertising claims, the general-interest feature will soon be duplicated by competition. This may well weaken its strategic usefulness for a smaller firm, while a larger firm may nonetheless consider it essential for maintaining leadership.

On the other hand, added devices of intense worth to one group of people in the general market can be of great value to the smaller firm. For example, a typewriter equipped with various accent marks would be in great demand by a limited number of people writing in foreign languages. Adding keys of this type might prove to be a wise move for a smaller concern, but uneconomic for a big company.

In short, features, too, have to be judged according to criteria which develop out of a look at a company's future prospects, its resources, and its objectives.

SCHEDULE OF ACTION

But the problem is larger than selecting a product or a set of new features. The schedule of action should provide for follow through. In full form it might contain these steps:

1. Start out with specifically defined objectives. Such objectives reduce the area of search and tend to make the entire program more efficient.

2. Begin with the company's existing business and work out from there. The more a product differs from the product the company knows best, the greater the danger and risks.

3. Make sure your new-product planning is customer-oriented rather than factory-oriented. Study and validate all basic assumptions before making extensive commitments. Recheck them as a precaution against obsolescence through market or competitive change if the time interval involved is long.

4. Carefully define and recognize the differences between present operations and the business which the company is entering with the new product. Efforts should be focused on launching the product into the market as it is, not as you may wish it were.

5. Maintain a careful schedule. Provide adequate time for market planning and market testing. Make your moves as slowly and deliberately as you can, and still keep ahead of competitors, so as to minimize risk and be able to gauge the market reactions over time.

6. Check results against forecasts as you go along, and take appropriate action when indicated.

BENEFITS OF POLICY

Some managers have expressed concern lest an orderly, quantitative, and qualitative set of measures—a formal policy, in other words—might limit the creativity of employees and douse the sudden flashes of intuition which have led to so many useful items. Actually, the reverse is true. Employees with ideas will have some guidelines to apply themselves, and they know that the final decisions will be made according to an impartial yardstick, not by the snap judgment of some manager higher up the line who got served cold coffee for breakfast that particular morning.

Furthermore, the greater range of possibilities and the orderly examination of them which the establishment and implementation of a product policy encourages is more likely to turn up a good answer — or answers — to the problem than a brainstorm.

It is true, of course, that a company can be successful without a formal product policy. But the rate of failure of new products and new features is so high that it seems unwise to ignore the potential of an organized and systematized approach. Furthermore, there are positive advantages to a well-understood, well-thought-out policy which should not be overlooked. It provides a frame for information top management needs on products; it gives executives a check on other control data; and it supplies a set of unifying goals to guide the whole organization. Viewed in this light, the rationalizing of a process that has been very much a "seat-of-the-pants" operation has much to recommend it.

►►►►►►►►►► THE RISE OF MARKETING IN PRODUCT PLANNING

E. RAYMOND COREY*

It may be useful to digress briefly at this point to ask what the term "product planning" means. In actual practice, it seems to involve dealing with a broad range of problems related to what a company makes and sells. At one end of the spectrum, product planning is concerned with the company's objectives and its over-all marketing strategy. At this end, we deal with such problems as: What are the basic functions that our product line is designed to perform? What are the groups and classes of customers for which this line is intended? Do we seek to serve our markets as full-line suppliers or limited-line specialists? Will we function primarily as a supplier of materials and components or as a manufacturer of end products? Will we attempt to take a position of technical leadership in our industry, or will we achieve greater success as a follower?

At the other end of the scale, product planning becomes concerned with the detail of carrying out the basic product policy. We deal at this end with such problems as: How many grades, models, and sizes do we supply in each product line? What exactly are the specifications of each item in the line? If Customer x requests certain modifications in the specifications to meet his particular needs, will we accede to this request?

By way of definition then, product planning is the determination of the company's basic product objectives, of what products the company will make and/or sell, and of what the specifications of these products will be.

DECISION-MAKING CRITERIA

Product planning decisions often involve investigation and judgment in three areas: What does the market want? Can our company be competitively effective in this market? What will our making and selling the new product contribute to our total opera-

Reprinted with permission from First International Seminar on Marketing Management, Business Horizons, *Indiana University, February 1961, pp. 81–83.*

Associate Professor of Business Administration, Harvard University.

tions? Let us consider each of these areas in turn.

What does the market want? The late Charles Kettering, a pioneer in the automotive industry, was once asked in an interview whether he believed that "if a man made a better mousetrap, the world would make a beaten path to his door." Kettering replied, "The people who have mice will." This observation is striking for its clear and simple wisdom. Kettering stresses the necessity for orienting product development effort to market needs. He also suggests in his rejoinder that, in analyzing markets, we need to be conscious of the fact that every market is made up of segments. Each segment consists of a group of customers having homogeneous needs and buying motivations.

Our first task, then, is to identify the specific market segments with which we are concerned and to determine market needs as precisely as possible. We are then able to ascertain, first, whether the product under consideration actually has a market and, if so, what its specifications should be.

Simple enough to say, but we often encounter obstacles in making these judgments. In the first place, the market we have in mind may not be able to articulate its needs if the idea of the product is relatively new. How far would we get, for example, in determining the potential market for private space vehicles by interviewing our potential customer—the man in the street? He has no way of knowing how such a product would fit into his pattern of living, if in fact it ever will. The same fundamental difficulty is present even

in investigating the needs for new products that might fit immediately into the customer's day-to-day activities.

Another difficulty often exists in identifying accurately those groups that will make the buying decisions and whose ideas may then determine product planning decisions. Take, for example, the dilemma of a manufacturer of heating and air-conditioning equipment who was interested in adding heat pumps to his line. The heat pump, based on the same principles of operation as the refrigerator, heats the home in the winter and cools it in the summer with the same unit doing both tasks. This equipment could be made in one large unit and installed in the house. Alternatively, it could be made in two parts with one in the house and the other outside. The choice involved such considerations as ease of installation, quality of performance, and noise levels. In attempting to resolve this question, the manufacturer recognized that homeowners, architects, builders, heating and plumbing contractors, and distributors would all be influential in buying decisions regarding the heat pump. It was unlikely, however, that each would appraise the relative advantages of the split and the integral designs in the same way. How, then, could he appraise the relative importance of these conflicting signals, and make a product design decision?

A third difficulty in analyzing markets for new products is presented by the changing and evolving nature of these markets. The market segments of which we speak may emerge only after a product is in commercial use for a period of time. Then different groups begin to exhibit distinguishing characteristics with regard to the purchase and use of the product. At the outset, however, market segmentation may be only a latent thing.

In the face of these problems, it may be difficult, but not impossible, to make some initial judgments regarding market needs. For lack of adequate market information, marketers and engineers may have to define, as objectively as possible, what market needs are likely to be. Interviews with a few potential customers, with the company's field sales engineers, and with representatives of technical trade associations may provide them with some broad guidelines. These ideas may be enough for a first approximation of the market to be served and the product to be supplied.

The further refinement of these ideas then may come through the experience gained in the initial marketing of the product. It may be useful to recognize that the beginning phases of market development, when the new product is actually being made and sold to commercial customers, are at the same time a part of the market research effort. Introducing the product commercially, in other words, is part of the very process of finding out what we need to know about where the market exists and exactly what it wants.

Can our company be competitively effective in this market? It is axiomatic that, in defining its basic purpose and objectives, a company should "lead from strength." It should attempt to do those things that it can do well. In dealing, then, with product plan-

ning questions that fall at the "policy" end of the spectrum, we need to relate the company's strengths to the requirements of the specific job a management undertakes if it elects to make and market the new product.

It then becomes pertinent to ask questions such as these: Are there few or many potential customers? Can they be reached through the company's existing channels of distribution? Will extensive technical and engineering service be required by customers? Will the company need to establish new manufacturing and warehouse facilities? Are the supplier's trade reputation and brand name important considerations in the eyes of potential customers? Will market share depend significantly on maintaining a position of technical leadership? Will market position depend on low price or on level of quality? Are existing customers also potential customers for the new product?

Answers to these questions may go a long way toward determining whether the particular assets, skills, and relationships the company possesses can be effectively employed in marketing the new product.

There is one other dimension, however, with which to deal in appraising a company's capacity for marketing a new product. This is the matter of management interests and orientation. The degree of enthusiasm—or alternatively, the degree of resistance—that is generated internally by the idea of adding a new product can be a critical consideration. The new product may, for example, compete against the existing line for certain applications. In such instances, it may be true that the sense of psychological commitments to the current line literally disqualifies the management from doing an effective marketing job with the new product.

What will our making and selling the new product contribute to our total operations? Instinctively, the first question asked regarding the addition of a new product to the line is: How profitable will it be? While this may be an appropriate first question, it is often not the key question. And very often a product planning decision is made not simply to increase profit but to accomplish some other objectives related to the business as a whole.

It may be desirable, for example, to add certain products to have a full line of products going to certain customer groups. Or the product may be added because the company's distributors want it and will turn to other sources of supply if the company does not add it to the line. Again, improvements in product specifications may be made simply to meet the threat of a competitor's improved product and thereby to retain market position.

On the other hand, new product ideas may be considered and rejected because of their potentially adverse impact on some part of the company's business. Making and selling the new product may put the company in competition with some present customers. Or selling the new product might seem to existing customers to be in conflict with the company's image. A manufacturer of electric fork-lift trucks, for example, who had claimed for years in his advertising that electric trucks were superior to gas trucks would face some difficulty in adding gas trucks to his line.

Judgments regarding the impact of a new product on the company's total operations are not easily made. For one thing, it is often not possible to apply quantitative measures in this area. Nevertheless, tough-minded and objective judgment is called for to avoid making decisions based on emotion and short-run considerations.

Product planning may be defined as the determination of the company's basic objectives, of what products it will make and sell, and of what the specifications of these products will be. Product planning as a marketing activity has gained greatly in importance in the last decade. Reasons for the increase are the high rate of technological development, the postwar wave of mergers and acquisitions, increasing competition in world markets, and the mounting costs of new plants. These factors have tended to increase both the number and the significance of decisions corporate managements must make regarding what products the company should make and sell. They have forced management to give increasing effort to the task of designing competitively effective product lines.

In making product planning decisions, the relevant factors seem often to fall in three areas of consideration: What does the market want? Can the company be competitively effective in this market? What will making and selling the new product contribute to the company's total operations?

►►►►►►►►►►► A MODEL FOR DIVERSIFICATION

H. I. ANSOFF *

1. PURPOSE OF THE PAPER

. . . The model presented in this paper is oriented toward the specific purpose of providing top management of a large corporation with a tool for making intelligent diversification decisions. Our purpose will be to make it a reasonably comprehensive and accurate mirror of reality without attempting, for the time being, to provide an algorithm for selection of "optimum strategies." The purpose will be to identify the variables which have a first-order influence on diversification decisions and to identify important structural relations among them. In the language of classical physics we appear to be dealing with a step which is intermediate between a "description" and a "model." If this effort is successful, the results should provide management with a means for making informed diversification decisions through a combination of computation and judgment.

2. PRODUCT-MARKET STRATEGIES

Many different definitions can be found for the term "diversification." For the purpose of this paper we will define it in terms of a particular kind of change in the product-market make-up of a company.

Let the *product line* of a manufacturing company be described by two sets of statements:

(a) Statement of the physical characteristics of the individual products (for example, size, weight, materials, tolerances, etc.) which is sufficiently complete for the purpose of setting up a manufacturing operation;

(b) The performance characteristics of the products (for example, in the case of an airplane, its performance in terms of speed, range, altitude, payload, etc.) which endow them with competitive characteristics on the markets on which they are sold.

For a definition of the "market" we can borrow a concept commonly used by the military—the concept of a mission. Let a *product mission* be a description of the job which the product is intended to perform.[1]

To borrow another example from the airplane industry, one of the mis-

[1] For our purposes, the concept of a mission is more useful in describing market alternatives than would be the concept of a "customer," since a customer usually has many different missions, each requiring a different product.

Reprinted with permission from Management Science, *Vol. 4, No. 4, July 1958, pp. 392–414.*

Director, Diversification Department, Lockheed Aircraft Corporation.

sions to which Lockheed Aircraft Corporation caters is commercial air transportation of passengers; another is provision of airborne early warning for the Air Defense Command; a third is performance of air-to-air combat.

In each of these examples the mission can be described in specific quantitative terms and performance of competing products can be evaluated quantitatively. In many other types of business which have less well defined product missions, such as "cleansing of the teeth and prevention of tooth decay," job specification and hence measurement of competitive performance is a great deal more difficult.[2]

Using the concepts of product line and product mission, we can now define a *product-market strategy* as a joint statement of a product line and the corresponding set of missions which the products are designed to fulfill. Thus, if we let π_i represent the product line and μ_j the corresponding set of missions, then the pair σ_{ij} : π_i, μ_j) is a product-market strategy.

Four commonly recognized business growth alternatives can now be identified as different product-market strategies. Thus, *market penetration* (See Fig. 1) is an effort to increase company sales without departing from an original product-market strategy. The company seeks to improve business performance either by increasing the volume of sales to its present customers or by finding new customers

[2] One is tempted to enunciate an appropriate Parkinson's Law to the effect that advertising budget spent on a product is in an inverse ratio to the precision with which its mission can be specified.

who have mission requirement μ_0. *Market development* can be identified as a strategy in which the company attempts to adapt its present product line (generally with some modification in the product characteristics) to new missions. For example, an airplane company which adapts and sells its passenger transport for the mission of cargo transportation engages in market development.

MARKETS PRODUCT LINE	μ_0	μ_1	μ_2 .... μ_m		
π_0	MARKET PENETRATION	MARKET DEVELOPMENT			
π_1					
π_2	PRODUCT DEVELOPMENT	DIVERSIFICATION			
π_x					

A Product-Market Strategy $\sigma_{ij}:(\pi_i,\mu_j)$
Overall Company Product-Market Strategy $\sigma_k\equiv\{\sigma_{ij}\}$

FIG. 1

A *product development* strategy, on the other hand, retains the present mission and pursues development of products with new and different characteristics which will improve the performance of the mission. *Diversification* is the final alternative. It calls for a simultaneous departure from the present product line and the present market structure.

Each of the above strategies describes a distinct path which a business can take toward future growth. In most actual situations a business will simultaneously follow several of these paths. As a matter of fact, a simultaneous pursuit of market penetration, product development, and market development is usually recognized as a sign of a progressive, well-run business. Pursuit of all three of these strategies is essential to survival in the face of economic competition.

The diversification strategy stands apart from the other three. While the latter are usually pursued with the same technical, financial, and merchandising resources which are used for the original product line, pursuit of diversification generally requires new skills, new techniques, and new facilities. As a result, diversification almost invariably leads to physical and organizational changes in the structure of the business which represent a distinct break with past business experience. In view of these differences, it is logical to inquire into the conditions under which pursuit of a diversification strategy becomes necessary or desirable for a company.

The question can be put in the following form. We can think of market penetration, market development, and product development as component strategies of the *overall company product strategy* and ask whether this overall strategy should be broadened to include diversification.

3. WHY COMPANIES DIVERSIFY

A study of business literature and of company histories reveals many different reasons for diversification. Companies diversify to compensate for technological obsolescence, to distribute risk, to utilize excess productive capacity, to re-invest earnings, to obtain top

management, etc., etc. One study of diversification (Ref. 2) lists a total of 43 reasons for diversification. Fortunately, all of these reasons can be interpreted in terms of a relatively small number of typical expected patterns of business activity for a given company.

A standard method used to analyze future company growth prospects is through the means of long range sales forecasts. Preparation of such forecasts involves simultaneous consideration of world-wide business trends alongside the trends in the particular industry to which the company belongs. Among the major factors considered are:

(a) General economic trends.
(b) Political and international trends.
(c) Trends peculiar to the industry. (For example, forecasts prepared in the airplane industry must take account of the following major prospects:

i. A changeover, which is taking place within the military establishment, from manned aircraft to missiles.

ii. Trends in government expenditures for the military establishment.

iii. Trends in demand for commercial air transportation.

iv. Prospective changes in the government "mobilization base" concept and consequent changes toward the aircraft industry.

v. Rising expenditures required for research and development.)

(d) Estimates of the company's competitive strength as compared to other members of the industry.
(e) Estimates of improvements in com-

pany performance which can be achieved through market penetration, product development, and market development.

(f) Trends in the manufacturing costs.

Such forecasts usually assume that company management will be aggressive and that management policies will be such as to take full advantage of the opportunities offered by the environmental trends. Thus, a long range forecast of this type can be taken as an estimate of the best possible results the business can hope to achieve short of diversification.

The results fall into three typical trends which are illustrated in Fig. 2. These trends are compared to a growth curve for the national economy (GNP), as well as to a hypothetical growth curve for the industry to which the company belongs.

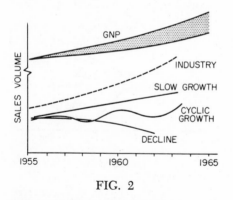

FIG. 2

One of the curves illustrates a sales forecast which declines with time. This may be the result of an expected contraction of demand, obsolescence of manufacturing techniques, emergence of new products better suited to the mission to which the company caters,

etc. Another typical pattern is one of cyclic sales activity. One common cause of this is seasonal variations of demand. Less apparent, but more important, are slower cyclic changes, such as, for example, peace-war variation in demand in the aircraft industry.

If the most optimistic sales estimates (which can be attained short of diversification) fall in either of the preceding cases, diversification is strongly indicated. However, a company may choose to diversify even if its prospects may, on the whole, appear favorable. This is illustrated by the "slow growth curve." As drawn in Fig. 2, the curve indicates rising sales which, in fact, grow faster than the economy as a whole. Nevertheless, the particular company may belong to one of the so-called "growth industries" which as a whole is surging ahead. A company may diversify because it feels that its prospective growth rate is not satisfactory by comparison to the industry.

Preparation of trend forecasts is far from a precise science. There is always uncertainty about the likelihood of the basic environmental trends, as well as about the effect of these trends on the industry. Furthermore, there is additional uncertainty about the ability of a particular business organization to perform in the new environment. Consequently, any realistic company forecast would include several different trend forecasts, each with an (explicitly or implicitly) assigned probability. As an alternative, the trend forecast may be represented by a widening spread between two extremes, similar to that shown for GNP in Fig. 2.

In addition to trends, long range plans must also take account of another class of events. These are certain environmental conditions which, if they occurred, would have a recognizable effect on sales; however, their occurrence cannot be predicted with certainty—they may be called *contingent* (or catastrophic) events.

For example, in the aircraft industry catastrophic forecasts may be based on the following environmental discontinuities:

(a) A major technological discontinuity (popularly described as a "breakthrough") whose characteristics can be foreseen, but timing cannot at present be determined. This would occur, for example, if a new manufacturing process were discovered for manufacture of high strength, thermally resistant aircraft bodies.

(b) An economic recession which would lead to loss of orders for commercial aircraft and would change the pattern of spending for military aircraft.

(c) A limited war which would sharply increase the demand for goods produced by the air industry.

(d) Sudden cessation of cold war (which was a subject of considerable interest a year ago).

(e) A major economic depression.

The two types of sales forecast are illustrated on Fig. 3 for a hypothetical company. Sales curves S_1 and S_2 represent a spread of trend forecasts and S_3 and S_4, two contingency forecasts. The difference between the two types lies in the degree of uncertainty associated with each.

In the case of trend forecasts we can

trace a crude time history of sales based on events which we fully expect to happen. Our uncertainty arises from not knowing when they will take place and the way they will interact with the business activity. In the case of contingency forecasts we can again trace a crude time history. However, our uncertainty is greater. We lack precise knowledge of not only *when* they will occur, but also of *whether* they will occur. In describing trend forecasts, we can assign to each a probability $p = p(t_0)$, whereas for contingency forecasts, the best we can do is to express its probability with $p = p(t_0, T)$, where T is the time at which the catastrophic event occurs. In going from a trend to a contingency forecast we advance, so to speak, one notch up the scale of ignorance.

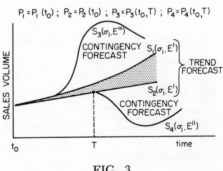

$P_1 = P_1(t_0)$; $P_2 = P_2(t_0)$; $P_3 = P_3(t_0, T)$; $P_4 = P_4(t_0, T)$

FIG. 3

In considering the relative weight which should be given to contingent events in diversification planning, it is necessary to take account not only of the magnitude of the effect it would produce on sales, but also the relative probability of its occurrence. For example, if a deep economic depression were to occur, its effect on many industries would be devastating. However, many companies feel safe in neglecting it in their planning because it is generally felt that the likelihood of a deep depression is very small, at least for the near future.

It appears to be a common business practice to put primary emphasis on trend forecasts. In fact, in many cases long range planning is devoted exclusively to this. Potential corporate instability in the light of contingency is frequently viewed either as "something one cannot plan for" or as a second-order correction to be applied only after the trends have been taken into account. The emphasis is on "planning for growth" and planning for contingencies is viewed as an "insurance policy" against reversals.

People familiar with planning problems in the military establishment will note here an interesting difference between the military and the business attitudes. While business planning emphasizes trends, military planning emphasizes contingencies. To use a crude analogy, a business planner is concerned with planning for continuous, successful, day-after-day operation of a supermarket. If he is progressive, he also buys an insurance policy against fire, but he spends relatively little time in planning for fires. The military is more like the fire engine company. The fire is the thing. Day-to-day operations are of interest only insofar as they can be utilized to improve readiness and fire-fighting techniques. It appears that in some important respects the business planning problem is the easier one of the two.

4. SALES OBJECTIVES

Analysis of forecasts is useful, not only for determining the desirability of diversification, it also indicates two basic goals toward which diversification action should contribute. These goals may be referred to as *long range sales objectives*. They are illustrated on Fig. 4.

The solid lines describe the performance of a hypothetical company before diversification (when its overall product strategy was σ_1) under a general trend, which is represented by the sales curve market $S_1(\sigma_1, E')$, and in a contingency represented by $S_1(\sigma_1, E'')$,

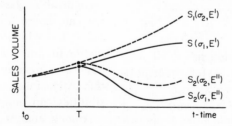

Growth Objective: $\dot{S}_1(\sigma_2, E') - \dot{S}_1(\sigma_1, E') \geqq \dot{\delta}(t)$

Stability Objective: $\dfrac{S_1(\sigma_1, E') - S_2(\sigma_1, E'')}{S_1(\sigma_1, E')} - \dfrac{S_1(\sigma_2, E') - S_2(\sigma_2, E'')}{S_1(\sigma_2, E')} \geqq \rho(t)$

FIG. 4

where E' and E'' describe the respective environmental conditions. The dashed lines show the improved performance as a result of diversification when the overall product-market strategy becomes σ_2.

The first diversification effect was to improve the growth pattern of the company. The corresponding *growth objective* can be stated in the form:[3]

$$\dot{S}_1(\sigma_2, E') - \dot{S}_1(\sigma_1, E') \geqq \delta(t)$$

The second effect desired of diversification is improvement in company stability under contingent conditions. Not only should diversification prevent sales from dropping as low as they might have before diversification, but the *percentage drop* should also be lower. The second sales objective is thus a *stability objective*:

$$\frac{S_1(\sigma_1, E') - S_2(\sigma_1, E'')}{S_1(\sigma_1, E')}$$

$$\frac{S_1(\sigma_2, E') - S_2(\sigma_2, E'')}{S_1(\sigma_2, E')} \geqq \rho(t)$$

As will be seen later, the two sales objectives can be viewed as constraints on the choice of the preferred diversification strategy.

5. UNFORESEEABLE CONTINGENCIES

So far our discussion has dealt with reasons and objectives for diversification which can be inferred from market forecasts. These objectives are based on what may be called *foreseeable* market conditions—conditions which can be interpreted in terms of time-phased sales curves. We have dealt with forecasts on two levels of ignorance: trend forecasts for which complete time histories can be traced and contingent forecasts, the occurrence of which is described by probability distribution. In problems dealing with planning under uncertainty, it is often assumed that trends and contingencies, taken together, exhaust all possible alternatives. In other words, if $p_0 \cdots p_n$ are the respective probabilities of occurrence assigned to the respective alternatives, the assumption is made that

$$\sum_{i=0}^{n} p_i = 1$$

Since this assumption leads to a neat and manageable conceptual framework, there is a tendency to disregard the fact that it is indeed not true, that the sum of the probabilities of the events for which we can draw time histories is less than one, and that there is a recognizable class of events to which we can assign a probability of occurrence, but which otherwise is not specifiable in our present state of knowledge. One must move another notch up the scale of ignorance before the possibilities can be exhausted.

Among analysts one runs into a variety of justifications for neglecting this last step. One simple-minded argument is that, since no information is available about these unforeseeable contingencies, one might as well devote his time

---

[3] Some companies (particularly in the growth industries) fix an annual rate of growth which they wish to attain. Every year this rate of growth is compared to the actual growth during the past year. A decision with respect to diversification action for the coming year is then based on the extent of the disparity between the objective and the actual rate of growth.

and energy to planning for the foresee-able circumstances. Another somewhat more sophisticated rationale is that in a very general sense, planning for the foreseeable also prepares one for the unforeseeable contingencies.

One finds a very different attitude among experienced military and busi-ness people. They are very well aware of the importance and relative prob-ability of unforeseeable events. They point to this fact and ask why one should go through an elaborate mock-ery of specific planning steps for the foreseeable events while neglecting the really important possibilities. Their substitute for such planning is con-tained in practical maxims for conduct-ing one's business—be solvent, be light on your feet, be flexible. Unfortunately, it is not always clear (even to the peo-ple who preach it) what this flexibility means.

An example of the importance of the unforeseeable class of events to busi-ness can be found in a very interesting study by the Brookings Institution

(Ref. 3). A part of this study exam-ined the historical ranking of 100 largest ranking corporations over the period of the last 50 years. An example of the mobility among the 100 largest is given in Fig. 5. It is seen that of the 100 on the 1909 list, only 36 were among the 100 largest in 1948. A major-ity of the giants of yesteryear have dropped behind in a relatively short span of time.

The lesson to be drawn from this illustration is that if most of the com-panies which dropped from the 1909 list had made forecasts of the foresee-able type at that time (some of them undoubtedly did so), they would have very likely found the future growth prospects to be excellent. A majority of the events that hurt them could not at the time be specifically foreseen. Railroads, which loomed as the primary means of transportation, have given way to the automobile and the airplane. The textile industry, which appeared to have a built-in demand in an expand-ing world population, was challenged

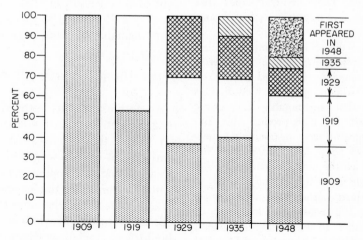

FIG. 5

and dominated by synthetics. Radio, radar, television created means of communication unforeseeable in significance and scope in 1909.

But the lessons of the past 50 years appear fully applicable today. The pace of economic and technological change is so rapid as to make it virtually certain that major breakthroughs comparable to those of the last 50 years, and yet not foreseeable in scope and character, will profoundly change the structure of the national economy.

This problem which, by comparison to planning under uncertainty, may be called the problem of planning under ignorance, deserves serious attention. A natural question at this point is, "Can any lessons be drawn from the preceding example with respect to the specific problem of diversification?" An indication of the answer is provided by the Brookings study:

The majority of the companies included among the 100 largest of our day have attained their positions within the last two decades. They are companies that have started new industries or have transformed old ones to create or meet consumer preferences. The companies that have not only grown in absolute terms but have gained an improved position in their own industry may be identified as companies that are notable for drastic changes made in their product mix and methods, generating or responding to new competition. There are two outstanding cases in which the industry leader of 1909 had by 1948 risen in position relative to its own industry group and also in rank among the 100 largest—one in chemicals and the other in electrical equipment. These two (General Electric and DuPont) are hardly recognizable as the same companies they were in 1909 except for retention of the name; for in each case the product mix of 1948 is vastly different from what it was in the earlier year, and the markets in which the companies meet competition are incomparably broader than those that accounted for their earlier place at the top of their industries. They exemplify the flux in the market positions of the most successful industrial giants during the past four decades and a general growth rather than a consolidation of supremacy in a circumscribed line.

This suggests that existence of specific undesirable trends is a sufficient, but not a necessary, condition in order to commend diversification to a company. An examination of the foreseeable alternatives should be accompanied by an analysis of how well the overall company product-market strategy covers the so-called growth areas of technology—areas which appear fraught with potential discoveries. If such analysis shows that the company's product line is too narrow and that its chances of taking advantage of important discoveries are limited, such company is well advised to diversify, even if its definable horizons appear bright.

6. DIVERSIFICATION OBJECTIVES

As formulated in Section 4, long range objectives have the advantage of generality; they serve as a common yardstick to any new product-market strategy which a company may contemplate. The price for this generality is a lack of specificity; the objectives provide no indication of where a company should look for diversification opportunities in the broad product-market field of the national economy. Nor do they provide a means for a final evaluation of the respective merits of different opportunities which compete for company attention. The objectives are mainly useful as minimal goals which must be attained in order to give a company desirable growth characteristics. As we shall see later, they operate as constraints in the final evaluation processes: only strategies which meet the long range sales objectives are admitted to the final test of the probable business success of the competing diversification strategies.

To complete the formulation of our problem, it remains to specify two things: a means of reducing a very large field of possibilities to a particular set of diversification strategies which deserve close scrutiny by a diversifying company, and a means for evaluating the merits of the respective strategies within this set.

Business literature employs a variety of terms to describe alternative directions which a diversification program can follow. A commonly encountered breakdown is into vertical, horizontal, and lateral diversification directions.

Each product manufactured by a company is made up of functional components, parts, and basic materials which go into the final assembly. It is usual for a manufacturing concern to buy a large fraction of these from outside suppliers. One way to diversify is to branch out into production of components, parts, and materials. This is commoly known as *vertical diversification* (or sometimes as vertical integration). Perhaps the most outstanding example of vertical diversification is

afforded by the Ford empire in the days of Henry Ford, Sr.[4]

Horizontal diversification can be described as introduction of new products which, while they do not contribute to the present product line in any way, cater to missions which lie within the industry of which the company is a member. The term "industry" is taken here to mean an area of economic activity to which the present activities of the company have a substantial carry-over of know-how and experience by virtue of its past experience in technical, financial, and marketing areas.[5]

Lateral diversification can be described as a move beyond the confines of the industry to which a company belongs. This obviously opens a great many possibilities, from operating banana boats to building atomic reactors. It can be seen that while definitions of vertical and horizontal diversi-

---

[4] At first glance it would appear that vertical diversification is inconsistent with our definition of a diversification strategy (see Section 2). It should be recognized, however, that the respective missions which components, parts, and materials are designed to perform are distinct and different from the mission of the overall product. Furthermore, the technology in fabrication and manufacture of these is again likely to be very different from the technology of manufacturing the final product. Thus, vertical diversification does imply both catering to new missions and introduction of new products.

[5] As is well known, the term "industry" is commonly used in several senses. Sometimes it is taken to mean a set of missions which have a basic underlying characteristic in common, such as, for example, the air industry, the automotive industry, etc. Sometimes the unifying notion is a common area of technology, such as electronics industry, chemical industry, steel industry, etc.

fication are restrictive, in the sense that they de-limit the field of interest, lateral diversification is permissive. Adoption of a lateral diversification policy is merely an announcement of intent of the company to range far afield from its present market structure.

How does a company choose among these diversification directions? In part the answer depends on the reasons which prompt diversification action. If a company is diversifying because its sales trend shows a declining volume of demand, it would be unwise to consider vertical diversification, since this would be at best a temporary device to stave off an eventual decline of business. On the other hand, if the trend forecast indicates "slow growth" in an otherwise healthy and growing industry, then both vertical and horizontal diversification would be desirable for strengthening the position of the company in a field in which its knowledge and experience are concentrated.

If the major concern is with stability under a contingent forecast, chances are that both horizontal and vertical diversification could not provide a sufficient stabilizing influence and that lateral action is indicated. Finally, if the concern is with the narrowness of the technological base in the face of what we have called unforeseeable contingencies, then lateral diversification into new areas of technology would be clearly called for.

An analysis of the sales trends impelling diversification can thus be used to formulate conditions which diversification possibilities must meet in order to fit the company requirements. These conditions can be termed as *diversifica-*

tion objectives. In contrast to sales objectives which set forth general growth requirements, diversification objectives specify types of diversification strategies which will improve the product-market balance of the company.

For example, in the light of the trends described for the aircraft industry, an aircraft company may formulate the following diversification objectives:

In order to meet long range sales objectives through diversification the company needs the following moves:

(a) a vertical diversification move to contribute to the technological progress of the present product line;

(b) a horizontal move to improve the coverage of the military market;

(c) a horizontal move to increase the percentage of commercial sales in the overall sales program;

(d) a lateral move to stabilize sales against a recession;

(e) a lateral move to broaden company's technological base.

Some of the diversification objectives apply to characteristics of the product, some to those of the product missions. Each objective is designed to improve some aspect of the balance between the overall product-market strategy and the expected environment. Thus, objectives (a), (b), and (c) are designed to improve the balance under the trend conditions, objectives (c) and (d) under foreseeable contingencies, and objective (e) to strengthen the company against unforeseeable contingencies.

It is apparent that a diversification strategy which is highly desirable for one of the objectives is likely to be less desirable for others. A schematic graphical illustration of this is presented in Fig. 6. The horizontal axis represents alternative diversification strategies in a decreasing order of affinity with respect to the present market structure (including both technological and business characteristics). In the air industry, which is going through a period of rapid technological change, the best promise for taking advantage of the growth trend seems to lie in the fields of vertical diversification into major system components or lateral diversification in adjacent areas of technology, such as electronics. The problem of sales stability could probably be best met through lateral diversification. However, horizontal diversification into new types of new products for the air industry is also desirable for this purpose. Finally, if its participation in the technological growth of the national economy is confined to one major area, an airframe company is well advised to diversify laterally as a means of acquiring a flexibility for unforeseen contingencies.

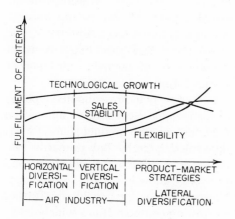

FIG. 6

Diversification objectives are useful for determining merits of individual cases. However, they do not provide a central orienting theme which can give shape and a sense of direction to the diversification program. Such theme must be sought in the long range objectives of the company.

7. LONG RANGE COMPANY OBJECTIVES

So long as a company confines its growth to changes other than diversification, statement of long range company objectives can frequently be confined to generalities: "growth," "flexibility," "financial stability," etc. However, when a break is contemplated with the past pattern of business, it becomes necessary to reduce the objectives to much more specific form. Questions, such as where the company is going, what unifying characteristics it should preserve as it goes through a period of change, should be answered before intelligent diversification decisions are made.

Sales objectives described in Section 4 provide part of the answer. However, these must be supplemented by a statement of the long range product-market policy.

A consistent course of action is to adopt a policy which will preserve a kind of technological coherence among the members of the product line with the focus on the products of the parent company. Thus, a company which is mainly distinguished for a type of engineering and production excellence would continue to select product-market entries which would strengthen and maintain this excellence. Perhaps the best known example of such policy is exemplified by the DuPont slogan, "Better things for better living through chemistry."

Another approach is to set long term growth policy in terms of the breadth of market which the company intends to cover. It may choose to confine its diversification to the vertical or horizontal direction, or it may select a type of lateral diversification which is circumscribed by the characteristics of the missions to which the company intends to cater. For example, a company which has its origins in the field of air transportation may expand its interest to all forms of transportation of people and cargo. "Better transportation for better living through advanced engineering," while a borrowed slogan, might be descriptive of such long range policy.

A greatly different policy is to place a primary emphasis on the financial characteristics of the corporation. This method of diversification generally places no limits on engineering and manufacturing characteristics of new products (although in practice, competence and interests of the corporate management will usually provide some orientation for diversification moves). The decisions regarding the desirability of new acquisitions are made exclusively on the basis of financial considerations. Rather than a manufacturing entity, the corporate character is now one of a "holding company." The top management delegates a large share of its product planning and administrative functions to the divisions and concerns itself largely with coordination and financial problems of the corporation and with building up a balanced "portfolio of products" within the corporate structure.

These alternative long range policies demonstrate the extremes. Most actual diversification case histories have taken a path intermediate between them; furthermore, neither of the extremes can be claimed to offer an intrinsically more promising road to success. The choice of policy rests in large part on the preferences and objectives of the management of the diversifying company, as well as on the skills and training of its people.

The fact that there is more than one successful path to diversification is illustrated by the case of the aircraft industry. Among the major successful airframe manufacturers, Douglas and Boeing have to date limited their growth to horizontal diversification into missiles and new markets for new types of aircraft. Lockheed has carried horizontal diversification further to include aircraft maintenance, aircraft service, and production of ground handling equipment. North American Aviation, on the other hand, appears to have chosen vertical diversification through establishment of its subsidiaries in Atomics International, Autonetics, and Rocketdyne, thus providing a basis for manufacture of complete air vehicles of the future.

Bell appears to have adopted a policy of technological consistency among the members of its product line. It has diversified laterally but primarily into types of products for which it had previous know-how and experience. General Dynamics provides a further interesting contrast. It is a widely laterally diversified company and, among major manufacturers of air vehicles, appears to come closest to the "holding company" extreme. Its airplane and missile manufacturing operations in Convair are paralleled by production of submarines in the Electric Boat Division, military, industrial, and consumer electronic products in the Stromberg-Carlson Division, and electric motors in the Electro Dynamic Division.

8. QUALITATIVE EVALUATION

In the preceding sections we have dealt with two basic factors which affect diversification actions. These are the long range objectives of the company and the more specific diversification objectives.

The problem now is to apply these to evaluation of diversification opportunities. Since the objectives are stated in both quantitative (sales objectives) and qualitative terms (diversification objectives and company product-market policy), it is convenient to construct a two-step evaluation process: first, application of qualitative criteria in order to narrow the field of diversification opportunities; and second, application of numerical criteria to select the preferred strategy (or strategies).

The long range product-market policy can be applied as a criterion for the first rough cut in the qualitative evaluation. It can be used to order a large field of opportunities (which each company can compile by using commonly available industrial classifications) into classes of diversification moves which are consistent with the basic character of the diversifying company. For example, a company whose policy is to remain a manufacturing concern deriving

its competitive strength from technical excellence of its products would eliminate as inconsistent classes of consumer products which are sold on the strength of advertising appeal rather than superior quality.

Each individual diversification opportunity which is consistent with the long range objectives can next be examined in the light of individual diversification objectives. This process tends to eliminate opportunities which, while consistent with the desired product-market makeup, are nevertheless likely to lead to an unbalance between the company product line and the probable environment. For example, a company which wishes to preserve and expand its technical excellence in, say, design of large highly-stressed machines controlled by feed-back techniques may find consistent product opportunities both inside and outside the industry to which it presently caters. If a major diversification objective of this company is to correct cyclic variations in demand characteristic of the industry, it would choose opportunities which lie outside.

The diversification opportunities which have gone through the two screening steps can be referred to as the "admissible set." A member of the set satisfies at least one diversification objective, but very probably it will not satisfy all of them. Therefore, before subjecting them to the quantitative evaluation, it is necessary to group them into several alternative overall company product-market strategies, composed of the original strategy and one or more of the admissible diversification strategies. These alternative overall strategies should be roughly equivalent in meeting all of the diversification objectives.

At this stage it is particularly important to make allowance for the unforeseeable contingencies discussed in Section 5. Since available numerical evaluation techniques are applicable only to trends and foreseeable contingencies, it is important to make sure that the alternatives subjected to the evaluation have a comparable built-in diversified technological base. In practice this process is less formidable than it may appear. For example, a company in the aircraft industry has to take account of the areas of technology in which major discoveries are likely to affect the future of the industry. This would include atomic propulsion, certain areas of electronics, automation of complex processes, etc. In designing alternative overall strategies the company would then make sure that each contains product entries which will give the company a desirable and comparable degree of participation in these areas.

A schematic description of the preceding steps looks as shown below.

9. QUANTITATIVE EVALUATION

So far we have been concerned with establishing a balanced relationship between the company and its business environment. An important remaining question is: "Given such relationship will the company make money, will its profit structure be more attractive after diversification?"

The measurement we seek might be called the *profit potential* of diversification. It should accomplish two purposes. It should compare the performance of the company before and after a given diversification move; it should also compare the performances of several alternative diversification strategies. In the light of the characteristics of the diversification problem discussed in the preceding sections, the profit potential should have the following properties:

(a) Since diversification is invariably accompanied by a change in the investment structure of the business, profit potential should take account of such changes. It should

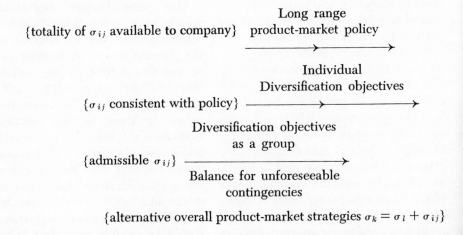

{totality of σ_{ij} available to company}

Long range product-market policy

$\longrightarrow$ $\longrightarrow$

Individual Diversification objectives

{σ_{ij} consistent with policy} $\longrightarrow$ $\longrightarrow$

Diversification objectives as a group

{admissible σ_{ij}} $\longrightarrow$

Balance for unforeseeable contingencies

{alternative overall product-market strategies $\sigma_k = \sigma_l + \sigma_{ij}$}

take explicit account of new capital brought into the business, changes in the rate of capital formation resulting from diversification, as well as the costs of borrowed capital.

(b) Usually the combined performance of the new and the old product-market lines is not a simple sum of their separate performances (another common reason for diversification is to take advantage of this inherent characteristic —to produce a combined performance which exceeds the sum of individual performances). Profit potential should take account of this non-linear characteristic.

(c) Each diversification move is characterized by a transition period during which readjustment of the company structure to new operating conditions takes place. The benefits of a diversification move may not be realized fully for some time (in fact, one of the common purposes of diversification into so-called growth industries is to "start small and grow big"). Therefore, measurement of profit potential should span a sufficient length of time to allow for effects of the transition.

(d) Business performance will vary depending on the particular economic-political environment. Profit potential must provide an overall estimate of the probable effect of alternative environments described earlier in this paper.

(e) The statement of sales objectives in Section 4 specified the general characteristics of growth and stability which are desired. Profit potential function should be compatible with these characteristics.

Unfortunately there is no single yardstick of performance among those commonly used in business practice which possesses all of these characteristics. In fact, the techniques currently used for measurement of business performance constitute, at best, an imprecise art. It is common to measure different aspects of performance through application of different performance tests. Thus, the earning ability of the business is measured through tests of income adequacy; preparedness for contingencies, through tests of debt coverage and liquidity; attractiveness to investors through measurement of shareholders' position; efficiency in the use of money, physical assets and personnel, through tests of sales efficiency and personnel productivity. These tests employ a variety of different performance ratios, such as return on sales, return on net worth, return on assets, turnover of net worth, ratio of assets to liabilities, etc. The total number of ratios may run as high as 20 in a single case.

In the final evaluation of a diversification opportunity which immediately precedes a diversification decision, all of these tests, tempered with business judgment, would normally be applied. However, for the purpose of preliminary elimination of alternatives, it has become common to use a single test in the form of return on investment, which is a ratio between earnings and the capital invested in producing these earnings.

While the usefulness of return on investment is commonly accepted, there appears to be considerable room for argument regarding its limitations and its practical application (See, for example, Ref. 7 and Ref. 8.) Fundamentally, the difficulty with the concept seems to be that on one hand it fails to provide an absolute measure of business performance applicable to a range of very different industries, and on the other, definition of the term "investment" is subject to a variety of interpretations.

Since our aim is to use the concept as a measure of *relative* performance of different diversification strategies, we need not be concerned with its failure to provide a yardstick for comparison with other industries, nor even with other companies in the same industry as the parent company. Similarly, so long as a consistent practice is used for defining investment in alternative courses of action, our concern with proper definition of investment can be smaller than in many other cases. Nevertheless, a particular definition of what constitutes profit-producing capital cannot be given in general terms. It would have to be determined in each case in the light of particular business characteristics and practices (such as, for example, the extent of government-owned assets, depreciation practices, inflationary trends, etc.).

For the numerator of our return on investment we shall use net earnings after taxes. A going business concern has standard techniques for estimating its future earnings. These depend on the projected sales volume, tax structure, trends in material and labor costs, productivity, etc. If the diversification opportunity being considered is itself a going concern, its profit projections can be used for estimates of combined future earnings. If the opportunity is a new venture, its profit estimates should

be made on the basis of the average performance for the industry.

In the light of earlier discussion, it is important for our purposes to recognize that estimated earnings depend on the overall product-market strategy, the amount of capital to be invested in diversification, the estimated sales volume, and the particular economic-political environment being studied. If we use previously employed notation and let P stand for earnings and I for the capital investment, we can recognize the determining influences on the earnings in the following *profit function:*

$$P = h(I, S, E, \sigma) \qquad (1)$$

As mentioned previously, a diversification move is accompanied by a change in the investment structure of the diversifying company. The type of change used in any given case, as well as the amount of capital involved, will depend on the resources available for diversification purposes, the particular product-market strategy, as well as on the method which the diversifying company selects for expansion of its manufacturing activities. The choice of the particular method of expansion (there are four basic alternatives: use of existing facilities, expansion, acquisition of controlling interest, and merger) is a part of the larger problem of business fit (See Sec. 10). For this reason it will not be discussed in this paper. We will assume that for each product-market entry an appropriate type of expansion can be selected (See Ref. 9).

The source of investment for the new venture may be one of the following:

1. The diversifying company may be in the fortunate position of having excess capital.

2. The company may be in a position to borrow capital at attractive rates.
3. It may be in a position to exchange part of its equity for an equity in another company (for example, through an exchange of stock).
4. It may decide to withdraw some of the capital invested in the present business operation and invest it in diversification.

Let us define the following:

σ_l Original product-market strategy of the company.

$\sigma_k = \sigma_l + \sigma_{ij}$ Overall product-market strategy resulting from the qualitative evaluation (where σ_{ij} is the diversification strategy).

$I(t)$ Total capital invested in the business in year t.

$i_1(t)$, $i_2(t)$, $i_3(t)$, $i_4(t)$ Investments made in σ_{ij} in year t from the four respective sources enumerated above.

$r(t)$ Prevailing interest rate for capital on the open market.

$k(t)$ Dividends paid out in year t.

Also let us make the following assumptions:

(a) That the diversification program may be spread over a period of time and that investments in diversification may be made yearly from time $t = 0$ up to t.
(b) That all four types of investment described on the preceding page may be made during this period.
(c) That if the company does not diversify, earnings of the company, in excess of paid out dividends, may be divided between additional investments in the company's prod-

uct-market line and investments in outside ventures.

(d) If the company diversifies, earnings in excess of dividends are all reinvested in the business either in the original product strategy σ_l or in the diversification strategy σ_{ij}.

To simplify notation, select a particular economic-political environment, a diversification strategy, and a specified sales volume so that Expression (1) becomes

$$P = h(I, S, E, \sigma) = h(I)$$

Let $P_0 = h_0(I)$ be profit earned by σ_l before diversification.

$P_1 = h_1(I)$ be profit earned by σ_l after diversification.

$P_2 = h_2(I)$ be profit earned by σ_{ij} after diversification.

Using this notation and the preceding assumptions we can write the *present value* of return on investment in the following form:

If the company does not diversify

$$R(t) = \frac{P(t)(1 + r)^{-(t+1)}}{I_p(t)}, \quad (2)$$

where $P(t)$ represents earnings for year t

$$P(t) = h_0 \left(I(t) - \sum_{\tau=0}^{t} i_1(\tau) \right) + r \sum_{\tau=0}^{t} i_1(\tau), \quad (3)$$

$I(t)$ is the total capital available to the business in year t

$$I(t) = I(0) + \sum_{\tau=1}^{t} P(\tau - 1)(1 - k(\tau)), \quad (3)$$

and $I_p(t)$ is the present value of the total capital which is in the business in year t

$$I_p(t) = I(0)$$
$$+ \sum_{\tau=1}^{t} P(\tau - 1)(1 - k(\tau))(1 + r)^{-\tau} \quad (3)$$

If the company does diversify, the present value of return on investment becomes

$$\bar{R}(t) = \frac{\bar{P}(t)(1 + r)^{-(t+1)}}{\bar{I}_p(t)}, \quad (4)$$

where $\bar{P}(t)$ represents earnings

$$\bar{P}(t) = h_1 \left(\bar{I}(t) - \sum_{\tau=0}^{t} \sum_{j=1}^{4} i_j(\tau) \right)$$
$$+ h_2 \left(\sum_{\tau=0}^{t} \sum_{j=1}^{4} i_j(\tau) \right) - r \sum_{\tau=0}^{t} i_2(\tau), \quad (5)$$

$\bar{I}(t)$ represents the capital

$$\bar{I}(t) = I(0)$$
$$+ \sum_{\tau=1}^{t} \bar{P}(\tau - 1)(1 - k(\tau))$$
$$+ \sum_{\tau=0}^{t} [i_2(\tau) + i_3(\tau)], \quad (5)$$

and

$$\bar{I}_p(t) = I(0)$$
$$+ \sum_{\tau=1}^{t} \bar{P}(\tau - 1)(1 - k(\tau))(1 + r)^{-\tau}$$
$$+ \sum_{\tau=0}^{t} [i_2(\tau) + i_3(\tau)](1 + r)^{-\tau} \quad (5)$$

Using (2) and (4) we obtain the improvement in return on investment in year t which can be brought about by diversification:

$$\Delta R(t) = \bar{R}(t) - R(t) \quad (6)$$

For a selected investment policy, $i_1(t)$, $i_2(t)$, $i_3(t)$ and $i_4(t)$ specified for $\tau = 0 \dots t$, ΔR can be computed

for each year for which forecasted data are available employing information normally provided in such forecasts.

The next step is to consider the return in investment in a time perspective. Completion of a diversification move by a company will normally span a period of time. During this period the return on investment should be expected to vary, and even drop temporarily below pre-diversification levels. In order to assess the full effect of diversification, it is, therefore, desirable to compute an average return over a period which includes the transition to diversifying operations and which extends as far as possible into the future beyond the transition.

In principle it would be desirable to measure the effects of diversification over an indefinite future (See, for example, Ref. 10). In practice this period will be measured by the time span for which long range forecasts are available.

Let N be a period which includes transition and for which forecasted data are available. Further, recall that ΔR was computed for a particular environment E and that usually several different forecasts will be available in order to take account of several probable environments. Let $E^1 \dots E^n \dots E^g$ be the environments considered by the company, each with an associated probability distribution $p^n(T)$ (See Sec. 3).

Then the expected average improvement in return to be derived from the diversified operations can be written in the form

$$(\Delta R)_e = \frac{1}{N} \sum_{n=1}^{g} \sum_{t=0}^{N} \sum_{\tau=t}^{N} \Delta R(E^n, \tau) p^n(\tau) \quad (7)$$

$(\Delta R)_e$ meets all of the conditions laid down for profit potential earlier in this section.

Recall that (7) is computed for a particular overall product-market strategy $\sigma_k = \sigma_l + \sigma_{ij}$, and that in the preceding section the totality of diversification possibilities was reduced to a set of such strategies, say $\{\sigma_k\}_m$.

The final step of selecting the preferred strategy through comparison of their respective prospect potentials can be stated as follows:

For a given increase in investment $\bar{I}_p - I(0)$ over a period from $t = 0$ to $t = N$ and investment policy $i_1(t)$, $i_2(t)$, $i_3(t)$, $i_4(t)$ for $t = 0 \cdots N$ specified for each σ_k, we can compute $(\Delta R(\sigma_k))_e$.

Recall that in Sec. 4 we stated long range sales objectives which require that certain minimum sales performance be shown for each E^n. Since (see Eq. 1 in this section) $(\Delta R)_e$ is a function of sales S, the long range sales objectives can be viewed as a constraint to be applied to $\Delta(R(\sigma_k))_e$.

Thus, the preferred overall company strategy σ_p is such that

$$[\Delta R(\sigma_p)]_e = \max_m (\Delta R(\sigma_k))_e \tag{8}$$

subject to the conditions that in the trend environment

$$\dot{S}_l(\sigma_k, E^1) - \dot{S}_l(\sigma_l, E^1) \geq \delta(t) \tag{9}$$

and for contingent environments E^n, $n = 2 \cdots g$, where g is the number of distinct environments considered in the forecast,

$$\frac{S_1(\sigma_1, E^1) - S_2(\sigma_1, E^n)}{S_1(\sigma_1, E^1)}$$

$$- \frac{S_1(\sigma_k, E^1) - S_2(\sigma_k, E^n)}{S_1(\sigma_k, E^1)}$$
$$\geq \rho^n(t) \tag{10}$$

10. INTERPRETATION OF RESULTS

The approach used above in arriving at the desirable diversification strategies is, of course, not rigorous in the mathematical sense of the word. The conceptual model is one of successive elimination of alternatives involving either application of qualitative criteria, or straightforward numerical comparisons. Mathematical notation has served more as a shorthand language than a tool of analysis. While straightforward, the required evaluations may involve some difficult practical problems, such as computation of capital investment or assignments of earnings to the respective members of the product line. Nevertheless, all of the required basic data are normally available in long range sales and financial forecasts.

The final numerical evaluation is recognizable as a form of the problem of allocation of resources under uncertainty. While expected value is used for the payoff function, the usual danger, implicit in the expected value approach, of unbalanced preparedness for alternative environments is anticipated through the requirement of a minimum performance level in each, as expressed in the sales objectives. Incidentally, since the sales objectives can be computed independently of $(\Delta R)_e$, they are not constraints in the usual sense of the word. They can be applied to the admissible set $\{\sigma_k\}_m$ before $(\Delta R)_e$ are computed. The method for providing against what we have called unforeseeable contingencies is not as satisfactory as it should be in view of the importance of this class of futures. A rationale and an accompanying quantitative evaluation are needed and these should be used to restate the problem of allocation of resources under uncertainty.

One of the reasons why a simplified approach was possible lies in the fact that we have dealt with only a half of the diversification problem. Our concern has been with what might be called *external* aspects of diversification. We have sought to select diversification strategies in the light of the probable economic-political environments and the long range goals of the company. We have not been concerned with the influence of the internal, organizational, and business characteristics of the company on the diversification decisions.

It happens that business performance of a company is determined both by external characteristics of the product-market strategy and internal fit between the strategy and business resources. The first of these factors is what we have called *profit potential* of the product-market strategy, the second is the *business fit* of the strategy with respect to the diversifying company. Profit potential measures potential earnings as a function of the economic-political environment, characteristics of the demand, and nature of the competition under the assumption that the diversifying company is capable of offering effective competition in the new product-market area.

Business fit tests the validity of this assumption. It is a measure of the company's ability to penetrate the new market. It is determined by the particular strengths and weaknesses which the company brings to the new venture, such as the capabilities and past experience in engineering, production, finance, and merchandising.

Business fit is only one of the important internal aspects of the diversification problem. Other aspects include organization for diversification, development of new product-market ideas, methods of corporate expansion, anti-merger legislation, problems of corporate control, etc. While the external aspects generally deal with the advantages to be derived from diversification, the internal aspects deal with assessment of costs and risks. The overall diversification problem is to balance these against one another.

Unfortunately, quantitative evaluation of internal aspects is even more difficult than for the external ones. Consequently, a usual approach to this part of the problem is to derive qualitative criteria which are added to those discussed in this paper.

An interesting discussion of the internal aspects can be found in Ref. 2 and Ref. 5. It is also the subject of forthcoming Ref. 9.

REFERENCES

1. J. Sayer Minas, "Formalism, Realism and Management Science," *Management Science* 3, 9–14 (1956).
2. Thomas A. Staudt, "Program for Product Diversification," *Harvard Business Review*, Nov.–Dec. 1954.
3. A. D. H. Kaplan, "Big Enterprise in a Competitive System," The Brookings Institution, Washington 6, D. C., 1954.

4. FEDERAL TRADE COMMISSION, "Report on Corporate Mergers and Acquisitions," Government Printing Office, Washington, D. C., May 1955.

5. CHARLES H. KLINE, "The Strategy of Product Policy," *Harvard Business Review*, July–August 1955.

6. DAVID BENDEL HERTZ, "Operations Research in Long-Range Diversification Planning," Special Report No. 17, Operations Research Applied (New Uses and Extensions), American Management Association, 1957.

7. CHARLES R. SCHWARTZ, "The Return-on-Investment Concept as a Tool for Decision Making," General Management Series AMA Pamphlet No. 183, American Management Association, New York, 1956. (42–61)

8. PETER F. DRUCKER, *The Practice of Management*. New York, Harper & Brothers, 1954.

9. H. IGOR ANSOFF, "An Action Program for Diversification," Lockheed Aircraft Corporation, Burbank, California, 1957.

10. JOHN BURR WILLIAMS, *The Theory of Investment Value*, Amsterdam: North-Holland Publishing Co., Printed in the Netherlands, First printing 1938, Second printing 1956.

11. AMA CONFERENCE HANDBOOK, *Mergers and Acquisitions: for Growth and Expansion*, Published for distribution at the AMA Special Finance Conference, October 31–November 2, 1956, Hotel Roosevelt, New York.

12. FINANCIAL MANAGEMENT SERIES No. 113, "Integration Policies and Problems in Mergers and Acquisitions," American Management Association, New York, 1957.

13. FINANCIAL MANAGEMENT SERIES No. 114, "Legal, Financial, and Tax Aspects of Mergers and Acquisitions," American Management Association, New York, 1957.

14. FINANCIAL MANAGEMENT SERIES No. 115, "A Case Study in Corporate Acquisition," American Management Association, New York, 1957.

15. W. F. ROCKWELL, JR., "Planned Diversification of Industrial Concerns," *Advanced Management*, May 1956.

16. W. E. HILL, *Planned Product Diversification*, William E. Hill Co., 660 Madison Ave., New York 21, N. Y.

17. WESLEY A. SONGER, "Organizing for Growth and Change," General Management Series AMA Pamphlet No. 171, American Management Association, New York.

18. HARRY R. LANGE, "Expansion Through Acquisition," Implementing Long-Range Company Planning, Stanford Research Institute, Menlo Park, Calif. (Speech given before Industrial Economics Conference, San Francisco, Jan. 21–22, 1957.)

►►►►►►►►►►►► THE STRATEGY OF PRODUCT POLICY

CHARLES H. KLINE*

T he first concern of most businessmen is the content of their product lines. No other problem of management affects profits more directly. Few problems require more constant attention from management.

Reprinted with permission from Harvard Business Review, *July–August 1955, pp. 91–100.*

Manager, Chemical Development Division, Climax Molybdenum Co.

Active executives make decisions almost every day that affect the product line in such matters as allocations of manpower, factory space, or sales effort. Frequently they must also decide major product questions—whether to undertake a new development project, to introduce a new product, or to eliminate an old one. Mistakes in any of these are usually costly, and may even be ruinous.

To help get better and faster decisions on problems of product-line content, executives in a number of manufacturing companies have developed formal product policies. These policies summarize the business characteristics which experience has shown successful products must have. In effect, each policy is a statement of long-range strategy that defines the means for a particular company to make the greatest over-all profits.

Experience has shown that a product policy serves these three main functions:

1. A product policy helps to provide the information required for decisions on the product line. It tells lower management and professional staffs of market analysts, research workers, and industrial engineers what top management needs to know. Furthermore, it provides a convenient framework around which this information can be organized.

2. Also, a product policy gives executives a supplementary check on the usual estimates of profit and loss. Even though modern techniques of market research, sales forecasting, and cost estimating are often surprisingly good, the data they provide are still only approximations.

It is often impossible to make any realistic financial estimates at all—for ex-

ample, at the start of a long-range research program. At other times available sales and profit data may not be significant. An unsatisfactory record for an existing product may reflect a basic mistake in product policy, but it may also be the result of poor organization, unsuitable sales and promotion, faulty design, or inadequate plant facilities.

An analysis in terms of a basic product policy shows up weak spots in the financial estimates and indicates imponderable factors that cannot easily be reduced to numbers.

3. Most important of all, a product policy guides and directs the activities of the whole organization toward a single goal. Only rarely are product decisions made solely by top executives. More often such decisions require the specialized knowledge of experts in many fields—research, development, engineering, manufacturing, marketing, law, finance, and even personnel.

The original idea for a new product may occur to an engineer at the laboratory bench, a copy writer in the advertising department, or a salesman in the field. Between the first concept and the final decision by top management to introduce the new product there comes a long series of investigations, analyses, research and development studies, pilot production runs, and marketing tests. This work is expensive and time-consuming, and it involves a great many people in the organization. To complete these indispensable steps as quickly and thoroughly as possible requires good teamwork and a clear idea of management's over-all policy.

A sound product policy, well prepared and well taught to all professional and supervisory employees, is thus an important tool for coordination and direction. It applies not only to those major decisions which are the ultimate responsibility of presidents and general managers but also to the many day-to-day decisions by which lower-level employees shape the course of a business.

ANALYZING RESOURCES

The first step in developing a product policy is to make a careful inventory of a company's resources along the lines suggested in Exhibit i. Every company is unique. As a result of its history, experience, and personnel it has certain strengths and certain weaknesses that distinguish it from other business organizations. The ideal product policy makes the best use of a company's strong points and avoids its weak points.

In this sense every business enterprise is specialized, so that it is best suited to perform only certain services or to produce only certain types of product. The product lines of many large and successful corporations are so extremely varied that this point is often missed. One well-known company makes everything from light bulbs to jet engines, and another has a product line ranging from flashlight batteries to synthetic fibers. Although at first glance it may seem difficult to relate such diverse products to a single product policy, closer analysis shows that they all have in common certain strategic business characteristics which are related to company resources.

DEVELOPING THE POLICY

It is these business characteristics that make up the elements of product

EXHIBIT I

INVENTORY OF COMPANY RESOURCES

Financial strength	Money available or obtainable for financing research and development, plant construction, inventory, receivables, working capital, and operating losses in the early stages of commercial operation.
Raw material reserves	Ownership of, or preferential access to, natural resources such as minerals and ores, brine deposits, natural gas, forests.
Physical plant	Manufacturing plant, research and testing facilities, warehouses, branch offices, trucks, tankers, etc.
Location	Situation of plant or other physical facilities with relation to markets, raw materials, or utilities.
Patents	Ownership or control of a technical monopoly through patents.
Public acceptance	Brand preference, market contracts, and other public support built up by successful performance in the past.
Specialized experience	Unique or uncommon knowledge of manufacturing, distribution, scientific fields, or managerial techniques.
Personnel	Payroll of skilled labor, salesmen, engineers, or other workers with definite specialized abilities.
Management	Professional skill, experience, ambition, and will for growth of the company's leadership.

policy. Individually they are all well known. Every business executive deals with one or another of them daily. But in developing a product policy he must look at all these strategic points together. Let us see how they fit into an over-all policy.

FINANCIAL STRENGTH

In many respects the most important characteristic of any business is the investment required to enter it. This investment includes the land, buildings, and equipment needed for the business; the required inventories of raw material, work in process, and finished stock; and the funds necessary to carry accounts receivable and provide cash for working capital.

These components of the total investment are all related to the volume of sales. Investment in inventories, receivables, and cash varies almost directly with sales. Even the investment in such fixed assets as land, buildings, and equipment must be scaled to the volume of product to be sold. Thus a given operation may require a high capital investment merely because the volume of sales will be large. Many merchandising ventures are of this type.

In manufacturing industries, however, capital requirements usually depend on process economics. Some products inherently require manufacture on a larger scale than others. EXHIBIT II compares the size of plant, as measured by the number of employees, in four types of establishment in the chemical process industries. As the exhibit shows, synthetic rubber and synthetic fiber plants are always large,

soya oil mills are usually of moderate size, and plants producing cleaning and polishing compounds are generally small. The typical synthetic fiber plant has a thousand times more employees than the typical cleaning and polishing compound plant. The difference in fixed plant investment is probably much greater.

Small companies with limited financial resources are restricted to businesses that require a relatively low investment. On the other hand, large and wealthy corporations have the choice of entering either high-investment or low-investment businesses—though experience has shown that such companies are most successful (indeed, sometimes only successful) in high-investment businesses, where large-scale operations do give them a competitive advantage.

In these connections, the observation made by Crawford H. Greenewalt, president of Du Pont, is significant:

There is much misconception also about the relationship between big and little businesses. . . . No little business could compete with us in nylon for the reason that no such business could bring together the capital and technical resources required for an efficient producing unit. We, on the other hand, have no interest in competing in spheres where we can make no substantial technical contribution, and there are many activities, particularly in the fields of marketing and distribution, that small businesses can do better than we. . . .

Let me cite an example. We make nylon yarn and sell it to whoever will buy. Your wife buys, let us say, a nylon blouse. Between the sale of that yarn and that blouse are the throwster who twists

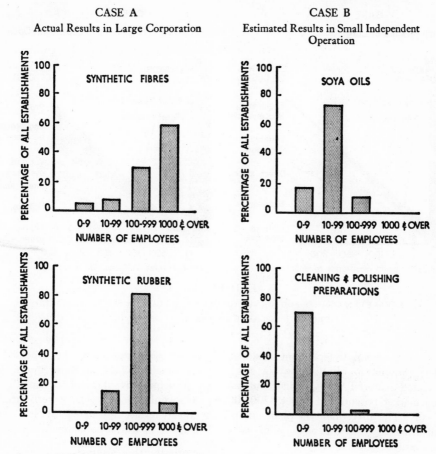

CASE A
Actual Results in Large Corporation

CASE B
Estimated Results in Small Independent Operation

Source: U.S. Census of Manufactures, 1947

EXHIBIT II

SIZE OF MANUFACTURING ESTABLISHMENTS FOR VARIOUS PRODUCTS

the yarn, the weaver who weaves it, the finisher who finishes and dyes it, the cutter who makes the garment, and the retail store that sells it. For the most part these are small businesses.[1]

As a general rule, the smallest economic unit that has the facilities to undertake a given operation performs

[1] From a speech reported in *Chemical and Engineering News,* October 10, 1949, p. 2896.

it most efficiently. That is why, when large companies enter low-investment businesses, they very often run into difficulties. To illustrate:

The breakeven charts shown in Ex-HIBIT III summarize the findings of a cost analysis of the manufacture and sale of a specialty product under two sets of conditions: (a) actual operating results in one of the largest corporations in the United States; and (b) the estimated

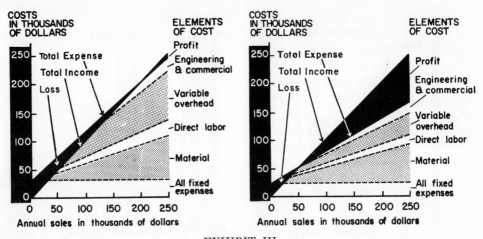

EXHIBIT III

BREAKEVEN CHARTS FOR MANUFACTURE OF SPECIALTY SEMIFABRICATED
PRODUCT IN LARGE AND SMALL COMPANIES

results in a small independent business.

The product in question was a semifabricated material with a small but assured market potential of about $200,000 annually. The investment in plant equipment necessary for this volume of sales was about $25,000.

As the left-hand chart shows, the large corporation needed a sales volume of $216,000 per year to break even on this product. The small company, however, could make money anywhere above the breakeven point of $55,000 in annual sales shown in the right-hand chart. At the breakeven volume of $216,000 for the large company, the small company would net $72,000 before taxes.

Comparison of the two charts shows that the lower costs in the small company would come partly from lower fixed charges, raw material and direct-labor costs, and commercial, administrative, and engineering expenses. An operating manager primarily concerned with this one product could reasonably be expected to make small savings in these items. But the principal advantage of the small company would be its far lower variable overhead costs, estimated at less than half those of the large company.

Actually this analysis was made by the large corporation after several years of poor operating results. When this cost study became available, the product was dropped.

SALES VOLUME

The financial strength of a company also influences the desirable level of sales for its products. A large volume of sales requires a large investment. For the reasons already mentioned, large companies are generally most successful in products with a large annual volume of sales, and small companies in low-volume specialty items. However, the acceptable range in dollars will obviously vary from one type of business to another.

Sales volume depends partly on the number of potential applications of a product, the number of potential customers, and the size of the area in which it will be distributed. These factors also determine the degree of stability in the sales volume. A product with only one application and relatively few customers is liable to sudden obsolescence and violent fluctuations in sales. Therefore most large companies seek products with broad markets and avoid items salable only to one or two customers, the government, or the armed forces. The small company can sometimes afford to take more chances, for it has more flexibility to turn around and adjust to changing circumstances.

DISTRIBUTION CHANNELS

Channels of distribution consist largely of intangibles. There may be some investment in warehouses, trucks, and offices, but these facilities may also be rented. In any case the fixed investment is generally small. Perhaps for this reason business executives sometimes overrate the flexibility of their distribution channels.

Engineers and production men are particularly apt to assume that a salesforce can always handle "just one more" product, regardless of its market. Even sales managers sometimes say that a product will "sell itself" or "take no effort." As a result, one of the commonest problems in business today is that of the single salesforce trying to cover too many markets.

Professor Melvin T. Copeland summarizes the problem this way:

Early in my research work in the field of marketing, I found that when a company was catering to two different markets, such as the consumer market and the industrial market, for example, better results typically were secured by segregating the salesforce into two groups, one for each type of market. It appeared that ordinarily a salesman could not be continually shifting back and forth between different types of buyers without having his effectiveness materially impaired. The buying habits and the buying motives of the two types of buyers were so different as to involve difficult mental shifts by the salesman. . . .[2]

Any new product has a great advantage when it can be sold to the same consuming groups as existing products. The new product benefits from the company's accumulated knowledge of the markets, close relationships with customers, and public acceptance which the salesforce has built up over the years.

On the other hand, a new product is at some disadvantage when it must be sold in entirely new markets. In this case the company must build entirely new distribution channels for the product. Sales executives must develop new sales and promotional concepts, hire and train a new salesforce, perhaps select new distributors, and ultimately win new customers. These steps are costly and time-consuming, and they may prove a steady drain on executive effort that could be better spent elsewhere.

[2] Melvin T. Copeland, *The Executive at Work* (Cambridge, Harvard University Press, 1951), p. 85.

Accordingly a product intended for an entirely new market should generally have other advantages strong enough to justify the risks involved in distribution.

EFFECT ON PRESENT PRODUCTS

A going concern cannot forget the products which are already earning assets.

Ideally every addition to the line should improve the profitability of present products. When a company such as Westinghouse develops a new electrical appliance, it increases the over-all demand for electricity and thus increases the market for its turbines, generators, transformers, and other power equipment.

Unfortunately, situations of this sort are rather rare. For practical purposes a proposed new product will be satisfactory as long as it does not hurt the sale of present products. Of course, the situation is different when a new product makes an old one obsolete. It is obviously better for a company to replace its own products than to let a competitor do so.

COMPETITION

In entering a new market a company should usually have some advantage over present and potential competitors in the field. At the least it should have no disadvantage.

The number and type of competitors a company will have to face in a new business generally depend on the capital investment required to enter the business. Where the investment is high, the number of competitors is fairly small, but they are usually strong, well entrenched, and difficult to dislodge.

On the other hand, where the investment is low, there may be so many small, relatively weak companies in the field that poor pricing practices prevent any one from making a reasonable profit.

Executives in some companies with national distribution make it a policy not to enter any new market unless they believe they have enough advantages over competition to capture at least 20% of the market on a sound pricing basis.

CYCLICAL STABILITY

Steady, nonseasonal demand is nearly always desirable in a product. It is desirable also to have a product that is relatively independent of fluctuations in the business cycle.

Capital goods and some consumer durable goods are particularly vulnerable to periods of depression. Some companies in these fields lay special stress on new products that go into consumer nondurable markets. These products include not only items sold to the ultimate consumer, such as paints, drugs, lubricants, or antifreeze, but also industrial materials sold to fabricators or processors of consumer goods—for example, tetraethyl lead to gasoline refiners or tin cans to food packers.

RESEARCH AND PATENTS

Research brings profitable new products and leads to strong patent positions. It can also be very expensive. Products which offer the opportunity for important technical achievement are generally most attractive to financially strong companies, especially those which already have large research staffs as corporate resources. Smaller companies tend to avoid businesses requiring much development. Many small companies operate in highly technical fields, but these are usually rather specialized.

The attitude toward research and development also varies from one company to another on purely strategic grounds, regardless of size. Some companies specialize in very technical products. They carry on as much research as they can afford, continually seek out new technical fields for development, and even abandon older products that have reached a fairly stable technology and are no longer protected by patents. Joel Dean describes one such company in these terms:

It is a fairly conscious policy of one of the large chemical companies to choose only those new products that have been developed by its product research organization and that are distinctive enough in both chemical and manufacturing requirements to be protected for some time to come. The counterpart of this policy is to abandon products when they have degenerated to the status of commonly produced commodities. The company advances to new monopoly positions as fast as economic progress wears down the walls of the old.[3]

In a company like the one just described any product that does not offer much opportunity for technical advances is not very attractive.

On the other hand, some companies concentrate on making old or relatively nontechnical products better and cheaper than any one else. Here the

[3] Joel Dean, *Managerial Economics* (New York, Prentice-Hall, Inc., 1951), p. 130.

emphasis is usually on expert low-cost production or aggressive merchandising. The company resources are primarily the production or sales staff, and the need for much research is an unfavorable factor.

RAW MATERIALS

In the event a company owns or controls a source of raw material, it has a resource which it should obviously use whenever possible. However, most companies must buy all or the greater part of their raw materials. These preferably should be basic commodities that are readily available in constant supply from several sources. They should also be free of any restrictive competitive control. Any raw material available from only one source is vulnerable to interruption by strikes, fires, bankruptcy, or other disasters— and even, on occasion, to the supplier's flat refusal to sell.

Distant and unreliable sources are also dangerous. For example:

One large company is a heavy consumer of Indian mica. Because of unsettled conditions in India and throughout the world, this company always keeps a protective inventory of about one year's supply. Since the total expense of maintaining an inventory for a year (including interest, taxes, insurance, warehousing, and losses) is about 20% to 25% of its cost, this company pays a heavy penalty for its unavoidable dependence on an unreliable source.

Freedom from competitive control is especially important for raw materials used in large quantities. Thus:

After World War II several chemical companies developed methods for polymerizing styrene to polystyrene. After spending considerable sums on technical developments, the companies all eventually abandoned these projects. Executives realized that they would have to buy styrene from the basic producers, who also made and sold polystyrene. As converters of a material under the control of competitors, they would be at the mercy of more integrated companies both as to supply and in regard to the relative price level of the two materials.

VALUE ADDED

The fate of those styrene projects calls attention to the strategic value of highly integrated businesses. The best measure of integration is the value added by manufacture — that is, the spread between the cost of raw materials and the total cost of making the product, expressed as a percentage of total cost. Where distribution costs are high, the value added by manufacture and distribution is a more appropriate measure.

A high value added means that the product demands a high plant investment or considerable expense in engineering, labor, or supplies. These requirements give producers greater scope for improving efficiency, reducing costs, and developing a superior product. Furthermore, all these factors represent capital requirements. For this reason a high value added by manufacture is usually more desirable for the large company and less important for the small one.

MANUFACTURING LOAD

In many types of manufacturing, executives have some freedom of choice in deciding whether to produce standard products that can be sold from stock or custom products made to the individual customer's order. Standard products sold in large volume can be made most economically with equipment specially designed for mass production. The heavy capital investment and high volume of sales make such products particularly suitable for large companies.

On the other hand, the smaller company with limited capital may find it more profitable to make custom products or to supply standard products in a larger number of grades, sizes, and finishes. This type of manufacture substitutes labor for expensive and inflexible plant equipment. Operating costs are higher but can sometimes be offset by higher prices. Furthermore, since the investment is smaller, lower margins may still give a satisfactory return.

The job-shop processing of industrial goods—for example, custom molding of plastics—is an example of diversified manufacturing load where the small company has a great advantage over the large. The production of fashion goods is another. Professor Copeland describes this situation:

From an administrative standpoint, style merchandising calls for rapid adjustment to continual and frequent changes in demand. Designing, purchasing, production, pricing, and sales have to be adjusted quickly to each change in a volatile market, and the various activities are so closely interdependent that they must all be adjusted almost simultaneously. Under these circumstances the activities of an enterprise manufacturing style merchandise are not sufficiently standardized or stable to permit the delegation of such decision-making to lieutenants. Hence, the small manufacturer who can constantly feel the pulse of the market and who can transmit his instructions directly and immediately to the operating forces is in a strategic competitive position. In such an industry the advantages of quick decision-making and speedy transmittal of decisions to operatives more than offset the economies which might otherwise be gained from large-scale manufacture.[4]

STATING THE POLICY

Even this brief review shows that different companies may take diametri-

[4] *Op. cit.*, p. 149.

cally opposite positions on each of a dozen or more points of product strategy. The contrast in over-all policy between two hypothetical companies is illustrated in EXHIBIT IV. Both companies are assumed to be manufacturers of synthetic organic chemicals and similar in all respects except one —size. In size they are assumed to differ by a factor of 1,000 as measured by their net worths. As the exhibit shows, this one difference is reflected in almost every aspect of their product policies.

EXHIBIT IV

EXAMPLES OF PRODUCT STRATEGY IN LARGE AND SMALL COMPANIES

Product Requirements	*Company A* Net Worth $500,000,000	*Company B* Net Worth $500,000
Capital investment	High	Low
Sales volume	Large volume	Small volume
	Mass markets	Specialized markets
	Many applications	Many to few applications
	National distribution	Local or specialized distribution
Similarity to present distribution channels	High to moderate	High
Effect on going products	Good to fair	Good
Competition	Relatively few companies	Few to many companies
	Sound pricing	Sound pricing
	Good possibility of securing a large percentage of the market	Desirable market position variable
Cyclical stability	High	High
Technical opportunity	Great	Moderate to small
Patent protection	Great	Great to none
Raw materials	Basic materials	Intermediate or basic materials
	Many suppliers	Many to few suppliers
Manufacturing load	Standard products	Standard or custom products
	Mass production	Specialized production
	Few grades and sizes	Few to many grades or sizes
Value added	High	High to moderate

In practice the differences between companies are never so simple and pronounced. Consequently the differences between product policies are often more elusive, though nonetheless real.

Whatever policy is adopted, it must generally be reduced to written form if executives and employees are to use it throughout a company. The statement of policy may be a series of short definitions, as in these excerpts paraphrased from the instructions of a large manufacturer of industrial goods:

1. *Sales volume*: Each product line should have a large potential volume of sales. It should be useful in a number of different applications and salable to a large number of customers. . . .

4. *Patent protection*: Each line should be well protected by patents arising from the company's own discoveries or acquired by purchase or other means. . . .

EXHIBIT V

EXAMPLES OF SUMMARY PRODUCT APPRAISALS BY A LARGE MATERIALS PROCESSOR

Case A: A Generally Favorable Pattern

	Rating				
	Very good	Good	Fair	Poor	Very poor
Sales volume	x				
Type and number of competitors	x				
Technical opportunity	x				
Patent protection		x			
Raw materials		x			
Production load		x			
Value added		x			
Similarity to major business				x	
Effect on present products			x		

Case B: A Generally Unfavorable Pattern

	Rating				
	Very good	Good	Fair	Poor	Very poor
Sales volume	x				
Type and number of competitors					x
Technical opportunity				x	
Patent protection					x
Raw materials		x			
Production load			x		
Value added		x			
Similarity to major business	x				
Effect on present products	x				

9. *Effect on present products*: Each line should improve the company's over-all sales and profit position. It should preferably help to promote the sale of the company's other products. If, however, it would hinder the sale of other company products, it should have a greater potential long-range profit than the products in conflict with it.

The statement may also be written up as a series of questions arranged as a check list. The following excerpts are paraphrased from such a statement developed by a well-known manufacturer of consumer goods, whose strategy was "to serve the market for non-durable household goods bought by large numbers of families with a fairly high frequency of purchase":

1. *Customer advantage*: Does the proposed product offer the customer an advantage?

  a. Is it superior to competition in a major property?
  b. If equal to competitive products in use properties, can it be sold profitably at a lower price?

2. *Mass market*: Is there a mass market for the product? . . .

6. *Stability*: Will the product be free of undue breakage or deterioration from normal handling in distribution? . . .

8. *Permissibility*: Will the product conform to applicable government regulations?

To summarize the appraisal of actual products against the product policy, one large materials processor supplements the formal statement with a simple check form. EXHIBIT V shows this company's summary appraisals of two proposed new businesses. In Case A, although the proposed business was quite different from the company's present lines, it did represent a favorable over-all pattern. In Case B, on the other hand, the over-all pattern was poor even though there were several favorable points, such as a general similarity to the present operations. The company in question developed Case A into a major new business but did not consider Case B further.

APPLYING THE POLICY

A product policy is especially helpful as a supplement and check on the usual estimates of profitability in three types of product activity: (a) development of new products; (b) vertical integration in manufacturing; and (c) elimination of old products.

NEW PRODUCTS

Research and development programs usually proceed stepwise, and in a completed project executives must make at least four major decisions:

1. To undertake preliminary exploratory research, either technical or commercial.
2. To launch a full-scale development program.
3. To build a pilot plant and conduct pilot market tests.
4. To build a commercial plant and put the product on the market.

If the development does not satisfactorily meet the requirements of the company's over-all product policy at each of these check points, it should be dropped or seriously changed.

Of course, at the start of an exploratory research program there will not be enough information for a complete analysis of the project. An important part of the development will be to obtain the needed information through marketing research, product research, and engineering studies. Nevertheless, early analysis of the information that is available can help prevent such wasted projects as those on the conversion of styrene already mentioned.

Executives can ensure proper consideration of product policy in development work by requiring a brief analysis of each project whenever they must authorize major operating expenditures. One company that controls research and development work by formal "development authorizations" has incorporated such an analysis in its standard authorization form. Despite some initial protests from the research department, the system has worked well for several years now.

INTEGRATION

Should a company make or buy a component part or raw material? Captive production gives certainty of supply, control of quality, and the possibility of substantial cost savings. It may also divert capital from more profitable end products and lead a company into unrelated fields in which it cannot operate efficiently. Furthermore a captive production unit lacks the spur of competition. It may produce only at high cost and lag behind in technological development.[5]

Analysis in terms of a company's product policy helps to indicate these dangers. In general, a company should produce its own parts or materials only when all three of these conditions are met:

[5] See Carter C. Higgins, "Make-or-Buy Reexamined," HBR March–April 1955, p. 109. —*The Editors.*

1. The raw material considered as a product by itself meets the requirements of the company's product strategy.

2. Internal consumption is large relative to the output of a plant of economic size—say, over 50%. (Otherwise the company is adding a new product, not primarily integrating.)

3. Production will give substantial savings—or profits, if the material is to be sold externally as well.

Somewhat similar considerations apply when a company decides whether to sell an intermediate product or to process it further toward the form in which it will finally be used. Each additional step in manufacture eliminates the cost of intermediate distribution, increases the value added by manufacture, and adds to total profits. However, further processing can also lead a company into fields where it cannot function as efficiently as its customers.

Here again an analysis in terms of product policy is useful. As a general rule, further processing is justified only when all three of these requirements are satisfied:

1. The new end product resulting from further processing meets the requirements of the company's product strategy.

2. The cost of the present product is large relative to the total cost of the new end product—say, over 50%.

3. The new processing step will improve the profitability of the over-all operation.

OLD PRODUCTS

The analysis of unsatisfactory products already made and sold is a less common but widely needed application of product policy. Some executives periodically review all product lines to eliminate obsolescent items and to prevent the diversion of effort on low-volume, relatively unprofitable products. For example:

After such a survey one company with annual sales of $40,000,000 eliminated sixteen different products with a total volume of $3,300,000. It also made a number of improvements in methods of handling the products retained.

Over the next three years the company's total sales increased by one-half and its profits by some twenty times. Among the many factors contributing to these spectacular increases, top executives have stated that dropping unsatisfactory products was one of the most important.

BUILDING FOR THE FUTURE

Besides helping the executive himself make better decisions on product questions such as those just discussed, a good product policy helps to build teamwork throughout the organization. If soundly conceived, clearly stated, and thoroughly understood by all supervisory and professional employees, the policy can be an important tool for control and coordination.

Finally, this approach to product strategy can also have a very dynamic effect in shaping the future development of a company. There is no need to take the present weaknesses for granted. If different resources and a different product strategy show greater promise for the future, then the analysis will indicate where the company must change and strengthen itself. On this basis management can take the constructive steps that are needed.

▶▶▶▶▶▶▶▶▶▶▶ DIVERSIFICATION: *watch the pitfalls*

R. W. DALZELL*

The road to product diversification can be rocky or smooth. But it's seldom easy.

And the pot at the end of the rainbow can hold ashes as well as gold. On the record, there have been more failures than successes in this business of introducing new products.

Success or failure can hinge on how many soul-searching questions the diversification bound company asks itself —and how many honest answers it comes up with.

NO CURE-ALL

The company that plunges in without a close look at all angles is like the fellow who tries to break the bank at Monte Carlo. The results are more likely to be disastrous than rewarding.

First thing to ask yourself is whether diversification is the only answer to your problem. It could be that the time, effort, and money would be better spent shoring up weaknesses in your present business area. Remember that diversification is no cure for manage-

Reprinted with permission from The Iron Age, *August 16, 1956, pp. 22–26.*

Business Research Group, Arthur D. Little, Inc.

ment shortcomings. It's more likely to aggravate the disease by generating new management challenges.

And don't be ashamed to back away if the proposition is not so rosy after close inspection as it looked at first glance. Too many times, managements have decided to enter a new business to justify the time and money spent on a program. Usually, these ventures lead to unhappy consequences.

Here are two basic areas you should look into before a new product is taken into the family:

1. What are the general objectives of your business as a whole? Do management and stockholders want to continue it on a long-term basis? Is capital buildup or current return more important to the owners? Are the stockholders in a mood to take on more of a risk than that involved in the existing business? Are there any operating characteristics of the business, such as seasonality, which should be remedied for the long-range good of the business?

These fundamental, long-term objectives should be clearly defined by management, of course, for general business planning. But it's particularly important that they be agreed upon before considering a new business venture.

2. Make sure you're doing as well as you should in your present business before shouldering new problems.

HOW TO DO IT

If answers to the foregoing questions don't rule out diversification, here's how to go about it:

The first step is to take stock of your corporate strengths—and weaknesses. These resources may be human or physical and include such factors as acceptance in specific markets, established distribution channels, design and engineering skills, plant facilities, natural resources, highly skilled management in a given business area, and many others.

In our experience, we have found that management, technical skills, distribution channels, and market acceptance are generally the most important resources.

Production facilities and know-how, particularly in the metal-working industry—are a resource. But diversification based on production resources alone is usually risky because of the highly competitive situation in most areas of metal fabricating.

STRENGTH VERSUS WEAKNESS

Production-oriented companies, particularly those whose operations have been concentrated in contract manufacturing, many times prefer to diversify by buying a going business. In this way they obtain ready-made sales organizations, market acceptance, product design skills, and the like.

It is just as important to assess weaknesses as it is to recognize strengths. Frank recognition of deficient areas, such as lack of merchandising or product engineering skills, need not lead to a negative decision regarding diversification. However, it can lead to a program geared to overcome them.

In adding up strengths and weaknesses the management group might well consider one more factor: It should determine whether there is any type of business even remotely related to the current one which it finds interesting and stimulating. This human interest factor has been a prime contributor to success in several company diversification programs. Of course, no matter how much enthusiasm is generated by this approach, the new venture should still make business sense.

PRODUCT GUIDEPOSTS

After you've found out where your strengths and weaknesses lie, your second step is to formulate a set of rules for a new product or line. Such yardsticks are invaluable both in directing product search and in evaluating opportunities. From a practical standpoint, you can't expect to find a product that will satisfy all your requirements. So it helps to separate the requirements in at least two groups, say, major and desirable. Products under consideration can then be judged on the basis of these yardsticks.

Once you've set up the yardsticks, the third step is to find a line or product to fit them. The new line or product can originate from one of three general sources (1) internal development, (2) product acquisition or (3) taking over a going business. But regardless of where they originate, new product areas should be screened and the possible range narrowed by exploratory research and evaluation with respect to product requirements. This process then should be carried on to a finer degree, identifying, exploring, and evaluating specific product lines within a chosen area.

It's possible that after a close look,

changes in certain standards, or the addition of others, will be justified. It is not too important that the original product rules first be strictly followed. But it is important to have and to use a set of standards which will provide objective guides for each major decision to be made. It's easy to become too enthusiastic over a product or company on its own merits and to overlook the fundamentals of diversification.

NARROWING FIELD

There are a number of tools available for use in product research. Probably the broadest is the Standard Industrial Classification Manual, published by the Executive Office of the President,

---

THREE WAYS TO ACQUIRE A PRODUCT

1. Internal Development: Internal development of a product and of the business organization needed to promote it is generally a high risk situation—unless it is related closely to existing management, design, engineering, and marketing skills and facilities. Employment of one or several key persons with extensive experience in the proposed new field makes the job easier.

2. Product Acquisition: Acquiring a license or other rights on a product available for manufacture and sale. This can some times provide a short-cut, particularly from a product design standpoint. However, in most instances it still requires substantial engineering, tooling, and market development investment.

3. Taking Over a Going Business: If the company is adequately evaluated and is operating at a reasonable profit in relation to contemplated investment, this course probably involves the least risk of any diversification method.

Bureau of the Budget, and obtainable from the Superintendent of Documents, U. S. Government Printing Office, Washington 25, D. C., at a cost of $1.25. This is a complete list of major classifications and types of manufactured products that are produced and marketed in the United States. It may well suggest fields which ordinarily would not come to attention.

For more directed search, directories and encyclopedias for many specific industries are available which furnish specific details on products and companies in, or serving, these fields. Trade magazines also provide information on new products and businesses, some of which are frequently available to a company with financial and other resources.

Once product search has been narrowed to a fairly specific product or market situation, discussions with distributors or even major users regarding their experience and needs are generally profitable.

Of particular interest to metal-working firms, a number of the basic metals producers, both ferrous and nonferrous, make available to potential customers the services of their market development departments.

DIVERSIFICATION PITFALLS

There have been more failures than successes in introducing new products. The major reasons for failures are:

Inadequate knowledge of markets and buying habits.

Inability to finance an adequate development program, particularly for market development. Market development costs often exceed those of development engineering, and facility additions or modifications.

Lack of appreciation of the market acceptance and general resources of competition—particularly where one or two companies control a given market. It is generally more difficult to enter a market dominated by relatively few companies.

Nonprofessional approach in management, design, and marketing. Many times, a highly qualified management and organization in its own field has failed in a new business area, simply because of lack of experience and/or adaptability in another type of business. For example, it is difficult for a firm in a field of highly engineered industrial products to utilize the same management philosophy, engineering skills, marketing approach, or manufacturing facility to serve even its current markets with a low-cost, volume-produced product.

HOW TO GET A DIVERSIFICATION PROGRAM OFF THE GROUND

Corporate Objectives—

Success or failure of a new product depends to a great extent on the amount of planning which precedes it. Before a specific product is even considered the company should first outline its corporate objectives, analyze its strengths and weaknesses and set up yardsticks for judging proposed new products.

Here is a step-by-step example of how a typical metalworking firm might go about it—pointing out the type of information needed to make a sound evaluation of a new business situation:

WHAT THE COMPANY WANTS TO DO

1. Maintain current operations at $10 to $12 million annual level, manufacturing heavy appliance components and plated novelty items for automobile supply jobber distribution.

2. Broaden the company's product line to reduce its present dependence on five contract customers for 50 pct of sales, and on automotive novelty items, which depend on fad acceptance, for 30 pct of total sales.

3. Develop or acquire a proprietary product line to enable the company to control its own markets and to reduce its dependence on contract manufacturing and private brand customers.

4. Invest surplus working capital, amounting to approximately $1.5 million, in business expansion to realize a minimum on investment of 20 pct before taxes.

5. Maintain an annual dividend rate of at least $5 per share to provide adequate income to beneficiaries of family trusts controlling 35 pct of outstanding stock.

6. Look forward to creating a public market for the company's stock to provide the family trusts as well as present equity management or its heirs with a greater degree of investment liquidity.

7. Retain equity management and family trust ownership of at least 51 pct of outstanding common stock. Since these interests now own 60,000 shares, or 80 pct of the 75,000 shares issued and outstanding, this would permit issuance of approximately 40,000 additional shares valued at $80 per share, or $3.2 million on a current book basis. This newly issued stock could be applied toward financing a sound diversification opportunity.

8. Provide over the long term a sound income-producing investment for family interests.

9. Assure present junior management members an opportunity for creating a satisfactory career in the business.

Once it has been decided that a diversification program will not conflict with long-range objectives, the company then must determine if it can successfully undertake a new line or product. This calls for a frank appraisal of company strengths and weaknesses.

STRONG POINTS

1. An aggressive and seasoned senior management team consisting of the president, vice president in charge of sales, treasurer, and vice president in charge of operations. All are between 50 and 55 years of age and are vitally interested in continuing their full-time management responsibilities.

2. Extensive metal forming and finishing skills and facilities including extrusion, die-casting, stamping, mechanical surface treatment, chrome plating, anodizing, enameling, and associated operations for the fabrication and finishing of ornamental metal products.

3. Excellent production management throughout the plant, including tool design, production scheduling and inventory controls, quality control, and cost accounting. The company is believed to have the lowest shop costs and rejection rate in the sharply competitive industry in which it operates.

4. High quality labor force, of approximately 500 people, which could be increased by 50 pct through drawing from the local area. Employee-management relations have been ex-

ORGANIZING A DEVELOPMENT PROGRAM

If you've decided to develop a new product internally, a development program, timetable, and budget should be set up before any major steps are taken. Here's what it should include.

1. Define the product in terms of function, price, services, and other matters of interest to the distributor and user.

2. Determine by market research: a. distributive and consumer acceptance, b. market potential, c. requirement for, and availability of distribution channels, d. pricing, discount, and financing practices, e. competitive structure and activity, f. long-term market trends, g. design and engineering features to maximize acceptance.

3. Complete design and produce prototype models.

4. Make final market tests.

5. Complete production engineering and prepare facilities.

6. Set up market development and distribution program: a. sales organization, b. advertising and sales promotion, c. other sales support, e.g. technical service.

7. Project investment, earnings, and cash flow over a three to five-year period.

cellent, with no strikes or slowdowns over the last ten years.

5. A high degree of acceptance as a source by major appliance manufacturers and by the automotive jobbing trade.

6. Through close association with the design groups of appliance manufacturers, a sense of styling of ornamental trim and hardware.

7. A centrally located, expandable plant location in a relatively favorable labor area (average plant wage $1.65 plus 12 fringe benefits) with approximately 35 pct of U. S. and industrial consumer markets within a 500-mile radius.

8. Some consumer acceptance as a producer of high quality automotive novelties, particularly in the male, 16-25-year-age group.

WEAK POINTS

1. Lack of an organized technical research activity. A metallurgist and a chemist, both of whom were employed approximately three years ago to develop new processes and products, have been totally absorbed with trouble-shooting problems in the plant.

2. Senior management pre-occupation with day-to-day duties. It is believed that much of this work could be delegated to more junior people in the organization over a 1- to 2-year period, thus freeing management for broader assignments.

3. A board of directors that provides management with little stimulation or outside viewpoint. It is comprised of the senior management group and two trustees representing other family interests.

4. A narrow sales organization comprised of a vice president in charge of sales and two sales engineers servicing the appliance accounts, and a sales manager and three field representatives servicing the chains and the automotive jobbing trade.

Knowing where its strong points lie, the company is now ready to form opinions on the type of product best fitted to its present operations. Realizing that no one product is ideal, it breaks product requirements into major and desirable needs.

MAJOR NEEDS

1. The new business should involve a proprietary product, or one which can be merchandised to the user as a finished unit bearing the company's own brand.

2. Required investment should range between $2 and $4.5 million and produce earnings of at least 20 pct before U. S. income taxes. The minimum limit is based on the company's requirement for a fairly substantial product line in relation to existing business potentials, and the maximum on cash and newly issued stock available for investment.

3. The new product line should have growth potential, both in respect to the total market and the company's participation.

4. The product line should be developed both from a technical and a market standpoint. It should not require a substantial pioneering effort by the company nor should operating losses be anticipated through a development period.

5. Diversification should probably be accomplished through acquisition of a going business with particular emphasis on securing product management, sales organization, product design and engineering, and research and development skills.

6. The product line should provide a basis for future expansion of the business through diversification.

7. The product should be such that "garage-shop" competition would be

SIZING UP A GOING BUSINESS

If you're thinking of buying a going business, examine it thoroughly before committing yourself. Here are three important steps.

1. An accountant should verify assets, liabilities, and earnings records.

2. Legal examination of indentures, corporate charters, stock restrictions, executive compensation contracts, and other pertinent legal documents related to assets, liabilities, and corporate equity rights and obligations.

3. An operational analysis to study those segments of business that will contribute in a major way to future profits. The following situations should be analyzed: management, market potential and trends, product strength, engineering evaluation, user and distributive acceptance, distribution, research and development, patent position, manufacturing, competition.

limited by substantial investment requirements.

8. The product may be either for use in industrial, commercial, or consumer markets. However, it is desirable that the market be comprised of a substantial number of customers, so that the loss of one or several would not materially affect the total picture.

9. The product line should capitalize on the company's knowledge of mass production of small and medium-sized metal forms, and their decorative finishing.

10. Research and development requirements for the new product line should be such that the same metallurgical, chemical, and mechanical

group could provide services for the company's existing business.

11. If a going business is acquired, the manufacturing facility should be within 150 miles of the company's present headquarters.

DESIRABLE NEEDS

1. The product line should not be sold on a seasonal basis.

2. The product line should not be subject to short term changes.

3. Distribution should be available through the automotive jobbing trade.

4. Manufacturing facilities should be somewhat similar to those in the existing plant to provide for exchange of overflow volume, particularly in respect to appliance components which have seasonal peaks.

5. Ideally, it should be feasible to house new manufacturing facilities in an expansion of the present plant, both to simplify management and staff co-ordination and to take advantage of local labor conditions.

part - 3

Developing New Products Internally

Stories of research and development pitfalls and of new product failures are legion. The decision by management to modify a product mix through the internal development of new products commits the company to a difficult and hazardous course of action.

Many firms are still experimenting and learning to find ways through the maze of barriers to successful new-product development. The problems involved are highly individual, diverse, complex, and unpredictable. It is not easy to draw meaningful generalizations about prerequisites to new-product success. There is no standard approach suitable to all companies.

However, some progress has been made in the search for general guides. Basic techniques and perspectives have begun to crystallize which are useful to many firms in diverse settings. The selections in Part 3 have been chosen to reveal them as clearly as possible. Specifically, these readings highlight four basic themes.

The first concerns the critical nature of "directed creativity." Certainly no development program can be better than the underlying ideas supporting it. In recent years a tremendous stockpile of scientific knowledge has been amassed in various stages of refinement. To exploit the lode, to reduce costly duplication of effort, and to build upon the base of accumulated knowledge is a task in itself. In addition to this need to keep abreast of accelerating technological change—merely to find and assemble known new-product information—progressive firms must also seek to create new ideas via fresh exploration and discovery. The market provides a possible clue. Prudent executives attempt to create products for market needs rather than wait for product designs to be frozen to find possible applications for them. While market research in the early stages of development is still not in widespread use, it is not impossible. Energetic market researchers are improving their techniques and are slowly coming to play a truly creative role in generating new-product alternatives. Of course, the bench scientist—with or without the guidance of market research—continues to fill the dominant creative role. Yet he, too, must be guided by management toward commercially practical ideas, toward an acceptable blend of fundamental and applied research, and toward some sort of dynamic program balance in new-product development efforts. Finally, all ideas for new products, whether originating in the laboratory or in the market, are not likely to be equally useful or suitable to any given company. Each management team needs an objective procedure for evaluating the raw ideas in order to screen out those toward which it can ill afford to devote the company's scarce resources.

A second central thread running through the following selections is that technical development and market development are twin streams in the overall development process needing close cooperation. They are truly handmaidens in modern new-product development. Interconnections between them are suggested in the accompanying Figure and are developed more completely in one of the readings. A continuous interchange between these two dimensions of develop-

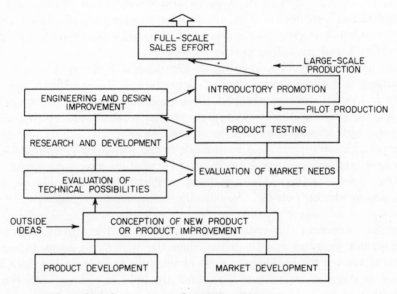

Source: Industrial Marketing, *September 1957, p. 180.*

FIG. 1

The interrelated processes of product and market development can be coordinated. Ideas are considered jointly and go on up the ladder if deemed worthy.

ment is crucial in an increasing number of situations. Without assurance that the two halves of development are neatly integrated, management is likely to be plagued by the persistent worry that the researcher's idea of a good product will not coincide with the consumer's notion of goodness once the item is commercially introduced.

Third, new-product development is a company-wide activity in which nearly every department has a vital interest. Researchers, engineers, designers, marketers, financial personnel, production people, lawyers, and others all have roles to fill. The success of development efforts depends heavily on how well each and every section understands and shoulders its responsibilities. All departments are potential contributors to new-product success; pitfalls may arise in any functional area. In a setting in which countless functions are simultaneously involved in an ongoing process, where daily relationships are difficult to comprehend, where jealousies and misunderstandings seem inevitably to develop, where normal channels of communication and chains of command are repeatedly in danger of being violated, coordination becomes a key word. To hold individuals accountable for fragmented activities, to provide effective interdepartmental liaison, to define and fix specific responsibilities and authorities, to provide for integration of a highly creative group endeavor without stifling individual imagination and while positively nourishing a dynamic innovating attitude—these are the tasks facing the organizer of new-product development work. Few organizational issues are more complex. In fact, one leading business educator reserves a case problem in the coordination of new-product development activity "to teach a renewed sense of humility to those students of organization who may have become prematurely and unduly confident of their organizing abilities."

The fourth theme is that close control over organized effort is essential to sound new-product development. In the transition from raw idea to finished product, two very scarce resources are consumed—time and money. Conflicts may arise over the need to expedite the development timetable and the need to reduce risk and proceed with caution. Objective control over both dollar and time expenditures is a prime requirement.

In short, while technical and scientific skills are important to new-product development, success or failure is very often tied directly to how well the total process is managed. The selections in Part 3, therefore, stress a managerial orientation to research and development problems. The opening readings are aimed at promoting an overall grasp of new-product development as a dynamic process. The second group of selections deals with the issue of creating an effective organization for pursuing this process. The third set of readings provides insights, perspectives, and approaches for locating, creating, and evaluating new-product ideas. The final readings in Part 3 are intended to impart a familiarity with some of the chief methods, procedures, and concepts for administering a controlled and coordinated program for the conversion of new ideas into potentially salable products.

A

An Overview of the Process

▶▶▶▶▶▶▶▶▶▶▶▶ CASE HISTORY OF A NEW PRODUCT

Business Week

E. I. du Pont's decision to go into large-scale production of plastic printing plates marks the end of one phase of a story that has been running almost a dozen years. It's a story with desperate moments and last-minute discoveries and tough decisions and frayed tempers. Yet it's the same kind of story that has occurred over and over again at Du Pont and will be repeated many times in the future.

The development of a new way of preparing printing plates is just one example of the logical, well-defined method Du Pont uses to bring new products into being. The route the new idea followed from its first vague beginnings to a commercial product is the same one previously traveled by nylon, Dacron, Mylar, urea herbicides, and the other Du Pont new developments. Even the name of the new plate-making material, Dycril, is in keeping with a company policy of giving its products brand names made up of euphonious but meaningless syllables to give them full copyright protection.

DU PONT'S BASIC AIM

Du Pont's pattern of new products development is rooted in the over-all task it has charged itself with—"to come out with entirely new products." Dycril meets this qualification easily. The traditional way of making a letter-press printing plate for a long press run is to take a mold of lead type and

Reprinted by permission from Business Week, *February 20, 1960, pp. 105–106, 108.*

engravings, and then make a copy of it by casting or electroplating. In contrast, Dycril turns to the photographic approach used in photoengravings and offset printing plates. The Dycril plastic plate is exposed to light through a photo negative of the material to be printed; ultraviolet light hardens the part of the plate it hits, leaving a relief image when the unexposed part is washed away chemically. The advantage of the new process is the speed with which a finished plate can be made and the ease with which complicated designs can be used. Chief disadvantage is that it costs substantially more than the conventional process. This problem is expected to lessen as volume of production increases. Some $6-million has been spent developing Dycril, $1½-million of it in the last year.

For a company to come up with a radically new idea like this, it has to be willing to sink lots of money into research—much of it perhaps fruitless in terms of the number of commercial new products that result. And Du Pont has been willing. Last year it spent $90-million on research, $15-million of it on fundamental research.

The big chemical company began doing its fundamental research in 1928, by investigating the how and why of molecule combustion into "giant" molecules, especially polymers. This led to nylon, which went into commercial production 11 years later.

SEARCH FOR IDEAS

Fundamental research is done by all 11 of the manufacturing departments at Du Pont, but it is the special interest of the Central Research Dept., a staff operation servicing all departments. About 80% of Central Research's time is spent on preproduct investigations.

Dr. Paul Salzberg, department head, and five of his key lieutenants sort out the written proposals submitted by the company's researchers for new lines of investigation, O.K. those which promise to be "really scientifically new." Another important consideration is the potential importance as an area of science to the company's future. A topic like astrophysics, for instance, may well be important, but isn't likely to get a go-ahead as a research project now because it doesn't seem related to Du Pont's lines. Even so, the company's management says 19 out of 20 projects never result in a marketable product.

VAGUE BEGINNING

A project is initially a one-man operation and is intentionally vague. When Dr. Louis Plambeck, Jr., began work on what turned out to be the plastic printing plate, for instance, all he knew was that he was interested in seeing how light could be used to form images by processes other than those used in photography. Du Pont held patents arising from some work done in this area, which is called photopolymerization, in the early 1940s. These provided a point of departure for the printing plate project. (The patents also served to block at least one other company that began doing research on light-sensitive printing plates.)

Most research done in Salzberg's department comes out of his budget, but in this case he was able to get the Photo Products Dept. to underwrite the investigation from the start.

In just about a year, Plambeck had narrowed his field of investigation down to the idea of making a printing plate. He was able to take a liquid, expose it to a pattern of ultraviolet light. The liquid hardened where the light hit it, and, when the rest of the solution was washed away with a solvent, a raised relief of the light pattern remained. When this point had been reached the fundamental research stage was over.

APPLIED RESEARCH

Salzberg's job now was to sell an operating department on underwriting further—"applied"—research, done either in his laboratories or in the department's own lab. In this case, the selling job was easy. Photo Products was excited about the new printing idea, decided to pick up further bills and let Plambeck continue with the research.

The applied research stage is the long one. As one Du Pont man put it, "the hardest work lies between the invention and the invoice."

During 1950 and 1951, Plambeck worked on various formulas, slightly different development techniques. Early in the game he could turn out good work for print or pen-and-ink drawings, but he ran into a lot of trouble with photographs, where a continuous shading of tones is necessary.

INDUSTRY ENTHUSIASM

At the same time, Plambeck was giving private demonstrations of the process. The first enthusiasm came from personnel at Du Pont's own printing plant in Philadelphia. Chicago Lakeside Press & Intertype Corp., maker of

phototype-setting equipment, and, later, the Philadelphia Inquirer also were impressed.

By the end of 1951, the technique had been developed to the point where a small brochure was prepared on the plastic plates for the Du Pont board, showing how the process could handle different kinds of copy. Early the next year, the first long run was made with the plates—90,000 copies of a purchase requisition form made for actual company use. The plate held up—and the bulk of the research work was transferred to the departmental labs. Central Research continued to iron out bugs in the plate, while Photo Products worked on techniques to manufacture it.

STUMBLING BLOCK

Then the general manager of the Photo Products Dept. made a decision that might have spelled the end of the product right there—he said he would not market the process in a liquid state or with a flammable solvent.

The project went back to Central Research. Plambeck, now with two other men working with him, then developed a putty-like form and finally, by 1953, arrived at his first solid-layer photopolymer printing plate. What was essentially the present product was in hand by 1955.

By this time the departmental sales division, responsible for all market research and product testing, had begun to get ready for the product. Men experienced in the printing industry were added to the payroll, and on their recommendations minor alterations were made in the plate. Constant tests were run at the company printing plant, and tests were then run in secret at a few selected job shops.

OFFICIAL DEBUT

Finally, in May, 1957, the company was ready to announce publicly the development of a light-sensitive plastic printing plate. Queries from interested printers poured in.

Often it takes persuasive salesmanship to get potential users to tool up to test a product the company may later decide not to market. With the printing plate, the sales division had just the opposite problem—how to pick from the myriad requests for test samples a few printers who would be able to give variety and accurate test controls, and yet not insult all those potential customers who were turned down.

Field results were promising. The technique was first demonstrated to the industry at large—to some 2,700 paid attendees at a letterpress forum in New York—in September, 1958. By then an option had been taken on a plant site, and the department was just about ready to ask top management approval to roll ahead with the product.

PRICE WORRY

Then one worry—fanned by a reaction at the letterpress forum—stopped the project cold.

That worry was price.

The manufacturing process then used required that the plate be sold for about $10 a sq. ft., and even with quantity production, the price seemed unlikely to go far below that. That was just too high, John M. Clark, manager of the Photo Products Dept. decided;

he sent the production men and laboratory experts back to work to come up with a new production process. If they couldn't come up with one, he said, the light-sensitive printing plate would die right then. There were a lot of hurt feelings and angry thoughts.

NEW PRODUCTION METHOD

There was another problem to be tackled, too. The plate was then being made by a batch method which limited its size. This hadn't been of much importance when development began, because the size was adequate for flatbed presses. But printers kept putting more and more of their work on high-speed presses using cylindrical plates; these needed bigger plates to operate at maximum efficiency.

It took about a year, but Du Pont engineers managed to replace the batch method of making the plates with a "more-or-less continuous flow" process which licked both the size and price problems. Now, although $10 a sq. ft. is the present price, volume production is expected to bring price reductions. Du Pont won't estimate just what these price cuts might be, but some users are hoping for a halving of the present price.

FINAL "YES"

With these problems overcome, the only step left was to ask the executive committee and the finance committee for more than $1-million to build a plant. Approval came early this year.

The new plant, which opens in mid-1961, will have a capacity of 1-million sq. ft.

Not all prospective new products get

the go-ahead for commercial production on the first trip to the executive and finance committees. Some are sent back for more research work to have specific bugs eliminated. Some products have made four trips to the committees before getting approval. Others have died on the way. And some requests have been rejected for reasons not connected with the quality of the product itself. Some Du Pont executives even remember one case where the committees turned thumbs down because there weren't enough manufacturers in the field—the company didn't want to court antitrust trouble.

EARLY DEATH

Few projects, however, die at this level—most that fail to make the marketplace are killed off much earlier. Sometimes even when the fundamental research has been promising, Salzberg has a hard time drumming up the departmental sponsorship necessary for further investigation. When Central Research turned up a polyvinyl fluoride with high tensile strength and high weatherability, for instance, the Fabrics & Finishes Dept. turned it down. Later Salzberg approached the Film Dept. and managed to spark an interest. That department has just announced plans to turn out the fluoride, brand named Teslar.

Sometimes no department will give the go-ahead. Then Central Research simply patents the discovery and waits. In the mid-1930s some polyurethanes were made in the lab, but none of the operating departments would spend any money to work further on them. Suddenly a dozen years later, upholstery foams turned out to be a hot item in the chemical industry, and the polyurethane patents were dusted off and carried on into applied research. But with a 17-year patent limit, the company tries to keep shelf time to a minimum.

Sometimes a department will drop a project in mid-stream. Du Pont has done a lot of laboratory work in developing a magnetic recording tape, for example, but dropped the idea when it came up with nothing much better than tapes already on the market.

THE MISSES

Getting to the field test stage or even into commercial production is no guarantee of success for a product idea.

The Photo Products Dept. had developed a line of phosphers to coat the inside of color television tubes, to go along with its line of phosphers for black and white tubes. The product was distributed to some makers in test quantities, then Du Pont decided to drop the television tube phospher business altogether. Too many set makers, it decided, were beginning to make their own phosphers.

In 1951, the company put on the market a color film for motion pictures, designed to make prints for films shot in a particular color process. This one suffered what one Du Pont scientist calls "technical obsolescence in a hurry." Shortly after the film was introduced, a new kind of color film came on the market which immediately put in a shadow the shooting process for which Du Pont was then making copy film.

NARROW ESCAPE

Even orlon—with a $25-million expenditure before commercial production began—came within a hair's breadth of being a flop. Artificial fibers can be made either in filament form—squeezed out in long strands—or in short staple lengths, which are then treated like cotton or wool natural staples. Orlon was conceived by Du Pont as a filament fiber for industrial textiles. But it never managed to catch on. Only the success of the orlon staple plant, opened a year later to produce the fiber for clothing textiles, saved the day.

DYCRIL'S CHANCES

Few think that the company's new plastic printing plates will have such a close call. On the other hand, few think that Dycril will take over all letterpress printing jobs. The extent of Dycril's impact on the printing trade depends in a large part on its eventual price—still an uncertainty. Other considerations are involved, too. So far, in limited use, there have been few complaints from printers about shortcomings in the plastic plates. But there have been worries about things that could go wrong. A chief source of concern, for example, is the fact that the plastic plate, unlike the metal one, cannot be changed or "corrected" after it has been made.

So now plastic printing plates, after a 12-year struggle to make the grade as a Du Pont new product, must take on the new challenge of winning acceptance in the tradition-bound printing industry.

▶▶▶▶▶▶▶▶▶▶▶▶ A PROGRAM FOR NEW PRODUCT EVOLUTION

BOOZ, ALLEN & HAMILTON

. . . The term "new product evolution" now has rather widespread acceptance and usage.

After examining several hundred companies' new products activities, conviction develops that there is a basic approach to the management process of new product evolution that is sound for most companies in most industries. Written here in terms of manufactured products, a similar process applies in service businesses and profit-making enterprises of all kinds.

It is clear that any pattern of approach for a new product program must be tailored to meet the unique characteristics of each company. However, this tailoring can be most effective when working from an established set of proven principles. The program described here identifies such principles.

It must be indicated that this investigation has been concerned with a carefully selected sample of companies —companies with heavy new product experience and high reputation. The conclusions presented, then, do not actually represent the total business com-

Reprinted by permission from Management of New Products, *Booz, Allen & Hamilton, 1960, pp. 8–18.*

munity, since they are based on the practices of relatively few companies that have successfully bridged some of the problem areas. Thus there is no intention here to represent majority practice, since "majority" practice is rarely "best" practice. The intent is to present the best practices wherever found.

Happily, new product practices are changing for the better. Much of what was found in a few companies only a few years ago has proved successful and is becoming the prevailing practice among well-managed companies.

The basic program outlined here is thus more of a review of accepted practice of prominent companies. Admittedly, even as accepted practice, the program may rarely achieve full effectiveness.

PRODUCTS DEFINED IN BUSINESS TERMS

If we accept that products are the medium of business conduct, then business strategy is fundamentally product planning. The "marketing concept" of business is within this basic philosophy.

When a company selects and develops a product, it is choosing the kind of business it is going to be. It is deciding what will be its customers, competitors, suppliers, facilities and skills, and the socioeconomic environment that will form the perimeter of its opportunity for success.

Chart 1 shows this concept—that products are, for all practical purposes, the business. Products occupy the middleman role between basic resources on the one hand and customers on the

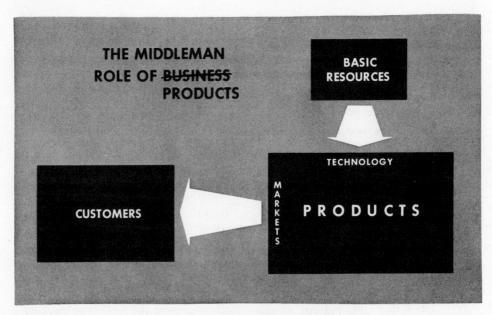

THE MIDDLEMAN ROLE OF ~~BUSINESS~~ PRODUCTS

BASIC RESOURCES

TECHNOLOGY

CUSTOMERS

MARKETS

PRODUCTS

Source: Management Research Department, Booz, Allen & Hamilton Inc.

CHART 1

other. A product has two key dimensions of *technology* (fund of knowledge, technical and otherwise, enabling the product to be economically built) and *markets* (to whom and how the product is to be sold, enabling profitable distribution). These two basic characteristics are inseparable. An invention is not a new product. A new product is something that can be made that people want to buy.

It seems wise, also, to point out a "new product" is defined here as a product that is new to the company. It may well have been made in one or more forms by someone else. Nevertheless, whenever the product is new to the company, the problems inherent are new to that management and it must be handled as a "new product."

So far, two major dimensions of new products have been identified, technology and markets. Now a third is added—product evolution—or the time it takes to bring a product into existence. This time span varies very significantly between products and industries—from weeks to years.

Chart 2 illustrates these three dimensions. As indicated by the arrow, a new products program starts with company objectives, which include product fields of interest, profit aims, and growth plans. The more specifically these objectives can be drawn, the greater guidance will be provided the new products program. For example, the company with the objective to grow ("no matter what field, so long as it is profitable") provides little, if any, guidance. On the

Source: *Management Research Department, Booz, Allen & Hamilton Inc.*

CHART 2

other hand, if an objective is set, for example, to operate only in the field of high quality electronic measuring instruments, a starting point for guidance has been established. Company objectives provide the framework for the new products program; the better framed they are, the better the new product guidance.

Finally, it seems clear that the new products activity is a complex and often sizable activity embracing the whole company. To manage such a complex activity it is necessary to break it into functions and stages that can be managed.

THE STAGES OF NEW PRODUCT EVOLUTION

The new product process can be broken down into manageable stages for planning and control. Study of case histories reveals that there are six fairly clear stages, although the labels for such stages vary from company to company.

These six stages [shown in Chart 3] are:

Exploration—the search for product ideas to meet company objectives.

Screening—a quick analysis to determine which ideas are pertinent and should be given careful investigation.

Business analysis—the expansion of the idea, through creative analysis, into a concrete business recommendation including product features and a program.

Development—turning the idea-on-paper into a product-in-hand, producible and demonstrable.

Testing—the commercial experiments necessary to verify earlier business judgments.

Commercialization—launching the product in full-scale production and

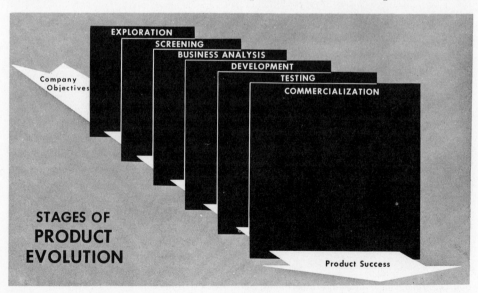

Source: Management Research Department, Booz, Allen & Hamilton Inc.

CHART 3

sale, committing the company's reputation and resources.

As earlier indicated, the stages may be called by different names appropriate to each company's industry, and they may be combined or subdivided. However, this six-stage pattern is most common and represents *the basic management process* before company, industry, organization or product variations are considered.

BASIC CHARACTERISTICS OF THE NEW PRODUCT PROCESS

The *decay curve for ideas* is characteristic of the process. This is the progressive rejection of ideas or projects of the new product process by stage. Viewed from top management perspective, the process of new product evolution moves through a series of management decisions. At each major control or decision point about half of these decisions (on the average) are negative, resulting in the elimination of the project or making major modifications before moving ahead.

Although the rate of rejection varies some between industries and more between companies, the general shape of the decay curve is typical. Chart 4 is the average decay rate for a sample of leading companies. As will be noted, it takes some 40 ideas in the collected universe to yield one successful new product.

Another characteristic of this process is that each stage is progressively more expensive as measured in expenditures of both time and money. Chart 5 shows

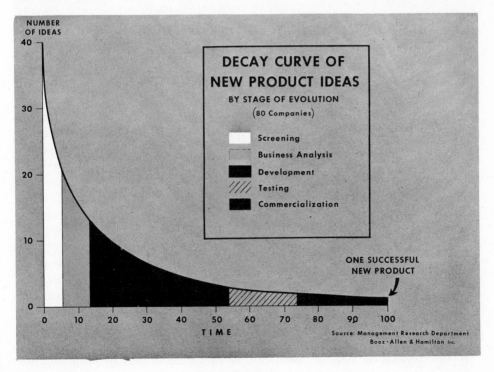

CHART 4

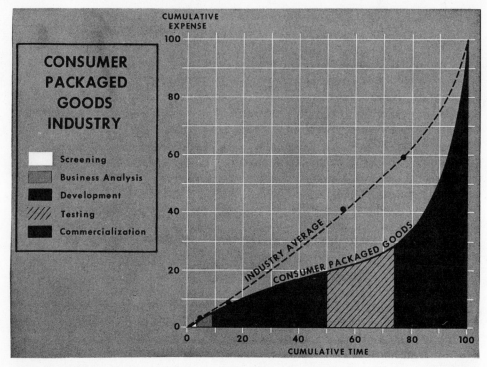

CUMULATIVE
EXPENSE

CONSUMER
PACKAGED
GOODS
INDUSTRY

☐ Screening
▨ Business Analysis
■ Development
//// Testing
■ Commercialization

INDUSTRY AVERAGE

CONSUMER PACKAGED GOODS

CUMULATIVE TIME

Source: *Management Research Department, Booz, Allen & Hamilton Inc.*

CHART 5

the rate at which expense dollars accumulate as time accumulates for the average project in a sample of leading companies. This illustrative chart is for consumer packaged goods; the dotted line shows an all-industry average of time and money expenditures.

These curves tend to understate the situation, especially for industries requiring heavy capital investment. Only expense dollars are represented in the curves; capital expenditures are not included.

THE OBJECTIVE OF NEW PRODUCT SELECTION

If this process is one of "product selection" there is a clear objective to

be achieved: to pick the best ideas for investing available new product time and money. To illustrate, in Chart 6 product ideas can be sorted against two grids, risk vs. payout. There are more high-risk than low-risk products; and there are more low-payout than high-payout. This probability sometimes leads to the belief that for an idea to have a high payout, it must, *ipso facto*, have high risk. However, management's purpose is to beat the probabilities by finding those rare ideas that are both low-risk and high-payout. This is the key to maximum yield on available manpower and resources.

Effectiveness in product selection can be measured in part by examining the degree to which projects in the com-

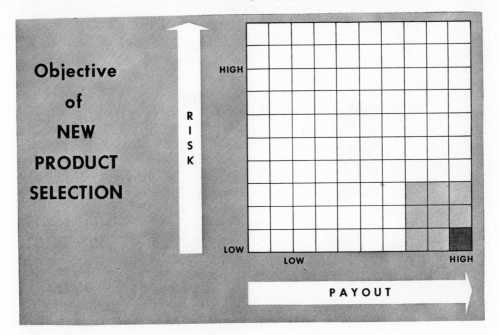

Objective of NEW PRODUCT SELECTION

RISK

HIGH

LOW

LOW

HIGH

PAYOUT

Source: *Management Research Department, Booz, Allen & Hamilton Inc.*

CHART 6

pany cluster at the lower right-hand corner of this chart. Most companies make a profit without approaching this degree of selectivity. However, profits tend to improve markedly in companies when management consciously seeks combinations of low-risk and high-payout, however rare.

THE NEED FOR MORE PRODUCTIVE UTILIZATION OF AVAILABLE MANPOWER AND MONEY

Most companies do make a profit just like most men do make a living. But men and companies vary greatly in their level of earnings. The rate of growth can be generally taken as a measure of relative success. Throughout history companies have prospered the most that, among other things, have purposefully channeled their available energies into the most productive tasks they could devise and have avoided waste of their resources on less productive tasks. Against this philosophy, the data can be examined again to see how much companies today are spending on unsuccessful new product projects. At risk of argument, let's call this "waste."

Of all the dollars of new product expense, almost four-fifths go to unsuccessful products; 70% of these waste dollars are in the "development stage." Thus, about seven out of eight development scientists and engineers may be said to be working on projects that will not be justified in terms of commercial usefulness (basic research is not included here). See Chart 7.

If management could decrease this

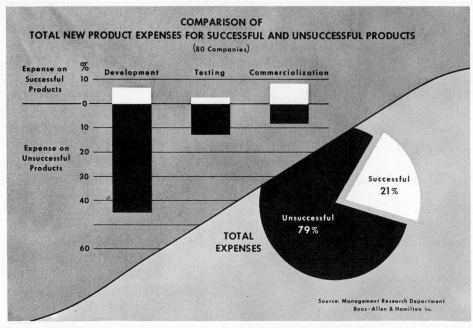

CHART 7

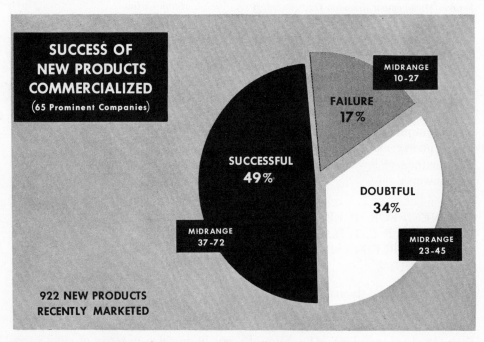

Source: Management Research Department, Booz, Allen & Hamilton Inc.

CHART 8

waste only slightly, it would in theory— and often in fact—greatly enhance its effective manpower in the new product process.

THE OPPORTUNITY FOR IMPROVEMENT IN NEW PRODUCT RESULTS

Management judgment in the new product process meets its final test at the last stage—commercialization. At this point, management has pronounced its product worthy and says so publicly and expensively. The record for an average of prominent companies is pretty good, considering the hazards (see Chart 8).

However, few companies can take comfort in this failure-success average of 50-50. (Most doubtful products drift into the failure column, unless redesigned in some way to make another "new product.") The failure rate of new products differs surprisingly little between industries, but there is a great difference in failure rates between com-

panies. This appears to be largely a reflection of the differences in management effectiveness. The range of success probability for new products is shown in the table.

POINTS FOR IMPROVEMENT IN A PROGRAM OF NEW PRODUCT EVOLUTION

The following list of points, made without comment, has helped increase success in many companies seeking to analyze, change and improve their new product programs.

EXPLORATION

1. *Determine the product fields of primary interest to the company.*

Analyze major company problems.
Evaluate the company's principal resources.
Identify external growth opportunities ready for exploitation—expanding markets, technological breakthroughs or rising profit margins.

PROBABILITY OF COMMERCIAL SUCCESS

	New Product Ideas	Product Development Projects	New Products Introduced
	Success Percentages		
All Industry Groups	2.4%	12.5%	49.0%
Chemical	2%	10%	47%
Consumer Packaged Goods	1%	6%	40%
Electrical Machinery	3%	17%	57%
Metal Fabricators	2%	14%	38%
Non-Electrical Machinery	2%	20%	52%
Raw Material Processors	4%	13%	60%

2. *Establish a program for planned idea generation.*

Identify idea-generating groups.
Give them a clear concept of the company's interest fields.
Expose creative personnel to idea-generating facts.
Conduct exploratory technical research.
Utilize team approach.
Minimize distractions from current problems.

3. *Collect ideas through an organized network.*

Designate an idea collection point.
Establish comprehensive idea-collection procedures.
Cover selected outside sources of ideas.
Solicit ideas actively and directly.
Consider each idea first on a "can-do" basis.
Treat the idea man with care.

SCREENING

1. *Expand each idea into a full product concept.*

Translate the idea into business terms.
Identify the key business implications of the product concept and its development.
Prepare a written proposal of the product idea.

2. *Collect facts and opinions, which are quickly available, bearing on the product idea as a business proposition.*

Select evaluation techniques to fit the specific idea.
Identify the best sources of facts and qualified opinions.

Use quick and inexpensive fact-gathering methods.
Apply strictly the principle of "diminishing returns" to fact-gathering.

3. *Appraise each idea for its potential values to the company.*

Estimate the magnitude of the profit opportunity.
Assess the investment, time and risk requirements.
Check the idea against other selection criteria.
Provide for subsequent review of ideas discarded or shelved.

BUSINESS ANALYSIS

1. *Appoint persons responsible for further study of each idea.*

Select a small product team, representing major departments that would be affected by the product.
Tailor team size and composition to the nature of the product.
Select team members on the basis of their self-interest.

2. *Determine the desirable market features for the product and its feasibility.*

Determine characteristics of the market and its trends.
Appraise both competitors and their products—existing and potential.
Conduct experimental market and technical research, within budget limits established for preliminary investigation.
Identify "appeal" characteristics that would differentiate and sell the product.

Establish feasibility of developing and manufacturing a product with these features.

3. *Develop specifications and establish a definite program for the product.*

Evaluate various business alternatives to determine desired product specifications.

Establish a timetable and estimate expenditures to evolve this product through succeeding stages.

Reduce the proposed idea to a specific business proposition in terms of time, costs, manpower, profits and benefits.

Get top management approval or revision of the product idea in terms of its specifications and program before authorizing the development stage.

DEVELOPMENT

1. *Establish development projects for each product.*

Explode the product proposal into as many projects as are required for administrative control.

Schedule these projects within the approved budget and timetable for the product.

Maintain the product team for company-wide coordination.

Pin-point responsibility of all team members and identify them in all reports and records.

Establish yardsticks for measuring performance and progress.

2. *Build product to designated or revised specifications.*

Exhaust available information.

Maintain security against outside information "leaks."

Continue market studies as a basis for enhancing product salability.

Hold to agreed specifications or make formal revisions by repeating the specification stage.

Keep top management informed; report promptly anticipated changes in objectives, schedule or budget.

3. *Complete laboratory evaluation and release for testing.*

Complete laboratory tests adequate to determine basic performance against specifications.

Provide checks and balances through organization and procedure to assure objectivity of product appraisal.

Apply commercial rather than scientific standards to determine product "release" point.

Prepare management report summarizing product description and characteristics; report project completion.

TESTING

1. *Plan commercial experiments necessary to test and verify earlier judgments of the product.*

Expand product team, if required.

Outline the nature and scope of commercialization phase.

Identify the major factors that must prove out to support successful commercialization.

Establish the standards by which product performance and market acceptance will be judged.

Plan test methods, responsibility, schedule and cost.

Construct a testing program and recommend it to top management for approval.

2. *Conduct in-use, production and market testing.*

Continue laboratory testing.
Design and test production facilities.
Submit products to customer use for "abuse" testing.
Conduct test marketing programs in line with plans for commercialization.
Survey company, trade and user reactions to the product and its commercialization program.

3. *Make final product decision; freeze design.*

Interpret test findings objectively; drop or modify products which fail tests.
Incorporate test findings in product design and commercialization plans.
Detail the program for full-scale production and sales with a schedule, budgets and manpower.
Recommend the product and its commercialization program, with full supporting data, to top management for final product decision.

COMMERCIALIZATION

1. *Complete final plans for production and marketing.*

Establish patterns for over-all direction and coordination of the product.
Expand product team to encompass all departments involved.
Designate individuals responsible for each part of the commercialization program.
Assure that these individuals work out all program details to fit coordinated plan.

2. *Initiate coordinated production and selling programs.*

Brief all participating personnel.
Maintain established program sequence and schedule.
Provide feed-back mechanisms for program corrections.

3. *Check results. Make necessary improvements in product, manufacturing or sales.*

Make design changes promptly to correct "bugs."
Work continuously for cost reduction and quality control.
Shape the product and its program to meet competitive reaction and changing internal pressures.
Maintain necessary team members until the product is a "going" commercial success, absorbed by established organization.

The management concepts outlined here "take some doing" to bring actual improvement in new product results. The vital "how to" factors are not easily generalized. The specifics of a program for one company, even if well understood, tend to be useless and often dangerous in another company.

CONCLUSIONS ON NEW PRODUCT EVOLUTION

In examining the management process of new product evolution, the conclusion is reached that heavy attention should be focused on the first three stages. As will be remembered, these are the "idea" or "concept" stages. Experience of major companies indicates that most products fail because the idea or its timing was wrong and not because the company lacked the knowledge on how to develop and commercialize the product.

The following points bear on the accent of the earlier stages of product evolution:

In the commercialization stage failures should occur rarely in well managed and adequately financed companies because successful companies know pretty well how to produce and sell. Such companies feel that their failures can usually be traced to an earlier stage and reflect weakness in the product concept itself.

The testing stage is the place to experience product failures. Still, too many products are killed in this stage after development for nontechnical reasons that could have as easily been anticipated before development (if given the same thought at that earlier time).

As for the development stage, experienced companies in R&D say, in effect, "Our men can develop anything. Show me enough sales and enough profit, and we'll spend the necessary time and money to develop it." Most *development* work, after all, should and does take place within technology largely understood at the outset of the project.

Therefore, well managed companies can concentrate with advantage on the early stages of determining "what should be developed." It takes just as long and just as much money to develop a million-dollar bust as a ten-million-dollar bell ringer. There are plenty of problems to solve in the world. The secret of success is to be working on the most useful ones.

►►►►►►►►►►► WHY NEW PRODUCTS FAIL

PHILIP MARVIN*

Nineteen out of twenty new products are failures. Not all of these failures are spectacular—the newly launched product may not sink immediately under the salvos of commercial warfare. It may just develop slow profit leaks that take it down to Davy Jones' locker before anyone is even aware that there's trouble.

Based on the experiences of a number of companies, there are six primary reasons why new products fail. Perhaps a seventh could be added—fear of fail-

Reprinted with permission from Machine Design, *November 23, 1961, pp. 109–111. Copyright 1961 by The Penton Publishing Co., Cleveland 13, Ohio.*

Division Manager, Research and Development, American Management Association.

ure. A new product program can develop slow leaks and finally founder merely because everyone's afraid to act —and take the chance of making a mistake. After all, no-one points a finger at those who stall for time.

These uncertainties can be avoided, and risks of product planning minimized. A lot can be learned by studying product failures, particularly these six main problems, as a basis for developing skill in avoiding the usual product-planning pitfalls.

1. TIMING WAS OFF

The best-planned programs can trip on timing. In new-product planning, few things seem more certain than the fact that there is a time and place for everything. Put another way, every part of a new product program must fit a master time schedule.

To illustrate the importance of timing, here is how one company missed a market by bad timing. The proposed new product was given the green light after careful appraisal and screening. It looked like a real money maker. It was a specialty item for the Christmas market, one accounting for 80 per cent of the sales of this type of item.

Two years was estimated as the time needed to develop the idea, get it into production and fill the pipelines between producer and consumer. But unforeseen difficulties arose and delays occurred. Because the importance of tying the product's introduction to the Christmas market was overlooked, delays weren't offset by extra efforts. As a result, the market was missed by six weeks—six weeks that cost a loss of 80 per cent of one year's sales.

In another case involving an industrial product, timing played a different role with equally costly consequences. One large manufacturer of electronic components planned to introduce a new tape-recording device adapted to visual images. Engineering development was allowed to lag. As a result, a competitor was the first to introduce apparatus which was quickly established as a recognized standard in the television industry.

Some delays can't be circumvented. No amount of attention paid to time schedules can prevent unforeseen factors from arising. This isn't the function of time schedules. Their job is to highlight dates that have an important bearing on the profit picture. Then, when delays do occur, it is possible to make a rapid appraisal of the probable cost of these delays, and to relate this cost to the cost of offsetting these delays with accelerated programs.

Either too much or too little, timed too soon or too late, can cause consequences of serious proportions. "Too little and too late" are some of the saddest words heard in discussions of new-product programs. Equally unfortunate is the opposite extreme of "too much and too soon." This can be costly too! Timing is the important factor in avoiding these bugaboos of product planning.

Timetables are vitally essential to the success of new-product development. Timetables should reflect recognition that dates are coupled to dollar signs, and that time periods are tied to costs. Compromises must be made, fitting the two together. Once this is done the importance of these decisions should not be forgotten. Too often, careful planning efforts, once completed, are treated as an incumbrance of the past rather than as a guide to the future. When this happens, all of the effort that has gone into planning is wasted.

Departures from timetables should be viewed with alarm. They should signal the need for prompt reappraisal of the program. Timing is too closely tied to profits to be neglected.

2. THE PRODUCT WASN'T PRACTICAL

Some good ideas just don't pass the test of commercial feasibility. It isn't always easy to distinguish between what can be done and what is commercially feasible. The difference between these two is the difference between profit and losses. It isn't enough to be able to produce the product; it must be possible to sell it at a profit. Overlooking this fundamental fact would seem to be almost impossible.

But the challenge of technical achievement sometimes has a temporarily blinding effect. Individuals who are otherwise quite objective in their outlook frequently fail to be objective when faced with the opportunity to score a technical triumph. From a business point of view, profits are the only ultimate triumph.

Failure to pass the test of commercial feasibility has come about in many ways. Here is a rapid rundown of some of the more familiar tales of woe: 1. "It was easy to produce one, but we ran into difficulty with production lots." 2. "It was a good product but it took us too long to tool up." 3. "We didn't realize how much it would cost to de-

velop the market." 4. "We didn't understand what our customers really wanted."

The ultimate test of commercial feasibility lies in the answer to two questions: 1. Can it be made? 2. Can it be sold at a profit? Affirmative answers are needed.

Industrial products and consumer items incorporating advanced engineering technology are particularly sensitive to the test of commercial feasibility. The challenge of technical achievement has already been cited as one of the reasons why new products are pushed to completion without weighing all of the factors. Beyond this is the difficulty of appraising the final product of highly complex technology until that product actually takes shape. Performance characteristics are often critical factors in determining commercial feasibility. In many cases these can only be determined by building prototypes.

3. CUSTOMER NEEDS CHANGED

New products are created and developed in a dynamic environment. Carefully conducted surveys may reveal specific customer needs. But these needs can change before sufficient time has elapsed to capitalize on them.

The time factor involved in making a profit on a new product can be quite long. Products must not only be created, produced and marketed. They must also enjoy a sufficient span of sales to build an attractive return on the investment. If the risk is great that the span of sales may be too short, it's a good idea to reappraise the situation.

Some years ago, a company concluded that there was a market for an automatic electric razor-blade sharpener. This was based on a carefully conducted study. By the time the product was developed, needs had changed. The price of razor blades had been drastically reduced. Ejector-type dispensers were available that eliminated handling sharp blades. The introduction of the electric shaver captured a portion of the potential market. The need to resharpen razor blades was largely eliminated.

One of the common errors in analyzing customer needs is to consider the survey completed once product development gets under way. During development stages, more than ever before, it is important to maintain vigilance over potential markets. The investment in a new product mounts steadily during the development phase. When factors arise that alter sales prospects, they should be detected as soon as they appear. Nothing is gained by adopting ostrich-like tactics. Burying one's head in the sand provides no protection.

Action that has been taken, and money that has been spent, can't always be salvaged. Early detection of new factors which change original assumptions prevents needless additional expenditures of time and energy. Programs can be altered to provide new direction. Resources can be diverted into more profitable channels.

Consumer needs are always changing. Steadily increasing watchfulness over these changes is needed as the investment in new products grows.

4. BASIC ASSUMPTIONS WERE FORGOTTEN

Every new product is based on specific assumptions. Here were some assumptions of one manufacturer in developing an automatic multipurpose machine tool: 1. An expanding market for automatic equipment. 2. An opportunity to increase profits by entering this market. 3. A desire to expand in this direction. 4. A willingness to accept the added burdens on management's time.

The Engineering Department embarked on the project. They came up with a special-purpose machine tool that integrated a time-consuming sequence of operations into one operation. The machine was marketed, not too successfully. For some time, management's energies were dedicated to making a success of this project. Everyone is familiar with the flurry of activities when a company attempts to achieve such goals. Sales and engineering conferences, dealer meetings, executive huddles occupy management's time to the hilt.

As frequently happens when the going gets rough, someone began to wonder how the company got into the muddle. Thinking back, some of the basic assumptions were recalled. In this case —an automatic multipurpose tool—to enhance future profits—in an expanding market. The tool as developed didn't fit. Basic assumptions had been forgotten.

It is easy to forget the assumptions on which decisions are made. Engineers and scientists get lost in the details of their work. They fail to check their directions periodically. They follow clues as they must, but fail to defer interesting leads that run counter to more immediate objectives. Salesmen and marketing men are prone to lose interest in longer range developments once the enthusiasm, kindled by a new idea, has spent its force. Management is distracted by day-to-day activities.

New products are frequently neglected until too late. They often stray far from original directions because basic assumptions were forgotten.

Basic assumptions shouldn't constitute such a rigid framework that they aren't adjustable to new intelligence as it develops. As knowledge and information develops that suggests changes in basic assumptions, the entire program, along with the basic assumptions underlying the program, should be reviewed. Changes should reflect new conditions and new needs. Basic assumptions should be altered only by aggressive, informed action. Changes should never be a by-product of neglect.

5. GOALS WEREN'T CLEARLY DEFINED

The driving force behind successful new products lies in well-developed corporation objectives. It's exceptional when executives are able to make a clear-cut statement of their companies' objectives. It's rarer still when these statements come to a common focus. Yet concentrated, co-ordinated effort depends on common goals. Lacking these, executives are apt to drive toward opposing ends.

The development group in one company spent sizable sums developing a diversified product line, while the sales group was concentrating on establishing a leadership position in a single industry market. In another case, a chemical company developed a food-processing operation subsequently judged too foreign to established business for further exploitation.

With odds as unfavorable as they are to the success of any new venture, new products should have the benefit of co-ordinated efforts within the company if they are to have any chance of success.

Product managers work most effectively when goals are clearly defined. These goals are linked to corporate objectives. Indeed, these product goals are one of the most important facets of corporate objectives. Nothing is more important to business success than a company's products. And a continuing flow of new products is necessary to inject added vitality into the company's product lines.

New products frequently fail because of conflicts of interests within the confines of the company's own operations. The reason: Confusion over objectives. When top management fails to establish objectives, this function is usurped by those in widely scattered activities at lower echelons. Goals established at these levels will be motivated by many factors, some good and some selfish. At best, they never achieve the objectivity and cohesiveness needed for successful new-product planning, production, and promotion.

6. PRODUCT COMPETED WITH CUSTOMERS' SALES

Products aren't always sold to ultimate consumers. Many middlemen may be involved between an initial sale and the final customer. A fiber producer sells to a yarn producer, who in turn sells to a knitting mill, whose customer may be a converter. The chain doesn't stop here. Converters sell to wholesalers, who sell to apparel houses, who sell to distributors. Apparel then passes to retailers and finally to ultimate consumers. There have been many customers for the original fiber. The fiber itself was probably produced from a chemical intermediary that had already passed through a number of sales sequences.

Thinking about new products is sometimes projected to things the company buys and sells. This is dangerous territory. Particularly so because thinking turned into action can have serious impact on presently profitable products.

Competing with customers, or suppliers, may prove costly. Successful business experience can't always be projected as profitably and as easily as thinking about greener pastures of customers and suppliers.

A company's customers and suppliers operate in markets having their own distinctive characteristics. In the various parts of the same industry, specialized experience and knowhow must be acquired. Technologies may also be different. It's a mistake to assume that it's easy to expand in any direction from an established spot. Reputation may help some, but profits will largely depend on good, hard work.

Invading territory of customers and suppliers is an act of commercial warfare. Retaliatory measures must be anticipated. In competing with customers for their markets, some of these customers may shift to other suppliers. This means lost sales that must be offset by additional orders from new markets yet to be exploited by relatively new selling teams. Customers and suppliers, in retaliation to encroachment, can expand their individual spheres of operation too! They will share equal opportunities for success.

Before developing new products that compete with customers or suppliers, the consequences of such steps should be carefully weighed. Potential gains should be based on an evaluation of retaliatory strategies of either a defensive or, more importantly, an offensive nature.

B

Organizing for Development

▶▶▶▶▶▶▶▶▶▶ HOW TO ORGANIZE FOR NEW PRODUCTS

SAMUEL C. JOHNSON AND CONRAD JONES*

. . . Certainly each manufacturing company is well advised to organize carefully its over-all program for the selection and development of new products.

LOCATION & RESPONSIBILITY

The selection and development of new products must, in the final analysis, be the responsibility of top management. Not only does the selection of products determine the fundamental nature of a business—its customers, competitors, and suppliers, as well as its internal facilities and personnel; but the product line establishes the limits of opportunity for maintaining and expanding a company, which can be no bigger and not much more profitable than the product fields in which it competes. Also, product plans are at the heart of competitive strategy; they are the starting point for over-all corporate planning, since they determine capital, personnel, and facility requirements.

Of course, top management cannot carry out such a responsibility by itself. The question is how to go about organizing for it.

NEED FOR CONTROL

A typical company shows many symptoms of the need for systematic

Reprinted by permission from Harvard Business Review, May–June 1957, pp. 49–62.

*Samuel C. Johnson is New Products Director, S. C. Johnson & Son, Inc.; Conrad Jones is an Associate in Booz, Allen & Hamilton, management consultants.

control of this complex activity, such as:

The executives who want new products, but do not know or cannot agree on what kinds of products to be interested in.

The inventors who do not know what to invent.

The laboratory crowded with development projects, but with few new products coming out, and too many of these not paying off.

The downhearted idea-man whose brain child was squashed for unexplained reasons.

The "floating" product idea that has been considered for years, but has never had a decision made on it.

The "bootleg" project in the laboratory that management does not know about.

The "orphan" project that goes on and on because nobody has given it the thought or had the heart to kill it.

The "bottomless hole" product that took three times as long and cost five times as much as expected, and finally got to market behind all other competitors.

The product with "bugs" that were hidden until 10,000 came back from consumers.

The "me too" product that has no competitive reason for existence.

The product that had the sales "engineered out of it."

The scientific triumph that turned out to have no market when someone thought to investigate it.

The sales force that jumped the gun ahead of production.

The sales force that was not "interested" in the added product.

No single existing department can be held responsible for these problems in the new product process; all are involved in it. If the rate of activity is more than a handful of projects—and

large companies count their development projects in the hundreds—top management simply does not have the time to assume direct supervision and coordination of all the tasks involved. Thus, more and more companies are reaching the conclusion that somebody must be put specifically in charge of the new product effort and held accountable for it.

SPECIAL DEPARTMENT

A number of leading companies have established "new products" or "product planning" departments. General Foods Corporation, General Electric Company, International Business Machines Corporation, and Burroughs Corporation are some of the well-known examples. Analysis of 58 such departments in larger companies shows that only 20% of them are more than four years old, and 50% have been organized within the last two years.[1] This is a short history, and little knowledge of these departments has reached the public in print.

Executives considering the establishment or operation of such a department have three fundamental questions to answer.

How can I define the new product function clearly enough to delegate responsibility?

How should I structure this department in my company organization?

How should this department be staffed, and how will these people operate?

Each company must find the answers, of course, in terms of its own unique characteristics and requirements. How-

[1] Booz, Allen & Hamilton, *Management Research Report, Management of New Products* (Chicago, 1956).

ever, there are fundamental concepts that can be drawn from the experience of others to provide a useful frame of reference. In the interests of brevity and consistency, we shall confine ourselves to illustrations from a single case study.

CASE STUDY

S. C. Johnson & Son, Inc., makers of Johnson Wax products, a company with a long history of product development, established its new products department about a year and a half ago. This company's experience cannot be said to be any more "typical" than any other, although all new products departments have much in common. But it is especially useful as a case study for the following reasons:

The company is large enough and active enough in product development to support specialization within the new products activity.

It is essentially a single division company and has a centralized administrative staff, which simplifies case study presentation.

The department was fully planned before installation, whereas many departments long in operation are still evolving their organization and procedures.

The concepts and plans for the department were documented and are available for illustrative purposes.

Over-all new product results have been good.

Since the analytical concepts and principles of organization described here have been applied effectively in other companies also, this case study may be useful generally to executives who are planning new product activities.

KEY PROBLEMS

The idea for the organization of a new products department at S. C. Johnson & Son, Inc., grew out of examination of the management problems inherent in new product activity.

An active and growth-minded company, especially in an industry characterized by products of relatively short life cycles, has many items in varying degrees of creation and exploitation. Every department of the company is involved in some degree and some way. At any given moment a cross section of the workday of the company would show a bewildering tangle of interrelated activities and decisions on new products. For example, during a late phase in the evolution of a new household insecticide, on a single typical day:

1. A chemist of the R & D department conferred in Washington with officials of the Department of Agriculture.

2. A merchandiser of the marketing department discussed labels with an outside designer.

3. A budget accountant of the financial department recalculated gross margin estimates based on new cost data supplied by the purchasing manager, who had received a formula revision from the development laboratory.

4. Technical service personnel tabulated findings from tests of product samples in use.

5. The vice president of production approved a tentative production schedule based on a sales estimate of the market research manager.

This diverse activity, multiplied by 100 or more projects, forms a maze in which it is all too easy to lose the thread of continuity. Problems breed rapidly

EXHIBIT I

CLASSIFICATION OF NEW PRODUCTS BY PRODUCT OBJECTIVE

→ INCREASING TECHNOLOGICAL NEWNESS →

↕ INCREASING MARKET NEWNESS ↕

PRODUCT OBJECTIVES	NO TECHNOLOGICAL CHANGE	IMPROVED TECHNOLOGY To utilize more fully the company's present scientific knowledge and production skills.	NEW TECHNOLOGY To acquire scientific knowledge and production skills new to the company.
NO MARKET CHANGE		**Reformulation** To maintain an optimum balance of cost, quality, and availability in the formulas of present company products. Example: use of oxidized microcrystaline waxes in Glo-Coat (1946).	**Replacement** To seek new and better ingredients or formulation for present company products in technology not now employed by the company. Example: development of synthetic resin as a replacement for shellac in Glo-Coat (1950).
STRENGTHENED MARKET To exploit more fully the existing markets for the present company products.	**Remerchandising** To increase sales to consumers of types now served by the company. Example: use of dripless spout can for emulsion waxes (1955).	**Improved Product** To improve present products for greater utility and merchandisability to consumers. Example: combination of auto paste wax and cleaner into one-step "J-Wax" (1956).	**Product Line Extension** To broaden the line of products offered to present consumers through new technology. Example: development of a general purpose floor cleaner "Emerel" in maintenance product line (1953).
NEW MARKET To increase the number of types of consumers served by the company.	**New Use** To find new classes of consumers that can utilize present company products. Example: sale of paste wax to furniture manufacturers for Caul Board wax (1946).	**Market Extension** To reach new classes of consumers by modifying present products. Example: wax-based coolants and drawing compounds for industrial machining operations (1951).	**Diversification** To add to the classes of consumers served by developing new technical knowledge. Example: development of "Raid" —dual purpose insecticide (1955).

in such an environment. However, the administrative problems that arise can be traced to these basic needs:

Classification—to determine what handling each kind of new product proposal ought to receive.

Coordination—to assure continuity and cooperation in evolution of each new product from idea to market introduction.

New knowledge—to provide information for decisions on products with which the company has had no direct prior experience.

Analysis of these needs leads to the concepts underlying new product organization.

CLASSIFICATION

A large part of the problem of assigning responsibilities has proved to be a simple lack of definition.

Just what is a new product? There are "improved products," "new uses," "new markets for old products," "related new products," "unrelated new products," "innovations," and other terms in common use. Identification of the new product function began to emerge at S. C. Johnson & Son, Inc., when the different kinds and degrees of product "newness" were related and defined so that responsibility for each kind could be sorted out and assigned. Definition rests on these concepts:

A "product" is conceived by the matching of a technology and a market and therefore has two principal "dimensions."

A product can be "new" in either one or both of these two dimensions.

"New"—for the purposes of company organization—means only that the product is new to this company.

The simplest classification of new products can now be drawn by arraying the broad technological and market objectives of the company against each other, by degrees of newness in two dimensions, as shown in EXHIBIT I. This chart unlocks the complex departmental relationships involved in the evolution of new products; different products are handled differently, in accordance with the kind of newness involved in each case.

This, then, is the first function of a new products department—to identify, isolate, and classify each new product idea. And this implies an objective, company-wide viewpoint.

COORDINATION

When the responsibilities of the marketing department and the R & D department are overlaid on the product classification chart, a large area of joint responsibilities shows up, as indicated by EXHIBIT II. Where there are joint responsibilities, there is a need for coordination of the people and activities involved—and it is exactly here, and here only, that the authority of the new products department is required.

Coordination means providing continuity for a new product through its full process of evolution, including:

Exploration—searching for ideas to meet company product objectives.

Screening—weighing technological, market, and other considerations which determine whether or not the idea is of interest to the company.

Proposal—analyzing and converting an idea into a concrete recommendation, and deciding to undertake a development project.

PRODUCT EFFECT	NO TECHNOLOGICAL CHANGE Does not require additional laboratory effort.	IMPROVED TECHNOLOGY Requires laboratory effort utilizing technology presently employed, known, or related to that used in existing company products.	NEW TECHNOLOGY Requires laboratory effort utilizing technology not presently employed in company products.
NO MARKET CHANGE Does not affect marketing programs.		Reformulation	Replacement
STRENGTHENED MARKET Affects marketing programs to present classes of consumers	Remerchandising	Improved Product	Product Line Extension
NEW MARKET Requires marketing programs for classes of consumers not now served.	New Use	Market Extension	Diversification

KEY: ▨ Research and Development Department   ▧ Marketing Department

▨ Joint Responsibility of R & D and Marketing Departments

EXHIBIT II
RELATIONSHIP OF NEW PRODUCT RESPONSIBILITIES BY DEPARTMENT

Development—turning an approved idea into a demonstrable and producible item.

Testing—conducting the product and market tests required to confirm earlier judgments and to finalize plans for production and marketing.

Commercialization—launching the new product full-scale in both production and distribution.

Coordination also means maintaining communication and directing the relationships of personnel in all company departments, as required in each phase of this complex evolution process; for every company department is involved in some way and to some extent in every one of these six phases. For example:

The development of "J-Wax," a combination cleaner and paste wax for automobiles, introduced successfully last spring, required decisions by the *marketing department* on the sales opportunity and the effect on automobile products already in the line; by the *R & D department* on the performance characteristics that could be achieved; by the *production department* on the adaptability of present machinery; and by the *administrative departments* on the availability of necessary working capital and personnel.

Only a few weeks of lost motion in the coordination of this product would have cost heavily in the competitive advantages resulting from the early introduction date actually achieved.

Thus a second and more fundamental function of the new products department is to guide the continuity of evolution for proposed new products from exploration to commercial products, and promote interdepartmental cooperation during each step of this process. And this implies independent status for the department, reporting to the chief executive officer.

NEW KNOWLEDGE

New product planning, operation, and analysis often require special investigation or activity beyond the present scope of the business, as indicated by Exhibit III. Proposed products that involve new technology or new markets require investigation of techniques and types of consumers that are outside the present body of recognized company knowledge. For example:

The development and marketing of "Raid," the dual purpose insecticide introduced by S. C. Johnson & Son, Inc., this past summer, involved the company deeply for the first time in the technology of insecticides and in the needs, habits, and purchasing patterns of the housewife in her battle against insects.

The R & D department and the marketing department do not usually have this kind of information and often have

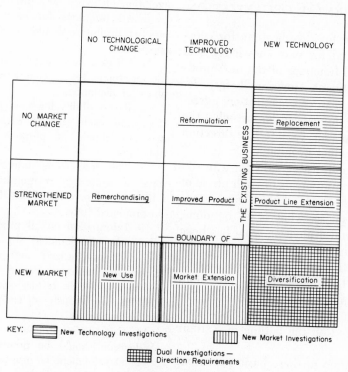

EXHIBIT III

REQUIREMENTS FOR INFORMATION OUTSIDE THE SCOPE OF
PRESENT BUSINESS

no time to get it. This is especially true in the screening phase, when the sheer volume of ideas to be considered would mean constant interruption of the scheduled work upon which the company's revenues depend.

So there is a third major function for the new products department—to conduct investigations in all phases of product evolution in which knowledge of new technology and new markets is required, as a supplement to the activities of the marketing and the R & D departments. And this implies a staff of specialists trained in technical, marketing, and business research.

DEPARTMENTAL ORGANIZATION

The need for classification, for coordination, and for new knowledge sets the general functions of the new products department. However, before developing a plan of organization, agreement must be reached on just what the requirements are for effective direction of new product evolution.

A minimum listing calls for a breakdown of requirements of each phase of evolution in terms of three basic steps for each phase—what is to be done, doing it, and evaluating what has been done. This breakdown yields only a sparse outline, but does provide a skeleton for the organizational provisions needed to meet these requirements. The executives of S. C. Johnson & Son, Inc., have agreed on the outline in Exhibit IV.

In addition to these basic provisions for each phase, all of the phases in new product evolution should be linked to-gether by added provisions for continuity, control, and completeness:

1. The originator or chief advocate of a proposed product idea should participate formally in all phases until the product is in full production and sale as an established product in the line.

2. The person who will be responsible for marketing the product should participate formally in development of the product, as well as its test marketing.

3. The person who is responsible for development work in the laboratory should participate in formulating design objectives and follow the production on through the testing phase.

4. One organizational unit should guide the complete process of product evolution on every new product.

5. All programs for each phase of product evolution should be spelled out concretely.

6. Check lists should be provided for the programs to be completed in each phase of evolution.

7. Responsibility for each phase, each step, and each task in each product's evolution should be pinpointed on one individual.

8. This responsible individual should have a reporting relationship through which interdepartmental coordination can be promoted fully.

9. Information on all product proposals under development should be consolidated, summarized, and re-evaluated in business terms at frequent intervals.

10. A full case history should be assembled continuously on each new product as it evolves.

11. Criteria for judgment at all points of decision should be pre-established.

12. Development of proposed products should be either actively in work or formally shelved.

EXHIBIT IV

REQUIREMENTS AND ORGANIZATION OF NEW PRODUCTS DEPARTMENT

Requirements for Effective Direction and Coordination of Product Evolution	*Organizational Provisions Needed to Meet These Requirements*
EXPLORATION PHASE	
1. Areas of company interest (in terms of potential products) clearly stated and widely understood.	1. A single executive charged with the specific responsibility to focus and coordinate searches for new opportunities in technology and markets.
2. Full and programed coverage of all productive sources of ideas.	2. Specialized personnel, free of responsibilities for present products, to conduct supplementary exploration of unrelated markets and technology in a neutral environment.
3. Complete capture of all ideas for proposed products to assure that each is considered.	3. A central collection station to record and process all ideas and the data supporting them.
SCREENING PHASE	
1. Standards for the measurement of proposed product ideas against company product policy.	1. Authority to determine the criteria and method by which each idea will be judged.
2. Complete and careful consideration of each idea by the persons best qualified to judge each screening factor.	2. Authority to select screening participants and to secure formal replies to specific questions.
3. Evaluation of ideas for their commercial value prior to committing development funds and manpower.	3. Skilled personnel to secure the data necessary for early commercial evaluation and to summarize all facts and opinions as a basis for deciding the disposition of each idea.
PROPOSAL AND DEVELOPMENT PHASES	
1. A management commitment of willingness to accept and utilize a product before development is begun.	1. Formal construction and authorization of a concrete development proposal, in business terms: a product of stated characteristics by a specific date, at an approved development cost.
2. Continuing liaison and agreement between marketing, R & D, other departments, and top management during the development phase.	2. Direction of the interdepartmental relationships required during development; preparation of regular summary status reports to top management.
3. Complete and realistic evaluation of the performance characteristics and market acceptance of the product developed.	3. Impartial review and audit of all new product data developed prior to top-management decisions based on these data.

EXHIBIT IV—*Continued*

REQUIREMENTS AND ORGANIZATION OF NEW PRODUCTS DEPARTMENT

Requirements for Effective Direction and Coordination of Product Evolution	*Organizational Provisions Needed to Meet These Requirements*
TEST MARKETING PHASE	
1. Opportunity to exploit all products developed, even if judged unsatisfactory for further commitment of company resources.	1. Perspective and personnel to acquire or dispose of products outside established company channels.
2. Complete and careful programing and control for test marketing, product testing, and early production.	2. Coordination and guidance of committee work and the preparation of progress reports to top management.
3. Complete and realistic appraisal of product, production, and market testing results.	3. Perspective to help establish evaluation criteria and review results impartially.

PLACE IN COMPANY STRUCTURE

Concepts and requirements, when merged, sketch a picture of a department which:

Reports to the executive vice president, in order to provide the stature and independence that are necessary for coordinating interdepartmental programs.

Participates in actual work in proportion to the degree to which a proposed idea or a product is new to the company.

Makes no decisions where responsibilities are clearly assigned to other departments.

Has authority to make required decisions and the budget to implement these decisions in areas where the responsibility is assigned to the department.

Draws on established departments as much as possible for their services in order to minimize duplications and conflicts.

Houses its own specialists as required, in order to discharge its specific duties without interfering with other divisions.

Provides its director with enough staff and freedom to participate in the broad affairs of the top planning committees of the company.

These characteristics call for a small department of specialists with a minimum of routine responsibilities. The operating departments of the company, particularly the marketing and R & D departments, should continue to carry the major work load in all product activities.

The new products department at S. C. Johnson & Son, Inc., reports directly to top management (see EXHIBIT v), rather than to R & D or marketing. Analysis of 47 departments in other companies shows this to follow majority practice, represented in 60% of the cases.[2]

OPERATING STAFF

The actual work on each project should be carried out by specific individuals drawn from as many departments as necessary. Each new proposal is unique in its requirements for development from idea to product, and therefore deserves a unique interde-

[2] Booz, Allen & Hamilton, *op. cit.*

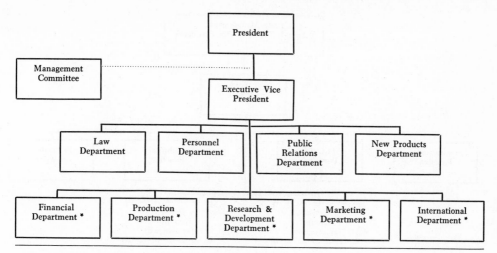

* At S. C. Johnson & Son, Inc., these large organization units are actually called "divisions." In this article they are called "departments" to avoid confusion for readers who might attach other meanings to the word "division."

EXHIBIT V.

PLAN OF TOP ORGANIZATION, S. C. JOHNSON & SON, INC.

partmental organization to nurture it. It would be impractical to staff the new products department with enough permanent employees to handle the full evolution of every proposed product.

At S. C. Johnson & Son, Inc., two kinds of "task forces" report to the new products director (see EXHIBIT VI). These are the principal vehicles for carrying forward new product activities in all departments:

1. *Sponsor groups* formulate a proposal and guide its development. Each group is formally charged, after the screening phase, with responsibility for successful development into a realistic product. The composition of the group is tailored to fit the specific product and its characteristics. Marketing, R & D, and the new products department are always represented; in addition, there may be one or two individuals drawn from other departments. To illustrate:

At the present time, there are nearly 40 sponsor groups, with a total of over 150 members from all company departments, each vigorously pushing forward the development of its product. Each group is guided and assisted by the new products department, which coordinates the activities through a member of its own staff assigned to each sponsor group.

The sponsor group is a key provision in the organization of this new products department. It is the device through which the department discharges its responsibilities in the proposal and development phases. It provides minimum interference with the established departments and maximum reliance on their existing personnel and services. It represents, in effect, formal recognition of relationships among people who either do or should work together in any successful product development.

2. *Product committees* are formally organized with regular meetings and agenda,

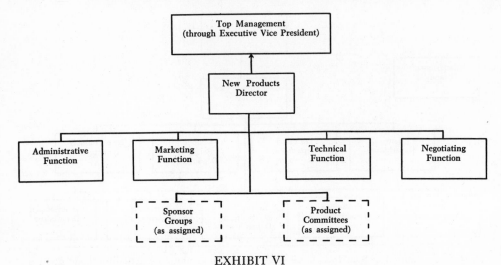

EXHIBIT VI

PLAN OF ORGANIZATION, NEW PRODUCTS DEPARTMENT, S. C. JOHNSON & SON, INC.

and have a large membership drawn from many departments—but the nucleus of each committee is the sponsor group that developed the product. The product committee is responsible for carrying a product, once developed, through to full-scale commercialization. At S. C. Johnson & Son, Inc., where test marketing is of major importance, the committee chairman is usually a product or sales manager.

For example, product idea #620 (a lightweight wax applier) is now in a product committee with this membership:

The staff designer from the development department.

A product manager from the advertising and merchandising department.

A project manager from the marketing research department.

An account executive from the advertising agency.

A buyer from the purchasing department.

An industrial engineer from the industrial engineering department.

The technical coordinator from the new products department.

The minutes of one week's conferences show that the product committee made these decisions:

Ordered production molds.

Recommended advertising copy and strategy (for top-management approval).

Established delivery schedule with suppliers.

Programed additional product-in-use tests.

The committee also coordinates all activities of product introduction to the point where line responsibility for the new product has been permanently established and is operating smoothly.

The importance of these task forces is attested by the fact that the phases of new product evolution have come in practice to be called the "sponsor group phase" and the "product committee phase."

FUNCTIONAL SPECIALIZATION

The over-all responsibilities of the new products department are broken down into four basic areas for purposes of internal organization:

1. *Administrative (internal)* — includes monitoring schedules, processing forms, maintaining records, and preparing reports.
2. *Marketing*—includes marketing research, analysis, and liaison with sales personnel.
3. *Technical* — includes technical research, analysis of technological factors, and liaison with R & D personnel.
4. *Negotiating (external)*—includes contacting outsiders for acquisitions, negotiations, patents, and product exploitation outside company facilities.

Of course, each member of the department participates in many sponsor groups and product committees and shares in a variety of cooperative tasks.

The responsibilities of each position are established in detail and the working relationships in each step of the total process defined. Similarly, the working relationships of the total department with each major department of the company are specified. Such detailing is important to effective operations, and must be tailored to each company. However, the broad division of responsibilities which is shown here is typical of other new products departments that have achieved a comparable level of specialization.

OPERATING PROCEDURES

Effective communication channels are essential to new product evolution. Organization of the new products department at S. C. Johnson & Son, Inc., has been planned to assure that these communication channels could be easily maintained within the formal lines of organizational authority required for control (see EXHIBIT VII).

The organizational responsibilities and working relationships have been given more specific expression by translating communications into procedures, with forms and records, for the conduct and control of new products activities. It is obvious that the detail of these procedures cannot be covered in the limited space of this article. It is especially regrettable that the roles of the production, financial, and several administrative departments cannot be described. All are highly important to a successful new product endeavor.

The established procedures—carefully built and integrated—retain considerable flexibility to meet changing circumstances. There is a constant recycling of phases and steps as events unfold, but the recycling is formal, and control is maintained by phase even in the ebb and flow of this creative process.

The most important single form is probably the "product proposal" (EXHIBIT VIII) which is the basis of management control. It is this document which is prepared by the sponsor group for top management authorization of each new product before development and through which subsequent progress is followed. This form, with its summary data, has the merit of being on one page, and the total company new product effort can be assembled in a loose-leaf book of a size conducive to frequent executive review. (Further data in considerable detail can be supplied as required at major decision points.)

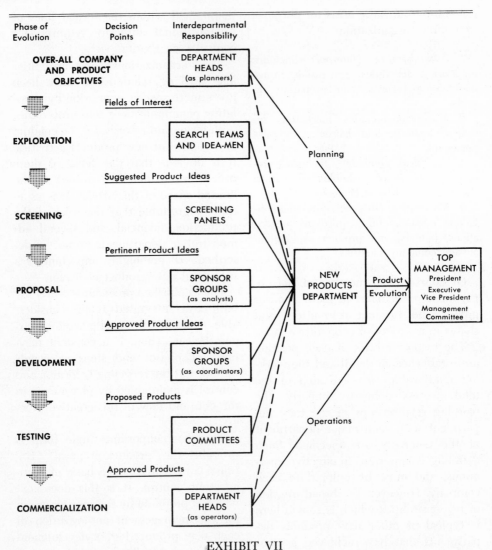

| Phase of Evolution | Decision Points | Interdepartmental Responsibility |

OVER-ALL COMPANY AND PRODUCT OBJECTIVES → DEPARTMENT HEADS (as planners)

Fields of Interest

EXPLORATION → SEARCH TEAMS AND IDEA-MEN

Suggested Product Ideas

SCREENING → SCREENING PANELS

Pertinent Product Ideas

PROPOSAL → SPONSOR GROUPS (as analysts)

Approved Product Ideas

DEVELOPMENT → SPONSOR GROUPS (as coordinators)

Proposed Products

TESTING → PRODUCT COMMITTEES

Approved Products

COMMERCIALIZATION → DEPARTMENT HEADS (as operators)

Planning

NEW PRODUCTS DEPARTMENT

Product Evolution

TOP MANAGEMENT
President
Executive Vice President
Management Committee

Operations

EXHIBIT VII

COMMUNICATIONS FOR EFFECTIVE NEW PRODUCT EVOLUTION

BUDGET ALLOCATION

Organization and control are most clearly illustrated in the acid test of allocating the product development budget. The budget is allocated and controlled so that the marketing department, R & D department, and the new products department each has its own budget for development work—though, of course, all laboratory projects are actually carried out under the administration of the R & D department, and all market testing under the marketing department.

The product development budget components, with requisitioning author-

EXHIBIT VIII
SAMPLE PRODUCT PROPOSAL FORM

S. C. Johnson & Son, Inc.

PRODUCT PROPOSAL

PRODUCT
PROPOSAL NO. 27

Type	Priority	Title	Date
Diversification	1	Space Deodorant	October 19, 1955

1. PROPOSAL OBJECTIVES: To develop a room deodorant in a pressurized container which performs in a manner which the housewife will recognize as being demonstrably better than competitive products. This is to be accomplished as follows:

   a. by neutralizing offensive odors rather than acting through olfactory desensitization and masking.

   b. by having a clean, fresh, low level odor (such as "the smell of the outdoors after a rain").

The product shall have a cost which will permit competitive pricing to yield a profit consistent with the company profit policy and shall be made with readily available materials and equipment.

2. ESTIMATED RETURN

A. Present Total Market Factory Annual Sales ... $ XX,000,000

B. Estimated Total Market in Five (5) Years ... $ XX,000,000

C. Johnson Target Annual Sales (Yr.) ... $ X,000,000

D. Estimated Annual Gross Profit % ... $ X,000,000

3. ESTIMATED INVESTMENT

A. Est. Sponsor Group Phase Costs ... $ XX,000

B. Product Committee Phase Costs ... $ XX,000

C. Introduction Costs ... $ XXX,000

D. Capital Expenditures ... $ XX,000

E. Total ... $ XXX,000

4. SCHEDULE

	Proposed	Actual
A. Approval of Product Proposal		Oct 31, 55
B. Development Start Date	Nov 7, 55	Nov 7, 55
C. Presentation of Development Report	Feb 17, 56	
D. Presentation of Test Market Plans	Mar 9, 56	
E. Presentation of Final Sales Plans	Aug 24, 56	
F. Full Sale Begins	Oct 1, 56	

5.

		BUDGET	
		Current Six Months to 7 1956	Next Six Months to 19
A. R & D (Inside)	$	X,000	$ X,000 $
(Outside)	$	000	$ 000 $
B. Mrktg. (Inside)	$	000	$ 000 $
(Outside)	$	X,000	$ X,000 $
C. Other (Inside)	$		$ $
(Outside)	$		$ $
D. Total	$ XX,000	$ XX,000 $	

6.

		Division
A. Chairman	W. M. Schmick	Mktg.
B.	C. T. Rood	R&D
C.	R. A. Graef	Adm.Mgt.
D.		
E.		
F.		
G.		

7. APPROVAL OF ITEMS INDICATED

All	Samuel C. Johnson		10-20-55
	New Products Director		Date
1, 4F, 5B	R. W. Carlson		10-25-55
	Marketing Vice President		Date
1, 4C, 5A	J. V. Steinle		10-28-55
	R & D Vice President		Date
1, 4, 5	H. M. Packard		10-31-55
	Executive Vice President or Management Committee		Date

A-4 Rev. 2

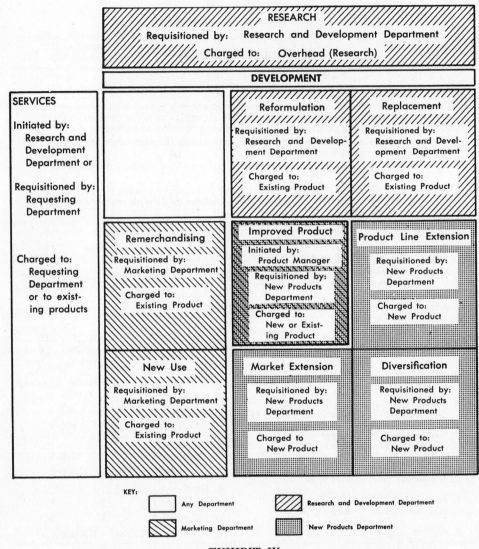

KEY:

☐	Any Department	▨	Research and Development Department
▧	Marketing Department	▦	New Products Department

EXHIBIT IX

BASIC COMPONENTS OF THE RESEARCH AND DEVELOPMENT BUDGET
(showing requisitioning authority and accounting procedure for expenditures)

ity and accounting procedure, are charted in EXHIBIT IX, along with the budget components for basic research and the service functions of R & D.

It should also be noted that S. C. Johnson & Son, Inc., has product man-

agers, or "brand managers," in its marketing department, who retain primary responsibility for their own product improvements. However, over-all control and coordination are exercised by the new products director, and the product manager is, in effect, a predetermined sponsor group chairman.

Only when the new products department function is conceived clearly enough to establish budget and accounting procedure for its area of responsibility is it practicable to consider that the organization has been defined.

CONCLUSION

Every management that is convinced of the importance of new products is faced with this question of how to organize the new product function. At S. C. Johnson & Son, Inc., the program has been placed under a new products department, which reports to top management. After a year and a half of operations, company executives see such noticeable benefits as these:

The total product strategy of the company has been clarified and is scheduled toward specific products, which is the only possible approach to realistic long-range company plans.

Enthusiasm of persons on product development teams is often lifted by the knowledge that management has already agreed to utilize the developed product and that management knows which individuals are working on it.

Sponsor group and product committee activities are developing broader management skills for individuals at all levels, and their group efforts are clearly stimulating more creative ideas.

The profit potential of projects is higher, because product selection standards have been upgraded and controlled toward the goal of maximum return on available resources and manpower.

Lost effort has been reduced, with a lower mortality of products after development, thereby relieving staffing pressures

in technical manpower and minimizing personal disappointments.

Top management has a more complete picture of the current new product status in factual, condensed business terms; decisions are more prompt and based on fuller information.

Management has been relieved of many part-time coordinating and supervisory requirements and has more time for analysis and judgment at critical decision points.

In addition to the ideas generated, development on a number of long-considered new products is finally crystallized, and so more new products than ever before are on the way to market.

The time required for a new product to go from idea to market place is noticeably faster because group work anticipates problems and devises solutions well in advance.

Products created are more successful because the sales features are designed into the product proposal by team thinking before a full-scale development project is ever begun.

It is not suggested that this particular new products organization is for universal application, set up as it is for a particular company. Here are some of the variations seen in other companies:

Larger multidivisional companies, for example, need a new product function in each division (to expand divisional markets and technology) and also at the corporate level (to generate products for new divisions). Smaller companies with lower levels of activity can coordinate directly by executive committee without a supporting new products department staff.

Companies in which strategy is dominated by merchandising factors sometimes locate the new product function in the marketing department. Companies that are dominated by technological factors sometimes locate it in R & D.

The size of the new product staff varies from one company to another, depending on company size, new product generation rates typical of its industry, and the competitive standing of the company in its industry at the time. Actual cases exist of departments from one to over two hundred men.

Nor should it be implied that this one dose of organization and control has provided full immunity from all new product aches and pains. Many specifics, vitally important to making gears mesh smoothly in actual operations, have been omitted in this article. It is especially important that the product teams, cutting across department lines, be administered to avoid the inherent problem of breaking down normal and healthy supervisory relationships.

However, the basic principles and the analytical techniques have stood the test of time and are applicable in a variety of manufacturing companies that seek bench marks for improved organization of their new product effort.

►►►►►►►►►►►► WHY MODERN MARKETING NEEDS
THE PRODUCT MANAGER

Printers' Ink

For every company with more than one product line, the intensely competitive conditions of marketing today pose a special organizational problem. The question is how to put the greatest marketing effort behind each product when there are so many products and markets. A growing number of companies are finding their answer in two words: product managers.

A harried management consultant reports, "A lot of our executive recruiting right now involves finding men qualified to work as product managers." He adds, "At the moment, we have more jobs than candidates."

Manager Ed Reynolds of American Management Assn.'s marketing division reports that recently his office has been getting more requests for information on product management than on any other issue.

It seems clear that the product manager is the man of the hour in marketing organization. Less clear is his role. He is many things in different ways. But for all companies, there is one common denominator: The product manager is their means of solving the complexities of modern marketing through a new form of decentralization.

The concept of product management is not new. Probably it originated (as have so many other effective marketing techniques) in the retail trade, in this case in the departmental buyer system used in department stores. Since no one person can reasonably be expected to determine all of the thousands of products a store must stock, and the merchandising programs for each, the store divides this basic responsibility among several departmental specialists.

Similarly, the product manager in a producing company is, by virtue of a reverse twist, assigned (within variable limits) the responsibility for selecting the products in his line and planning the marketing of them. He is, to a variable degree in different companies, a deputy chief marketing executive. He supervises for one of several product lines those functions supervised by the chief marketing man for all of the company's products.

BREEDING GROUNDS

Every product manager performs many duties in connection with his products, but his efforts usually center mainly in one functional area, the orientation generally being determined by industry category. There seem to be three basic types of product-management organization:

An advertising (and sales promotion) orientation is most common among consumer companies, like Procter & Gamble, where advertising is such a large and critical part of the marketing program.

In the industrial field, where customer relations and service are paramount requirements, sales (and technical service) get the PM's major attention. At Du Pont, for example, a PM may report upward through four or five levels of sales executives.

The third, and most comprehensive kind of product manager—as well as the most rare—is the kind who is more correctly called a general manager. He is found in the largest companies, like General Electric, which has more than 100 product departments or "profit centers." Each is headed by a general manager responsible for everything about his products from manufacturing to marketing—with supervision from above.

However he functions, the product manager is old for some companies, but new for most. Except for a handful of larger companies, those that now use PMs have done so for five years or less. Among the exceptions are P&G and Johnson & Johnson, which have had PMs for 25 years or more. Neil McElroy, board chairman at P&G, started as a product manager with the company. PMs of other companies have become top executives, too.

This is one of the many benefits companies have found in product manager organization. The position is, among other things, an excellent training ground for promising young executive candidates, for it generally involves them in every area of company operation—finance, production and marketing. It has already served as a launching pad for marketing-minded young men interested in rising to the top of their company, and it seems certain to produce many more company leaders.

But these are future benefits—for the company and for the executive. The major reasons for the growing interest in product managers are more urgent. Product management offers:

Concentrated fire power in each market segment, through centralized planning responsibility. Obviously (assuming competence) four men, each working on one product line, can do a more complete job than one man spreading his talents over four product lines.

Greater efficiency through greater liaison and coordination. It is not only the growing number of product lines that complicates the marketing process, but also the growing number of functions (marketing research, product planning, etc.) required for each. What might be a tangled web of activities around a product is often synchronized by the presence of a product manager.

Increased profitability, through savings from improved efficiency and a stronger position in the market. General Aniline & Film estimates that its product manager system has meant millions of dollars to the company in the three years since the system was installed.

COMMON TRAITS

In a study of companies with product managers, *Printers' Ink* found wide variations. Probably lack of experience best explains the difference in individual company operations revealed by the study. But differences there are. For example, the same job carries different titles, duties, responsibilities, authority —and status—in different companies. But there are also a number of common denominators.

For one thing, product management seems to work as well for industrial as for consumer companies. Just as much if not more enthusiasm for the system exists among industrial firms. For another, there is an apparent accent on youth. Most PMs seem to be business-school graduates who have had a brief baptism by fire in line marketing operations—perhaps as field salesmen—before moving into their positions. And for a third, few companies sharply delineate the PM's area of operations, as between line and staff function; most give him heavy responsibility, though not with commensurate authority. And almost all are still grappling with the problem of how to center profit responsibility on the PM without giving him control of price-cost-profit factors (though almost every company gives him some voice on these matters).

Unquestionably, the most common characteristic of companies working with PMs is *change*. A company makes changes as it learns more about how best to use the system, as pressures from changing markets force new needs, as the experience of other companies suggests new forms. And there is every indication that for all these same reasons, additional change may be expected as experience broadens. To illustrate the range of experience and change, *Printers' Ink* selected three companies that represent the three basic kinds of product management operation.

Kimberly-Clark's consumer division (Kleenex, Delsey, Kotex, etc.), which has used PMs since June 1956, reflects the advertising orientation of many consumer PMs. Merck's chemical division, which has used PMs for about

14 years, typifies the company whose accent is on sales and technical service. Raytheon's government equipment and systems division, which has used PMs since the mid-'50s, takes the general manager approach.

ORIENTATIONS—1

Kimberly-Clark has seven brand managers in its consumer division, six handling one brand each and the seventh two. Their work is supervised by products manager Harry J. Sheerin, who reports to the marketing services manager, Eugene Olson, along with

sales promotion manager James Arnold and budget control manager August Hillem.

There are two other marketing units operating as independent departments within the division and reporting to the corporate senior vice-president (L. E. Phenner) who heads the division. A divisional sales force handles all products in the field. A marketing planning and research department includes among its divisional functions the testing of new products.

Each brand manager is responsible for drawing up complete marketing programs for his brand. But, says a

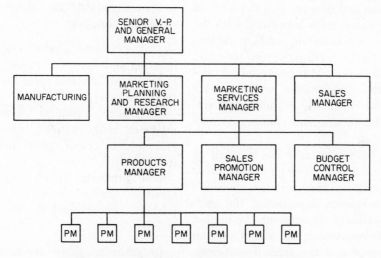

ACCENT ON ADVERTISING: KIMBERLY-CLARK CORP.,
CONSUMER DIVISION

Special boxes for advertising agency account executives and supervisors would make this chart complete. For, while advertising as a function isn't shown, it is nevertheless the single most important responsibility of the seven brand managers. They are essentially advertising managers for their brands, and spend about 75 per cent of their time on advertising and promotion problems. But they also have basic responsibility for planning and coordinating all marketing activities connected with their products. They report through a products manager, and work closely with all related functions to develop complete marketing plans for their brands. There is one sales force serving all brands.

company spokesman, "The brand manager spends 75 per cent of his time on advertising and promotion campaigns—creating, budgeting and getting approval."

There is no divisional advertising department. The brand manager serves as ad manager for his products, working with an account executive of one of the company's two ad agencies, Foote, Cone & Belding, and Doherty, Clifford, Steers & Shenfield.

In addition, the brand manager is responsible for recommending marketing objectives for his brand, planning marketing strategy, drawing proposed budgets, initiating new projects and programs and coordinating the work of all functional units concerned with the production, financing and marketing of the product. He must also maintain communication with management and with the departments working with him, and constantly evaluate performance and recommend changes as necessary.

The brand manager has no staff of his own, but may draw on the resources of advertising agencies, the division's sales promotion department, the marketing research department, the budget control department, the manufacturing department and the sales department. The brand manager has a definite responsibility for the profitability of his line, but no price-making authority and no profit accountability.

ORIENTATIONS—2

The chemical division of Merck & Co., Inc., one of four divisions in the company, reflects the importance of sales in industrial marketing generally and in the chemical industry specifically. Each of the five product departments making up the chemical division has its own sales force.

Typically, the general products department, which sells a variety of additives to food packers and processors, is headed by a marketing director—R. W. Hayes—who is also the sales manager. This department—like the other four in the chemical division—is organized in two units, sales and product management. Hayes reports directly to division president W. H. McLean.

Under R. G. Valerio, who holds the odd-sounding title of manager of product management, are three product managers handling:

—meat products (meat curing, fermenting and flavor-enhancing products for meat packers and spice houses who serve packers);
—enrichment products (enrichment mixtures, bulk vitamins, amino acids, etc., sold to cereal, grain and baking industries);
—food products (citric acids, bulk vitamins, amino acids, etc., sold to packers, canners and the frozen food industry).

In addition, there are a technical service manager and one assistant product manager.

Each product manager is a staff member whose primary function is to "plan for the growth and profitability of his markets."

The emphasis on markets, rather than products, is important. It indicates a growing trend among industrial companies toward serving the needs of their markets rather than simply selling

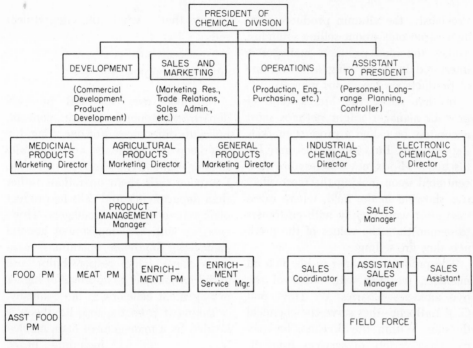

Sales-oriented PMs: MERCK & CO., INC., Chemical division

Like many other industrial marketing companies, the chemical division of Merck puts its major emphasis on field sales and service in distributing a constant flow of new products to various markets. The PM is concerned primarily with markets rather than products, and his basic objective is to draw plans that will help the sales force fully to penetrate the various markets for which the PM is responsible. The divisional organization reflects this sales orientation. Each of the five product departments of the division, like the general (food) products shown on this chart, is organized into two units: planning, through the product managers; and field operations, through a separate sales force for each department. In addition, the division staff includes a sales and marketing function which, apart fom marketing research for all departments, provides a number of varied sales support activities for each department.

products on hand to various customers. This is, of course, the essence of true marketing.

In several cases, the same products are handled by different product managers. It is their job to know their markets thoroughly and to exploit the possible uses for the products of the company.

This policy represents a major change in the orientation three years ago from the product orientation that had existed.

Previously, the vitamin products manager cared only about selling vitamins. Today, the food products manager is interested in developing a broad line of products for use in his markets.

In that sense, the Merck type of product manager might perhaps most accurately be called a product marketing manager. But, true as this may be, his major efforts nevertheless are concentrated upon making the most effective showing in the field, where salesmen must work closely with customers to demonstrate the values of the products they are selling.

The product manager is his own ad manager, working with either of the two agencies—Charles W. Hoyt and C. J. LaRoche—that serve the chemical division. Within the division, he may call on a variety of services from divisional departments, including product development and sales and marketing, the latter a sizable unit providing marketing research and a variety of sales support, including sales service, sales administration and sales control.

Further emphasizing the primary role of sales in its marketing efforts is the fact that the general products department, under the assistant sales manager, has two staff planning aides. The entire effort is organized to strengthen the position of the man who has to sell the customer.

Merck's chemical division has undergone many changes in its product management operation, but none so far-reaching as the switch in orientation from products to markets. Further changes are expected—one probably in the name of the general products department to food products department

(since that's what the department sells).

ORIENTATIONS—3

Raytheon uses the GE product-department general manager concept, but with differences. For one thing, the Raytheon departments are generally smaller than GE's. And for another, Raytheon calls them operations rather than departments, and calls its product managers operations managers. However, as with GE department general managers, Raytheon operations managers have wide responsibility and authority—subject to approval of higher management echelons in the company.

Taking it from the top, Raytheon is headed by a management team labeled "executive offices," including board chairman Charles F. Adams, president Richard E. Krafve, and senior vice-president Percy L. Spencer. The company has 12 operating divisions, most of which are organized into two groups, government and commercial, headed by group vice-presidents, with the other divisions reporting directly to the top. Operations are organized within divisions headed by general managers.

Because of its rapid past growth and continuing expansion, Raytheon has experienced somewhat more organizational change than many other companies. Management structure may vary within the same group and even within the same division—as modifications of the basic forms are made to meet specific conditions.

The government equipment and systems group headed by vice-president D. D. Coffin has three divisions: equip-

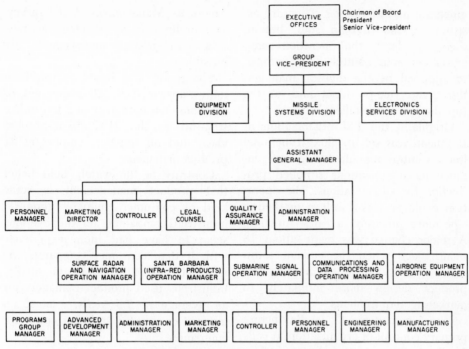

THE PM AS GENERAL MANAGER: RAYTHEON CO.,
GOVERNMENT EQUIPMENT DIVISION

Raytheon calls its product departments "operations," its product managers "operation managers." Although there are variations in actual practice among the operation managers in Raytheon's 12 operating divisions, they are generally given full responsibility for their product lines. That includes manufacturing and engineering, though some operations may have no production facilities of their own, and purchase manufacturing elsewhere within the company or outside. A Raytheon operation manager may have more responsibility and authority than most PMs. But his activities are carefully supervised and controlled by three layers of management above him, at division, group, and corporate levels. This chart, focused on the organization of submarine signal operation manager W. Rogers Hamel, illustrates a typical operation manager's reporting relationships upward through three other management levels, and downward through his own staff.

ment, missile systems, and electronic services. The equipment division has five operations managers reporting to general manager Glenn Lord. In addition, reporting through assistant general manager Fritz Gross are six divisional staff functions, including a marketing director who provides staff aid to operations managers in such

areas as advertising, sales promotion and product planning.

Some operation managers have sizable staffs of their own. For example, within the equipment division, which has five operations, W. Rogers Hamel, manager of the submarine signal operation, has eight functions reporting to him, including manufacturing, engineering and marketing. They are assisted by the division staff, but in theory at least, the operation manager's decisions control—albeit subject to approval by the division manager, the group vice-president and, at the top, the "executive offices."

Originally the PM organization at Raytheon was set up along functional lines. Central manufacturing and engineering organizations supplied production for all operations. The operation manager was purely a marketing —or more precisely, a sales—function. A major change was made about 18 months ago when the current setup was established to tie engineering and product design more intimately to marketing requirements.

"Area management" is Raytheon's primary concept of organization. It calls for the building of complete manufacturing operations to serve various areas of the world with Raytheon products. But this would seem to put the currently decentralized "operation" type of product management in conflict with the basic organizational concept.

The result could be a move toward something like the Merck operation, with product managers responsible for serving markets rather than simply selling products, and without responsibility for production. But that is speculative. What remains certain is that Raytheon, like all companies, can expect further change in its structure and methods of product management.

ORIGINS AND DUTIES

How do these three cases measure up against the experience of other companies? Some comparisons with an American Management Assn. survey, as a preliminary to organizing its new course in product management, are possible.

The survey was based on questionnaires answered by 20 companies or divisions—ten consumer and ten industrial—all in the $100-million-or-more class, and all together employing 77 product managers.

Contrary to the widely held belief that product management is some kind of consumer company gimmick, industrial companies, on the average, seem to have had more experience with it than consumer companies. At least, of the companies in the survey, industrials used product managers for an average of 7.5 years, against an average of only 6.3 years for consumer companies.

Several pertinent questions are illuminated if not definitively answered by the survey.

Where does the product manager come from? Generally from some other marketing job within the company. More consumer PMs (87 per cent) than industrial PMs (52 per cent) moved into their posts from other marketing positions; but more industrial PMs (78 per cent) were promoted from within, consumer companies having recruited 43 per cent of their PMs from outside. (Incidentally, 38 per cent of the industrial PMs came from engineering or research and development jobs—fields that produced none of the consumer PMs.)

What are his responsibilities? They vary widely between consumer and industrial companies. Companies were asked to list primary responsibilities of their PMs. All of the industrials listed first, "Recommends additions and deletions to the line"—a reflection of the importance of market needs over product selling. Nine out of ten added sales forecasting and sales promotion. And eight out of ten noted that their PMs determine product specifications, participate in sales planning. Further reflecting industrial emphasis on sales is the fact that while all 20 companies (industrial and consumer) noted that their PMs made periodic fact-finding field trips, eight out of the ten industrial PMs "assist in selling key accounts"—a function listed for none of the consumer PMs. And all industrial PMs are required to counsel regional or district sales managers, as against only 80 per cent of consumer PMs.

All consumer companies grouped advertising, sales promotion and marketing research at the top. Eight out of ten added "expense budgeting."

How does he operate? Some of the confusions about the PM system can be laid to lack of sufficient experience with it. For example, 60 per cent of the consumer companies choose to designate their PMs as line executives, when in fact some of them exercise little line control and actually perform planning and advisory duties usually designated as staff. Probably the most realistic approach to the question of line or staff designation is offered by those two out of ten consumer companies that reported they make no distinction—for they most clearly suggest the fluidity of the situation.

Again, 60 per cent of consumer and 50 per cent of the industrial companies reported that they give their PMs "price making authority." But, almost all added some qualification that renders that authority something more like the authority to make serious price *recommendations*.

ANSWERABLE TO . . . ?

There is greater clarity about and uniformity of policy on other operational points. All companies require their PMs to prepare sales forecasts and price-cost-profit budgets. Similarly, all give their PMs periodic operating statements for their product lines. On the matter of ad and promotion budgets, 80 per cent of the consumer companies and 55 per cent of the industrials give PMs the authority to determine or approve both, and another 30 per cent of the industrials give this authority for one or the other.

Incidentally, as for the number of products for which a PM is responsible, the range is from a consumer average of 1.4 to an industrial average of 10.2 —the larger figure, however, including a greater variety of sizes and designs of industrial products. (One company that noted its PMs handle an average of 203 products might have more accurately said they each handle that many items instead.)

What are his reporting arrangements? Generally, the product manager reports to a higher marketing executive, though this is more common in consumer companies, wherein he reports to either a marketing director (40 per cent), chief product manager (30 per cent), merchandising manager (20 per cent), or ad manager (10 per cent). Among industrials, eight out of ten report to general managers of their divisions.

Beyond that level, the PM is closer to general management in industrial than in consumer companies. Sixty per cent of the men to whom the product managers report in industrial companies themselves report to either the president, executive vice-president or division manager. In consumer companies only 30 per cent report to general management. The rest of the PM supervisors in both categories report to another marketing executive, either the marketing vice-president, director of marketing or general sales manager.

WHAT'S AHEAD?

Whatever validity these findings have, they are true only for today. Even now, the companies studied by *Printers' Ink* and AMA are very likely planning or making changes in their product management organization. And every change is directed toward improving the system. For with all the confusions and experimentation, there seems no doubt that the product manager system is here to stay.

Here and there the validity of the PM operation is questioned. For example, president Grant Horsey of Salada-Shirriff-Horsey, which doesn't have product managers, wonders whether the young, relatively inexperienced men frequently appointed as product managers can reasonably be expected to carry the heavy load of responsibilities they are given. But such questions seem to be answered by the experience of those companies that rely on product managers. These companies recognize the problems, and work constantly to balance the realities. And, apparently, they seem certain that they are doing the right thing. *Printers' Ink* found no company now using product managers that is willing to abandon a system that many consider the best means yet devised to put their best foot forward in every one of their markets.

➤➤➤➤➤➤➤➤➤➤➤➤➤ ORGANIZATION FOR NEW-PRODUCT DEVELOPMENT?

E. J. MCCARTHY*

INTRODUCTION

In recent years a great deal of attention has been directed to new-product development. The failure rate on new products is so high (four out of five) that management has been avidly searching for panaceas. One panacea frequently advanced is some kind of committee organization.

Reprinted from The Journal of Business, *April 1959, pp. 128–132, with permission of the University of Chicago.*

*College of Commerce, University of Notre Dame.

This paper will argue that (1) organization is not a very important factor in new-product development and that (2), although organizational plans may facilitate successful product development, such plans will be fruitless unless accompanied by a dynamic innovating attitude on the part of both top management and the whole company organization.

METHODS OF ORGANIZATION

There are six different methods of co-ordinating new-product development, classified as to the person or department that does the co-ordinating: (1) a facilitating committee (usually top management); (2) a member of management, perhaps assisted by a co-ordinator or a committee; (3) the research or engineering department; (4) the sales department; (5) a new-product development department reporting to the director of research; and (6) a new-product development department reporting to management. The last method, a new-product development department reporting directly to top management, is the one generally being suggested in current literature. This approach usually requires coordination (through committees!) with all the various divisions of the company.

A review of the various methods makes it obvious that, except for the first one, a committee method is not required at all. However, it should also be emphasized that a committee approach could be used for all six approaches.

CURRENT HYPOTHESIS ON ORGANIZATION FOR NEW-PRODUCT DEVELOPMENT

The hypothesis that some type of committee organization is necessary for successful new-product development is stated or strongly implied in most discussions on this topic. Many firms have had success facilitating new-product development with the committee form of organization, and it certainly would be foolhardy for any management to delay adopting such a form if it would insure results. In a well-written article Johnson and Jones indicate that a majority (60 per cent) of companies do use some kind of committee organization for new-product development.[1] In a democracy the majority is considered to be right, and therefore the implication seems to be that the committee form of organization is most successful. The failure rate of four out of five new products, however, suggests that many companies are having difficulties and that perhaps the committee form of organization is not the whole answer.

One well-known company using the first method—a top-management committee—where the benefit of top-management group thinking, planning, and co-ordination should facilitate the easy flow of new products (at least if one considers the committee plan as a cure-all) has been notoriously unproductive of new products. Another company, the Stauffer Chemical Company, has had considerable success with new-product

[1] Samuel C. Johnson and Conrad Jones, "How to Organize for New Products," *Harvard Business Review*, May–June, 1957, pp. 49–62.

development without any committees. The president directs activities and delegates responsibility. Organization is of little importance to him, as he believes that there is no such thing as a "textbook organization."[2]

In view of the high failure rate among companies using some kind of committee organization in the main, it would seem prudent to reject the implied hypothesis that committee organization is necessary for successful new-product development.

ALTERNATE HYPOTHESIS

In place of the rejected hypothesis, the following one is advanced: Successful new-product development requires *constructive action* on the part of top management as well as all personnel and is *not* directly a function of the method of organization in use. What is really involved in this hypothesis is the difference between "constructive action" and "defensive action."[3] Constructive action is that action taken by a group of individuals who are working together in an enthusiastic way. It means that everyone who is concerned with the new product is working with a positive attitude of overcoming all the problems or obstacles on the way to achieving the final objective. Individuals working together with a constructive attitude are willing to work independently as well as in co-operation with others and usually do a little more than is normally required. This

is the kind of action expected at General Mills, Inc.

A product development manager in the Jell-O Division of General Foods feels that the product development job requires "a real infatuation with the challenge of developing new and better consumer products."[4] The new products manager for General Foods' Perkins Division goes further: "New product progress is . . . a matter of character—individual and corporate. It is a management frame of mind. It must permeate the entire organization. It is a mixture of imagination, optimism and drive."[5]

Contrasted with constructive action is defensive action, which involves a "wait and see" or "let's think about this some more" attitude. People taking defensive action usually work together formally, especially if there are committees, but each individual takes steps to make sure that he is not responsible in the case of failure. Such "organization men" are more interested in being right than in making an effort to contribute toward the over-all company objective. In one well-known but stagnant company, a member of the top-management new-product committee, while describing its methods, indicated that "sensible ideas don't come up often enough to cause *trouble*."

At Texas Instrument Company there has been a real effort made to minimize the "NIH" (not invented here) factor—

2 "Stauffer: A Feel for the Future," *Business Week,* July, 1958, p. 49.

3 W. E. Anklam, "Impatient Patience," *Progress thru Research,* VIII, No. 1 (Fall, 1953), 8–10.

4 Benjamin M. Hines, "The Product Manager and New Product Development Manager," *Tide,* May 23, 1958, pp. 52–54.

5 Stephen M. Barker, "Introducing New Products: Some Observations," in R. L. Clewett (ed.), *Marketing's Role in Scientific Management* (Chicago: American Marketing Association, 1957), p. 83.

the attitude of "you invented it; you make it work."[6] The company has found that it cannot afford any working at cross-purposes in its research program.

Similarly, at Calco Division of American Cyanamid Company it was found that successful product development

requires *mutual confidence, mutual help* and *successful teamwork*. There must be a clear understanding of objectives, means for *unhampered exchange of thought* and a UNITED EFFORT not only on the part of technical personnel but also of all departments of the business. . . . Successful new product development requires . . . a tremendous cooperative effort.[7]

The difference between constructive and defensive action is not easy to recognize in an organization, and obviously all men and all organizations do not fall into either one of the two extremes. It certainly is possible to have a very dynamic top management and a very defensive organization which in total probably would not accomplish too much. The reverse is probably not so likely, however, that is, a very defensive top management and a dynamic organization. Really successful innovating companies seem to have a dynamic top management not at all like a $300,000,000-a-year, New York-based company where the research chief "growls that the company president hasn't the slightest concept of what we are doing or why."[8]

One of the complicating factors in coordinating a new-product development program is that there is a gradual shift in responsibility as the project develops from the laboratory through engineering and production to sales.[9] Apparently, in some companies, new-product development is merely an extra job which each of the departments must accomplish in addition to its regular and, it feels, more important activities. Each department is a separate little empire to itself, and any infringement upon departmental rights or activities is resisted. Some departments are "fat and lazy" as a result of currently profitable lines of products and really do not want new problems, or costs of new-product development, allocated to their accounts.[10] In such situations it is easy to see why an easy flow of new-product development projects would be difficult. The companies are strongly departmentalized, and each executive is protecting his domain. Apparently, there is no one, or no desire, to inhibit this action.

In many companies, however, this shift in responsibility is easily handled because each job is merely a part of the over-all company effort to develop and market new products. Everyone is working toward a common goal. Management is strongly innovation-minded and is willing to take risks and incur costs as long as the company is pulling together and doing its best. As noted

[6] "Research Packed with Ph.D.'s," *Business Week,* December 22, 1956, p. 58.

[7] K. H. Klipstein, "Philosophy of New Product Development," *Chemical and Engineering News,* XXVI (June 7, 1948), 1691–93.

[8] "Splurge of Research Is Piling Up New Problems for Management," *Business Week,* January 4, 1958, p. 49.

[9] Elliott S. Higgins, *New Product Development* ("Studies in Business Policy," No. 40 [New York] National Industrial Conference Board, Inc., 1950), pp. 15–16.

[10] J. A. McFadden, Jr., "Organizing New Product Development," *NACA Bulletin,* March, 1956, p. 834.

above, Hans Stauffer, president of Stauffer Chemical Company, is much interested in developing new products and new areas even at the risk of great loss. He has consistently pushed into new areas before they were obviously marked for success. Organization to him is of little importance.[11]

At Minnesota Mining, well known for successful innovation, it is felt that "the most important ingredient in successful new-business development is *people.* . . . [There] an atmosphere is created which encourages freedom of movement in exploring new business areas."[12] Minnesota Mining uses not one but four (Nos. 3–6) of the six organizational methods listed above, frequently without the aid of facilitating committees. It might be criticized for using so many different approaches. However, if the criteria for judging good organization is successful and profitable innovation, then it is not so easy to criticize the Minnesota Mining operation. It seems to get results.

Analysis of the philosophies and organizational methods of many companies leaves one with the feeling that company philosophy on new-product development is more important than the organization to carry it out. Perhaps the will to innovate must be present throughout the organization before the method of organization or mechanical aids, such as check lists, can be of much help in developing new products. Anthony reached an analogous conclusion regarding the work of research

laboratories. He found that the formal controls may be almost identical in poorly managed and in well-managed laboratories.[13] He concluded that the difference came in the way that the controls were used. In this case, it is the company attitude or philosophy toward innovation which may determine how successful the organization procedure will be.

The preoccupation in the literature with how to organize a new-product development department rather than with the philosophy of innovation may be due to the fact that the authors (and perhaps their companies) have the proper philosophy. Some special organization plan has helped those who write about this phase of the problem, and they are eager to pass on their experience to others. However, the importance of the proper outlook, because it is so natural to them, is ignored.

When an aggressive organization looks at new-product development as a company-wide activity, the method of organization and co-ordination may be of some importance. In a large company some type of committee plan may facilitate communication. Also check lists may serve as mechanical reminders. The organization plan or the administrative tools should not be given credit for the successful new-product development program, however. They are merely facilitating tools.

Theoretically, a hypothesis cannot be "proved," but the arguments presented above strongly support the proposed

[11] "Stauffer: A Feel for the Future," *op. cit.*

[12] Arthur G. Janssen, "The Organization and Use of a New-Business Development Division," *Tide*, May 23, 1958, pp. 58–59.

[13] R. N. Anthony, *Management Control in Industrial Research Organizations* (Cambridge, Mass.: Harvard University Press, 1952).

hypothesis: Successful new-product development requires *constructive action* on the part of top management as well as all personnel and is *not* directly a function of the method of organization in use. In the face of the evidence, it would seem that the burden is upon the "organizers" to show that organization is more than a facilitating mechanism.

CONCLUSION

New-product development cannot be systematized. Organizational plans may facilitate successful new-product development; but real success requires that top management's dynamic innovating attitude be instilled into and felt by the whole company. A caretaker or administrator type management cannot expect to have spectacular results with new-product development just because it has a committee or department for such purposes. Top management and the whole organization must be interested and willing to take chances and to do things which are out of the ordinary, because the development of new products is not ordinary business. When such an organization is built, then and only then should management become preoccupied with organization charts and controls. The "best-planned" organization in the world still may not come up with enough "sensible ideas . . . to cause *trouble*."

C

Generating New Product Ideas

▶▶▶▶▶▶▶▶▶▶▶ SELECTING THE RESEARCH PROGRAM:
a top management function

C. WILSON RANDLE*

RESEARCH
AS AN ECONOMIC NECESSITY

Within recent years, research has been fast becoming a basic economic necessity. Its increasing necessity has been dictated by the prevailing characteristics of our economic system, characteristics which have teamed up to cause a rather steady pressure on business profits.

The most influential of these characteristics are a growing competitiveness, steadily rising costs, and shortening product life cycles. It is no coincidence, then, that much industrial

research is aimed directly at overcoming these unwelcome business influences.

For example, the major purpose of research among manufacturing industries is to generate **new products** where the profit margins will be greater over longer periods because of accruing competitive advantages.[1]

Another primary purpose of research

[1] For all manufacturing, 48 per cent of the research effort goes into new products, 41 per cent into improving present products, and 11 per cent into developing new or improved processes. (*Business Plans 1958–1961*, McGraw-Hill, Department of Economics, 1958, p. 8).

Partner, Booz, Allen & Hamilton.

is to improve present products—often described as "defensive" research. This is research primarily aimed at maintaining or improving market position.

The third purpose is to develop new or improved processes, with the intent of reducing costs or improving productive effectiveness.

All, of course, hinge on creating greater profitability. There are few tasks of more fundamental magnitude than those already mentioned.

This thought has been well expressed by a prominent business executive who has stated:

Research and development, in this era of unprecedented technological activity and progress, may have a more important bearing on the future of a business than any other major effort in which the company is engaged.[2]

It seems clear, then, that many businesses today fail or succeed, depending on the effectiveness of their research. The number of businesses that fall into this category is increasing daily. Thus, R & D is fast becoming the insurance for tomorrow's business.

This critical dimension of research, plus the long acknowledged growth incentive provided by it, makes the attention of top management to the research program mandatory. Perhaps this can be better emphasized by considering that the research program determines what products the business will have. Determining the products literally determines what the business will be in the future. Therefore, if

[2] Wallace McDowell, "Company Policy and Research Management," American Management Association, 1955, p. 9.

management gives up leadership of the research program, it gives up leadership of the enterprise.

RESEARCH AND THE PRODUCT LIFE CYCLE

The shortening life cycles of products bears significantly on the proper planning of research by top management. Analysis shows that every product tends to pass through a rather well defined life cycle.

Most products go through a period of introduction, or market entry, which is slow in sales results. The product then catches on and enters a period of rapid growth, followed by a period of maturity where sales still increase but not at so fast a rate.

The growth period is followed by a saturation period where the competitive lead has been eliminated. Other companies have initiated production, and supply tends to outstrip demand. From this point product sales move into decline.

Although the general shape of this cycle tends to remain rather constant for all products, the length of the cycle tends to vary rather significantly between industries and products.

As a generality, basic and producers' goods industries tend to have longer cycles. The closer the product comes to the consumer and the vagaries of the market place, the shorter the cycle becomes. Thus, steel and machine tools may have life cycles of 25 to 50 years. The cycles of pharmaceuticals, cosmetics, or grocery products may range from one to four years.

From this life-cycle concept come

two major influences on the management planning of research. First, the apex of the profit-margin curve is reached far sooner than the apex of the sales-volume curve.

This is an often overlooked phenomenon. Management tends to plan around the sales volume rather than the profit yield of the product. If this normal inclination is followed in planning for new products (the province of R & D), the company invites profit deterioration. The reason is clear. By the time that sales start to fall off significantly, profits may be lean indeed, if existent at all.

PRODUCT PROFIT PERFORMANCE

The first fundamental of planning that grows out of the life-cycle concept, then, is to key the planning to product profit performance rather than sales volume. From this concept grows the necessity for having an inventory of new products whose introduction and commercialization can be timed to produce a series of interlocking profit waves which sustain company growth and success. Only top management has the perspective and leverage to ensure this result.

The second planning consideration emanating from the life-cycle concept is that the length of the cycle almost dictates the amount of effort and expenditure that is required for R & D. Businesses having short product life cycles must give greater accent to research and development.

The machine tool manufacturer, for instance, can live a more leisurely research life and may spend only a very small percentage of his sales dollar on research. On the other hand, the drug manufacturer must vigorously pursue his research program, spending perhaps five to seven per cent of sales on R & D. The alternative may be economic extinction.

Therefore, the degree of pressure created by the length of the product life cycle largely accounts for some industries spending less and others more on research.

It can logically be concluded that companies with short product life cycles will have to put more planning effort and investment into R & D than those companies favored with longer cycles. Top management should consider this a cardinal principle.

RESEARCH MORTALITY

The rather high mortality rate of research projects is another factor commanding top management's attention to the research program. There tends to be a fairly close correlation between the mortality of these projects and the life-cycle concept.

Those industries closer to the consumer and with shorter product life cycles tend to have greater research project mortality. Those at the other end of the industrial spectrum have the lowest project mortality. In both cases, however, the project mortality rate seems higher than can be justified.

It is understood, of course, that the nature of the scientific task has inherent hazards that make some mortality inevitable, and also that some companies may be willing to stand a very high mortality to achieve a single breakthrough or "business making" result.

A recent research study completed by Booz, Allen & Hamilton disclosed that, in the average industrial situation, approximately two-thirds of the R & D projects designed for a market appearance will never reach the market place.[3]

No matter how you look at it, this is a situation deserving attention. The money dimensions alone are significant. The average annual cost per scientist and engineer may range from $17,000 to $35,000, depending upon the industry involved.[4]

Thus, money dissipated by high project mortality can be significant. But even more important, a high mortality rate may retard the over-all research effort, cripple the growth impetus of the business, and cause severe profit erosion.

The reasons for this high mortality are various, but one thing seems clear. Few projects fail because of technical reasons. By and large, the technical ability of R & D personnel is excellent. Most research projects fail because the project concept was wrong in the first place. For example, the project did not fall within company fields of interest, the timing was bad, or people didn't want to buy the resulting product. In most cases, these bad research investments spring from faulty project selection.

Thus, it is again seen that top man-

[3] *The Management of Research and Development,* Management Research Department, Booz, Allen & Hamilton, Chicago, 1958, p. 13.

[4] These figures include the salary of the scientist or engineer, the salaries of technicians and supporting workers, laboratory supplies, and a proper overhead loading factor. They do not include the cost of equipment or the facility.

agement's attention to the research program can yield highly significant dividends in enhanced research effectiveness, and hence yield better business profits.

SELECTION OF THE RESEARCH PROGRAM

What goes on in research inevitably affects every area of the company. The products emerging from research (in the absence of merger or acquisition) will shape the future contour of the business. For all practical purposes, the products are the business.

It stands to reason, then, that the selection of the research program should be a total integrated company task, with final approval resting with the chief executive. The organization for project selection should implement this concept.

It seems particularly appropriate to mention here the growing importance of marketing in project selection. Many companies in today's competitive environment are finding it increasingly easier to make new products than to sell them. Consequently, these companies tend to work from the market place back to research rather than the opposite. They find what products need to be developed and then develop them. Since this development role rests with research, the major influences today in project selection are marketing and research.

Most companies have organized to reflect these two major functions in selecting the research program. Some, however, have neglected to reflect, in organizing to select research projects, the importance of other company areas.

The inclusion of other company functions may be a virtual necessity. For example, the emergence of a new or improved product frequently generates a new tooling requirement. This may be a major influence. As a consequence, many companies include engineering in the program selection group.

Almost as frequently, finance is included. The capital and expenditure requirements of a new or improved product are many times of great moment. The uniqueness of company operations may dictate the inclusion of other company functions—such as advertising or purchasing—but the four areas cited (research, marketing, engineering, and finance) appear to be a minimum nucleus with which to provide the experience and background necessary for effective and far sighted selection of the research program.

This selection group, of course, provides the variety of viewpoints necessary for appraisal of a project proposal. The final decision on the projects selected rests with the chief executive, who cannot often delegate the decision. He can never delegate his responsibility for the decision, for the consequences rest squarely on his office.

This is the generality of the matter. Specifically, there are some nine steps which can be invoked to improve the research program selection process.

1. IDENTIFY COMPANY FIELDS OF INTEREST

It is just as easy to come up with pertinent as it is impertinent product ideas. Put it another way. People can be just as creative within defined limits as they can all over the landscape.

A careful delineation of company fields of product interest will go far in providing proper and effective dimensions within which to generate product ideas. The more specifically these fields can be defined, the more direction will be provided. For example, if a company's interest is to grow in whatever field is profitable, strong pay-out product ideas are hard to come by. On the other hand, if a company is interested in only a single field of endeavor, such as electronic instruments, product ideas come much easier.

Identifying company fields of interest is thus a primary step in making project selection more effective.

2. COMMUNICATE FIELDS OF INTEREST

Management needs next to communicate the company fields of interest to personnel most likely to get new product ideas. This is necessary if there is to be "directed creativity." New idea persons or areas may vary somewhat from company to company. In general, the marketing and R & D people are most prolific with pertinent ideas (see

TABLE I

SOURCES OF NEW PRODUCT IDEAS
71 MAJOR COMPANIES

	Per Cent of Ideas
Marketing	32.4
R & D	26.5
Top Management	13.1
Customers	10.6
New Products Department	6.7
Manufacturing	3.7
All Others	7.0

Source: Management Research Department, Booz, Allen & Hamilton, 1959.

Table I for sources of new product ideas).

3. BUILD IDEA COLLECTION SYSTEM

Most businesses have enough new product ideas with which to work. However, both quantity and quality of ideas will improve with an idea collection system. Almost always there are a number of good ideas rattling around in the business which have not been nailed down or expressed.

To set up a collection system, the company first should designate an idea collection station or point. Many times people with ideas don't know where to take them.

A direct route to this collection point should be designated. Ideas melt away when subjected to multiple transmission through a complex organizational structure. Expecting ideas to come up through an organization just as authority moves down is a false hope.

Although it may appear an organizational heresy, it is recommended that the idea route be direct to the collection point rather than through supervisory levels. Otherwise, many ideas, maybe the best ones, will be choked off by supervisors who do not have sufficient knowledge for a qualified judgment.

Finally, ideas have to be actively solicited. As nearly as can be determined, there is little correlation between garrulity and creativeness. The quietest man in the company may be the most creative. Ideas have to be sought. Many will not gravitate to the collection center.

4. SCREEN THE IDEAS

Since both manpower and financial resources are usually limited, most com-panies cannot afford to develop all or most of the new-product ideas collected. Indeed, most companies cannot afford even thorough investigation of all ideas. Management should thus employ here, as it does elsewhere, the "greatest probability" approach. What ideas—quickly and inexpensively identified—offer the most promise?

This approach means certain screening criteria must be set up to drop out quickly new-product ideas of least promise. It is almost a toss-up as to whether company "fields of interest" or the estimated range of profit yield should be the first screening measure. Certainly, these are both primary persuaders. If ideas pass these tests, they can be screened against the feasibility —in a broad sense—of developing, manufacturing, and marketing the product. These major screens quickly get the bulk of the ideas out of the way so that attention can be paid to those with considerable promise.

It again should be emphasized that the screening group should be composed of representatives from each of the key company areas. No single area has the necessary experience or vision to levy effective unilateral judgment against the ideas available.

5. EXPAND PERTINENT IDEAS INTO A BUSINESS CONCEPT

With pertinent new-product ideas at hand as a result of screening, each idea now needs to be given rather detailed study and scrutiny. After the screening, each idea needs to be specifically evaluated. The best step at this point is to expand the idea into a business concept.

Most new-product ideas are either

fragmentary or simply technical considerations. Ideas in this form are difficult, if not impossible, for management to judge validly regarding their business propriety. A new-product idea as a business concept would involve, at a minimum, the development schedule, an estimated range of money to be spent, the estimated range of profit yield, and the company benefits to be derived other than direct profit yield.

Wise companies usually figure their "pay back" on the minimum range of profit yield, since there is enough risk already without extending vulnerability.

Most new-product ideas will drop out under the test of a full business concept. Remaining ones should be fully studied. At this point, some companies employ a product study team or task force to carry out the full investigation. Needless to say, full scrutiny of the ideas will cause many more to be dropped.

6. SELECT PROJECTS
AND ESTABLISH THEIR PRIORITY

Each remaining new-product idea now has been expanded to a business concept and fully investigated. Some companies find it advantageous to summarize findings and investigation in a "management" report. At any rate, the product idea should be described so that top management can assess it along with others and make a decision on which projects should be developed and in what order.

7. BUILD SPECIFICATIONS
FOR EACH APPROVED PROJECT

To this point, we have dealt in product ideas or concepts. Much emphasis has been put on the correct formulation of these concepts because here the payout is greatest. If the concept is right, the research program will be right. If the concept is wrong, no amount of technical ingenuity can assure success.

The next step is to provide research with the guidance needed to keep the development of the product in line with top management decisions. This step involves agreement on a time schedule for development, the money to be spent, and the desired design and performance characteristics to be engineered into the product. The latter will be in order of priority, for probably all cannot be achieved.

Research now has time, money, and product characteristics perimeters within which to carry out the development. These are the guide lines to be followed if the activities of research are to be integrated effectively with other functions of the business and thus assure product success.

8. RECYCLE FOR ADDITIONAL
AUTHORIZATION OR REVISED
SPECIFICATIONS

It is obviously impossible to foresee all of the problems and roadblocks R & D may encounter while the project is in the development process. However, it is clear that R & D must not violate the imposed project perimeters on its own. If it encounters circumstances that make it necessary to violate limits of time, money or product characteristics, the impending decision as to whether to continue the project is re-cycled to the organizational unit responsible for bringing a total company view into focus.

Now new limits may be set and the integrative process for other company areas revised. On the other hand, management may decide to kill the project to prevent further expenditures against an improbable product success. The company must be firm and nonemotional at this point. Money and manpower expended from here onward rise very rapidly.

9. CONTINUE EVALUATION AS DEVELOPMENT ENSUES

Research may operate well within imposed limits yet still not develop a pertinent product. Successful companies today maintain a continuing evaluation of the product evolution within R & D. As research clothes a concept with the physical characteristics constituting a product, marketing or sales must be constantly answering the question: Will the design, characteristics, and performance being achieved make the product sell?

Manufacturing, in a similar fashion, must determine whether the materials, design and performance are compatible with production possibilities. Engineering should constantly scrutinize the research project to be sure the right kind and amount of tooling will be ready at the right time. As projects develop, finance must be aware of tooling expenses, capital outlays, commercialization expenditures, and other monetary requirements and meet these needs effectively.

Thus, evaluation of evolving products within R & D is not simply a matter of technical inspection but rather must be looked at in terms of the management implications involved. Unless this is done, inappropriate prod-

ucts will be developed, useless money and manpower will be spent, and the future of the enterprise may possibly be jeopardized.

CONCLUSION

The worries of the chief executive are many. All functions naturally clamor for his attention, and he cannot attend to all. He must choose those, which in terms of his own company are the most vital to business health and growth. Research and development meets these qualifications in the majority of prominent businesses. As Duer Reeves of Esso Research has said:

Many companies and many industries realize today that technology is an important raw material in their operations. It is no longer like the frosting on the cake but is a critical element in their diet. The effectiveness of industrial research can affect a company's competitive position, its future growth, its employee relations, its public relations, and almost everything else connected with what the company does.[5]

It is for this reason that selecting the research program is a top management responsibility which cannot be otherwise delegated.

Our basic theme is that when R & D fails to meet its objectives, with consequent detriment to the company, it is more often because of the concept than technical reasons. Poor concepts are derived from faulty project selection. Faulty project selection results from lack of proper management of the selection process.

A properly managed selection proc-

[5] Maurice Holland, *Management's Stake in Research*, 1958, p. 75.

ess requires an orderly organized approach with two dominant accents. *One,* in selecting the research program, a total integrated company viewpoint should be employed rather than the unilateral decision of any one company function. *Two,* realization must be paramount that selecting the research program means deciding the future course of the business, and this can only be a top management decision.

These two accents will tend to be reflected in an improved profit and loss statement—which even the most pessimistic businessmen will admit is a nice spot to be affected.

►►►►►►►►►►►► GUIDEPOSTS IN DEVELOPING
A NEW PRODUCTS PROGRAM

ROBERT J. WILLIAMS*

It's not very difficult to distinguish between a Hemingway and a hack writer or between a Picasso and a house painter. Some people believe they can even distinguish between pure and applied research. The basis for all these distinctions is the contrast between an activity which is motivated by a desire for remote gains and glory; and one which is motivated by a quest for more immediate personal profit.

Something of this same distinction can be applied in the area of new product development. Some firms, for example, distinguish between "basic research," which has as its objective the creation of new substances or radically new products, and "customer applications research," which attempts to adapt existing products to the varying needs of the consumer. In some R & D programs, the major emphasis is on "research"; in others, on "development." Some programs are planned for an efficient short-term payoff, while others are meant to provide returns over a longer period.

THE CHOICE

For the sake of uniformity, we will use the terms "laboratory-oriented" and "market-oriented" to refer to two contrasting types of new product programs.

Each company must choose the type of development program best suited to its objectives, or must decide how to allocate its resources between the two. For this reason let us review the two programs in some detail, to see the

An address delivered before the New York Chapter of the American Marketing Association, April 17, 1963. Reprinted by permission of the author.

Director, Marketing Intelligence, Edward Dalton Co., Division of Mead Johnson & Co.

workings of each and to determine the risks and rewards involved in the choice.

In the laboratory-oriented new products program the scientist-inventor is the key figure. He is a person of unusual scientific accomplishments, hired because his professional interests parallel those of his company. He is usually encouraged to pursue his own interests and to develop products which he thinks will provide his company a profit advantage. The fruits of his labors are passed on to the marketing man who must then determine a basis on which the invention can be profitably and effectively marketed.

The market-oriented new products program, on the other hand, is one in which the creative marketing expert is the dominant figure. He is hired because of his ability to identify market vacuums and consumer needs that his company can profitably fill. When he has identified a marketing opportunity, he writes the functional specifications for the new product and passes them on to the scientist. The laboratory man must then do his best to engineer a product which fits the marketing specifications.

The type of program which exists in a company carries with it a particular relationship between the man in the white smock and the one in the grey flannel suit. Sometimes this relationship grows out of a deliberate choice of one or the other of the two types of development programs we have been considering. More often, however, a pre-existing set of social relations determines the type of new products program employed.

"Pecking orders" between scientists and marketing men tend to become established by accidents of tradition, or in attitudes of a key individual. A new products program then often grows out of such status considerations. Only rarely does a rational decision establish the basis for cooperation between Mr. White-smock and Mr. Grey-flannel. This is unfortunate, since the type of program developed has definite economic consequences for any company, and should, therefore, be based on a more rational and deliberate decision-making process.

EFFECT ON TYPE OF NEW PRODUCTS GENERATED

The choice of a laboratory- or market-oriented program will have a decided effect on the type of new product which a company brings to market. Historically, the giant steps in new product development have occurred within laboratory-oriented programs. For example, we would classify as "laboratory-oriented" the research programs which produced the electric light, penicillin and nylon. Neither Thomas Edison nor Sir Alexander Fleming sought the advice of a marketing expert to direct their research efforts. It is doubtful too that any marketing man wrote the specifications for a substance that could be woven, molded, blown, extruded, machined, and made into an array of fabrics ranging from sheer stockings to heavy carpets. These spectacular and revolutionary discoveries were inventions of individuals working, in a sense, "outside" of their markets.

The new products which issue from a market-oriented program are usually less dramatic, "evolutionary" changes. A marketing man may perceive the need, for example, for a filter on cigarettes, a ball applicator for a deodorant, premixed cake ingredients, or a pouring spout on a soap package. None of these, obviously, qualifies as a product "breakthrough." Yet, innovations such as these have had marketing significance sufficient to bring fame and fortune to the companies that produced them.

A marketing man working for an oil lamp company around the turn of the century might well have perceived a consumer need for cleaner-burning lamp fuel, larger reservoirs, and a device for instantaneous ignition with greater safety than that afforded by an open flame. He may thus have written functional specifications for improved fuel products and better lamp design, but it is unlikely that he would have invented the electric light. Nevertheless, until he was up-staged by Mr. Edison, the marketing man could have given his company a considerable competitive advantage by stimulating the development of small but quite desirable changes.

In summary, revolutionary new products, which virtually redefine a company's business and exert a profound social effect are likely to emerge only from a laboratory-oriented new products program. The countless minor changes which strengthen a company's leadership in a defined field by better adapting its products to the needs of its customers are most likely to issue from a market-oriented new products program. Obviously, the two programs differ in the pay-off-per-new-product-marketed. They differ also in the cost-per-new-product as well as in the degree of risk involved.

EFFECT ON COSTS AND PAY-OFF

Lower costs and lower risks favor the market-oriented program. In it, the marketability of a new product is virtually assured before development work is begun. Indeed, the proper stimulus for physical development of a product in a market-oriented program is evidence of the marketability of a particular product concept. Laboratory work in a market-oriented program is directed toward specific goals and is never speculative. The new products suggested by such a program very rarely involve great technological strides and so are unlikely to appear as scientific "breakthroughs." They are more likely to be extensions of present technology, or modifications of existing products for greater convenience or increased effectiveness.

A laboratory-oriented research program must commit large sums of money to providing the facilities and man power for much speculative "basic" research. New products which issue from this research may or *may not* be marketable—even if the research itself is well conceived and properly executed. For example, suppose the efficiency of energy conversion in the electric light bulb had been 5 per cent less than it actually was. Suppose Fleming's molds turned out to be a specific cure for parrot fever rather than an antibiotic to combat many infections. Or what if the tensile strength of nylon were just a little bit less than it actually is. These great products might now be merely laboratory curiosities. The margin between success and failure is incredibly slim, and no one can predict with certainty on which side of this margin the outcome of a particular research project will fall. Because we hear largely of the successes and seldom of the failures, we may lose sight of the fact that failure is the more common outcome of such research ventures. This means that the company committing itself to a laboratory-oriented new products program must be ready to underwrite the cost of many failures for each research effort that results in a marketable product.

The market-oriented new products program also requires research, some of which may end in failure. In this case, however, the first investment is in *marketing* research, dealing mainly with concepts and ideas. Its cost, and the cost of the company facilities required to support it, is modest by comparison with laboratory research.

A company that chooses to allocate a major portion of its new products research effort to laboratory-oriented activities must accept the fact that profit flow from year to year will be quite uneven. Even the best of laboratory research programs cannot be counted on to produce a sensational new product breakthrough every year. However, when a breakthrough *does* occur, the profit advantage, for a while, may be enormous. Thus, the profit flow from a laboratory-oriented new products program takes the form of occasional tidal waves.

A market-oriented new products program, however, *can* be counted upon to generate product improvements or innovations in service on a fairly regular schedule—perhaps three or four a year. Profits from any individual development may not, however, be "enormous." Thus, the profit flow would take the form of a series of regular ripples.

OPERATIONAL DIFFERENCES

The contrast in costs and risks between the two types of programs can be illustrated by a specific example. Let us suppose that we conceived of a synthetic hamburger. In a market-oriented program the marketability of such a product would be evaluated as a concept in a marketing research project requiring three or four months time and an expenditure of a few thousand dollars. The same study could accommodate a dozen or more additional concepts without adding significantly to time or cost requirements. If no basis for profitably marketing such a product could be found through market research, the concept would be dropped and efforts directed toward other possibilities. Only a small investment is lost if the idea is abandoned at this point.

If it appears, however, that such a product *could* be marketed, provided it were given certain features, then the concept can be presented to the development laboratory, which in turn can attempt to create the physical product. If, on theoretical grounds, the product is not technically feasible, then the idea can be dropped—still with only a small amount of money lost. On the other hand, if the idea is theoretically sound, physical development work in the laboratory can commence. But the laboratory work is now directed toward a specific product with a known market potential. At this point, substantial development costs are incurred, but the risk of product failure in the market place has been considerably reduced.

In a laboratory-oriented program the procedure would be somewhat different. On the basis of a new theoretical development or process discovery, the laboratory researcher perceives the technical feasibility of producing a synthetic hamburger. He proceeds to develop a product. Depending on the technical obstacles he encounters, the costs of his research project may range from a few hundred dollars to several hundred thousand dollars. His work may require several months or several years. When he emerges with the synthetic hamburger product, it may or *may not* be acceptable to the consumer. As long as the inventor follows his own inclinations, without deliberate communication with marketing people, some of his inventions must be expected to have little or no market value —even though they may be spectacular technical achievements.

The pro's and con's of both types of new product development programs may be summarized as follows:

The laboratory-oriented program yields spectacular rewards for the rare product breakthrough. The rewards are so great that a single success can pay for many failures. But the costs of such a program are high, the pay-off irregular, and the risks great. The major costs of laboratory-oriented product development are necessarily incurred before the marketability of the product is assayed.

The market-oriented program, on the other hand, yields smaller but substantial rewards for minor product improvements and adaptations to the customer's needs. The costs are relatively low and the pay-off more predictable. And major investments are incurred only after an indication of marketability has been secured.

MAKING THE CHOICE

The conceptual separation of the two types of new product programs is merely a convenience undertaken for the sake of discussion. In reality, it is difficult to find a pure case of either type. As was suggested above, the mix between the two types of programs within any particular company is more likely to be determined by the status relations existing between the scientist and the marketing man, than by a rational decision based on the growth needs of the company. It might be worthwhile to consider the factors on which a more rational decision might be based.

The choice between a laboratory-oriented or a market-oriented new products program will depend on the gambling instincts of a company's management, the size of the company, the proportion of its total resources channeled into new product programs, and the markets within which the company competes. However, none of these factors should exert the major influence. The most important consideration should be management's own definition of its future business.

Management may choose to define its business in one of two ways. A business may either be defined in terms of its control of a raw material and technology, or it may be defined in terms of the services which it performs for its customers. For example, the Standard Oil Company appears to have defined its business in terms of a raw material and a technology—oil and oil refining. Procter and Gamble, on the other hand, seems to define at least a part of its business in terms of a service to consumers—helping women to clean the house.

Each of these definitions results from what a company identifies as its principal unique asset. Standard Oil has considerable investments in oil fields, and thus is in the *oil* business. Procter and Gamble Company might identify as a principal unique asset its reputation among consumers and its skills in marketing, and thus it is in the *house cleaning* business.

Some companies have more than one business, and different segments of the business may be differently defined. For example, U. S. Rubber with its sizable investment in rubber plantations, must define a segment of its business in terms of a raw material and technology. However, the U. S. Royal Tire Division, with a considerable interest in dealerships and marketing skills, defines its business as "keeping something between your car and the road." These two segments within the business would necessarily react with different enthusiasms to the discovery of an effective synthetic material for tires.

But how do these definitions influence the type of new products program appropriate for each company? Given its definition as an *oil* company, Standard must seek growth through new uses

or new applications for oil. If oil should be outmoded as a source of power by atomic energy, then an *oil* company would be pressed to develop new uses for its raw material, perhaps as a basic chemical. What such a company needs to know is how its particular raw material can be made useful in new ways. Clearly, more can be learned about this in the laboratory than in the market place. The kind of growth opportunities such a company should be seeking require a new products program with considerable emphasis on laboratory-oriented activities. Then, once a product has been created in the laboratory, marketing skills will be required to assess its saleability.

Procter and Gamble, on the other hand, having defined its business as "helping women to clean house," will seek growth opportunities by finding new ways of serving the housewife. It will attempt to develop products that solve cleaning problems, and lighten the burden of household chores. Such a company has only a minor committment to raw materials. When soaps are outmoded by detergents, or powdered detergents by liquids, it simply seeks sources for obtaining new raw materials. The growth opportunities which such a firm seeks require a new products program with heavy emphasis on market-oriented activities. The type of information needed is that which concerns the housewife's cleaning problems and her probable reaction to new ways of solving them. More can be learned about this in the market place than in the laboratory. But once the cleaning problem has defined the need for a new product, technical skills will be required to develop its physical properties and make production feasible.

In summary, a company may define its business in terms of a particular raw material and technology, or in terms of marketing knowledge and type of service. It is this definition that determines where that company seeks its growth opportunities. And the nature of the growth area determines whether its new products program should be laboratory-oriented or market-oriented.

If the company's committment to a particular raw material or technology is great, then that company must undertake basic research in applications and uses of the raw material. It would thus require a laboratory-oriented new products program. On the other hand, if the company's principal asset is in a franchise or set of marketing skills, then that company must undertake research to understand the customer needs which create its markets. It will require a market-oriented new products program.

DEFINING THE BUSINESS

Since the choice of a type of new products program depends so much on how company management defines its future business, this definition becomes one of management's most serious tasks. Tradition, sentiment, and personal taste will, of course, affect the form of this definition. The nature of the company's principal strengths, as was suggested above, should also be a most important consideration. A company's strength may be in access to a raw material, exclusive control of a manufacturing process, a uniquely effective

marketing or sales organization, highly developed skill in communicating with a particular market segment, or perhaps simply an extraordinary reputation for a particular kind of performance. The definition of a company's future business is, of course, a key consideration in planning its strategy for growth.

No business can grow at its optimum rate if it is defined *only* in terms of raw materials or technical expertise—that is, with complete indifference to its markets. Such a definition is simply a description of *present* operations. At the very least the raw material supplier must make himself aware of the current applications of his product. Further, a definition in terms of materials or process should be eschewed unless the company has some measure of *exclusive* control over the source of supply, or patents or other protection on the processing techniques. For example, a company that owns a measureable share of the world's oil resources can realistically define itself as being in the *oil* business. At the present time, however, no one can own a measureable share of the world's plastic supplies, and no one controls the forming or processing techniques applied to plastics. Therefore, it would seem unwise for a company to define itself as being in the *plastics* business, even if plastic is very important in its present operations.

On the other hand, a business *can* define its future exclusively in terms of offering a particular service—that is, with complete indifference to raw materials or manufacturing skills. It is possible, for example, for a company to contract for all of its manufacturing requirements. Such a company could be extremely nimble in adjusting its operations to the changing demands of the market place. It would be constantly seeking new raw materials and new processes that would improve its service to its customers.

These considerations suggest a procedure for arriving at a definition of your company's future business. Tradition, access to materials, technical skills, and reputation suggest an area of service to consumers. Improving and extending this service, adding technical skills and new materials as may be necessary, provides the impetus for growth of the business.

ORGANIZING FOR NEW PRODUCT DEVELOPMENT

A company with a substantial interest in a raw material must protect that interest by organizing for new product development which extends the uses and applications of that material. Such a company must allocate a portion of its development funds to what we have called a "laboratory-oriented" program.

However, every company must seek growth opportunities which improve its service to its customers. Thus, every company must allocate a portion of its development funds to a "market-oriented" program. For some companies this portion may be very close to 100%.

How should a company organize to accelerate new product development? An answer which, until recently, seemed to be quite reasonable is, "enlarge the laboratory and hire some more scientists." This discussion is intended to suggest an equally reasonable alternative . . . "budget for more marketing research and hire some creative marketing talent."

►►►►►►►►►►► CREATIVE DEVELOPMENT OF PRODUCT ALTERNATIVES

Market Facts, Incorporated

E very product class[1] has a number of physical characteristics that can be reasonably well

[1] For purposes of discussion, a product is thought of in the restrictive sense of its physical or tangible characteristics, rather than in the broader sense, which would also

include the entire bundle of services the consumer buys (whether purchased at a supermarket, etc.). Furthermore, this paper will deal essentially with consumer goods in which the physical characteristics are dominant as compared to the prestige characteristics not directly related to the other physical product characteristics.

Reprinted with permission from Product Research Methodology: A Critical Review Based on Experimentation with Alternative Methods, *Market Facts, Incorporated, pp. 4–30.*

defined. For example, if a manufacturer were contemplating marketing a new synthetic detergent, he would be concerned with a number of characteristics that would determine the final composition of his product: the amount of suds generated, the cleaning power on a number of specific kinds of textiles, the effect of the product on the hands, rinsing qualities, and perhaps others.

Since the manufacturer's product may assume any given variation on each of these characteristics, it is obvious that the number of different products that he could develop is virtually infinite. As a result, it is customary for the manufacturer to select from this large number of possible varieties two or three variations. From these, one is eventually selected as being the most desirable.

It could certainly be argued that this first phase, that of developing a limited number of product alternatives, is the most crucial step of all. *However successful the second phase (of selecting the one product alternative to be marketed) certainly this final selection can be only as good as the best of the two or three alternatives that were tested.*

This brings one to the question of possible weaknesses in product research methodology in this first phase of product development.

In developing any product—whether new or existing—the manufacturer must decide first *which particular attributes of the product he should include or change.* In many cases it is simply not feasible to change all aspects of the product. The automobile maker could

conceivably change everything from rear bumper to front bumper, but the financial executives of the company would have to see a good deal of evidence on the resulting sales increases before approving such a move.

Furthermore, there may be a *critical relationship between various product attributes;* that is, the manufacturer may not be able to change one attribute without affecting other characteristics of the product. For example, the soap maker who thinks his product should be less harsh on the hands must also consider what effect such a change might have on the soap's cleaning power—in the opinion of the ultimate user.

The manufacturer has a number of criteria he might use in deciding which attributes he might change. We would expect him to be genuinely concerned with the *general importance* of each attribute to consumers, both in causing them to use the product class in general, as well as in differentiating between brands, and we would think the manufacturer would be very much interested in the specific weaknesses of his product in the eyes of various segments of the consuming public.

Yet product research is often inadequate to serve this purpose.

It can be put very simply. *Management's inadequate use of marketing research as a tool for the initial development of product alternatives may be attributed to the fact that it is unaware that marketing research practitioners have at their disposal the tools of analysis needed to make a contribution.*

To a large extent, the techniques frequently employed to uncover consumer attitudes toward products are considered outmoded in other areas of the study of consumer motivation. One very conventional approach is to simply ask consumers the perennial product research questions: "What do you like about this product?" and "What do you dislike about it?"

A critical appraisal of the kinds and validity of information uncovered using these approaches may be helpful in indicating why some managements have no great amount of confidence in marketing research as an aid to creative product development. Here are some of the weaknesses of these conventional approaches:

1. *Highly generalized findings* When one relies on the "what do you like about the product?" approach, he is quite often forced to maintain a level of generality in his reports that is so high as to be of questionable value to management.

For example, the researcher may report that a certain percentage of the population did not like the "cooking qualities" of his utensil. While this may be of some usefulness to the manufacturer considering specific changes in his product, one is forced to admit that it is far less than optimum information.

Part of this high level of generality may logically be attributed to the inability of the consumer to be as articulate and self-conscious as we might have wished. On the other hand, some good part of this generality may be a function of the questioning approach, the type of personnel used, and the nature of the statistical analysis of this information.

2. *Ambiguity of the findings* Quite apart from the high level of generality encountered in the conventional questioning approach is the difficulty one has in interpreting the findings.

For example, often not more than 5 or 10 percent of the population comment voluntarily on any given product attribute. In fact, let us assume that we are an automobile manufacturer and that we find that 10 percent say they do not like the "quality of the body construction" on our automobile and that 5 percent make this comment about a competitor's product.

Ignoring the level of generality involved in "quality of the body construction" and the problem of statistically significant differences, one is faced with some rather crucial questions when interpreting these data:

a. What of the 90 or 95 percent of the consumers who did not mention "body construction"? Can we interpret this to mean that they were generally very happy with that product attribute or, *were they so engrossed with the more "important" or perhaps obvious characteristics that they simply did not state their attitudes on this particular attribute?*

b. Can we assume that our make has inferior "body construction" because twice as many consumers mentioned this? Or, *is this differential caused by the fact that the owners of the competitive make verbalized more easily on some other attribute?*

If these conventional research methods have real shortcomings, if more advanced techniques are available, and if there is good reason to believe that marketing research in many companies is not currently playing a substantial role in this initial product development, why are these methods still used to a considerable extent?

It can only be said that marketing research practitioners are either quite willing to accept the limited role of simple testing of product alternatives after they have been developed, or quite complacent in their product research activity under what appears to be the illusion that conventional methods are quite satisfactory.

At this point it seems appropriate to describe an analytic approach which avoids some of the shortcomings of the conventional approach. The method— let's call it the analytic motivational approach—strives to measure not only *what* product attributes are important to the consumer, but *how* important these attributes are in determining product or brand selection.

The method calls for a series of attributes to be scaled or rated by the consumer. The procedure involves several distinct steps:

1. Determining which attributes or characteristics should be submitted to the consumer for scaling
2. Developing the appropriate measurement techniques
3. Administering the scale to consumers
4. Checking the reliability of the scaling
5. Ascertaining the importance of the attributes in the consumer's product selection

THE SELECTION OF ATTRIBUTES

Without judging the results of a study in advance it is difficult—or impossible—to say which particular product attributes are most likely to influence consumer acceptance of the product. Therefore, the goal of the preliminary selection process should be to develop for consideration the entire range of consumer attitudes toward a product—to examine every actual or imputed product attribute which could conceivably affect a consumer's decision to accept or reject it.

These are some of the sources which can be mined for this type of material:

1. The manufacturers' knowledge and experience in the product field. Any systematic research should be preceded by discussion with the manufacturer's technical and marketing staff to determine what the product was designed to do and what are its major competitive advantages or disadvantages.

2. Current and past advertising for the product as well as for competitive products. A content analysis of the advertising claims—explicit or implicit— for products in this class will often provide important clues for consideration.

3. The researchers' own experiences with consumer attitudes toward similar products. These will often suggest avenues of exploration which have been ignored by the manufacturer or advertiser.

4. Intensive preliminary depth in-

terviews with consumers. A constant concern of the product planner is that his laboratory criteria on given attributes may not coincide with the consumer's. Depth interviewing is very helpful in suggesting not only the specific characteristics that are important, but also the ways in which consumers formulate opinions of various products on these given characteristics.

How much preliminary open-ended interviewing should be done? In view of the objective of the preliminary work—to bring to the attention of the researcher product attributes which may be relevant to consumers—the sample size is frequently determined on a judgment basis. New factors are listed as they arise in the interviewing and the interviewing cut off when it ceases to be productive of anything new.

Statistically, a guide for determining the sample size for this preliminary open-ended interviewing might be:

1. A criterion is set up for determining whether an attribute is significant enough to be included in the questionnaire. Such a criterion might be for an attribute that would be mentioned by 10 percent of the *population* (rather than the sample) or more to be included in the questionnaire.

2. The sample size has to be so large that the probability of including at least one person who mentions the characteristic is, say, 95 percent.[2]

----

[2] On the assumption of random sampling from the population, the number of interviews required for a 95 percent probability of including any one factor with an incidence of 10 percent or more is determined by:

Let us assume now that the researcher has gone through all these steps and is at a stage of the investigation where he has developed a comprehensive list of product attributes. Before he can actually embark on the task of obtaining consumer evaluation of these attributes he has to face these problems:

1. How can he be certain that he has included all of the relevant attributes . . . that his list is exhaustive?

2. If the researcher follows his inclination and includes *all* the items or attributes that he considers necessary, the chances are that he will have problems on his hands with both interviewers and respondents because of the excessive length of the resulting questionnaire.

Actually, one is never completely certain that everything has been considered. What one can do is to organize all these attributes into general

----

$$\sum_{k=1}^{n-1} \binom{n}{k} (0.1)^k (0.9)^{n-k} \geq 0.95$$

$$1 - (0.9)^n \geq 0.95$$
$$n \geq 29$$

Perhaps a more realistic model of the depth interviewing situation would involve the consideration that not all attributes that are relevant to a consumer would necessarily be mentioned in a depth interview. Therefore, one might wish to restrict consideration to attributes that have a probability of, say, 0.5 or more of being mentioned. In other words, assume that even if this attribute is relevant to a consumer, it is not sufficiently close to consciousness to be mentioned more than half the time. With the appropriate modification in the above formula, this leads to a sample size of $n \geq 58$.

categories that will enable him to analyze the question logically and spot areas where information may be missing. A grave danger of such organization is that it often presents the temptation to ignore items which do not conveniently fit into the pre-established categories.

One method of organization involves classifying the statements by their level of generality. As an example let's consider a partial list of product attributes which might be used in evaluating a make of automobile:

Pleasant to ride in
Roomy
Rides level
Little sway
Accelerates smoothly
Seats the right height
Door well placed
Window well placed
Correct inside width
Tunnel not too high
Little engine vibration
Smooth-riding
Comfortable interior
Good performance
Low gas consumption
Good acceleration at high speeds
Good acceleration from stand-still

The levels of generality in this light are quite clear (see below).

A useful scheme for looking at such attributes is to categorize attributes or items according to whether they may be considered *user benefits* or *product attributes*. The specific product attributes can then be grouped according to the user benefits with which they are associated. Thus, in the scheme above, the general categories—"pleasant to ride in" and "good performance"—are user benefits. The items under each benefit are the product attributes which are presumably causes of these benefits. In this kind of classification the same product attribute could conceivably be related to several different user benefits.

In general, the functions of any scheme of organization are that the attributes are considered logically and systematically and the risk of overlooking important areas is minimized.

A logical organization of attributes also aids in approaching in a systematic way the task of eliminating items which are dispensable because they are repetitive or not relevant to the problem at hand. For instance, suppose that the list of attributes above appeared in a study primarily concerned with the design of automobile interiors—rather than with the riding characteristics. Nevertheless, one might

Pleasant To Ride In		*Good Performance*
Smooth Riding	*Comfortable Interior*	
Rides level	Roomy	Low gas consumption
Little sway	Seats the right height	Good acceleration at high speeds
Accelerates smoothly	Door well placed	
Little engine vibration	Window well placed	Good acceleration from stand-still
	Correct inside width	
	Tunnel not too high	

argue against dropping the section dealing with smooth riding because it would be informative to understand the *relation* between respondents' judgments on the smooth riding characteristics and interior comfort.

On the other hand, one would be justified in dropping from the study the *detailed* items which appear under the smooth riding category. If, in fact, the study showed that the car was having serious problems along the lines of smoothness of ride, the attribute "smooth riding" should be enough to call attention to the fact and another study could be designed to develop this specific area more efficiently.

In approaching the problem from this point of view, the researcher is making the practical decision to restrict the scope of the study so as to obtain more valid information about the questions that are most relevant to the product decisions that have to be made.

In addition to organizing the attributes in some systematic fashion, another approach to reducing the length of the list of attributes or items to reasonable size is to determine by means of preliminary testing whether items which *seem* to refer to different attributes are in fact different. If two stimuli are related in such a way that almost everybody tends to react in exactly the same way to both of them, then clearly one of them can be eliminated without any significant loss of information.

The decision as to whether the items are close enough in meaning to warrant dropping one of them can be made on the basis of a cross-tabulation of one of the items by the other. In the example below, the decision might well be made to drop the item on attribute B, since it correlates highly with attribute A.

	This Percent of Those Rating the Product on Attribute A		
Rated the Product on Attribute B	*Very High*	*Medium*	*Very Low*
Very high	83	12	5
Medium	10	80	10
Very low	7	8	85
	100	100	100

If the number of items is large and there is the possibility of a number of close decisions a casual inspection may not be enough. It may become advisable to compute correlation coefficients or some other measure of association.

THE MEASUREMENT TECHNIQUES

Having determined the list of attributes to be evaluated, the decision must be made as to how the evaluation should be done. For instance, what kind of rating scale should be used? There has been extensive discussion of the theory and techniques of scaling in the psychological literature. For the present, let us confine the current discussion to pointing out some basic limitations which are present in the use of scales.

The most fundamental limitation in using rating scales as a means of measuring attitudes toward product attributes is that many attitudes are not scalable[3] at all. Two people may have completely different attitudes about the healthfulness of a certain food and the difference may revolve about the circumstances under which the food is healthful rather than whether it is more or less healthful. Putting it another way, food A may be considered to be healthful under one set of circumstances and food B under another; whereas any kind of scaling of one food as more or less healthful than the other may not make sense.

An analysis by means of which complex attributes are broken down into simple ones will often result in a series of attributes which are individually scalable. However, even when one is dealing with scalable items, these two basic limitations should be borne in mind:

1. Most attitudes do not have a well-defined neutral point or well-defined extreme point. This may be so because the "true" scale of attitudes is really open at both ends. For example, there is probably no point at which one can say it is impossible to be more "uncomfortable." Nor is there a point of medium comfort. On the other hand, it is difficult although perhaps not impossible to define the exact dividing line between comfort and discomfort.[4]

There seems to be a definite advantage in avoiding scales with a neutral

[3] The best-known approach to determining the scalability of attitudes is Gutman's scalogram analysis. See *Measurement and Prediction*, Stouffer *et al.*, Princeton, 1951.

[4] Techniques for determining a neutral position on an attitude scale are discussed by Gutman in the reference given above.

position available to the respondent. The neutral position encourages a loss of information from the respondents who actually lean on one side or the other but who adopt a neutral position in order to avoid a decision. This objection is less valid with scales ranging from "too much" to "too little" where there is a neutral position corresponding to "just right."

However, the avoidance of the neutral position does involve two problems:

a. An element of error may be generated by the scattering of neutral opinions throughout the other scale positions. In general, one suspects that this error is nonrandom, since a person whose overall attitude toward a product or brand is favorable will tend to rate it favorably on individual attributes toward which he actually has no opinion.

b. Forcing a respondent to take a stand about an attribute on which he actually has a low degree of interest or awareness often creates resentment which has an adverse effect on the validity of his scaling of other attributes.

In order to resolve these difficulties, Market Facts has adopted the expedient of using scales with an even number of scale positions but with an "absolutely no opinion" inconspicuously placed on the rating sheet and available as a "no decision haven."

2. There is no exact or uniquely correct way of defining the distance between two points on a scale. The difference between "somewhat com-

fortable" and "very comfortable" may be much greater for one person than another. Or, the distance from "somewhat pleasant" to "very pleasant" may be much less than the distance from "somewhat painful" to "very painful."

The operational meaning of the scale positions can be arrived at only on the basis of an analysis of the results of the scaling. The rationale of such analyses will be discussed later. At this point it would be well to point out that a scale in which all respondents tend to cluster in one or two adjacent scale positions yields less information than one which allows for a greater range of expression. Thus, a six-point scale ranging from "doesn't get floors clean *at all*" to "gets floors *very* clean" may not yield as much discrimination among a group of floor-polishes, all of which are above minimum performance standards, as will a six-point scale ranging from "does a fair job of getting floors clean" to "does a superlative job of getting floors clean."

In the extreme case differences between products or brands may be too small on the scale being used to yield any discrimination and yet important enough in practice to be a factor in consumer behavior. In such cases it may be desirable to use rating devices which place the emphasis on the differences between brands in order to force discrimination.

For example, one may wish to use a question or a sorting device which singles out only one brand—as best, or worst, on an attribute—and yields no information about the other brands. Detecting discrimination between

brands may be much more critical information than can be obtained from an assignment of scale positions which results in a tie for all brands.

QUESTIONNAIRE AND SCALE ADMINISTRATION

Part of the solution of this conflict between the need for detail and the requirements of a questionnaire of reasonable brevity lies in the area of questionnaire construction and administration. Some of the considerations which govern questionnaire length are:

1. The intrinsic interest of the product or subject matter. An interesting questionnaire will obviously seem shorter than one about dull or irksome subjects.

2. The physical handling of the questionnaire or of the questions. Respondents who rebel at answering a long list of tedious questions, or who react negatively to a page full of fine print, may be agreeable to sorting or marking cards, or expressing their attitudes by gamelike devices which have a certain amount of appeal.

3. It may be possible to buy the respondent's time by means of a gift. The response error may be reduced by such a device. This could conceivably improve the study sufficiently to justify drawing funds from other phases of the study.

A major advantage of using scaling techniques in interviewing is that the questionnaire can be made self-administering to a great extent, thus reducing the possible effects of interviewer bias. This does not eliminate the problems involved in obtaining accurate field work. It merely shifts their focus to these considerations:

1. *The mechanics of questionnaire administration should be as simple as possible.* The problems of handling all the material, such as cards, scales, should not be so complex as to obscure the task itself.

2. *Instructions to the interviewer and the respondent must be very clear and explicit.* These instructions should be profusely illustrated by worked-out examples, and the respondent should be asked to do a few test items in order to check his understanding of the technique.

3. *Interviewers should be thoroughly indoctrinated in the requirements for this type of interviewing.* The interviewer must be trained in a new role, making it as easy and inviting as possible for the respondent to go through the scaling procedure without injecting herself into this situation. This may be difficult for interviewers who are accustomed to open-ended or the conventional type of structured questionnaire. The interviewer may find it difficult to restrict herself to dealing with procedure rather than with subject matter.

Assuming that all the desirable measures have been taken to train interviewers adequately, and to assure that the respondents understand the scaling technique, there will still be problems of ambiguous items, of respondents who fail to get the idea, or who refuse to cooperate, of cheating by interviewers, and many other problems which make it essential to institute systematic checks of reliability.

RELIABILITY CHECKS

Without going into the subject of reliability and validity of questionnaire data—a subject which has been discussed at great length in the statistical and psychological literature—it would be well to point out a few devices which are available to detect some of the common types of unreliability encountered in handling scaling data.

1. *Departures from randomness* Frequently it seems desirable to include a fairly large number of scaling items on the same questionnaire. One limit to the number that can be included is respondent fatigue or boredom. If the items are listed randomly to begin with, it is reasonable to assume that fatigue or boredom will tend to manifest itself in one or both of these ways:

a. Too little variation in response from item to item. Extreme cases can be detected visually by a quick examination of the questionnaires as they are edited. Market Facts has found such screening to be worthwhile.

b. Systematic drift from one position of the scale to another as the questionnaire proceeds. These can be detected by tests of randomness, such as *run tests,* tests based on the mean square successive difference, or simply the difference between average scores on the first items and the last ones.

2. *Consistency checks* Consistency checks should be provided by adding items deliberately designed to check

consistency. An examination of correlations between similar items provides additional consistency checks.

Some caution should be exercised in interpreting such correlations. Seemingly low correlations between apparently similar items may be caused by the fact that statements which appear similar to the researcher are actually being perceived as different by the consumer. It may be necessary to depth interview a sub-sample of respondents to determine whether this is the case.

3. *Dispersion* If the questionnaire involves scaling several products on a variety of attributes, it would be desirable to have some measure of discrimination among brands. Market Facts has used the following technique with some success for measuring reliability and for item analysis. It is based on the assumption that we are dealing with a series of bi-polar scales with several brands being rated on each scale, and with a numerical value assigned to each scale position.

a. Set up some measure of dispersion for ratings by a respondent of all the brands on any one attribute or item. In most cases, the range —highest score minus lowest score —will be an adequate measure. This range would measure the respondent's tendency to discriminate between brands on a given attribute.

Thus, assigning 1 through 6 to the scale positions below for facial tissue brands from left to right, the Item Respondent Range would be $4 - 1 = 3$.

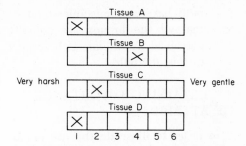

b. An average of a respondent's range over all items is a measure of the respondent's tendency to discriminate between brands on a variety of attributes. An extremely low value indicates that all brands are being rated equally on all or most attributes.

A further examination will generally make it possible to decide whether it is a genuine failure to discriminate or whether it is poor technique. Thus, a tabulation by interviewer of mean ranges per respondent may show that one interviewer's work has a high frequency of low mean ranges because of an error in interviewing technique.

Extremely high mean ranges should also be examined to determine whether respondents mistakenly used the end positions only—a frequent happening if the respondents have been inadequately instructed.

c. A mean range is obtained for a given attribute by averaging ranges on this attribute for all respondents. An exceptionally low item mean range indicates that the attribute in question does not discriminate among different brands. This presents the possibility that either the statement of the attribute has been misunderstood or that all the brands are actually perceived as similar with respect to this attribute.

ASCERTAINING IMPORTANCE OF ATTRIBUTES

In order to illustrate the use of analytical techniques as a creative tool in product research, let us examine a somewhat simplified product problem:

The manufacturer of a cake mix has reason to believe that he needs to modify his product to win greater consumer acceptance. On the basis of extensive preliminary exploration of his problem he feels that the areas that may be causing the greatest difficulty are:

Taste factors

Is the cake too sweet or not sweet enough?

Is it too spicy or not spicy enough?

Physical properties

Is it too moist or too dry?

Too fine or too coarse in texture?

Package

Does it make too large or too small a cake?

The task of determining the exact changes that should be made in all five problem areas—sweetness, spiciness, moistness, texture, size—is extremely complex. He would do well to get a "fix" on his problem first by determining which of these problem areas is sufficiently important to warrant attention—important in the sense that a product change in these areas is likely to have an appreciable effect on consumer acceptance.

To get such a "fix" he has findings available in the form of consumer ratings showing the acceptance of his product in terms of all the attributes under discussion, as illustrated on this type of rating device as shown below.

For purposes of analysis, let's assume a seven-point scale and assign numerical values to the boxes ranging from −3 for the box on the extreme left to +3 for the box on the right. In general a higher positive value will indicate a higher degree of the attribute—a rating of +3 on sweetness means *too sweet*, a rating of 0 means just right in sweetness.

How can this kind of data best be used? One approach might be to examine the consumer ratings of each of

Cake Mix A

Very much prefer a competitive product	Very much prefer it to competive products
Not sweet enough	Too sweet
Not spicy enough	Too spicy
Too dry	Too moist
Too coarse in texture	Too fine in texture
Too small a cake	Too large a cake

		Percent Who, on Each of These Attributes:					
Gave Mix A This Scale Value		*Overall Prefer- ence*	*Sweet- ness*	*Spici- ness*	*Moist- ness*	*Fine- ness*	*Size*
More of the attribute	+3	10	10	—	—	10	5
	+2	15	16	—	5	12	10
	+1	15	22	10	10	15	20
	0	30	20	75	40	25	35
	−1	20	20	15	30	12	20
	−2	8	8	—	15	12	5
Less of the attribute	−3	2	4	—	—	4	5
Average rating		*0.33*	*0.36*	*−0.05*	*−0.40*	*0.21*	*0.10*

these items. Let's assume that these are available in this form. What inferences can be drawn from these data as shown above?

One might be tempted to infer that mix A is somewhat too *sweet*, that it is just right in *spiciness*, not *moist* enough, it is too fine in *texture*, and that the *package* is too large.

However, before rushing off to change the product in all directions it would be well to examine what further guidance can be obtained by a closer analysis of the data—specifically by *relating the evaluation of specific product features to overall acceptance.*

This type of analysis can best be illustrated by the table shown below.

This table can be summarized by a graph showing the relation of the average preference score to the rating of sweetness.

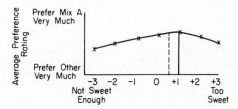

An examination of this relation between overall preference and sweetness when combined with the sweetness rating will in fact point to quite different actions than would be indicated by the sweetness ratings alone. Thus, the graph suggests that it is

	Consumers Who Gave Mix A This Rating on Sweetness						
	Not Sweet Enough −3	−2	−1	0	+1	+2	*Too Sweet* +3
Expressed This (Average) Degree of Preference	−0.20	0.01	0.20	0.27	0.41	0.29	0.19

better for the mix to be a little too sweet than "exactly right" in sweetness. In fact, one might say that the correct sweetness level is the one which has the highest preference—the maximum point on the sweetness-preference curve. This "ideal" sweetness level is designated by the solid line on the graph. The actual sweetness rating level is shown by the dotted line on the graph.

It further appears that errors in the direction of making the product too sweet are not as bad as errors in the direction of not making the product sweet enough. Since preference does not fall off as rapidly when the product is too sweet as it does when it is not judged sweet enough, it appears that mix A is really close to the right level of sweetness. Thus, no change in sweetness is indicated—except possibly in the direction of greater sweetness rather than less.

Let's examine what action is indicated with respect to some of the other

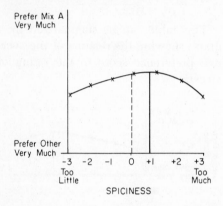

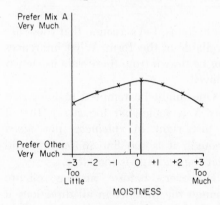

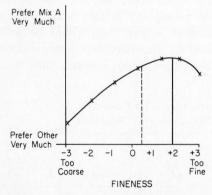

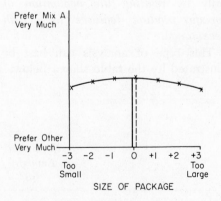

Dotted line indicates actual rating level.
Solid line indicates ideal or optimum rating level.

OVERALL PREFERENCE RELATED TO ATTRIBUTE RATINGS

attributes. The preceding graphs indicate the relation between the degree of overall preference for mix A and the evaluation of mix A with respect to each of the attributes. This relation when considered together with the rating for the attribute (shown by the dotted line on each graph) indicates what changes—if any—are called for with respect to that attribute. In each graph the full vertical line indicates the "ideal" level of each attribute. The dotted line is the *actual* rating level for mix A on that attribute.

As an illustration of the possibilities of this analysis, let us interpret the significance of the "spiciness" graph.

SPICINESS

The consumer's overall acceptance of the product will be affected only if she thinks the mix is *very* much overspiced. Her preference will not be very much affected by the relatively minor variations of spiciness—particularly if they are in the direction of less spiciness.

Product A is actually not spicy enough. However, an increase in spiciness would have relatively little effect on overall preference. Too great an increase would be worse than none at all. A possible management decision on the basis of this evidence might be that since the addition of spices would add to the cost of the product, any changes may be ruled out at this time.

The reader is recommended to try his hand at an analysis and interpretation of the graphs illustrating the relations of the remaining attributes to overall preference. The conclusions will be seen to be quite different from those inferred from a superficial analysis.

For the sake of simplicity of exposition, many complexities have been bypassed in this discussion. For example, no reference has been made to possible interrelations between the individual attributes. Such interrelations should be considered in setting up and testing the final product alternatives. The function of the above analysis is to delimit the areas of suggested change. The actual choice of the specific alternatives and the selection among them could conceivably require complex consideration of experimental design.

An often-overlooked aspect of product testing is the identification of characteristics of consumers that, in combination, discriminate those who prefer, for example, brand A from those who prefer brand B. The discriminating characteristics may be attitudes, as measured by scales, or demographic characteristics, or both. One method of analysis that achieves this is the linear discriminant function. This technique has not yet been widely applied in product testing, but it is worthy of serious experimentation.

In reviewing briefly the comments on marketing research and its role in the first and creative phase of product research—the development of product alternatives—several things might be said:

1. The *creative* phase is probably the key step in product development.

2. Marketing research's role in this

phase is very often a limited one. This might be explained by possible shortcomings in methods that are conventionally used.

3. The analytic-motivational method offers great promise of aiding in the creative phase of product determination.

►►►►►►►►►► LOCATING IDEAS FOR NEW PRODUCTS

GUSTAV E. LARSON [*]

HOW DO MANUFACTURERS FIND IDEAS FOR NEW PRODUCTS?

Once a manufacturer has checked over his operations and decided that he wants to find and develop one or several new products, the search for ideas begins.

Before selecting a particular new product possibility for development, it is probably wise to assemble and compare several good ideas. If this is done, the chances of making a good product choice will generally be improved.

The quantity and quality of product ideas a manufacturer will be able to assemble for consideration will depend in part upon how well he knows where and how to look for practical possibilities. As shown in the following pages, ideas come from all types of sources including Government agencies, research laboratories, executives, sales force, customer suggestions, and many others.

HOW 25 MANUFACTURERS LOCATED IDEAS FOR NEW PRODUCTS

Company	New Product	Source of Idea
Machine tool builder.	Machine for textile industry.	Examination of machinery needs of noncustomer industries. For example, the company knew that the textile industry didn't use lathes; it reasoned, however, that the industry might use certain machines which could be produced by a manufacturer of machine tools. After a thorough study of the textile industry the company selected four textile machines for manufacture.

Reprinted from Developing and Selling New Products, *U. S. Department of Commerce, Office of Domestic Commerce, Washington, D.C., 1950, pp. 3–12.*

[*]*Marketing Division, Office of Domestic Commerce, U. S. Department of Commerce.*

HOW 25 MANUFACTURERS LOCATED IDEAS FOR NEW PRODUCTS—*Continued*

Company	New Product	Source of Idea
Meat packer.	Onion soup.	Executive's wife.
Do.	Canned chicken product.	Salesman.
Manufacturer of industrial equipment.	Steam-producing unit.	Advertised sale of manufacturing rights.
Tin plate converter.	Bread box.	Market research agency assigned to study new product possibilities.
Electric appliance manufacturer.	Foot warmer.	Customer inquiries.
Manufacturer of golf equipment.	Golf bag "toter."	President of company.
Manufacturer of service equipment for garages.	Hoist for garage.	Garage mechanic contacted during survey of product users.
Chemical company.	Deodorant for garbage.	Advertising agency, which learned of local use.
Chemical and film company.	Detergent.	Laboratory.
Die casting company.	Line of dejuicers.	Company executives.
Manufacturer of plastic product.	Film viewing device.	Inventor.
Manufacturer of kitchen utensils and gadgets.	Kitchen gadget.	Register of patents available for licensing or sale. (U.S. Patent Office.)
Chemical products company.	Insecticide.	List of Government-owned patents available for licensing.
Manufacturer of office equipment and machinery.	Index device, envelope opening device, pencil gripper.	Office managers. Also jobber and wholesaler catalogs.
Canner.	Apple juice.	Food broker.
Appliance manufacturer.	Electric bottle-warmer.	Customers.
Film company.	Film.	Engineer.
Landscape supply and equipment company.	Fiber glass blanket to place around tree to keep down weeds and retain moisture in soil.	Register of patents available for licensing or sale.

HOW 25 MANUFACTURERS LOCATED IDEAS FOR NEW PRODUCTS—*Continued*

Company	New Product	Source of Idea
Container manufacturer.	Reuse container.	President of company (noticed waste of materials).
Plumbing equipment and supply manufacturer.	New washer.	Sales report.
Manufacturer of hardware.	Bedroom door knockers. Also miniature jewelry door knockers.	Executive in considering idea of reducing size of regular door knockers.
Pottery manufacturer.	New vase.	Museum exhibit.
Plastic products company.	Plastic shield for wall light switch.	Inventor.
Do.	Film slide viewer.	List of needed inventions published by a bank.

SOURCES OF IDEAS FOR NEW PRODUCTS

A good first step for manufacturers actively seeking new products is to prepare a list of sources which can yield practical possibilities. The following checklist includes most of the major sources for all types of new product ideas. The list is good for all types of firms, whether they are manufacturers of consumer or of producer goods.

Not all of these sources will necessarily be used by any one company. Each, however, can use the checklist as a guide in setting up a list of best idea sources fitted to specific company interests and products. How to do this is discussed on the pages directly following the checklist.

A CHECKLIST OF IDEA SOURCES FOR YOUR COMPANY

In making up an idea checklist tailored to your company's interests, be as specific as possible, and include all helpful information. For example, company A's special checklist includes the following information about two trade associations:

1. Trade association Y has a laboratory located at . . . . The association laboratory technicians are thoroughly familiar with the machinery and equipment requirements of the X industry. See technicians in regard to leads to possible equipment needs and improvements.

2. Trade association M has carried on research on products which might be manufactured from X waste materials. May be able to locate ideas for new products from director of research laboratory located at . . . .

The company's listing of Government agencies provides the following details:

1. Patent Office. The Register of Patents Available for Licensing or Sale

may have several patents available in this field which might be purchased. (Several large corporations in the same field as this company have placed large numbers of patents on the Register.) We may find some usable machinery items available for licensing.

2. Patent Office. G o v e r n m e n t-owned patents. Federal Government has been active in this field. Has a number of patents available for licensing which should be examined.

3. Patent Office. Dedicated patents. Check to see if there are any dedicated patents which might suggest a product new to our company.

4. Call on Navy Department for possible new developments resulting from Navy wartime research. Also find out if Navy has any special product interests in the field we are studying. Navy may be a good customer for some of products we have in mind.

CONSULTING SOURCES FOR IDEAS

Just how do these sources yield helpful ideas? Probably the best way to answer this question is to cite the experiences of three companies which examined many of the sources in making surveys for new products.

MANUFACTURER OF OFFICE EQUIPMENT AND MACHINERY

The management had decided that several new products were needed. Although the company had its own engineering division which had developed new product ideas in the past, in this instance it was felt that an outside consultant should be engaged

to make an additional search. The company's management believed that a consulting agency would not be as likely to limit the range of their search as would their own engineering staff accustomed to thinking along a few product lines.

This company engaged a management consulting firm which examined most of the idea sources listed in the foregoing checklist of major sources for new product ideas. The take-off point in the survey was to make a study of the firm's own staff and records. After interviewing company executives, salesmen, design engineers, and other office and field personnel, and studying sales reports, the consulting engineers then launched an extensive field study.

In the field, the consulting firm first called on jobbers to get leads on types of office equipment and supplies which were sold in greatest volume. While calling on jobbers the engineers examined catalogs of competing firms. These catalogs suggested several products which were at least new to the inquiring firm.

The next step was to call on about 50 office managers in the immediate area to find what their particular office work problems were. The consultant also made a study of which jobs were done by machine, and which by hand, and the time and labor required to do the various jobs. After obtaining many suggestions from the office managers as well as their own studies of office operations, the investigators talked to secretaries and clerks to get any additional suggestions they might have. Thus, several practical ideas were ob-

CHECKLIST OF MAJOR SOURCES FOR NEW PRODUCT IDEAS

I. Company staff, record, experience

Research and engineering staffs.

Sales staff.

Market research department.

Sales reports and other records.

Employee suggestions.

Customer suggestions, inquiries, and complaints.

II. Distributors

Brokers.

Factory distributors (manufacturers' agents).

Wholesalers or jobbers.

Retailers.

III. Competitors

Customers of competitors.

Competitors' products.

Mail order catalogs.

Exhibits and trade shows.

Foreign products.

IV. Miscellaneous

Inventors.

Patent attorneys and brokers.

Firms going out of business.

Manufacturers of parts and accessories.

Suggestions from public (or industry) as result of advertising.

University and institute laboratories.

Commercial laboratories.

Industrial consultants.

Management engineers.

Product engineers.

Market research agencies.

Advertising agencies.

Trade associations—executives and laboratory personnel.

Trade magazine writers and editors.

V. Government agencies

Government agencies and publications are important sources of ideas for new products. Some of the chief Federal Government agencies and publications helpful in this respect are described here. . . .

(1) United States Patent Office, Department of Commerce:

(*a*) *Register of patents available for licensing or sale.*—This reservoir of available patents is a good source of new product ideas. Some patents on the Register may be used with the consent of the owners or on payment of royalty; many may be purchased outright.

(*b*) *Government-owned patents.*—The Federal Government develops and patents many processes and products. Such patents are available on nonexclusive royalty free licenses and are announced in periodic listings issued by the Patent Office.

(*c*) *Dedicated patents.*—No license to make, use or sell is required to use a dedicated patent. No royalty need be paid, and no formality is required to make full use of the patent.

NOTE.—For information about (*a*), (*b*), and (*c*) write to United States Patent Office, Washington 25, D. C.

(*d*) *Official Gazette, United States Patent Office.*—This weekly publication of the Patent Office, an important source of ideas for new products, lists patents added to the Register of Patents Available for Licensing or Sale; also patents granted, including designs and reissues.

(2) Office of Technical Services, Department of Commerce:

This office has a record of Government originated and enemy-acquired research which may suggest new product possibilities. Lists of acquisitions appear in the Bibliography of Scientific and Industrial Reports.

(3) Other sources:

Various other Federal agencies and state agencies may suggest new product possibilities in certain fields. For example, the research findings of the laboratories of the Department of Agriculture and of the state universities have suggested new product possibilities in many instances.

(4) Publications:

Publications of some Government agencies also are of value in suggesting product ideas which are new to a specific company. Examples of Department of Commerce publications useful in this way are: A Source of New Product Possibilities for Manufacturers; Standard Commodity Classification, volumes 1 and 2; and Statistical Classification of Domestic and Foreign Commodities.

tained from personnel actually using office equipment.

This user-research yielded several good ideas for new items. But the study of user needs represented only one phase of the company's search job. New product ideas were also obtained from the Register of Patents Available for Licensing or Sale, trade literature, trade magazine editors, trade associations, the Army and Navy, and several other sources.

MANUFACTURER OF SIGNS AND DISPLAYS

A small manufacturer of signs and displays carried out his own search for new products as he was unable to afford the services of a consulting firm. First he obtained all possible ideas from within the company and from distributors of his product. He then made a limited field survey of customers actually using his line. As a result of these two steps, he found several ideas which appeared to have good possibilities.

Several additional suggestions resulted from the following letter sent to the United States Patent Office:

Please place our firm on the mailing list of the Register of Patents Available for Licensing or Sale. Also, please send us any patented items (available for licensing or sale) which might be manufactured in our present plant. We are engaged in:

A. The manufacturing of signs, displays, and advertising specialties:
   1. Types:
     Interior and exterior
     Electrical and nonelectrical
     Fluorescent
     Animated
     Itinerant
   2. Materials:
     Wood
     Glass
     Plastics

Paper and paperboard
Fiberboard
B. The distribution of these products and allied items by—
Jobbing and wholesaling
Mail order
Specialty salesmen

In reply the Patent Office forwarded descriptions of more than 50 patents (available for sale or license) which might be suitable to the firm's facilities. Among the patents listed were:

Pat. 1,863,220—Card holder for rotary card display devices.
Pat. 1,875,321—Advertising card display device.
Pat. 2,282,305—Aerial advertising apparatus.
Pat. 2,300,180—Changeable price sign.
Pat. 2,383,725—Changeable exhibitor.
Pat. 2,400,330—Portable display table.

The above letter indicates the type of information the Patent Office should have when lists of available patents are requested in one product field. But if a company will go further and also state the types of products it is equipped to manufacture (other than its regular line), the Patent Office can then expand the list to include other product possibilities.

TIN-PLATE CONVERTER

This company felt that there must be some product into which it could put its material and labor which would bring greater profits than the metal boxes it was manufacturing.

To assure selection of a product which would have a good market, both for a short and a long term, the company hired a market-research agency to determine specific products that would offer the best new-product opportunities for the company.

After eliminating several product fields, the market research agency settled on metal housewares as the field best suited for comprehensive market study. The agency studied in considerable detail such things as the number and kinds of prospective buyers for breadboxes, wastebaskets, step-on garbage cans, and other metalware kitchen items.

Details were also obtained on prices customers were accustomed to pay for the houseware items, what consumers liked and disliked about items already on the market, what new products consumers would like, and where consumers were accustomed to buying such products.

The survey results indicated that consumers would buy a certain type of bread box. On the basis of these findings this company decided to design a new type of bread box to meet the expressed consumer interest. From the facts obtained, the company learned approximately how the bread box should be designed, at what price it must be sold, and through what channels it could profitably be marketed.

This new product has now been successfully sold for many months.

SUGGESTIONS FOR UNDERTAKING A SURVEY

Each manufacturer will want to develop survey plans suited to his particular product interests, budget, and knowledge of usefulness of the various sources suggested. Likewise, most probably will begin their search for ideas by first examining sources within the company.

After this step has been taken, it probably will pay for most companies to consult sources which from their experience they know and feel would be most likely to produce good results. Many will find, too, that it will pay them to include in their investigation an examination of available patents as such material constitutes the single greatest reservoir of ideas available in any one place. In so doing a letter to the Patent Office probably should precede actual investigation of material on file in Washington.

Field surveys of present customers is one of the best ways of assembling usable product ideas. Many companies have found such surveys to be so effective that they repeat them at regular intervals, usually annually. One company interviewed men on the job, including mechanics, chief engineers, and plant managers. Time and cost studies were also made to spot promising opportunities for new machinery. When the study was completed the company had obtained many useful opinions, ideas, and information on industry practices and problems, all of which suggested several ideas for new products.

When carrying out a customer study keep in mind that there are often three types of users who can contribute helpful information and ideas. These are: (1) men on the job who use and operate the equipment; (2) job supervisors; and (3) company executives responsible for quantity and quality of output and for approving new-equipment purchases.

It also has been found that wholesalers, retailers, manufacturers' agents, and brokers constitute some of the most fertile of all sources of ideas for new products. For example, in the food and grocery industry, the broker constitutes a major channel for distribution to wholesale buyers of all kinds. Hence he is familiar not only with the products of his principals but also with all other similar or related products in his market as well as the product demands. He often can quickly advise the manufacturer seeking ideas as to what items are needed, as well as the advantages and disadvantages of existing products. Because brokers, being paid commissions only, are interested in sales, their suggestions for new products generally are practical ones having sales possibilities, but they may not necessarily prove to have profit possibilities. In the same way retail buyers and wholesalers in many lines of goods can give practical counsel on proposed new products.

ORGANIZING TO FIND NEW PRODUCTS

Many manufacturers faced with frequent new-product development problems have organized for the job of finding and appraising new-product ideas. Such organization has taken the form of new-product planning committees, departments, or divisions which generally have the chief responsibility for finding new-product possibilities. The important work that such groups can do, when given complete authority to act, is illustrated by the following examples.

A company, manufacturing machine tools, after deciding that it wanted new products to manufacture, appointed a new-products planning committee. Each member was freed of all regular work and gave his entire time to the job of finding and analyzing new products. The committee was made up of three sales managers, two engineering department members, and one economist. The chairman had had long experience with both the manufacturing and sales problems of the company. As a direct result of committee work, and after screening more than 3,000 product ideas, the company has now added several successful new items in the capital goods field.

In a large milling company, the responsibility for finding ideas falls on four groups: The sales department, officers of the corporation, the technical research laboratory, and the new-products division. In establishing the field of responsibility, the management places a part of the burden upon each of the groups. Any one may do some preliminary work in running down the merits of a new idea, but before the ideas receive more than a cursory check they are turned over to the new-products division for consideration.

The new-products division, under management's direction, is not, therefore, alone responsible for the development of new ideas, but it thus assumes leadership in that direction. Within the new-products division, selected personnel, with extensive training in several fields, are charged with keeping abreast of new fields and new developments. Its staff is continually combing all sources of ideas such as colleges, research laboratories, competitors, foreign developments, and others.

In many companies, laboratories serve as the focal point for obtaining ideas for new products. For example, in one large food-manufacturing company, ideas are first originated by the regular laboratory staff, technicians, chemists, bakers, and office personnel. But as the new-product program gets under way the laboratory reaches out for suggestions from members of the sales division, national advertising agencies, home economists, housewives, or, in fact, anyone from whom a good idea can be obtained. This company reported that many ideas came from such sources as retailers, brokers, and its own sales staff.

SMALL FIRMS

While small firms seeking new products generally are not in a position to organize committees or divisions to handle the search, many find that a better job can be done if one individual is given the primary responsibility for locating ideas. He may spend part or full time on the job, depending on the importance of new products to the firm. Naturally, the selection of the right individual for the job is all important.

TYPES OF IDEAS WANTED

As there are many different reasons for searching for new products no hard and fast rules about the types of products to look for can be laid down. A company generally will be on the safest ground if it looks for products that relate to its chief strengths. Ideally, the new product should be one that can be manufactured by the present labor force with existing equipment, sold by the sales force to the same classes of customers, and advertised and promoted in much the same manner as the present line. The farther a new product moves away from this ideal, the less likely it is that it can be profitably added to the operations of the average company.

There are, of course, many exceptions to the above generality. Some manufacturers seek to diversify their lines and investments. But even in such cases, manufacturers generally try to add new lines that are compatible with existing manufacturing operations, established distributing channels, or that will supplement existing lines with items of outstanding design. Often many of the products which are added for diversification are developed because of their basic interrelationship with regular lines. For example, a manufacturer of agricultural machinery and equipment uses certain parts and motors in building conveyors, trucks, small tractors, wagons, and other farm machinery. When seeking new products this manufacturer might want to add such end products as would require the same motors and possibly some of the same parts, such as frames and wheels, which are already being used in the firm's present line.

Furthermore, a manufacturer would not always turn down a new product merely because it did not fit his manufacturing facilities. If his sales set-up was right, the product might be profitably manufactured somewhere else.

Or, if the product had unusually good sales and profit potentials it might even be worth the expense of building a new sales organization and purchasing new equipment and machinery, if such expansion was necessary. But most firms usually want new products which can be distributed through their regular sales outlets by their established system of selling.

PRESENT LINE VERSUS NEW PRODUCT

Many manufacturers have gone ahead with new-product programs only to learn that they would have been better off had they concentrated those extra dollars and efforts in developing their present lines. So, before moving into a product development program perhaps it is well, at least, to check to see if such steps as the following may not be the best means of increasing company profits:

1. Find new uses for established products and advertise such uses to increase sales.
2. Find new markets—concentrate on areas or types of customers where coverage is low in relation to sales potential.
3. Improve appearance of product or product line.
4. Improve styling of product or product line.
5. Improve packaging.
6. Improve display material such as counter cards, streamers, exhibits, mechanical demonstrators, movies, slide films, and cutaways.
7. Simplify product as means of re-

ducing sales price and opening new markets.

8. Train salesmen and dealers to do a better job of selling.
9. Find unprofitable customers and try to improve their profitability. In some cases, it may be well to eliminate unprofitable customers.
10. Find more profitable customers and concentrate greater sales efforts on such outlets.
11. Weed out unprofitable products (must be watched carefully so as not to destroy line completeness; frequently it is possible to combine models, leave out tricky features, and end up with a shorter but sufficient line).

►►►►►►►►►►► FISHING FOR FACTS

TED STANTON*

...How can U.S. industrial firms cope with the growing mountain of scientific information being produced by the world's laboratories and research centers?

Every 24 hours enough technical papers are turned out around the globe to fill seven sets of the 24-volume Encyclopaedia Britannica. And the output is rising every year. This year's crop: Some 60 million pages or the equivalent of about 465 man-years of steady around-the-clock reading.

Hidden away in this glut of literature are thousands of ideas for new products and for cost-saving processes of all sorts. Yet, the laboratory scientist, busy with work of his own, no longer can find enough hours in the day to keep up with all that is published in his field. Even staying on top of the indexes and abstracts of these papers has become an insurmountable task for the lab man. One result is that company after company has found itself duplicating research work that others already have done and fully chronicled.

A NEW PROFESSION

The solution an increasing number of the larger corporations are trying is to free some of their experienced research and development men completely from laboratory or so-called bench chores and to put them full time to reading. As "information scientists," these men perform a variety of useful functions, from keeping project teams abreast of the latest competitive developments in their research areas and helping avoid duplication of past work to suggesting new projects for investigation.

Helping the trend along has been the development of elaborate mechani-

Reprinted with permission from The Wall Street Journal, *December 20, 1960, pp. 1, 8.*

**Staff Reporter of* The Wall Street Journal.

cal and electronic systems for filing and retrieving scientific information. But, as Henry C. Longnecker, manager of the science information department of Smith Kline & French Laboratories, Philadelphia, puts it, "Just having the information available is not enough. Maintaining our competitive position requires the proper and timely use of the information by trained men." Smith Kline & French maintains a special staff of 15 information specialists, nearly all with Ph.D. degrees, who participate as advisers and co-planners in each R. & D. project the big drug company undertakes.

The Du Pont Co., Merck & Co., the Convair division of General Dynamics Corp. and Lockheed Aircraft Corp. are others with formal information programs aimed at aiding the bench scientist and keeping him from being buried under the flood of scientific literature.

ATTRACTING A CROWD

One of the most ambitious of these ventures, being carried on by Esso Research & Engineering Co., a unit of big Standard Oil Co. (New Jersey), is attracting a steady flow of visitors from other corporations anxious to pick up ideas on the management of scientific information.

Esso's program is centered in a Technical Information division, staffed by 50 men and costing more than $1 million a year. The core of the division consists of 15 senior scientists, all Ph.D.'s and all with several years prior experience in various Esso research projects, both as team members and as directors of project teams. These men are backed by a supporting cast of junior scientists and library technicians to conduct searches of background literature for specific projects and to prepare reports and abstracts.

"Our prime job is to stimulate the men on the bench," says William T. Knox, the soft-spoken Georgian who heads Esso's information division. "We don't relieve the technical man of his responsibility; we try to help him use his time most efficiently by acting as an intermediary between his problem and the available information."

What prodded Jersey Standard into full-time information research? According to Mr. Knox, an internal survey in 1956 revealed a surprising feeling of inadequacy on the part of the company's scientific personnel. Most of the research men believed they weren't sufficiently up-to-date in their own fields, had insufficient opportunity to benefit from possible "cross-fertilization" from other fields and weren't even adequately informed of past or current work within the company itself. When management heard this it acted quickly.

Savings were not long in showing up. One technical monograph from Sweden, coming to an information researcher's hand, saved an Esso laboratory in Tulsa a month-long exploratory program, budgeted at thousands of dollars. In another case, more than 100 chemical compounds scheduled for examination were swept from test schedules after a literature review by a researcher revealed that similar test work had been done by others.

The division has initiated important projects, too. Recently, an information researcher was going through the literature in search for an answer to the problem of settling refinery dust. In reading the various ways in which heavy petroleum residues such as asphalt have been used for laying dust on roads, he suddenly had what Mr. Knox calls "a happy flash." As a result, Esso is now actively promoting the use of a petroleum mulch to protect the roots of newly planted grass and farm crops from wind erosion and loss of moisture.

REQUISITES FOR A JOB

The success of a corporate information program, of course, hinges mainly on the ability of the individuals entrusted with carrying it out. In recruiting his staff three years ago, Mr. Knox set down several requisites.

"I wanted men who had the confidence of management, men who would be listened to," he says. "Their evaluation of data had to be considered sound and they had to be thoroughly familiar with company programs."

Another vital requirement: Initiative and imagination. "We wanted people who could tie data together, formulate a program, then get it launched. And they had to be able to communicate," Mr. Knox says.

"Talking a scientist, busy with his own problems, into tackling another with no sure chance of success is a big job," Mr. Knox says with a small smile. "At this stage our people have to be as much salesmen as scientists."

DEVELOPMENT LAG

Another aim of the researchers is to insure that research relevant to their field from other, seemingly unrelated scientific disciplines doesn't go unnoticed and unused. An extreme example is the lag in the development of gas chromatography, now widely used in the petroleum industry. A chromatograph is used to constantly monitor product streams. The chromatograph measures chemical components of gases or vaporized liquids by bleeding off a portion of the stream and depositing it on a special chemical coating. The chemicals in the gas separate and solidify, then flake off from the coating and are measured.

The process of chromatography was discovered around the turn of the century by Michael Tswett, a Russian botanist. Experiments in gas chromatography began in 1930 but lapsed until 1941 when the idea was revived in a technical journal, only to disappear again until 1949. It wasn't until the mid-1950's that the method gained widespread use in the petroleum industry, replacing more costly, time-consuming methods of gas analysis.

To illustrate how the Esso program works, follow the path of one piece of information that came into the office recently. It was a 20-page paper given at a chemists' meeting in Texas. Mr. Knox read it through and found on the last page a casual one-sentence reference to a new catalyst. He passed it along to Dr. Isidor Kirshenbaum, one of his research men, with an "Are we interested?" note attached.

"WORTH A LOOK"

"I turned it over in my mind a couple of hours and finally came up with a possible application," Dr. Kirshenbaum says. "Then I talked with the head of one of Esso's laboratory teams and broached my catalyst. He thought it was at least worth a look."

Whether it will pan out may take months or even years to determine, "but at least it didn't get by us," Mr. Knox observes.

Was Dr. Kirshenbaum tempted to go back into the laboratory and personally test the new catalyst? "Definitely not," he declares. "And that's one of the major advantages of my job. I don't have to get involved in the day-to-day concerns of individual projects or even a small part of them."

"It's this freedom of choice," he adds, "that makes the work much more stimulating to me than working in a lab. Anything I think the company is interested in, should be interested in or, within limits, anything for which I think there may be some vague future possibility, I can pursue if I choose."

Dr. Kirshenbaum calculates he goes through more than 6,000 scientific abstracts a year and finds perhaps two or three a week of interest to the company, or to himself for further consideration. On top of this, he attends professional meetings, takes advanced courses, maintains personal contact with scientists in and out of the company and keeps up-to-date through extensive correspondence.

Playing a vital role in many corporate information research programs is their mechanical mate, information retrieval. Esso estimates it has over 1.5 million file cards on all types of technical literature stored away as well as about 75,000 feet of microfilm. Mr. Knox is looking forward eagerly to a few years from now when he believes machines to both scan and translate foreign technical works will be in common use. "The machines appear to be the best solution to the growing body of foreign language publications," he says. It's estimated that more than one third of all technical and scientific publications now are printed in Russian, Chinese or Japanese, languages in which only 2% to 5% of American scientists are at home.

The Russians, with about 50,000 people assigned to information retrieval work, have gone far more extensively into the translation of foreign journals than have Americans, either in private industry or in government research centers. But Esso's Mr. Knox observes that the Soviets still face the basic problem of information: Getting it into the hands of the bench scientist in a form he can use efficiently.

Dr. J. P. Nash, director of research for Lockheed's Missiles & Space division, cites one difficulty with translations. One of his men got word that a Russian technical journal had printed a lengthy paper dealing with the specialty he was working on. For weeks the Lockheed scientist waited for a translation to be made by an outside agency. When the document finally arrived, it was a retranslation of a paper the scientist himself had given many months earlier.

►►►►►►►►►►►► A RATING SCALE FOR PRODUCT INNOVATION

BARRY M. RICHMAN*

In an increasingly dynamic environment resulting in more rapid innovation and product obsolescence, a more precise method must be found to improve the chances of success in the introduction of new products. Poor product planning has resulted in poor product decisions. This situation can be corrected by the application of more scientific tools and techniques in the screening and selection process. This article considers such tools and techniques.

What determines the success of a new product in terms of over-all profitability to the company? Most executives would probably agree that the success a new product enjoys is directly related to the nature and extent of the competitive advantage in a market that has a demand for this class of product. It is the result of price and product differentiation with respect to specific attributes, characteristics, and features—tangible or intangible—that gives one product a greater degree of acceptance within a certain segment of the market. The degree of profitability, therefore, could be said to result from two major factors: (1) the nature and extent of competitive advantage; and (2) the size of the market segment where the advantage is appreciated and transferred into consumer preference and hence profitable sales.

In selecting new products, many companies have a tendency to estimate success and profitability in some ad hoc manner without systematically analyzing competitive advantage as it relates to consumer acceptance. A profit target is established without carefully considering whether it is realistic in terms of the company's talents, resources, and capabilities, or whether this product possesses the characteristics necessary to achieve this profit goal.

Considering the extremely high failure rate[1]—as compared with the successful development, commercialization, and marketing of new products by most companies—it appears that there is much room for improvement in the selection and screening procedures now in use. The approach presented here entails the quantification of qualitative considerations in a systematic and structured manner. In this way decisions will be more meaningful since the crucial factors to be analyzed will be ranked and assigned weights and

[1] For current figures see *Management of New Products* (New York: Booz, Allen & Hamilton, 1960), p. 14.

Reprinted with permission from Business Horizons, *Indiana University, Summer 1962, pp. 37–44.*

Lecturer in Management and Marketing, Graduate School of Business, Columbia University.

values. This will by no means supplant management judgment or completely eliminate the environment of uncertainty; however, it will offer a more scientific approach to the decision-making process. A case example will be used to illustrate the practical utilization of the tools and techniques.

The term "new product" will refer to an innovation or to a product addition already marketed by other companies. It should be noted that the screening process to be presented can also serve as a useful tool in evaluating company acquisitions and mergers.

SCREENING AND SELECTION

In order to arrive at a proper decision concerning new product additions, a company may best approach the problem by deducing specific integral elements from broad general factors until a meaningful profit estimate can be made. The initial factors that should be considered are:

1. Total potential market for this class of product and the related determinants of demand (It is assumed that the company has the proper tools and techniques for such forecasting.)

2. Company talents, skills, capabilities, and resources.

3. Competitive environment and the company's position in the industry.

Before the company can arrive at any meaningful estimate of profitability, it should, by use of the second and third factors, define and deduce the optimum competitive advantage the new product may enjoy. This is so because the nature and extent of competitive advantage depend on all of the company resources in relation to the competitive environment and the company's position in the industry. The nature and extent of the competitive advantage, in turn, define the size of the market segment within the total potential market. Only when competitive advantage and size of the related market segment are determined can a realistic profit estimate be made.

TOOLS AND TECHNIQUES

An effective tool and certain techniques are required to determine (1) whether the company is in a position to endow the new product with the necessary features that would result in profits, and (2) what type of advantage the company can most readily provide. The selection of product ideas and new products should be limited to those that can be translated into the necessary competitive advantage, which in turn can be transferred into a minimum desired level of over-all company profits. It is felt that new product proposals may best be screened and evaluated by use of an evaluation matrix (to be discussed later), which reflects product fit and compatibility with the company.

INITIAL SCREENING

The screening process begins with the inception of the product idea, which may originate from both internal and external sources. The company may wish to consider the idea in terms of any special reasons it may have at that time for adding new products. At different times in the life of a company some product ideas may be of greater significance than others. For example, the company may be more interested in replacing obsolete products than in expanding its line, or it may be interested in adding a new product that will balance the seasonal nature of its operations. Whatever the case, it will be assumed that management wants to pursue the product idea for purposes of development and commercialization. If there are clearly some insurmountable obstacles and limitations, such as lack of funds or legal considerations, the product proposal will be eliminated at an early stage. The study will relate only to new products where no such obstacles are apparent.

In some cases the company will adopt a new product regardless of its fit with respect to the company as a whole, for reasons of opportunism and large profits in the short run. The products to be considered here, however, will be only those that have long-run implications for the company inasmuch as they would become a permanent part of the organization, at least for the foreseeable future.

EVALUATION MATRIX

The evaluation matrix has two major functions and involves a two-part analysis. First, it is concerned with ranking and weighting the various spheres of company performance in relation to the over-all future success of the company. This will serve as a guideline in determining the nature of the competitive advantage the new product may offer. Second, it indicates the degree of product compatibility in relation to these spheres of performance by the assignment of values, thus reflecting

the over-all product fit with the company as a whole. The over-all result derived by the application of this tool is reflected in one quantitative figure. An estimate of profitability is not provided for in this matrix. Such an estimate, however, would evolve directly from the findings and conclusions resulting from the application of this tool.

The following hypothetical example will illustrate the practical application of the evaluation matrix.

CASE STUDY: THE MATRIX IN ACTION

A large manufacturer of a wide line of photographic equipment, cameras, projectors, and other related supplies is considering the addition of a transistor radio to its product line. The company has undertaken a preliminary study of the total market potential for this class of product, and at present the management believes that the idea should be pursued and translated into a product with specific characteristics. The company must decide whether an expenditure is warranted for the development and eventual commercialization of a line of transistor radios.

By concentrating its efforts on certain determinants of demand relating to consumer preference, the company may be able to obtain an adequate share of the market through demand manipulation, and perhaps even alter the conditions of the market. This would, of course, be within the limits set by various uncontrollable factors such as population and level of incomes. This focus on specific determinants of demand would result in a differentiated product that would offer certain advantages over competing products in a particular segment of the market. An analysis of the nature of major strengths of the company is required for this purpose.

SPHERES OF PERFORMANCE

The success and survival of this or any other company depend on the magnitude and extent of the over-all competitive advantage enjoyed. The competitive advantage is derived from the extent and nature of the company's resources and the utilization of these resources along with the talents and skills present in the company. The totality of this competitive advantage depends on the performances and contributions in different spheres of operation. These spheres, although not completely independent and mutually exclusive, can be subdivided for the sake of analysis. Each one has varying degrees of significance in terms of over-all company success. In ranking and assigning weights to the individual spheres, the company must consider all its resources with respect to the particular sphere of activity and in relation to the competitive environment.

The greater the competitive advantage the company has in a specific sphere, the greater would be the assigned weight, since it would be more significant in relation to over-all company success. In most cases the weights assigned would reflect the historical development of the company in terms of talent, know-how, and resources. It is the future relationship that is important, however, and a planned major change of emphasis in terms of the significance of some spheres should be reflected in the assigned weights. The total of the assigned weights should always equal 1.0, which is a reflection of the over-all company performance and success. This ranking and assignment of weights should also reflect the company's relations with various interest groups such as distributors, suppliers, creditors, and unions. This in turn indicates the ability to achieve a maximization of contributions to the company at minimum cost.

ASSIGNMENT OF WEIGHTS

In this company there are six operational or functional spheres in which success and performance are determined by the extent and nature of company capabilities and resources, and the effectiveness of company policies with respect to the utilization of these resources. In addition, there are two nonoperational spheres that must be considered since they play a role in determining over-all company success. Most companies would probably lend themselves to a somewhat similar breakdown. The spheres and their weights in this particular company follow:

Marketing (.20) This industry is highly marketing oriented, and the company feels that its capabilities and talents in this sphere are above average in relation to competition. This appears to be a major area in relation to over-all company success, and the company plans to capitalize further on its flair for promotion, strong brand name, and broad quality product line. Worldwide distribution and servicing of the products are probably major strong points. The company provides guarantees for its products and, although few of the retail outlets are owned by the company, good relations and servicing are expected to prevail in the future.

Research and Development (including design, styling, engineering, and market testing) (.20) Along with marketing, this operational sphere is expected to be the most integral with respect to future success. The company is a leader in the industry in terms of design, styling, and ability to develop durable products with special features that permit precision and ease of handling. In several cases the company obtained patents for products and plans to do the same in the future.

Personnel (.15) The company expects to maintain a slight advantage with respect to managerial talent as a result of its recruiting, selection, training, and compensation policy. It is expected that high morale will continue among employees, provided that the organizational structure is not disrupted too quickly or too extensively. The company expects good union relations to continue, but no competitive advantage is anticipated in this respect.

Finance (.10) The majority of the firms in this industry are financially strong, as is this company. No distinct competitive advantage is expected to be derived from this area.

Production (.05) While this company has modern methods and processes of production enabling the output of durable and high quality goods, no distinct competitive advantage is anticipated in terms of cost or know-how.

Purchasing and Supply (.05) The company does not anticipate any special advantage with respect to cost or the attainability of special materials.

Location and Facilities (.05) Although this is a nonoperational sphere, it should be considered since it contributes in varying degrees to the overall success and performance of a company, but especially so if the company has a preferred location in terms of cost or special access to supplies and markets. The location of this company offers no distinct advantage, and its facilities are not expected to result in any competitive advantage in the future.

Company Personality and Goodwill (.20) This nonoperational sphere can be treated independently even though it has evolved as a result of the performances in other spheres. It would be more significant in an industry dealing in highly differentiated products than in an industry dealing in products with a high degree of standardization. This sphere relates to the character, traditions, customs, and personality of the company, as well as its reputation and clarity of identification in the minds of its employees and consumers. This in essence reflects loyalty and consumer preference.

This particular company feels that its future success and performance depend greatly on its character, image, and personality. It has developed pride among its employees and a reputation for dependable, durable, and high quality products. The company has won consumer confidence by standing behind its products with guarantees and warranties.

A management team should be responsible for ranking and assigning weights, and the field of operations research presents some approaches that can be utilized. The most applicable one appears to be the Standard Gamble Technique for measuring utilities.[2] This technique could be extended and applied to determine the quantitative weights of each sphere based on subjective appraisals.

PRODUCT ATTRIBUTES

In translating the product idea into an actual product that offers optimum competitive advantage, the company must consider its areas of major strength. It is best to select products that do not divert company attention from the structure of its over-all success pattern. Since this company is highly marketing oriented and has a flair for sales promotion, the company need not offer an advantage in terms of price. In order to capitalize fully on its reputation and personality, the company feels that the transistor radio, if adopted, should derive its advantage through innovistic style and design, high quality in terms of durability and

tone, and a guarantee at least as good as those offered by competitors.

It is felt that a very compact, durable, high quality transistor that would also give a good, clear tone in an automobile would appeal to travelers, especially those who travel abroad and rent or buy foreign cars, which are seldom equipped with radios. Many of these travelers would be the consumers of existing company products. Such a radio could probably command a higher price than competing products but a price somewhat lower than car radios.

It is necessary to consider whether a transistor radio with the above attributes and features can be effectively developed and marketed by the company, in light of all its resources. In addition, it must be determined whether the new product ties in with future company operations. The better the fit, the greater the probability of achieving the desired competitive advantage without hindering the over-all success of the company. If it is ascertained that the product has a good fit and can derive the desired competitive advantage, a meaningful estimate with respect to the scope and extent of consumer preference, and hence profitability, can be made.

It should be noted that in many instances the new product being screened may already be a developed product rather than merely an idea. In this case, many of the attributes of the product must be taken as given. The company could then influence the extent of competitive advantage only through price or its promotional policy. The degree of product fit and com-

---

[2] See, for example, David W. Miller and Martin K. Starr, *Executive Decisions and Operations Research* (Englewood Cliffs, N.J.: Prentice-Hall, Inc., 1960), pp. 69–72. The use of this technique may be facilitated by regrouping the above spheres into broader spheres and then subdividing this grouping and repeating the process.

patibility with the company should still be determined in order to decide whether the new product ties in with the future over-all success and performance of the company and whether the company is capable of successfully undertaking its commercialization. If there is a poor fit, the likelihood of deriving an increase in over-all company long-range profits would be highly questionable.

ASSIGNMENT OF VALUES

The new product proposal reflecting the desired attributes and characteristics should be analyzed in terms of compatibility with each separate sphere, and with the company as a whole. This is best accomplished by assigning values that reflect the product fit in each sphere. In each case a value between 0.0 and 1.0 is assigned depending on the degree of product fit with respect to the policies, resources, and other features of the sphere under consideration. Near-perfect fits call for values approaching 1.0, and very poor fits have values approaching 0.0. The assigned values in each case are multiplied by the assigned weights, and all the net results are added, thus reflecting over-all product fit in one quantitative figure.

Marketing (.9) The company believes that the proposed product fits in well with anticipated marketing policies and activities. The same channels of distribution, outlets, and sales promotion policies can be utilized. The company expects it to appeal to many of the same customers as the old products do. The company has the ability to effectively promote the significant product attributes and features. In addition, the radio will not upset the pricing policies of the company or replace any part of its product line. The brand name of the company does not tie in perfectly with the new product, but it is felt that there is some degree of compatibility in this respect.

Research and Development (.7) The company feels capable of developing, designing, and testing a transistor radio that would possess the tangible attributes necessary to obtain the desired competitive advantage. Although the company is confident that it can obtain the required basic skills, the services of some outside experts will be necessary. This will also call for some new research and development activities, but they are not expected to disrupt or hinder the other necessary activities and policies of this sphere. It is unlikely that a patent can be acquired for this product.

Personnel (.6) The necessary labor and executive resources can be obtained, although some additional training will be required. There will be some organizational disruption, but this is not expected to be of a very significant or serious nature. There is no anticipated change in the area of industrial relations.

Finance (.9) The necessary funds for development, commercialization, and promotion of the new product are readily attainable at favorable terms. Furthermore, it does not appear that expenditures for other important pur-

TABLE 1

EVALUATION MATRIX—PRODUCT FIT

Sphere of Performance	(A) Relative Weight	(B) Product Compatibility Values											(C) A × B
		0	.1	.2	.3	.4	.5	.6	.7	.8	.9	1.0	
Company personality and goodwill	.20							x					.120
Marketing	.20										x		.180
Research and development	.20								x				.140
Personnel	.15							x					.090
Finance	.10										x		.090
Production	.05									x			.040
Location and facilities	.05				x								.015
Purchasing and supply	.05										x		.045
Total	1.00												.720*

* Rating Scale: 0–.40, poor; .41–.75, fair; .76–1.0, good. Present minimum acceptance rate: .70.

poses will be restricted. Only if the product is highly unsuccessful will dividend payments have to be curtailed.

Production (.8) A new production line will be required, but no difficulty is expected. The processes used for other products will not be disrupted. The company anticipates using the same extent of mechanization and specialization that it uses in the manufacturing of several other items.

Purchasing and Supply (.9) Several of the existing sources of supply can be utilized, and a few new ones will have to be obtained. Materials required for the development and production of the transistor radio are readily obtainable.

Location and Facilities (.3) The company will have to acquire new facilities in a new location, preferably near one of its existing plants, because the present facilities have no excess capacity for this purpose. A special location is not required, however, and the company is confident that it can obtain a fairly desirable location.

Company Personality and Goodwill (.6) It is felt that the new product does not coincide exactly with the company image and personality. The transistor radio is not actually a related or complementary product, but the management has a reputation for being aggressive rather than conservative, and therefore the addition is not expected to endanger company reputation and loyalty in the future. Since the transistor radio is expected to derive its main advantage through promotion, quality, dependability, and design, the goodwill built up by the company will in some respects be compatible with the new product.

PRODUCT FIT

The results of the new product evaluation are presented in Table 1. It can be seen that the net figure obtained for the over-all product fit is .720, which places the product high up in the "fair" category in terms of compatibility with the company as a whole. (The maximum rating of 1.0 indicates a perfect fit.) The company may have differing minimum cutoff rates at different periods of time in light of economic and other conditions. In cases where consideration is being given to several new products, the company would be inclined to give priority and preference to those with the highest ratings.

The minimum cutoff rate could best be determined through experience by evaluating actual new product success in relation to product fit indicated during the screening stage. It is also possible to reflect back and consider what the product fit of currently successful products would have been in the idea and screening stage. Some type of post-completion audit could expand the usefulness and accuracy of this tool.

By selecting new products with a good over-all fit, the company can increase the probability of effective development and successful commercialization. Those products with the best fit are the ones most likely to succeed in terms of over-all profitability, since the company is capable of providing the necessary promotion, product attributes, and features in terms of competitive advantage. While the purpose of this paper is not to estimate profitability, a meaningful estimate could evolve once the company knows the nature and extent of competitive advantage desired in terms of the total potential market, and is confident of achieving this advantage. The estimation of profitability would be the last step in the screening process before a decision for adoption or rejection is reached. This would be preferable to a situation in which the company establishes a somewhat arbitrary profit target without analyzing and evaluating whether the new product will possess the attributes necessary for a great enough competitive advantage, and hence attainment of the profit goal. Nor should the company fail to consider the new product in relation to the skills, capabilities, and resources of the company, and its impact on anticipated over-all company success and performance.

With the utilization and application of the tools and techniques presented, management may be in a position to make more meaningful decisions with respect to new product additions. The approach outlined could also be useful for teaching purposes as a guide to the implications and problems that relate to the area of product planning.

In practice, it is evident that the above tools and techniques would not necessarily be utilized in a manner identical to the one presented. However, the approach could be adapted to fit many company situations relating to the screening and selection of new product ideas and new products.

D
Coordinating and Controlling Development

▶▶▶▶▶▶▶▶▶▶▶ COORDINATING TECHNICAL AND MARKETING
RESEARCH

B. F. BOWMAN*

A considerable amount of material has been written on this subject, so these currents are neither original nor revolutionary. They do represent, however, a sound, practical and effective program. Each part flows in and out of many areas of corporate responsibility and—if each is properly directed and coordinated—falls into its proper contributing slot like the pieces of a neatly made jigsaw puzzle.

This paper should be prefaced by three statements of a qualifying nature:

First, these comments deal largely with how things should be done, rather than how they are conducted during actual operations today. This is because companies have different organizational structures; some even have different identifying names for similar departmental operations.

Second, new products rather than existing products are used for the basis of discussion and illustration. This is

Reprinted with permission from Cost and Profit Outlook, July 1954, pp. 1–4.
*Vice-President, Huron Milling Company.

because new products usually present a far greater variety of problems. At some time or another, they are the cause of just about every conceivable type of problem situation affecting both technical and market research; and what is more important, they require the fullest resources of both of these important functions.

Third, this paper is presented not as the work of an expert in either marketing research or technical research but by one who heads up a sales department. From this observation post, it is possible to view the many instances of interlocking responsibilities which are so essential to successful product development as the product comes up the road toward the intersection where the sales department takes over.

With those preliminary comments, let's now look objectively at this important subject of coordination between technical and marketing research.

We must first define the objectives of a coordinated relationship between these two important tools of marketing. In other words, why must there be coordination? Aside from the more or less general and basic premise that every phase of corporate action must be meshed in with all others, there are some special needs for unusual sharpness in the coordination of these two major contributions.

On the one hand there are technical people who are a fertile source of knowledge. They are bacteriologists, chemists, biochemists, physicists, and their tools are benches, glass tubes, Bunsen burners, flasks, compressed air,

spray driers, tanks, and many large volumes of books. They know—or they are supposed to know—or at least they can find out—what happens when you put certain materials together and treat them by certain methods and processes. They are sometimes inclined to be intrigued simply with interesting phenomena rather than with how to put something costing 28 cents in a package to sell for 56 cents. Yet they are willing and eager, and, most important, they possess curiosity and imagination. They must be given every possible help to enable them to convert that curiosity and imagination into ideas and facts. This help can come in a very major way from market research.

On the other hand, market research people utilize techniques or methods of gathering facts—statistical and otherwise—which can be resolved into guideposts for action in the areas of product development, pricing, economics, and many others. They give constructive suggestions concerning methods which are based on objective viewpoints. It has been said that market research is as essential to successful corporate operations as radar is to successful navigation. This I firmly believe.

So we can only conclude that if corporate growth and diversification are to be accomplished successfully, it is imperative that these two areas of contribution be closely related. If we wish to reduce this objective to its simplest form, let us say that market research is a decisive factor in helping to translate technical research into the language of day-to-day corporate operation. In brief, market research can help bridge the gap between sales and science.

Now that we have indicated why this coordination is necessary, the next question is, what are the problems in accomplishing it? In other words, who is to coordinate? Any consideration of coordinating these two contributing areas must necessarily raise the question of organizational structure. Later on I shall refer to some charts which show the principal areas where market research and technical research must be pulled together.

To maintain maximum effectiveness, coordination must be accomplished by a corporate area which is unrelated either to market research or technical research. A separate department or individual must be charged with the responsibility for guiding a product from the idea stage until it is a full-fledged, regular product being sold through the company's regular channels of distribution—or of course, until enough attention has been given to the project to warrant a decision to defer or terminate development. Separate responsibility obviously is not practical in some companies, especially in smaller ones, but it is the ideal procedure. Let's examine some of the arguments for the assignment of separate responsibility:

To begin with, as a product or project moves through the various departments which contribute to its development, there is a continuous shift of responsibility which depends upon the current stage of development. Thus no

one department can be responsible for deciding when its contribution is to be activated or, for that matter, when it is terminated.

Next we are faced with the matter that all product development jobs do not proceed in the same pattern of events or present the same problems. This of course means that a department or individual outside of each contributing department must resolve the problem of which departments are to be consulted during the development process.

Finally, it is important to bear in mind that people and not machines are involved. Their temperaments, attitudes and methods must be recognized if they are to render maximum contributions.

There must be a melting-pot into which the contributions of all corporate experts can be brought together. Obviously this raises the question concerning the distinction between authority and responsibility in the coordinating area. This can perhaps be disposed of in a general way, however, by stating that the coordinating department is effective largely because of its ability to advise others about what is to be done, but at the same time, carefully refraining from telling each department how to do it.

Now, after we have considered why we must have coordination between technical and marketing research—plus some ideas concerning who is to do it —the most important question of all is: how is it to be done? What are the best techniques and methods to pull together effectively and to make coherent the brain-power of market research and technical research?

Most of you have read articles and books with checklists of matters to be resolved in a coordinated development program. As a matter of fact we once prepared a chart containing a list of fifty-six separate factors; the underlying concept was that when we started with Item 1 and ended with Item 56, we would have automatically covered all possible development problems. The next day three unlisted problems arose on one project alone; consequently the all-important checklist was consigned to the wastebasket.

Coordination of development work is not only complex but it is also costly because it involves so many phases of business operations. It is my belief that the problem can best be approached by an analysis of the areas where coordination is essential, rather than by a checklist or lengthy itemization of "things to be done today."

Analysis of some of the elements within each broad area should also be attempted.

I believe that the charts best illustrate these broad areas and also spotlight the decisions which must be resolved before the project's development proceeds to the next area.

Area I, or Phase I, is concerned with the product idea—or the origination of the suggestion for the new product.

The top half of our Chart I outlines the contribution of technical research while the lower half suggests the contribution or material which could be made available by market research. Certainly both market research and technical research are two of the most fertile sources of new product ideas. Product ideas come from many sources: from research, sales, manufacturing, outside suggestions, stockholders, management, and members of the Board. Ideas for products derived through technical research result from:

	I IDEAS			II INVESTIGATION EXPLORATION			III RESEARCH AND DEVELOPMENT
TECHNICAL RESEARCH	Experimentation Mechanical development Related technical departments Technical solution of existing problems Outside sources		TECHNICAL RESEARCH	Technical possibilities Scientific problems Technically practical Availability of men and facilities Fit present processes or require new equipment		TECHNICAL RESEARCH	Product characteristic and design Performance Formulation Basic or applied research Competitive products Stability Costs Processes
DECISION AREA		Selection for Phase II	DECISION AREA		Authorization for Phase III	DECISION AREA	Authorization for Phase IV
MARKET RESEARCH	Interpretation of sales, advertising, and related marketing data Outside sources		MARKET RESEARCH	Thorough preliminary commercial evaluation		MARKET RESEARCH	Market potential Market requirements Cost and profit aspects Share market goals Competition Selling techniques

Experimentation
Mechanical development
Related technical departments
Outside sources
Technical problems, the solution of
 which gives rise to a new idea

Market research is an equally fertile source of ideas as a result of its collection and analysis of sales, advertising and related marketing data plus its awareness and contact with valuable outside information sources. In addition, market research plays a key role by making preliminary appraisals to aid in the choice or selection of products worthy of further development. Even a relatively simple survey can uncover weaknesses in a proposed product before more serious appraisals are conducted and certainly before actual development operations are launched. For example, market research can with relative ease determine whether the proposed product will be priced too high, whether dealers or channels of distribution are already overstocked with competing products, or whether similar or better products are already available at a lower price.

The area of decision involved in this first phase is basically a matter of the selection of a product worthy of study in the second area of decision. This second area (Chart II) is concerned with the investigation or exploratory phase. It is here that a comprehensive analysis of the product idea begins. The technical research people must carefully investigate each factor listed below:

> Technical possibilities
> Scientific problems
> Technically practical?
> Availability of men and facilities
> Fit present processes or require
> new equipment?

At the same time, market research must assume its major responsibility

	IV TESTING		V INITIAL SALES AND MANUFACTURING	
TECHNICAL RESEARCH	Process development Pilot plant production Preliminary plant production Process costs Control methods Ingredient specifications		**TECHNICAL RESEARCH**	Aid to production in manufacturing Product specifications for procurement Control
	DECISION AREA	Authoriza- tion for Phase V		DECISION AREA	Product moves into regular operation
MARKET RESEARCH	Pilot marketing: Panel tests Consumer tests Market tests Review of previous evaluations Appraisal of sales potentials and marketing plans		**MARKET RESEARCH**	Thorough review with sales and advertising of: product potentials suggested techniques consumer reaction technique in approach to the actual marketing

of acting for both sales and management. They must conduct a commercial evaluation of the product idea to provide adequate answers to such questions as: will the product fit our established channels of distribution; will the product fit our established sales method; what is the present market total; what is the potential market total; and, assuming certain product and market characteristics, what share market could we anticipate?

Sales estimates of course must receive special attention. Not only must estimates of sales potential be as precise as possible, but such estimates must also be continuously refined and reviewed up to the point of actual manufacture and distribution.

A realistic final decision in this second phase must involve careful consideration of three corporate activities. First, production must agree that the product is practical to produce from the viewpoint of manufacturing. Second, the technical research department, after its investigation, must agree that the product is technically sound. Third, the sales department, represented by market research, must agree that sufficient market is available and that the product can be sold. This three-part group can either decide to go ahead with Phase III of the overall project if it has the authority, or send its recommendations to management. In either event, commitment of capital or real investment results only after an affirmative decision in Phase II.

Phase III (Chart III) is concerned with research and development. This is where the real investment begins.

On the technical side, a program must be activated which requires a commitment of men, equipment and hours. The key factors involved are:

Product characteristics and design
Performance
Formulation
Basic or applied research
Competitive products
Stability
Costs
Processes

Market research must initiate studies involving the following matters:

Market potentials
Market requirements
Costs and profit aspects
Share market goals
Competition
Selling techniques

Even though this third area is probably the most important, no special comment is necessary except to state that it is probably the crucial point in the entire development program. Eternal vigilance is necessary if the resources of the two departments are to be molded into the production of a product worthy of testing. Obviously, the major decision area necessary in Phase III is management's approval to proceed with product testing.

Our fourth chart is concerned with the area of product testing. From the technical side the following factors are most important:

Process development
Pilot plant production
Preliminary plant production
Process costs

Control methods
Ingredient specifications

On the market research side, the logical move is into the operation of pilot marketing which might include panel testing, consumer testing or market testing, depending upon the scope of the problem and the nature of the product. There must also be a review of all previous evaluations and a reappraisal of sales potentials and marketing plans as were mentioned previously.

In essence, the completion of Phase IV signals the end of product development. Certainly before the fifth area is entered there should be a carefully conducted review of the entire project with particular emphasis devoted to profit considerations, market opportunities, adaptability to company policy, availability of production facilities, requirements of funds both in terms of capital investment and working inventory, and the timing which might affect the sales department.

The fifth phase, outlined in Chart V, deals with initial sales and manufacturing efforts. Coordination between technical research and market research is still vitally important. Technical research must aid production and manufacturing in the development of specifications for procurement, and the establishment and finalization of quality and product control methods. Market research must thoroughly review sales, advertising and product potentials. They must also consider proposed techniques for introduction, consumer reactions, and proposals concerning marketing strategy. The relationship between technical research and market research is perhaps less significant in this fifth area than in those preceding it; yet, both are still responsible parties to the overall program and their efforts must be coordinated.

Obviously the decision area resulting from Phase V is to move the product into regular corporate operations. These five areas hold key positions into which must be fed both market intelligence and technical intelligence. Observation of the five areas as a whole emphasizes not only the complexity of product development but also the importance of continuity in this system. Specific illustrations were intentionally avoided because of the wide variety of possible product projects and the dynamic nature of emphasis requirements. However, these charts illustrate the complexity of problems of coordination, the necessity for coordination, and the rewards resulting from derivation of maximum contribution from the unification of efforts when all aspects are closely integrated.

When the project moves beyond these five areas, emphasis is devoted primarily to marketing. Although the subject of marketing new products is an extensive one, it is obviously not a part of this paper.

In addition to a multi-level program of coordination between technical and market research, there is one more ingredient necessary or no degree of success is likely. Behind all this activity there must exist correct and well-balanced management philosophy. This philosophy must be one of patience, willingness to invest men, time and money, and a sincere willingness to make the best possible objective decision based largely upon what the technical people and marketing people can communicate and recommend.

There may be disappointment on the part of some of you that a more precise method of coordination was not outlined. However, anything like a comprehensive list would involve just about everything that makes a business run. But there is logical common sense step-by-step coordination which pulls together all the pieces of the development project, as it is guided by market research intelligence and formulated by technical research and intelligence so that it results in a well built and carefully constructed product with a maximum chance for success in the Sales Department's list of products.

▶▶▶▶▶▶▶▶▶▶▶ COORDINATING DESIGN AT THE EXECUTIVE LEVEL

ARTHUR N. BECVAR*

I should like to discuss with you some reasons why design is one of the determining elements of success in a product, and how the method of handling it by coordinating design at the executive level affects the results.

In the General Electric Company, we have found that "design" is extremely important to the sale and satisfaction of the product. "Design," however, is a term that is used freely and means many things to many people. In the manufacturing plant, "design" applies to the engineering area, but the general public considers design as incorporating both the outward manifestations of engineering and the appearance characteristics of a product. Consequently, "good design" is beneficial to a product because it insures greater satisfaction to the customer, and also it helps the manufacturer sell his product. "Good design" expresses the quality and excellence of a product. For example, the mechanical parts of a product can be excellent, but if some of the structure does not reflect the same quality, such as a thin door or flimsy latch, the whole product is not considered of high quality level by the average consumer. The whole unit is judged. The public recognizes only the outward appearance of good engineering as part of design through quiet operation, long life, ease of control, and ease of maintenance.

It is interesting to consider what a product would be like if designed solely by the engineer, the manufacturing

Reprinted with permission from Advanced Management, *January 1953, pp. 77–79.*

Manager, Product Planning, General Electric Company.

man, the finance man, the product service man, the salesman, or the industrial designer. "Good design" requires the collaboration of each of the above men. If design is dictated by any one of them, a distorted product would result because each specialist would unconsciously emphasize his own area of work. It is important that all concerned with the product start on equal terms at the inception of the program so that each can argue for and agree upon the necessary contributions of each other. The final coordination must be guided at management level to balance and properly weigh each factor.

You will remember in the early days of our company, we produced a refrigerator called the "Monitor Top." The unit was mounted on the top. From an engineering viewpoint, this was and still is a very sound engineering principle. The cleanability of this design and its appearance soon pointed to the customer preference of putting the unit in the base and making a simple straightforward cabinet that would fit into the present concept of a kitchen.

You may be interested to know how we are set up to meet this problem of coordinating design in our company. In our Major Appliance Division, this coordinating responsibility is assigned to a Manager of Product Planning, both at the staff and department levels. They are responsible for the following:

I. Establishing pricing objectives
II. Preparing and maintaining a competitive analysis
III. Preparing a product plan that sets commercial specifications
IV. Using market research and consumer research to pretest our products
V. Coordinating time schedules and objectives

WHAT PRODUCT PLANNING IS

One of the most important elements in the major appliance business is having a product that is equal to or in advance of competition measured by consumer acceptance. It must be available at the proper time and be manufactured and sold to yield a reasonable profit.

It is a continuous collection, recording, and evaluation of all product information. Everyone in our business contributes the talents, ideas, and the facts related to our products. As you see in this chart, it is the funneling of this collection down to a specific product plan that integrates the marketing requirements with engineering development and manufacturing methods to consumer needs at the prices he will pay. Pricing, competitive features, new technology, new features and appearance are analyzed and focused on "next year's product."

During this funneling process, a line is drawn, and a specific product plan for five years is recorded. The product plan is fluid in the projected years, but as it approaches the present model year, it becomes a locked-up program with a definite time schedule starting with specifications, development, laboratory evaluation, consumer pretest, final design, tooling, and production. It does not stop there, for "Nothing is accomplished unless it goes to Mrs. Consumer. She likes it; she wants it; she buys it; she's satisfied!"

We are continuously finding out through market research the objectives that will satisfy the market. These specifications are then turned over to specialists who develop these requirements into the design, engineering, and manufactured product. This is when the appearance designer, the engineer, and the manufacturing man develop the best solutions to contours, textures, safety elements, convenience aspects, sales appeal, and ease of maintenance and service of the product.

It seems that products pass through the following stages in their lifetime: pioneering, competitive, retentive, and declining.

We can all appreciate that design is relatively more important in certain products than it is in others. No product escapes the influence of good design. Good design is considerably more important in the competitive and retentive stages principally because they

are the periods when all things are most equal, and it is then that the customer is influenced by "good design."

What happens when a new product is introduced to the market in terms of public acceptance? Initially, if it contributes a real consumer service and need, it rises high in public acceptance. But that unique spot is held for only a short time because competition very quickly moves in and equalizes the gain. Thus, it starts to decline until another basic change makes it rise again in public acceptance. Competition again equalizes it, and, thus, this general curve is followed during the life of the product.

Major changes usually involve new tools and plant layout; consequently, these basic changes are introduced not every year, but about every three to five years. It becomes imperative to use other methods during the "in between" years to build up public acceptance.

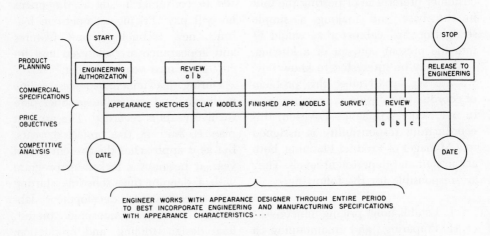

FIGURE 1

TIMING CHART

These are the years when it is necessary to have advanced features added, new appearance with minor tool changes, and color changes to spark-up the product.

This timing chart gives you an indication of the kind of thing we are relating to our Product Planning programs to make sure that our lines will be new and fresh and exciting and appealing every year (see Figure 1).

Our executives realize that the modern marketing organization requires a high degree of sensitivity to changing conditions and an ability to adjust quickly to them. Marketing dictates that the product be suited to market conditions at a specific time and at a specific price, and with product qualities which will meet volume reaction in the market satisfactorily.

ORIGIN OF PRESENT APPEARANCE DESIGN POLICY

Appearance Design is an important function, necessary in the development of consumer goods if it is to gain volume acceptance. This department in the General Electric Company is, therefore, responsible to the executive in charge of marketing through the Manager of Product Planning.

During the first 30 years of its existence, the General Electric Company manufactured products whose appearance had little effect on the volume of sales in its products.

Pioneers in our company like Thomas Edison and Charles Steinmetz were interested in the "application of electricity" to devices which would generate, transmit and use electricity in industry. This was done without too much regard to the appearance of the apparatus.

In the 1920's, Gerard Swope, then President of the General Electric Company, recognized the fact that the continued growth of the electrical industry would be dependent on the application of electrical equipment in the home as well as in industry. Therefore, he decided that more attention would have to be paid to the development, engineering, and manufacturing of consumer goods, such as home appliances.

In the early years of the development of such home appliances as the refrigerator, range, washing machine and flat iron, General Electric's greatest interest continued to center around the objective of making sturdy and serviceable appliances with efficiency and performance the chief criteria of good design.

Appearance Design specialization within the General Electric Company began in 1928 with one industrial designer and a very small staff. The results of this man's efforts to improve the appearance of consumer goods met with such good acceptance that the staff and facilities were gradually increased in size and scope.

Soon this Appearance Design Department was asked, because of increased competition in industrial lines, to make appearance recommendations on some of the company's capital goods equipment, such as electric locomotives, turbines, motors, instruments and other diversified products manufactured by the various divisions of the company. As the value of appearance design study became better recognized, Appearance Design departments were established in various divisions of the company. From the one man retained on appearance design problems, the personnel has developed into a well-staffed company department in each division of the company.

RESPONSIBILITY FOR CARRYING OUT PRESENT APPEARANCE DESIGN POLICY

In each division of the company, there is a Manager of Appearance Design, responsible to the Manager of Product Planning. He is responsible for the appearance recommendations on the products of that particular division. However, to insure insofar as is possible and desirable, a General Electric family likeness among our products, the Manager of Product Planning of the overall company marketing services division promotes the interchange of information for controlling and coordinating these objectives.

Within each operating division of General Electric, Appearance Design works most intimately with Product Planning, Marketing Research and Engineering.

Product Planning is primarily an analytical function involving the determination of what products will most profitably meet market needs. Market demands and competitive conditions are constantly changing and require corresponding modification of the product. The customer has shown in his selection of products that his purchase is influenced by the effect of pleasing design. Utility products such as those that are used in the kitchen and laundry must have eye appeal as well as utility, since they have become more closely related to the living area. With an open-floor plan becoming more popular in American houses, all the equipment must be attractive and contribute to enjoyable surroundings.

These buying trends also extend to non-luxury lines of products. Capital goods equipment now is placed in attractive, colorful factory areas and is subject to the same appearance design study.

Marketing Research continually checks the product for consumer acceptance. New ideas and designs are tested on groups of people in various geographical locations, and varied income groups to determine whether a new design has what they want and desire.

Engineering is responsible for the basic design of the product, its materials, construction, and performance. General Electric scientists and research engineers are continually pioneering new materials, processes, and new product functions for better living at less cost.

During the past 30 years, the American consumer has, in his selection of products, given evidence of his desire for good design. Today the consumer's interest in the appearance of a product has increased to the point where manufacturers of consumer goods must devote as much attention to characteristics of color harmony, fitness and simplicity, as to new features of performance and utility. Major redesigns are undertaken when new technology has shown the way to obtain improved designs giving greater value to the consumer. It is the function of Appearance Design to make these products attractive and most suitable functionally.

To obtain the necessary eye appeal, the Appearance Designer must give due consideration to other factors affecting the consumer—convenience of use, care and simplicity of operation of the product.

In the schedule of planning our products, Appearance Design works with Engineering before the mechanical design is frozen to get the best location of controls and operating features from the user's viewpoint. Under the stimulus of Appearance Design, basic structural changes may be indicated to achieve a harmonious appearance. It has often happened that a structure is worked out which is both new and economical as the result of the engineering search to find a new technique to accomplish both objectives. Harmonious coordination with engineering and the exploring of all approaches make possible the most favorable relationship of forms and components to get the best appearance.

APPEARANCE DESIGN ORGANIZATION

Since the General Electric Company is engaged in producing both capital and consumer goods, I should like to give you an example of how Appearance Design functions in one division of the company: namely, the Major Appliance Division, which produces ranges, freezers, water heaters, dishwashers and sinks, washing machines, dryers and ironers, and refrigerators.

The Appearance Design Department is composed of the following creative personnel: Designing Manager and Designers of each line of products. Also two model shops, one manned by sculptors devoted to creative clay or plastacine modeling and the other manned by skilled model makers, working in plaster of Paris, metal, wood, plastics and finishing techniques —a total of 46 people.

A separate section of Advance Appearance Design is devoted to "projected design," that is, product designs of the future. The design approach in this activity is one toward the "ideal design" disregarding our current limitations imposed by present engineering or manufacturing facility considerations. This type of design has value in stimulating new thinking; fundamental, even radical approaches to product function. This is product insurance for the future.

The Appearance Design Department is a self-liquidating type of operation, the cost being billed to each department for the work done on an hourly basis. Since it is a service which each department can buy, and not one that is arbitrarily assessed against them, the constant yearly growth of the department shows that this is a very satisfactory means of operation.

A small number of industrialists have considered that Appearance Design efforts are simply a move to add trim or ornamentation to a product without any purpose. Some have expressed the thought that the cost of industrial design and the increase in price for the addition of these design features are not justified.

We believe that the form and function of our appliances are well integrated and represent sound design principles. I should like to point out that for a volume market of mass manufacture, the cost of appearance design is negligible. We do, however, recognize the very serious problem especially as it pertains to changes of design which mean extensive retooling in the face of small production.

APPEARANCE DESIGN PROCEDURE

Let me give you an example of how we handle the design of a product that requires a yearly design change. This is the routine of our procedure for initial product planning.

Product Planning calls a meeting with Sales, Engineering, Manufacturing and Appearance Design to determine the objectives of the new line and to establish a product plan.

New engineering developments, required features, costs, and general appearance objectives are discussed. Dates are established that determine the schedule of appearance design in relation to engineering drawings, test models, pre-production runs and production dates. This meeting establishes a very realistic program of all the requirements to produce a new product at a specific date.

With this information, appearance design sketches are made and many design themes are drawn in rough form. This is a search for new design approaches, new concepts; and this is really the important period of concentrated design expression. These design ideas are all reviewed in order to select two or three ideas for further development.

At times, we have made up finished perspective drawings of the designs for discussion with representatives of Sales, Manufacturing, and Engineering. However, we have learned from past experience that beautifully colored perspective drawings can be very misleading in evaluating a design. Consequently, our design procedure requires three dimensional study. The design ideas are translated into full size clay models.

Only in this clay form can we properly analyze the proportion, contour, texture and character of the design. These studies are reviewed with engineering and manufacturing to determine whether they are within the limits of electrical and mechanical requirements.

Finished full size models are then made. This final step of design work is the most important, for here we translate the design concepts into its most refined form, the actual object to evaluate. Consequently, we insist on the highest degree of model craftsmanship and every detail is given the ultimate designer's touch. The plaster of Paris parts are finished with every degree of contour subtlety and then surface-painted to perfection. All metal trim and accessory parts are hand fashioned by expert metal workers. The result is always the finest expression of craftsmanship that it is possible to produce.

We feel that much effort should be expended on this final model, for this represents the product goal. It gives manufacturing a prototype desirable to achieve.

The appearance is thoroughly tested for consumer acceptance. It must be determined that the new model has acceptance in relation to present production and in relation to competition.

Sometimes a conflict occurs between what the designer regards as right and what the public thinks it wants as evidenced by samples of opinion taken by Market Research. Perhaps this conflict is only a matter of timing. A design is presented, for example, that Research indicates is not at the moment most popular, but under market stimulation becomes so because it is "basically right." Our efforts are always directed toward the objective of meeting the requirements of the real arbiter of American design: namely, the customer.

This model is then revised with the department manager, who in turn, submits it to the "Product Review Committee" as one he feels meets all the market conditions.

The "Product Review Committee" is a management committee, consisting of the staff managers of marketing, sales planning, product planning, engineering, manufacturing, and the comptroller. This committee reviews all aspects of each product to be produced. Upon receipt of their approval, manufacturing drawings are released. Thus, not only is the basic engineering tested to insure its efficiency, but the marketing qualities are tested to be sure that the product will sell.

SUMMARY

I have emphasized the functioning of the marketing plan within the General Electric Company because our design policy is so closely related to the marketing objectives. It is our belief that our products must be designed with a purpose and that purpose is to meet a specific market, at the right price, with the most desirable product qualities. These elements form the guide posts for Appearance Design. You can have the best product in the world, but if it does not combine the basic engineering technology with the right marketing characteristics, the mass of customers will not want it.

The responsibility of design is important when we recognize its place in the marketing plan necessary to distribute quality products to mass markets.

I believe with conviction that we who are concerned with coordinating design at the executive level are in a position to make a great contribution to the industries with which we are associated and to the pleasure and satisfaction of the customer users of our products.

►►►►►►►►►►► THE EXTENT OF ENGINEERING
RESPONSIBILITY

LAWRENCE M. PATRICK*

Basically, the main function of the engineering department is to provide products which the company can produce at a profit. Such products may be proprietary items developed solely within the company; they may be developed under contract to other firms or government agencies; or they may be obtained on a production contract after being brought to the production stage by some other company.

In addition, the manager of the engineering department is often included on the policy committee, and must be instrumental in establishing policies concerning the future direction which the company's business will take. In this capacity it is necessary that he evaluate engineering or production programs which are initiated by management or are suggested to management from outside sources. Often this evaluation is merely a matter of pointing out obvious flaws, while in rare cases the product is so ideally suitable that it requires no technical evaluation. Normally, a complete analysis of performance, appearance, reliability, and production cost is required which is then integrated into a complete report containing similar analyses from other departments.

Assistance to the sales department often requires a considerable amount of engineering time, especially if the company is engaged in research and development work of a technical nature with relatively small production. In this type of work, unless the salesmen are technically trained, they can make only the initial contact. Thereafter it is necessary for an engineer to meet with the customer's engineers to establish the exact requirements and to convince the customer that the company is in a position to meet the requirements economically and in the specified time. In addition to the customer contact, which often involves an appreciable amount of travel time, a technical proposal must also be prepared by the engineering department. If the sales potential is great enough, it may even be advisable to conduct some experimental work to prove the feasibility prior to negotiating the contract. While all these aids to the sales department are certainly essential, they are also time-consuming to a point not often realized by management. Furthermore, this work with

Reprinted with permission from Developing a Product Strategy (*Elizabeth Marting, editor*), *AMA Management Report No. 39, American Management Association, Inc., 1959, pp. 191–200.*

Assistant Professor, Department of Engineering Mechanics, Wayne State University.

the sales department often carries the highest priority and cannot be scheduled accurately, which can upset the entire engineering schedule. Experience will dictate the amount of time to allocate to sales, but there will always be unforeseen sales work to upset the schedule.

Liaison between engineering and research and between engineering and production can also require much more time from the engineering staff—and, in particular, the engineering manager —than is expected. This is especially true when unforeseen difficulties arise in going from the breadboard model to the prototype stage or from the prototype to production. In the latter case, the pressure from management is often great enough to give a project precedence over others in which the engineering is still not complete. When this occurs, the engineering delivery schedule suffers. These problems are not so likely to arise unexpectedly in a small company, since there is closer contact and often an overlap of duties.

The role of the engineering department varies widely in different companies. There are many firms in the Detroit area, catering primarily to the high-production automotive industry, which employ one or two engineers out of a total employment of a thousand or more. On the other hand, Ryan Industries[1] has an Engineering Department of 45 employees out of a total employment of approximately 400. In-

cluded in the Engineering Department are the engineers, draftsmen, technicians, and modelmakers. This comparatively high ratio of employees in the Engineering Department is due to the rather complex nature of the electromechanical and electronic equipment developed for industry and government agencies combined with the usual short-run production of such equipment. With these products a great deal of engineering time is spent in sales and development prior to production.

In general, however, a new product project is routed through a company's engineering department according to this 14-step outline, with variations to fit the peculiarities of the job. The degree to which each of these items is followed in detail will depend upon the individual job.

1. PROJECT EVALUATION

When a project is under consideration or has been decided upon, a complete analysis by the engineering department will be of great value to management and also to engineering itself. Preparing the report will bring out questionable points and result in a comprehensive understanding of all its aspects. Some indication of the market potential is essential. If the product is a complex, special electronic control, the engineering department can probably provide an adequate estimate of the market potential. In the case of a consumer product, some other department may be in a better position to determine the potential, or outside help from one of the organiza-

[1] The author was formerly Chief Engineer and Director of Research at the Ryan Industries, a Division of Textron, Inc.

tions which make such surveys may provide the answer.

The risk involved in developing a marketable article at a reasonable price is an important consideration. Depending on the stage of development at the time the article is turned over to engineering, there may be some question as to whether it is functionally feasible. Further, if it can be made to function satisfactorily, will it last long enough, will it be safe, and can it be made at an attractive price?

For example, if the product is for a customer or is of a nature which requires completion by a certain date to meet a seasonal demand, it is necessary to see how it will fit into the established schedule of the department. One pitfall to be avoided is that of counting on hiring all new personnel to take over a new job that will not otherwise fit into the schedule. It is better to assign some of the employees of known ability to each job and spread the new employees around on the established jobs where they will be working with or under experienced employees. After the new employees have proved themselves, they can be assigned to duties commensurate with their ability.

No matter what the potential of the product is, if it will not fit into the plant's operation it should probably be avoided. Chemical processing does not fit into an electronics plant, and a product comprised primarily of stampings is not suited to a screw machine plant. An exception to this rule occurs when there is a desire to diversify the operation of the plant.

The total investment required to bring the project to profitable fruition should be set forth in bold type. Granted that the product may eventually prove profitable, if there must be too great an investment prior to any return it will have to be shelved.

A complete study of all competitive products — including comparisons of price, sales appeal, reliability, performance, and annual volume—is invaluable in evaluating a product. After all these data have been assembled, they must be used as the basis for recommendations as to the proposed product.

2. ESTABLISHMENT OF SPECIFICATIONS

The importance of complete, detailed specifications cannot be overemphasized. Any time spent in compiling written specifications that cover every detail, from performance to reliability, will be regained many times over. True, verbal instructions might be adequate to develop a high-speed microfilm camera for a particular application, but as many as 70 pages might be needed to cover a piece of electronic countermeasures equipment for the Air Force.

Even with comprehensive specifications there can be different interpretations; so it is desirable to maintain close contact with the customer— whether it is one's own company or an outside company. If, during the program, some of the specifications are found to be too stringent, a request for deviation should be made; and, if this is granted, a specification amendment should be initiated immediately. Any delay can only cause hardship and the danger of penalties for non-performance in extreme cases.

3. BUDGET PREPARATION

After a job has been approved, it is necessary to prepare a budget under which the engineering department must operate. If the undertaking is highly experimental in nature, it may be appropriate to establish the budget in phases. A small exploratory project can be set up to obtain information on the unknown features of the job, and the results used to determine whether it is still desirable to undertake the project. If so, a budget for its completion can be established with greater accuracy. Most companies use standard forms which are tailored to their particular needs and include provision for all the normally anticipated costs.

It is advisable to have the engineers and technicians who will be assigned to the job assist in the estimate, since this provides the best over-all results and also tends to make the individuals expend a little extra effort to keep within the estimate they have established. The engineering manager then must weigh the estimate against the historical cost of similar work in the past. Experience soon shows which employees provide an accurate estimate and which do not. Practically everyone underestimates the time which will be required to accomplish his own part of the job. Deviation may range from 25 to 200 per cent, with 50 to 75 per cent being a fairly reasonable figure.

Once the budget has been established, a continuing record of the costs must be kept in order to determine whether the original estimate was correct. An important point to note here is that an actual record of the costs does not mean anything unless it is accompanied by an accurate estimate of the status of the project. For example, it means nothing to know that half of the budget is expended if the percentage of work completed is unknown. If the budget is to be exceeded by a large amount, this should be pointed out to management as soon as it is recognized, so that the whole program can be re-evaluated to determine whether, in view of the higher than anticipated costs, it is advisable to continue or whether the project should be dropped.

Management in any case should be kept informed, through periodic reports, of the progress of all projects from both the technical and cost standpoints so that plans can be made accordingly.

Any reasonable budget for a new product must have a provision for contingencies, which usually takes the form of adding a certain amount—say, 20 per cent—to particular areas of expense. This percentage is sometimes added by each person working on the budget—without, however, being set out as a separate item. When this happens, it is possible to pyramid the contingency factor to a point where it makes the entire program unattractive.

4. ENGINEERING PROGRAM OUTLINE

A complete engineering program outline, like the complete specification, is an invaluable means of establishing

462 ► *Coordinating and Controlling Development*

the magnitude of the program and provides an accurate basis for coordinating it with other programs in the department. While a few general points can be established for all programs, each one in turn can be outlined in detail.

  a. *General approach.* By the time a job has reached this point, at least one means of accomplishing it must have been set forth in order to evaluate it, prepare the budget, and so on. If it has progressed through the research section and some sort of model is available, the approach is obvious; it is simply a matter of refining the model and proceeding with the following steps. On the other hand, if it is a special machine or other design job, it is necessary to review the general approach and consider others so that the best one can be chosen.
  b. *Detailed approach.* The general approach is broken down into parts that can be attacked individually. If different employees or groups are assigned to the parts, the job will move faster and particular emphasis can be placed on those parts which are likely to cause trouble. An accurate schedule can be derived from the breakdown.
  c. *Experimental program.* Design data may have to be obtained from some simple models.
  d. *Preliminary design.* A layout of the product with all the component parts early in the design will prove useful in correlating the work on the individual com-

ponents and will prevent basic interferences.
  e. *Stress analysis.*
  f. *Final design.* This will be an evolution of the preliminary design and will incorporate all the details as they are completed. Product appearance is given particular attention, as are choice of materials, heat treatment, protective coatings, and decorative finishes.
  g. *Model shop work.* A crude working model, accurate to all functioning details but not necessarily a dressed-up model, is usually prepared. It incorporates all the final design features.
  h. *Model testing.* This involves a complete performance test.
  i. *Prototype design.* Changes dictated by the model testing are incorporated into the prototype design. They are usually made on the model first to see that they accomplish what they are supposed to.
  j. *Prototype fabrication.*
  k. *Prototype testing.*
  l. *Production design.*
  m. *Release for production.*
  n. *Liaison with production.*

5. PERSONNEL ASSIGNMENT

One person should be made responsible for the entire program, with adequate supporting help to finish it on schedule. His title is usually "project engineer," which in large companies often entails greater responsibility than that of vice president in charge of engineering in small companies. The project engineer in a small company often does layouts in addition to the more theoretical work.

6. EXPERIMENTAL PHASE

The experimental phase starts early, lasts right through to the final product design, and in some instances continues after the product is released—developing improvements for the next model.

In all development work there comes a time when progress reaches a point of diminishing return beyond which it is uneconomical to proceed. For the most part, engineers tend to be perfectionists, a tendency which can lead to financial disaster if not curbed. The engineering manager, together with the project engineer, must usually decide when to freeze a design, even though some small improvements might result from continuing with the development. However, before freezing the design, he of course must be satisfied that it meets all the specifications.

7. PROTOTYPE DESIGN

A prototype is constructed for the purpose of determining whether the final functional design is acceptable, and should be as near to the finished product as possible, short of making extensive tooling for fabricating it. A good model shop can produce a prototype, with no tooling or only a minimum of temporary tooling, which is almost identical to the product that will be made from production tooling.

The advantages of making the prototype similar to the production article are many. From a functional consideration, any difference can lead to a malfunctioning of the production article which is often difficult to pinpoint and can be costly to overcome once the production setup is complete. Even a difference of appearance can have an adverse effect; poor appearance detracts from the model's usefulness in advance sales work or surveys, while a better-than-finished-product appearance can lead to disappointment in the final product.

8. PROTOTYPE TESTING

Unlike the experimental model test, which was aimed primarily at checking performance, the prototype tests should be as comprehensive and complete as possible. They should include (where applicable) performance, environmental, shock, vibration, and life tests.

It must be decided whether to conduct the tests in the plant or have a commercial testing facility conduct them. Testing equipment is often expensive and sometimes must be designed for the particular application. If there is enough testing to warrant the purchase of the test equipment, there are distinct advantages to conducting the tests internally. In the event of failure, the contributing causes can be determined, and sometimes the test can be stopped prior to failure and corrective action taken. Also, if the test equipment is available, numerous tests can be made on components and experimental models which will decrease the likelihood of the final unit's failing.

No matter how carefully planned, simulated tests do not always duplicate actual field conditions, and even tests that are considered more stringent than operating conditions will not always prove adequate. Therefore, whenever possible, actual service tests should be included in the testing program, but not to the exclusion of the simulated tests unless all extremes of service operation can be achieved.

9. PRODUCTION DESIGN

Any flaws found in the prototype should be corrected, and the corrections incorporated into the production design. The design should be slanted toward whatever type of production the plant is best suited for, and whatever tooling is required to achieve the most economical production. With the type of product manufactured at Ryan Industries, tooling for production usually costs considerably more than the total development, engineering, and prototype costs. The ratio will be dependent upon the type of product and the amount of production.

The engineering manager must decide on the direction the design will take insofar as the tooling requirements are concerned. Future potential should be considered, although this should be a deciding factor only with the concurrence of management, since the additional production may never materialize and the consequent excessive tooling cost will provide grounds for criticism.

Appearance must be given due consideration at this point, along with any other factor which might cause a change later on. After the production design and tooling are completed, changes are often prohibitively expensive and will be made only in an emergency unless they are of a minor nature and require no tooling change.

10. PREPRODUCTION MODEL TESTING

The preproduction model differs from the prototype in that it is made with parts from production tooling, although it may not be made on the assembly line. Normally the same tests will be used as for the prototype, and no troubles are expected. If any are encountered, they are usually attributable to variations between the two units, which, as previously pointed out, should be kept to a minimum.

11. APPROVAL FOR PRODUCTION

When the preproduction model is satisfactory, the engineering manager approves the drawing for production. This is a duty which should not be taken lightly, for once approval is given, the production department sets the wheels in motion to buy raw material, vended items, and outside services. Costs then mount rapidly. Production facilities and personnel are assigned, and any reason for stopping the wheels is likely to cause trouble.

12. LIAISON WITH PRODUCTION

In getting a new job into production, there are always problems which require an interchange of information between engineering and production. Some of them involve changes in parts or tolerances as a result of poor tooling. It then becomes the duty of the engineering manager to decide whether the changes can be tolerated or whether the tooling must be reworked. Other changes may be requested to ease the assembly problem. In any case, liaison must be handled with tact, and the over-all cost to the company should be the determining factor in deciding upon changes. It is easy to sidestep this responsibility by insisting that all parts be within tolerance, but such an attitude can lower profits or result in a loss.

13. TESTING OF PRODUCTION ARTICLE

The tests on the preproduction model are usually considered to cover the production article, except for the performance testing necessary to see that the production assembly is satisfactory. Tests at varying intervals during production are made to keep a constant check on all phases of production.

14. QUALITY CONTROL PROCEDURE

While it is necessary to keep costs down by accepting out-of-tolerance parts occasionally, if this practice is carried to extremes it can lead to a general degradation of workmanship. Consequently, the quality control sec-

tion must reject any item that is out of tolerance by any amount. After rejection, production can request a deviation which may be allowed by the project engineer or the engineering manager. It is absolutely essential that quality control reject all parts even slightly out of tolerance, and just as essential that the engineering manager give quality control complete backing in this respect.

It is up to the engineering manager to establish the operating procedures best suited to the particular circumstances of his company. In the case of a small company they will usually be more flexible than in a large company. The important thing is to have some plan in operation and make it available to all employees, preferably in written form.

►►►►►►►►►►► MANUFACTURING CAN MAKE OR BREAK
YOUR NEW PRODUCT

KEVIN MCLOUGHLIN*

CASE 1 – FAILURE

A small manufacturer of brass valves decided it could produce a power lawn mower to take up slack in regular business.

Besides the fact that lawn mowers

require a different sales force than industrial valves, another problem arose when production started. The company began making lawn mowers as soon as it could — before it analyzed all the potential problems.

Factory management became in-

Reprinted by special permission of Factory Management and Maintenance, *November 1954, pp. 132–135. Copyright by McGraw-Hill Publishing Co., Inc.*

*Advanced Development Planning Department, International Business Machines Corporation, New York. (This article is based on the author's experience as a management consultant prior to joining IBM.)

volved in "fighting fires" — handling lawn mower production problems as they appeared. Result was production of valves got tangled, too. So badly that the company abandoned the lawn mower to avoid losing its valve business.

CASE 2 — FAILURE

A manufacturer of sterling silver flatware decided to introduce a new pattern with a gold insert. The pattern was designed, dies were made, manufacturing was started. Samples went to the salesmen. The new product was launched. It clicked — and orders rolled in.

But the method of assembling the gold insert wasn't completely satisfactory. Manufacturing had underestimated the time required to perfect it. Deliveries stopped during problem solving. That gave a competitor time to take over. When the new product finally reappeared, it got lost in the shuffle.

CASE 3 — FAILURE

Another company's research produced a new, super-secret papermaking process. The company quickly set up full-scale production facilities in a completely walled-in, remote part of the plant.

Trouble developed immediately, because the process required atmosphere control. And that wasn't possible in the location. So the process had to be relocated. *Result*: extra expense; time lost getting the new product to market.

CASE 4 — FAILURE

A manufacturer of automotive replacement parts decided to add a group of related products. An inventory of finished products was to be carried at the factory.

Planning for the new products overlooked volume of in-process inventories required. Production areas became glutted with new parts and components, causing delays and safety hazards. Before the situation was corrected, there were many grievances and even threat of a strike.

If any one of the four new-product failures cited above was pinned onto the sales department, the pinner-onner was wrong. The real blame in each case lay with manufacturing — which simply hadn't understood the role it plays in the development of new products. Manufacturing has certain prime responsibilities it must recognize—and accept. I've lined up a baker's dozen. Let's talk about them.

SELECTION OF PRODUCT

Before a product is adopted by the company, the manufacturing department should pass on the suitability of present production facilities, cost of tooling, additional equipment required, cost estimate, quality and safety considerations.

At this stage it is not enough to talk in generalities. You should be prepared with statistics on all operations, plant, and equipment that will enable you to evaluate the practicability of taking on the new product. You must know limitations of operator and machine performance that can be anticipated. You must consider how the new product can be fitted in with present production both in time (scheduling) and in space (plant layout).

You should anticipate problems arising out of differences between this proposed product and what you are accustomed to producing. And know whether they are serious enough to recommend rejecting the product.

You should have enough detail in hand to give a fairly accurate estimate of how long it will take to develop manufacturing methods and tool up. And you should have in mind whom you can spare and depend on to do this work.

PILOT RUN

You may assign an assistant or a methods engineer to take complete charge of the pilot run, but you should follow it closely yourself. By having one man responsible for all processes in the pilot stage, you will be able to tie them together and achieve greatest over-all manufacturing economy, with least cost of time and money for development.

During this stage, keep close to the man you put in charge. Meet with him daily. See that all the bugs are shaken out, so that the production run will not get off to a false start.

Look for minor design changes that will not adversely affect the finished product, but will facilitate manufacture and reduce cost.

Remember, every problem you solve during the pilot run is a problem that will not bother you during the production run. Every problem you do not anticipate and dispose of now will grow to much greater proportion when you are producing in large quantity. Then its solution will upset plans and schedules (not to mention your people). And cost you more not only in company dollars and cents but also in personal time and grief.

PLANNING FOR PRODUCTION

Your greatest responsibility is planning the production run. That includes procurement of raw materials; manufacturing processes and methods; personnel; tooling, equipment, and layout changes; schedules; control of in-process inventory. All these items of planning will land on you at the same time, so there is no use in attempting to assign them priority.

PROCUREMENT OF RAW MATERIALS

While the purchasing agent may be responsible for procuring raw materials and components, and the traffic agent for seeing that they arrive on time, they cannot plan quantities or schedules without your advice. Tentative schedules that may be set up far in advance of the production run in order to prepare the suppliers for your demands, may have to be changed when detailed planning indicates changes in schedules. Specifications may have to be changed.

PROCESSES AND METHODS

It may be the practice in your company for the engineering department to indicate the manufacturing procedures. Nevertheless, your knowledge and experience are needed here.

TOOLING AND EQUIPMENT CHANGES

Generally, any new equipment purchased for a new product should be as versatile as possible, and still perform the operation. In spite of the best possible planning, the new product may not be a success. In that case you will be much better off with equipment you can use for producing something else. There are exceptions, of course. If economies of production and contracts cover the entire amortization of the machine, then a special-purpose tool is justified.

Important thing in purchasing machinery for a new product is to determine how long it will take to liquidate its cost. You may have the initial competitive advantage with your new product, but experience shows that within two years you will have to fight serious competition with reduced prices and costs, and a better product. Sometimes your competitor will be able to drive you out of the market completely. Before this can happen, the entire development cost of the new product, including the equipment purchased for its manufacture, must be paid off to avoid a loss. Some companies will not purchase equipment for manufacturing a new product unless they can foresee its paying for itself within a year, others within six months. Probably the majority set the time at two years.

LAYOUT CHANGES

When a new product is introduced into the factory, its volume, path or plan of flow, and space requirements may necessitate changes in plant layout. At any rate, the fitting in of the new product and its in-process inventory should be planned well in advance of the date of manufacture. Failure to do this frequently results in disruption of not only the schedule for the new product, but also the schedules and costs of other products being manufactured in this same area. It is not simply a matter of finding a place for any new machinery that may be needed. It means fitting the entire production pattern of the new product in with the pattern of all other plant activities.

PERSONNEL SELECTION

Any rearrangement of personnel, of course, will result in at least temporary reduction of efficiency in present production operations. But it is important to select most carefully the supervisory, technical, and operating personnel who individually and as a team promise to give the new product its best opportunity to succeed in the shop. Be sure each one is intelligent and adaptable to change. Convince them of the importance of their part in making the new product a success. Select them with a view to greatest cooperation within the group. Give them as much of your time as they need to get started. Encourage them to come to you early in the run with problems, and with their suggestions for improvements.

PRODUCTION SCHEDULE

All the variables must be taken into account in planning the production schedule—rates of performance by different machines and operators; quality of raw materials; interruptions in service, such as electric power; rates of rejection by inspection. On top of all this, you can expect variations in the basic schedule imposed by sales demand and availability of raw materials and labor.

It's a difficult assignment, but you must plan it before starting a full-scale run, and usually before all the probable variations are known. The sales department must make delivery commitments, or it cannot sell the product. It then becomes of greatest importance to ride herd constantly on every process, machine, and person, until the production schedule has steadied down into a smooth, regular flow. This responsibility cannot be delegated. There are no surefire cure-alls for the headaches of scheduling.

PROCESS INVENTORY CONTROL

In many companies this is a problem. There is a constant running battle between the manufacturing department and the accounting department on the subject of in-process inventory. The former finds it easier to work with a large inventory between processes (subject only to limitations of space), because such an inventory of banks between processes tends to take care of temporary dislocations of the production schedule in individual operations. The latter, on the other hand, is conscious of working capital tied up in such an inventory, and the risks and financial burden associated with such an allocation of funds. This is a consideration demanding coordination between the two department heads.

The manufacturing head should restrict his inventory requirements to what is necessary, plus some safeguard against unforeseen temporary dislocations. The inventory of work in process will stagnate unless he keeps it under constant review, and solves the problems of uneven production flow, as far as possible, by attention to the production processes themselves. The financial officer should inform himself of the details of location of inventories so he can form a reasonable judgment of their necessity from a practical manufacturing point of view.

COST REDUCTION

Cost reductions fall into two categories—(1) those that require changes in manufacturing processes only, and therefore do not require approval outside the manufacturing department; (2) those that affect the product itself, by changes in design, material, quality or performance, and must therefore be passed upon and accepted by other departments because of their possible effect on sales, service, returns, safety hazards, etc.

Nearly all designs may be simplified without adversely affecting their functions. After the product has passed the pilot run, you can see chances to redesign parts for fewer and simpler operations, or to use interchangeable parts for more than one model. Sometimes you can combine parts so as to simplify subassembly or final assembly. Redesign may let you work with easier tolerances without affecting the product's operation, thus reducing the number of rejects.

Reducing sizes of parts and finished products, without interfering with performance, can cut costs, too. Often you will be able to see these opportunities in the plant more readily than they can be seen in the engineering office or in the salesroom.

Refinements in manufacturing processes that do not involve the performance or appearance of the product need not be discussed here. We only need say that the greatest opportunities for making such changes are to be found during the early life of the product in the factory.

QUALITY

In many cases there is a tendency to build too much quality into new products, rather than too little. This is understandable. The designers seek a perfect performance under adverse conditions of product use, and therefore design for as few failures as possible. In preproduction testing, flaws are discovered and corrected by upgrading design and quality of parts. Records are kept of rejects and reasons for them. The inspection department works toward eliminating rejects not only of finished assemblies but also of individual parts that may never be seen. Parts whose proper functioning may not require, for example, the finely polished, scratchless surfaces that the inspectors insist on. In one company making gun-recoil mechanisms, many man-hours are spent polishing by hand a large helical coil spring that is to be located inside an oil-filled steel cylinder.

You will find it difficult to meet competition on cost if you excel materially in quality. The customer will eliminate products that are below his quality requirements; he will also eliminate products that are above his price standards. So be sure your quality standards are practical.

SAFETY

This factor is stressed today more than it used to be, partly because of court findings against manufacturers of unsafe products or unsafe processes. Failure to study the hazards inherent in the product itself or in the processes of making it may result in large lawsuits against the company, and in rejection of the product by the buying public—consumer or industrial.

Manufacturing has a good opportunity to correct safety hazards in the product before it reaches the market. In making the parts and assembling the product, operators and foremen can observe conditions that might cause injury. If these cannot be eliminated by change in design, the product should be clearly labeled to show what they are. Among possible sources of such hazards are spring-loaded assemblies, sharp edges, exposed moving parts, electrical wiring, and hot surfaces. You must expect that the customer will not use the product as an expert mechanic would.

Within the factory there may be a danger of injury and organic poisoning, and the additional hazard of fire, explosion, corrosion, etc., during manufacturing processes. You probably have your own safety and accident-prevention campaign. Don't overlook the unusual, however, like the women workers who were poisoned beyond help by radium in a watch dial factory, or the man whose physical make-up was completely changed by absorbing female hormones through his skin while mixing them.

Consideration of the additional cost of avoiding serious hazards during manufacturing may sometimes lead to skipping an otherwise promising product. It is your responsibility to bring such dangers and costs to the attention of the product committee before large development expenditures have been made.

►►►►►►►►►►► BAYESIAN STATISTICS AND PRODUCT DECISIONS

PAUL E. GREEN*

In today's fast-moving technology the need for good decision making in the development of new and improved products is only too apparent. Typically, development of a new product from invention to commercialization is expensive and fraught with uncertainty regarding both technical and marketing success. On the one hand, it is not uncommon to find that development costs exceed discovery costs by fifteen or twenty times. On the other hand, the ratio of products successfully commercialized to total products placed on the market (let alone those that reached at least some stage of development) has been variously quoted as ranging from one in five to one in twenty.

As apparent as the need for improved decision making in this area is, there has been a dearth of good analytical techniques for dealing with the uncertainties that plague the development manager. While the product developer can (and usually does) enlist the aid of such data gathering services as market, process, and cost research, a formal apparatus for integrating these various sources of information has been conspicuous by its absence.

In recent years, however, a growing body of quantitative procedures for dealing with decision making under uncertainty has emerged from the disciplines of applied mathematics, statistics, and the behavioral sciences. Under the generic title of "statistical decision theory," these techniques show promise for assisting the decision maker in making rational choices under uncertainty. One of the most relevant and

Reprinted by permission from Business Horizons, *Indiana University, Fall 1962, pp. 101–109.*

* *Market planning and market research activities with E. I. du Pont de Nemours and Company.*

complete sets of tools is known as Bayesian decision theory. The pioneering development of this approach, as applied to business problem solving, is credited to Rôbert Schlaifer.[1]

The purpose of this article is to show the relevance of the Bayesian approach to product development decision making. More specifically, we shall illustrate how these techniques can be used to help answer two persistent questions related to each stage in the development of a new product:

1. Should we make a decision *now* (with respect to passing a product along to the next development stage versus terminating the project), or should we *delay* this decision until some future date, pending the receipt of additional information regarding the new product's chances for commercial success?

2. Given a decision on *when* to make the decision, *what* action ("go" versus "stop") should we take?

The power of the Bayesian approach as applied to these basic questions is described in two parts. First, we shall review the nature of the costs associated with moving too slowly versus too quickly through the product development process. Second, an illustrative

[1] Robert Schlaifer, *Probability and Statistitcs for Business Decisions* (New York: McGraw-Hill Book Co., Inc., 1959). In addition, two excellent expository articles dealing with a description of Schlaifer's work are: Harry V. Roberts, "The New Business Statistics," *Journal of Business,* XXXIII (January, 1960), 21–30, and Jack Hirschleifer, "The Bayesian Approach to Statistical Decision—An Exposition," *Journal of Business,* XXXIV (October, 1961), 471–89.

case will show how these groups of costs can be introduced within a Bayesian framework to guide both the "when to" and "what to do" classes of decisions. However, the richness of Bayesian statistics goes well beyond the scope of this illustration. The concluding section of this article discusses some of the more general aspects of Bayesian decision theory.

TIME-RELATED COSTS

The ultracautious decision maker tends to incur sizable costs when he delays each development decision until he has assembled enough information to make the choice patently clear. These costs are partly associated with time and partly associated with the cost of the information gathering activity itself (which also takes time to accomplish).

An illustration should make clear the nature of these time-related costs. Assume that a new chemical product has reached the development stage where the company must either (1) decide now whether to construct a semiworks unit or to terminate the project, or (2) delay, pending the receipt of additional information regarding the anticipated outcomes associated with the alternative to proceed. Apart from sunk costs (that is, historical costs, not relevant from an economic standpoint), termination at this point would result in a payoff of zero. The decision to proceed, however, is related to a series of future decisions up to and including commercialization before a positive payoff could be forthcoming. From the standpoint of delay, the decision maker should be concerned with how these conditional payoffs would be expected to change between now and some future time for viewing the same set of choices that he presently faces. Moreover, in multistage decisions, a present commitment does not demand that the project be continued in subsequent periods, should later information suggest project termination.

If the decision maker decided to delay his choice, pending the receipt of additional information, it should be clear that at least three groups of costs can be associated with delay.[2] First, as a function of delay time, the present value of all future revenues attendant with commercialization would be reduced as a consequence of delaying the start of the receipt of these revenues until a more distant time. This type of delay cost merely gives recognition to the time value of money.

Second, also as a function of delay time, the present value of all future revenues attendant with commercialization could be lowered as a consequence of the increased risk of competitive imitation or supersedure of the product (at the hands of competitors or conceivably of a future product of the decision maker's own research organization).

Finally, gathering the information obviously costs money and incurs time

for its development. If one assumes some linear relationship of money spent for information with the period required to obtain the information, then this cost also can be associated with the time variable.

Certain implications obviously stem from the preceding listing of delay costs. If required target rates of return are low (that is, a low opportunity cost of the company's capital exists), and/or the threat of competitive retaliation is low, and/or the costs of data gathering are low, a relatively small penalty is attached to delay. Conversely, when these costs are high, a larger penalty is attached to the delay option.

On the other side of the coin, an impatient decision maker who eliminates or gives short shrift to vital steps of information gathering runs the risk of incurring sizable costs associated with acting under a high degree of uncertainty (and perhaps costs associated with "crashing" the program, that is, telescoping development steps, as well). The behavior of these groups of costs can be viewed as a function of time, which, in turn, is a function of the amount of information collected.

Again, discussion of the preceding illustrative problem should make clear the nature of the costs associated with moving too quickly. Building a semiworks is related to a series of future actions leading to ultimate commercialization. In point of fact, however, these future actions may never be undertaken. The decision maker may delay any single decision while awaiting new data and, in multistage decisions, he will frequently have the opportu-

[2] In the case of interdependent activities, a fourth category of cost could include the penalty associated with delaying some other necessary activity not in the project directly affected, that is, equipment design groups might not be able to switch efforts easily over to another job, thus incurring costs of transition.

nity to reevaluate the venture before making subsequent commitments.

Thus, the decision maker must view the change in payoff associated with the go versus no-go decision now versus the payoff associated with delay of this decision, pending receipt of additional data. Why collect additional data at all? Additional data would be collected for the purpose of reducing the variance associated with the estimated distribution of payoffs related to acting now. A simple example should clarify this concept.

If the option to build the semiworks now is a "sure thing," that is, no matter what information that could conceivably be developed on, say, potential sales, could change the decision, then it is obvious that additional information (cost-free or not) is irrelevant. On a more realistic basis, however, some potential sales levels (say, zero sales) would obviously favor the option of no-go. The essence of this concept can be expressed in Bayesian terms as the expected[3] cost associated with acting under uncertainty. That is, the difference in payoff between taking the best act now (in the light of current uncertainties) and taking the best act under perfect information about future events represents the expected value of perfect information; and, hence, the upper limit that the decision maker should spend for addi-

tional information if it could be collected immediately and would be without error.

Other things equal, it is clear that when the costs of uncertainty are large the decision maker could suffer by moving too rapidly to the next stage of the development process. On the other hand, if the costs of wrong decisions are low, he should move rapidly.

It is thus implied that gathering additional information would at least reduce, if not eliminate, the cost of uncertainty; otherwise the information would not be gathered. It is further implied that time and money would be spent on the information gathering activity until the sum of the expected costs associated with information collection and delay and the expected costs of acting under uncertainty was minimal. Otherwise, a shorter or longer delay period would produce lower expected total costs. Figure 1 represents conceptually the behavior of the costs associated with moving too slowly versus moving too quickly with respect to some stage in the development of a new product.

APPLYING BAYESIAN THEORY

While the preceding remarks have focused on the nature of the costs associated with moving too quickly versus too slowly at any stage in the development process, we must still illustrate how Bayesian decision theory utilizes these costs to provide a rationale for answering both the "when to" and "what to do" questions. The fol-

---

[3] The adjective "expected" is applied here in the usual statistical sense. That is, expected costs are weighted averages found by multiplying each admissible cost by the probability of incurring it and then adding these products. The weights (probabilities) sum to unity.

lowing illustration is deliberately simplified to deal with the simplest of cases, a one-stage choice.[4]

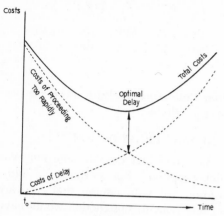

FIGURE 1

BEHAVIOR OF TOTAL COSTS: PROCEEDING TOO RAPIDLY VERSUS TOO SLOWLY

Assume that a point has been reached in the development of a new product regarding whether or not a semiworks should be constructed now versus delaying this decision (pending receipt of further market information). To be more explicit, three options will be considered:

1. Build a semiworks versus terminate project now
2. Delay this decision until one period (year) into the future

[4] In more realistic (but more complex) illustrations, a multistage decision process—for example, pilot plant to semiworks to commercial plant with possible information steps in between—may have to be used. The techniques of dynamic programming are frequently appropriate here. See R. Bellman, *Dynamic Programming* (Princeton, N.J.: Princeton University Press, 1957).

3. Delay this decision until two periods (years) into the future.

Options 2 and 3 imply, of course, that better marketing information than now exists could be secured over the next year or two and that the more extensive this inquiry, the better the quality of the information. However, the development of the additional marketing data will cost something itself and will delay subsequent steps toward commercialization.

Some present marketing information, which is rather imprecise, indicates that four alternative forecasts of potential sales, given commercialization, bracket the possible levels of future sales. Subjective probabilities[5] have been stated for the occurrence of each forecast and, given each forecast, it has been possible to calculate the payoff, given commercialization. These data are noted in Table 1 where F_i stands for each sales forecast deemed admissible nad $P(F_i)$ stands for the likelihood that the decision maker assigns to the occurrence of each forecast.

Under the go alternative, Table 1 indicates that if forecasts F_1 or F_2 ac-

[5] The term subjective probability refers to the degree of belief the decision maker wishes to assign to the occurrence of each admissible event. This degree of belief is expressed numerically along a scale ranging from zero to one and reflects the experienced judgments of the decision maker. All weights are assigned so as to obey the postulates of probability theory. For a full discussion of the so-called school of personalistic or subjective probability, see the excellent book by L. J. Savage, *The Foundations of Statistics* (New York: John Wiley & Sons, Inc., 1954).

TABLE 1

CONDITIONAL PAYOFFS AND EXPECTED VALUES
(in millions of dollars)

Acts	F_1	$P(F_1)$	F_2	$P(F_2)$	F_3	$P(F_3)$	F_4	$P(F_4)$	EP
Go	−$12	.15	−$1	.30	$5	.45	$10	.10	$1.15
No-go	$ 0	.15	$0	.30	$0	.45	$ 0	.10	$ 0

tually occurred, negative payoffs (in present value terms) would result, while under the more optimistic forecasts, F_3 or F_4, payoffs would be positive. According to the Bayesian approach the expected payoff (EP) of the go option is found by summing over the product of each payoff times its probability. The present value of future returns of the no-go alternative (termination) is, of course, zero.[6] In this oversimplified problem situation, the decision maker—in the absence of the opportunity to collect additional market information—would go with the project, that is, construct the semiworks. The expected payoff associated with this alternative is $1.15 million.

More realistically, however, the decision maker frequently has the option of delaying his decision pending the receipt of additional data regarding the occurrence of the alternative sales forecasts. These additional data will cost something to collect, delay construc-

[6] A project payoff of zero, on a present value basis, would imply that the project's cash flow back (over its anticipated life) would just be sufficient to pay back all cash outlays and to earn some net rate of return, say 10 per cent, on the present value of those outlays. Adoption of the no-go alternative thus assumes that other projects exist that could just earn this return; an opportunity cost concept is involved here.

tion time, and rarely, if ever, be perfectly reliable.

ONE-YEAR DELAY OPTION

We shall first consider the one-year delay option.[7] For purposes of illustration we will assume that a delay of one year in construction would have the following results: (1) the cost of delayed revenues amounts to payoffs that are only 91 per cent of the for-

[7] Although not explicitly shown above, it is relevant to note that the expected value of perfect information (EVPI) is $2.10 million. As mentioned earlier, this provides an upper limit on funds that could be spent on the collection of additional data, which could be collected immediately and would forecast perfectly which event would actually occur. To obtain EVPI, subtract the expected payoff of the best act in the light of current uncertainties from the expectation of the payoffs associated with the best acts (given the actual occurrence of each event):

EVPI = [.15 ($0 million) + .30 ($0 million) + .45 ($5 million) + .10 ($10 million)]−$1.15 million.

The result is $3.25 million −$1.15 million, or $2.10 million.

This calculation may be interpreted as follows. If the decision maker could purchase a "perfect" forecasting device that would tell him which event would actually occur, it is clear that before the purchase he must still apply his prior probabilities as to which event the device would indicate; he would then be able to take the best act associated with the event specified.

mer payoff (interest rate equal to 10 per cent annually); (2) the firm's market share would drop from 100 per cent, under the no-delay case, to 75 per cent because of the resulting greater lead time for competitive imitation; and (3) the cost of collecting additional information concerning future sales would be $150,000. However, information obtained at this early stage of development is assumed to be only 70 per cent reliable. That is, if the market survey results indicate f_1 (namely, that forecast F_1 will occur), there is a 30 per cent chance that this information could have been assembled if the true underlying sales potential were not F_1 but really F_2, F_3, or F_4.

All of the assumptions of our simple expository case can be summarized in Figure 2, which should be examined by working from right to left. To illustrate, the upper branch (do not delay) summarizes the results of Table 1. The conditional payoffs under each forecast, given go, are −$12 million, −$1 million, $5 million, and $10 million. Multiplying these payoffs by their respective probabilities and summing the results yields, of course, the expected payoff of $1.15 million. Since this is clearly higher than the $0 associated with no-go, this latter alternative is blocked off, and the best alternative, *given no delay,* is go.

However, the second main branch of the tree is still to be evaluated. The conditional payoffs, −$10.91 million, −$0.91 million, $3.41 million, and $6.82 million at the extreme right of the lower branch, reflect the penalties associated with (1) the discount pen-

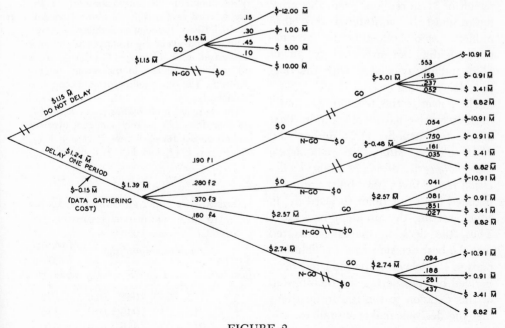

FIGURE 2

BUILD SEMIWORKS—TERMINATE PROJECT NOW VERSUS ONE-PERIOD DELAY

alty for delay and (2) the effect on the firm's market share, due to delay if the product were successful (see author's note).

If the market survey information indicates f_1 (that forecast F_1 is the best estimate), then, as noted earlier, some probability exists that this survey information could have been developed if the true underlying sales forecast were not F_1 but F_2, F_3, or F_4. If f_1 *is* observed, however, the best action to be taken after the survey is no-go—terminate the project. Hence, the go alternative branching from f_1 is blocked off. Similar results pertain to survey results f_2. Under survey results f_3 and f_4, however, the resulting best action is to build the semiworks. On an expected payoff basis, collecting the additional information produces a gross payoff of $1.39 million. From this gross figure must be subtracted the $0.15 million cost of collecting the information, yielding an expected payoff of $1.24 million associated with the one-year delay option.

The power of this technique is found in the recursive nature of solution. That is, the two payoffs, $1.24 million and $1.15 million, *summarize completely the whole series of moves along the decision tree.* Moves have been optimally planned from this point forward by, in effect, solving the problem backward. Thus, the decision maker is assured that the best decision now (which happens to be delay one period) has been derived by considering the relationship of this decision to the future decisions that the decision maker visualizes.

AUTHOR'S NOTE: Notice that several sets of new probabilities appear along the subbranches of the lower main branch of Figure

2. These probabilities are derived by application of Bayes's theorem, a central tenet of this approach. We shall need to compute marginal, joint, and posterior probabilities. Their meaning will be made clear in the computations to follow.

First we consider the calculation of the *marginal* probabilities, .190, .280, .370, and .160 appearing beside the market survey results f_1, f_2, f_3, and f_4, respectively. These calculations are shown in Table 2. The cell entries represent joint probabilities (the probability assigned to the joint occurrence of each survey result f_i and each underlying event F_j). For example the joint probability of survey result f_1 and event F_1 occurring is found under the oversimplified assumptions of our problem, by multiplying the conditional probability, $P(f_1|F_1)$, by the prior probability, $P(F_1)$, which the decision maker assigned to F_1; .70 x .15 = .105. The conditional probability of observing survey result f_1, given the fact that the true underlying forecast is F_2, is assumed equal to .10. (Similarly, for the sake of simplicity, the probability of obtaining the survey result f_1 if the true forecast is F_3 or F_4 is also assumed to be .10.) Hence the joint probability of survey result f_1 and event F_2 occurring is, by way of illustration, $P(f_1|F_2) \cdot P(F_2) = .10$ x .30 = .030 as shown in the second column of row f_1. The other cell entries are computed analogously.

The *marginal probabilities* f_1, f_2, f_3, and f_4 are then found by merely summing over the column entries for each row—$P(f_1) = P(f_1$ and $F_1) + P(f_1$ and $F_2) + P(f_1$ and $F_3)$

TABLE 2

MARGINAL AND JOINT PROBABILITIES UNDER THE ONE-PERIOD DELAY OPTION

Survey Results	Joint Probabilities				Marginal Probabilities
	F_1	F_2	F_3	F_4	
f_1	.105	.030	.045	.010	.190
f_2	.015	.210	.045	.010	.280
f_3	.015	.030	.315	.010	.370
f_4	.015	.030	.045	.070	.160
	.150	.300	.450	.100	1.000

$+ P$ (f_1 and F_4) or $.190 = .105 + .030 + .045 + .010$. Also note that the marginal probabilities, found by summing over rows for each column F_j, are simply the prior probabilities that the decision maker had originally assigned to the occurrence of these four events.

We can next proceed to the calculation of the *posterior probabilities*, $P(F_i|f_i)$, and to a brief description of how Bayes's theorem can be used to derive them. These calculations are shown in Table 3.

TABLE 3

POSTERIOR PROBABILITIES UNDER
THE ONE-PERIOD DELAY OPTION

Survey Results	Posterior Probabilites				
	F_1	F_2	F_3	F_4	Total
f_1	.553	.158	.237	.052	1.000
f_2	.054	.750	.161	.035	1.000
f_3	.041	.081	.851	.027	1.000
f_4	.094	.188	.281	.437	1.000

Table 3 can be explained as follows: Under the assumptions of our problem it was noted that each survey result was deemed to be only 70 per cent reliable in correctly "calling" the event assumed to be most strongly associated with it. Suppose, however, that we really did observe a particular survey result, say f_1. Under our assumptions it is more likely that event F_1 "caused" this specific result than events F_2, F_3, or F_4. Still, the other events could have caused this result. We would like to reason backward, so to speak, in order to determine how likely it is that F_1 was the underlying event, now knowing that f_1 has occurred.

Given that we have observed f_1, it is clear that only the joint probabilities along row one of Table 2 are now relevant. We would next wish to partition the total (marginal) probability associated with f_1 (.190) among the four events, F_1, F_2, F_3, or F_4, which could have produced this survey result. Hence the first row of Table 3 is derived by merely dividing each entry in Table 2 (.105, .030, .045, and .010) by the marginal probability (.190) associated with f_1. In summary, *before* observing f_1 we would have assigned

the prior probabilities .15, .30, .45, and .10 to events F_1, F_2, F_3, and F_4, respectively. *After* having observed f_1 we would then revise these probabilities to .553, .158, .237, and .052, respectively, so as to reflect the fact that the observance of f_1 was deemed more likely under F_1 than under F_2, F_3, or F_4. Analogous considerations apply to the calculation of posterior probabilities shown in the remaining rows of Table 3.

Bayes's theorem formalizes this notion in terms of the following formula:

$$P(F_i \mid f) = \frac{P(f \mid F_i) \cdot P(F_i)}{\sum_{j=1}^{n} P(f \mid F_j) \cdot P(F_j)}$$

In terms of our problem, the posterior probability assigned to, say, event F_1, given that survey result f_1 was observed, is:

$$P(F_1 \mid f_1) = \frac{.105}{.105 + .030 + .045 + .010}$$
$$= \frac{.105}{.190}$$
$$= .553$$

The appropriate marginal and posterior probabilities (as derived in Tables 2 and 3) appear along the subbranches of the lower main branch in the tree diagram of Figure 2. We can now proceed to discuss which act we would choose, given the occurrence of each admissible survey result.

TWO-YEAR DELAY OPTION

We now consider the third option: delaying the decision pending a two-year inquiry into the sales potential of the product.[8] In this case we will assume that: (1) cost of deferred rev-

[8] Numerous other combinations could be evaluated ranging from the case where construction of the semiworks and start of the marketing studies are begun simultaneously through various degrees of overlap in timing. No new principles would be involved. Payoffs would, of course, reflect the cost of project "takedown and salvage" if the marketing survey results were to indicate a change in action from go to no-go after construction had already been started.

enues amounts to payoffs that are only 83 per cent of the payoffs under the no-delay case; (2) the anticipated market share would drop to only 50 per cent of the market; (3) market survey costs increase to $300,000; but (4) the reliability of the resultant information increases to 90 per cent.

Figure 3 summarizes this second analysis. The upper main branch of the decision tree, covering the no-delay case, is exactly the same as that in Figure 2. All payoffs and probabilities in the lower main branch, however, are adjusted in accordance with the changed assumptions just enumerated by developing tables analogous to Tables 2 and 3. Solution of the problem again proceeds from right to left, always choosing the best alternative for each subbranch of the tree.

The upshot of this analysis is that the two-year delay option produces a lower expected payoff than the no-delay option. In other words, the costs associated with delaying the venture more than outweigh the gains expected through increased reliability of the sales information. For this reason the lower branch of the tree is blocked off in Figure 3.

In summary, it has been shown, via the preceding simplified examples, how costs associated with delay can be balanced against the costs associated with the higher costs of uncertainty related to moving a development along too quickly.

The preceding illustrative case has touched upon some aspects of Bayesian decision theory but has by no means exhausted the many facets of this ap-

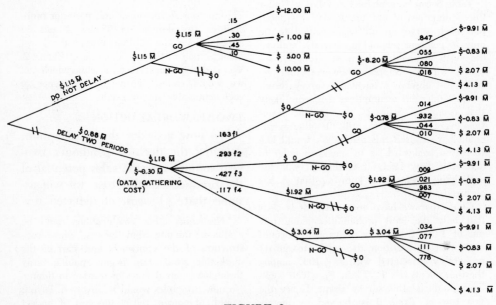

FIGURE 3

BUILD SEMIWORKS—TERMINATE PROJECT NOW VERSUS TWO-PERIOD DELAY

proach.[9] As could be inferred from our preceding illustration, the Bayesian approach to decision making under uncertainty provides a framework for explicitly working with the economic costs of alternative courses of action, the prior knowledge or judgments of the decision maker regarding the occurrence of states of nature affecting payoffs, and the conditional probabilities of observing specific events, given each state of nature.

The Bayesian approach to decision making under uncertainty provides a rich set of techniques for dealing with

[9] A full and lucid description of these features can be found in *Probability and Statistics for Business Decisions*.

the complex problems that attend new product development. This is not to say that the relevant probabilities used in this approach can be developed easily or quickly. Rather, granting that decisions must be made in any event Bayesian analysis represents a rational procedure for including all relevant data and for dealing explicitly with the gains versus costs associated with the option to "purchase" new information bearing on the problem. Coupled with ancillary techniques such as computer simulation and sensitivity analyses, it seems fair to say that this set of tools constitutes the most powerful analytical apparatus of its class currently available to the product development manager.

➤➤➤➤➤➤➤➤➤➤➤ THE PERT/COST SYSTEM

Special Projects Office, Navy Department

I. PROJECT MANAGEMENT

Early in the development of the Polaris Missile Program, the Navy Special Projects Office recognized the need for an integrated management system. As an early step in this direction, the Program Evaluation and Review Technique (PERT) was developed to aid in the planning and control of time schedules in the Polaris Program. Since its introduction in 1958, the PERT technique has re-

ceived widespread interest and voluntary adoption throughout American industry as a significant improvement in project planning and control.

In addition to its use in schedule planning and control, the network concept in PERT provides the framework for treating a wide range of project management problems. Recognizing this fact, the Navy Special Projects Office is currently extending the PERT technique to include the elements of cost and technical performance.

Reprinted, with minor omissions and changes, from An Introduction to The PERT/Cost System for Integrated Project Management, *Special Projects Office, Navy Department, October 15, 1961.*

II. THE PERT/COST SYSTEM

A. WHAT IT IS

PERT/Cost is an integrated management system designed to provide managers with the information they need in planning and controlling schedules *and* costs in development projects. The system provides information in various levels of detail, thereby satisfying the needs of contractor management as well as the customer. It is designed both to mesh with existing management systems and to provide valuable new information.

The PERT/Cost System consists of a Basic Procedure for planning and control, and two closely related supplements setting forth more advanced planning procedures. The objectives of the PERT/Cost System are summarized in Figure 1.

B. WHY IT IS NEEDED: LIMITATIONS OF CONVENTIONAL TECHNIQUES

The illustration in Figure 2 demonstrates the limitations of conventional planning and control techniques for determining project time and cost status, and for relating costs to progress.

Figure 2 contains a standard milestone chart accompanied by its corresponding rate of expenditure display.

The open triangles in the illustration are the milestones or events which are scheduled to be completed at a future time. The closed triangles are milestones already completed.

The development work of Project "X" is planned for a nine month period with six milestones scheduled throughout that period. The milestones scheduled during the first three months were the only ones completed at the time this report was prepared.

The budget for Project "X" for the first three months was $100,000, and, in terms of the data represented in Figure 2, the manager would conclude that the project was on schedule and on budget.

Project "X", however, is actually in serious difficulty. In order to identify this difficulty, it is necessary to develop different kinds of information than that which is presented in Figure 2.

PERT/COST SYSTEM

The Basic PERT/Cost Procedure	Assists project managers by providing information in the varying levels of detail needed for planning schedules and costs, evaluating schedule and cost performance, and predicting and controlling time and cost overruns.
The Time-Cost Option Procedure (Supplemental)	Displays alternate time-cost-risk plans for accomplishing project objectives.
The Resource Allocation Procedure (Supplemental)	Determines the lowest cost allocation of resources among individual project tasks, to meet a specified project duration.

FIGURE 1 OBJECTIVES OF THE PERT/COST SYSTEM

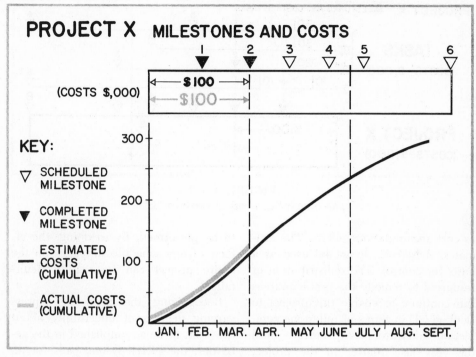

FIGURE 2

CONVENTIONAL MILESTONE AND BUDGET DISPLAY

A closer examination of Project "X" would have revealed significant information on a number of tasks that contribute to the accomplishment of the Project work (See Figure 3).

In task (I), milestone 1 was scheduled to be completed in February. Originally, $10,000 was estimated to achieve milestone 1, and $10,000 more for performing additional work on task (I) during the remainder of the first quarter. In task (II), milestone 2 was scheduled to be completed on 31 March at a cost estimated to be $20,000. Though tasks (III) and (IV) have no milestones scheduled during the first quarter, $30,000 was estimated to be spent on each of these tasks for ongoing work during the first three months. Thus, the total first quarter budget for Project "X" is $100,000.

As the project proceeded, task (I) expended funds and completed work as planned. Task (II), however, encountered difficulty. $50,000 was spent instead of the $20,000 estimated in order to accomplish milestone 2 on schedule. The added $30,000 came, in fact, from tasks (III) and (IV), which sacrificed labor and other resources to task (II). Thus, tasks (III) and (IV) face probable schedule slippages or cost overruns when attempting to meet their milestones later in the project year. Yet, in terms of the standard control techniques, all appeared to be fine.

Although conventional estimating procedures may require the preparation of estimates for all the tasks in a project, these tasks generally will not serve

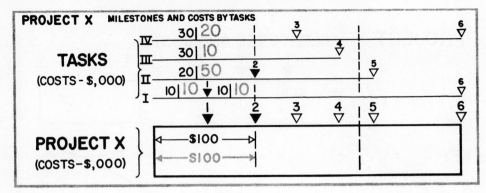

FIGURE 3

THE INDIVIDUAL TASKS IN PROJECT "X"

as cost accumulation centers. The estimates, therefore, cannot be used as a basis for control. The redistribution of resources to remedy the problem areas can continue to enable this project to "look good" in terms of milestone completion and rate of expenditure until the very last quarter in the project when it would be too late for effective corrective action.

The PERT/Cost System sets forth a procedure to identify critical schedule slippages and cost overruns in time for corrective action.

III. THE BASIC PERT/COST PROCEDURE

A. THE NETWORK AND TIME ESTIMATES

The first step in the PERT/Cost System is the construction of a network consisting of the activities (project tasks) to be performed, and the events or milestones to be attained.

The network reflects the carefully developed plan for accomplishing the project, and identifies the interrelationships and interdependencies in the work

to be performed. By so doing, the effects of any schedule slippages on the entire project can be readily determined.

Recognizing the need to express varying degrees of uncertainty about the work to be accomplished in the activities, the PERT system calls for an optimistic (t_o), most likely (t_m), and pessimistic (t_p) time estimate for each activity. From these estimates a statistically "expected" time estimate (t_e) is calculated.

In the example shown in Figure 4, the "Subsystem Tests" activity time estimates are:

$$t_o = 6 \qquad t_m = 7 \qquad t_p = 14$$

The calculated t_e is 8 weeks. The longest path through the network is called the critical path. Any shortening of total project time must be accomplished by reducing the duration of the longest path. The critical path may be shortened by applying more effort to critical activities or by replanning the network to eliminate certain tasks or to perform more activities in parallel. Thus the network focuses management attention on those areas where corrective action is most needed

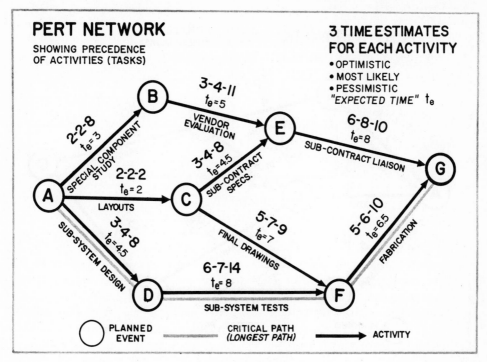

PERT NETWORK

SHOWING PRECEDENCE
OF ACTIVITIES (TASKS)

**3 TIME ESTIMATES
FOR EACH ACTIVITY**
• OPTIMISTIC
• MOST LIKELY
• PESSIMISTIC
"EXPECTED TIME" t_e

2-2-8 $t_e = 3$ — SPECIAL COMPONENT STUDY

3-4-11 $t_e = 5$ — VENDOR EVALUATION

6-8-10 $t_e = 8$ — SUB-CONTRACT LIAISON

2-2-2 $t_e = 2$ — LAYOUTS

3-4-8 $t_e = 4.5$ — SUB-CONTRACT SPECS.

3-4-8 $t_e = 4.5$ — SUB-SYSTEM DESIGN

5-7-9 $t_e = 7$ — FINAL DRAWINGS

5-6-10 $t_e = 6.5$ — FABRICATION

6-7-14 $t_e = 8$ — SUB-SYSTEM TESTS

◯ PLANNED EVENT

▬▬▬ CRITICAL PATH *(LONGEST PATH)*

──➤ ACTIVITY

FIGURE 4

THE NETWORK OF "EXPECTED" TIMES

$t_e = \dfrac{t_o + 4t_m + t_p}{6}$; to find the longest path through the network, the series sums of t_e values are compared.

and can do the most good. In Figure 4 the critical path is shown by the gray line. All other paths on the network are called slack paths.

B. COST ESTIMATES

After the network has been prepared and time estimates developed for the network activities, the manager will establish a schedule. This schedule will be based on the critical path calculations, the directed dates and the manager's judgment concerning the goals to be established for accomplishing the activities.

Once the schedule has been estab-

lished, resource estimates to perform each cost significant segment of the network (activity or group of activities) as scheduled are obtained. These estimates are then converted to total dollar estimates.

Figure 5 shows the PERT/Cost network with the scheduled time and estimated cost for each activity.

C. ACTUAL TIME AND COSTS

Actual costs and times are collected separately for each cost significant segment of the network. These actual time and cost inputs are compared with estimates to indicate the project status.

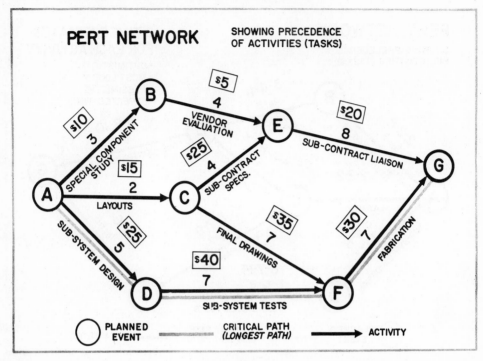

PERT NETWORK — SHOWING PRECEDENCE OF ACTIVITIES (TASKS)

FIGURE 5
THE SCHEDULE/COST NETWORK PLAN

Figure 6 contains the sample network with estimated *and* actual time and cost information.

In the example shown in Figure 6, the completed activities thus far include activities A-B, A-C, and A-D. Although activity A-B has consumed one week more than scheduled, it is on a slack path and the slippage will have no effect on the total program duration. This activity was budgeted for $10,000 and actually required only $8,000, a $2,000 underrun. Activity A-C was completed on budget and on schedule. Activity A-D encountered difficulty and incurred a $10,000 overrun in cost and a one week slippage in schedule. The schedule slippage in this path required immediate management attention since A-D is an activity on the critical path.

Note also that activity B-E and C-E have consumed both their time and budget, yet are incomplete. New estimates to complete are required for these activities.

D. ESTIMATING FORM

The PERT/Cost estimating form (See Figure 7) is used to develop the type of data needed for preparing the time/cost network plan for a project. Only the information appearing in the top half of this form is used until a satisfactory time plan and schedule have been determined. Once the schedule has been established, manpower and material estimates are entered in the manner indicated on the bottom half of the form.

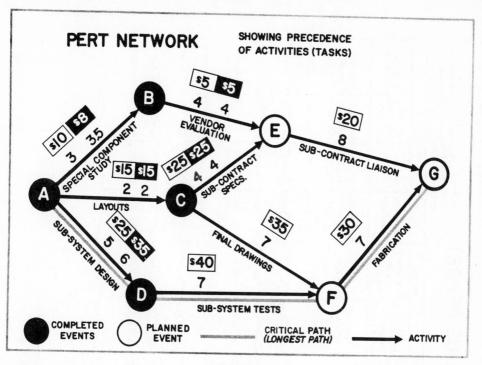

FIGURE 6

THE SCHEDULE/COST NETWORK, PLAN AND STATUS

PERT/COST ESTIMATING FORM

DATE PREPARED 23 June '61

ACTIVITY DESCRIPTION *Design Simulator No.5*		ACTIVITY ACCOUNT NO.	72345-01	PERT TIME EST. (IN WEEKS)	
BEGIN EVENT NO. 191	END EVENT NO. 193	RESPONSIBLE UNIT	5410	OPTIMISTIC	5
BEGINNING EVENT DATE 10 July '61	ENDING EVENT DATE 18 Aug '61	ESTIMATOR	RJK	MOST LIKELY	6
		APPROVED	TLM	PESSIMISTIC	10
TYPE ENTRY 1	SCHEDULED ELAPSED TIME 6 WKS	DATE APPROVED	6/27/61	EXPECTED ELAPSED TIME	6.5

MANPOWER SKILL	ESTIMATED DIRECT MANHOURS BY MONTHS ELAPSED TIME												TOTAL MAN HRS.	SUMMARY OF PURCHASES		
	MONTHS													CODE	DESCRIPTION	$
	1ST	2ND	3RD	4TH	5TH	6TH	7TH	8TH	9TH	10TH	11TH	12TH				
D	200	60											260		DIRECT MATERIAL	
E	200	320											520	61	ENG. DEV. MATERIAL	400
M	180	360											540		TOOLING MATERIAL	
S	80	40											120		TEST EQUIP. MATERIAL	
															INSP. EQUIP. MATERIAL	
															COMPUTER	
															SUB CONTRACT	
															TOTAL PURCHASES	400

FIGURE 7

THE PERT/COST ESTIMATING FORM

PERT TIME AND COST STATUS REPORT

Project _____
Contract No. _____
Month Ending _____

	IDENTIFICATION			TIME STATUS					COST STATUS			
	Begin Event No.	End Event No.	Activity Account No.	Expected Elapsed Time (te)	Scheduled Elapsed Time (ts)	Scheduled Completion Date (Ts)	Latest Allowable Completion Date (TL)	Activity Slack (TL−Ts)	Contract Estimate	Actual Costs	Latest Revised Estimate	Overrun/(Underrun)
BASIC By Activities	165	168	71829-01	5.0	5.0	9/8/61	8/25/61	−2.0	$20,000	$25,000	$30,000	$10,000
	168	182	71829-02	10.0	10.0	11/17/61	11/3/61	−2.0	35,000	18,000	30,000	(5,000)
	165	182	71829-03	8.0	8.0	9/15/61	11/3/61	7.0	15,000	6,000	25,000	10,000
(Direct Costs Only)									70,000*	49,000*	85,000*	15,000*
FIRST SUMMARY By Individual Hardware Items	165	182	71829	15.0	15.0	11/17/61	11/3/61	−2.0	70,000	49,000	85,000	15,000
									◆105,000	◆74,000	◆128,000	◆23,000
(Total Costs)									175,000*	123,000*	213,000*	38,000*
SECOND SUMMARY By Major Hardware Categories	051	325	718	30.0	30.0	1/26/62	1/12/62	−2.0	500,000	300,000	600,000	100,000
(Total Costs)												

Notes:

◆ = Indirect Costs
* = Totals

FIGURE 8

THE TIME AND COST STATUS REPORT WITH BASIC AND SUMMARY DATA

The breakdown of manpower by skill categories provides the data needed to indicate the manpower requirements of the project. Conversion of manhours and material to total dollars is accomplished by applying the appropriate labor and overhead rates.

Note: A contractor may use his existing accounting procedures for accumulating estimates and actual cost information used by the PERT/Cost System. What is required of the existing procedure, however, is that each activity or group of activities to be costed separately be identified by an accounting code.

E. TIME AND COST STATUS REPORT

The PERT/Cost System provides time, cost and resource reports for various levels of management. Some of these reports are shown on the following pages.

A typical comprehensive status report is one which combines time and cost information (See Figure 8).

The Time and Cost Status Report is a basic output of the PERT/Cost System. It is designed to assist the project manager in evaluating over-all time and cost progress and in pinpointing those activities which are causing schedule slippages or cost overruns, either actual or potential. The system permits this form to be printed in several degrees of data summation so that appropriate detail is presented to each level of management.

(The concept of summary reporting with detailed back-up reports applies to all PERT/Cost outputs.)

F. MANPOWER REQUIREMENTS REPORT

This is a typical report that identifies the monthly manpower requirements to perform the project on schedule. The report is presented by total manpower and by individual manpower skills. An "Activity Slack" column provides the manager with a ranking of activities in the order of their importance to completing the project on schedule. The Manpower Requirements Report is intended to point out those periods in the life of a project when manpower requirements for certain skill categories will exceed the availability, or where substantial idle time appears in the plan. This report will assist the line

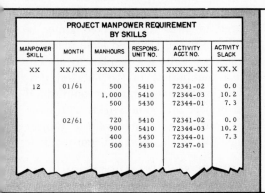

PROJECT MANPOWER REQUIREMENT BY SKILLS					
MANPOWER SKILL	MONTH	MANHOURS	RESPONS. UNIT NO.	ACTIVITY ACCT. NO.	ACTIVITY SLACK
XX	XX/XX	XXXXX	XXXX	XXXXX-XX	XX. X
12	01/61	500	5410	72341-02	0.0
		1,000	5410	72344-03	10.2
		500	5430	72344-01	7.3
	02/61	720	5410	72341-02	0.0
		900	5410	72344-03	10.2
		400	5430	72344-01	7.3
		500	5430	72347-01	

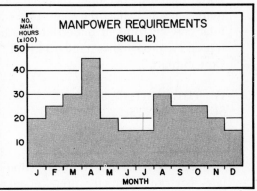

FIGURE 9

MANPOWER REQUIREMENT REPORT AND HISTOGRAM

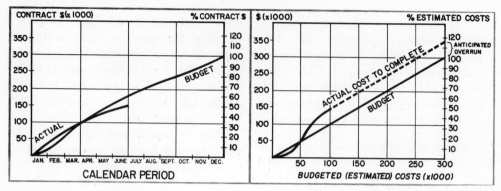

FIGURE 10

RATE OF EXPENDITURE

FIGURE 11

COST OF WORK

manager in leveling out peaks and valleys in his manpower loading plan.

G. RATE OF EXPENDITURE AND COST OF WORK REPORTS

These two summary reports, usually in graph form, present the manager with the over-all cost status of the project. The Rate of Expenditure Report, Figure 10, indicates the rate at which costs are budgeted and incurred over time. The Cost of Work Report, Figure 11, relates budgeted and actual costs to the amount of the work performed and indicates the estimated costs to complete the project. Together, these reports establish periodic funding requirements and show the trend toward total cost overruns or underruns. Both reports are prepared as standard PERT/Cost outputs.

IV. THE PERT/COST SUPPLEMENTS

A. THE TIME-COST OPTION PROCEDURE

Most proposal requests today stipulate that the contractor prepare only one time-cost plan to complete the proposed project by a directed completion date. Although this "Directed Date" plan may be based primarily on a timed military requirement, the factors of cost and technical risk are frequently of major importance in selecting a particular development plan. With only a single time-cost alternative to consider, neither the customer nor the contractor can determine that a directed date plan is the "best" combination of time, cost, and technical risk for a particular project.

The Time-Cost Option Procedure calls for the preparation of three alternate time-cost plans for accomplishing the project. (See Figure 12.) At least one of these plans will be prepared to meet the Directed Date. In addition to the Directed Date plan, the procedure calls for: a plan to accomplish the project in the shortest possible time, and a plan for accomplishing the project in a time which will allow the contractor to achieve the project objectives in the most efficient manner.

B. THE RESOURCE ALLOCATION PROCEDURE

In a development project, there frequently are various levels of resources

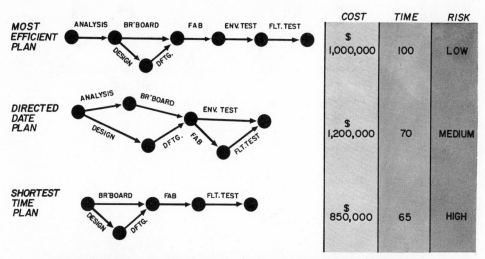

				COST	TIME	RISK
MOST EFFICIENT PLAN	ANALYSIS BR'BOARD FAB ENV. TEST FLT. TEST DESIGN DFTG.			**$ 1,000,000**	100	LOW
DIRECTED DATE PLAN	ANALYSIS BR'BOARD ENV. TEST DESIGN DFTG. FAB FLT.TEST			**$ 1,200,000**	70	MEDIUM
SHORTEST TIME PLAN	BR'BOARD FAB FLT.TEST DESIGN DFTG.			**$ 850,000**	65	HIGH

SELECTION OF THE "BEST" PLAN DEPENDS ON THE RELATIVE IMPORTANCE OF COST, TIME AND RISK IN EACH PROGRAM

FIGURE 12
THREE TIME-COST OPTIONS

that can be applied to each activity. It is important for the manager to recognize what effect the different applications will have on the total time and cost of a project, especially when a speed-up or stretch-out is being considered.

The Resource Allocation Procedure identifies the specific allocation of resources for each activity that will yield the lowest total cost for one or more specified project durations. To do this, the procedure calls for alternate resource/time estimates for performing each activity in the project.

The steps followed in this procedure are similar to the ones illustrated in Figure 13 and summarized below.

1. Construct network.
2. Obtain alternate time-cost estimates for each activity.

3. Select the lowest cost alternate for each activity.
4. Calculate the critical path and compare to directed date (duration).
5. If critical path is too long, select higher cost, shorter time alternates on critical path activities. These alternate points are picked where the ratio of increased cost to decreased time is least.
6. Repeat Step 5 until length of critical path conforms to directed date.

V. SUMMARY

The PERT/Cost System is directed toward the dynamic management of projects by the *contractor*, as well as toward the timely, accurate reporting

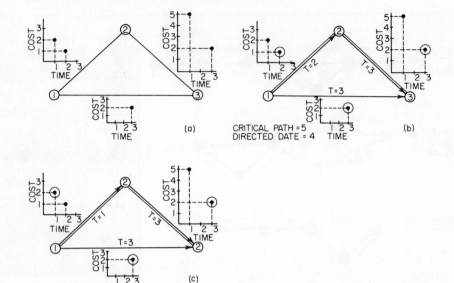

FIGURE 13

A SUMMARY OF THE RESOURCE ALLOCATION PROCEDURE
a. Procedural Steps 1 and 2
b. Procedural Steps 3 and 4
c. Procedural Steps 5 and 6

of project status to the *customer.* The System specifies techniques and procedures to assist *project managers* in:

Planning schedules and costs
Determining time and cost status
Forecasting manpower skill requirements

Predicting schedule slippages and cost overruns
Developing alternate time-cost plans
Allocating resources among tasks

PERT/Cost provides an integrated framework for effective management decisions.

part ► 4

Launching New Products

No clear line of demarcation establishes the point where new-product development ends and new-product marketing starts. There is much overlapping as well as a close interconnection between the two functions. A great deal of marketing work is begun long before the technical development phase is completed, and some of it may commence even before the new-product idea is crystallized.

Attention to the marketing effort must be devoted as early in the development process as is practicable: unless a new product can ultimately be sold at a profit, the development process itself is pointless.

There are numerous difficulties in the marketing of new products. Many can be avoided by rigorous thinking and systematic planning. Blind adherence to pat formulas which may have worked for past products is often a short cut to failure. Accordingly, the readings in Part 4 have been selected to underscore conceptual and procedural aids to the successful launching of new products. Some of the readings supply provocative springboards for discussion and original exploration; none is offered as a definitive or conclusive roadmap to new-product success. Purely descriptive and mechanistic "how to" readings have been de-emphasized. The selections in Part 4 have been classified into four groups:

1. *Preparing and approving the candidate product for commercialization* Early in the marketing phase a brand name may have to be created for the new entry. Perhaps various legal checks may be needed. The product may have to be subjected to rigorous technical and/or use testing to establish evidence of appropriate performance and to provide provable claims to be used in promotion. At some point in the process, a full-dress management review of the new product's past, present, and future will usually be needed to establish whether the new product is to be entered on the market at all—and when.

All these critical preliminary marketing and premarketing issues are discussed in detail in the first group of readings. The "go" or "no go" decision, of course, may also be predicated on strategic marketing considerations covered in succeeding selections of Part 4.

2. *Major building blocks in marketing strategy* Given the decision to devote time and energy and money to preparing a marketing program for the new product, the second group of readings focuses on the individual elements of the marketing mix as they relate to the special case of new products. Packaging, the first major strategic element to be treated here, is increasingly coming to be a market-oriented function—much more than mere product protection is required of today's packages. In pricing, too, a strategic choice must be made whether to charge high or low *initial* prices in the market segments selected for entry. In the area of marketing channels, the planner often has literally dozens of different selling methods and alternative distribution setups from which to choose. Finally, appropriate promotional methods to overcome the special problems and to achieve the unique goals of new-product introduction must be designed. Thus the chief ingredients of the marketing mix—package, price, distribution, and promotion—are individually treated from the new-product point of view.

3. *Formulating an overall plan* The third set of readings deals with the formulation of overall strategy incorporating all of the interrelated elements of the marketing mix. To ensure that these ingredients are properly blended into a total plan of action, some conceptual foundations must be laid. Relatively little has been empirically established about the new-product adoption process.[1] Until more is known, we must lean heavily upon the insights, concepts, and hypotheses advanced by more theoretical writers. As a minimum, the notions expressed and developed in this group of selections should provide general guidance in defining market targets and estimating potentials, help in establishing orders of priority for penetrating multiple end-use market segments, offer suggestions for setting objectives and tasks for new-product launchings, and develop inferences and implications for timing and pacing introductory efforts aimed at achieving a better-integrated total program.

4. *Program testing, implementation, and review* In the final selections, stress is placed on the key role of test marketing, on the need for thoroughness and attention to marketing details, on additional questions of timing market expansion, on the importance of rapidly diagnosing failures, on methods of monitoring customer acceptance and competitive responses, on means of predicting new-product success, and on alternative ways of evaluating overall new-product results at the completion of this complex process.

[1] For some provocative preliminary research, see *The Adoption of New Products: Process and Influence* (Ann Arbor, Mich.: Foundation for Research on Human Behavior, 1959).

►►►►►►►►►►► A

Clearing the New Product
for Commercialization

►►►►►►►►►►►► HOW TO PICK A NAME FOR A NEW PRODUCT

ROBERT N. MCMURRY*

One of the most promising yet least exploited phases of merchandising today is the development of appealing *product names*.... A well-chosen name can be a great asset; a poorly chosen one a liability. The ideal product name. . . .

① Implies that the product will satisfy an acutely felt need. Example: "Eversharp" for a pencil;

② Is easy to spell and remember: "Duz" for a cleanser.

③ Attention value: "My Sin" for a perfume.

④ Quality connotation: "Suave" for a man's hair dressing.

⑤ Pleasant connotations: "Beauty rest" for a mattress.

It is possible to take a coined name with no connotations and by the expenditure of large sums of money create desired associations. Typical is "Kodak." It has become a generic term for certain types of cameras. On the other hand, it has required a half century and the investment of millions of dollars in advertising and other promotional activities to bring this about.

Reprinted with permission from Sales Management, *August 15, 1954, pp. 102–105.*
McMurry, Hamstra & Company.

Many companies apparently give scant thought to product names. The majority are innocuous and pedestrian, constituting a means of identifying the product to public and trade, hardly more. They have little value in merchandising the item. Typical cases are those in which the company's name is incorporated with that of the product. Example: "Swift's Premium Bacon." The manufacturer's name often lends prestige to the product and aids in its promotion to a minor extent.

Other names are less fortunately chosen, particularly those designed to imply scientific or medicinal attributes, as in the pharmaceutical field, and are serious offenders against some or all of the five characteristics a good name should possess. Typical is the name "Anti-phlogistine," which, while it may suggest the presence of medicinal qualities, is neither easy to remember nor spell, has no particular attention value and no inherent connotations, favorable or unfavorable. As in the case of "Kodak," it can be given meaning by advertising, but this is costly and time-consuming.

Some names have meanings to certain, often limited, groups, not to the market as a whole. An example is "Iso-vis," a lubricating oil. This name means "constant viscosity" to an engineer. To the average layman it has no specific meaning. Asked what the name suggests to him, the layman may respond to the clang association of the word "iso" and report "ice." The technical meaning of the name escapes all but a small number of lubrication engineers, and its sound implies an element no one wants in a lubricating oil—ice.

There are names simple to remember, with appreciable impact. However, their connotations are confusing, inappropriate, or suggest something vaguely unpleasant. An example of this is "Clabber Girl," name for a baking powder. Undeniably an arresting name, easy to remember and spell, it nevertheless fails to suggest that the product is an aid in baking. More disturbing, the name conjures up a blurred image. What is a "Clabber Girl"? She does not come sharply into focus. The ideas associated with "clabber" are far from appealing. What finally emerges is the image of a pallid, doughy, glabrous, sticky creature who lacks glamour and is even slightly revolting. In a more obvious manner, a name such as "Klassy Kut Klothes" suggests cheapness and lack of product prestige.

THE AUTHOR PICKS SOME SAMPLES

1. These are names which may confuse the purchaser because they are not appropriate to the product:

Glasstex (batteries—The B. F. Goodrich Co.)
Permaglas (glass-lined water heaters and tanks —A. O. Smith Corp.)
E-Z-Do (wardrobes and chest accessories— Decorative Cabinets Corp.)
Flat-As-A-Pancake (gummed papers—Brown-Bridge Mills Co.)
Hi Low Witchery (brassiere—Exquisite Form Brassiere, Inc.)

2. These are names which imply that the product will deliver the results the purchaser seeks:

Bisquick (flour—General Mills, Inc.)
Wear-Ever (cooking utensils and foil—The Aluminum Cooking Utensil Co., Inc.)
Day-Glo (fluorescent colors—Switzer Bros., Inc.)
Week-At-A-Glance (date book—Nascon Products, Div. of Eaton Paper Corp.)
Ever-Ready (safety razors—American Safety Razor Corp.)

Kno-draft (adjustable air diffusers—Connor Engineering Corp.)

Cut-Rite (waxed paper—Scott Paper Co.)

Foam Shave (men's products—The Mennen Co.)

Keepsake (rings—A. H. Pond Co., Inc.)

Mum (deodorant—Bristol-Myers Co.)

My-T-Fine (desserts—Penick & Ford, Ltd., Inc.)

End-O-Corn (foot comfort—End-O-Corn)

Kantwet (crib mattress—Rose-Derry Co.)

3. These are names which are hard to remember and pronounce:

Analgestic (cream and pre-tape dressing—Larson Laboratories, Inc.)

Estrogenic (hormone cream—Helena Rubinstein, Inc.)

Elastic Naugahyde Royalite (plastics—United States Rubber Co.)

Rock-a-file Modular (office furniture—Rockwell-Barnes Co.)

Arsenoferratose (medical—Garret Lab., Inc.)

Dia-Pape-sin (milk—The Sterling Products Div. of Sterling Drug, Inc.)

4. These are names which at least tend to identify the product:

Elecom (electric computors — Underwood Corp.)

Ekotape (recorder-reproducer—Webster Electric Co.)

Double-flow Aquatower (cooling tower—The Marley Co., Inc.)

Roto-Clene (air filter—American Air Filter Co.)

5. These are meaningless names which can be given significance through advertising:

Tri "55" Clad (new motor to reduce installation costs—General Electric Co.)

Kordek (case binder—Corn Products Refining Co.)

Superex (high temperature block insulation—Johns-Manville Corp.)

Tocco (high frequency melting furnaces—Ohio Crankshaft Co.)

Echo (ladies' scarfs—Edgar C. Hyman Co., Inc.)

Foamglas (cellular glass insulation — Pittsburgh Corning Corp.)

Parlon (chlorinated rubber to withstand coolants and lubricants—Hercules Powder Co.)

Alfrax (B1 aluminum oxide brick for insulation and low heat loss—The Carborundum Co.)

Mullfrax (electric furnace mullite shaper for load strength—The Carborundum Co.)

Noa Noa (new perfume created by Helena Rubinstein, Inc.)

Hi-Hat (peanut cooking oil—Planters Nut and Chocolate Co.)

Dorex (air recovery — Connor Engineering Corp.)

6. These are meaningless names which have been given significance through advertising:

Arm & Hammer Brand (baking soda—Church & Dwight Co., Inc.)

Enna Jettick (shoes—Dunn and McCarthy, Inc.)

Zerex (anti-freeze—E. I. du Pont de Nemours & Co. [Inc.], Polychemicals Dept.)

Zippo (lighter—Zippo Manufacturing Co.)

Nucoa (margarine—The Best Foods, Inc.)

Va-Tra-Nol (nose drops—Vick Chemical Co.)

Electrolux (refrigerators—Servel, Inc.)

Scotchlite (reflective sheeting — Minnesota Mining & Mfg. Co.)

Argyrol (medical and ointment—[A. C. Barnes Co.] Zonite Products Corp.)

Arrow (collars, shirts and cravats—Cluett, Peabody & Co., Inc.)

Aunt Jemima (pancake and buckwheat flours—The Quaker Oats Co.)

Crystal Domino (sugar—The American Sugar Refining Co.)

Cuticura (toilet preparations—Potter Drug & Chemical Corp.)

Dutch Boy (white lead and paints—National Lead Co.)

Educator (saltines—Megowen Educator Food Co.)

Gold Medal Kitchen-Tested (flour — General Mills, Inc.)

Paper-Mate (pen—Paper-Mate Co., Inc.)

Heirloom (sterling—Oneida, Ltd.)

Zerone (anti-freeze—E. I. du Pont de Nemours & Co. [Inc.], Polychemicals Dept.)

Actually, a well-chosen name has tremendous value in merchandising a product. It often is as effective as pages of copy in telling prospective users what it is, what it does, and to what extent it is a quality product. This is in addition to its merits as an attention-getter and an easy-to-recall "friend in need."

It is probable that many of the best product names are the result of intuitive inspiration, as are many successful advertising themes. This does not preclude the development of effective names on a more empirical, or scientific, basis. In most cases a combination of inspiration and science undoubtedly yields the best all-around name.

Scientific development of a name requires a number of steps. For example, in the search for a name for a lubricating oil. . . .

1. Needs the product is expected to satisfy were explored. Five hundred motorists and truck operators were interviewed as to:
   a. their preferences among various brands of lubricants;
   b. their reasons for these preferences;
   c. their requirements for a lubricating oil;
   d. their ideas of the qualities a lubricating oil should possess.

2. A study of existing names of lubricating oils was made with the same group to ascertain:
   a. what names are known (have good attention and recall value);
   b. what names are preferred and why;
   c. what these names suggest to motorists and truck operators.

3. A list of names was compiled for testing purposes from: (This is where intuition and inspiration are important.)
   a. contests among employes and the public;
   b. company's advertising agency;
   c. an analysis of existing names.

4. These names were checked by the company's legal, advertising, and marketing departments to:
   a. eliminate those already in use or covered by copyrights;
   b. eliminate those too similar to existing trade names;
   c. eliminate those already in use with unrelated products or obviously inappropriate (too long, too difficult to spell, unsuitable connotations, etc.).

5. The remaining names were then tested with a new group of approximately the same size to determine:
   a. extent to which they suggested or implied that the lubricant would satisfy the user's most pressing needs;
   b. extent to which they could be easily spelled and remembered;
   c. extent of their attention value;
   d. extent to which the name suggested quality in the product;
   e. extent to which associations clustering about the name were acceptable and would rouse a desire to purchase the brand.

Successive screenings reduced the nearly 200 names on the original list in this study to a maximum of ten. This was in no way an indication that many of the names eliminated did not meet the criteria. A number, such as "Koolmotor" and "Permalube," met the criteria, but were already in use. In view of this, the name ultimately recommended, "Superlube," was in the nature of a compromise.

Since discovery of *the* name for a product may be in part fortuitous, the application of scientific methods to its choice cannot guarantee a name with all of the desired attributes. Possibly a flash of brilliant intuition will be equally fruitful in many instances. The only problem in most cases is: Who is to have this brilliant flash of intuition? Furthermore, is it really as brilliant as it may seem? Will a name conceived in this manner accomplish all that is expected of it? No matter how apt and appealing a name may appear, it should be checked against the five criteria set forth here.

Most companies make an appreciable investment in every new product they launch. Frequently they fail to recognize the role played by the product's name. It is of course not the only factor to make or break a product's acceptance. But the increment it can contribute, while intangible, can be substantial. Regardless of the seeming appropriateness and appeal of a projected name, it should be carefully tested for its true efficacy, at least in terms of the five principal criteria of a successful name. "Duz" is almost certain to be more efficacious in selling the product than "Clabber Girl."

►►►►►►►►►►►► A BASIC GUIDE TO LEGAL PROBLEMS IN NEW PRODUCTS

JOHN W. BOHLEN*

When a company is trying to find or develop a new product, a number of legal problems can arise. Many of these can be avoided if some of the pitfalls are known in advance, as well as basic legal facts.

On certain occasions, companies ask the public or select outside groups to submit new product ideas. Here there is an implied obligation to pay fair value if you use a submitted idea. The submitter or a court may put a much higher value on it than you may feel is proper.

Moreover, the claim can be made that the idea was submitted to you in confidence. Unless you can prove that you already were aware of the idea, you may be in real difficulty.

Where a confidential relationship is established and a company cannot prove it already knew of the idea, the company cannot use the idea, even though it is unpatentable or was known to many others. The result of these decisions is that the plaintiff could exact a fancy price or prevent the defendant company from using the idea,

Reprinted with permission from Industrial Marketing, *November 1958, pp. 69–73.*

Although the author is in the legal department of the Radio Corporation of America, he has emphasized that the views expressed are those of a lawyer in private practice and should not necessarily be construed as those of RCA.

whereas other companies may be in a position to use it freely.

Consider some other problems:

1. A number of people may suggest the same or similar ideas.

2. They may suggest ideas on which your people are already working.

3. They may suggest ideas which are presently impracticable, but which later can be made to work.

In any of the above cases you may find yourself subjected to claims or suits.

IDEAS FROM CONTESTS

Public solicitation of new product ideas is sometimes cast in the form of contests. Contest rules are designed to protect you by setting forth the limits of your obligation. Sometimes this is effective.

The rules should state clearly that, in return for a chance to win a prize and your impartial judging of the entries, all the ideas submitted shall become your sole property. The decision of the judges shall be final. Obviously you must retain records showing that all entries were fairly judged.

LIMIT CONTESTANTS

You will reduce your risk if you can narrowly limit the type of new product idea that is the subject matter of the contest, and also by limiting the group which is eligible to compete. For instance, the contest might relate only to ideas concerning improvements of tape recorders and be open only to school teachers and school administrators.

Such limitations show that the contest is not merely a sham method of "picking the brains" of the general public, and make it easier to prove that the judges were competent to fairly judge the contest.

COMPLETELY UNSOLICITED IDEAS

A dangerous source of new product ideas is the unsolicited idea submitted by an outsider. Most everyone is familiar with the letter, addressed to a company, that starts "Dear Mr. President: The other night it occurred to me that it would be to your company's advantage to make a fountain pen that would automatically follow its owner wherever he may go." This type of letter also is apt to end up with expressions of admiration for the company. Sometimes the writer is frank to say that he would expect payment for his idea if it were adopted.

FAIR VALUE

Here again the dangers are that, if you use the idea, you may have to pay what a court or jury finds is its fair value. You may open yourself to a claim that a confidential relationship has been established. The risks are real and the mere nuisance value of handling claims that may arise usually far outweigh the benefits of making a practice of examining these unsolicited suggestions.

Some companies feel the risks are so great that they make every effort to return these suggestions with as little internal handling as possible. Others, for public relations reasons, notify the submitter of the precise conditions under which they will examine the idea further. Still other companies simply trust to luck.

PROTECTING THE COMPANY

Assuming you want to be cautious, how can you protect your company? You should be able to show that:

No confidential relationship has arisen.

Your company did not review the idea until it reached an agreement as to the basis for compensation, if any.

Internal procedures should be established assuring that the suggestion will have the minimum possible circulation within your company.

Your people should receive dated printed instructions to the effect that they should not read submissions further than to determine that a new product idea is being submitted.

Suggestions should be returned with a covering letter stating the reader read only to the point where the writer's purpose became obvious.

Such replies should be kept in a central office or location.

CENTRAL OFFICE

Another plan is to have the person receiving the new product send suggestion letters directly to a central office with a covering letter explaining how far he read the letter. This central office then can return the suggestion, accompanied by a form of agreement to be signed by the person submitting the idea if he wants the company to look further into the suggestion.

The above agreement would provide that if your company examines the idea it will do so only on the understanding that it incurs no liability and that no confidential relationship is thereby established. It should state that if the company decides to pay anything for the idea, the amount shall be the company's sole discretion and that the amount shall in no event exceed a specified sum.

KEEPING A RECORD

Opinion varies as to whether a facsimile should be made of the suggestion letter. If one is made, it should be made by a non-technical person and should be filed in a place where operating people do not have access to it. By keeping a record of these ideas, you prevent people submitting them from claiming that they told you more than in fact they did. With adequate records, you are often in a position to show that the idea was incomplete or lacked practical value. If you later are sued, you also may be able to show that:

Many people had previously submitted the same or similar idea.

The idea lacked novelty and was widely known.

You did not rely on the idea in developing your new product.

The form of these suggestion letters generally shows that you did not seek a confidential relationship—the idea was simply thrust upon you. The worst thing to do is to circulate these ideas for careful review by engineering and management personnel before you have effectively limited any possible obligation to the person submitting the idea.

PATENT INFRINGEMENTS

Having determined your new product and while developing it and preparing it for market, you should consider whether it may infringe on someone else's patents. It would serve no purpose to discuss the complex rules that determine whether or not the Patent Office will issue a patent on an alleged invention. It should be borne in mind, however, that the Patent Office will only issue a patent after it has made an examination to try to determine whether the claimed invention is actually new.

It may be several years between the time that a patent is applied for and the time that it is issued. Even when the Patent Office issues a patent, this does not assure that that patent is valid. It can be attacked on a number of grounds, among the most usual of which are:

The patent has been anticipated by a prior patent.

The invention claimed was previously known and used.

The invention claimed actually was lacking in invention.

TWO TYPES OF PATENTS

Patents are of two general types:

1. The first type comprises "any new and useful process, machine, manufacture or composition of matter, or any new and useful improvement thereof."

2. The second type [consists of] patents on designs. These patents are granted for original and ornamental designs for an article of manufacture, which serve a useful purpose by enhancing the value or salability of the product, but which are not necessary to its functioning.

A U.S. Letters Patent confers upon its owner for the term of seventeen years the right to exclude others from making, using, or selling the invention throughout the U.S. This means he may deny others the right to use it; he may sell it or grant licenses under it. If the patent is merely an improvement, the patent owner may find that he has to obtain a license under basic patents, in order to be able to use his own invention. Design patents are granted for terms of three and a half years, seven years, or fourteen years.

SEARCHING PATENTS

Now, in the manufacture and marketing of a product there is always the possibility that you may infringe on a patent. If so, you may be prevented by injunction from continuing to make or sell the product, or you may be presented with a claim or be sued for money damages on account of the infringement.

It is wise to have a patent search made by a patent attorney or a patent agent before you incur manufacturing costs. While no one is infallible, such patent practitioners are the people most likely to discover whether there are prior patent claims that your new device might infringe. They might also conclude that what appears to be an adverse patent is in fact invalid.

Obviously no search can disclose what patents may issue in the future. There is therefore always the unavoidable risk that you will proceed in good faith, only to find that months or even years later a valid patent may be issued covering the very product you have been making and selling. This can come about because it takes considerable time to process a patent application through the Patent Office. In addition, time may have elapsed between the date of invention and the date on which the inventor first applies for a patent.

PATENT PENDING

The familiar phrases "Patent Pending" and "Patent Applied For" do not necessarily mean that a patent will ever issue. They are intended to serve as a warning and, indeed, they are sometimes misused in order to frighten potential competitors away from copying the device. Here, again, the patent practitioner may be able to reach a conclusion as to the likelihood of a patent actually issuing.

In any event you ordinarily will not be subject to an injunction nor liable in damages for having made or sold a product *up to the time that a patent issues.* (Exception: where the defendant is told of the invention in confidence before the patent is issued.)

If there is an adverse patent situation you are automatically in an area of risk. How great the risk may be will depend upon such factors as:

Whether the patent is of questionable validity.

Whether it is a pioneer patent.

Whether it contains broad or narrow claims.

How soon it will expire.

SEEKING A LICENSE

It may be concluded that it is wiser to seek a license rather than face patent litigation. Are there risks in proceeding to market while negotiating for a license? Certainly there are, but speed may be all-important. The risks may have to be run.

The atmosphere of the negotiations may at the outset lead you to believe that they ultimately will be successful and that the price will not be exorbitant. Patent lawyers or patent agents can be of real assistance in such negotiations. They are trained to evaluate the strengths and weaknesses of each party.

You may wish to consider another solution: that of designing around the patent and thus avoiding it. Of course you will not know in advance whether your efforts will be successful nor can you accurately predict the cost. Here, too, the patent practitioner may be very helpful.

COPYRIGHTING

Leaving the subject of patents, let's discuss the allied subject of the copyrighting and commercial use of works of art.

You can obtain copyright protection for "works of art"—and they don't necessarily have to have high artistic worth. This can apply to such things as statuettes, vases, and designs. The fact that you intend to use the work of art as a commercial item does not bar it from copyright protection.

Copyright protection is not lost simply because you use the copyrighted work of art as an integral part of a commercial product, such as incorporating a statuette as part of a lamp, applying a design on fabrics, etc.

The advantages of securing a copyright over a design patent in these cases are that it can be secured in a few weeks, there is no investigation as to priority and similarity of your design in relation to the designs which may have been created or copyrighted by others, and copyright protection extends for an initial period of twenty-eight years—renewable for an additional identical period.

ADOPTING A TRADEMARK

A new product is often more salable under a new trademark. If you decide to adopt a new trademark you should consider whether your needs are best served by one that is legally strong from the moment of its adoption or whether it is to your commercial interest to adopt one that, at the start, is relatively weak.

Legally strong trademarks are those which are fanciful or arbitrary. In other words they do not resemble words with ordinary dictionary meanings and they are not hackneyed in the sense that they have been widely used by others, though for different types of goods. For instance, the coined words, "Kodak" and "Dramamine" are strong trademarks. . . . However, it will take more time, effort, and money to firmly associate such trademarks with your product in the public mind. This may not be commercially worth the effort if you do not expect a lasting market for the new product.

So-called "weak" trademarks become legally as well as commercially stronger with proper and continued use. If you adopt such a mark and it appears to be effective, you will naturally make continuous use of it. The trademark thus can become as legally strong as those trademarks which are strong from the beginning.

Examples of legally weak trademarks are such laudatory expressions as "Acme," "Superior," or descriptive trademarks such as "Load-Easy" for tape recorder tape reels.

FOREIGN MEANINGS

You certainly don't want to adopt a word which has an offensive meaning in a foreign language; i.e., "Mist," which in German means "manure." "Nescafe" was the butt of a widely circulated joke in Mexico. In Spanish, the instant coffee became *"No es cafe"*—"Is not coffee!"

Before you adopt a trademark you should have a trademark and trade name search, in order to avoid infringement suits. Thus you also can avoid having to abandon a trademark in which you have invested considerable amounts.

KEEP IT QUIET

Be secretive when you plan to adopt a new trademark. In the United States and the so-called common-law countries, trademark rights are acquired only by using the mark on the goods when you sell them.

In civil-law countries, such as the South American countries, mere registration of the trademark establishes ownership. Therefore, if someone learns of your plans, they may be able to pirate the trademark either in the United States or elsewhere.

Having adopted the new trademark you will want to protect it. Real protection is afforded by registering the trademark in the Patent Office, which establishes proof of the time you first used the mark and is of great importance in permitting you to sue for damages. Because of the heavy possibility of piracy in civil-law countries, you will very likely want to register it in these foreign countries as soon as you have used it in the United States.

MARK THE GOODS

After the trademark is registered, apply a trademark registration notice on the goods. There are several forms, among them "Reg. U.S. Pat. Off." and the Spanish version, "Marca Registrada." In the U.S., where space does not permit using a long form the statutory symbol consisting of the letter "R" inside a circle is used.

The registration notice should appear not only on the goods but in connection with use of your trademark in your advertising. This notifies and warns others that you claim the trademark.

By showing your trademark in a distinctive lettering, in quotes, or in a different color from the rest of the text, you can strengthen your trademark position. Avoid using your trademark in a generic or dictionary sense.

Never substitute your trademark for the common name of the product. Instead use it as an adjective to describe your brand of that product; for example, "Vaseline" petroleum jelly.

LABEL PROTECTION

You may wish to have a distinctive new label created for use on your new product, or an original design made for its container or wrapping. These can be protected by copyright. Similar protection is available for advertising and promotional material.

▶▶▶▶▶▶▶▶▶▶▶ PRODUCT TESTING: *everybody's doing it*

MELVIN MANDELL[*]

American industry is going in for testing in a big way. Ever since World War II, when many manufacturers were obliged to conform to detailed and comprehensive Government test specifications, companies have been off on a testing binge. And it's all to the good. Unusual field conditions, the competitive one-year redesign cycle, and the greater need for

Reprinted with permission from Dun's Review and Modern Industry, *April 1958, pp. 40–42 and 137–39.*

[*]*Industrial Editor,* Dun's Review and Modern Industry.

reliability (in products ranging from missiles to home appliances) make careful product testing more necessary than ever.

Here are some of the new factors that are forcing industry to pay more attention to meaningful testing:

The consumer, both in the home and in the factory, demands and expects evidence of product testing. The shortage of good servicing people to cope with complicated gadgets is intensifying this demand.

Unmanned military vehicles (with safety factors sharply reduced to save weight) must be reliable—there's no human driver around to correct for errors. Parts must be carefully tested to insure reliability.

Industry is now investing enormous amounts of capital in production machinery and office equipment. It can't afford downtime on huge production machines or giant data-processing computers. Hence the extensive testing, usually of production runs.

New destructive forces such as nuclear radiation, ozone, and acoustic vibration have been discovered or are now more fully understood. Tests to determine whether products can resist these new forces must be developed. And when man invades space, still other destructive forces will undoubtedly call for new product tests.

Some giant retailers have established or are establishing testing labs to check the goods they sell. Examples are Sears Roebuck, Montgomery Ward, J. C. Penney, and R. H. Macy.

Public utilities, as, for instance, in Philadelphia, are testing home appliances for safety.

Both industry and the public have become more aware of testing as the result of a wave of accidental deaths directly traceable to poor product testing or bad design that could have been corrected by proper testing. The electrocution of a two-year-old baby by a TV set was one example.

Yet despite all the talk about testing, some manufacturers still don't bother with it, either because they are ignorant of test procedures or because they don't appreciate the need and the potential benefits.

Fortunately, to meet the demand for better and more intensive testing, the whole art of testing is advancing. Older techniques, such as nondestructive, accelerated-life, and simulated-environmental testing, are keeping step with the march of technology, and techniques are being developed to cope with newly discovered destructive forces, such as stress corrosion.

ACCELERATED LIFE TESTS

At the ever-increasing pace of product development today, accelerated life tests are becoming more and more significant. Manufacturers no longer have several years for thorough field-testing of prototypes. Often, if the new product isn't marketed quickly, it will be obsolete before it has a chance to get started.

Fortunately, the well-known techniques of accelerated life testing are improving steadily. For example, five years ago it took 144 hours of testing to judge whether a coat of paint would last one year. Today, this test takes only eight hours, with a comparable drop in test costs.

MANY KINDS OF TESTS

Sample testing to destruction is accepted procedure on mass-produced goods. But when the product is a huge, one-of-a-kind piece of equipment, testing to destruction is out of the question. The solution is one of the many nondestructive tests, like the use of plastic models and stress-coating to reveal undesirable stresses, X-rays and ultrasonics to detect subsurface faults, and ultraviolet and magnetic dust techniques to reveal surface weaknesses.

Extremes of temperature are the most common environments duplicated in the laboratory. But other field conditions reproduced under control are: high altitude, salt spray, high humidity, fungus, dust, shock, thermal shock, thermal cycling, acceleration, wear, mechanical and acoustic vibration, nuclear bombardment, and combinations of all these. The costs of simulation run from a few hundred dollars for a one-cubic foot "cold box" to millions for a nuclear materials testing reactor or the huge new environmental chamber installed by Douglas Aircraft.

As field conditions become more strenuous, we uncover destructive forces that, in some cases, were never known before. For example, back in 1952, when the engines on the prototype B-52 were run up to full power for the first time, mysterious cracks

appeared in wings and tail surfaces in about fifteen minutes. Boeing engineers soon found that the intense noise produced by the jets was the destructive force. Since that time the destructive power of intense sound waves has been well established. The acoustic vibration (which is completely unrelated to mechanical vibration) not only weakens structures but also causes electronic equipment to go haywire. To test materials, structural parts, and equipment for their ability to resist acoustic vibration, every aircraft manufacturer and many electronics companies have constructed ingenious noise makers supplemented by elaborate instrumentation. The largest and loudest "noise rooms" run up to hundreds of thousands of dollars.

The Space Age will make even greater testing demands on airframe makers. They will have to duplicate forces and environments that we can't even imagine now. However, the versatility of test facilities seems to be keeping up with the technological race. The minimum speed—32,400 mph—needed to escape from the earth's gravitational field was recently achieved, for one-tenth of a second, at the Air Force's test-center wind tunnel in Tullahoma, Tennessee.

Because of its traditional concern with reliability, the aircraft industry has long been devoted to extensive and expensive testing. Other industries often copy its methods. But some of the test facilities are so costly that no one company can afford them. In these cases, cooperative facilities, like the giant wind tunnel at California Tech, are sometimes built. This cooperative approach to expensive facilities could be the answer for other industries.

ESTABLISHING A TEST DEPARTMENT

If you don't have a test department, or if you want to reorganize the one you have, you should first hire a competent, experienced, and well-trained test engineer to run your lab. An upgraded technician or a cast-off design engineer won't do.

In fact, test engineers, a practical and detail-conscious breed, are becoming a separate branch of engineering. Recently, one special group organized its own national professional society, called the Institute of Environmental Engineers.

Small companies are at a disadvantage in setting up test labs, because it is no longer possible to hire a single jack-of-all-trades to handle all technical problems. Each technical specialty is growing in complexity. Now industry needs teams of test engineers who know how to use costly, specialized devices and supervise tests that cross scientific and technical boundaries.

At a certain point, however, the big company loses the advantage of bigness in setting up a lab. When one of the nation's largest appliance manufacturers built a complex of plants making a number of different products, a central testing lab was constructed. In a short time, the company discovered that the problems of scheduling all the diverse products of the area at one lab were overwhelming. It took longer and

longer to get products tested. The solution was to construct a test lab for each division. The decentralized labs seem wasteful of men and materials, but they were the only way to insure adequate and rapid testing.

Although the director of a test laboratory must have the imagination and ingenuity to invent unusual test procedures and testing machines, it's helpful to know that there are several organizations in the country that also develop standard test procedures. In textiles, the American Association of Textile Chemists and Colorists in Lowell, Massachusetts, is an excellent source. Consumers' Research in Washington, N. J., often supplies information on its test methods to manufacturers on request. Some of the procedures developed by the American Society for Testing Materials, Philadelphia, apply to end products, such as paint.

Many of the thousands of test specifications prepared by the Armed Forces apply to products that are essentially commercial equipment with a coat of khaki paint. These specs could be adapted for nonmilitary use. The many nonprofit and independent test labs are also sources of test procedures.

The National Bureau of Standards tests many end products for the Government, and the results used to be available to the public. But ever since the famous Astin affair in 1953, involving a very questionable battery additive, the NBS has adopted the politically expedient policy of keeping mum about its testing of consumer products.

WHERE TO REPORT

If possible, a test lab manager should report directly to top management. If the test lab is under Production, there is always the possibility that the test manager will be pressured into approving a below-spec production run. If the lab is part of Engineering and Development, there is some risk that the test engineer will not adopt a sufficiently critical attitude toward new designs.

One danger that many test lab managers warn against is undue influence from the sales department. Under pressure from sales managers to provide something new each year, many companies hastily add new attachments or accessories to their products. These parts should be thoroughly tested by the company, even if the basic design of the product is not affected.

Having the test manager report directly to the higher echelons doesn't help, however, if the man he reports to isn't qualified to interpret the results or hasn't the time to study the report. Of course, for easy interpretation, the report should not be a bleak mass of statistics, but should be related to the market. For example, merely listing all leakage currents from an electrical or electronic device doesn't tell much if the individual currents are not related to state, underwriter, or industry standards for prevention of shock.

The independent test laboratory plays a many-faceted and vital role in product testing and can be useful to all types and sizes of manufacturers. For the small company, it provides complete or supplementary test services, designs test procedures, or acts as a consultant when a company is setting up its own lab. For the large manufacturer, the independent lab handles temporary overloads, helps keep the company lab on its toes by checking its tests, and performs acceptance tests on large equipment (with seller and buyer often splitting the costs of the test).

Many manufacturers hire independent test services as a marketing aid. A tag bearing a seal of approval is attached to the product or a note is added to the brochure or catalog page. A reputable lab strictly controls this use of its name.

CONSUMER TESTING

Another reason for careful product testing is the increase in testing by independent consumer groups, large retailers, and trade associations. The number of consumers influenced by Consumers' Research (Washington, New Jersey) and Consumers Union (Mt. Vernon, New York), is growing each year. A bad rating in the magazines published by these two organizations can cut sales among an influential group of urban buyers. A good rating can sometimes help establish a stronger demand for a new product.

If a manufacturer receives a bad rating from one of the consumer test magazines, he needn't sit stewing. Frederick J. Schlink, head of Consumers' Research, is quite willing to talk over the rating and suggest changes to improve the product. The lab machines and test methods of Consumers' Research have been adopted in many instances by industry. Similarly, if any manufacturer questions the test results of Consumers Union, he will receive a complete test procedure on request.

If a manufacturer receives a good rating from the testing magazines, he is not permitted to publicize the fact or use the names of these organizations in his ads. But some companies have been getting around this prohibition by buying a number of newsstand copies of the magazines and giving one to each distributor or door-to-door salesman.

TESTING BY RETAILERS

Dealing with the test labs of the giant retailers is another matter. Here, huge orders are involved. Recently, one of the big mail-order houses had to settle a claim for $120,000, because a power tool it sold fatally shocked a user. Manufacturers can expect these retailers to rely even more on their test labs.

The test procedures used by these labs are also available on request. R. H. Macy's Bureau of Standards, which tests for the nation-wide chain of stores associated with Macy's, frequently confers with the manufacturers of goods it tests, according to Daniel Chaucer, laboratory manager.

Trade associations are also becoming more aware of testing (although none has gone so far as the Japanese camera industry, which has set up a lab to test and certify each lens). The Air Moving and Conditioning Association, for example, inspects the test laboratories of member companies. Companies whose labs are approved are given the right to attach a seal to their products.

THE FUTURE OF TESTING

If, in the future, computers are for the most part directing high volume plant operations, it's only reasonable to assume that considerable high-volume product testing will also be run by computers. Already, test data collected during the flights of new missiles and aircraft are computer-analyzed. But as testing grows inevitably more complicated, experienced and resourceful test directors will be increasingly in demand and increasingly hard to come by—a reflection of the general shortage of good technical people.

Good product testing costs money and takes time. Even so, it doesn't insure perfect performance. Nor does it replace field testing or proper operation and good maintenance. But it's still a lot cheaper than replacing guaranteed parts, taking back the merchandise, or losing customers, a lawsuit, and your reputation.

►►►►►►►►►► 146 REMINDERS FOR LAUNCHING THE PROMOTION OF A NEW OR REDESIGNED PRODUCT

Printers' Ink

THE PRODUCT AUDIT

1. Determine all the sales points.
2. Segregate sales points by appeal to:
   a. The distributors: (1) Jobbers. (2) Dealers.
   b. The consumer.
3. Make a comparative audit of sales points with leading competing products.
4. Does the product lend itself to multiple uses?
5. Is the guarantee correct? Do we need a new or different guarantee? Is a guarantee desirable?

PRODUCT ACCESSORIES

6. Is the labeling in keeping with the product design?
7. Should the label be more informative?
   a. To fit into modern consumer thinking?
   b. To aid retail clerks in selling?
   c. To emphasize main sales points to consumers?
   d. To comply with the law?
8. Is a special shipping carton needed for better shipping or to advertise the product in transit?
9. Is the consumer package adapted to the retail outlets?

10. Is the consumer package effective in window, shelf, and counter display?
11. Is the consumer package effective in advertising illustration?
12. Is the consumer package effective on television?
13. Is the consumer package suitable for automatic vending?
14. Does the consumer package sell the product?
15. Is the consumer package as advanced in design as the product?
16. Are instruction sheets needed?
17. Are instructions sufficiently clear?
18. Do the instruction sheets take full advantage of the new design features?
19. Are the sheets styled to be as modern and practical as the newly designed product?

THE MARKET

20. Who will use the product?
21. Does the new design open up possibilities of new groups of prospects?
22. How will the income status of logical prospects affect the merchandising?
23. What are the growth possibilities of the product?
24. What is the present consumption of products of this type? Will the new design increase the consumption? Can we forecast by how much?

25. Who are the important factors in merchandising the new design? (Jobbers, dealers, salesmen, etc.)

26. What has been the past influence in the market of such factors as style, quality, service, durability?

27. Will the new design change the weight of these factors?

28. When is the best time of the year to introduce new designs?

29. Should we bring out the new design at a time when the trade is unaccustomed to new designs, or should the trade trend be ignored?

30. What competition will the new product face?

31. Is the competition design-conscious?

32. Is the new design a pioneer in its field or is it being used because competitors have set the new design pace?

33. Will it be desirable, in introducing the new design, to change price, discount, allowance, and other similar policies? (Often a sweeping change in design gives excellent opportunity to inaugurate long-needed reforms in such policies.)

34. Will the new design open up possibilities for getting new distributors or more distributors?

35. Is extension of distribution set-up, assuming it is possible, desirable?

36. Is introduction of the new design going to make possible dropping undesirable outlets?

37. How long can the design be maintained without a major change?

38. How will the new design affect servicing policies of manufacturer, jobbers, and dealers?

39. What is the relation of the newly designed product to the rest of the line?

40. Will it necessitate radical redesign of other products in the line?

THE REPLACEMENT PROBLEM

41. If the product is radically different in design from a product it supersedes, what arrangements should be made to clear out old merchandise before new design is introduced?

42. Can we shift merchandise among the dealers so that stocks are equalized in an area? (Dealers with overstocks of old product transfer some of their stock to dealers who are understocked, and so on until stocks are cleaned out.)

43. Can special sales drives clean dealers out of old merchandise before new design is introduced?

44. How much will it cost to accept turn-ins of unsold old stock and credit against purchase of new design?

THE SALES DEPARTMENT

45. How should the new design be introduced to the sales force? Sales convention, sales meetings, by mail, by branch managers, or by some other method? Or by several methods?

46. Will the salesmen need special education to get the most out of selling the new design? If so, what is the most effective and economical method of doing the educational work?

47. Will special material be needed in this educational program?

48. What methods will be most effective in stimulating salesmen to put full drive behind the new design? Sales contests, revised compensation system, special quotas, or other methods?

49. What changes in salesmen's equipment will introduction of new design necessitate?

a. New sample cases?
b. Miniature models?
c. Films and film-showing equipment?
d. Drawings and blueprints?
e. Pictures of new designs?
f. Advertising portfolio?
g. Demonstrating equipment?
h. Visual sales presentation?
i. Other new equipment?

50. What part will branch managers play in the introduction of the new design?

51. What will missionary men do in introduction of the new design?

52. Will it be desirable for salesmen to hold meetings with jobber salesmen?

53. Should regular salesmen do clerk-education work? Or will it be desirable to use missionary men for this?

54. What methods can be used to keep up salesmen's interest in the new design after their first enthusiasm has worn off?

55. Will it be desirable to ask salesmen to cooperate in drawing up the most effective sales program to move the new design?

56. Is the manufacturer overlooking any opportunities to get the salesmen enthusiastic about new design?

THE JOBBER

What methods will be used to get jobber cooperation?

57. Jobber meetings?
58. Meetings of jobbers' sales forces?
59. Special promotion campaign directed at jobbers?
60. Work of individual salesmen with individual jobbers?

61. Will special sales material be needed in working with jobbers?

62. Will special deals be desirable?

63. How can jobbers be shown the opportunity that the new design gives them to open desirable new outlets?

64. Will the new design present any new warehousing or shipping problems to jobbers? If so, how can these be solved most effectively?

65. If the new design simplifies warehousing and shipping problems, how important is this fact as a sales argument with jobbers?

66. How can jobbers cooperate to help solve the replacement problem?

67. Will jobbers' salesmen need special sales equipment in selling the new design? If such equipment is not necessary, will it be desirable?

68. If it is not against jobber policy, should special stimulation methods and devices be used to encourage jobbers' salesmen to get behind the marketing of the new design?

69. Will jobbers and their salesmen cooperate in placing special advertising material promoting the new design? Should they be offered special inducements for doing so?

70. Will the new design make possible the opening of new jobber outlets?

THE DEALER

What methods will be used to get dealer cooperation?

71. Dealer meetings?
72. Meetings of dealers' clerks?
73. Special promotion directed at dealers?
74. Work by the manufacturer's missionary men?

75. Work by the manufacturer's regular salesmen?
76. Work by the jobbers' salesmen?
77. Deals?
78. Special advertising material:
   a. Counter displays.
   b. Window displays.
   c. Other types of store displays.
   d. Direct-mail material to be mailed either (1) by dealer, or (2) by manufacturer for dealer.
   e. Mats, electros, etc.
   f. Printed material (folders or booklets) for counter distribution.
   g. Informative labeling designed to help clerks.
   h. Special material tailored to self-service outlets.
79. Material designed particularly for dealer clerks.
80. Business-paper advertising.
81. Advertising portfolios shown to dealers by manufacturer's or jobber's salesmen.
82. Films to be shown to dealers.
83. Premiums.
84. Will the new design present any special storage problems? If so, how can these be most effectively solved?
85. If the new design simplifies storage problems, how can this fact be most effectively capitalized?
86. Does the new design lend itself to departmentalization in the store? (That is, setting up a special department or counter in the store where the product is sold.)
87. If the product is already being sold departmentally, is the dealer material on the new design planned to get the most out of this?

88. Will the new design lend itself better than the old to cross-selling?
89. What is the best method of doing the replacement job (see 41–44) with dealers? Is the replacement plan designed to give the dealer a fair break on his returns so that there will be no ill-will?
90. Does the product lend itself to demonstration? If so, will dealers cooperate in furnishing demonstration space or furnishing demonstrators?
91. Are special dealer inducements (allowances) desirable, if they come within Robinson-Patman requirements?
92. Can special promotions in department stores be built around the new design?

EMPLOYEES (OTHER THAN SALESMEN)

Is it desirable to get employees enthusiastic about the new design? If so, what methods can be used?

93. Employee magazine?
94. Factory and office posters?
95. Posting of advertising reproductions in factory or office?
96. Pay-envelope enclosures?
97. Meeting of employees?
98. Making employees salesmen of product in own community?

STOCKHOLDERS

How will new design be featured to stockholders? Via:

99. Dividend enclosures?
100. Special emphasis in annual or semiannual reports?

101. Special mailing to stockholders?

102. Special offer to stockholders whereby they actually purchase the product through the company?

103. Coupon or similar plan that will send stockholders to retail outlets to purchase the product?

THE CONSUMER

What media shall be used to reach the consumer?

104. Newspapers and farm papers?
105. Magazines?
106. Other periodicals?
107. Radio and television?
108. Car or bus cards?
109. Outdoor?
110. Theater programs?
111. Window displays?
112. Counter displays?
113. Store displays?
114. Novelties?
115. Booklets, folders, or similar printed material?
116. Direct mail?
117. Catalogs?
118. Motion pictures?
119. Other media?
120. Shall the newly designed product be sampled?
121. Is a premium plan desirable for the introduction?
122. Is a contest plan desirable?
123. Should the product be demonstrated in the retail store or in the home?
124. Should other methods be used to take the story of the new design into the home?
125. Has the new design a news value of interest to consumer publications?

126. Is the merchandising plan so designed that it gives a complete, uninterrupted follow-through from manufacturer, through jobber and dealer, to the consumer?

THE ADVERTISING

127. Does the new design lend itself to a new advertising appeal?
128. Does it require a drastic reconsideration of medium policies?
129. Does it require new copy treatment?
130. Does it require new art treatment?
131. Is the new art treatment thoroughly in harmony with the new product design?
132. Does the present trade mark need redesigning?
133. Is the present advertising agency adequate to do the merchandising of the new design?
134. Shall the new design be made the exclusive basis of the new advertising campaign or should other appeals be featured?
135. Does the present slogan fit the needs of the new design or is a new slogan needed?
136. What features of the new design should be emphasized?
137. Are any inexpensive methods of promotion being overlooked?
   a. Package inserts?
   b. Envelope enclosures?
   c. Letterheads?
   d. Envelopes?
   e. Shipping cartons?
   f. Trucks, salesmen's cars, freight cars?
   g. Factory display space seen by consumers?

h. Reception room?

i. Shipping and mailing labels?

138. Does the advertising overemphasize design at the expense of performance features?

139. Should the copy be pre-tested?

140. Does the advertising capitalize on the fact that the company has always been a design pioneer?

141. If the company has not been a design pioneer, does the new advertising emphasize the fact that the company is now assuming leadership?

142. Are the advertising and sales-promotion efforts properly meshed?

143. Is the advertising appropriation sufficient to do the promotion job?

144. Is a new method of determining the appropriation needed?

145. Should a reserve fund be set up in order to keep the administration of the appropriation flexible?

146. Is the appropriation properly safeguarded against encroachments of expenses that are not justifiably charged to advertising?

►►►►►►►►►►► WHAT ARE THE SIGNS THAT TELL A COMPANY WHEN *NOT* TO LAUNCH A NEW PRODUCT?

Printers' Ink

A constant theme in conversations about marketing is new-product development. Though dozens of new products and variations on old products debut every day, most of them are short lived. A lot of time, effort and money are put into the launching of new products that should never have left the experimental stages.

In the grocery field, for example, about 80 per cent of the 6,000 or so new products introduced annually fail. While many companies are aware of these statistics and take care to minimize the possibility of failure for their products, few are as careful as they should be.

The following is a true story of a new product which *didn't* get to market. For competitive reasons, identities are hypothetical.

Last January, the Xavier Co., a leading manufacturer of grocery items, got a suggestion from its sales department: Why not put out a ready-mix for goodies? There seems to be an increasing demand for them.

On investigation, Xavier's new-products department found that the goody mix market was indeed growing and profitable. At the time, only two firms were getting the major share of the business (the Able Co. and Baker, Inc., see chart). The market held growth potential, and the share "held by all others" seemed an attractive target.

Since the company already made a cookie mix and packaged nuts, which many housewives combined to make goodies, a one-package mix would simplify the procedure and very likely broaden the company's market beyond the scope of the two separate products. Also, Xavier found it could compete with the leaders on price and quality, and have the additional advantage of its famous name.

Consumer surveys revealed strong acceptance for goody mixes, and both the other major manufacturers were building good volume. Everything pointed to the advisability of marketing this new product.

From here, the procedure followed the normal company routine of new-product development. First, the new-products department gave the laboratory the specifications for the mix. Basically, it had to be better than goody mixes already on the market, and better than a combination of the company's own cookie mix and packaged nuts.

The lab technicians worked on these specifications for months before they came up with a product that could pass the standards of the test kitchen. After the test kitchen approved the proposed product, it was distributed for a blind consumer test. A panel of more than 1,200 families tried the mix without knowing which company had produced it. Relatively few consumers did not respond favorably. Most of their comments ranged from "excellent" to "very good."

FULL-SCALE PLANNING GETS UNDERWAY

By this time, a product manager had been appointed to handle the new item. Cost accounting had already computed its costs. Plans for an advertising campaign were well underway. The ad department and Xavier's agency developed a program that ranged all the way from newspaper, radio and television ads down to label design and store displays.

A test market was selected. The pro-

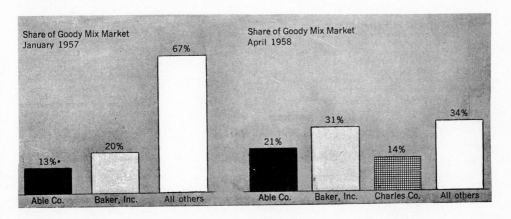

A TIGHTER MARKET CHANGES A COMPANY'S NEW PRODUCT PLANS

duction department then began arrangements to run test batches and iron out any production kinks. The company's engineering department surveyed the need for new or additional requirements.

Up to this point, the money spent on the new product was negligible. From now on, each step in the marketing process would be costly.

But the market picture suddenly changed. (See chart.) What had been an open market tightened up as the major competitors strengthened their grip. Instead of anticipating a share of market based on uncommitted customers, Xavier would now have to plan on fighting to win away part of the market share held by its chief competitors, the Able Co. and Baker, Inc. To make the prospects for success in launching the product even more formidable, a new competitor, the Charles Co., moved into the field.

THE PICTURE CHANGES

A *pro forma* profit and loss statement, which had been prepared on the basis of the initial market data, had indicated that marketing the new mix would require extensive investment, and that it would be some time before the break-even point would be reached. Such an investment had been valid at that time, but now the picture was changed. Rather than take a chance with the new product, Xavier decided to write off its relatively small investment, and forget about the marketing of goody mixes for the time being.

One day, the goody mix market may present new opportunities. When it does, Xavier will be ready with a good product. For now, the company is holding its fire and saving funds that might otherwise have gone into an uphill fight with only a limited chance of success.

►►►►►►►►►► B

Key Elements of the Marketing Mix

►►►►►►►►►►► PLANNING YOUR PACKAGE

W. H. ENZIE*

Too often, a package is designed and put into production with little or no consideration given to marketing problems and opportunities. The marketing man, in turn, may become impatient with the package designer's timetable because he is unaware of the many steps that must be taken to develop a package structure and design that provides adequate product protection, is marketing oriented, and which also can be produced at a cost that permits the product to be priced competitively.

It is reasonable to assume, too, that administrative executives concerned with costs may question the need for substantial expenditures for market research, laboratory testing, and other costs involved in package planning and development.

This article is intended, therefore, to provide proper perspective in the planning and development of packages for everyone in industry who is, in one way or another, concerned with product packaging.

Package planning, as it is known to-

Reprinted with permission from "Modern Packaging Encyclopedia '62," Modern Packaging, November 1961, pp. 26–29.

Manager, Packaging Development and Procurement, General Foods Corporation.

519

day, represents a relatively new technology in the manufacture and merchandising of foods, clothing, drugs, instruments and the many other items that flow from our production complex. In the early 1900s, there was little choice of packaging materials except for wood, natural fibres, glass and tinned steel cans. Marketing of consumer products as we now know it, with a multitude of consumer items competing for the shopper's attention and often in self-service stores, did not exist and there was less need for package planning with consumer appeal in mind.

The packaging of foods and drugs undoubtedly involves more problems and factors to be considered than is the case with other products. In planning packages for nonfood items, many of the criteria established for planning of food packages will, of course, be applicable. A logical point of departure in gaining a fresh perspective on package planning for any product is, therefore, a review of package planning as it should be conducted in the field of foods.

More than 100 years ago, the first "canned" foods were supplied to Napoleon's soldiers, and later became civilian consumer items. Actually, they were packed in glass jars. The "tin can" came later. Glass still has protective properties no other material can match or exceed, and glass containers will be with us for the foreseeable future.

They do, however, have shortcomings as used in today's large-scale food processing and marketing. Some of these shortcomings have been reduced

through research, and others may yield to some degree as the result of future developmental work. Fragility presents problems in high-speed packing lines. Glass containers can be mass-produced economically only in a cylindrical shape, and this shape wastes about 25% of the space in a shipping carton or on a store shelf. Glass is heavy and increases shipping costs. Jars are more difficult to handle than many newer types of packages, and labor costs in food stores thus are affected. The curved surface does not provide as effective display of product identification, and the label may be turned to the rear when shelved.

Long ago, too, the can took its rightful place on grocery shelves alongside the glass container. Being cylindrical, it shares that shortcoming with the glass jar. Also, it will dent and it lacks transparency. Its strength and light weight are major assets. Both glass and metal containers are low in cost and have been so maintained by continuance of manufacturing efficiencies.

The volume production of paper cartons and containers at reasonable cost gradually nudged the barrels and bins out of the food stores, and bulk display of flour, sugar, crackers and other consumer items eventually gave way to the more sanitary and convenient individual carton which we know today.

In recent years, the availability of new, flexible materials has permitted packaging to take rapid forward strides. The introduction of many new foods, or foods in new forms—frozen foods, cake mixes, ready-mix desserts, for example—has required the improvement of older-type packaging materials, the use of new materials, and in some cases the wedding of several different materials. Packaging has become a complex science and today's packages are being engineered by experts from many fields working together.

EARLY PLANNING ESSENTIAL

The importance of early review of all known factors to be considered in developing packaging for new or improved products is increasingly recognized, especially in the field of consumer products. Package development goes hand-in-hand with product development, and no longer can the package be regarded as just simply a convenient means of enabling a product to be transported from where it is produced to where it is sold or consumed.

A successful technique for a practical approach to package planning is to separate the over-all job into three categories:

1. Marketing considerations
2. Product protection
3. Economic factors

The next step is to establish a list of criteria for each of these categories against which packaging concepts can be measured. To accomplish this, it is necessary first to establish what is expected and needed in a package for the particular product involved.

Using these criteria, logical and economic packaging concepts can be evaluated to provide the optimum combination of properties, design characteristics and production cost to meet the packaging requirements established for the product.

MARKETING CONSIDERATIONS

Thousands of products, both old and new, are competing for a position on food store shelves and there is not room for them all. The product that wins against others in the race is the product that has been both developed and packaged so it actually is marketing oriented.

The success of package planning, therefore, depends on identifying all important criteria that enter into marketing considerations. Since the first sale of the product must be to the retailer, factors important to him always must be given early consideration in package designing. These include:

1. Shelf stacking characteristics and shelf space required
2. Ease of price marking
3. Quantity of packages per case
4. Ease of case identification
5. Ease of removing packages from case for shelving
6. Pilferage protection achieved through package size and design, especially where small items have relatively high value
7. Resistance to package failure or product spoilage

CONSUMER CONVENIENCE

Having made sure that the package and case conform to the retailer's requirements, full attention then must be given to consumer reactions to the package. If the product does not move and turn over at a rate profitable to the retailer, it soon will lose its position on store shelves.

A thorough understanding of how

and where the product is used is a most important factor in establishing packaging criteria. Misconceptions or inadequate information concerning ultimate use of the product, and the steps the consumer must go through to use it, can spell failure for that product. Thorough analysis and understanding of consumer use is needed to identify clearly the advantages of one type of package over another. Examples of this:

1. Will special opening, pouring or reclosure devices make it easier to use the product?

2. Are the package size and shape suitable for storage facilities normally found in the home?

3. Is the package easy to carry, easy to handle, easy to open?

4. If directions for preparation or use are important, are they easy to read and readily understandable?

5. Can the package provide extra use convenience, such as boilable bags for heating foods, or aerosols for ease of use?

6. Are there secondary use possibilities such as packing the product in glass containers that can later be used as juice glasses, or in plastic containers that later can be used for refrigerator food storage?

7. Is the package able to be disposed of readily?

Display Shelving and store lighting conditions vary considerably from store to store, and from one store section to another.

In self-service stores especially, graphic design of the package is of great importance. Under all lighting and shelving conditions, the package must do a selling job, and this calls for the best in design. The product must be identified quickly and easily, even when stacked flat. The price must be easy to locate and read, and design should provide eye-catching qualities important in producing impulse sales. The basic structural design of the package must provide the graphic designer with the opportunity to produce such a package.

Usually, the package should be planned to be recognizably better than competitive product packages. In a section where a variety of competitors' packages are "shouting" for attention through busy design and riotous colors, a plainer, quieter package may stand out. Conversely, where a line of products has traditionally been sold in packages that are drab and ultra-conservative, a package with a modern design may attract the impulse buyer.

Optimum image A deciding factor in considering a new package may be the product image already established in the consumer's mind.

Knowledge of consumer attitudes in this area is invaluable in planning a package acceptable to consumers, and considerable consumer research may be necessary.

Since this is an involved phase of package planning, only a few of the questions that should be raised are outlined here to suggest the part the product image should play in package planning.

1. Should the package suggest by design a deluxe or premium product, or does a theme of economy and practicality fit the marketing concept?

2. Might use of a radically new packaging concept create barriers against consumer acceptance? For example: edible films are available for wrapping foods, but is the consumer ready to "eat the package," and would the cost of educating the consumer to try to accept the edible film be worth-while?

3. Does the proposed size, shape, or type of bottle for a food, say salad dressing, conjure up an image of a different type of product—such as a shampoo?

4. Would a food product packed in an aerosol container meet with resistance because of consumer identification with insecticides or shaving creams?

These are but a few of the possibilities that must be considered, analyzed and, if possible, tested through consumer research in developing the new package.

PRODUCT PROTECTION

Since the first requirement of packages is to deliver the goods to store shelves and consumer cupboards in good condition and at lowest cost, the important new materials available today should be considered.

Food manufacturers today work closely with paper companies, chemical manufacturers and producers of other packaging materials, such as plastics and aluminum foil. Many of these suppliers have applications research laboratories to work out packaging problems in cooperation with independent package design firms and with the packaging laboratories of their customer-manufacturers. Frequently there is a wedding of several materials to provide the exact properties needed.

An example of such an approach will suggest the possibilities of modern packaging technology.

A dry salad-dressing mix, made in six different flavor combinations, contains spices and seasonings. The mixes have delicate fugitive flavors that must be retained within the envelope until the consumer is ready to use the mixes in preparing salad dressings. For this line of products, a five-layer flexible package was developed.

The outer layer is a reverse-printed cellophane laminated to paper to protect it and to enhance the appearance of product identification, and a full-color illustration. The paper is used to provide package strength and rigidity. It is laminated, in turn, to aluminum foil by means of a thin, extruded film of polyethylene. Lastly, the inside of the foil is coated with a vinyl lacquer. The foil provides an effective flavor barrier needed to retain the flavors of the product, and also is an effective barrier against moisture. The plastics on either side of the foil protect it from losing its barrier characteristics while being formed, filled and distributed. The vinyl lacquer used on the inside is compatible with the food with which it is in contact. Additionally, it is heat sealable.

In this package, each material was selected to provide certain needed properties, functions or economic qualities. The results have been highly successful—as proved by shipments of millions of cases over an extended period.

Sometimes new ideas provided by makers of packaging materials are excellent except for one thing—they are not marketing oriented. The manufacturer of foods and other consumer goods must always consider the product image that has become established in the consumer's mind. To deliver an established product in a form unfamiliar—and perhaps unacceptable—to the consumer is to invite marketing disaster.

Other good packaging ideas may not turn out to be usable because they are not suitable for high-speed production lines.

When planning a package in cooperation with a manufacturer of packaging materials, there must be a combination of knowledge in which the packaging expert combines his knowhow in the field of materials with the production and marketing skills of the consumer goods manufacturer.

SPECIAL PROTECTIVE FACTORS

There are special factors to consider in planning a package for product protection. These include:

Water-vapor protection Products requiring water-vapor protection fall into two categories: dry products and products having high moisture content. The first, such as cereal, crackers or dehydrated foods, needs a barrier to keep water-vapor out of the package. The second, such as frozen foods, bread or tobacco, needs a barrier to prevent loss of moisture.

Protecting a product from water-vapor transfer—in or out—usually increases package costs in ratio to the degree of protection needed. It is important, therefore, to establish the optimum level of protection required for any particular product.

The critical moisture level must be determined for a dry product, taking into consideration the levels at which caking, toughness or odor development occur.

Shelf life required of the product also must be considered. Since water-vapor transfer is a function of time, the expected shelf life must be taken into consideration in establishing the degree of protection required.

Climate is a factor, too. The degree of protection needed against water-vapor transfer is higher in the humid climate of southern Florida or the Texas Gulf Coast than in the northern states. Similarly, protection against drying out of product or package may be needed in certain areas during cold winter weather. Sometimes it is more economical to provide a special package for products shipped to the southern region, while a less costly package can provide a sufficient protection for the product to be sent to other parts of the country.

While available test data can be a guide to selection of packaging materials to provide the required degree of protection from water-vapor transfer, nothing can take the place of actual field tests.

Packages made in the laboratory

will, in many cases, provide considerably more protection than when machine-formed and subjected to the rigors of production packing, shipping and handling.

Greaseproofness The degree of grease protection required can usually be identified by laboratory testing. To provide the required level of protection in production runs, the effects of physical treatment of the packaging material during the set-up must be considered because the operation can have a pronounced effect on grease-barrier properties.

Infestation Products subject to insect infestation must be protected through use of proper packaging materials and structural design of the package.

Strength The physical strength of a package must be sufficient to stand the normal mechanical hazards of shipment and distribution: impact, shock, crushing and vibration. Climatic conditions and standard use cycles also are factors to consider.

There are numerous test methods that can be used in the laboratory to develop a package with the required strength specifications.

Pilferage With the increase in self-service stores in recent years, pilferage has become an ever-present problem. Especially in the case of small items which have relatively high value, the package should be so designed that its size or shape will help to discourage pilferers.

Odor Products subject to ready odor loss or pickup should be protected by materials with low rates of gas transmission. The manufacturer of products that readily absorb odors has no assurance that his products will not be stored or displayed next to odoriferous products, and this is another reason why he must provide adequate protection.

Contamination In packaging foods, drugs or cosmetics, full consideration must be given to safety. Safety is of utmost importance and is under the constant scrutiny of the Government. Where there is the slightest possibility for migration of any components of the package into the product, extra attention must be given to assure safety. There are plastic films, for example, which are excellent materials for containing many products. There is, however, a question that when in contact with certain foodstuffs migration might take place. If so, these materials should not be used for such foods until exhaustive animal feeding tests have established that it is safe to do so. Avoidance of contamination must be kept in mind when any planning and selecting of coupons or premiums is being done.

This is an area in which there can be no compromise or guesswork. The package planner must know.

Gas transmission The presence of oxygen with some foods can cause development of off-flavors and odors. The elimination of oxygen is necessary, therefore, for extended shelf life of such products. In some cases, such as in packaging dry-frozen or freeze-dried products, it is necessary to expel all oxygen from the package and replace it with an inert gas, usually nitrogen. Metal and glass provide the maximum level of protection against gas transmission—in or out—in the finished package. Flexible packaging materials, such as foil, have excellent gas-barrier properties in the flat, but may lose some of these properties in the package-forming operation. When these materials are used, this must be taken into consideration.

Effect of light Many products require protection against light. Foils, opaque plastics, paper, metal and colored glass provide such protection, and can be specified according to product needs.

ECONOMIC CONSIDERATIONS

Packaging costs are, of course, a factor that must be considered to a greater or lesser degree, depending on the product. In the case of an expensive instrument, a metal-cutting tool, an electronic component, or a piece of jewelry, the cost of the package itself may be relatively unimportant. In fact, an expensive-looking package may be a factor in making sales. Moreover, it is false economy to save pennies and sacrifice protective properties in designing a package to contain costly products such as those mentioned above. An adequate package must be provided regardless of extra cost.

For mass-produced consumer goods such as foods, however, cost of the container is of great importance, especially in the light of price competition and small profit margins.

Over-packaging and under-packaging can be unnecessarily costly. An important factor in relating package design to costs is, therefore, accurate identification of the kind and degree of protection required.

Some of the factors to be considered when evaluating the economics of any package are:

Costs of packaging materials
Costs of fabrication of the package itself
Usability of existing equipment in forming and filling
Added or reduced manpower
Inventory, shipping and storage costs
Requirements of an adequate case to contain the packages
Refunds and allowances for damaged products
Obsolescence factors indicated by known or anticipated trends in materials, machinery, methods and marketing requirements.

Because there are so many and such complex factors to be considered in developing or improving a package, the goal should be to arrive at a design that provides the best combination of marketing effectiveness, product protection, and costs.

The final measurement of effectiveness of a complete package or of package components is always in commercial experience. No commercially effective package can be designed to give 100% performance under all conditions. It is, however, necessary to find a design that represents the optimum in protection, consumer acceptance and packaging costs.

NEW DEVELOPMENTS

Each day, new packaging ideas and new materials are becoming available to those who are responsible for package planning.

New types of aerosol propellants are being developed to be compatible with various food contents. This could open up whole new fields of packaging possibilities.

New uses are being found for the newer materials. Foam styrene, for example, has been widely used to provide protection against impact and shock in packaging expensive tools and instruments, and other industrial products. Today it is being molded into containers for cosmetics and jewelry, not only for the protection it provides but also for the eye appeal that stimulates sales.

Aluminum containers with pull tabs for quick and easy opening already are here. Frozen orange concentrate and sardine containers are two examples of their use.

As new methods of preserving foods come into wider use, new packaging problems, new materials and new methods will appear.

Aseptic packaging already is here on a limited scale. This packaging technique permits foods to be shipped and stored without dehydration, refrigeration or freezing. The flexible packaging material is sterilized by chemicals, the food by cooking—and the two brought together under sterile conditions.

Dehydro-freezing and freeze-drying each present new packaging requirements and, as these preservation processes come into more extensive use, an entire new phase of packaging may develop.

►►►►►►►►►►► HOW TO PRICE A NEW PRODUCT

JOEL DEAN*

Pricing new products is important in two ways: It affects the amount of the product that will be sold; and it determines the amount of revenue that will be received for a given quantity of sales. If you set your price too high you will be likely to make too few sales to permit you to cover your overhead. If you set your price too low you may not be able to cover out-of-pocket costs.

Reprinted from Edward L. Anthony (editor), Management Aids for Small Business, Annual No. 3, Small Business Administration, Washington, D.C., *1957, pp. 9–16.*
*Joel Dean Associates and Professor of Business Economics, Columbia University.

WHAT IS DIFFERENT ABOUT NEW PRODUCTS?

New products that are novel require a different pricing treatment from old ones because they are distinctive. No one else sells quite the same thing. This distinctiveness is usually only temporary, however. As your product catches on, competitors will try to take away your market by bringing out imitative substitutes. The speed with which your product loses its uniqueness will depend on a number of factors. Among them are the total sales potential, the investment required for rivals to manufacture and distribute the product, the strength of patent protection, and the alertness and power of competitors.

Although competitive imitation is almost inevitable, the company that introduces a new product can use price as a means of slowing the speed with which competitive products are placed on the market. Finding the "right" price is not easy, however. New products are hard to price correctly. This is true both because past experience is no sure guide as to how the market will react to any given price, and because competitive products already on the market are usually significantly different in nature or quality. Therefore, in setting a price on a new product you will want to have three objectives in mind:

1. Getting the product accepted.
2. Maintaining your market in the face of growing competition.
3. Producing profits.

Your pricing policy cannot be said to be successful unless you can achieve all three of these objectives.

WHAT ARE YOUR CHOICES AS TO POLICY?

Broadly speaking, the strategy in pricing a new product comes down to a choice between (1) "skimming" pricing, and (2) "penetration" pricing. There are a number of intermediate positions, of course, but the issues are clearer when the two extremes are compared.

Skimming pricing Some products represent a drastic departure from accepted ways of performing a service or filling a demand. For these a strategy of high prices, coupled with large promotional expenditure in the early stages of market development (and lower prices at later stages), has frequently proven successful. This is known as a skimming price policy. There are four main reasons why this policy is attractive for new and highly distinctive products:

First, the quantity of the product that you can sell is likely to be less affected by price in the early stages than it will be when the product is "full-grown" and competitive imitation has had time to take effect. These early stages form the period when pure salesmanship, rather than price, can have the greatest influence on sales.

Second, a skimming price policy takes the "cream of the trade" at a high price before attempting to penetrate the more price-sensitive sections of the market. This means that you can make more sales to buyers who are willing to pay high prices for a product they want, and at the same time build up experience useful later in hitting the larger mass markets with tempting prices.

Third, you can use this as a way to feel out the demand. It is frequently fairly easy to start out with a high price which some customers may refuse, and reduce it later on when the facts of the product demand make themselves known. But it is often difficult to set a low price initially and then boost the price to cover unforeseen costs or to capitalize on a popular product.

Fourth, high prices will frequently produce a greater dollar volume of sales in the early stages of market development than will a policy of low initial prices. When this is the case, skimming pricing will provide you with funds for financing expansion into the larger volume sectors of your market.

Penetration pricing Nevertheless, a skimming-price policy isn't always the answer to your problem. Although high initial prices may safeguard profits during the early stages of product introduction, they may also prevent quick sales to the many buyers upon whom you must rely to give you a mass market. The alternative is to use low prices as an entering wedge to get into mass markets early. This is known as penetration pricing. This approach is likely to be desirable under the following conditions:

First, when the quantity of product sold is highly sensitive to price, even in the early stages of introduction.

Second, when you can achieve substantial economies in unit cost and effectiveness of manufacturing and distributing the product by operating at large volume.

Third, when your product is faced by threats of strong potential competition, very soon after introduction.

Fourth, when there is no "elite" market—that is, a class of buyers who are willing to pay a higher price in order to obtain the latest and best.

While the decision to price so as to penetrate a broad market can be made at any stage in the product's life cycle, you should be sure to examine this pricing strategy before your new product is marketed at all. This possibility should certainly be explored as soon as your product has established an elite market. Sometimes a product can be rescued from a premature death by adoption of a penetration price policy after the cream of the market has been skimmed.

The ease and speed with which competitors can bring out substitute products is probably the most important single consideration in your choice between skimming and penetration pricing at the time you introduce your new product. For products whose market potential looks big, a policy of low initial prices makes sense, because the big multiple-product manufacturers are attracted by mass markets. However, if you set your price low enough to begin with, your large competitor may not feel it worth his while to make a big production and distribution investment for slim profit margins. For this reason, low initial prices are often termed "stay-out" prices. In any event, you should appraise your particular competitive situation very carefully for each new product before you decide on your basic pricing strategy.

FACTORS YOU SHOULD ANALYZE IN SETTING A PRICE

Once you have decided on your basic pricing strategy, you can then turn to the task of putting a dollars-and-cents price tag on your new product. In order to do this you should analyze at least five important factors:

1. Potential and probable demand for your product.
2. Cost of making and selling the product.
3. Market targets.
4. Promotional strategy.
5. Suitable channels of distribution.

DEMAND

The first step in estimating market demand is to find out whether or not the product will sell at all—assuming that the price is set within the competitive range. That is, you should find out whether or not the product fulfills a real need, and whether enough potential customers are dissatisfied with their present means of filling that need. To do this, you need some measurement of the total potential market for the new product and all its competing substitutes. Then you need to estimate the portion of this total that your product is likely to get.

Following that, you should determine the range of competitive prices. This will be easier when substitutes are relatively similar to your product, or when your customers are familiar with the cost and quality of substitutes and buy primarily on the basis of performance, rather than on the basis of impulse or emotion.

The next step is to try to judge the probable sales volume at two or three possible prices within the price range. The best way to do this is by controlled experiments checking sample sales at different prices. A second best way is by a close examination of the sales volume of other similar products which potential customers might buy.

Finally, you should consider the possibility of retaliation by manufacturers of displaced substitutes. If your new product hits any one of your competitors hard enough, you may be faced with price retaliation. The limit to this price cutting is set by the out-of-pocket cost of the price-cutting competitors. Therefore, knowledge of the out-of-pocket cost of making competing products will be helpful in estimating the probable effects of a particular price.

COSTS OF MAKING AND SELLING

Before going ahead with your new product, you should estimate its effect on your investment, your costs, and your profits. First, you should estimate the added investment necessary to manufacture and distribute the new product. This investment should include estimates of increased working capital that will be required at various sales volumes. Then you should estimate the added costs of manufacturing and selling the product at various possible sales volumes. Frequently, the most satisfactory way of developing these estimates is to calculate *total* costs with and without the new product, rather than attempting to arrive at *unit* costs right at the start. The difference can then be assigned to the new product. Allocations of overheads that you are already incurring should not be assigned to the new product because they will be the same whether or not you go ahead with the addition to your product line.

In building up your two sets of cost and investment figures—one showing the situation *without* the new product, and the other showing the contrasting situation *with* the new product added to your line—be sure to take into account *all* pertinent items. It often happens that companies which lose money on new products have run into trouble because of unanticipated costs or investment requirements which have absorbed most or all the profits realizable from the new idea.

New product costs may be segregated into half a dozen main categories:

1. Direct labor.
2. Materials and supplies for production.
3. Components purchased outside.
4. Special equipment (such as jigs, dies, fixtures, and other tools).
5. Plant overhead.
6. Sales expenses.

Direct labor Methods of estimating direct labor may be built up in one of three ways: (1) You can compare each operation on each component with accumulated historical data, from your files, on similar operations for similar components. (2) You can develop a mockup of the proposed workplace layout, and actually time an operator who performs the series of manufacturing operations, simulated as accurately as possible. (3) You can apply one of several systems of predetermined, basic-motion times which are currently available from private sources. Make certain, however, that you include any added time used for setup work, or needed to take the item from its trans-portation container, perform the operations, and return the item again to its transportation container. When the total direct labor time is determined, multiply it by the appropriate labor rates.

Materials and supplies for production In developing reliable cost figures for materials and supplies, make a methodical list of all requirements. Having listed everything in an organized fashion you can enter the specifications and costs on a manufactured-component estimate form. Remember to include any extra costs which may be incurred as a result of requirements for particular lengths, widths, qualities, or degrees of finish. Allowances for scrap should also be made as accurately as possible and corrected by applying a salvage factor if the scrap can be sold or reused.

Components purchased outside In the case of parts purchased from other concerns, place your specifications with more than one reliable supplier. Get competitive bids for the work. But in addition to price considerations, be sure you give proper weight to the reputation and qualifications of each potential producer. Moreover, if you use a substantial volume of purchased parts you may want to use a "plus" factor above the cost of the components themselves to cover your own expenses involved in receiving, storing, and handling the items.

Special equipment Take careful precautions against making a faulty analysis of your expense and investment in special jigs, dies, fixtures, and other tools which you need to produce the new product. To avoid trouble in this area make a table showing all cases where special equipment will be needed. The actual estimating of the costs of such equipment is best done by a qualified tool shop—your own if you have one or an outside organization. Here again, competitive bidding is an excellent protection on price. Do not include costs of routine inspection, service, and repair; these are properly charged to plant overhead.

Plant overhead The overhead item may be estimated as a given percentage of direct labor, machine utilization, or some other factor determined by your accountants to be the most sensible basis. In this way you can allocate satisfactorily charges for administration and supervision, for occupancy, and for indirect service related to producing the new product. Overhead allocations may be set up for a department, a production center, or even, in some cases, for a particular machine. In calculating plant overhead make certain that in setting up your cost controls, your accountants have not overlooked any proper indirect, special charges which will have to be incurred because of the new product.

Sales expense As in the previous cost categories, the critical element is the *added* sales expense which the new product will involve. To make sure you have included everything, it is often helpful to deal with these expenses in several segments. The following is a simplified checklist: (1) salaries, com-

missions, and traveling expenses; (2) advertising and sales promotion; (3) transportation; (4) credit and collection expenses; (5) warehousing and storage; (6) sales overhead expenses—including office expenses, insurance, depreciation, and the like. Other lists could, of course, be developed, but for greatest usefulness they should be kept as simple as possible and should be organized in terms of the specific selling activities which a company has.

Your estimates of sales revenue at various potential volumes can now be compared with your estimates of added costs at those volumes. The difference will be the added profits of introducing the new product. Although costs themselves probably should not be used as the sole basis for setting price, you should not go into any venture that doesn't produce a rate-of-return on the added investment which (1) is adequate to compensate for the added risk and (2) is still at least as high as the return you could get by investing your money elsewhere. If no price that you set will provide enough revenue to produce an adequate profit over your added costs, then you should either drop the venture, try to cut costs, or wait for a more favorable time to introduce the product.

MARKETING TARGETS

Assuming that the estimates of market demand and of cost and investment have been made, and that the profit picture looks sufficiently rosy, you are now in a position to set up some basic goals and programs. A decision must first be made about market targets—that is, what market share or sales volume should be aimed at? Among other factors, you probably should consider what effect sales expansion in varying amounts will have upon your costs, what effect it will have upon investment requirements, whether or not your existing organization can handle the new product, how it fits in with the rest of your present product line, and so forth. These decisions should be made after an objective survey of the nature of your new product and of your company's organization and manufacturing and distributive facilities.

PROMOTIONAL STRATEGY

Closely related to the question of market targets is the design of promotional strategy. As an innovator, you must not only sell your product, but frequently you must also make people recognize their need for this kind of product. Your problem here is to determine the best way of "creating that market." You must determine the nature of the market and the type of appeal that will secure prompt acceptance by potential buyers. And you should also estimate how much it will cost you to achieve this goal.

CHANNELS OF DISTRIBUTION

Frequently, you'll have some latitude in your choice of channels of distribution. But the channel you pick must be consistent with your strategy for initial pricing and for promotional outlays.

Penetration pricing and explosive promotion, for example, call for channels which can make the product widely and promptly available. Otherwise you waste advertising money or lose the effect of mass-market pricing. Distribution policy also involves how much you want dealers to do in pushing your product, the margins you must give them to get this push, and the degree of exclusiveness of territory and of inventory the dealers insist on.

YOUR DECISION

These are the factors you should analyze in setting a price. Estimating these factors shrewdly and objectively requires specialized training and experience. But good estimates will make your pricing realistic and successful. Pricing cannot, of course, be established by any cut and dried formula. Combining these factors into a pricing policy requires judgment. In the last analysis you must pull together all the estimates of the experts, and arrive at your own decision. It's your money and you're the boss as to how the business is to be run. You will want to make sure that your pricing analysis is guided by sound assumptions, and that the activities of any specialists you use are all geared toward the same end—an effective marketing and promotional program in which the price will meet the objectives of market acceptance, competitive advantage, and profits.

►►►►►►►►►►►► WHAT TYPE OF DISTRIBUTION SETUP
FOR THE NEW PRODUCT?

JOHN ALLEN MURPHY[*]

Since the problem to be met in introducing a new product is likely to vary somewhat in each case, actually scores of different selling methods are used. From these I have selected the methods most generally followed for analysis in this article:

1. USE PRESENT SALES ORGANIZATION AS FAR AS POSSIBLE

In introducing a new product a company should use its present sales organization in so far as it is feasible. . . .

Obviously companies cannot always be making over their sales organizations as they do their lines. If they were to have special salesmen or different distributors or separate marketing channels for each new product, their selling structures would soon become top heavy. Where it can be done, therefore, the best practice is to let the present sales organization take on the new product.

Note that I specify "where it can be done." Unfortunately it cannot always be done. In fact, it can be done with reasonable assurance of success only under very definite situations. Usually such a favorable situation exists when the new product does not depart too widely from the manufacturer's present business. If it is the same general type of product and is sold through pretty much the same trade channels, there is, as a rule, no reason why the regular salesmen cannot sell it. . . .

On the other hand, if a concern departs entirely from its accustomed field with its new product, it may be necessary to employ different selling methods to put it over. . . .

Whether for better or worse much of the product expansion now taking place is of the diversification type. That is, it is spreading companies out into new businesses and into markets that they never penetrated before. All that a company has to do now-a-days is to pursue its by-product opportunities, and before it realizes what is happening, it is operating in a number of industries.

. . . Of course companies that do expand in this way are compelled to diversify their selling methods as well.

But when the average company adopts a new product program, it is best for it not to get too far from its base. In most businesses this leaves plenty of room for expansion and also for a safe degree of diversification. . . .

The point is that a closely knit business is easier to handle, not only from the selling standpoint, but in every other way. Usually a company adds

Adapted by permission from Sales Management, *April 1, 1948, pp. 44–46, 48, 50.*
[*]*Marketing Counselor and former Associate Editor of* Printers' Ink.

new products to round out its line, to take the place of declining items, to increase volume or to make for more economical and more efficient operation. Its purpose will be defeated unless it utilizes as much of its present organization as it can.

2. SPECIAL SALES ORGANIZATIONS FOR NEW PRODUCTS

Often a new product has to be sold differently when it is being introduced than it does after it has been established. A special type of salesman is required to introduce the thing. Then after the market has accepted it, its selling can be turned over to the company's regular salesmen.

Often the new product demands salesmen with missionary zeal. It is necessary to have men who not only can break down resistance for their products, but who can create enthusiasm for them.

In selling a new product it is also important that the salesman be allowed to concentrate. If he has too many articles to sell he cannot do justice to the article being introduced. For this reason many concerns delegate the introduction of a new product to some of their regular salesmen, letting them give full time to the assignment for a few months or longer. In other cases, regular salesmen are obliged to give the first part of their sales presentation to new products.

Of course the idea of missionary salesmen, for both new and old products, is as old as the hills. But it is still as good as ever. . . .

This type of new product selling is employed extensively by chemical manufacturers. They have sales staffs that devote their entire time permanently to introducing new products. These men are usually chemical engineers, who are experts in the application of the products they are selling. They introduce the new line, stay with it for two or three years, or until the "bugs" have been eliminated from its uses. Then they turn it over to the regular salesmen and tackle another new product.

These introductory salesmen may have a roving commission. That is, they will go anywhere if there are prospects in sight. The regular salesmen, on the other hand, are likely to be territorially located. Often the "introducers" specialize. They are paper mill specialists, swimming pool specialists or specialists in the application of plastics, or specialists in any of the numerous branches of this amazingly ramified business.

Some of the regular salesmen may specialize also. Usually, however, they handle all industries in their territories. In many cases the territory has a principal industry. The salesman in that territory just naturally becomes a specialist in that industry. The Detroit salesman, for example, would eventually become an automotive specialist, even though he knew very little about the industry when he entered the territory.

3. THE INDUSTRIAL PRODUCT

The system of selling new products which chemical companies use is the system that is used quite generally in introducing new products to industry. Of course there are many variations in method. But the nucleus of all systems is the salesman. Almost certainly a new product can be sold to industry only through the manufacturer's own salesman. There are exceptions—but they are few. Mill supply houses and independent representatives of various types cannot be expected to bear the entire brunt of introducing a new industrial product, unless there is something about it that commands ready acceptance.

The trick in introducing an industrial product is to do problem-selling. That is, to show how the product can solve the prospect's production problems or contribute in some other way to the efficiency of his business.

4. PRE-TESTING THE NEW PRODUCT

. . . a market study should ordinarily be made before the new product is launched. This should be done principally for two reasons: to find out if there is a market; to determine how the market should be sold. A cross-section study of the contemplated market usually will satisfactorily answer both questions.

Large retail buyers are especially helpful in giving advice on a proposed product. I have often taken samples of such products to chain store and department store buyers and merchandise men and always have been rewarded with valuable suggestions. They will give suggestions as to price, packaging, show cards, etc. They give an idea as to the number of units that should be packed in a package and what sizes there should be. It is significant that new products some-

times do not register with the trade because it is necessary to make too large an investment to try them out. At the outset, it is well to hold down the initial investment as low as possible. Often they will explain why the product cannot be sold, at least without making certain changes. Sometimes they will tell why similar products failed to go over in the past. . . .

A market study also should explore information as to the channels through which retailers prefer to buy such products. It should also reveal how manufacturers in similar lines sell their goods.

5. FRIENDLY DEALERS

Manufacturers who are close to their dealers are in fortunate position when they are introducing new products. Generally a friendly dealer will readily accept a new product from a manufacturer who has been cooperating with him—if the product is in the dealer's line. Of course, the proposition may require some selling, as retailers do not take on everything that even a favorite supplier may ask them to buy. Anyway, experience has proven that when a manufacturer brings out a new item, his present dealers are likely to be the first to stock it. In this way numerous new products are introduced exclusively.

. . . The best part of introductions of this kind is that they generally can be handled by a company's regular salesmen. Often they fill in seasonal valleys and tighten up slack all along the line.

Of course, what I said about friendly

dealers also applies to jobbers and special distributors who are already cooperating with the manufacturer.

6. OWN STORES, OWN DEPARTMENTS

The manufacturer who has stores of his own or his own departments in other stores has no difficulty in getting distribution for a new product in these outlets. . . .

7. MANUFACTURERS' AGENTS

In a number of cases manufacturers have done a good job in selling new products, especially to industry. The manufacturer's agent is about the best way to cultivate a thin market territory. These agents have been tending strongly toward becoming specialists in catering to the predominant industry in their community. . . .

They will often take on a new product if it seems to meet an obvious need in their field.

However, they will be inclined to shy away from a product the need for which is not apparent or for which they have to do all the preliminary educational work. Too often they claim they lost the agency after they did a back-breaking job in introducing a new device.

8. MAIL ORDER

When individuals or small concerns originate new products, they seem to be increasingly disposed to market them through mail-order methods. . . . A favorite medium is Sunday newspaper magazines. Dozens of products, from musical bears to fishing rods, have been advertised. Direct mail, also, is being used in this effort.

After an individual has stormed conventional trade channels with his new product, he could be so discouraged that mail-order selling would seem easy to him. But it is not so easy as it looks. The trouble is that these advertisers think that they can insert a few advertisements and then sit back and watch the orders flow in. Unfortunately, seldom does it happen that way. To make a success of selling by mail requires a persistency of effort and a brilliant follow-up that few advertisers are willing to give. . . .

9. FAIRS, BUSINESS SHOWS

Many a product has been introduced at fairs and shows. The automobile is the most conspicuous example. It is generally conceded that the Automobile Show played a major part in popularizing the automobile to the American public.

Scores of trade shows of different kinds are held throughout the country each year. At these affairs numerous new products receive their initial kickoff. For instance, . . . the annual Toy Fair is held in New York City. Hundreds of new toys are unveiled at this event each year. In this industry the Fair is regarded as the best place and the best way to introduce a new toy. Large attendance indicates extent of buyers' interest.

10. ESTABLISHED PRODUCT SPONSORS NEW PRODUCT

It is a common practice to let the company's established product usher the new product into the market. This is done in a number of fields.

. . . In these cases the buyer gets the new product free or at a special price when he buys the old product.

Often a company with a well established, respected name lets its name carry the new product into the market. . . . This is an effective way of introducing a new product, provided the advertising is backed up with adequate sales follow-through.

11. GETTING MANUFACTURERS TO JOB YOUR NEW PRODUCT

There is a tendency for manufacturers to job products that they do not themselves manufacture. This is done for various reasons: to fill in lines, to give salesmen more to do, to make more economical operation possible. . . .

The maker of a new product might have difficulty to get big concerns to job an unknown article. However, if the new product serves an obvious usefulness, it may be possible to make such an arrangement.

12. LICENSING

If the sponsor of a new product can license it to other manufacturers, he will save himself a lot of grief in building his own market. Licensing arrangements are fairly common, although it must be admitted that few products or processes lend themselves to this type of marketing. D.D.T., the insecticide, . . . is an example of the kind of product that [was] appropriate for licensing.

13. SHALL YOU SELL YOUR MACHINE OR THE PRODUCT THAT IT MAKES?

The inventor of many a machine has been confronted with this question. There are several big industries that started with the invention of a machine. Had the inventor tried to market his machine rather than the product which it manufactured, it is hard to say what would have been the fate of these industries.

The inventor of the machine for shredding wheat is a case in point. He fooled around for several years trying to market his machine. Not until a company was organized to make Shredded Wheat, and not a wheat shredding machine, did the business begin to go places.

NO ONE ANSWER

CONCLUSION

Finally we are led to the conclusion that there is no one best way to sell a new product. Actually, there are scores of ways to sell a new product, all of which may be good ways under certain given conditions.

In some other cases several of these ways might be successfully used at the same time. Different ways can be used in different fields and in different territories and under different situations. It all depends on what the preliminary analysis reveals, on what competition is doing, what the trends are in the field being entered, and what the experience of other manufacturers with similar new products has been.

►►►►►►►►►►► PROMOTING NEW ENTRIES

THOMAS L. BERG[*]

The question of how best to promote a new product is a controversial issue with few clear answers. However, it seems safe to begin with a few basic propositions:

1. The hoary theory of the "better mousetrap" and the popular "hoopla and ballyhoo" school of merchandising have largely been scrapped in actual practice.

2. It is now widely acknowledged that no advertising or promotion campaign can be relied upon to sustain successfully an inferior product over the long pull; the product must itself be good.

3. The sheer *rate* of new-product launchings in recent years has produced changes in the methods used to promote new entries, i.e., a changing promotional environment has required the development of new tactics.

4. Because of their very newness, new products—those in the introductory or growth stages of the product life cycle performing an entirely new function or an old one in a different way—clearly pose different problems, require different objectives and planning approaches, and call for different promotional techniques than do established items.

KEY PROBLEMS

Basically, the main problems in promoting new products relate to two facts: (1) there is a good deal more *buyer resistance to new products* than is commonly recognized, and (2) much *risk and uncertainty* are involved in the promotional task facing new entries to the market.

Today's new-product prospect has been variously described as coy, gunshy, skeptical, bashful, disinterested, fearful, suspicious, reluctant, and procrastinating. The seller faces a fundamental problem of resistance to innovation and change in getting his offering accepted. Changes in attitudes, customs, habits, traditions, and consumption practices are involved in the adoption process. Reluctant consumers must be wooed, and the best ways to romance them are sometimes far from clear. A cacophony of counterclaims compete for attention. The promotional task involves more than simple consumer education as to product function and desirability: it must often induce basic behavioral changes in a high-noise atmosphere.

To draw upon a long-familiar example, rapid initial acceptance was once erroneously predicted for instant coffee.

Reprinted with permission in a slightly modified form. Published under the title "Managerial Aspects of New-Product Promotion" by The Business Quarterly, *Spring 1963, pp. 52–61.*

[*]*Graduate School of Business, Columbia University.*

Sales growth expected on the basis of a strong convenience factor took a long time to materialize. Strong initial resistance to instant coffee was explained as follows: (a) G.I.'s, who were first introduced to "instant" products during World War II, carried a deep-seated dislike for them back to civilian life, (b) some early products were actually inferior in flavor and conveyed few real user satisfactions, (c) during wartime rationing, soluble coffee came to be perceived only as an "emergency" supply, and (d) the image of laziness was stamped on the housewife who took short cuts to coffee making. It took *time*—and a great deal of product improvement, sampling, and other promotion—to overcome the objections to this product. New uses (such as using instant coffee for ice-cream flavoring) and new markets (such as hospitals, other institutions, and those individuals just coming into the coffee-drinking-age brackets) had to be painstakingly developed to lay the groundwork for the widespread use of these products that we know today.[1]

The trade—as well as the end user—may offer strong resistance to new items. Acceptance must be won at all links in the marketing chain inside and outside the producing firm. To gain distribution in the face of numerous rival new-product offerings requires the careful cultivation of trade buyers to win their support and acceptance of essentially unproved items. Shelf space, which must often be wrested from ma-

[1] "Overcoming Resistance to New Type of Product," *Printers' Ink*, March 29, 1946, pp. 24–26, 80–81.

ture products, has become a critical variable.

Coupled with this resistance factor in ultimate and intermediate markets are the high risk and uncertainty facing the promoter of new products. There are typically many unknowns in successfully promoting new entries. Acceptance levels and rates are often unpredictable in the crucial early stages. The uncertainty of public and trade reaction makes the estimating of sales volume and possible return on investment questionable. Rational expenditure planning, in turn, is difficult. Planners may be kept in the dark for significant periods until product use-patterns, advantages, and limitations slowly make themselves known. There may be no good way to get a realistic profile of potential customers early in the game. Planning, in short, may be based more on guesses and assumptions than on hard facts.

But these problems of resistance and uncertainty need not inhibit planning. In fact, it is precisely in unstable and indefinite situations such as this that systematic and rational planning is most needed. The basic problems can be greatly reduced with the right sort of planning, organizing, and controlling. Assumptions clearly and explicitly stated in the early stages are more susceptible to later double-checking. An orderly diagnosis as a prelude to prescribing specific promotional techniques is superior to blind gimmick-grasping and sole reliance on compulsive flashes of inspiration. Strategic decisions can and must be made to support a sound choice of promotional methods and provide the basis for effective follow-up on their use.

STRATEGIC DECISIONS

While a keen sense of timing and an awareness of market dynamics are indispensable in promoting new products, tactical maneuvering can be done with more assurance if a basic framework for action can first be erected. Among the important planks in such a platform are these:

1. Stake out an appropriate promotion planning period.
2. Establish clear sales objectives.
3. Fix the overall promotion budget.
4. Clarify payout policy.
5. Decide on the pace of market penetration desired.
6. Provide for continuity and flexibility in promotion.

Planning period The promotion plan should be forward looking enough to cover fully the introductory phases and should embrace a sufficiently long additional period to establish market performance of the new entry. In some cases, the horizon for promotion planning can be geared to distribution expansion plans. While the initial planning period may be as short as three months or as long as five years, perhaps most companies still make definite programs to cover a period of six months to one year beyond the beginning of market testing.[2] Later revised plans are

[2] "Most Advertisers Plan New Product Program a Full Year Ahead," *Printers' Ink*, April 5, 1946, pp. 31–32, 94.

extended as market penetration is achieved.

Sales objectives Many promotional decisions of a detailed nature hinge on estimates of unit sales volume and dollar revenues. To justify *any* advertising and sales promotion at all, there must be a certain minimum sales volume available. Although it is difficult to forecast future sales accurately without a past sales record to go on, companies with long experience in other new products can at least make rough estimates.

The variables affecting sales volume targets are many. Fragmentary information on market potentials, probable competitive action, and other external factors artfully combined with internal considerations will govern projections on sales volume. Because of production pressures on the scale of sales operations, *minimum* volume levels to assure survival at break-even operations can be established from engineering estimates. An audit of corporate financial resources may help establish the *maximum* volume the firm can afford to shoot for. Within this range, volume must be set high enough to support minimal advertising and to interest dealers in stocking the new item. Although the commitment may require courage, a statement such as this will prove helpful: "Our sales target at our planned price of one dollar per unit is 150,000 units in the first year."

Initially, preset volume levels expressed in dollars and units may be all that should be attempted. Sooner or later, however, competitors are likely to appear, so market-share objectives may also have to be established. As competitive inroads are made, market shares may have to be stabilized at some acceptable "floor" by promotional and other means. If concrete figures on needed market share cannot be set, it may prove possible to state aims in terms of a *range* of acceptable values. A new dentifrice, for example, might be introduced with the object of "being established by March first with a market share somewhere between 15 and 30 percent."

Promotional budget A decision must be made as to how much available money can be devoted to promotion. Both underspending and overspending must be avoided. Introductory costs are usually heavy, and an assessment of the risks involved has to be made. Estimates of promotional elasticity—how responsive sales volume is to promotional outlays—are necessary in determining aggregate expense. The notion of "opportunity costs" must be applied, for every dollar spent on promotion represents a foregone opportunity to apply financial resources in other areas.

Perhaps the surest way to determine the size of the appropriation is to use some sort of task method in combination with a percentage of expected sales.[3] The procedure is to determine the promotion task, set explicit goals, and then spend enough to do the job.

A first step in assessing the promotion task is to identify those critical

[3] "What Size Advertising Budget for New Product?" *Printers' Ink*, March 29, 1946, pp. 31–32, 78.

factors in the situation from which constructive inferences can be drawn. Surveys of end-use and competitive factors, trade conditions, and an evaluation of what the new product really is can be useful. Consumer products typically require more promotion than industrial goods; items sold through self-service outlets usually place a larger share of the marketing burden on advertising and sales promotion than those sold by clerk-service and direct-to-consumer methods. Budgets for trade media can be set on the basis of the number of retailers and wholesalers to be reached. The degree of enthusiasm for the new product inside and outside the company may be considered. Past experience is a useful guide to what it takes in each territory to do the job. The effect of the new item as a traffic builder for the rest of the line could be analyzed and the budget set on the basis of anticipated sales plus some imputed promotional value for the volume builder. As a minimum, the promotional budget must be large enough to test out the real potential for the new product.

The budget may be set to reach a pre-established volume within some stated time period. In certain cases, a percentage of expected sales is used as a limiting or control factor rather than as a determining factor. In others, production capacity acts as a limiting factor, with the promotion budget based on a percent-of-sales of total capacity. If advertising is controlled at some preset ratio to expected sales, a higher than normal percentage figure may be used to reflect the fact that the new product may require a greater per-unit promotional punch than established items. Such budgetary controls may be based either on dollar volume or on physical units, e.g., 3 percent of dollar sales, or 5¢ per case.

Payout policy Payout policy refers to the period of time needed for a new product to break even. Although closely linked with the planning premises discussed above, a strategic choice must explicitly be made whether (a) to view promotional spending as an *investment* to achieve long-term goals with no profit expected in the immediate future, or (b) to view outlays as a *current expense* and attempt to make the new product self-sustaining from the start. Three citations may serve to establish the importance attached to this issue by business executives.

According to Alfred M. Ghormley—president of the Carnation Company, makers of evaporated milk and other products—Carnation has to invest $3 million to $5 million in a new product before it begins to make money for the company. Thus, a new product must have longevity "because your big payout comes after the heavy promotion costs at the beginning have been absorbed. If the product can't maintain its momentum over a long life, then the initial promotion costs eat up the profits."[4]

Robert H. MacLachlan, product manager for Lever Brothers, has noted that payout periods vary widely from company to company and industry to industry, with some large firms using

a pay-as-you-go policy. He has urged more familiarity with the idea of a product life cycle as an aid in determining when a new product will reach its maximum point of profit and volume.[5]

Sponsor magazine notes a departure from the "long steady pull" techniques and a new emphasis on "short-term high-horsepowered campaigns" for products that are here today and may be gone tomorrow—due to diminished brand loyalty, cascading new product entries of competitors, and shorter product life cycles. This refers most appropriately to products like toiletries, which are often short-lived—ranging from a few years for toothpastes to a few months for some cosmetics. "Investment spending tactics, by which advertisers poured back all profits on a new product into additional advertising over a period of several years, are being carefully reconsidered. At one time P & G allowed as much as a three-year payout on a new product, before expecting profits. Nowadays . . . payouts must be shorter or the competition will kill you."[6]

At some point you must get your bait back. Payback policies are reflected in the choice made between penetration and skimming initial price policies. They directly affect the choice of promotional media, e.g., pay-as-you-go tactics may call for self-liquidating premium offers in preference to high-

[4] "New Lines Make Carnation More Contented," *Business Week*, February 22, 1958, pp. 106–107.

[5] "Call Benefit to Consumer Vital Aspect of New Product Design," *Food Field Reporter*, April 10, 1961.

[6] "Avalanche of New Products Change Ad Tactics," *Sponsor*, September 20, 1958, pp. 34–35.

cost sampling. The period is influenced by fear of competitive retaliation (which shortens the payout period), by patent protection (permitting longer periods), by the rate of new-product development to be financed by the company (a high rate requiring shorter payout periods), and similar factors.

Penetration rate To effect a smooth transition from a new product to a solidly established one, the time-shape of the promotional campaign must be tailored to mesh with initial strategies chosen for pricing and distribution. Among the key decisions is this: Should national coverage be attempted at once, or should a more modest start be made on a local or regional basis with wider distribution gradually attempted one market at a time?

A saturation send-off may be called for to get the jump on rivals or to discourage competitors altogether. Rapid market coverage, coupled with penetration pricing and explosive promotion, may be appropriate for the dramatically new product with eagerly awaiting buyers. Large initial advertising budgets, high-impact media, and eye-stopping copy and layout are tactical correlates of this strategic choice.

By way of contrast, a slow market-by-market approach may be taken. Many firms, having gone overboard on some new product only to find that they have greatly underestimated promotional costs, now resist the natural temptation to move too quickly in gaining geographic coverage. A slower and more intensive approach toward achieving deep penetration in one zone be-

fore moving on to the next may be dictated by the need for caution in the face of high risk. Slow penetration rates permit the marketer to gather information as he feels his way, allows time for testing to uncover flaws and weak spots in promotion planning, and encourages timely adjustments to plans as they are needed. Slow penetration permits better geographical maneuvering, with the total new-product campaign assuming the form of multistage tactical evolutions. Some companies invade each local market with almost battle-plan precision and attention to detail. In such cases, each market may be thoroughly softened up by promotional bombardment prior to entry.

Slow penetration is correlated with skimming price policies and highly selective approaches to trade channel policy. It permits a "save your gunpowder" approach to administering the promotion budget, with a smaller percentage of the appropriation devoted to initial advertising when this may be dictated by short payout policies. "Teaser" advertising copy can be used to advantage, although some national media cannot be economically employed with such a strategy. Slow penetration rates may be required if the company or brand name is not well known and respected in markets selected for entry, if the product is so radically new as to require a long time for it to be worked into new consumption patterns, or if the item is so superficially new as to invite buyer skepticism.

Slow penetration may permit more attention to the synchronizing of promotion plans and distribution coverage. Advertising and promotion must "break" at precisely the right time. In recent years, both a leading beauty aid and a candy bar were heavily promoted to consumers before pipelines could be adequately stocked. The net results were disgruntled consumers and dealers and a waste of promotion money. Promotion intended as a device for securing initial stocks in trade channels, of course, may be needed. Trade ads, for instance, may be needed to produce inquiries leading to prospect lists. Often the promotion must be keyed to trade shows and exhibits with fixed dates, timed to coincide with seasonal deadlines, or otherwise strategically paced to get maximum mileage from the promotion dollar.

Production considerations are often important in determining market penetration rates. If the plant can supply only 15 percent of the total market, then only 15 percent of the market can be penetrated, and this forces consideration of the *sequence* in which markets are to be entered. Which area is to be first and which is to be next, which outlets are to be opened first and which are to be next, and similar priorities and schedules must be determined. Constraints imposed by delivery problems may be restrictive. One company, for instance, found that in order to guarantee quick delivery on a new product, precedence had to be given to only ten prime markets before national distribution could follow.

Payout policies, sales volume objectives, budgetary limits, and other factors also serve as constraints in determining penetration rates. For example, a "snowballing" ad expenditure geared to market-by-market distribution may be dictated by the need to finance promotion from current revenue even though promotion-minded executives might personally prefer "smash-and-follow-up" or "level expenditure" strategies for promotion.

Continuity and flexibility It may seem paradoxical to strive for both consistency and change in planning the promotion of new products, for these objectives conflict with each other. Yet some balance is needed to avoid both underplanning and overplanning.

Promotion planning is inherently something of a dynamic programming problem. Advertising strategy must be somewhat fluid and geared to the estimated life cycle of the new product. Since promotional tasks and objectives may change as the product moves from unknown entity to established item, promotional budgets, advertising appeals, and the media mix may require compensatory adjustments. Flexibility is also needed to adapt promotion plans to totally unexpected conditions which may develop. A new item may be hotter than expected, and production capacity may become so overtaxed that out-of-stock conditions may require temporary cutbacks in promotion. The reverse may be true if the item turns out to be cold. If there are high risks and many unknowns associated with the new product, special care must be taken to allow for operating flexibility by avoiding unnecessary commitments.

On the other hand, some consistency and continuity are often built into promotion plans. No purely arbitrary changes in the media mix should be made, for instance, unless intended as part of a planned experiment. An awareness of the importance of repetition and of lagged responses to promotion may underlie the continuity goal. That new-product advertisers lay some stress on this objective is reflected in the fact that they are sometimes reluctant to alter promotional appeals and media once a plan is established, and in that they sometimes deliberately hold down initial promotional costs in order to ensure the establishment of a rate of expenditure which can be consistently maintained. Hand-to-mouth administration of the promotion budget may be avoided through such means as splitting the budget equally by months for nonseasonal products.

Although there may be merit in the preplanning of promotional continuity, plans must also be forward looking enough to contain special provisions for flexibility. The media mix, for example, can be set to vary at different times in the campaign, e.g., by using more trade media in the announcement period at the start of a campaign and scheduling more consumer media for later periods. Built-in provisions for periodic review and/or continuous monitoring of results can be specified ahead of time. Special allowance for contingencies in expenditure planning can be set up in advance. Elastic plans for more or less promotion can be reserved for use as the situation develops. While plans are made farther ahead, commitments can be held to shorter periods. A "cushion" for special promotions may be set aside for hypos aimed at sluggish markets, or sliding scales of various kinds can be used in budgeting, e.g., in the event sales exceed a certain sum, advertising can be increased or decreased on a preset percentage basis.

If attention is devoted to promotion planning very early in the new-product development process, flexibility and continuity are more likely to be achieved in proper proportion.

Strategic decisions, such as the six discussed above, provide a promotion planning framework serving several purposes. They clarify basic objectives which shape the scale on which promotion is to be conducted, the degree of futurity involved, and the sources from which promotional funds are to be drawn. They provide broad criteria for selecting specific promotional alternatives. They serve as standards for measuring the success of new-product promoting. This framework, in short, contains many clues to program design —the detailed plan follows directly from these beacon lights whenever they can be translated into specific criteria for blueprinting elements of the advertising and sales promotion campaign.

BLUEPRINTING THE CAMPAIGN

A promotion plan for new products must cover at least the following four steps:

1. Crystallize specific campaign requirements.
2. Formulate the promotional message.
3. Determine the advertising media plan.

4. Supplement advertising with sales promotion devices.

Campaign requirements The concrete objectives of new-product promotions are many and varied. It may be necessary to inform, to educate, to persuade, or to enthuse prospective buyers about the merits of the new entry. Or the purpose may be simply to test customer reaction to the product. For example, a publicity release might provide a quick test or couponed ads and trade show exhibits could be used to pull inquiries. Promotional targets have to be established, and these, of course, may differ from ultimate market targets—as in the case where "tastemakers" are appealed to in initial efforts.

In most cases, the overriding promotional aim is to get *initial acceptance.* While the chief function of early promotion is simply to get the customer to try the item, the role of the product itself is to *retain* the customer through its performance characteristics and user benefits. Thus, the product must live up to the promises made for it and may even be designed from the outset with specific promotable claims in mind.

Because there are many kinds of buyers in most trade channels, it is necessary to identify promotional requirements for each link in the marketing chain. Promotional "push" as well as "pull" is needed in most situations, and balanced coverage is required at all links without overlooking a single trade level. Company salesmen, the distributor and his personnel, the dealer and his employees, and each end-use market must be individually considered to identify the pressure points where promotional leverage is to be applied.

Promotional message Since advertising and sales promotion are communications problems, the message to be transmitted to designated "receivers" in the marketplace must be carefully defined. The message consists of both the promotional copy and the way in which that copy is laid out and presented. In order to crystallize ideas most sharply, copy should be determined before layout. Layout, pictures, headlines, and other elements of the advertisement can later be designed to make customers aware of the copy and to direct and hold their attention to it.

For some new products, a dramatic appeal in a news type of announcement may do the trick. More often a basic dilemma is present: Although you must be "different" when you have a new item, customer resistance may be encountered if you are *too* different. Basically, the prospective buyer must be shown a real advantage to establish his interest, desire, and preference. Since desire and preference is based on belief that the product will actually fill a need well, product performance must often be clearly demonstrated in advance through advertising copy.

A thoroughgoing product-and-market analysis is the starting point for determining product claims and copy slants. If there are known dissatisfactions with substitute products not present in the new item, these plus-features can serve as major sales points to be exploited in copy. The results of technical product testing and use testing are major talking points. Once these selling points are identified, they should be segregated by their appeal to each link in the trade channel before finished copy is developed.

At some point, a dominant central theme must be originated to serve as an integrating device to tie all elements of the advertising and sales promotion plan into a unified "package." This central theme is usually built around one or more basic human wants or needs closely associated with the product. The value of the theme will be directly dependent on the strength of the incorporated appeal in terms of its ability to motivate buyers and on the size of the buyer group susceptible to the appeal.

Automobile seat belts provide an interesting illustration of the care and imagination needed in creating appeals. For years, sellers of these safety devices have been met with a curious public apathy and few sales. Indeed, some marketers felt the seat belt was a "nonsalable" product. But the Midas Company, a manufacturer of auto parts, thought the product could be sold with fresh selling appeals. According to Gordon Sherman, Midas president, "Social consciousness can play a larger role than self-preservation in the sales of a product primarily designed to save lives. At first glance, seat belts seem to have their strongest selling point in simple self-preservation. In the field, however, we found this sales message working against us. There is a naïve bravado on the part of the

man in the street that leads him to give more consideration to what his fellow man thinks than to the basic safety offered to him and his family."[7] When the copy slant was shifted to emphasize children and families and when "nonsafety" social appeals were stressed, sales of seat belts increased. Now, the copy reads, "Let seat belts do the baby-sitting for you," and "Their use eases fatigue, helps the driver remain more alert, and controls the effect of centrifugal force on turns." Because they are more positive in tone and approach, these are stronger than self-centered safety appeals.

Advertising media Each advertising medium requires certain conditions for its effective use. The choice of media depends on the nature of the product, the market, and the message. Basically, the media problem is first to define the market and then to decide which media will reach that market most effectively and efficiently. Readership and audience data, cost-per-thousand logical prospects, and similar information are needed to resolve the choices.

However, the framework of strategic decisions discussed earlier imposes strict limitations on media selection. For example, media which are much more costly than others may be declared ineligible on budgetary grounds. Where promotional budgets are small, special budget stretchers, such as free publicity and cooperative dealer ads, may be used. Some media produce results more quickly than others, and

[7] "Selling a 'Nonsalable' Product," *Sales Management*, February 2, 1962, pp. 75–78.

their use may be suggested by short payout policies. If a slow area-by-area market penetration pattern is followed, the decision maker has a narrow choice of media in the early stages and a constantly expanding range of alternatives as the boundaries of market coverage are pushed out. Media choices must, of course, be geared to the outlet patterns employed. A strong commitment to continuity might dictate that a fixed list of media be used throughout the entire new-product campaign.

Beyond broad decisions on the types of media and the individual media within each class to be used, a wide range of detailed decisions must also be made. Since the calculation of space and time costs is a necessary step to breaking down the appropriation, issues relating to number and timing of ads, size of advertisements, black and white versus color, and similar issues must be resolved. These, too, will be influenced by strategic constraints.

Sales promotion devices Every salesman knows the value of a good "close" in personal selling. Sales promotion devices perform essentially the same function for advertising. Despite effective messages in appropriate media, advertising may not produce positive buyer action on new products. "Most of the difficulties encountered in introducing a new product stem from the consumer's reluctance to part with his money for something he hasn't bought or used before."[8] Sales promo-

tion devices for new products are intended to reduce or eliminate the risk to the buyer or to offer special inducements to achieve sampling and first product trials.

Although it would be impossible to list all the techniques in use today for promoting new products, the major ones can be visualized as occupying different rungs on a ladder of increasingly strong incentives. First are the simple *confidence builders.* Testimonials, seals of approval from respected testing laboratories, guarantees, return privileges, consignment sales, combination offers which permit the new product to ride the coattails of a well-established complementary item, and similar techniques may provide sufficient extra incentive to move the less timid prospect to action. Next in increasing strength of inducement is the *bargain.* Coupons, premiums, trade-in offers, outright price reductions, and special deals—two for the price of one, one case free with five, one-cent sales—are representative of this group. Third, are the *no-charge* alternatives. Free goods given to dealers, samples distributed by mail or crew to households, and free trials for limited periods are strong inducements to product sampling since they require no cash outlay on the part of the trier. The strongest inducement of all is to *pay the customer* to try the new product. Cash or merchandise awards for consumers and push-money for dealers are examples of this extreme form of inducement.

Many considerations will influence the choice of a specific technique. Among the major criteria are these:

---

[8] "Special Offers to Introduce New Products," *Printers' Ink,* April 26, 1946, pp. 40–41.

1. *Cash outlay required.* Free samples, for instance, can be distributed only in the case of inexpensive items, while the cost of distributing any sample by crews in rural markets may be prohibitive. Sampling is usually more expensive than couponing.

2. *Legality.* Some forms of sales promotion are taxed, licensed, restricted, or forbidden in certain states and localities.

3. *Flexibility and control.* It is usually easier to shut off a special deal after the introductory period than it is to increase price. Coupon offers can be made with definite expiration dates.

4. *Product characteristics.* Products appealing to the basic senses of sight, touch, taste, and smell are most suitable for physical sampling. Thus, toothpaste—which can quickly be judged on the basis of flavor, feel, sudsing action, and after-taste—is an ideal product for small-quantity sampling. Where product reliability and performance cannot be promptly determined by the customer, something like a guarantee may be a more suitable inducement.

5. *Impact on the trade.* Coupons are difficult to store and count at retail levels, slow check-outs, and invite misredemption. Special deal packs compound inventory problems. Dealer preferences, administrative headaches, and the ease of merchandising the promotion to the trade in a manner which will ensure dealer and jobber cooperation are important factors.

6. *Possibility of repeat purchase.* Sales promotion devices to induce new-product sampling are most suitable for items which are rapidly consumed and replaced by the buyer. Overly large free samples keep the buyer out of the market too long. Special devices to stimulate repurchase after the initial product trial—such as the "repurchase value offer," where the customer uses the boxtop of his first package as part payment on the second —may be used. The greater the cash outlay required of the customer, the greater the customer interest and involvement in a near-normal buying process is likely to be, and this fosters repeat buying. Deals are said to produce a substantially lower repeat rate than other sales promotion devices because they invite the fickle bargain hunter. Coupons probably accelerate sampling and speed up customer responses more than outright price reductions.

These are the major elements of a new product promotion. Long before the program is blueprinted, however, an administrative base must be laid down for its evolution and control. Advance organization and coordination among all members of the promotion team is a key to success. Project teams, task forces, brand managers, sponsor groups, and other organizational approaches may be employed. Close cooperation from the advertising agency is essential, for the agency can help in clarifying new-product aims and requirements and translate them for creative and media departments. The agency is usually appointed prior to test marketing and may even be designated at the inception of the new-product idea.

When the Colgate-Palmolive Company decided to come out with "Baggies," clear plastic bags on a tear-off roll used as food wraps, it appointed Street and Finney of New York as the agency. Nineteen different agency staff members helped to aid and advise Colgate in a number of ways. They offered suggestions on the physical nature of the product itself and its possible uses—name, box size, design, price, quantity of bags per box, size of bags, ease of handling, potential customers, protective qualities. They gathered marketing information on both Baggies and competitive products—retail attitudes, allowances and discounts, price-off deals, displays, spot advertising, salesforce materials, shelf facings and positions, promotions. They developed a complete advertising, sales promotion, and publicity campaign, including the creation and production of six TV commercials, and offered suggestions to Colgate's own production department on supporting sales promotion material.[9] This is illustrative of the help that may be extended by a cooperative agency.

An energetic agency, top management interest, crystal-clear strategic concepts, a well-oiled organization backed by solid research at critical stages, and close attention to all elements of the campaign blueprint are essential to the successful promotion of new entries.

[9] "Partners: Agencies, New Products," *Printers' Ink,* April 13, 1962, pp. 31–32.

▶▶▶▶▶▶▶▶▶▶C

Formulating Over-all
Marketing Strategy

▶▶▶▶▶▶▶▶▶▶▶ HOW CONSUMERS TAKE TO NEWNESS

Business Week

The preoccupation of manufacturers and merchandisers with new products is by now a recognized part of . . . selling. Competition, tremendous productive capacity and skills, and aggressive merchandising techniques have pushed producers and marketers further into new lines, new models, and new features, brand new products.

Does the consumer—target of much of this activity—have as cogent reasons for accepting all these innovations as the manufacturers have for making them?

What are the basic situations in which he will buy a new product or a new feature?

Can you pinpoint the kind of consumer who is likely to go for an innovation?

Can you show any real correlation between innovations and changes in your sales curve?

What hazards lie in wait for the manufacturer?

Will the consumer continue to support the trend to newness? How can you make him continue?

Reprinted with permission from Business Week, *September 24, 1955, pp. 41–42, 44, 46.*

FORUM OF EXPERTS

These were the questions that came out of a conference at Ann Arbor, Mich., sponsored by Consumer Behavior, Inc. . . . This group, organized in 1952, aims to promote basic research into how a consumer behaves and why. Supported mainly by corporate gifts (Consumers Union got it off to its start), it tries to pool the resources of psychologists, anthropologists, sociologists, economists, marketing research experts, and business to establish a true science of consumer behavior.

. . . The problem it had set itself was consumer reactions to innovation and obsolescence. Representatives from such companies as Ford Motor Co., General Electric Co., General Foods Corp., Household Finance Corp., Goodyear Tire & Rubber Co., as well as from the universities and professional market research organizations, tackled the problem in a program where the theoretical and practical attempted to come to terms.

THE BASICS

On the theoretical side, Michael Halpert and Wroe Alderson, both of Alderson & Sessions, Inc., research consultants, set out to formulate the situations in which a consumer may buy something new. They indicated what the merchandiser was up against in putting an innovation over, and how—broadly—he might hit a bullseye.

"Occasions for purchase" They summed up the eight "occasions for purchase" in which a consumer acts.

In all of these situations the consumer is presumed to have a "cultural inventory," indicated by the letters a to x, representing the whole range of products available for consumption. No one consumer is likely to own all the items, but he is aware of them.

The simplest kind of purchase occurs when a consumer buys x because he has run out of his supply of x. Or, tired of x, he may buy w—about which he already knows something.

With the third type, he gets right into the field of innovations. This is when x has failed him—and there's a new, supposedly better product on the market, say a better grade of gasoline. Or he may try an old product to which something new has been added—as TCP was added to Shell's gasoline.

Up to this point, the consumer has been thinking only in terms of improving an inventory he already understands. With the next step begins the task of persuading him that he should enlarge his inventory to satisfy wants he hasn't felt before. This occurs when the product is radically different from anything yet offered. It may be complicated by requiring a supplementary new product. The new automatic washing machines, for example, brought forth a special detergent. . . .

Alderson and Halpert stressed the sociological aspects of the consumer's reactions to this kind of product. Some consumers will take to it because they are leaders; they want to be first to own the latest. Others are followers; they will hang back till the innovation has made some headway. This is a phenomenon that every new appliance manufacturer and every fashion creator is well aware of.

Making consumer bite Given these basic situations, how do you get consumer acceptance of an innovation? The consumer has two bases for choice: the product itself, and the claims made for it.

On the product, say these experts, the differences between it and an established product must be discernible. The product must be identifiable. And it must be reproducible.

On the claims, ideally they should be meaningful, plausible, and verifiable. In effect, a new product is "an offer to solve a problem"—often a problem the consumer hasn't been aware of. How meaningful the product can be made depends on the urgency of the problem and how much doubt the consumer has that the product will meet the contingency. He might ask, for example, whether he really must have a color TV, how often he will watch it, how much added pleasure it will give him—and whether it will do the job.

If the manufacturer can establish the meaningfulness of an innovation, the next step is to make the claims plausible. Here the three forces to work with are credulity, authority, and scientific proof. If the product is replacing an old one, the consumer has the old one to use as a yardstick to measure the new. If it is a radical innovation, he will judge it on the basis of claims: Does it come up to its advance billing?

The stress varies Different kinds of innovations require different stresses. In a simple improvement, it is particularly important that the difference between the old and the new be discernible; otherwise there's no excuse for it. In cases of adding a new element, identifiability is important—as when water softener is added to a soap. In utterly new products, product claims must take a big share of the sales task. Convincing the consumer that he wants the new offering is the marketer's big job.

WHO REACTS?

Eva Mueller, of the University of Michigan's Survey Research Center, got down to cases in attempting to pinpoint where the innovations market is likely to be found. She stressed that her findings so far are tentative, in some cases the survey sample was too small to be statistically significant. But the findings pointed to some interesting clues.

Income factor First, up to a point, interest in new features on household appliances—and in the newer appliances—grows with income. On a basis of 2,027 families surveyed, only 30% of those in the under-$3,000 group expressed an interest in new features; 40% of those in the $3,000 to $4,999 group did so; and 45% did in the $5,000 to $7,499 group. There was a slight drop-off in the $7,500 and over bracket—possibly because this is the group that is most likely to have the newest anyway.

The study indicates that even owners of fairly new appliances, in good condition, are responsive to new features —though here the number of cases was small. Last June, 19% of the people who had refrigerators not more than five years old and in good condition planned to replace them; 23% of those who bought in the last year had had such refrigerators.

New features apparently helped spark this interest. A resurvey of 855 respondents who owned a fairly new refrigerator (five years or less) showed that 5.5% who had expressed an interest in new features had bought in the following year; only 1.9% of those who had expressed no interest had bought.

Gauging "innovation-mindedness"
The study came up with a kind of gauge for "innovation-mindedness."

This was based on the interest expressed in the latest features on traditional appliances, on the ownership or plans to buy the newer appliances (garbage disposal units, home freezers, air conditioning, for example), and on the consumer's evaluation of the new ones as "useful," or merely "luxury" items. On this basis, the study finds that the great bulk (58%) of the innovation-minded consumers fall in the age group 35 to 54; that those families where there were children were most receptive; and those who had a high school or college education responded the most.

Significantly, the degree of innovation-mindedness seems to correlate di-

Which Customers Are Likely to Go for Innovations in Household Appliances?

By Income Group

- ☐ Under $3,000 .... 6%
- ☐ $3,000-$4,999 ....23%
- ☑ $5,000-$7,449 ...... **39%**
- ☐ $7,500 plus 30%
- ☐ No response 2%

By Age Group

- ☐ 18-34 years 28%
- ☑ 35-54 .... **58%**
- ☐ 55-64 ....10%
- ☐ 65 and over 3%
- ☐ No response 1%

By Family Status

- ☐ Single 8%
- ☐ Married, no children 20%
- ☑ Married, children **69%**
- ☐ Other 3%

By Financial Outlook

- ☑ Income up, expect rise. **27%**
- ☑ Income steady,
  expect rise **23%**
- ☐ Income steady,
  no change expected.....19%
- ☐ Income unsteady,
  expect worse 15%
- ☐ Income up,
  no change expected..... 8%
- ☐ No response 8%

Data: University of Michigan Survey Research Center.

rectly with how a consumer feels about his financial status. The largest chunk (27%) of those who were innovation-minded fell in the group whose income has been going up and who expect further improvement; next largest (23%) were among those whose income has been steady and who expect to do better. Those with less cheerful prospects were less eager for the new.

WILL IT LAST?

If these findings continue to hold up under further investigation, all this has important implications for business. Apparently, whether the trend to new things continues depends to a considerable extent on how prosperous people are, or think they are going to be. That a fairly recent acquisition of a new appliance doesn't discourage interest in still newer features seems to push further into the background that old bogey, saturation—as so many manufacturers have hoped it would.

Findings from Robert Eggert, marketing research manager of the Ford division of Ford Motor Co., point in the same direction. They credited the major model changes throughout the automotive industry with a great part of this year's unprecedented car output and sales. Specifically, he cited the case of the 1952 Ford—the first year in which it used a one-piece windshield. Some 17% of Ford owners mentioned visibility as one of the features they liked that year—whereas competitor A, with the traditional windshield, rated only 2% mentions for visibility. Sig-

nificantly, Eggert reported, next year, when the competitor also had a one-piece windshield, only 2% of Ford owners mentioned visibility.

Incentives Eggert added these factors as terrific incentives to change: rising births, the active market of teen-agers, increased leisure.

In the U.S., especially, strong winds are blowing to make the trend to innovation prevail. Harvard's Samuel A. Stouffer pointed to some: the technological development of recent years (including credit selling); the country's immense area, the consumer's mobility. Stouffer earlier had cited the rapid postwar new family formation as an important stimulus to breaking with tradition.

Both Robert Giraud of the University of Geneva and George Katona of the University of Michigan's Survey Research Center pointed out that in Europe the pressure has traditionally been in the other direction. There the consumer wants quality and permanence.

Difficulties But there were plenty of warnings that the road to progress is rugged. Arthur C. Nielsen, Jr., of A. C. Nielsen & Co., pointed out that among companies he had studied, 10% found it took from three to four years to reach a point where they felt that a new product was going to take; 30% reported two to three years; only 10% said it took less than six months.

Nielsen granted that a new product takes hold faster today than in the past —thanks in good part to television.

►►►►►►►►►►►► THE PROCESS OF MARKET ACCEPTANCE

JOHN A. HOWARD*

A brief analysis of the typical process by which a new product becomes accepted in the market sets the stage for discussion of methods of measuring the demand for new products. Although this analysis will be confined to a radical innovation such as the home refrigerator, it will apply to mild innovations as well. The only difference is that mild innovations make less of an impact on buyer behavior when accepted. Also, the analysis will be in terms of consumer goods, but the same thing occurs with slight modification among industrial products. Industrial buyers are subject to habit, too; they differ from consumer buyers mainly in that competition may force change more quickly. Also, industrial buyers are typically better informed.

When the product is first introduced, sales are usually small. Consumer habits change slowly, but also the product is inferior to the one that will ultimately emerge. These improvements come more rapidly in the early years of a product's life. As experience is gained in production, first, costs decline, then price is reduced, which is important because the lower price is essential to reaching the mass market. At the same time, related services and products are developing, which

enhance the usefulness of the product to the consumer. Refrigerator sales were probably stimulated by the development of year-round, greengrocery departments.

Factors modifying the speed of market acceptance may be such things as the level of economic conditions, vested interests, and the socioeconomic groups constituting the market. Consumers are probably less willing to try new products in depression periods because their income is lower than the level they had come to consider essential and because they may be less inclined to accept the risks involved in buying an untried product. The speculation that declining consumer incomes discourage acceptance of innovation has been alluded to. . . . Some suggestive empirical evidence is contained in Table 1. Although the evidence is by no means conclusive, it is the only attempt that has come to the attention of the author to test this important hypothesis empirically. The table merely shows that among household goods, including appliances, people with favorable income expectations used to be associated with innovation-mindedness. It could be, for example, that people with favorable expectations are more inclined to buy. Consequently, they have been shop-

Reprinted with permission from Marketing Management: Analysis and Decision. *Richard D. Irwin Inc., 1957, pp. 248–252.*

*Professor of Marketing, Graduate School of Business, Columbia University.

TABLE 1

RELATION BETWEEN ATTITUDES TOWARD INNOVATIONS AND PEOPLE'S PAST
AND EXPECTED FINANCIAL SITUATION°

Past and Expected Financial Situation	Innovation-Minded†	Intermediate†	Not Innovation-Minded†
Income has been going up— further improvement expected	27%	18%	10%
Income has been going up— no change expected	8	10	6
Income has been steady— improvement expected	23	14	13
Income has been steady— no change expected	19	29	32
Income has been unsteady or going down, or family expects to be worse off	15	23	25
Not ascertained	8	6	14
Total	100%	100%	100%
Number of cases	179	421	163

° Based on urban re-interview sample of 855 cases; report on past and expected financial situation as of June, 1954:

† The three attitude categories are based on the following criteria:

1. *Interest in the latest features on the traditional appliances.* Being interested in new features and naming one or more specific appliances is a positive response. Not being interested in new features is a negative response.

2. *Owning, planning to buy, or having considered purchasing a new appliance.* Owning or planning to buy one of the new appliances is a positive response. Having only considered buying is a pro-con response. Neither owning nor having considered it is a negative response.

3. *People's evaluation of new appliances as "useful" or "luxury."* The answer "useful" is a positive response. Answers such as "partly useful, partly luxury" are pro-con responses. The answer "luxury" is a negative response.

The questions were: (1) "Has your family income been quite steady during the past few years, or has it been going up, or going down, or changes from time to time?" (2) "A few years from now, would you think you and your family will have a better position and income than you have now, or will you be in about the same situation or even in a less satisfactory situation? Why do you think so?"

SOURCE: Eva Mueller, "The Desire for Innovation in Household Goods," in Survey Research Center, University of Michigan, *Consumer Behavior* (New York: New York University Press, 1957), Vol. III, Table 14.

ping in anticipation of the purchase and have familiarized themselves with product features.

If certain groups are affected ad-versely by a new product, they may retard its development. Borden considers that this happened in foam rubber for mattresses where the established mattress makers and retailers are alleged to have limited its acceptance.

The upper socioeconomic groups are probably more inclined to change because of their relatively better communication patterns and facilities, but this has yet to be documented under modern mechanical methods of communication, particularly television. Small-group theory is currently being applied to the problem of innovation and some interesting conclusions have been drawn. For example, the rate of adoption of a new drug by physicians has been analyzed.[1] The drug industry is characterized by a high rate of product innovation and obsolescence. The research procedure was to interview a sample of doctors and to ascertain the date of their first prescription of the new product by examining drugstore prescription records.

At the time "gammanym" was first made available, it had two important older competitors.[2] Within 15 months, 87 percent of the general practitioners, internists, and pediatricians interviewed in four selected cities had introduced it into their practice, although only 50 percent of them were writing

[1] The study, carried out at the Bureau of Applied Social Research of Columbia University by James S. Coleman, Elihu Katz, and Herbert Menzel, is to be published in book form. For a preliminary statement see Herbert Menzel and Elihu Katz, "Social Relations and Innovation in the Medical Profession: The Epidemiology of a New Drug," *Public Opinion Quarterly,* to be published. The results reported here were presented in a paper read at the meetings of the American Sociological Society in September, 1956.

[2] "Gammanym" is a fictious name used to protect the identity of the company.

more prescriptions for "gammanym" than for either of its competitors. With this knowledge of the speed with which "gammanym" was accepted in these communities as a background, the next question is, "What was the actual process of diffusion?"

In order to investigate this question, it was decided to include, as far as possible, all the doctors practicing in the specialties concerned in the communities covered. Actually 85 percent of these doctors were included in the sample. The interpersonal networks, or "sociograms" as they are sometimes called, were determined by asking each doctor for the names of three colleagues in answer to each of the following questions:

1. Whose advice did he seek about questions of therapy?
2. With whom did he discuss cases or therapy during an ordinary week?
3. Whom did he see most often socially?

The results for each question, for example, could be something like the sociogram shown in the figure. In this diagram, each circle represents a physician, who is identified by a code number. An arrow pointing from Circle 03 to Circle 50 means "Dr. 03 named Dr. 50 as one of his frequent partners in the discussion of cases." According to their positions in the sociogram, doctors were divided into the two groups, "well integrated" and "isolated." It was found that doctors who were well integrated into the network tended to accept the drug much more rapidly than did the isolated. They also accepted it at an accelerating rate, while

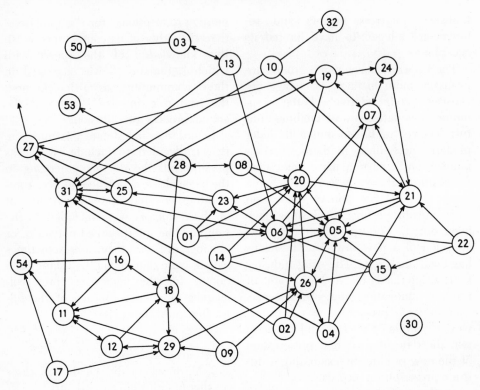

SOCIOGRAM OF DOCTORS

the isolated ones accepted it at a more nearly constant rate. These results are consistent with the hypothesis that integrated doctors learned of the drug through contacts with doctors who had already begun to use it, while isolated doctors had to depend more on formal communication media.

As a check upon the conclusion that social networks were effective in speeding innovation, "pairs" of doctors were determined. They were "pairs" in the sense that one or both named the other as an adviser, a partner in discussion of cases, or a friend. From an analysis of the time at which each member of the pair began using the drug it was concluded that the early users (first six months) tended to use it soon after any associates who had already adopted it. Among the later users, there were more and more discrepancies between the behavior of each member of a "pair." By the end of a year the relationship between the "pair" idea and first usage of drug disappeared. A possible conclusion is that, in the early period, the doctors needed reassurance from their colleagues in adopting the new drug since prescribing the drug involved heavy responsibility. Once the drug was well established, the reassurance was no longer needed. In substance, according to this interpretation, it was a case of a social network providing its function of "sharing the responsibility."

Of a more immediate marketing interest is that the innovators made more use of professional sources of information (professional journals and medical meetings) than did their colleagues, but not of commercial sources (drug salesmen and house organs of drug companies). Also, of the three relationships mentioned (adviser, case discussion, and friends), it is only among friendship relations that brand as opposed to generic product was discussed. (Several brands of the new product "gammanym" had been released in rather quick succession.)

Explorations of the drug-study type should provide insights into the role of social relations and the flow of information in changing consumer purchasing habits. From this should emerge hypotheses that can guide the individual company in making estimates about the relative demand for alternative new products.

▶▶▶▶▶▶▶▶▶▶▶ FOUR STEPS TO RESEARCH TRANQUILITY

Sales Management

Why is it so many bright and shining new products hit the market with a sickening flop? The specific reasons are as many and varied as the pebbles on the beach.

But nearly all these reasons have one thing in common: Somewhere along the line, somebody was wide of the market. It may have been in judging demand . . . or in designing an appeal to which the market would be receptive . . . or in building answers to market needs into the product itself. Almost never does a product fail because the product research was sour.

But market research seems to lay an egg more often than not.

Certainly it's not because nobody tries. Sometimes management is at fault. It becomes confused when faced with the task of setting market potentials, and important factors just get lost in the fog. Sometimes market research is to blame. It may get the techniques right, but concentrate so much on statistical methodology that it never does come through with terms and procedures that management can understand and interpret. Or, for that matter, research methods may become so bloated that costs grow out of line with the value of results, and accuracy is sacrificed for economy.

What is needed, it seems, is a compromise system, a standard operating procedure that incorporates accurate, complete and only essential research within a framework easily understood and interpreted by marketing management.

A model of one such system has been created by Seymour Kroll, the

Reprinted by permission from Sales Management, *April 20, 1962, pp. 17–18.*

former manager, market research, for the Wood Products Division of Weyerhaeuser Co. (and now a consultant), who gained a certain measure of fame with his theories of experimental marketing. . . . This model system is designed for use in setting market potentials for two kinds of new products: the new product which merely replaces an old product (another brand of soap flakes) and the new product which not only replaces an old one but which, because of its great superiority, also jacks up total market demand (transistors). The third kind of new product, the all-new, no-previous-market kind (Metrecal), requires interpretation that is a bit too spiritual to be formularized.

Mr. Kroll's model system has four parts:

1. *Determining end-use potential (EUP)* This is the broad look. This means determining the volume of all products the market is currently consuming for a specific end use. Many, if not most, products will have more than one EUP inasmuch as they have more than one basic market. Example: The market for a new residential siding product is being determined. This product could be used on single-family dwelling units and on apartment houses; thus, two EUP's must be determined. In this step it is also necessary to determine the degree of penetration of different types of competing materials.

2. *Determining the market segment potential (MSP)* Each end-use market will be held by a variety of competing products. Many of these, however, will be somewhat different from the others in function. Although they all do the same basic job, characteristics will vary and make some more suitable than others under certain circumstances. The market must be thoroughly analyzed to determine the characteristics (price, strength, appearance, etc.) that make each competing product desirable under certain conditions, and the degree to which buyers will forego one desired feature (say, looks) for another (lower price).

3. *Setting product potential* Once the market segments are known, and once the new product is completely planned (right down to price), it will be possible to stack the new product against the segments to see in just which parts of the total market the new product can compete. Of course, if it is to penetrate any of these segments, it must displace older or existing products to some degree. Therefore, it is also necessary to make a detailed study of the marketing strategies and techniques used by competitors. It is also necessary to determine in this step whether or not the product will expand the market, and how much.

4. *Finding company potential* This final step involves looking at product potential in the light of corporate policy, geographic, distribution or other restrictions, as well as determining the effects of probable competitive moves and market changes.

This S.O.P. certainly cannot solve the problems of long-range forecasting, of market investigation, of certain cause-and-effect relationships, or of many other very tacky qualitative research problems. But it does give step-by-step direction to research. It does give management an easily understand- able scorecard to follow. It does permit a certain amount of calculated leeway in setting research expenditures. And it does guarantee that all the bases will at least be covered.

►►►►►►►►►►► WHAT IS "NEW" ABOUT A NEW PRODUCT?

CHESTER R. WASSON[*]

Consider the case of the soup-maker who, by freezing, was able to develop commercial production of soups which previously had to be fresh-prepared—an oyster stew among them. Estimating that the market potential might be approximated by the average relationship between frozen and canned foods, he tried his soups in a single test market. The oyster stew sold out so fast that he had to withdraw it from test until he could expand production facilities even for this one market.

Or take the case of the industrial manufacturer who developed a silo-like forage storer, capable of increasing livestock production profits substantially if properly used. Yet when put into distribution through experienced dealers in heavy farm equipment, it lay dormant for more than four years. In fact, no appreciable market headway was made until it was taken out of the hands of what had seemed to be a logical channel for any kind of farm equipment.

Then, consider the business executive with soap-and-cosmetic experience who acquired rights to a promising soil improver. Trade checks indicated that consumers liked it very much, and an impartial laboratory test indicated technical properties of substance. Put into a few test garden stores with no more than nominal advertising, sales seemed satisfactory. Nevertheless, jobbers would not take it on, and when direct sales to a wider group of dealers was tried, none of the outlets developed any major volume. Even though both amateurs and professionals who have tried it like it, and come back for more, and in spite of the fact that the economics of its use is reasonable and that theoretical demand seems attractive, the executive is about to write it off after four years of trying.

THE DIFFERENCE LIES IN WHAT IS NEW

All three cases are simple examples of a too prevalent failure to analyze

Reprinted with permission from Journal of Marketing, July 1960, pp. 52–56.

[*]Drexel Institute of Technology.

the "what's new?" in the new product . . . to make sure that marketing strategy, channels of distribution, and available resources are compatible with the elements of novelty in the new product. The ease or difficulty of introduction and the characteristics of the successful marketing strategy depend basically on the nature on the "new" in the new product—the new as the customer views the bundle of services he perceives in the newborn.

Take the oyster stew—what was really new, the stew itself? In "R" months, oyster stew has been traditional in homes and restaurants from Boston and San Francisco to What Cheer, Iowa . . . from the Waldorf-Astoria to Harry's Diner. Assuming adequate quality in the commercial product, oyster stew was an old and welcome dinner-table friend. Was the idea of commercial preparation new? For oyster stew, yes, of course, but not for soup. Just look at the facings in the gondolas of any supermarket, or at the empty cans in the trash of any restaurant.

Of course, the idea of a frozen soup was new, but not the concept of frozen prepared foods. Food-store freezer cases had indeed established the association of fresh-quality taste with freeze-processing. But to the consumer, the only "new" aspect about frozen oyster stew was the greater availability and convenience implied in "frozen." With this particular item, the probability of great development might have been anticipated and prepared for in advance.

The silo and the soil improver, by contrast, looked deceptively similar to known items. But actually both embodied, for the consumer, radically new ideas; and both required extreme changes in user habits and user ways of looking at familiar tasks.

The forage storer looked like the familiar silo from the outside, but really embodied a new principle of preservation whose major benefits would be realized only when livestock were taken off pasture and barn-fed harvested forage the year around. Adoption of the device meant, in effect, adoption of a radically new pattern of work organization, and even of farm buildings in some cases.

No matter how great the promised benefit, such a major turnabout of habits requires a great deal of personal selling to get even the more venturesome to try it. Traditional farm-equipment channels are not prepared to carry out the prolonged and intensive type of pioneering personal sales effort and demonstration required. A reasonable degree of success began to accrue only after the manufacturer realized these facts and made the necessary changes in his selling plan.

Likewise, the soil improver resembled other growth stimulants in that it was sold in large bags and had a granular appearance. But the method of use was entirely different from, and more difficult than, the methods of surface application common to most growth stimulants in garden use. It had to be dug in, to be physically intermixed with the soil. In addition, the benefit was an unfamiliar one, and perhaps not easily believable—simple soil aeration. True, in cultivation, all gardeners practice aeration; but they think of weed killing, not aeration, when they hoe their gardens.

With such a product, success can reasonably be expected only after a strong educational campaign based on intense advertising, wide publicity, and personal contacts with consumer groups such as garden clubs and women's clubs. The resources needed were far in excess of those available in a "bootstrap" operation.

THE TONI EXAMPLE

Determination of the novel aspects of a new product is no simple mechanical process. What is new depends on what the prospective consumer perceives, or can be brought to perceive, in the new product.

Determining such potential aspects requires a high order of imagination, and spectacular successes such as the Toni Home Permanent are due in no small part to the introducer's skill in pinpointing the nature of the novel aspects of the product, and devising the kind of marketing strategy needed to fit the various types of "new" elements in his product.

When the Harrises first introduced Toni, they clearly perceived that their key problem was to gain credibility for the idea of a safe and satisfactory "permanent wave" done in the home. Home curling of hair was an old custom, but the home-produced curl had always been very temporary. Permanent waves had been available, and proven, for nearly thirty years, but only at the hand of a skilled hairdresser, and in a specially equipped beauty parlor. With the perfection of the cold-wave lotion, a true home permanent became possible, using a technique not very different from those already in use for temporary home curling. The principal benefit was one for which the times of the middle and late 1940's were ripe —a major saving in cost as compared with the professional job.

The problem was to gain credibility for the safety and the effectiveness of the product claiming the benefit (Toni) —a problem requiring intense selling effort. The Harris strategy consisted of: persuading the girl behind every cosmetic counter in town to use a kit herself before it went on sale; making sure that every cosmetic counter had a stock before the day of introduction; working one town at a time, putting the maximum advertising effort behind the introduction; plowing back all income into further advertising until market saturation was accomplished; and then using funds from established markets to open new ones.

If, on hindsight, this solution seems to have been the obvious, it should be noted that Toni was not the first coldwave home permanent—merely the first successful one. The forgotten competitor, who was really first, never appreciated the intensity of consumer education that would be needed, and had so little success that his product is remembered by few.

WAYS A PRODUCT CAN BE "NEW"

In how many ways can a product be new? Of course, each case should be analyzed on its own. Nevertheless, there are at least thirteen possibilities which should be considered:

A. Six novel attributes are positive, in the sense that they ease the job of introduction:
  1. New cost—or, better yet, price —if lower.
  2. New convenience in use—if greater.
  3. New performance—if better, more dependable and in the range of experience of the prospect—if believable.
  4. New availability, in place, or time, or both (including anti-seasonality).
  5. Conspicuous - consumption (status symbol) possibilities.
  6. Easy credibility of benefits.
B. At least four characteristics make the job more difficult, slow up market development, and usually make it costlier:
  7. New methods of use (unless obviously simpler).
  8. Unfamiliar patterns of use (any necessity for learning new habits in connection with performance of a task associated with the new product).
  9. Unfamiliar benefit (in terms of the prospect's understanding).
  10. Costliness, fancied or real, of a possible error in use.
C. Three others are ambivalent in their effect—that is, the effect on market development probably depends not only on their exact nature, but also on the cultural climate at the moment. However,

extreme unfamiliarity would probably be negative in effect:
  11. New appearance, or other sensed difference (style or texture, for example).
  12. Different accompanying or implied services.
  13. New market (including different channels of sale).

The oyster stew had four of the six positive characteristics (only lower cost and conspicuous consumption omitted), and no negative ones. The silo and the soil improver had all of the negative attributes listed, and only performance among the positive. Toni had cost and performance in its favor, and marketing strategy involved an overwhelming attack on the negative aspects (fear of error and credibility of results).

The ambivalence of style should be obvious to those who have followed automobile history. The turtle-shaped DeSoto of the 1930's was one of the most spectacular design failures of history. The design was "too radical" for the motorists of that era. Twenty years later, the very similar appearance of the Volkswagen "beetle" proved no deterrent to the initiation of a radical reorientation of the American automobile market. And while the Volkswagen brought into that market items of dependable performance, greater convenience in use, and a lower cost than had been available for some time, one element in its success was the recognition of the necessity for continuing the availability of an established implied service in the sale of the car—ready availability of parts and service. Volkswagen entered no area until it had made certain of a high-grade service network in that area.

A FOURTEENTH CHARACTERISTIC

Omission of a possible fourteenth characteristic—new construction or composition—is purposeful. This characteristic is neutral—that is, it has no consumer meaning except to the extent that it is identified with, or can be associated with, one or more of the consumer-oriented characteristics listed above.

All that is new in any product is the package of consumer-perceivable services embodied in it. The innovator leads himself astray who analyzes the novel in his newborn in terms of physical and engineering attributes.

AN EXAMPLE IN TELEVISION

The physical similarity of color TV to black-and-white TV probably led the electronic industry to expect, erroneously, that color-set introduction would parallel the "mushroom" market development experienced with black-and-white. Physically, the parallel was certainly there. Color adds a new dimension to the signal received, just as the picture added a new dimension to the radio signal. But black-and-white television was not, for the consumer, a simple extension of radio. To the family, and most especially to the children, it was a vastly more convenient theater—it was "movies in the parlor." In an era in which children were being granted almost everything they asked for, the pressure for ownership soon became overwhelming. And to add to that pressure, the black-and-white tele-

vision set required an unmistakable and quite conspicuous symbol of possession—the distinctive aerial. Black-and-white television never had to be sold—it was bought.

Color television, however, to the consumer, *is* simply an extension of black-and-white, which he already owns, and to which he is thoroughly accustomed. The mere idea of an added color dimension has only potential interest to the adult, and probably little to the child. Programs, moreover, are fully compatible—the owner of the color TV set can talk about no program the black-and-white neighbor has not been able to see.

Color television's one positive characteristic is thus simply better performance—a degree of better performance which has not as yet acquired much value in the eyes of the consumer. Offsetting this are the factors of higher cost, questions as to perfection of color TV, and a benefit that is relatively unfamiliar, so far as the experience of most prospects is concerned.

If color television is to become dominant, it will have to gain acceptance the way most other home appliances have—by "hard" direct-to-customer personal selling, probably operating through selective retail distribution, backed up by strong advertising and shrewd publicity that will build up the latent added value of color reception into kinetic reality.

THE OLD CAN BE NEW

Even the well-established can be "new" so far as the buyer is concerned. The pharmaceutical industry is well aware that when its ethical formulations can be made available for over-the-counter sales, new sales vistas can be opened by a new sales effort. Ecko discovered that an invention of the 1890s could gain quick success when reintroduced to the modern market (the case of the one-hand egg-beater). And one of the most interesting research results the author ever had was the discovery that a minor product which a client had been making for over fifty years needed only a different kind of sales effort, including a new channel of sale, to turn it into a promising new major product in the industrial-component field.

MARKET MANAGEMENT OF INNOVATION

Skilled management of the innovation phase of the enterprise is, increasingly, a prerequisite to business success. Today's fast-moving markets pay best profits to firms in the van of those with product improvements and new products. In some industries, even mere survival depends on constant, successful new-product introduction. New-product success follows only when the marketing plan is suited to the innovational characteristics of the individual product, as the customer views it, or can be brought to view it.

Really consistent success in the marketing of innovations requires an all too rare understanding that the extent and nature of the new is not measurable in terms of the physical specifications of the product nor in the logical blueprint of the service. The nature of the new is in what it does to and for the customer—to his habits, his tastes and his patterns of life.

Some aspects of the new product make familiar patterns of life easier, cheaper, more convenient, or otherwise more pleasant. These aspects aid speedy introduction and adoption. Other aspects of the innovation require new patterns of life, new habits, the understanding of new ideas or ways of looking at things, the acceptance of the difficult to believe, or the acquisition of new tastes. The latter require the maximum concentration of marketing energy, to add enough value to the strange service to counterbalance the pain of the new idea.

Finally, some characteristics can be positive, negative, or neutral, dependent on the trend of the cultural climate. The current valence of these must be carefully evaluated at the time of introduction, and the marketing plan, or even the product design, fitted to the value determined.

Skillful development of new-product marketing plans would thus seem to consist of three basic steps:

1. Careful analysis of the positive and negative aspects of the specific product.
2. Maximum exploitation of the improvements in the familiar embodied in the product, to gain added value necessary to overcome the negative aspects.
3. Application of the maximum promotional effort in countering the negative aspects and lending value to the new and unfamiliar.

▶▶▶▶▶▶▶▶▶▶▶ DESIGN OF THE MARKETING PROGRAM FOR A NEW PRODUCT

G. T. BORCHERDT[*]

Before getting into the aspects of designing a marketing program for a new product, I thought it might be well for me to give you a little background about the kind of business in which we are engaged in the Polychemicals Department of Du Pont. This may help you understand why I'll be somewhat vague in some areas that perhaps are of major concern to you, and on the other hand, appear to go overboard in considering some of the finer points related to our problems, not necessarily of great concern to you. I hope, however, that I adequately touch on the significant points because my main objective in this presentation is to relate them in a fashion that describes an integrated program.

Our Polychemicals Department manufactures and markets "Zerone" and "Zerex" anti-freeze, a wide range of agricultural chemicals and various bulk chemicals such as adipic acid, methyl alcohol, and ammonia. On the plastics side, we are heavily involved in the polyethylene business, in fluorocarbon polymers, and a variety of nylon and acrylic plastics resins. We produce some semi-finished forms as well as finished forms of plastic products.

For this discussion I have chosen the plastics area for considering the design of a marketing program for a new product. I feel that here we can delineate specific factors in a very orderly and common-sense manner—and in addition we are dealing with what is now a profoundly important area in coming to grips with commercialization of new products.

In Figure 1 I have depicted in simplified form the sequential flow of materials as a plastic is produced, shipped to a customer for molding or shaping with the shaped object then following typical channels until it reaches its point of ultimate consumption or use. You will note that I have made a basic distinction between uses of the product that end up in producer equipment and those that are ingredients of consumer items. Depending upon the extent of this split, the over-all product involvement can be profoundly influenced, because, as you well know, consumer goods purchases and capital goods purchases can be and very often are markedly out of phase. I have flagged this in the diagram by showing that the machinery involving the product ceases to flow at the point at which it is used, whereas the ingredient portion of the

Reprinted with permission from Marketing's Role in Scientific Management (*Robert L. Clewett, editor*), *American Marketing Association, 1957, pp. 58–73.*

[*]*Manager of Marketing Analysis Section, Polychemicals Department, E. I. du Pont de Nemours and Company.*

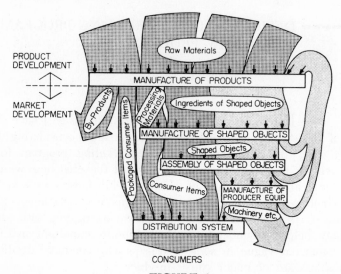

FIGURE 1

TYPICAL FLOW OF PLASTIC PRODUCT

consumer item flows beyond this point. Although not shown in this simplified diagram, producer equipment, of course, can and usually does flow into the various other stages of manufacture. In this connection I have shown items produced by the customers, and their customers in turn, flowing back to the basic manufacturer of the product. This, I feel, can be a very important point to recognize inasmuch as valuable information can be obtained within your organization as to performance of items made from your products. You will find as I go along, that recognition of factors involved in the distribution through the stages indicated on this chart become principal points in my discussion, in particular the end-use factors involved. Also the factors shown on the left-hand side of the chart involving product development needs become important to recognize in the over-all design of the marketing pro-

gram as these factors relate to the market development segment of the program.

Since I have selected a new plastic product for the discussion, let's take a look at what's been happening to plastics. Figure 2 shows the history of growth of plastics resins. This is an arithmetic scale in which the quantity in pounds for 1956 was a little over four billion and in dollars about two billion. Now, some pretty learned gents did a little projecting back in 1942, and look what they came up with. How wrong can you be by relying on historical trend projections? The point which I want to emphasize here—and as a matter of fact this is the heart of my whole presentation—is that in designing our program we must consider primarily what it is that can be achieved as a result of bringing this product on the market, rather than simply transcribing what has happened in the past

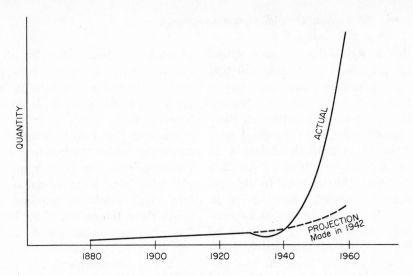

FIGURE 2

HISTORY OF GROWTH OF PLASTIC RESIN

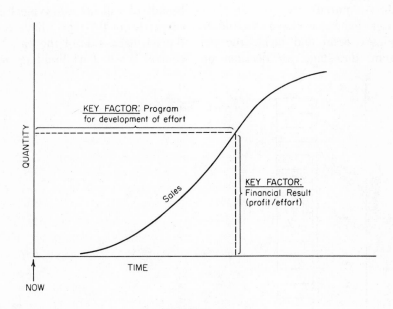

FIGURE 3

BASE FACTORS IN DESIGN OF MARKETING PROGRAM FOR THE NEW
PRODUCT

to other materials that we have chosen to call plastics. I think you will find that the approach constitutes fundamentally the application of straightforward common sense, although there are undoubtedly some pretty knotty problems to face in development of the various components of the program and what can be achieved by it.

To set the stage, I have shown in Figure 3 the basic factors to be considered. Obviously, it is necessary to predict quantity of sales we feel we can realize as time goes on. The key factors in achieving these will be how we expect to deploy our effort in the marketing program—and resulting from this, whether or not it is worth while. In other words, can we predict an attractive profit position in relation to the effort required?

... Let's assume we have a candidate new plastic resin and tackle the job of setting the stage for decision on commercialization. Naturally, the first question we ask as the new plastic emerges from the test tube is "what's it good for?" So, in Figure 4, I've shown a quantity bar which describes, and I emphasize the word "describes," the extent to which the product is technically suitable for use. Or more simply, what can you make out of it and how much would be required if you made these things out of it? In doing this we must consider specific end uses, and since we are considering whether or not it is worthwhile to commercialize the product, the size of the markets for these end uses must be built up. Since our tools for doing this are statistical data available from government and trade association sources and the like, it is inevitable that a first broad cut will fall into typical industry categories of the type I have shown on the left-hand side of the bar. Now, of course, if we don't build up much of

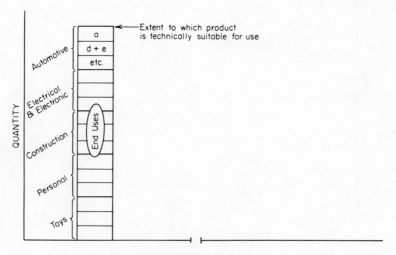

FIGURE 4

SIZE OF MARKET POSSIBILITIES

a bar here, it is unlikely that we should be faced with designing a marketing program.

We are undoubtedly going to be competing in many of the end-use areas with other materials either now being used or, though not yet on the market, also technically suitable. And so, we immediately start matching this new product against these other materials to judge where the new product will do a better job. In Figure 5 I have added, therefore, a second bar depicting the extent to which the product is technically preferable for use. Now I want to emphasize at this point that we have not yet come to grips with the costs associated with the use of the product. We're just trying to find out where, because of its end-use properties, it will do the best job. You will notice I've dropped out some of the end uses in two areas, the automotive and the construction areas, as a pos-

sible typical situation faced with a new plastic resin. Thus, it may be possible to use it for a structural part, but if you really had your choice, and cost was not a factor, you would prefer to stick with steel or concrete, or possibly even wood. Now, I think this second bar with the data backing it up is a pretty important piece of information to have around. It is an important guide to indicate incentive for doing research and development to overcome cost barriers involved in the use of the product. It tells you what could be fair game for sales efforts in the event that you could do something about costs.

But we haven't considered costs yet and we still have a way to go in making up our minds as to what we should be able to do in the way of sales if we commercialize this product. So, let's take a next step and consider the impact of selling price on the size of these market possibilities.

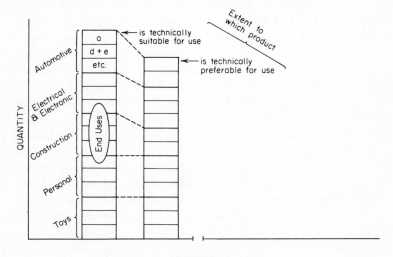

FIGURE 5

SIZE OF MARKET POSSIBILITIES

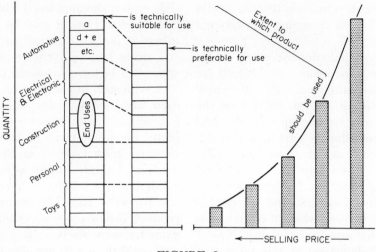

FIGURE 6

SIZE OF MARKET POSSIBILITIES

In Figure 6 I have added to the picture the market size depicting the extent to which the product should be used over a selling price range. Here is where the problem really gets complex because you will remember from the first figure that a plastic resin can go through several stages of fabrication before its real value as a potential end product has been assessed. Basically, the economic aspects of utilizing this material must be built into the overall picture in order to build the bars of "should be used" over the "selling price" range. The bar to the far right is, of course, equal to the far left bar, since at a sufficiently low selling price the product should be used wherever it is technically suitable for use.

Now, at this point I want to emphasize that in no way do these quantities representing size of market possibilities tell us how much we can expect to sell. We still have quite a way to go before we are ready to tell our management

how much we expect to be able to sell. These quantities, documented by the data used in their development, basically provide us with a tool—and possibly one of the most basic tools— to start consideration of the design of the program with its attendant expected sales result. In the next series of figures, I am going to try to depict the basic framework in which this information behind the "should be used" bars fits with respect to the consideration of various alternative courses that we could take.

In the first figure of this series (Figure 7) I have switched around the ordinates of the last figure showing the line of the "should be used" against "selling price" with selling price on the vertical and volume on the horizontal ordinates. In Figure 8, I've detailed the end-use market pattern by the various market areas associated with the built-up volume. Thus, at a high selling price we may have a single use in the auto-

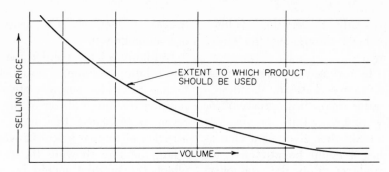

FIGURE 7

FRAMEWORK OF MARKET POSSIBILITIES

motive area and perhaps a couple of end uses in the electrical and electronics area where the specific properties of this new product have high economic value. Particularly in the construction, personal, and toy areas other competitive products beat out our new product if it must sell at a relatively high price. But as we go down in testing the effect of selling price, D and E uses, or use areas, come in in addition to the A, B, and C areas. Nothing more emerges from the electrical and electronics area, but an F use pops up in the construction area. Still no personal or toy items, but these later come in as we go down to relatively low selling prices, and of course

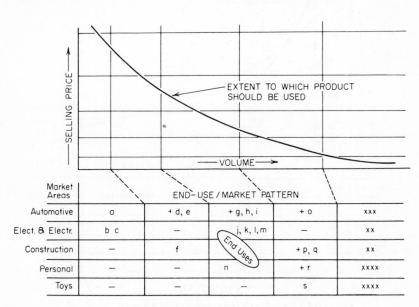

Market Areas	END–USE / MARKET PATTERN				
Automotive	a	+ d, e	+ g, h, i	+ o	xxx
Elect. & Electr.	b c	—	j, k, l, m	—	xx
Construction	—	f	*End Uses*	+ p, q	xx
Personal	—	—	n	+ r	xxxx
Toys	—	—	—	s	xxxx

FIGURE 8

FRAMEWORK OF MARKET POSSIBILITIES

build up rapidly to very high volume levels, perhaps throughout the entire market area.

Now, I feel we are starting to recognize some factors basic to the design of a possible marketing program for this new product. But, as yet I've shown nothing that gives us a clue as to whether it could be attractive for us as a producer to put the product on the market. Undoubtedly, while we've been building this market possibility picture we have been developing cost and investment information on the manufacture of the product, and we probably have a pretty good idea of what it's going to cost us to manufacture it. Moreover, it is likely that the unit costs and unit investments in production facilities will be quite sensitive

to scale, particularly at the early stages of volume growth.

In Figure 9 I have added the typical line relating volume of production to selling price for an attractive profit position for the producer of the plastic resin. As indicated, this figure depicts a region of mutual incentive when you relate the line showing the extent to which the product should be used in the market with the attractive profit position line. In graphic form, it depicts whether or not there is likely to be mutual incentive on the part of potential users of the product and on the part of the producer for commercialization. If these lines don't cross, it seems quite unlikely there is any sound economic reason for putting the product on the market.

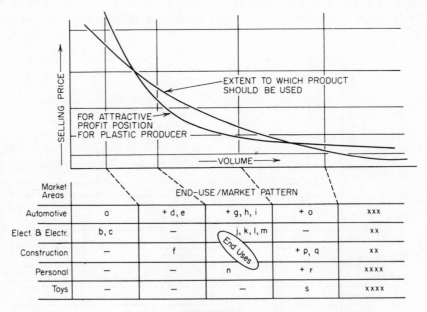

FIGURE 9

FRAMEWORK OF MARKET POSSIBILITIES AND AREA OF
MUTUAL INCENTIVE
(producer vis-a-vis user)

Perhaps you can now see my reason for associating the lower portion of the chart on end-use market pattern with this selling-price volume picture. We immediately begin to get some clues as to the nature and kinds of end uses on which we can put marketing effort and expect enthusiastic response in the market areas, depending upon our pricing plans. Of perhaps greatest importance, it indicates the order in which we will promote uses with the recognition of planting the seeds for future promotions as selling prices may trend down with increased volume of production. However, bringing this up at this stage is really premature because we have not yet come to grips with deciding what our sales volume can be in the face of these opportunities, and whether or not we can capitalize on

them will depend upon the effectiveness we can achieve in a marketing program.

Referring again to Figure 3, we must put together the program for deployment of effort in terms of cost in relation to the profit to be realized by achieving sales. Another way of putting it, shown on Figure 10, is that if we start a marketing program we must, within an acceptable time, reach the point at which sales dollars are sufficient to cover our marketing costs, our manufacturing costs, and provide us with an acceptable profit. I have shaded the profit area and the marketing cost area as they are the key points in today's discussion. Arriving at manufacturing costs is usually straightforward, and we are likely to know these within acceptable limits.

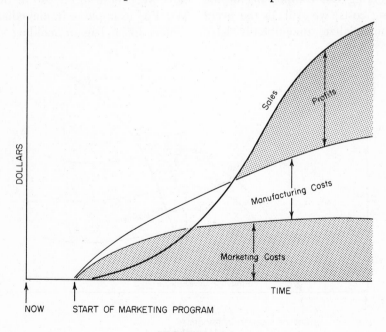

FIGURE 10

SALES VERSUS COST

I've said nothing yet about forecasting our sales. Actually, we still are not in shape to forecast. There are likely to be more market possibilities than we can possibly go after within the limitations of our marketing facilities. Consequently, we must select from the alternatives facing us. It behooves us to consider very carefully the costs of attempting to develop the various markets, if we are to select the most attractive approach. Accordingly, on Figure 11, I've translated the previous figure into one depicting profit/effort relationship showing typical components of a marketing program for a plastic resin, which add up to a total marketing cost which must be related to the total profits derived from sales volume achievable.

Considering the components of the marketing costs, we will, in the event we commercialize, undoubtedly have continuing costs associated with research on improving and modifying the product. I have indicated this on the figure as product development cost. There will be costs connected with working out ways in which to fabricate the end-use items. This is inevitable, even though we may not be making the actual end-use item ourselves. Our salesmen will be working with the customers, such as molders and extruders, whose customers may be assemblers, as indicated on my first chart. Thus, there will be what I've called here customer development costs. There will also be distribution costs. Obviously, there can be wide variations in the compositions and costs of these individual components depending upon the particular end uses involved and how we choose to engage in the market. For example, our immediate customers for a bag of molding powder

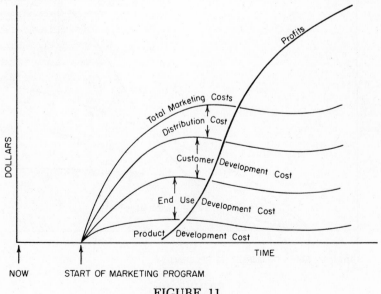

FIGURE 11

PROFIT/EFFORT

may, in a captive sense, carry right through to the end-use area in some uses, and we, therefore, may have very minor costs involved in end-use development with some uses. In some areas a great deal of work may be required in this end-use area, with our immediate customers merely picking this up with very little effort on their part. Or, if the end uses are predominantly in areas where a significantly new distribution approach must be involved, perhaps even to the extent that we have to be organized to handle distribution, this area may be of particular importance. Plastic pipe is an example here, where, if we elect to manufacture and distribute pipe and are not already in the pipe business, we will have real additional distribution costs. My point is that the specific end uses must be studied individually and the profit to result must be related to the efforts required in order to decide on our marketing program. Inevitably we will find that there are possibilities for selling the product, some of which might be quite substantial in volume, but in which there is not a very attractive profit-effort relationship, at least for early market development.

So, let's assume that we have really "cased the joint"—looked over the various alternatives for sales possibilities— and have decided within the individual areas what we could accomplish if we went out to develop these areas. On Figure 12 I have put together these data from the standpoint of volume, where the bar shows the market possi-

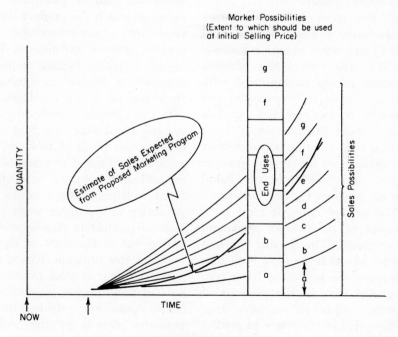

FIGURE 12
PROJECTED SALES RESULT

bilities—that is, the extent to which the product should be used at the initial selling price. The faint segments of the stacked line chart indicate, in an accumulative fashion, what we believe we can accomplish as time goes on in each of these end-use areas to give an over-all framework of total sales possibilities. Then, through a selection of the most attractive ones from the standpoint of profit in relation to effort, we have finally arrived at an estimate of the sales that we believe we can realize from our proposed marketing program involving the various components of product development, end-use development, etc. Finally, we have made a forecast—but you'll notice I've previously called it an estimate of sales. It can only become a forecast upon decision to commercialize.

Well, that covers a lot of territory and obviously a great deal of soul searching and rather precise considerations. We have a marketing program to propose to our management with the sales volumes to be expected and the profits to be expected. At first glance, it looks like our job is done, but I would like to bring up one further point which I feel is very important to recognize and build into the initial marketing program for this new product. The cost of doing it must be a component of the over-all marketing costs predicted. This is that we had better be sure that we have built into our program the procedure for a continuing evaluation of the progress of the venture. Although we have done everything within our power to predict results and plan our efforts, there is no question that we will face road blocks, and that as new information develops,

we may have to make some rather profound changes in the way we operate. In other words we need to project while formulating the initial program, the procedure and the facility with which to carry out the procedure of continuing analysis of market position.

On the last figure (13) I have summarized the sales volume considerations previously developed but shown now in the form they will take if we commercialize the product and build its market. What I've done here is to "straw man" the position we will be in in the future (as indicated by the future "now" legend on the figure) from the standpoint of the marketing analysis requirements to assist the marketing organization in its continuing marketing decisions. Thus, I've divided our market possibility bar of extent to which the product should be used into three inevitable areas; namely, size of possibilities in uses already established, those under development but not yet established, and those not yet under development but still conceptually sound. Just as we are now faced with projecting the position we will be in as to initial selling price at the time of commercialization, we will at this future "now" time be faced with projecting a future market possibility at a possible lower price as scale of production may increase, and so the bar at the right of the figure indicates this situation. I have flagged again the total of sales possibilities in light of these market possibilities, and have assumed we're up to date on the attractive areas to go after, and therefore, have put in the estimates of sales expected.

Now, you may ask why bother to

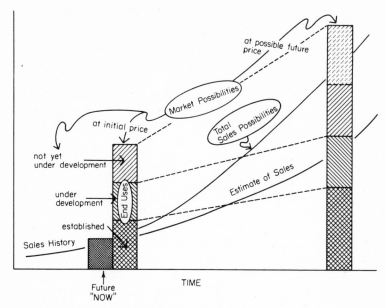

FIGURE 13

POSITION IN EVENT COMMERCIALIZATION UNDERTAKEN

show this future position requirement for analysis at the time we're designing the initial program? My reason is this— any continuing program on a new plastic resin comprises deployment of field salesmen to extend sales in established uses, the deployment of development technologists to get new markets started and, inevitably, the involvement of research and development technologists to test ideas and concepts for market soundness. And so, the opportunities to which these three stages of development are cued are separated in my figure. Of course, to be able to do this we must build into our marketing program an analysis procedure which will give us adequate knowledge of the stages of the end-use developments— and we'd better have it, with its costs, built right into our initial design.

I hope I've been able to lead you through my maze. Quite obviously what I have shown is a marketing analysis. Also, quite obviously, no single organizational segment of a marketing team can do the entire job. A variety of skills and experiences are required. In fact, what I have attempted to depict is the result of the entire marketing team's deliberations. Much of the factual market data can be developed by staff marketing research or marketing analysis teams, but ultimately it takes the operating marketing people to say just how they will do it and what it will cost, and this is as it should be. They will be responsible for achieving the result and, accordingly, in my opinion, should say what they expect to achieve. The design of the marketing program for a new plastic product must certainly be a team effort.

▶▶▶▶▶▶▶▶▶▶ D

Testing, Executing, and Evaluating the Program

▶▶▶▶▶▶▶▶▶▶▶▶▶PUTTING THE PLAN INTO ACTION

GEORGE P. BUTLER, JR.*

The sales v-p of a big industrial tool manufacturer reviewed his new product plan (below) with some pride. Then he succumbed to a very normal, human desire—to get his show on the road.

"We're ready to move," he decided. "We want to get this new product line out before competition gets the jump on us. We have a good, basic sales plan. All the major decisions are made. The remaining details will get taken care of."

The sales v-p had provided for everything, he thought. The new tool line was really new, had a solid com-petitive edge, was priced competitively, and packaged to sell. Market tests had produced excellent results. Sales train-ing, advertising and promotion, tech-nical service, everything had been planned.

But let's see what actually happened.

Even though the salesmen were all fired up to sell the new line, the results were most disappointing. The salesmen found the prospects keenly interested, but not ready to buy. Despite encour-aging interest in introductory sales presentations, few orders were written in the follow-up sales calls.

Reprinted with permission from Sales Management, *August 5, 1960, pp. 36–37, 94.*

St. Thomas Associates, Inc., Management Consultants.

The only bright spot in the entire effort was in the test market area, where customers appeared to be really satisfied.

The sales v-p simply couldn't understand why his "good, basic sales plan" had failed. Later, the difficulties were traced to three major causes, all of them missing links in the sales plan. The plan had made no specific provision for the following factors:

1. Planned sequence and timing of events.

2. Comprehensive internal communications.

3. Up-to-the-minute, objective progress measurement.

Many new products that are brilliantly conceived go down as failures in the market place—because one or all of these three management techniques are not given enough attention by the sales executive.

In sales planning, the sales executive finds an appropriate challenge for his combined creative, managerial and

A SALES PLAN CHECKLIST FOR YOUR NEXT NEW PRODUCT

☐ MARKET TEST
extensive enough to be reliably indicative?
sufficiently good results?

☐ SALES VOLUME OBJECTIVES
developed realistically?
agreed upon by all responsible?

☐ MARKETING BUDGETS
determined for all functions?
accepted as sufficient for each task?

☐ PRE-SELLING PROGRAM
effective advertising campaign prepared?
related sales promotion programs planned?
all necessary literature designed and approved?

☐ FIELD SELLING
introductory prospect list prepared?
sales policies determined and understood?
most effective sales points selected?

sales training program developed?
technical customer service provided for?

☐ PRODUCT DESIGN
fulfills customer needs?
has competitive advantages?

☐ MARKET RESEARCH
sufficient present demand?
continuing demand?

☐ DISTRIBUTION
channels selected for optimum marketing efficiency?
adequate inventory of all items on hand?

☐ PRICE AND DISCOUNT STRUCTURE
good consumer value?
sufficient to motivate distributors?
adequate company profit?

☐ PACKAGING AND PUT UP
right for the customers' needs?
convenient for shipping and inventory?
convenient for display and installation?

marketing skills. It is probably the most imaginative element of his job and, like anything imaginative and creative, it is often highly stimulating. The unfortunate fact is, however, that creativity and stimulation do not normally go hand in hand with the thoroughness and attention to detail required to make a sales plan pay off in a highly competitive situation.

As competition in all markets gets keener, the emphasis on careful and thorough sales planning increases. Today there is always someone ready to exploit a missing link or slip-up in a competitor's sales plan.

Too often the stimulation and creative satisfaction felt by the author of an ingenious sales plan turn out to be the plan's worst enemies. It is in this frame of mind that the sales executive is most prone to push for immediate action. He usually gets his way, too, because the rest of the organization falls under the spell of his enthusiasm.

Many successful sales chiefs who mastermind sales plans themselves have come to realize that creative planning and attention to detail call for divergent talents. These men have hired assistants, usually men experienced in exhaustive projection of detail and methodical review and revision of timetabled action plans.

But, in this case, the sales v-p had overlooked this "detail." Let's see what went wrong with his sales plan.

SEQUENCE AND TIMING OF EVENTS

Several basic differences were found between the company's approach to its test market and to its general market. One was that sales development in the test market had followed a carefully sequenced program of action. But, in the national sales plan, sequence and timing had not been given full-fledged status as elements of the plan. The sales v-p had considered timing a part of implementing the plan but not an integral part of the plan.

On the other hand, in the limited test market project, the market research manager, who was an old hand at detailed programming, had devised a careful action plan for approaching each individual prospect. Separate phases of the plan were assigned to individuals, with target completion dates that were carefully sequenced, as follows:

(a) Exploratory market development interview with prospect to establish his interest and willingness in participating in the test market program —interview to be conducted by area salesman.

(b) Technical conference between company and prospect engineering people to develop details of product test—to be handled by salesman.

(c) Installation — supervised by salesman and a technician.

(d) Periodic follow-up — by sales and technical service people to ensure proper functioning of product and to obtain performance data.

But, when the product was introduced to the national market, the sequence of events was haphazard rather than programmed. Sales training, for example, had not progressed far enough to enable the salesmen to do an effective job of presenting the engineering features of the product in their introductory sales calls. Technical service men were too few to follow up promising sales leads, and there was no program for their participation in introductory sales calls.

The initial advertising break, which included some engineering testimonial data from satisfied test market customers, had met with a few publishing delays and consequently was launched after, rather than before, the initial direct selling effort. Therefore, an ad theme designed primarily to presell was being used to overcome a lack of customer technical education — a job it was not designed for, and was poorly equipped to do.

INTERNAL COMMUNICATIONS

Another shortcoming in the sales plan: The absence of specific provision for internal communication among persons and departments responsible for various elements of the plan. Rapid and comprehensive cross-communications are particularly important during the product introduction period. This is when relatively small problems, if known immediately, can be corrected before they grow into major obstacles.

For example, the engineering personnel working on product applications for test market customers were not instructed to inform the sales force of their findings. But, if this cross-communication had been planned, the sales force would have been far better equipped to furnish prospects with the technical assistance required to make

purchasing decisions. Also, if the delay in the ad schedule had been foreseen and reported immediately, initial sales efforts could have been postponed and thus made much more effective.

UP-TO-THE-MINUTE PROGRESS MEASUREMENT

Every sales plan should provide for up-to-the-minute progress measurement. Its primary purpose is to pinpoint immediate needs for corrective managerial action.

Had this been provided for in the original sales plan, the sales v-p's attention would have been focused immediately on any element of the plan not up to schedule. Periodic progress reports would have been his basis for proceeding as planned, or for adjusting or revising plans.

In addition to being timely, progress reports must be objective and accurate.

For example, when prospects interested in the product were not given the technical information required to appraise a particular application, they were unwilling to go to any effort to get it. They felt such information should come from the manufacturer. Although some salesmen knew they lacked adequate technical training and product application data to sell the product, they were not inclined to report this information because it tended to reflect on their own abilities. Therefore, the sales v-p was not made aware of this problem. And such a problem — requiring men to report against themselves — could not have been caught unless the sales v-p, or another objective person, had been in a position to observe the problem first-hand.

This example emphasizes that it is vital for progress—or the lack of it—to be measured by management that is objective and not directly responsible for the progress being appraised.

So we see that, despite the apparent thoroughness of the sales v-p's plan, all important decisions had not been made, and details that were supposed to fall into place did not take care of themselves.

The most unfortunate result of the missing links in this otherwise sound sales plan happened as a result of a competitor's alertness. This competitor, learning that all was not well with his adversary's sales progress, exploited the opportunity by contacting the same customers and hinting that he had a new product under development which would obsolete all existing products. This introduced just enough doubt into the minds of prospects to cause them to hesitate over making any purchases until all new developments were on the market.

The moral of this story: Today's sales plans must be more thorough than ever. They must have built-in provision for immediate feedback of the information required to make fast adjustments when necessary.

It is no longer adequate to rely on an intuitive feeling that a plan is good and therefore will work. Details, unfortunately, have a way of not working themselves out. In fact, details are more inclined to follow Murphy's Law, the ancient marketing axiom which says: "That which can go wrong, will go wrong."

►►►►►►►►►► TEST MARKETING OF NEW CONSUMER PRODUCTS

FRANK LADIK, LEONARD KENT, AND PERHAM C. NAHL*

Probably the most important purpose of test-marketing programs is to aid in evaluating opportunities for new products.

Of course, the term "new" may have a number of different meanings. Some new products never have been offered to consumers, while others represent simply a change in form, content, or perhaps packaging. Sometimes the term "new" has been used when the only change has been one in marketing approach. Whatever the precise meaning, in each case it has offered a challenge to the marketing team, including advertising, to do a more effective selling job.

Because of increased emphasis on

Reprinted with permission from Journal of Marketing, *April 1960, pp. 29–34.*

**All from Needham, Louis and Brorby, advertising agency.*

new-product programs and the corollary emphasis on test marketing, a set of general procedures and limitations is presented in this article. These can be of assistance in the design, control, and evaluation of test-marketing programs.

Each test-marketing situation is unique. Each client, brand, product, and market situation will make somewhat different demands on a test-marketing program. Therefore, the intent is to cover only the more basic principles of test marketing, recognizing that these principles cannot always be strictly adhered to in actual operations.

TEST MARKETING IN INTRODUCING A NEW PRODUCT

In any organized new-product program, there is a screening process which begins with the elimination and selection of potential products or variations at the "idea" stage and continues through the various stages of development until finally the "new" product is considered ready for sale. More and more companies are reducing the risks of faulty marketing decisions by first offering the product on a limited basis.

It is axiomatic that product acceptability should be thoroughly tested through the laboratory and through consumer research before the product is offered for sale. Consumer research can indicate whether or not consumers "like" the new product, can pinpoint some of their likes and dislikes, and can provide comparisons of the new product with those already being sold. However, the only way a manufacturer or distributor can *really* know whether consumers will buy the product is to

offer it for sale. If done on a limited basis, the marketer stands to benefit from the test program, even if the introduction is not successful.

A successful operation not only provides a "go ahead" for broadening the introduction, but also sound information for planning and launching the expanded program. It is not enough to know whether consumers will buy the brand. It is also important to know how much the consumer will buy, how often, and what profit this volume will yield.

If the test operation shows negative results, the marketer conserves his capital and other resources with a minimum adverse effect on the company's reputation, and gains information and experience that will prove valuable later.

Test marketing, then, involves offering the product for sale in a limited geographic area (or areas), resembling as nearly as possible the expanded market in which the product eventually may be sold. A program of test marketing must be carried out with a methodology and on a scale which will permit reasonably accurate projection of its results.

Such tests should be conducted when the potential financial loss to the company through new-product failure, or through the failure of a market plan or approach, is significantly greater than the cost of the proposed test-marketing procedure. This assumes not only that the new product is potentially important to the manufacturer or distributor, but also that any variables to be tested are of such significance that measurable variations in results may be expected.

WHAT CAN BE LEARNED THROUGH TEST MARKETING?

Answers provided by test marketing obviously will vary as test objectives vary. However, market tests can be designed to provide the following different types of information:

1. Rather than merely showing whether a product can be sold at a profit, test marketing can and should be used to indicate *maximum profitability*. It is not enough to establish that a previously decided upon minimum share of the market can be attained with a specific level of selling, promotional, and advertising expenditure. Effective test marketing should help establish the optimum combination of volume, marketing expenditure, and profit. While sales goals and expenditure levels frequently are set on the basis of judgment, it is usually impossible to forecast accurately the share or volume potentials of a new product.

2. Test marketing provides an opportunity for determining the *market profile of a new product*. This includes characteristics of consumers, the way the product is used, frequency of use, and purchase history . . . including frequency of purchase, who buys, who makes buying decisions, etc.

3. Test-marketing performance offers an opportunity to evaluate the *effectiveness of a marketing program* (or of alternative marketing programs), particularly in the areas of securing trial and usage of the product and evaluating amounts expended for advertising and promotion.

4. While *copy testing* along the lines of believability, understanding, and copy-point registration normally is completed prior to test marketing, the test operation provides an opportunity for further checking of these factors.

5. Test marketing can provide up-to-date *trade information* which contributes to the evaluation of the test-market operation through the use of special audits and surveys. Information, both for the test product and for competitive products, can be gathered on trade attitudes, trade allowances and discounts, price-off deals, displays, spot-advertising expenditures, promotions, distribution and out of stock, inventory situations, shelf facings and positioning, and sales-force performance and requirements.

6. Test marketing offers an opportunity to obtain from *consumers* a wide variety of information relevant to the test operation, including facts, opinions, and attitudes concerning the test product and competitive products.

HOW MUCH CAN BE TESTED?

There is a practical limit to the number of market programs, or variations, which can be tested at one time. This limit is for the most part economic. From a research point of view, it is possible to test almost any number of variables or groups of variables, including such things as different price levels, sizes, media combinations, advertising themes, and consumer and dealer promotions.

However, principally because of cost considerations, an expanded program to cover many of these variables is not practicable. A minimum number of test variations will hold losses to a minimum if the product or marketing variations prove unsuccessful.

On the other hand, should the product or marketing variations prove successful, additional information probably will be desired and required. This additional information usually can be determined more efficiently (faster and at less cost) during the conduct of the original test series.

QUALIFICATIONS CONCERNING TEST MARKETING

If test marketing is to be conducted, there are certain conditions which must be met before test results may be used with confidence:

The objectives of the test must be *specific* and *well defined*. The test must be well *designed*. It must be well *supervised* and *analyzed*.

The following points also need to be considered for a program of test marketing:

1. Product or program variations must be large enough to provide for measurable differences in results within the budget and time requirements.

2. When seeking advertising and promotional expenditure levels, it is desirable to test at least two variations—a maximum and a minimum. All too frequently, an expenditure level for testing is selected on a rather arbitrary estimate of what is affordable, based on anticipated sales and earnings. Typically, estimates of sales and earnings are conservative; for this reason many products never have an opportunity to show their true potential. Only through

testing more than one expenditure level can a reasonable estimate of a product's potential be determined.

3. All important variations to be tested should be tested, if practicable, at the same time (although different markets may be required).

4. If a new variation is to be tested, and the results compared with those of a previous test of another variation, it is desirable that both be tested concurrently. This is to eliminate possible differences due to the time factor.

5. All factors other than those being tested should be held as constant as practicable, and allowed for in evaluating results.

6. Criteria for action should be established, at least in general terms, prior to testing. Often market findings during the test period will indicate a need for modifying previously established criteria.

HOW LONG IS THE OPTIMUM TESTING PERIOD?

One of the most serious and potentially expensive errors facing the test-marketing program is the temptation to utilize short cuts. And one of the more frequent and dangerous of these is the cutting short of the test run.

Test marketing has been defined as a method of reducing future marketing risks, and thus represents a form of marketing insurance. This insurance, however, is not without its costs. These costs, or premiums, take many forms, including the expenditure of money, time, and effort in carrying out an introductory marketing program; the exposure of a new product and its marketing program for all competitors to see and analyze; and commitments to the trade.

All of these are "premiums" paid for this form of marketing insurance. To reduce seriously the length of the test run is to pay these premiums in full without realizing the full insurance protection.

The actual length of the test-marketing program should vary, of course, according to the type of product, consumer buying frequency, the nature of the industry and competition, and the activities being tested. However, there are some general rules:

1. In introducing new products, particularly in the grocery-products field, it is best generally if test periods run at least six months. This much time is usually necessary to evaluate brand progress properly. However, if dealing or couponing continues through much of the introductory period, then in all probability the test period should be extended to allow a "normal" sales level to come about.

2. If there is to be an evaluation of advertising campaigns in connection with the market test, the concept of cumulative effect through repetition requires that the test be run considerably longer than the usual product-acceptance test. It may well be necessary to run the test as long as a year.

3. For promotional tests, the governing time factor should be the time required for consumers to return to normal buying patterns after their exposure to "deal" merchandise.

Of course, there are substantial pressures exerted—both within and outside the company—as the test progresses, which agitate for a decision before a decision is justified.

INTRACOMPANY PRESSURES

The drive and competitive spirit which contribute to successful management and aggressive sales policies frequently are characterized by a restlessness and an eagerness to "get going." This restlessness may not only be responsible for setting test machinery in motion before it has been adequately prepared, but may also be responsible for premature interpretation of test data.

Another pressure, perhaps one of the most difficult to combat, results primarily from an unwillingness to accept negative test findings. This lack of objectivity is understandable when it is remembered that by the time the product has been in the test-market stage for some time, management probably has made a considerable investment in ideas, talent, time, money, and facilities.

Still another form of intracompany pressure comes from members of the sales force not participating in the test. For any number of reasons, including rumors of test-market successes, this group may actively solicit, and in some cases demand, premature expansion of the marketing program.

The carrying out of a reliable test operation rests in no small part on the successful resistance to such pressures.

MARKET PRESSURES

There are numerous market pressures, including reputed advantages of market leadership and competitive challenge for market position. Sometimes there is opportunity in the face of weak demand for present products. Others are consumers' loyalty to established brands, and the "bandwagon."

Management, in its earnest desire to be first, or its desire to protect brand position and franchise, or in the face of a slackening demand for its regular products, is sometimes so impatient that it will rely upon preliminary test results. If management believes that competitors will respond quickly and that consumer loyalty to any one brand is a fleeting thing, the temptation is to expand the marketing program beyond the test stage before the facts warrant this.

Perhaps the most dangerous form of pressure from the outside comes from trade sources. Wholesalers and dealers, not a part of the original testing program, may hear about a particularly promising new product and exert great pressure on management to "get on the bandwagon." These pressures may be hard to resist, especially where excess production capacity or excess sales capacity exists.

Since even the most expertly conducted test-marketing programs cannot prove conclusively that a product will be a success, it is not difficult to understand management's willingness to go along with the various pressures exerted upon it. The best that can be hoped for is that, after committing substantial sums to testing and paying the premiums for marketing insurance, management will view the pressures as objectively as possible.

HOW MANY TEST MARKETS ARE REQUIRED?

There is no fixed answer to the question of how many test markets are required in a test-marketing operation. As the number of test markets for a given variable increases, accuracy increases. And, as the number of markets increases, the cost of testing increases. Obviously a compromise must be reached between the accuracy required in the test and the amount of money to be appropriated for the testing operation.

Disregarding the matter of money available, there are several basic considerations which help to determine the minimum number of markets to be considered:

1. There should not be fewer than two markets for each variation to be tested. This does not include control markets—markets in which the variables to be tested are held constant or allowed for.

2. Where the purpose of the test is to estimate the sales potential of a product which is to be distributed nationally, markets in at least four geographic areas should be used.

3. As the significance of the variables to be tested decreases, the number of markets necessary to reflect the effect of these variables increases. Thus, it is likely that where variations are minor, it may not pay to test market them. The determination of which of two secondary copy phrases is more effective in building volume is an example of the type of variable it probably would not pay to market test.

These considerations, relating to the number of markets required, represent an ideal. In practice, the economics of the test situation usually compels a reduction in the number of markets. The extent of this reduction is, quite naturally, a managerial decision. Care should be taken, however, that management does not pare the number of markets to be used to a point where confidence levels may not be reliable.

CRITERIA FOR SELECTING TEST MARKETS

Because of the necessity for projectability and comparability of test-market results, markets selected for use in the testing operation should meet certain requirements. Depending upon the purpose of the test, not all of these may receive equal weight, but the list which follows includes most of the generally accepted criteria:

1. The market or markets should not be over-tested. On the other hand, there may be instances when using a market with a "track record" should be considered.

2. The market should have normal historical development in the product class.

3. The market should represent a typical competitive advertising situation.

4. The market should not be dominated by one industry.

5. State capitals, highly industrialized areas (where shut-downs could seriously impair buying power), college towns, and other areas where population characteristics not normal to the product's target market usually should be avoided.

6. Projectability of results is an important factor. Therefore, the markets selected should represent different geographic regions where varying conditions of use might influence sales.

7. The markets selected should be relatively independent, with little strong outside media competition and relatively little of the test market media circulation going outside the areas. The same principle applies to the movement of the product class being tested.

8. The markets should have a media pattern which conforms closely to the proposed national media plan. For example, TV set saturation should be close to the U. S. average.

9. Markets selected should not be too small to provide meaningful results nor so large that testing becomes too expensive in terms of the results expected.

WHAT SORT OF MEASUREMENTS ARE NECESSARY?

Specific research methods and their timing will vary with the objectives of the test-marketing program. This again emphasizes the importance of establishing precise test objectives in advance of the test operation.

Fundamentally there are two types of measurements made in market-testing operations: (1) consumer studies involving usage, habits, reaction, etc., to the brand in question; and (2) sales measurements involving the brand in question, other "company" brands which might be affected, and selected competitive brands or products.

When measuring consumer usage, habits, and reactions to the brand, interviewing is usually conducted in four stages, which may, of course, be combined.

1. The "base" stage—interviewing during this stage takes place immedi-

ately before the primary distribution phase of the test-marketing program. Its purpose is to establish reference points for use in future analysis.

2. The initial trial stage—interviewing during this stage takes place fairly shortly after the beginning of the test. Its primary purpose is to determine preliminary levels of trial attained.

3. Preliminary usage and reaction stage—interviewing during this stage takes place periodically during the progress of the test. Its purpose is to determine early usage levels and reactions to the product. This stage may phase into the final stage.

4. Final stage—interviewing during this stage frequently takes place about six months after the test has been in progress. Its purpose is to determine current usage levels and reaction to the product after continued exposure.

The in-home interview is probably the most satisfactory method of obtaining the above information. However, telephone interviews or mail questionnaires may be used with relative success.

Sales measurements for most products are satisfactory only if made on a retail-store audit basis. Shipment data are satisfactory only for long-term analysis because of distortions due to filling pipelines and fluctuations in inventory levels. And shipment information does not determine the effect on competition.

Store audits at four-week intervals are generally the most satisfactory sales measurements at the retail level; monthly audits are less desirable because of variations in the number of business days from month to month. If store-audit information is to be obtained, audits should begin at least four weeks prior to the beginning of the market test in order to establish a base for measuring the product's impact on its competitive environment.

BENEFITS OF TEST MARKETING

No practical program of test marketing can predict with absolute certainty the success or failure of products in the market place. Nevertheless, properly planned and executed test-marketing programs do represent an important means of examining the growth and profit potentials of a company's products.

The benefits are worthwhile either when the product survives, or when the results are negative. Survival should contribute to greater profitability of the expanded operation through information and experience gained under actual marketing operations. In addition to enabling management to proceed with greater confidence and possibly to effect indicated revisions, a successful test provides evidence to help "sell" the company's own organization and trade on the product.

When a test has negative results, this is a small price to pay for a sound investment. There are, of course, instances where test marketing is not feasible; and in these cases judgment must prevail, even as it does in many phases of a sound test-market program.

►►►►►►►►►►► EARLY PREDICTION OF MARKET SUCCESS
FOR NEW GROCERY PRODUCTS

LOUIS A. FOURT AND JOSEPH W. WOODLOCK*

Many leading American grocery manufacturers derive from one-half to three-fourths of their sales from items that did not exist prior to World War II. Yet a survey of 200 large packaged goods manufacturers reveals that four out of five new products placed on the market after 1945 failed.[1] A reliable method for early selection of the most promising fraction of innovations would eliminate much of the loss now incurred on failures.

This article reports progress in early prediction of success or failure for new grocery store items. The data were obtained from National Consumer Panel records for national launchings, but the method is applicable to consumer panels in test markets.

The time required for prediction by this method depends upon the average interval between purchases for repeat customers. It can be only a few weeks for a new brand of margarine, but is nearly a year for cake mixes. This contrasts with older methods, using sales volume alone, in which the median time required for decision of new product success has been estimated at 19–24 months after completion of full-scale launching.[2] The new method has been applied to items in the following product classes:

Shortening cake mixes	Ready-to-eat cereals
	Food drinks
Foam cake mixes	Canned fruit
Frosting mixes	Scouring pads
Specialty desserts	Detergents
Cookie mixes	Pet foods
Margarine	

These predictions depend upon the collection and efficient use of detailed information on the factors underlying sales. Sales volume for any item is the product of number of customers times frequency of purchase times size of purchase.

Observation of each of these components is required for our method of prediction, plus a further analysis: separation of initial from repeat purchases, and observation of the developing structure of repeat buying. All this information can be obtained from a consumer panel.

[1] *New Product Introduction*, U.S. Small Business Administration, Management Series No. 17 (Washington, D.C.: Government Printing Office, 1955), p. 63.

[2] Arthur C. Nielsen, Jr., "Consumer Product Acceptance Rates," in *Consumer Behavior*, edited by Lincoln H. Clark (New York: Harper, 1958).

Reprinted with permission from Journal of Marketing, *October 1960, pp. 31–38.*

Both from Market Research Corporation of America, Consumer Panel Division.

Consumer panel analysts often have examined the penetrations and first repeat buying ratios of new products.[3] By penetration is meant the proportion of households that make an initial purchase of an item; by first repeat ratio is meant the fraction of initial buyers who make a second purchase.

Once the initial hurdle of attracting triers has been passed, this ratio is the most important single clue to the future success of an innovation. Reasonably high values for this ratio are a necessary (but not a self-sufficient) condition for success. In our experience repeat ratios below 0.15 (that is 15 out of every 100 triers) almost always spell failure; some very successful items convert as many as half of all triers into repeat purchasers. This facet of the observation technique makes possible identification of the very successful and very unsuccessful at a reasonably early stage.

The new elements in the method reported here are the following:

1. Experience with a large number of earlier new products is used to pre-determine the general functional form or shape of the cumulative penetration as a function of time. Observations of penetration for the particular new product are then used to determine its unique constants. Having estimated these constants, we can then extend the penetration as far into the future (for the same market) as desired.

2. The first repeat ratio is applied to

[3] Stanley Womer, "Some Applications of the Continuous Consumer Panel," *Journal of Marketing,* Vol. 9 (October, 1944), pp. 132–136.

this extended penetration curve to derive a cumulative first repeat purchase curve.

3. Subsequent repeat ratios as needed are similarly applied in turn. These are the ratio of third purchases to second, fourth to third, etc. The actual number of such ratios used depends on the frequency of purchase. The values used for these ratios are not merely those achieved to date, but are estimates for later periods, allowing each group of buyers an opportunity to make a repurchase.

4. The time intervals between purchases and the average size of transactions are observed, the latter separately for new and repeat buyers, and applied to obtain volume estimates. This separation is sometimes vital, for repeat customers may buy the large economy size or in multiple units, while triers may start cautiously.

PENETRATION PREDICTION

As indicated above, extension of penetration from observed periods through prediction periods establishes the framework for volume prediction for grocery products.

There are products such as durable goods, novelties, and certain cosmetics, whose marketing depends solely or mostly upon one-time sales for the particular style or model. For such products, penetration is the entire story; with suitable modifications the procedures indicated here can be applied to such products.

Observation of numerous annual cumulative penetration curves shows that (1) successive increments in these curves decline, and that (2) the cumulative curve seems to approach a limiting penetration less than 100 per cent of households—frequently far less.

A simple model with these properties states that the increments in penetration for equal time periods are proportional to the remaining distance to the limiting "ceiling" penetration. In other words, in each period the ceiling is approached by a constant fraction of the remaining distance.

Such a model is illustrated in Table 1 and in Figure 1, where the ceiling, x, is 40 per cent, and the constant of proportionality, r, is 0.3. In the first time period, the number of new buyers is $0.3(40-0) = 12$ per cent. In the second time period, the number of new buyers is $0.3(40-12) = 8.4$ per cent. Each increment is simply $1-r$ times the preceding increment.

Ratios of successive increments in penetration, such as 8.4/12 or 5.9/8.4

in Table 1, are fast simple estimates of $1 - r$.[4] These ratios can be averaged and applied to the last observed increment repeatedly, to extend penetration as far as desired. This model turns out to be somewhat too simple, but its basic properties remain usable.

To be more realistic, consider the fact that different buyers purchase a product class and its individual brands at widely differing rates. Experience shows that, when buyers are grouped by purchase rates into equal thirds, typically the heavy buying third ac-

[4] Efficient estimates of $1 - r$ and x and a generalization of this model are the subject of a paper presented to the Stanford meeting of the Institute of Mathematical Statistics, August, 1960, by Professor Frank Anscombe of Princeton University. He points out that successive increments can be considered as drawings from a multi-nomial distribution and presents maximum likelihood estimates of $1 - r$ and x that are also sufficient statistics; that is, they utilize all the pertinent information in the observations.

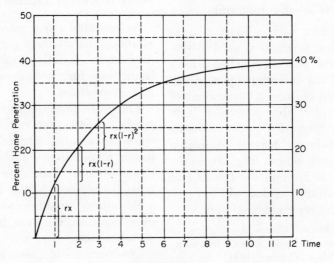

FIGURE 1

NEW BUYER PENETRATION—ASSUMED (x,r model)

TABLE 1

SIMPLE x,r PENETRATION MODEL

Example: $x = 40\%, r = 0.3$

Time Period	Increments in Penetration	
	Formula	*Numerical Example*
1	$r(x - 0) = rx$	$0.3(40) = 12$
2	$r(x - rx) = rx(1 - r)$	$0.3(40)(0.7) = 8.4$
3	$rx(1 - r)^2$	$0.3(40)(0.7)^2 = 5.9$
i	$rx(1 - r)^{i-1}$	$0.3(40)(0.7)^{i-1}$

counts for 65 per cent of the total volume, the middle third for 25 per cent, and the light third for only 10 per cent. This means that, if transaction sizes are equal, heavy buyers make 6.5 purchases for every one of a light buyer, while medium buyers make 2.5, the total averaging 3.3.

If the original x,r model is applied to each of these thirds separately, this difference in purchase frequency will be sufficient to induce a remarkable "stretch-out" effect in the decline of increments of penetration for all buyers combined. This effect is sufficiently pronounced that the penetration model can be improved for the purpose of predicting a year ahead by assuming that increments of penetration approach a small positive constant, k, rather than zero.

A seemingly plausible alternative explanation for this behavior, panel turnover, is ruled out by observations of penetration stretch-out in subsamples chosen so that their composition does not change during the period of observation.

This second model is illustrated in Figure 2, where total penetration approaches a line whose value (at point t

after i time periods) is $x_o + ik$. We can convert our data to observations appropriate to the simpler two-parameter model by subtracting k from observed increments. The x in this simpler model then becomes the x_o of the x,r,k model. Like x and r, k depends upon the individual item and its retail availability.

An empirical rule has worked rather well for estimating k: let k be one-half the increment of new buyers during the fourth average purchase cycle. The effect of subtracting too large or too small a k (when this is the largest source of error) is to produce characteristic serial correlation in the deviations of observations from the fitted curve of penetration. Too small an estimate for k causes the extreme (first and last) observed penetrations to exceed the fitted values, and those in the middle to be less than fitted values. Too large a k produces a reverse (excess) curvature.

Thus a means exists for detecting and correcting a mistake in the estimation of k. Typically k is a small number, of the order of 0.2 per cent per month, or 100,000 households for a nationally distributed grocery product. Actually k has not exceeded 200,000 in our experi-

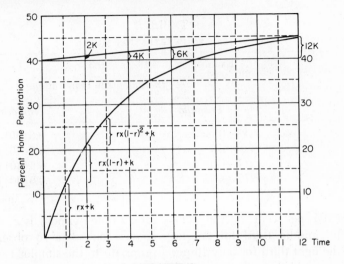

FIGURE 2

NEW BUYER PENETRATION—ACTUAL (x,r,k model)

ence, nor is the model very sensitive to small errors in k.

PREDICTIONS OF SALES

If sales volume in a second period is to be estimated from observations on sales in a first period, several assumptions are required. In market areas to be predicted:

1. Distribution will not shift greatly from the level existing at the end of the first period.

2. Promotional expenditures will not be substantially different in the second period from those during the latter part of the first period.

3. Prices will not change markedly.

4. Neither the product nor the package will be changed.

5. Competitive activity will not differ strikingly.

A shift in a single one of these observable factors should cause the pre-

diction to be off in a predictable direction. A sixth assumption might be added—that the manufacturer does not know the prediction and hence does nothing to alter it. Altered behavior, of course, is a large part of the value of predictions, and failure for this reason is truly success.

Markets grow by deepening—through acquiring new triers and through developing repetitive buying in the original areas. Markets also grow by entry into new areas. Thus, the first assumption of constant distribution has the double burden of meaning steady availability in the old areas and of warning that new areas must be estimated as a separate procedure.

In an effort to predict as early as possible, we may want to use an observation period during which distribution is still increasing. This problem of gradual regional introduction can be minimized by observing various regions or markets separately.

The second assumption acknowledges that the costs of introductory promotions typically exceed levels that are profitable to maintain later. Hence, it is assumed that future promotion will be near current levels in the regions of earliest introduction—that is, levels current in those regions at the time of prediction.

PREDICTION OF REPEAT RATIOS

The fraction of new buyers who have made a second purchase by the end of an observation period is necessarily an under-estimate of those who will ever make a repeat purchase—for some have not yet had an opportunity to repeat.

This error can be substantially reduced by omitting the most recent new buyers from the denominator of the repeat buying ratio estimate. Omission of those purchasing within the most recent one or two average purchase cycles works well empirically. The first new buyers of an item are typically heavy buyers of the product class. Their average purchase cycle is about one-half that of all buyers. (Compare 6.5 purchases with 3.3 for all buyers.) Thus, for equal observation times, the average purchase cycle of repeat buyers to date will be a smaller fraction of the eventual average if the product is purchased infrequently. Such products will require omission of two average purchase cycles' increments of new buyers while omission of one may suffice for frequently purchased product classes.

In practice, the decision to use one or two purchase cycles can be guided by the trends in the two repeat ratio estimates that result. Typically the trends converge as information accumulates.

Similar remarks hold for estimation of the proportion of second-time buyers who will ever make a third purchase, etc.

As might be expected, each successive purchase increases the probability of still another purchase. This is similar to the phenomenon noted by Alfred Kuehn for successive purchases of established brands; each consecutive purchase of a brand increases the probability that the next purchase by the household will be the same brand.[5] Here the purchases do not have to be consecutive. Intervention of purchases of other brands merely prolongs the time until a given number of buyers make their n^{th} repeat purchase. While these interventions are important for some purposes, they need not be considered here.

EXAMPLE OF APPLICATION

Table 2 illustrates the process of obtaining estimated ratios for one product, and Table 3 their application. Together they present one case history in which data for a preliminary observation period were used to predict purchases and volume in a second period.

The first column of Table 2 represents the observed number of purchases through the end of the observation period, in this case a year. The fourth-

[5] Alfred Kuehn, *An Analysis of the Dynamics of Consumer Behavior and Its Implications for Marketing Management,* unpublished Ph.D. thesis, Graduate School of Industrial Administration, Carnegie Institute of Technology, 1958.

TABLE 2

DERIVATION OF REPEAT RATIOS

Buyer Type	No. of Purchases During Observation Period (000's)	Average Interval Until Next Purchase (months)	No. of Cycles in Lag	No. of Purchases in Observation Period Less Lag	Repeat Ratio
New buyers	6,021	2.41	2	4,472	
1st repeat	2,170	1.72	1	1,932	0.485
2nd repeat	1,076	1.43	1	917	0.559
3rd repeat	591	1.20	1	550	0.645
4th repeat	326	1.19	1	282	0.593
5th repeat	223	1.19	1	190	0.797
Over 5	627				3.300

column purchases are observations through somewhat shorter periods. While 6,021 new purchases were made in the first year, only 4,472 had been made 4.82 (2 × 2.41) months before the end of the year. Only these are assumed to have had an adequate opportunity to make a second purchase. Similarly, although 2,170 first repeat purchases were made within the first year, only 1,932 had been made 1.72 months prior to the end of the period, and only these are regarded as having adequate opportunity to make a second repeat purchase.

The first repeat ratio, 0.485, is obtained by dividing 2,170, the number of first repeat purchases, by 4,472, the number of new purchasers who had an adequate opportunity to make a first repeat purchase. Second repeat and further ratios are obtained by using single cycle lags. Thus, 0.559 is the ratio of 1,076 to 1,932. Each new product has its own set of ratios. Comparison with ratios of other new products aids in the evaluation of a new item.

The final line in Table 2 represents a grouping of all purchases beyond the fifth repeat rather than the much smaller number of buyers. The value 3.3 is obtained by dividing 627 by 190. It is not mandatory that this ratio be used as the estimate of future purchases beyond the fifth repeat; work is in process to evaluate this ratio as a function of time.

The ratios in the final column of Table 2 are applied sequentially to the estimated number of new buyers reached by the end of the second period—in this example, 8,141. (This number comes from the application of the second penetration model—r,x,k.) Thus, 8,141 × 0.485 equals 3,948, the number of repeat buyers by the end of the second period. Similarly, 0.559 × 3,948 yields 2,207, the number of second repeat buyers. It can be objected that these repeat ratios should be applied to lagged values of the previous waves of buyers. This is true, but in most instances the differences that result are minor because the cumulative

TABLE 3

ESTIMATED AND ACTUAL PURCHASES $(r,x,k$ model)

Buyer Type	Estimated No. at End of Prediction Period (000's)	No. in Preliminary Observation Period (000's)	Difference or Estimated Addition in Prediction Period (000's)	Actual Addition (000's)
New buyers	8,141	6,021	2,120	2,544
1st repeat	3,948	2,170	1,778	1,523
2nd repeat	2,207	1,076	1,131	858
3rd repeat	1,422	591	831	569
4th repeat	841	326	515	398
5th repeat	671	223	448	283
Over 5	2,214	627	1,587	1,711
Total purchases	19,444	11,034	8,410	7,886

buying curves are rather flat and parallel by the end of the second period.

The first column of Table 3 shows these estimates of purchases by type through the end of the second or prediction period. The second column, repeated from Table 2, shows actual purchases through the observation period. Because the method produces estimates on a cumulative basis through the end of the second period, it becomes necessary to subtract the actual results at the end of the first period to establish net additions during the second period.

The third column is the difference in the first two and represents predictions for the second period—again in this case a year.

The final column of Table 3 reports the actual number of buyers of each type in the second period as reported by the National Consumer Panel.

From the structure of Table 3, it can be seen that errors in prediction of one type of buyer may be partially compensated by offsetting errors for other types of buyers. In this example, underestimates for new buyers and repeats beyond 5 help to compensate for overestimates of the first 5 waves of repeats. In this sense the entire procedure is rather insensitive to error in individual details.

Multiplication of new buyers by their average transaction size, 1.05, and repeat buyers by theirs, 1.09, and adding, yields a total estimated package volume of 9,082,000 in the second period, or a predicted decline of 23 per cent. Actual volume was 8,604,000—down 27 per cent.

The example shown in Tables 2 and 3 is by no means the most accurate in our collection of case histories. It was chosen to present in detail because it illustrates difficulties as well as success in prediction.

Table 4 summarizes estimates that were made for this and six other prepared mix items. Two marketing considerations deserve emphasis in considering such estimates:

TABLE 4

COMPARISON OF PREDICTIONS WITH ACTUAL RESULTS FOR SEVEN PREPARED MIX ITEMS

Product	2nd Period Volume Change		1st Period Repeat Volume as % of Total	2nd Period Repeat Volume as % of Total	
	Estimate	Actual		Estimate	Actual
1	+ 5%	+ 1%	35%	64%	61%
2	−23	−27	47	77	69
3[a]	−40	−58	38	65	58
4	−51	−46	33	60	55
5	−53	−48	34	50	50
6[b]	−56	−48	46	76	74
7	−59	−59	24	47	c

[a] Loss in distribution
[b] Product reformulated
[c] Not determined

Items in Table 4 represent five different introduction times, four different price levels, and three different first-period volumes. In the two instances where actual change differed from predicted change by more than five percentage points, the stated assumptions were violated.

1. Is the total volume predicted sufficient for profitable operation?

2. Is a sufficient part of that volume expected to come from repeat customers?

New buyer volume can be expected to deflate substantially through time. Repeat buyer volume is the ultimate determinant of success or failure.

These marketing considerations suggest that comparisons of predicted and actual results should be directed in the first instance to these questions:

1. Is the total volume estimate reasonably accurate?

2. Is the proportion of that volume from repeat customers predicted closely?

APPLICATION TO MARKET DEVELOPMENT

The foregoing method presents a reliable and easily usable prediction model for test markets or initial national marketings. It has the desirable feature of separating the very good and the very bad quickly. Intermediate cases can be observed for fairly long periods of time. In evaluating these longer observations, the model makes effective use of many previously neglected aspects of the cumulative marketing information available from panels.[6]

Finally, the model acts in a diagnostic capacity for failures. Too few triers might be due to the limitations of the promotional campaign or some limiting aspects of the labeling, naming, or use

[6] A different but complementary approach to new product evaluation using other aspects of panel information is contained in "The Dynamics of Brand Loyalty and Brand Switching," a paper by Dr. Benjamin Lipstein at the 5th Annual Conference of the Advertising Research Foundation, September 25, 1959, New York City. In particular, Dr. Lipstein's technique reveals the source of new buyers in terms of their earlier purchases.

suggestions. Too small a repeat ratio implies that something is wrong with the product or the entire concept. Too long an interval between purchases demonstrates the need for large numbers of triers if product volume is to reach a reasonable level. This suggests the advisability of rapid introduction and greater stress of multiple uses—if any are available.

Of course, this work is too new for all possible difficulties to have been encountered yet. Regional variation in product acceptance is one problem; this can be handled by treating regions as separate markets. Development of a small but very loyal hard core of multi-repeat buyers is another problem. Tracing through many waves of repeat buying rather than grouping beyond some selected level permits treatment of this type of problem.

▶▶▶▶▶▶▶▶▶▶ HOW TO EVALUATE COMPETITIVE MOVES BEFORE IT'S TOO LATE

CHARLES G. BROWN[*]

The usual method of determining the effectiveness of your own company's consumer product offerings is through the use of store audits. Store audits provide total sales volume, market share, pricing, inventory levels, markup, and retailer sales profit per dollar invested in inventory. Nielsen, Audits and Surveys, Burgoyne, Selling Research, etc., have conducted retail audits for years; they provide excellent marketing data, and their contribution to manufacturers has been well established.

Store audits are difficult to set up, in that the samples of stores may not be representative of the market, i.e., more and more of the larger supermarkets, particularly chains, simply do not allow store auditing of any kind;

some supermarkets have private-label brands while others do not; they are difficult to administer over time due to an enumerator error, trans-shipments, lack of sustained cooperation, misplaced invoices, etc.; they are not inexpensive if you want to determine what happens in the "long run."

Over the past 6 or 7 years, we have been using a method of quickly determining the effectiveness of our own innovations and particularly those of our competitors in the test-marketing stage through a system we call "time-sampling." In one long sentence, it is the shelf count and recount of various sizes and brands within a given product category, conducted continuously during heavy traffic periods in high-volume retail grocery stores.

Reprinted with permission from Food Business, *April 1962, pp. 26–28.*

[*]*Assistant to the Vice President of Product Planning and Marketing Research, Purex Corp., Ltd.*

Perhaps it might be more clear if I cited an example. The soap and detergent business is a most competitive one. It is composed of several large, highly marketing-oriented, major manufacturers and a number of smaller sectional and regional manufacturers. Anything the majors do in the way of test marketing new products, innovations, etc., is naturally of tremendous interest to the remainder of the industry.

In the last year or so, the industry has anxiously watched the majors test market heavy-duty detergents in both tablet and water-soluble pack form. . . . The tablet is simply a pre-measured, approximately 1″ x 2″, pressed tablet of laundry detergent that the housewife places in the washing machine. The water-soluble pack is a pre-measured polyvinyl chloride package of laundry detergent that dissolves when the housewife places it in the washing machine. Both forms represent substantial convenience to the housewife.

These changes in form presented several questions to the industry:

1. Will the change in form increase total industry volume, or simply rearrange type and brand shares?
2. Will the change in form more seriously affect packaged powders or liquids, and within these 2 types, the high, the middle, or the low sudsers?
3. Will the housewife pay the increased price for the change in form after the novelty wears off?
4. Will the water-soluble pack be accepted by the housewife more readily than the tablet product or vice versa?

Obviously, you can come up with a list of marketing questions as long as your arm, but coming up with the right answer to any one of them *while the types are in the test-marketing stages* can be most helpful to any manufacturer who must determine whether or not to market one of the 2 forms, or some other form.

The day one of the major competitors started to sell his brand of detergent in a water-soluble package to the trade in several test markets our salesmen reported it. This was on a Monday. By Wednesday it had been decided that the innovation was interesting enough to warrant obtaining a "before," "during," and "after" share figure.

The immediate problem was to obtain a "before" figure *prior to the water-soluble pack obtaining actual store distribution.* Store audits were out of the question, in that (1) they could not be set up quickly enough and (2) the test markets had major chain stores accounting for a substantial share of business that would not permit physical store audits. Inasmuch as we are primarily interested in market-share changes, this was a tailor-made job for "time-sampling."

On Thursday morning one of the product research managers from the Purex marketing research department met with an individual marketing research supervisor and 5 enumerators (interviewers or auditors) in one of the test cities and outlined the time-sampling procedure. Forty high-volume supermarkets located in representative socio-economic areas were visited and a sample of 20 stores was selected.

Each of the 5 enumerators was assigned 4 supermarkets to cover.

At 3:00 p.m. on Friday afternoon, at the beginning of the highest traffic period of the week, each enumerator visited his first store, made a small purchase in order to become a bona-fide customer, and proceeded to count the shelf stock of the various brands and sizes of detergent. The count included special displays and any other stocking areas where the consumer could purchase any brand. It did not include the water-soluble pack because the brand was not on the shelf yet in the "before" period. The count of shelf stock took about 7 minutes, and the enumerator then proceeded to the second, third, and fourth stores to do exactly the same thing.

Upon completion of the 4 stores, the auditor returned to his first store at about 4:00 p.m., recounted the shelf stock, then repeated the auditing approximately every hour thereafter, with the last audit at 8:00 p.m.

On Saturday, commencing at 11:00 a.m. and continuing through 5:00 p.m., the procedure was repeated. At the end of 2 days' auditing, the universe of purchases totaled over 3,000 units, and from this universe the sales by type, size, and brand were readily tabulated.

In this particular instance, it was possible to obtain "before" audits for 2 consecutive weekends prior to having the water-soluble packs actually on the shelf, available to the consumer.

After the water-soluble pack had obtained good distribution and the advertising promotion appeared to be just past its peak, another weekend audit was taken, followed by 2 more at monthly intervals. Subsequent audits at later intervals were also taken as competitors introduced tabletized products in the same test market.

Thus we were able to determine what we felt we needed to know about the entry of both the water-soluble pack and tablet form of detergent into the market, quickly, economically, and with a reasonable degree of accuracy: quickly, because the time-sampling method was set up in 2 days; economically, because costs have run between $400 and $500 per weekend measurement for 20 stores, and we could obtain a measurement at any time without having to measure continuously, as might be required with store audits; with a reasonable degree of accuracy because the sample stability from day-to-day and period-to-period was very high.

Time-sampling can be used on virtually any kind of promotional activity and works well on relatively fast-moving items sold through retail outlets that are easy to count. When restocking occurs, it must be readily discerned and that particular sales movement audit taken out of the compilation. The time interval between audits in this particular instance was about one hour, but it could have been shorter in the case of faster-moving products like beer, bread, or margarine, or longer in the case of slower-moving items.

Time-sampling is representative of *sales and share* during the high-traffic periods covered in heavy-volume stores and allows the manufacturer the versatility of measuring the effectiveness of hot weekend specials or other promotional activity on his own or competitive brands. It can measure sales share off an end gondola vs. the shelf sales share per number of facings, difference in sales share caused by pricing differences, etc.

By using time-sampling we are able to determine the effectiveness of these competitive innovations and give good direction to promotional activities of our own. In this particular instance, we supplemented the share change information produced from time-sampling with telephone surveys to determine consumer awareness, consumer initial trial, consumer characteristics, and consumer acceptance or rejection. Obviously, this gave us a pretty good idea

of the housewife's initial and sustained actions to detergent in water-soluble packs and tablets.

In the example cited, we were concerned with the effectiveness of competitive offerings. Time-sampling can also be used to measure packaging changes, size changes, cents-off labels, one-cent sales, etc.

If your company sells relatively fast-moving products through grocery stores, the next time you have need to measure brand-share changes, changes brought about by either your company's promotional activities or your competitor's, try time-sampling. You may be able to have the answer Monday morning.

►►►►►►►►►►► NEEDED: MORE RESEARCH ON THE FLOW OF GOODS FROM FACTORY TO CONSUMER

Printers' Ink

S o m e w h e r e around $10,000,000 a year is spent on taking the nation's purchasing pulse.

Yet research men feel that the biggest gap in their work is in measuring the flow of goods from the factory to the consumer's hands. And it is a significant gap, for when the "pipeline" clogs with unsold goods, the whole economy is affected.

On a less broad scale, the fortunes of every company are dependent on having production in tune with de-

mand, and on maintaining its competitive position in the market.

It's not a simple problem. Consumers are unpredictable beings at best. Still, some ingenious work is being done in this field—and there are some notable failings.

I. THE WELL INFORMED

The men who make and sell products that consumers buy and use, often do the best job of keeping track of the market. They have to. Store audits are one of the methods they use. Here are some of the people who compile them:

A. C. Nielsen Company, the oldest and best known in the field, runs a Food Index, Drug Index, Pharmaceutical Index, and has just launched a Camera Index. Nielsen's Drug Index checks on one out of every 58 sales made in a drug store of the products his clients are selling. To do that, every two months his store auditors check the shelves and invoices of 750 drug stores serving 800,000 families. Their findings are processed at Neilsen's Chicago headquarters, and separate reports prepared for every client that show the share of the market for his product and its relation to competing products. Reports are made every two months.

The Nielsen Food Index audits 1,600 stores serving 500,000 families, and covers more than 3,000 brand items. One weakness is that A&P and Safeway do not allow Nielsen auditors in their stores.

A. C. Nielsen Jr., president, sums up the value of the reports this way:

The indexes are designed and operated to do the triple job of keeping over-all management, sales management and advertising management continuously and factually informed so that each may operate with greater efficiency toward producing more sales and profits.

Audits and Surveys, a newcomer to the field, issues a National Total-Market Audit every two months. Based on a carefully-devised probability sample, it checks 1,500 stores of *all types* for some 34 clients whose products include vacuum cleaners, television sets, phonographs, ball-point pens, fountain pens, auto waxes, films, hair sprays, home permanents, shampoos, face creams, deodorants, insecticides, razor blades, furniture polishes, table salt, cold remedies, and oil filters for cars.

The A&S report is usually in the client's hands six weeks after the audit is completed, but the organization can move faster for special situations. For instance, A&S gives weekly reports on cold remedies during the winter, and on insecticides during the summer.

Three of its clients—Gillette, Simoniz and S. C. Johnson—compare the A&S product-audit reports with figures on factory sales and wholesaler inventories, so they know precisely how their products are moving, and what is in the pipeline at any given moment.

Critics complain that the audits do not give a picture of the price at which goods are being sold, or the sizes of packages being bought, or a measurement of advertising effectiveness.

These criticisms are usually leveled by partisans of consumer panels. The two best known of these panels are:

The Market Research Corporation of America's National Consumer Panel. Composed of 6,000 families throughout the United States, the panelists jot down in a diary every purchase they make, the price paid, size bought, where it was bought, how much, and a multitude of other data.

J. Walter Thompson's panel, in operation since 1929, has many similarities, but differs chiefly in that its panelists keep their diaries on a monthly rather than weekly basis. As in M.R.C.A.'s consumer panel, the panelists get $50 worth of merchandise a year for keeping the diaries.

Critics of the panels, usually store-audit partisans, say the diary system turns panel members into "professional" consumers, and that there is no check on the accuracy of the records kept by each of the panelists.

The consumer panels do not measure the same thing that Nielsen, and Audits & Surveys do.

"What we measure is how she buys, not why," says Dan Connell, eastern regional director of M.R.C.A.

Thus, M.R.C.A. supplies its clients every month with data on brand share, brand-share trends, brand switching, channels of distribution, qualitative characteristics of the kind of people buying a given product and, when compared with promotional efforts, it gives a measure of advertising effectiveness.

PROFILE DETERMINES MEDIUM

As Donald Longman, Thompson's director of research, puts it:

"If we can identify more precisely the characteristics of a market for a product, then it is easier for us to settle on a medium for reaching that market, and on what we ought to say to them."

Connell feels that this "portrait" of purchasers is particularly significant. One of the large cereal manufacturers, for instance, learned from consumer-panel reports that the market for its most important product was concentrated in the 12- to 18-year age group, probably because its historic advertising theme appealed to teen-agers. The company wanted to attract the 6-to-12 group too, and included in its promo-

tional efforts a premium aimed at that group. The panel reports, used to adjust that weakness, showed that it succeeded.

To supplement its consumer-panel information, M.R.C.A. also conducts a quarterly check among a sample of 1,700 food stores to obtain information on brand distribution and inventory, and makes more intensive studies of distribution in 23 large-city markets.

Whatever the weaknesses of store audits and consumer panels, the fact remains that they are the best yardsticks available for gauging what is happening in the market place in the sale of soft goods to the American consumers.

Other types of products would have easier going if they used similar measures.

II. THE LESS INFORMED

Paradoxically, the biggest gap in information on the flow of goods to the consumer is in the area that has the greatest effect on the economy as a whole—hard goods.

Most trade associations keep statistics on industry sales, and by reckoning his own sales against those of the whole industry, the manufacturer can estimate what his share of the market is. But there is much more that he doesn't know, particularly whether the goods he has sold to wholesalers are piling up there, or whether they are back-logging at the retail level.

Lack of this knowledge can have disastrous effects, as television-set makers learned in 1951 when they watched an estimated $200,000,000 in profits evaporate under the weight of inventory pile-ups.

Rolling happily along at an annual production rate of 8,000,000 sets, the television industry was blissfully unaware that retailers had some 1,500,000 unsold sets on hand. Factory and wholesaler inventories brought the total to nearly 2,250,000.

Result: two out of three production lines had to be closed down and production cut back to a level of 3,000,000 sets a year.

The debacle caused thoughtful appliance-industry leaders to explore some means of finding out what was going on in the retailers' shops.

ELECTRONIC INDUSTRIES ASSOCIATION

Today, television and radio manufacturers and wholesalers channel weekly sales and inventory figures to the Electronic Industries Association's research department in Washington, which is headed by William F. E. Long. Audits & Surveys supplies the figures on what is happening in the retail outlets monthly, and the industry knows where it stands by the middle of the following month.

"We've got the finest marketing-data department of any trade association on earth," an E.I.A. spokesman boasts. "There's been no television or radio inventory pile-up in the current recession. We knew what was happening, and our members adjusted their production to demand."

Makers of air conditioning units are not so well informed. The Air Conditioning and Refrigeration Institute does keep figures on year-end inventories, but the only up-to-month information available is just on the factory sales of compressor motors, not even completed units. The industry in its short history has been continually plagued by overoptimistic sales forecasts.

One source of information that appliance makers do have on retail sales is the return of warranty cards from purchasers. But this is a very inaccurate measure, largely because it gives no indication of where sales are taking place and in no way reflects the stocks on hand on retailers' or wholesalers' shelves. Makers of electrical ranges, refrigerators, electric blankets, automatic coffee makers, electric skillets, and such, are also fond of using this method to measure their markets.

In the hotly-competitive automobile business, a thorough but somewhat slow job is done on measuring what is taking place in the car dealers' show rooms.

Production is charted weekly by Ward's Automotive Reports, and sales are kept track of by R. L. Polk and Company. For this information, the latter must check on car registrations with the motor bureaus of key states. There is a lag of about six weeks between the time a sale takes place and when the information is back in the hands of the motor makers in Detroit. Ward's then publishes a weekly box score on the market position for each model.

The Automobile Manufacturers Association also publishes sales reports at ten-day intervals that go to one or two top officials in each company. The reports are treated with about as much secrecy as plans for the hydrogen bomb.

Having the information and acting

on it are two entirely different things. One research man notes that the auto business is subjected to tremendous pressures from conflicting directions, and traditionally tries to out-sell its competitors regardless of the cost.

With so much at stake in the important hard-goods field, the obvious question is why aren't the auditing techniques used in soft goods applied to this field too?

TURNOVER TOO SMALL

Nielsen answers: "Most hard goods move slowly. We need a sufficient volume to produce valid index figures. For example, women buy refrigerators on the average of once every ten years or so. To obtain sufficient data to analyze, we would have to check a large number of dealers over a long period of time, and the cost would be prohibitive."

Solomon Dutka, president of Audits & Surveys, disagrees. He notes that his firm began checking vacuum cleaners recently for General Electric, and is exploring the possibilities of auditing auto parts for another client. He thinks there will be a great growth of research concerned with the flow of goods into consumers' hands in the years ahead.

"I am constantly amazed at how intelligent American businessmen are," he says. "When they realize they need something, they don't hesitate to get it."